Jewish Spirituality and Divine Law

THE ORTHODOX FORUM

The Orthodox Forum, convened by Dr. Norman Lamm, Chancellor of Yeshiva University, meets each year to consider major issues of concern to the Jewish community. Forum participants from throughout the world, including academicians in both Jewish and secular fields, rabbis, *rashei yeshiva,* Jewish educators, and Jewish communal professionals, gather in conference as a think tank to discuss and critique each other's original papers, examining different aspects of a central theme. The purpose of the Forum is to create and disseminate a new and vibrant Torah literature addressing the critical issues facing Jewry today.

The Orthodox Forum
gratefully acknowledges the support
of the Joseph J. and Bertha K. Green Memorial Fund
at the Rabbi Isaac Elchanan Theological Seminary.

The Orthodox Forum Series
is a project of the Rabbi Isaac Elchanan Theological Seminary,
an affiliate of Yeshiva University

Jewish Spirituality and Divine Law

EDITED BY

Adam Mintz and Lawrence Schiffman

Robert S. Hirt, Series Editor

THE MICHAEL SCHARF PUBLICATION TRUST
of the YESHIVA UNIVERSITY PRESS
NEW YORK

Library of Congress Cataloging-in-Publication Data

Orthodox Forum (12th : 2000 : New York, N.Y.)
Jewish spirituality and divine law / edited by Adam Mintz and Lawrence Schiffman.
p. cm. -- (The Orthodox Forum series)
Papers from the 12th Orthodox Forum held in New York, N.Y., Apr. 2-3, 2000.
ISBN 0-88125-865-2
1. Spiritual life--Judaism--Congresses. 2. Orthodox Judaism--Congresses. 3. Spiritual life--Judaism--History of doctrines--Congresses. I. Mintz, Adam. II. Schiffman, Lawrence H. III. Title. IV. Series.
BM723.O78 2000
296.3'82--dc22

2004018125

Manufactured in the United States of America

Published by
KTAV Publishing House, Inc.
930 Newark Avenue
Jersey City, NJ 07306
Email: orders@ktav.com
www.ktav.com
(201) 963-9524
Fax (201) 963-0102

Contents

SECTION FOUR

Spirituality and the Arts

SECTION FIVE

Spirituality in Education

SECTION SIX

Spirituality and Prayer

SECTION SEVEN

Other Volumes in the Orthodox Forum Series

Rabbinic Authority and Personal Autonomy
edited by Moshe Z. Sokol

Jewish Tradition and the Non-Traditional Jew
edited by Jacob J. Schacter

Israel as a Religious Reality
edited by Chaim I. Waxman

Modern Scholarship in the Study of Torah:
Contributions and Limitations
edited by Shalom Carmy

Tikkun Olam:
Social Responsibility in Jewish Thought and Law
edited by David Shatz, Chaim I. Waxman,
and Nathan J. Diament

Engaging Modernity:
Rabbinic Leaders and the Challenge of the Twentieth Century
edited by Moshe Z. Sokol

Jewish Perspectives on the Experience of Suffering
edited by Shalom Carmy

Jewish Business Ethics:
The Firm and Its Stockholders
edited by Aaron Levine and Moses Pava

Tolerance, Dissent and Democracy:
Philosophical, Historical and Halakhic Perspectives
edited by Moshe Z. Sokol

Contributors

Judith Bleich is associate professor of Judaic Studies at Touro College in New York City. She has written extensively on modern Jewish history.

Alan Brill was ordained by the Rabbi Isaac Elchanan Theological Seminary and received his PhD from Fordham University. He is assistant professor of Jewish mysticism and thought at Yeshiva University and founding director of Kavvanah, a Center for Jewish Spirituality. He is the author of *Thinking God: The Mysticism of Rabbi Zadok of Lublin*.

Erica Brown is the scholar-in-residence for the Jewish Federation of Greater Washington and director of its Leadership Institute. Formerly, she served in that capacity for the Federation of Boston. She did her undergraduate studies at Yeshiva University and continued her graduate work at the University of London and Harvard University. She was a Jerusalem Fellow and is a faculty member of the Wexner Heritage Foundation. She has been teaching Jewish adult education for sixteen years and has lectured widely in the United

States, London and Israel in addition to having written extensively in journals of education and Jewish Studies, and has chapters in *Jewish Legal Writings by Women* and *Torah of the Mothers*. She is the author of the forthcoming book, *The Sacred Canvas: The Hebrew Bible in the Eyes of the Artist.*

Shalom Carmy teaches Jewish Studies and philosophy at Yeshiva University and is Consulting Editor of *Tradition*. He has published extensively on Jewish thought and biblical studies. He is the editor of two volumes in the Orthodox Forum series, *Modern Scholarship in Talmud Torah: Contributions and Limitations*, and *Suffering: A Jewish Perspective.*

Yaakov Elman is professor of Jewish Studies at Yeshiva University. He is the author of *Authority and Tradition* and *The Living Prophets*. He is a prolific writer on talmudic literature, biblical interpretation, and ḥasidic thought.

Steven Fine is the first incumbent of the Jewish Foundation Chair of Judaic Studies and is head of the Department of Judaic Studies at the University of Cincinnati. He received his doctorate in Jewish History from the Hebrew University of Jerusalem, and his MA in Art History from the University of Southern California. He is the author of *This Holy Place: On the Sanctity of the Synagogue During the Greco-Roman Period*. His *Sacred Realm: The Emergence of the Synagogue in the Ancient World* accompanied an exhibition of the same name which he curated at Yeshiva University Museum and was awarded the Philip Johnson Award for Excellence in Published Exhibition Catalogues by the Society of Architectural Historians. Dr. Fine is a founding editor of *AJS Perspectives: The Newsletter of the Association for Jewish Studies* and is also the editor or co-editor of a number of critically acclaimed volumes in his field, including the forthcoming *Liturgy in the Life of the Synagogue*.

Robert S. Hirt serves as the series editor of The Orthodox Forum publications, and as Senior Adviser to the President of Yeshiva

University. Since 1991, he has occupied the Rabbi Sidney Shoham Chair in Rabbinic and Community Leadership. In 1987, Rabbi Hirt – who formerly directed the University's array of Holocaust studies programs – co-edited Shimon Huberband's critically acclaimed book on the Holocaust, *Kiddush Hashem: Jewish Religious and Cultural Life in Poland During the Holocaust.* He has also contributed to *Tradition, The Journal of Orthodox Jewish Thought,* and other educational publications.

Arthur Hyman is dean of the Bernard Revel Graduate School and Distinguished Service Professor of Philosophy at Yeshiva University. He is a specialist on medieval Jewish and Islamic philosophy and on Maimonides. He is former president of the American Academy for Jewish Research and of the Society for Medieval and Renaissance Philosophy. Currently, Dr. Hyman is a member of the Council of the World Union of Jewish Studies and a member of Averroes Opera, the disseminator of all the works of Averroes. He is the author of numerous articles and editor of *Maimonidean Studies*, an international journal devoted to Maimonides research, and has authored (among other works) *Philosophy in the Middle Ages: The Christian, Islamic, and Jewish Tradition.*

Daniel J. Lasker is Norbert Blechner Professor of Jewish Values at Ben-Gurion University of the Negev, Beer Sheva, where he teaches medieval Jewish philosophy in the Goldstein-Goren Department of Jewish Thought. Professor Lasker is the author of four books and over a hundred other publications in the fields of Jewish philosophy and theology, the Jewish-Christian debate, Karaism, the Jewish calendar, and Judaism and modern medicine.

Aharon Lichtenstein is Rosh Yeshiva at Yeshivat Har Eẓion and the Gruss Institute of the Rabbi Elchanan Theological Seminary. He is a frequent contributor to books and journals of contemporary Jewish thought.

Naftali Loewenthal is a lecturer on Ḥasidism at Jews College in

London, England. He is the author of *Communicating the Infinite,* published by Chicago University Press.

Vivian Mann is Morris and Eva Feld Chair of Judaica at The Jewish Museum and advisor to the Masters Program in Jewish Art and Material Culture at the Graduate School of the Jewish Theological Seminary. She has created numerous exhibitions and their catalogues. Dr. Mann's many articles and lectures cover a broad range of topics in medieval art and in the history of Jewish art. Dr. Mann has been the recipient of numerous fellowships and awards.

Adam Mintz is a Visiting Lecturer at the Allen and Joan Bildner Center for the Study of Jewish Life at Rutgers University. Previously, he served as rabbi of Lincoln Square Synagogue and associate rabbi of Congregation Kehilath Jeshurun in New York.

Lawrence H. Schiffman is chairman of New York University's Skirball Department of Hebrew and Judaic Studies and serves as Ethel and Irvin A. Edelman Professor of Hebrew and Judaic Studies. He is also a member of the University's Hagop Kevorkian Center for Near Eastern Studies and Center for Ancient Studies. He is the author of many books and articles on the Dead Sea Scrolls, Jewish law, and rabbinic Judaism.

Moshe Sokolow is professor of Bible and Jewish education at Yeshiva University, director of the Intensive Training Program for Day School Leadership, Azrieli Graduate School of Jewish Education and Administration of Yeshiva University, and the editor of *Ten Da'at: A Journal of Jewish Education*, and *Texts & Topics: A Teachers' Guide to Limmudei Kodesh.*

Chaim I. Waxman is professor of sociology and Jewish studies at Rutgers University. Among his books are *American's Jews in Transition, American Aliya: Portrait of an Innovative Migration Movement*, and *Jewish Baby Boomers.*

Series Editor's Preface

We are delighted to introduce the 10th volume in The Orthodox Forum Series, Divine Law and Human Spirituality, edited by Dr. Lawrence Schiffman and Rabbi Adam Mintz. The editors of the volume have skillfully guided the formulation and exploration of the spirituality theme across a wide range of disciplines.

The Orthodox Forum Series has become a significant resource for scholars, advanced students and serious laymen seeking clarification of major intellectual and theological questions facing the Jewish people in the modern world.

At a time when Jewish identity and commitment are being challenged by apathy and ignorance of primary sources, it is critical that clear exposition of our classical values be widely disseminated by knowledgeable leaders in a thoughtful and engaging manner.

We are confident that the community will warmly welcome this timely volume.

October 2003 Robert S. Hirt
(editor's introduction 10-8-03)

Introduction

Adam Mintz

In 1989, the Orthodox Forum was established by Dr. Norman Lamm, then President of Yeshiva University, to consider major issues of concern to the Jewish community. Academicians, rabbis, *rashei yeshiva*, Jewish educators and communal professionals have been invited each year to come together for an in-depth analysis of one such topic. This group has constituted an Orthodox think tank and has produced a serious and extensive body of literature.

In the spirit of its initial mandate, the Forum has chosen topics that have challenged Jews and Judaism throughout history. One of the themes addressed in this series is the numerous confrontations that have existed, both in past eras and in the present time, between the central principles of Orthodox belief and practice, on the one hand, and the widely-accepted values of the contemporary secular society. In the 1992 Orthodox Forum, which examined the tension between rabbinic authority and personal autonomy, Dr. Moshe Sokol pointed out that this tension between authority and personal autonomy which is a central problem for Western religions generally "can be a particularly sharp problem for Jews who maintain a commitment to the observance of *halakhah*."[1]

Similarly, spirituality, the topic of the conference held in the year 2000, presents, on first consideration, an apparent clash between spirituality and law and breaches the divide between the subjectivity inherent in the one and the objective requirements of practice and belief essential to *halakhah*. In addition, the seeming New-Age faddishness of spirituality stands starkly against the deep historical roots of the Jewish tradition. In a passage quoted by several of the volume's contributors, Dr. Lamm formulated the delicate balance between law and spirituality:

> The contrast between the two – spirituality and law – is almost self-evident. Spirituality is subjective; the very fact of it inwardness implies a certain degree of anarchy; it is unfettered and self-directed, impulsive and spontaneous. In contrast, law is objective; it requires discipline, structure, obedience, order. Yet both are necessary. Spirituality alone begets antinomianism and chaos; law alone is artificial and insensitive. Without the body of the law, spirituality is a ghost. Without the sweep of the soaring soul, the corpus of the law tends to become a corpse. But how can two such opposites coexist within one personality without producing unwelcome schizoid consequences?[2]

The risks of producing the "ghost" and the "corpse" and the need for coexistence and integration are issues that have confronted Jews for centuries.

The primary purpose of the conference and this resulting volume has been to demonstrate through a spectrum of diverse views, that spirituality and Orthodox Judaism are actually not hostile to one another, but, to the contrary, complement and enrich one an-

---

[1] Moshe Sokol, "Preface", in *Rabbinic Authority and Personal Autonomy*, edited by Moshe Sokol (Northvale, NJ, 1992), p. xii

[2] Norman Lamm, *The Shema: Spirituality and Law in Judaism* (Philadelphia, 2000), p. 6.

other. The issue is first approached from a historical perspective, in essays dealing with ancient Judaism, the medieval period and the contemporary period. The following essays then consider the interplay between spirituality and traditional Judaism in synagogue art and in prayer. Essays by Rabbi Aharon Lichtenstein and Dr. Chaim Waxman frame the discussion and present an overview of the wide-ranging philosophical and sociological implications of the topic.

In an attempt to guarantee that our society's current search for spirituality is not overlooked, a colloquium was added to the conference to address the role of spirituality within our synagogues and *yeshivot*. Rabbi Daniel Cohen, Cantor Sherwood Goffin, Rabbi Nathaniel Helfgot, Dr. David Pelcovitz and Prof. Suzanne Last Stone explored the possibilities for spirituality in our institutions focusing on the "Carlebach phenomenon" and the perceived need for enhanced spirituality in Orthodox institutions. While the intention was not to produce a written record of the colloquium, it served to enhance the conference and helped to maintain the delicate balance required between the theoretical and the practical.

In the first essay of this volume, Rabbi Aharon Lichtenstein defines both the values and the risks of spirituality and law. He utilizes Maimonides' distinction between law, which relates to the public sphere, and spirituality, which is highly personal, as the basis for his understanding of the terms. According to Rabbi Lichtenstein, while we must abandon neither, we also must achieve the proper balance between the two. Spirituality provides expression for the *halakhah* while *halakhah* prescribes necessary forms and constraints to our spiritual impulses. We have to prevent our commitment to the minutiae of law from robbing our actions of meaning and feeling just as we must be careful not to allow our desire for spirituality to cause us to ignore those laws considered non-spiritual.

Rabbi Lichtenstein concludes his paper with an analysis of the contemporary Jewish scene. He sees the risks inherent in the move toward excess spirituality both in the realm of prayer and Torah study. He writes, "I'm afraid, however, that votaries of current spirituality often tend to erode the status of *yirah* (awe); and, together with it, the status of the very essence of *yahadut*: *kabbalat ol malkhut shamayim* (acceptance of the yoke of heaven) and *kabbalat ol mitzvoth* (acceptance of the yoke of commandments)." Is this fear reasonable or is this critique of contemporary spirituality too harsh? The remaining articles in the volume provide the necessary background to consider this question.

Professors Lawrence Schiffman and Yaakov Elman explore the uses of spirituality in the ancient period, concentrating on the eras of the Bible and second temple and of the Talmudic period. Professor Schiffman focuses on the approach to religion, which centered on the Temple and its service and how this religious expression evolved as people began to move away from the Temple. Professor Elman examines human spirituality as it was construed in the rabbinic era through a study of specific incidences and testimonies of key Talmudic figures.

Professors Brill and Lasker examine spirituality in medieval literature. Professor Brill argues that the study of Kabbalah is crucial in order to add meaning to *mitzvot* and Torah. He takes issue with those who exclude Kabbalah from the canon of Judaism or advocate for finding certain aspects of Kabbalah outside the normative framework of Judaism. Professor Lasker begins his paper by stating that, "Medieval Jewish philosophers did not have a specific concept of human spirituality in its modern usage." He goes on to present two models of medieval philosophy's understanding of the soul and its place in establishing a relationship between man and God. The ability to frame spirituality in the world of medieval terminology and thought allows us to begin to formulate a definition of spirituality that is relevant in different historical and cultural settings.

Professors Fine and Mann further expand the scope of the discussion with an exploration of spirituality and the arts. Professor Fine examines the mosaics found within synagogues of the fourth through sixth centuries CE. While the use of mosaics was common in public places during this period, the presence of these mosaics in synagogues and the later opposition to this artistic representation in the synagogue points to a spiritual aesthetic that was both communally and culturally driven. Professor Mann traces the rabbinic attitude towards Jewish ceremonial art. While rabbinic opposition points to the potential distractions caused by these works of art, certain rabbis were also sensitive to the spiritual value of decorative ceremonial objects especially within the synagogue setting. These surveys broaden our appreciation for the role of spirituality beyond the intellectual world.

Having presented a picture of the historical, intellectual and cultural images of spirituality, the challenge remains how to understand these images and how to transmit them to others. Rabbi Moshe Sokolow and Erica Brown explore the experience of teaching spirituality. Rabbi Sokolow presents a model for the introduction of spirituality in Jewish day schools and yeshiva high schools. Spirituality must play a role in the formulation of the school's vision as well as in its curriculum and teacher's training programs. Ms. Brown looks at the field of adult education and points out a unique educational problem – namely that adults tend to be interested in acquiring new information and are not especially interested in seeking the spiritual value of this information. She shares with us her experiences in the field and her strategies for overcoming this obstacle and transmitting this spiritual essence to a class of adults.

The challenge of transmitting spirituality is particularly relevant in the arena of prayer. Professor Hyman explores the Maimonidean position on prayer and concludes that according to Maimonides, spirituality is part of the process of prayer but that ultimately it plays only a minor role in the complex halakhic and philosophic definition of prayer. Professors Bleich and Lowenthal trace the evolution of spirituality and prayer in the nineteenth and twentieth centuries. Professor Bleich looks at the Reform innovations to the synagogue service and the response of the Orthodox who attempt to maintain the tradition while incorporating the needs of the spiritual. Professor Lowenthal examines the innovations of the Hasidic community in the realm of spirituality as a response to the potential encroachment of the modern world into the Jewish community. His emphasis on the value of spirituality for the youth, especially the girls in the early days of the Bais Yaakov movement and in the Chabad community, provides an important perspective on the relevance and importance of spirituality in pre-war Eastern Europe. Professor Carmy concludes the discussion on prayer and spirituality by posing the question, "Can thinking about prayer improve the quality of our prayer?" He goes on to examine prayer in the context of the religious and halakhic philosophies of both Rav Kook and Rav Soloveitchik.

The final essay in the volume by Professor Waxman is entitled "Religion, Spirituality and the Future of American Judaism" and explores the sociology of spirituality in America today. He claims that spirituality is a manifestation of the privatization of religious practice today in which people are moving away from institutions and looking for personal expressions of religious observance. This phenomenon has served to weaken the traditional institutions of Judaism. Waxman argues that what is needed is for our institutions to provide avenues for spirituality thereby enabling the quest for spirituality to be realized within traditional Judaism and not outside of it.

Professor Waxman's paper provides an appropriate segue from our discussion of the past to the necessity of developing a plan for the future. Contemporary Jewish society has much to gain from an appreciation of this subject as seen through the variety of vantage points presented in this volume. Yet, at the same time, modern culture introduces its own challenges and unique personality that must be addressed by the committed Jew. Rabbi Lichtenstein articulates this challenge at the conclusion of his paper:

> This brings us, finally, back to our primary problem: How to attain optimal fusion of divine law and human spirituality, committed to both while eschewing neither. We live by the serene faith that it can be done. We refuse to believe that we are doomed to chose between arid formalism and unbridled sensibility…The apocryphal remark attributed to an anonymous *hasid*, מתנגדים דאווען נישט – אין צייט; חסידים דאווען – נישט אין צייט (Misnagdim daven not, but on time; Ḥasidim daven, but not on time) is both facile and tendacious. It is also false. It is our mission to assure that legalists and spiritualists both pray – on time.

The volume has been compiled with the hope that it will contribute to the realization of that mission.

I would like to take this opportunity to acknowledge those people who have been instrumental in the completion of this volume. The project has been spearheaded by Dr. Norman Lamm, Chancellor of Yeshiva University and convener of the Orthodox Forum. My own spiritual development is a product of his many years of leadership and I am honored to participate in this project. Rabbi Robert Hirt, Senior Advisor to the President, Yeshiva University, is deeply committed to the mission of the Forum and the dissemination of its material. Rabbi Hirt has provided guidance and direction for me since my first day at Yeshiva College and his invitation to participate in the Orthodox Forum and to co-edit this volume is just one of the many things for which I am grateful. Mrs. Marcia Schwartz's gracious assistance has made this job significantly easier and I am thankful to the members of the steering committee for their involvement in developing and formalizing this challenging topic. Miriam and Yonatan Kaganoff served as editorial assistants and were instrumental in the preparation of the manuscripts for publication. Finally, it was a pleasure to co-edit this volume with Professor Lawrence Schiffman; his passion, expertise and experience made this process an enjoyable and enlightening one for me.

Section one

1

Law and Spirituality: Defining the Terms

Rabbi Aharon Lichtenstein

Spirituality, as concept and reality, revolves around three distinct elements. In one sense, it denominates a kind – or, if you will, a level – of existence. In a primitive context, this might crudely refer to a physical essence, albeit more rarefied than gross carnal being. In a more sophisticated vein, it bears metaphysical import.[1] At the highest plane, it is of course identified with the *Ribbono shel Olam*. He is, Himself, pure spirit, "אין לו דמות הגוף ואין לו גוף" ("He has not semblance of a body nor is He corporeal"), and not subject to the vicissitudes of matter:

> וכל הדברים האלה אינן מצויין אלא לגופים האפלים השפלים שוכני בתי חומר אשר בעפר יסודם אבל הוא ברוך הוא יתברך ויתרומם על כל זה (רמב"ם יסודי התורה א:יב).

[1] See Edwyn Bevan, *Symbolism and Belief* (Boston: Beacon Press, 1957) [the Gifford Lectures of 1937], pp. 151–60.

> All these states exist in physical beings that are of obscure and mean condition, dwelling in houses of clay, whose foundation is in the dust. Infinitely blessed and exalted above all this, is God, blessed be He (Maimonides, Foundations of the Torah, 1:12).

Moreover, He is a source from which emanates a derivative spirit, as it were, such as "dove-like sat'st brooding on the vast abyss, and mad'st it pregnant":[2] ורוח א-לקים מרחפת על פני המים ("the spirit of God hovered over the face of the waters"). At a second, categorically inferior, plane, it denotes a plethora of immaterial entities, differently conceived in various cultural traditions. These, for us, may be angelic "שהמלאכים אינם גוף וגויה אלא צורות נפרדות זו מזו" (יסוה"ת ב:ד) ("the angels are nevertheless not corporeal and have no gravity-like bodies which have weight"), or demonic: "והגוף הזה", says Naḥmanides of a demon, "הוא רוחני יטוס לדקותו וקלותו באש ובאויר" (ויקרא יז:ז) ("The body [of these demonic creatures of two elements] is of a spiritual nature; on account of its delicacy and lightness it can fly through fire and air"). But whatever the moral state, the metaphysical state is purely spiritual.

At yet another plane, however, we encounter spirituality within the context of the physical. In a very limited sense, it has even been taken by some to include the animal world. The term, "רוח הבהמה" ("the spirit of the beast"), is of course familiar from the *pasuk* in *Kohelet*; and Naḥmanides, in particular, took pains to stress the significance of this aspect as a spiritual category, and not merely as a reference to one of the four elements, in Aristotelian terms, or to a molecular entity, in modern usage. Maimonides had totally dissociated the human spirit from the animal, emphasizing that the terms, נפש ורוח ("soul and spirit"), have totally different referents with respect to both:

---

[2] *Paradise Lost*, 1:21–2, based on BT *Ḥagigah* 15a, "כיונה המרחפת על בניה ואינה נוגעת (Like a dove that hovers over her brood but does not touch them)".

> ואינה הנפש המצויה לכל נפש חיה שבה אוכל ושותה ומוליד ומרגיש ומהרהר אלא הדעה שהיא צורת הנפש ובצורת הנפש הכתוב מדבר בצלמנו כדמותנו ופעמים רבות תקרא זאת הצורה נפש ורוח ולפיכך צריך להזהר בשמות, שלא יטעה אדם בהן וכל שם ושם ילמד מענינו (יסוה"ת ד:ח).
>
> Nor does it [i.e. the human "form"] refer to the vital principle in every animal by which it eats, drinks, reproduces, feels, and broods. It is the intellect which is the human soul's specific form. And to this specific form of the soul, the Scriptural phrase, "in our image, after our likeness" alludes. This form is frequently called soul and spirit. One must therefore, in order to avoid mistakes, pay special attention to the meaning of these terms which, in each case, has to be ascertained from the context (Maimonides, Foundations of the Torah, 4:8).

Naḥmanides, by contrast, taking note, *inter alia*, of the capacity for feeling and reflection cited but discounted by Maimonides, repeatedly insists upon recognizing a common factor. Thus, he explains that the pre-Noahide prohibition against carnal consumption was grounded upon concern for the bestial *nefesh*:

> כי אין לבעל נפש שיאכל נפש כי הנפשות כולן לא-ל הנה, כנפש האדם וכנפש הבהמה לו הנה, ומקרה אחד להם כמות זה כן מות זה ורוח אחד לכל ועל הדרך היוני שיראוהו חוקריו מן השכל הפועל התנוצץ זיו וזוהר צח מאד ובהיר וממנו יצא נצוץ נפש הבהמה והנה היא נפש גמורה בצד מן הפנים ולכך יש בה דעת לברוח מן הנזק וללכת אחרי הנאות לה והיכר ברגילים ואהבה להם כאהבת הכלבים לבעליהן והכר מופלא באנשי בית בעליהם וכן ליונים דעת והכרה (ויקרא יז: יא).
>
> One creature possessed of a soul is not to eat another creature with a soul, for all souls belong to God. The soul of man, just as the soul of the animal, are all His, "even one thing befalleth them; as the one dieth, so dieth the other; yea, they have all one breath" (Ecclesiastes 3:19). Now in the opinion of the Greek philosopher [Aristotle], as interpreted by those who scrutinize his words, it was out of the Active Intellect that there emitted a very fine and bright flash and glitter of light, from which came forth the spark which is the soul of the

> animal. It is thus in a certain sense a real soul. It therefore has sufficient understanding to avoid harm, and to seek its welfare, and a sense of recognition towards those with whom it is familiar, and love towards them, just as dogs love their masters, having a wonderful sense of recognition of the people of their households, and as, similarly, pigeons have a sense of knowledge and recognition (Leviticus 17:11).

Nevertheless, Naḥmanides obviously assumed the uniqueness of the human spirit, singularly derived from divine aspiration – ויפח באפיו נשמת חיים ("He breathed into his nostrils the breath of life");[3] and it is upon man – in Browning's phrase, "half angel and half dust, and all a passion and a wild desire" – that the conception of physically based metaphysical spirituality centers.[4] Within our own tradition no less than in that of religious humanism, in general, the themes of man's dual origin and dual nature – whether dichotomized or integrated, in conflict or in harmony – are both common and central, almost to the point of being platitudinous; and, asserted or assumed, they seem to posit spirituality as the defining quality of human existence.

From spirituality as fact we move, second, to spirituality – here, purely human – as attitude and approach. We are, of course, all bound by physical limitations, impelled by instinctual drives, and constrained by socioeconomic needs. Montaigne's trenchant observation, put in the mouth of Raymond Sebonde, that man aspires for the stars and all the while cannot rise from his toilet seat, is universally applicable; and *Ḥazal*,[5] we recall, took note of Pharaoh's arrogant folly in pretending otherwise. However, the balance between astral aspiration and anal bondage may be variously struck. Individuals and societies can establish priorities. They can succumb to the weakness of the flesh, the appetite for affluence, or the lust for power, or

---

[3] See Naḥmanides, Gen. 1:28 and 2:7.

[4] In this connection, extensive discussions of the nuanced differences of נפש, רוח, נשמה, particularly in light of Kabbalah, are, of course, relevant.

[5] See *Tanḥuma*, Exodus 7:15.

they may seek to transcend them. A spiritual life, in this sense, is one which seeks to maximize spiritual achievement and to advance the distinctly human aspect of personal and communal existence – of man as *ẓelem E-lohim*, "the human face divine;" of man as a moral and intellectual being, of man as a creative *ruaḥ memallela* ("spirit which speaks"), capable of esthetic perception and expression. For secular moralists, the issue is simply one of the quality of mundane life – although for them, too, existence *sub specie aeternitatis* is a value. From a religious perspective, the priority of *ḥayyei olam* over *ḥayyei shaah* is a crucial aspect of the spiritual agenda.

Thirdly, spirituality denotes a mode of experience and activity, a quality of personality which finds expression not only in what is pursued, but how. In part, it relates to perception, to the degree of supra-materiala being ascribed to observed reality. Thus, the mythological view of nature – fauns, satyrs, maenads, and all – is more spiritual than the scientific. Analogously, Carlyle's theory of history is more spiritual than Marx's; the Rabad's view of the afterlife less spiritual than Maimonides'. Even more critically, anthropomorphism – particularly, insofar as it relates to corporeality rather than to emotions – is not only theologically repugnant but spiritually deficient.

Primarily, however, at issue is sensibility and expression. A spiritual person is one who not only perceives reality as spiritual, but experiences it as such. He is one who relates himself and his situation to the world of pure spirit – transcendental, in religious terms, or cultural and/or national, secularly conceived;[6] and who can give his sense of that relation a given cast. That cast encompasses a cluster of elements: ethereality, vitalism, dynamism, inwardness,

---

[6] The general editors of the series of volumes, *World Spirituality*, published over the last fifteen years, shy away from a clear definition of the term. However, in the preface printed at the beginning of each volume, they present, "as a working hypothesis," the following: "The series focuses on that inner dimension of the person called by certain traditions 'the spirit.' This spiritual core is the deepest center of the person. It is here that the person is open to the transcendent dimension; it is here that the person experiences ultimate reality." The concluding statement gives the term a purely religious cast; and, indeed, the series is subtitled, "An Encyclopedic

feeling, personal expression, imagination. The emphasis is experiential and, hence, significantly subjective. Beyond the inner sense, and the inner voice, we may also note – and this factor has attained increased popularity in current parlance – the mode of its expression. What is intended is not necessarily verbalization but, rather, more physical means of rendering the spiritual – dance, song, vehicles of exuberance, passion, and enthusiasm; not quite the Dionysiac, but in that general vein. In this respect, the Romantics' preference for music over visual art, or the Baal ha-Tanya's grading a *niggun* without words above one with a text (although he regarded "a *niggun* without a *niggun*" as loftier still) may be viewed as reflecting spiritual sensibility.

Given this account of spirituality, we are confronted with the question of its relation to the halakhic linchpin of our religious world – and, hence, derivatively, of its relation to ourselves. As regards the first two senses of the term, with respect to which the spiritual is juxtaposed with the material, there is, of course, no problem. There have undoubtedly been schools of thought that have perceived both the cosmos and man in more purely spiritual terms than *Yahadut*, ascribing, mystically or philosophically, an almost ethereal character to the whole of reality, and virtually denying the empirical. And there are certainly cultures which, far more than our own, have denigrated the material, as either, in Plato's terms, metaphysically flaccid, or, with Augustine, as a *massa perditionis*, corrupt and corrupting. The central tradition of *hashkafah* has never gone this far. As the leading modern figures, in particular, have emphasized, it has adopted neither pole of James' familiar dichotomy, world-acceptance or world-rejection, and has opted, instead, for world-redemption. Nevertheless, the fundamental affirmation of spirit, as fact and value, is central to traditional Jewish thought; and whatever controversies have flared over the degree of centrality – and they have been significant – have arisen within the parameters of clearly accepted spiritual priority.

If we have a problem, it obtains with respect to our third aspect – the spirituality of sensibility and expression. *Prima facie*, here, too, there is no conflict. We rightly regard the focus upon inwardness as endemic to any meaningful religion, and it was clearly and succinctly articulated by *Ḥazal*: רחמנא ליבא בעי ("The Merciful One desires the heart").[7] Further, the purgation envisioned in the familiar midrash as the *telos* of *miẓvot*, לא ניתנו המצות אלא כדי לצרף את הבריות ("The precepts were given only that man might be refined by them"),[8] is unquestionably spiritual. Beyond this, we can also heartily espouse the spirituality of exuberance. Maimonides, regarded by classical *maskilim* as the paragon of restrained rationalism, was emphatic on this point. After describing the festivities of *simḥat beit hasho'evah*, he concludes *Hilkhot Lulav* with a ringing affirmation regarding the performance of *miẓvot* in general:

> השמחה שישמח אדם בעשיית המצוה ובאהבת הא-ל שצוה בהן עבודה גדולה היא וכל המונע עצמו משמחה זו ראוי להפרע ממנו שנאמר תחת אשר לא עבדת את ה׳ א-לקיך בשמחה ובטוב לבב[9] וכל המגיס דעתו וחולק כבוד לעצמו ומתכבד בעיניו במקומות אלו חוטא ושוטה ועל זה הזהיר שלמה ואמר אל תתהדר לפני מלך וכל המשפיל עצמו ומקל גופו במקומות אלו הוא הגדול המכובד העובד מאהבה וכן דוד מלך ישראל אמר ונקלותי עוד מזאת והייתי שפל בעיני ואין הגדולה והכבוד אלא לשמוח לפני ה׳ שנאמר והמלך דוד מפזז ומכרכר לפני ה׳ וגו׳ (לולב ח:טו).
>
> Rejoicing in the fulfillment of a commandment and in love for God who had prescribed the commandment is a supreme act of divine worship. One who refrains from participation in such rejoicing deserves to be punished, as it is written, "Because you did not serve the Lord thy God with joyfulness, and with gladness of heart" (Deut. 28:47). If one is arrogant and stands on his own dignity and thinks only of

History of the Religious Quest." I can appreciate this inclination but I feel that, on the subjective plane, aspects of spirituality may also manifest themselves within a secular context.

[7] BT *Sanhedrin* 106b. Our text reads הקב"ה instead of רחמנא but Rashi appears to have had רחמנא, and, when cited, this is the prevalent text.

[8] *Bereshit Rabbah*, 44:1; familiarized by Maimonides, *Guide* 3.26, and Naḥmanides, Deut. 22:6.

[9] The ordinary, and more literal, interpretation of the *pasuk* explains בשמחה ובטוב

> self-aggrandizement on such occasions, he is both a sinner and a fool. It was this that Solomon had in mind when he uttered the words, "Glorify not thyself in the presence of the King, (Prov. 25:6)." Contrariwise, one who humbles and makes light of himself on such occasions, achieves greatness and honor, for he serves the Lord out of sheer love. This is the sentiment expressed by David, king of Israel, when he said, "And I will be yet more vile than this, and will be base in mine own sight (Sam. II 6:22)." True greatness and honor are achieved only by rejoicing before the Lord, as it is said, "King David leaping and dancing before the Lord, etc. (Sam. II 6:16)" (Laws of Lulav 8:15).

The statement stands opposed not only to the patrician critique of Mikhal,[10] royal daughter and wife, but to Appolonian restraint, or Philistine decorum, in general.

And yet we do have a problem – one which, moreover, we ignore at our peril. It may perhaps best be delineated by noting elements frequently regarded as opposed to spirituality. The spiritual is often contrasted with the material, the formal, and the intellectual[11] – all three being viewed as relatively external when compared to, in Hamlet's phrase, "that within which passeth show." Yet all three figure prominently within the halakhic order. Even pietists who trumpet

לבב ("with joyfulness and with gladness of heart"), as referring to a situation during which there had been no *avodat Hashem* whatsoever. Maimonides – followed by Rabbenu Baḥye, *ad locum*, takes it to denote a mode of service.

[10] The gravity of her remark is underscored by *Ḥazal*'s statement that her subsequent barrenness was its punishment; see BT *Sanhedrin* 21a. However, Gersonides, Sam. II, 6:20, suggests a more rational interpretation – i.e. that David's passion for her waned as a result of the incident.

[11] Of course, spirituality may assume an intellectual cast, contemplative or even discursive, in the form of *amor Dei intellectualis* or in the quest for knowing God, in accordance with David's counsel to Shlomo – ודע את א-לקי אבי ("Know the God of my father"); and, in our world, the two very different and yet related examples of Maimonides and Ḥabad spring to mind. Nevertheless, broadly speaking, spirituality is often associated with more conative and emotional modes of experience.

the priority of *ḥovot ha-levavot* acknowledge the critical role of *ḥovot ha-eivarim*. Technical *shiurim* abound in numerous areas:

> כל מדת חכמים[12] כן הוא בארבעים סאה טובל בארבעים סאה חסר קורטוב אינו יכול לטבול בהן (כתובות קד.).
>
> All the standards of the Sages are such. In [a bath of] forty *se'ah* [for instance] one may perform ritual immersion; in [a bath of] forty *se'ah* minus one *kortob* one may not perform ritual immersion (BT *Ketubot* 104a).

And, finally, the central, almost anomalous, place assigned to *Talmud Torah* hardly requires evidential prooftexts.

The potential for attenuated spirituality clearly exists, then. Our adversaries have, of course, gone further, contending that this potential has indeed been realized. From non-Jewish and from Jewish sources, the charge has been leveled since, at least, the dawn of Christianity. The critique of Pharisaism touched upon duplicity and insincerity, but at its heart – in the Pauline version, particularly – lay the broadside attack upon legalism and the juxtaposition of letter and spirit. The theme, commingled in Protestant writings with the opposition of faith and works, has reverberated since, with some contending that the lapse of halakhic Judaism is not accidental but endemic. In the modern period, this criticism has been particularly honed by existentialists. For Dostoyevsky's spokeswoman in "Notes from the Underground" as for Buber, programmed religion inevitably stultifies spirituality. For Berdyaev,[13] these stand opposed, by definition, inasmuch as normative service implies the servitude which he regards as anathema to the spiritual life.

These charges are familiar, and they have served as the focus

---

[12] The term, מדת חכמים ("standards of the Sages"), with reference to the specific example of *mikveh*, may suggest that the requirement of forty *se'ah*, for a person who can be fully immersed in less, is only *mi-di-rabbanan*, as apparently assumed by the Me'iri – M. *Mikva'ot* 2:1, 7:1; but cf. 1:7 – and possibly the Rosh, *Hilkhot Mikva'ot*, the end of sec. 1. The principle enunciated certainly applies *mi-di-oraita*, however.

[13] See, particularly, his *Slavery and Freedom*, *passim*.

of considerable polemic. Our concern, however, is not with what we say to our adversaries – we certainly are not inclined to dance to their fiddle – but with what we say to the *Ribbono shel Olam* or to ourselves. For the antinomy is real and the tension immanent. Apart from the material, formal, and intellectual factors already cited, other divisive elements might be mentioned. As Maimonides[14] noted, law is formulated with reference to the public; spirituality, by contrast, is highly personal. In a related vein, law is, by definition, normative, and, hence, objective, while the spiritual is presumably subjective, and more contextually oriented. Above all, while *halakhah* may be perceived as constraint – it establishes a floor for the religious life and both provides a basis and points a direction for progress towards the attainment of values, moral and religious – it may also be seen as imposing a ceiling; as clipping the wings of soaring aspiration. This sense is perhaps most keenly felt within the modern context. The backdrop of much current spirituality is, after all, Romanticism; and the Romantics were, both deeply subjective – art was, for them, not so much descriptive mimesis as self-expression – and, as T.E. Hulme[15] complained, persistently expansive.

Given the dichotomy, our message and our challenge is clear. We shall abandon neither the normative nor the experiential pole. On the one hand, as committed Jews, we have neither the right nor the desire to reject *halakhah*. We know that it is the fountainhead of collective *Yahadut* – initiating with שם שם לו חק ומשפט ("There He made for them a statute and an ordinance") at Marah,[16] and culminating in the covenantal commitment at Sinai and Arvot Moav. It is the essence of national existence within our homeland – ראה למדתי אתכם חקים ומשפטים כאשר צוני ה׳ אלקי לעשות כן בקרב הארץ אשר אתם באים שמה

[14] See *Guide* 3.34.

[15] See his essay, "Romanticism and Classicism"; reprinted in *Criticism: The Major Texts*, ed. W.J. Bate (New York: Harcourt, Brace, 1952), pp. 564–73.

[16] Exodus 15:25. Rashi, following the *gemara* in BT *Sanhedrin* 56b – with respect to the general concept, although the details vary – explains that the *mizvot* commanded at Marah were an earnest of subsequent Torah, part of which was revealed earlier. However, Naḥmanides, *ad locum*, contends that, *al derekh ha-peshat*, the *ḥok u-mishpat* in question were civil and moral ordinances, אינם חקי התורה והמשפטים אבל

לרשתה ("Behold I have taught you statutes and ordinances, even as the Lord my God commanded me, that ye should do so in the midst of the land whither ye go in to possess it") – and not only there. It is, equally, the linchpin of personal *avodat Hashem*. אי אתה בן חורין להיבטל הימנה ("you are not free to withdraw from it") – but even if one were, there is no inclination. A Jew certainly experiences the *Ribbono shel Olam* as Creator and Redeemer, ה' צורי וגואלי; but, first and foremost, he encounters Him as ultimate Commander, before whom he stands in servile bondage; with respect to whom, בטל רצונך מפני רצונו ("Nullify your will before His will") is the *alpha* and *omega* of religious existence. In full-throated song we wholeheartedly pronounce אנא עבדא דקודשא בריך הוא ("I am a servant of the Holy One, Blessed is He"). We are not abashed by the contrast between sonship and servitude prevalent in much Christian theology; and we are not tempted by the sirens holding out the promise of secularized humanistic Judaism, *à la* Erich Fromm's *Ye Shall Be as Gods*. We implore *avinu malkeinu*, or plead אם כבנים אם כעבדים ("whether as children or as servants"), in one breath. And we know full well that it is דבר ה' זו הלכה ("the word of God is the law") which links us, with bonds of love and awe, to our Master, and it is that which grants us ultimate freedom: אין לך בן חורין אלא מי שעוסק בתורה ("There is no freer man than one who engages in the study of the Torah").

On the other hand, we dare not, and we may not, forgo spirituality, as either value or mode. Its significance is dual. First, it ennobles and purifies human personality, as such, a quality to be admired even irrespective of specifically religious ramifications. This point was vividly brought home to me some years back when one of the Rothschilds, wholly devoid of halakhic commitment, came to visit the Rav. I asked him later how the visit had gone, and he responded, "You know, he is a spiritual person;" and I noted that this was meaningful to him.

Second, it brings a person closer to the *Ribbono shel Olam* – and, hence, to His service. As a religiously oriented individual enhances his spirituality, he becomes increasingly sensitized to the presence of *shekhinah*; and we recall that a constant sense of that presence, שויתי ה' לנגדי תמיד ("I place God before me constantly"), was posited by the Rama, in the very opening codicil of *Shulkhan Arukh Oraḥ Ḥayyim*, as an overarching principle of religious existence, כלל גדול בתורה ובמעלות הצדיקים אשר הולכים לפני האלקים ("a major principle of the Torah and among the attributes of the righteous that walk with the Lord").

What is needed, clearly, is balance; and it is that which, within the parameters of tradition, has been sought. As might have been anticipated, *a priori*, it has historically been variously formulated, within different movements or cultures and by different masters; and, at times, there has been alternation, with the pendulum, swinging between relative pietism and legalism. Some of this variety has been traced by my late brother-in-law, Professor Yitzchak Twersky *zt"l*,[17] and, most fully – albeit, by and large, from a less traditional perspective – in the two volumes, *Jewish Spirituality*, in the series on *World Spirituality*;[18] and much will surely be amplified by forthcoming papers at this Forum. The point is that we need not be surprised. On so critical an issue, should we expect, ought we prefer, uniformity? What we should seek is assurance that whatever emphasis is predicated be determined not by the weakness of the secondary factor, tepid religious experience or shallow normative consciousness, but by the strength of the dominant.

What we need, however, is more than balance, with its connotation of respective checks and equilibrium. We need mutual, genuinely reciprocal, fructification. On the one hand, the spiritual is to inform and enrich the material and the intellectual. To this end, we need to have recourse to two elements. First, we have to develop our own selves as spiritual beings. To the extent that we are sensitive, generally, we shall enhance the capacity for being sensitive, reli-

הנהגות ויישובי המדינות ("The expression does not refer to the statutes and ordinances of the Torah, but rather to the customs and ways of civilized society").

17 See his essay, "Talmudists, Philosophers, Kabbalists: The Quest for Spirituality in the Sixteenth Century," in *Jewish Thought in the Sixteenth Century*, ed. Bernard Dov Cooperman (Cambridge, MA: Harvard University Press, 1983), pp. 431–59; and, in a broader vein, "Religion and Law," in *Religion in a Religious Age*, ed. S.D. Goitein (Cambridge, MA: Association for Jewish Studies, 1974), pp. 69–82.

18 Vols. 13–14 in the series, ed. Arthur Green (New York: Crossroads, 1986–1987).

giously. Shallowness and aridity in one area leave their mark along the whole front. Secondly, we can harness specific halakhic categories. Quantitativeness is, as the Rav[19] stressed, an intrinsic feature of halakhic existence. This element is natural and understandable. It manifests itself, in part, in a concern for *shiurim*, proper units of time and space; and, in part, in awareness of the number and/or duration of *mizvah* performances. This aspect is fundamentally highly positive – although at times one finds that fretting over requisite qualification may, regrettably, drain attention from the interactive religious character of the act. However, it needs to be counterbalanced, on purely halakhic grounds, by the qualitative dimension, by awareness of not only how much we do or how many *shittot* we consider, but of how we do, as regards both the motivation and the character of performance.

To take a relatively narrow example, we might note the *gemara* in *Yoma* with respect to *keriat shema*: הקורא את שמע לא ירמוז בעיניו ולא יקרוץ בשפתותיו ולא יורה באצבעותיו ("He who reads the Shema may neither blink with his eyes, nor gesticulate with his lips, nor point with his fingers") – this being subsumed, as the Rif explains, under the rubric of the guideline cited in the *sugya* subsequently, ודברת בם עשה אותן קבע ואל תעשם עראי ("'And you shall speak of them,' – do them seriously and not casually"). Moreover, on the basis of the *Yerushalmi*,[20] Naḥmanides[21] expands the requirement for *keva* to *berakhot*, generally, this view being subsequently codified in *Shulkhan Arukh*;[22] and the concept of focused concentration can surely be applied to *mizvot* at large. To take broader categories, the qualities of *ahavah* and *yirah*, normatively obligatory at all times, should, if woven into the fabric of a halakhic performance, enrich its substance.

Naḥmanides held that the Torah itself had assigned a specific *mizvah* to the task of qualitative enhancement. Maimonides, it will

[19] See איש ההלכה – גלוי ונסתר (ירושלים: תשל"ט), עמ' 45–65.

[20] See M. *Berakhot* 2:5; זאת אומרת שאסור לעשות מלאכה בשעה שיברך, ("This means that it is forbidden to do work at the time one recites the blessings [of *Shema*]").

[21] See *Milḥamot Hashem*, BT *Berakhot* 9a (in the Rif).

[22] See *Oraḥ Ḥayyim*, 183:12, 191:3.

be recalled, interpreted ולעבדו בכל לבבכם ("serve Him with all your heart") as referring to daily *tefillah*. Naḥmanides, however, held that this obligation was only *mi-di-rabbanan*. Hence, he offers an alternative, and far more comprehensive, interpretation of the phrase and of the norm:

> ועיקר הכתוב ולעבדו בכל לבבכם מצות עשה שתהיה כל עבודתנו לא-ל יתעלה בכל לבבנו כלומר בכונה רצויה שלימה לשמו ובאין הרהור רע לא שנעשה המצות בלא כונה או על הספק אולי יש בהם תועלת כענין ואהבת את ה' א-לקיך בכל לבבך ובכל נפשך ובכל מאדך שהמצוה היא לאהוב את ה' בכל לב ולב ושנסתכן באהבתנו בנפשנו ובממוננו (ספר המצות, עשה ה').
>
> The essential meaning of the Scriptural phrase, "to serve Him with all your heart," is the positive commandment that every one of our acts of divine service be performed absolutely wholeheartedly, i.e., with the necessary full intent to perform it for the sake of His name, and without any negative thought not that we perform the commandments without proper intentionality, or only on the chance that they may bring some benefit – in the spirit of the commandment "You shall love the Lord your God with all your heart, soul and possessions" means that the commandment is to love God with the totality of our hearts, and that we should be prepared to risk our lives and possessions on account of our love. (*Sefer ha-Mizvot*, Positive Commandment 5)

I do not know to what extent the *kavvanah* demanded by Naḥmanides coincides with intentions and mindsets familiar from his own subsequent mystical tradition. But it is the overall thrust which, for our purposes, is crucial.

Other *rishonim* lacked this fulcrum. Unquestionably, however, the burden of this passage is consensual. It is, after all, implicit in the demand for *ahavah*, which ought presumably suffuse our total standing as *ovdei Hashem*. In this connection, it is important to emphasize that the contribution of spirituality to our service of God is not confined, *ad hoc*, to moments of *mizvah* performance.

It pervades our entire existence – as persons, generally, and as religious beings, specifically. The reinforcement of our spiritual aspect enhances the realization of ויהי האדם לנפש חיה ("and man became a living soul") – rendered by Onkelos as רוח ממללא ("spirit which speaks") – in the wake of ויפח באפיו נשמת חיים ("He breathed into his nostrils the breath of life"); and this realization is the basis of our standing before our Master. I presume few are today capable or desirous of striving for the spiritual level which Naḥmanides placed at the apex of *miẓvah* performance:

> והעוזבים כל עניני העולם הזה ואינם משגיחים עליו כאלו אינם בעלי גוף וכל מחשבתם וכוונתם בבוראם בלבד כענין באליהו בהדבק נפשם בשם הנכבד יחיו לעד בגופם ובנפשם כנראה בכתוב באליהו וכידוע ממנו בקבלה (ויקרא יח:ד).
>
> But those who abandon altogether the concerns of this world and pay no attention to it, acting as if they themselves were not creatures of physical being, and all their thoughts and intentions are directed only to their Creator, just as was the case of Elijah, [these people] on account of their soul cleaving to the Glorious Name will live forever in body and soul, as is evidenced in Scripture concerning Elijah and as is known of him in tradition…(Leviticus 18:4).

Rightly or wrongly, this otherworldly strain does not resonate well with modern readers, of almost every ilk. But acknowledgement of the fact that spirituality, as a quality of soul, is likely to bring even the average person closer to the *Ribbono shel Olam* can and ought to be widespread.

Conversely, *halakhah* enriches spirituality; and this, in at least two major respects. First, its prescribed forms and technicalities, while undoubtedly constraining, and meant to constrain, in one sense, are liberating in another. With respect to many *miẓvot* mandated procedure frees the individual from groping for means to flesh out a ritual initiative, and enables him to pour all of his spiritual energies into the religious experience proper.

As a case in point, we may briefly examine prayer. Votaries of spirituality complain frequently about the standardized text of the *siddur* and lament the devaluation which has occurred, historically, in the institution of voluntary *tefillat nedavah* or in the impetus toward innovative *ḥiddush davar* in compulsory prayer. The lament is understandable. In some cases, standardization does indeed undermine the inwardness which constitutes the essence of prayer, and this tendency surely needs to be resisted. There is, however, another side to the coin. With reference to Rabbi Eliezer's statement in the Mishnah in *Berakhot*, העושה תפלתו קבע אין תפלתו תחנונים (כח:) ("One who makes his prayers rote; his prayers do not constitute pleas"), the *gemara* seeks to define *keva*; and, *inter alia*, cites the joint response of Rabba and Rav Yosef: כל שאינו יכול לחדש בה דבר (כט:) ("Whoever is not able to insert something fresh in it"). This is, presumably, a manifesto for spirituality in *tefillah*. Yet, the *gemara* immediately cites Rav Zeira's comment: אנא יכילנא לחדושי בה מילתא ומסתפינא דלמא מטרידנא ("I can insert something fresh, but I am afraid to do so for fear I should become preoccupied") – presumably, not only as a biographical tidbit, but as a general caveat and guideline. Maimonides' formulation that uniformity in *berakhot* was instituted in order that:

> שיהיו ערוכות בפי הכל וילמדו אותן ותהיה תפלת אלו העלגים תפלה שלימה כתפלת בעלי הלשון הצחה (תפלה א:ד),
> an orderly form would be in everyone's mouth, so that all should learn the standardized prayer, and thus the prayer of those who were not expert in speech would be as perfect as that of those who had command of a chaste style (Laws of Prayer 1:4),

is relevant not only as concerns those who can barely express themselves but, equally, with respect to anyone who has difficulty in formulating and experiencing simultaneously.

And the same may be suggested, *mutatis mutandis*, with respect to some other *mizvot*. How much spiritual energy would be wasted every *seder* night, if one had to improvise the evening's structure and content, even if it were done in advance? How much distraction from the experiential substance of *yom teruah* would ensue if we had to invent anew the texts and themes of the day's prayers and *teki'ot* every Rosh Hashanah? The *halakhah* has entitled us by confronting us with the existent and demanding that we cope with its challenges.

Secondly, however, the contribution of *halakhah* to spirituality extends beyond the removal of barriers or the diversion of energy from one task to another. It consists, primarily, in a positive and substantive vein, in bonding ourselves to its Author, in deepening and intensifying our relation to the *Ribbono shel Olam*. Encounter with Him and His will in every area, almost at every step; attention riveted upon understanding and implementing His directives; awareness of His pervasive presence in all walks of life; the constant challenge to free, and yet obedient, decision – all of these impact significantly upon our religious being and upon our link to *shekhinah*. That link, in turn, impacts profoundly upon our total spiritual life.

Admittedly, however, while this interactive reciprocal fructification exists at the general plane, its realization at the personal level requires some effort. The key is an awareness, in-depth awareness, of one critical point. We have spoken of the confrontation and possible conflict of law and spirituality in general terms; and, indeed, in the abstract, the specter of legalism looms large. However, as committed Jews, we do not regard the issue abstractly, and we do not deal with *a* legal system. We deal with *devar Hashem*, with divine will as expressed in ordinances and incorporated in *the* legal order of *halakhah*. When this fact is fully absorbed and integrated, we sense that we do not just encounter a codex but a vivifying presence; that vitalism and dynamism derive from clinging to our Commander and Legislator – ואתם הדבקים בה' א-לקיכם חיים כלכם היום ("You who cleave to God your Lord, you are all living today"); that He, and, derivatively, His revealed will, is the wellspring of effervescence, מקור מים חיים ("the source of living waters"); and that, consequently, divine law and human spirituality can interact positively within our own selves. However, where this conviction is jaded, and awareness of the transcendental character of *halakhah* superficial, the sense of conflict may penetrate.

Of course, recognition of the uniqueness of *halakhah* as *devar*

Hashem does not necessarily assure the strain of interactive balance I would encourage. If illustration be necessary, I might cite – on the authority of a person whose veracity I consider unimpeachable – a story concerning a certain *adam gadol*. On one of the *yamim noraim*, he (out of deference, I omit his identity) noticed that one of his sons stood for *Shemoneh Esreih* considerably longer than he had. He approached him, and asked to see his *maḥzor*. Upon leafing through it, he observed laconically: "Strange, we both have the identical text, and yet it takes you so much longer." I have the highest regard for the person in question – *kotano avah mimotnai*; but the story is chilling. Without this recognition, the problem is greatly exacerbated, however.

The Rav *zt"l* was keenly – and, at times, painfully – aware of this problem. The awareness is already very much in evidence in *Ish ha-Halakhah*. He knew fully the critique leveled at the world of Brisk – particularly, in Y.L. Pereẓ's "Bein Shnei Harim" – as being coldly aspiritual; and, in a work idealizing its tradition, he takes up the cudgels in response.

> האם משולל הוא איש ההלכה? כל אותה התפארת של החוויה הדתית הגועשת והסוערת הבוערת בלבת אש קודש, שאיש הדת האכסטטי רגיל בה?...הפועם רגש של כמיהה ועריגה לה' בנשמתו של איש ההלכה?
> Is halakhic man devoid of the splendor of that raging and tempestuous sacred, religious experience that so typifies the ecstatic *homo religiosus*? … Is it possible for halakhic man to achieve such emotional exaltation that all his thought and senses ache and pine for the living God?

And his reply is unequivocal:

> איש ההלכה מוכשר וראוי להתמכר לחוויה דתית נאדרה בקודש, על כל צביונה ושיכלולה. ברם ההתלהבות הדתית הכבירה באה אליו אחרי ההכרה, אחרי שרכש לו כבר ידיעה בעולם האידיאלי של ההלכה ובבואתו בעולם הריאלי. ומתוך שחוויה זו באה אחרי ביקורת חריפה והסתכלות עמוקה וחודרת, הרי היא גדולה ביותר.[23]

[23] איש ההלכה – גלוי ונסתר, עמ' 74.

> Halakhic man is worthy and fit to devote himself to a majestic religious experience in all its uniqueness, with all its delicate shades and hues. However, for him such a powerful, exalted experience only follows upon cognition, only occurs after he has acquired knowledge of the *a priori*, ideal halakhah and its reflected image in the real world. But since this experience occurs after rigorous criticism and profound penetrating reflection, it is that much more intensive.[24]

Educationally, however, this sequential approach seems neither feasible nor desirable. It is, at best, suited for only an elite coterie.[25] Subsequently, in any event, as his pedagogic experience expanded, some of the Rav's early confidence waned and gave way to a sharper sense of the difficulties involved as well as to a measure of frustration. His basic faith in the interaction of *halakhah* and spirituality, and his personal quest to attain and to inculcate it, never wavered. But he recognized increasingly that the path was tortuous and that if the goal were to be attained, significant effort would need to be invested.

I have discussed, primarily, the possibly corrosive impact of halakhic living upon spirituality, and of the need to address the issue. We need, however, to be no less sensitive to the reverse – the dangers posed by a bent for spirituality upon full Torah commitment. These dangers are multiple. First, there is the possibility that a thirst for the spiritual will issue in disdain for what is perceived to be non-spiritual. The latter might be "pure" *Talmud Torah*, dismissed either out of anti-intellectualism, or out of passionate moral and religious fervor. In this connection, one of course recalls the polemical preface to *Ḥovot ha-Levavot* – parts of which, incidentally, Reb Hayim Brisker did not hesitate to brand as *apikorsos*.[26] Or it might be rote and shallow performance of *mizṿot*. The outcry against *mizṿat*

---

[24] *Halakhic Man*, trans. Lawrence Kaplan (Philadelphia: Jewish Publication Society, 1983), pp. 82–3.

[25] The question of broad application hovers over the essay, generally, but especially so with respect to this point.

[26] This was related to me by the Rav.

anashim melumadah has, of course, been the staple of pietists and moralists throughout the generations; and, in the modern era, it has united the *mussar* movement and *Ḥasidut*. However, its impact may be a two-edged sword. At the personal level, it may inspire more spiritual observance; or, it may, contrarily, lead one to abandon observance entirely, inasmuch as technical performance is deemed meaningless anyway. And, at the interpersonal plane, it may lead to demeaning the ordinary Jew, routinely but tepidly enacting his halakhic commitment. There is, to be sure, a democratic streak in certain spiritual movements – in Romanticism, generally, and in *Ḥasidut*, particularly: appreciation, if not idealization, of the child, the untutored, even the simpleton, and their naive faith. However, these may also engender an aristocracy of their own. Rousseau's or Chateaubriand's admiration for the primitive and their contempt of the *bourgeois* were two sides of the same coin.

We, as committed Jews, cannot, however, dismiss "mere" observance. Quite apart from the mystical quality ascribed to a *miẓvah* by the *Nefesh ha-Ḥayyim*, the impact upon the personal Jew and his modicum of *avodat Hashem* remains significant. Back in the nineteen-sixties, Professor Twersky addressed a student body at Yeshiva University and argued that, if forced to choose between Mendelssohn's adogmatic ritual observance and Buber's non-halakhic spirituality, he would opt for the former. At the time, I challenged this thesis, contending that a ritual act, wholly devoid of a faith infrastructure,[27] entailed neither a *maasseh miẓvah* nor a *kiyum miẓvah*. I abide by that position; but, if we are dealing not with adogmatic observance but with superficial, and yet belief-based, action, we cannot delegitimize it.

A second danger, already noted *en passant*, pertains to attitudes toward the material. As secularism serves as a leveling ideology in one vein – it recognizes no ultimate difference between times, places, persons, or objects – so spirituality can democratize in another. Where the focus upon spiritual essence is exaggerated,

[27] Whether indeed Mendelssohn went so far in his rejection of any normative duty to believe, I do not here presume to ascertain. The discussion at the time was predicated upon the assumption that this was the case.

the danger of minimizing material halakhic status increases. This is of particular relevance with respect to the land of Yisrael. One recalls the stir raised here a decade ago by remarks attributed to the Lubavitcher Rebbe, that while *olotekha u-shelamekha* could only be offered in the *beit ha-mikdash, aliyotekha u-shelemutekha* could be attained universally.

Somewhat akin to this factor, lurks a third danger – perhaps best noted by reference to the *issur* of *sheḥutei huẓ*. The prohibition against slaughtering and offering sacrifices anywhere but in *mikdash* appears in the Torah twice – but in very different contexts and, presumably, with different import. In *Re'eih*, in accordance with a dominant motif of that *parshah*, it is related to enshrining *beit ha-beḥirah*, wherever it may be, as the unique locus of sacrificial worship:

> השמר לך פן תעלה עלתיך בכל מקום אשר תראה. כי אם במקום אשר יבחר ה׳ באחד שבטיך שם תעלה עלתיך ושם תעשה כל אשר אנכי מצוך (דברים יב:יג–יד).
>
> Take heed that you do not offer your burnt offerings at every place that you see; but at the place which the Lord will choose in one of your tribes, there you shall offer your burnt offerings, and there you shall do all that I am commanding you (Deuteronomy 12:13–14).

That status would be impaired by diversification and the existence of competing centers; hence, evidently, the proscription.[28] In *Aḥarei Mot*, on the other hand, *sheḥitat huẓ* is forbidden in order to avoid continued drift to the worship of alien spiritual entities; ולא יזבחו עוד את זבחיהם לשעירם אשר הם זונים אחריהם (ויקרא יז:ז) ("They shall no longer sacrifice their sacrifices unto the satyrs, after whom they go astray"). That heretofore prevalent practice verging upon idolatry is henceforth interdicted.[29]

[28] The incessant and unsuccessful battle (רק הבמות לא סרו, "only from the high altars they did not desist") against local altars during the period of *bayit rishon* presumably revolved around this issue.

[29] This point is reflected in a comment which appears in *Vayikra Rabbah, ad locum,*

Spirituality, analogously, poses a potential threat on both fronts. First, its creative and dynamic aspect may exert a centrifugal thrust, issuing in alternative modes of religious experience and expression which, if insufficiently integrated, may rival normative categories. Secondly, the spiritual impulse may be adulterated, religion becoming tinged with superstition or vestigial magic, spirituality degenerating into spiritualism or its equivalent.

Finally, alongside the religious, there looms a moral danger. Excessive spirituality, possibly tinged by otherworldliness, may lead to averting one's gaze from mere material suffering. We are, of course, enjoined to emulate the *Ribbono shel Olam*, המגביהי לשבת, המשפילי לראות בשמים ובארץ ("Who is enthroned on high yet deigns to look down upon heaven and earth"); but the lesson of Rav Yoḥanan's familiar observation כל מקום שאתה מוצא גבורתו של הקב"ה אתה מוצא ענוותנותו (מגילה לא.) ("Wherever you find the greatness of the Holy One, Blessed be He, there you find His humility" [BT *Megillah* 31a]), can be all too easily lost. And inordinate spirituality may accelerate that loss.

I regard none of this as cause for discarding spirituality. It remains an indispensable component of the religious life. These

---

to the effect that *korbanot* were to serve as a means of weaning the community away from idolatry:

> לפי שהיו ישראל להוטים אחר עבודת כוכבים במצרים והיו מביאים קרבניהם לשעירים...והיו מקריבין קרבניהם באיסור במה ופורעניות באה עליהם אמר הקב"ה יהיו מקריבין לפני בכל עת קרבנותיהן באהל מועד והן נפרשין מעבודת כוכבים והם ניצולים (כב:ח).
>
> Because Israel were passionate followers after idolatry in Egypt and used to bring their sacrifices to the satyrs...and they used to offer their sacrifices in the forbidden high places, on account of which punishments used to come upon them, the Holy One, blessed be He said: "Let them offer their sacrifices to me at all times in the Tent of Meeting, and thus they will be separated from idolatry and be saved from punishment," (22:8).

The phrase, באיסור במה (in the forbidden high places) is puzzling, but I presume that it, too, refers to the *issur* of *avodah zarah*. It might be noted that this text was cited by the Maharam Al Askar, as a possible source for Maimonides' rationale for *korbanot* in his *Guide*, 3.32, 3.46. See *She'eilot u-Teshuvot Maharam Al Askar*, sec. 117, p. 302.

are, however, reasons for nurturing and honing it carefully; and, together with the caveats against arid legalism, constitute an overriding challenge for optimal personal realization in the quest for integrated *avodat Hashem*. If we had to decide between pallid normative observance and non-halakhic spiritual dynamism we would, as commanded beings, unhesitatingly, albeit regretfully, opt for the former. But does anyone imagine that the *Ribbono shel Olam* confronts us with such a cruel choice? Our aim, duty and aspiration both, is the conjunction of spiritualized *halakhah* and disciplined spirituality; the fusion which enables us to realize the poetry and prose of ideal Jewish existence.

The topic of this paper, as well as of this conference, is, in every sense, timeless. Yet it bears, additionally, a clear immediate relevance, in light of the recent upsurge in spirituality within the Western world, generally, and our own Jewish sector, particularly. I take it this was a factor in the choice of the topic and, hence, that, in conclusion, I should presumably address myself – with specific reference to the Jewish scene – to the current scene somewhat. I must confess that I cannot claim extensive intimate contact with the phenomenon, but I trust that I can nonetheless address myself to several significant issues regarding it.

The most palpable manifestation of this movement, in public perception, is exuberance and enthusiasm – particularly, within the context of prayer. Songfests, midnight dancing, Carlebach *kabbalat Shabbat* – these are among the hallmarks. In seeking to assess this development, I am convinced that, on the whole, its effect has been salutary – especially in the lay community. The verve and the excitement felt by many in the course of more visibly "soul"-oriented *tefillah* stand in marked contrast to the pallor and desiccation which characterized many *batei knesset* a decade ago. Carping critics sometimes object that the vibrant hour of *kabbalat Shabbat* is, for many, merely a faddish island within an otherwise tepid and possibly "yuppie" existence. Possibly. I have no way of judging; and who has designated me to evaluate the depth of other people's sincerity? Be this as it may, an island is also not to be lightly dismissed; and, beyond that, I find it difficult to believe that the interlude leaves no imprint upon the totality of personal spirituality.

When I gave vent to this evaluation in Jerusalem recently, some listeners responded with a measure of surprise. "*Et tu, Brute*?" They needn't. In a talk before a group of *rabbanim* close to twenty years ago, entitled, by way of adaptation, "Spirit and Spirituality," I stressed the need for a much greater injection of *ruaḥ* – within our educational institutions, particularly. Again, in an address before the Educators Council of America in 1985 – recently disseminated by the Israel Koschiẓky Virtual Beit Midrash of Yeshivat Har Etzion – I stated: "I spoke before about a passionate concern for Torah. The key, indeed, is the passion – passion which is important in its own right as a component of *avodat Hashem*, and passion which holds the key to the development of other components.... In order to attain that, we, as educators, should be ready to sacrifice – and even sacrifice considerably – a measure of objective intellectual accomplishment." I have since recurred to this theme, periodically; so I feel perfectly consistent in asserting that, for the bulk of the purveyors and participants of current spirituality, the net religious result is indeed positive.

There are, however, several reservations – some, major. First, as regards the perception of spirituality. We are all in favor of enthusiasm and would find it difficult to believe that, in the age of Locke and Shaftesbury, the term had negative associations. However, we must beware of conditioning our definition or conception of spirituality upon enthusiam and its external expression. Does anyone question the spirituality of George Fox and his quietist Quakers? Is Byron more spiritual than Wordsworth – the Wordsworth who defined poetry as "emotion recollected in tranquility;" he who taught us to approve "the depth and not the tumult of the soul;" he who could attest, in concluding the "Ode on the Intimation of Immortality," "To me the meanest flower that blows can give / Thoughts that do often lie too deep for tears?" On the contrary, nothing is more unspiritual than confining the world of the spirit to its outward expression, to *Sturm und Drang* at any level. Was not this part of the message of the famous counsel of Carlyle, the patron-saint of Victorian spirituality, "Close thy Byron, open thy Goethe?"

Second, the question of the balance of innovation and tradition needs to be carefully considered. I am not certain as to whether or how far the Rama's dictum, ואל ישנה אדם ממנהג העיר אפילו בניגונים או בפיוטים שאומרים שם (או"ח תריט:א) ("A person should not deviate from the local custom – even in the matter of the particular tunes or liturgical poems that are traditionally recited there [*Oraḥ Ḥayyim* 619:1]") applies to ordinary daily or Shabbat prayer. After all, the Rama waited until *Hilkhot Yom ha-Kippurim* to pronounce it. But the issue as such, relating not only to the *niggunim* but to the overall atmosphere of *tefillah* and its locus, needs to be confronted, judiciously and sensitively.

The more critical concerns lie, however, beyond the purview of the practical aspects of conduct in the *beit ha-knesset*, and touch upon major cruces, especially as they impinge upon the *dati le-umi* Torah community. By way of example, in one of the more "spiritual" *yeshivot hesder*, the assembled *ẓibbur* burst into dance in the midst of *tefillat Yom Kippur*. It was subsequently explained that – and the rationale is even more perturbing than the event – inasmuch as they dance on *Simḥat Torah*, why differentiate. Clearly, whoever can offer such a rationale has no idea of the genuine import of *Yom Kippur* – and probably also has no idea of the import of *Simḥat Torah*. Surely, he has erased from his consciousness the *gemara's* explanation for the omission of *hallel* on *yamim noraim*:

> אמר רבי אבהו אמרו מלאכי השרת לפני הקב"ה רבש"ע מפני מה אין ישראל אומרים שירה לפניך בר"ה וביום הכפורים אמר להם אפשר מלך יושב על כסא דין וספרי חיים וספרי מתים פתוחין לפניו וישראל אומרים שירה (ר"ה לב:).
>
> R. Abbahu stated: The ministering angels said in the Presence of the Holy One, blessed be He: Sovereign of the Universe, why should Israel not chant hymns of praise before Thee on New Year and the Day of Atonement? He replied to them: Is it possible that the King should be sitting on the throne of

> justice with the books of life and death open before Him, and Israel should chant hymns of praise? (BT *Rosh ha-Shanah* 32b).

In this instance, not the halakhic calendar but personal inclination dictated the day's mood.

Even more seriously, misguided spirituality distorts *Talmud Torah*. In another yeshiva, students are encouraged to adopt, as do their masters, quasi-mystical interpretations for apparent halakhic discussions in the *gemara*. And this, in the name of a presumably spiritual quest for *penimiyut ha-Torah*. Spatial metaphors regarding what is higher, deeper, or inner are used congenially to suggest a greater degree of truth, value, or sanctity which the method presumes to attain. The spiritual impulse in this connection is dual. Spiritually, advocates of Maimonides' rejection of literal anthropomorphism admire it for two reasons. First, it issues in a purer conception of divinity, as opposed to grosser renderings. Quite apart from the result, however, there is a strain of spirituality in the process. A metaphorical or allegorical reading is not so fettered or shackled by the text, and relatively untrammeled imagination can be brought to bear upon its explication. Here, too, analogously both elements are at work. A *penimi* analysis of שנים אוחזין בטלית or שור שנגח את הפרה enables one to soar far above the dull sublunary sphere of garments and cattle to a firmament of celestial reality. Second, the liberating enterprise, *per se*, by dint of its very nature, provides an exhilarating stimulus. For those who countenance the validity of these insights, *ashrei ha-maamin*. But those of us who were trained to deal with halakhic *realia* in their own terms, are chagrined by the harnessing of misconceived spirituality, in order, literally, לגלות פנים בתורה שלא כהלכה ("to produce an interpretation of Torah that is contrary to *halakhah*").

Most serious, however, are the dangers which lurk in a relatively abstract realm. Religious spirituality expresses itself, primarily, in two areas. The first, at which we have already glanced, is that of forms of worship and modes of expression. The second is focus upon the nature and degree of adhesion and linkage to the transcendental order, in general, and to the *Ribbono shel Olam*, in particular. In its more extreme form, this tendency is reflected in various mystical traditions, particularly Oriental ones. In a lesser vein, however, it remains a significant component of more moderate religious outlooks.

Per se, the aspiration for linkage is of course positive, provided that awareness of the absolute chasm separating man from his Creator is not jaded. Where the sense of the "wholly other" is eroded, the striving for fusion can become highly dangerous, even more so from a Jewish perspective than from a Christian one. The Gaon's critique of the *Tanya*, in this respect, is familiar; and it is paralleled by Barth's rejection of Schleiermacher's Romantic theology. The natural bent of spirituality in religion very often expresses itself, however, precisely in diminishing the sense of chasm and engendering a feeling of familiarity. Of many of its votaries, particularly in the current vogue, one might invoke the *gemara*'s rhetorical query, חב־רותא כלפי שמיא? (ברכות לד.) ("Can one behave familiarly with Heaven?" [BT *Berakhot* 34a]).

In seeking to trace the roots of our current spiritual vogue, we should no doubt look, in part, to some universal factors, inasmuch as the phenomenon extends beyond our borders. However, if we should focus upon insular sources, particularly within the *dati le-umi* community here in Israel, unquestionably the figure of Rav Kook[30] would loom prominently. His personality and his writings have left an indelible imprint upon that community, and reinvigorated spirituality is surely part of his patrimony, as it was central to his life and works; and for this we are all in his debt. Some would contend that he is also, unwittingly, responsible for some of the excesses. I do not feel qualified to judge; but it is a fact that those whom I would regard as having gone overboard regard themselves as his progeny. Be this as it may, it is essential that we grasp the seriousness of this issue.

---

[30] A recent collection of essays surveying various aspects of Rav Kook's thought was entitled, *Rabbi Abraham Isaac Kook and Jewish Spirituality*, ed. Lawrence Kaplan and David Shatz (New York: New York University Press, 1995). See, especially, the essays by Jerome I. Gellman, "Poetry of Spirituality," and Norman Lamm, "Harmonism, Novelty, and the Sacred in the Teachings of Rav Kook."

We are not just dealing with some moot theological abstraction. At issue is the character of man's relation to the *Ribbono shel Olam*. Much of what now passes for spirituality implicitly presses for the demotion of *yirah* in the interest of *ahavah*. C.S. Lewis has somewhere observed that most people don't want a Father in Heaven, but rather a Grandfather. Some would prefer a mate. This, for traditional *Yahadut*, is critical. This is hardly the place to examine this crucial issue in depth, but one point needs to be clarified emphatically. To be sure, Ḥazal decried the inferiority of *avodah mi-yirah*, but never *yirah* itself. As a motive for the religious life and the performance of *miẓvot* in general, love is pre-eminent; but as an integral component of the inner religious life, as one aspect of man's experience of God and his relation to Him, fear or awe takes its place alongside love. The selfsame Maimonides who, in the concluding chapter of *Sefer Mada* denigrates *avodah mi-yirah*, posits reverential awe in the second chapter of that treatise as a positive commandment; and he goes so far as to state that *ahavah* and *yirah* can jointly spring from the same contemplative experience. Indeed, one might suggest, without paradox, that one could fulfill the *miẓvah* of *yirah*, impelled by *ahavah*.

It is entirely possible that, even as specific *miẓvot*, love is superior to fear or even awe; and this is perhaps suggested by Naḥmanides'[31] celebrated explanation of why *assei doḥeh lo ta'asseh* ("a positive commandment overrides a negative one"), or by Maimonides'[32] statement that practical *miẓvot* were intended to engender *yirah* and the

---

[31] See his comment on *Exodus* 20:8:

ולכן מצות עשה גדולה ממצות לא תעשה כמו שאהבה גדולה מהיראה כי המקיים
ועושה בגופו ובממונו רצון אדוניו הוא גדול מהנשמר מעשות הרע בעיניו.

It is for this reason that a positive commandment is greater than a negative commandment, just as love is greater than fear, for he who fulfills and observes the will of his Master with his body and his possessions is greater than he who guards himself from doing that which is not pleasing to Him.

It is noteworthy that the discussion is placed within the context, and with reference to the categories of servitude.

[32] See *Guide*, 3.52.

philosophic knowledge communicated by the Torah to instill *ahavah*. However, the place of *yirah* as a cardinal aspect of our normative religious life is beyond question. It constituted the central motif of *maamad har Sinai*; in *Ḥazal*, religious commitment is generally denominated *yirat shamayim*; and we say daily, ויחד לבבנו לאהבה וליראה את שמך ("unite our hearts to love and fear Your name").

I'm afraid, however, that votaries of current spirituality often tend to erode the status of *yirah*; and, together with it, the status of the very essence of *Yahadut*: *kabbalat ol malkhut shamayim* and *kabbalat ol miẓvot*. In Israel today, in certain circles much is heard of *hitḥabrut*, as linkage, but little of *hitḥayvut*, as obligation. Only recently, I heard of the Bar Miẓvah of the son of a local spiritually inclined rabbi, at which the homiletic parlance was suffused with linkage and self-realization but nary a word about yoke or bondage. Or to take a published example, what is one to make of the following affirmation by Rav Shagar, regarded as bearing affinity to current spiritual circles:

> האמונה בהלכה, כמו גם אמונת חכמים בהקשר זה, אינה נובעת בהכרח מכך שיש לי הוכחה שהם היו החכמים הכי חכמים. מקורה בסוג של אינטימיות – התורה והיהדות זה אני! הבחירה שלי בעצמי היא בחירה בתורה, במסורת. לא לחנם הביעו חכמים במדרשים רבים את אהבתם לתורה במטפורות הלקוחות מחיי איש ואשתו. הכרה זו, שבפי חז"ל נקראת קבלת עול מלכות שמים נותנת את האופציה למגע עם האין־סוף, בהיותה מוחלטת וראשונית.[33]
>
> Belief in the *halakhah*, like the belief in the Sages in this connection, does not necessarily derive from being sure that these sages were the wisest. Rather, its source is a kind of intimacy: Torah and Judaism – this is I! My choice of myself *is* the choice of Torah, of tradition. Not for nought did the Sages, in so many *midrashim*, express their love of Torah through the metaphor of conjugal life. This realization – which the sages term "the acceptance of the yoke of Heaven" – affords

[33] Cited from an extensive interview with him, published in *De'ot*, 3 (February, 1999; שבט, תשנ"ט), p. 12.

> the possibility of contact with the Infinite, in that it is absolute and primal.

And to think that this exercise in narcissism is to be equated with *kabbalat ol malkhut shamayim*!

Still more worrisome – hopefully atypical, but still a chilling straw in the wind – I found a conversation to which I was recently privy. Towards the end of a wedding of a *ḥatan* from a markedly spiritual yeshiva – during which the dancing proceeded with admirable gusto – I overheard one of his peers confidently reassure another:

> בעצם, אתה לא צריך לקנא בא-לקים, מפני שאתה הוא. רק החלק שבנו שעושה רע אינגו א-לקים; אשר לכל השאר, אתה הוא.
>
> Actually, you don't have to envy God, because *you are He*. Only the part of us that does evil is not God. As for the rest, you are He!

I may not be quoting verbatim, but the citation is close to that; and the substance of the remarks is utterly accurate. I was confronted by the obvious question: Was there any connection between the gusto and the blasphemy, no less grievous for being innocent? I am convinced that there is no necessary link, but cannot be certain about specific cases; and this leaves room not only for thought but for concern.

We are confronted, then, with significant difficulties. The benefits of the current wave of spirituality are many and diverse; and, if such matters can be quantified, I repeat that, on balance, they outweigh the reverses even within our own Orthodox camp. However, some of its manifestations – particularly, ideological flotsam and jetsam – are truly worrisome; and with these we need to cope.

This brings us, finally, back to our primary problem: How to attain optimal fusion of divine law and human spirituality, committed to both while eschewing neither. We live by the serene faith that it can be done. We refuse to believe that we are doomed to choose between arid formalism and unbridled sensibility. We reject both Leibowitz and Buber. But that faith needs to be energized, and to that end, we need to harness effort and commitment. The apocryphal remark attributed to an anonymous *ḥasid*, מתנגדים דאוונען נישט – אין צייט; חסידים דאוונען – נישט אין צייט ("*Mitnaggedim* pray not – but on time; Ḥasidim pray – but not on time") – is both facile and tendentious. It is also false. It is our mission to assure that legists and spiritualists both pray – on time.

Section two

Spirituality Across Intellectual History – Ancient Period

2

Jewish Spirituality in the Bible and Second Temple Literature

Lawrence H. Schiffman

INTRODUCTION

The topic this paper seeks to investigate can theoretically be understood in various ways. Whatever approach may be taken to this topic, it is a given that the "spiritual," in any phase of the history of Judaism, must be intimately related to the commandments which stand at the center of Jewish life.[1] These commandments, in all periods of Jewish history, ought to be seen as the platform upon which the spiritual or religious experience must be built. What we seek to understand is how the spiritual dimensions of meaning or significance impact on the individual Jew as he or she participates in a variety of religious or

[1] Cf. G. Scholem, *On the Kabbalah and its Symbolism,* trans. R. Mannheim (New York: Schocken, 1965), pp. 5–31.

even mundane activities. We hope to show that the spiritual aspects of Jewish life are deeply imbedded in the biblical tradition, and that these same trends were continued into Second Temple times and further developed, thus forming an essential aspect of the conceptual framework that is evident in classical rabbinic literature.

But such a study requires that we attempt to better define what we mean by "spirituality." Let me try my hand, in the hope that my definition can serve as the basis for the paper that follows:

Jewish spirituality involves the quest for a meaningful religious life, involving both the distinctive belief system and required halakhic observances which together constitute the authentic Jewish experience. The quest for spiritual fulfillment in a Jewish context is an attempt to experience a connection with the divine through the application of theological beliefs to the observance of the commandments and to all phases of daily life. It is the self-transcending aspect of our Jewish life, in which we attempt to develop greater and greater sensitivity to the presence of God as it can be manifested in ourselves, our community, the Jewish people, our fellow humans, and the natural world. The true seeker of the spiritual will necessarily feel a sense of progress in his or her religious life as it becomes increasingly transcendent.[2]

This working definition should make clear that we do not intend to treat here the complex phenomenon of biblical prophecy or the nature of mystical experience, which in the Bible are overlapping categories but which are clearly separate in Second Temple times. Prophecy and mysticism are essentially elite phenomena which represent a bridging, to some extant, of the gap between humans and God. In prophecy, the bridge is traversed by God who searches out His creatures with whom He seeks to communicate.[3] In mysticism, it is lowly mankind that attempts to transcend its earthly existence

[2] Contrast A.E. McGrath, *Christian Spirituality* (Oxford: Blackwell, 1999), pp. 1–7 which deals also with the differences between spirituality and mysticism.

[3] A.J. Heschel, *The Prophets* (Philadelphia: Jewish Publication Society, 1962), pp. 439–46.

and come closer to God.[4] We seek, however, to investigate the religious – better, spiritual – paths that are open to average Jews and which form the core of their religious life.

This "spirituality" is what Max Kadushin called "normal mysticism," by which he meant the average Jew's experience of God.[5] This experience he saw as private and incommunicable to some extent. In his view, the experience of God takes place through belief in fundamental Jewish concepts and practices which endow with holiness our everyday existence. Such experiences of God are non-theurgic in character and are tied to ritual occasions.

While such experiences are available to all Jews, some individuals will have greater appreciation of the divine. But an awareness of God is expected to be attained by all Jews. One of the functions of *halakhah,* in his view, is to level the playing field, making such experiences available to every Jew – not only to the elite.[6]

"SPIRIT" IN BIBLICAL AND SECOND TEMPLE LITERATURE

Spirituality is seen by some as a foreign import into traditional Jewish discourse, probably because of its trendy nature in our society. But in fact, it has deep roots in biblical tradition. Let us not forget that the medieval term *ruḥaniut* ("spirituality," as opposed to *gashmiut,* "materiality") has as its basis the use of *ruaḥ,* "spirit," in the Bible and later Jewish literature. This aspect, as we hope to show, is intimately connected with the manner in which the Bible describes the non-physical aspects of the human being.

This is an area that has been greatly misunderstood. It is commonplace in most modern scholarly literature to state that the biblical person was a corporate entity, and that there is no division of

[4] G. Scholem, *Major Trends in Jewish Mysticism* (New York: Schocken, 1941), pp. 3–14.

[5] M. Kadushin, *The Rabbinic Mind* (New York: Jewish Theological Seminary of America, 1952), p. 194.

[6] Kadushin, pp. 201–14.

body and soul in the Bible.[7] Such a division is said to exist only in Second Temple literature, and is said to be due to Hellenistic influence. Whereas the notion of a body/soul duality – in which body and soul vie for control over one another – is indeed Hellenistic, the notion of a spiritual aspect of the corporate person is already very clear in biblical times.

A variety of biblical passages testify to the notion that the soul is an entity in and of itself. The soul itself (*nefesh*) was assumed to be in the blood (Lev. 17:11) or was identical to it (Gen. 9:4–5; Deut. 12:23). The soul was understood to be the seat of the animal functions as well as affections or emotions, such as love or fear, and of desire – hence of the individual conscious life. Hence, *nefesh* can denote the personality or even the person. Upon death the soul leaves the body but retains a degree of self-consciousness and knowledge after death.[8]

Additional passages speak of a more complicated "anthropology." This view is based primarily on Gen. 2:4–3. Here, material form, when animated by the spirit, becomes a living soul. When God breathes the *nishmat adam* into man, he becomes *nefesh ḥayyah*. The *nishmat ḥayyim* is also called *ruaḥ ḥayyim*, the spirit. This spirit – the essence of life, is part of the human corporate personality. Thus we have a *ruaḥ*, the power of life, which when joined to the body, leads to the presence of a *nefesh*, a soul, the personality of the individual. If the *ruaḥ* leaves, as at death, the soul ceases to be a living soul and continues its existence in the netherworld, *Sheol*. The *ruaḥ*, the life force, however, returns to God.[9]

Essentially, when the *ruaḥ* and *nefesh* are conceived as one, we arrive at the first body/soul conception that we described above. Hence, in some texts *ruaḥ* is essentially identical with *nefesh*.[10] It should be apparent that doctrines of resurrection such as appear in Ezekiel (37:1–14) and Daniel (12:2, 13), presuppose the afterlife of the soul and its immortality. While the nature of these concepts is

[7] P.W. Porteous, "Soul," in *Interpreter's Dictionary of the Bible*, vol. 4, pp. 428–9.
[8] R.H. Charles, *Eschatology* (New York: Schocken, 1963), pp. 37–40.
[9] Cf. Charles, pp. 41–3.
[10] Cf. Charles, pp. 44–7.

beyond the scope of this paper, we note that they are very different from the cognate concepts of the Greeks.[11] It was the biblical conception of the spirit that lay at the root of Second Temple period developments, not the Hellenic notions.

These concepts underwent considerable development in Second Temple times. Josephus (*War* 2:162–4; *Ant.* 18:14–16) testifies to differences of opinion about the idea. He says that the Pharisees accepted the idea, whereas the Sadducees rejected it.[12] He also states that the Essenes believed in the immortality of the soul (*Ant.* 18:18, *War* 2:154–158),[13] as did the Dead Sea Scrolls.[14]

It was in the Hellenistic domain, especially, that the soul and the body became competing elements, a concept somewhat at variance with the biblical notion. In this view, found in 2 Maccabees[15] and extensively in the works of Philo, one meets an almost neo-Platonic view in which the soul struggles valiantly against the physical body to attain virtue, in our case observance of God's law.[16] This approach had great influence on the entire subsequent history of Judaism,[17] but for our purposes, we should note that it leads to the corollary notion that spirituality can be attained best by restraining

---

[11] Charles, pp. 142–56.

[12] He claims in *War* 2:163 that the Pharisees believed in transmigration of the souls of the good and eternal punishment of those of the evildoers after death. But in *Ant.* 18:14 he states that all souls are subjected to subterranean reward or punishment depending on their deeds.

[13] In *Ant.* 8:154–7 he puts forward a very Hellenic notion of the afterlife, assuming that the souls of the good rise up out of the prison of the body for eternal reward, while those of the evildoers are punished in a Hades-like existence.

[14] See E. Puech, *La croyance des Esséniens en la vie future: Immortalité, résurrection, vie éternelle? Histoire d'une croyance dans le Judaïsme ancien*, vol. II (Paris: Libraire Lecoffre, 1993), pp. 327–692.

[15] Puech, vol. I, pp. 85–92.

[16] Cf. H.A. Wolfson, *Philo, Foundations of Religious Philosophy in Judaism, Christianity and Islam* (Cambridge, MA: Harvard University Press, 1968), vol. I, pp. 360–423.

[17] J. Guttmann, *Philosophies of Judaism, The History of Jewish Philosophy from Biblical Times to Franz Rosenzweig* (Philadelphia: Jewish Publication Society, 1964), pp. 84–133.

the physical aspects of existence.[18] Such concepts became prominent among various Second Temple groups, most notably in the Essenes as described by Philo and Josephus.

In the Dead Sea sect (whom most scholars identify with the Essenes), the *ruaḥ* of the individual takes on a different role.[19] It is essentially identical to what the Rabbis call the *yeẓer*, following Gen. 6:5.[20] Two *ruḥot*, good and evil, operate both within each individual and within the cosmos, competing with one another for dominion.[21] This is totally different from the Hellenistic approach. In the Dead Sea Scrolls, body and spirit are one, and both together are either good or evil. Even with the radical ethical dualism[22] and the concomitant notion of predestination[23] present in the sectarian scrolls, the spiritual is never cast as an opponent of the physical.

The concept of spirit or soul in biblical literature, as we have seen, developed in various ways in Second Temple literature, to some extent under Hellenistic influence. It was this soul/spirit that was the forum for the individual's experience of God and holiness as it was understood and described in early Jewish literature. When we speak of spirituality, we deal with the intersection of this aspect of human existence with the divine. The soul, the essence of human

[18] We have not included asceticism in the study that follows. For a survey, see S.D. Fraade, "Ascetical Aspects of Ancient Judaism," in *Jewish Spirituality,* vol. 1, *From the Bible through the Middle Ages*, ed. A. Green (New York: Crossroad, 1989), pp. 253–88.

[19] A.E. Sekki, *The Meaning of* Ruaḥ *at Qumran* (SBL Dissertation Series, no. 110; Atlanta, GA: Scholars Press, 1989), pp. 95–144, 193–219.

[20] Cf. G.F. Moore, *Judaism in the First Centuries of the Christian Era: The Age of the Tannaim* (Cambridge, MA: Harvard University Press, 1966), vol. I, pp. 479–93; E.E. Urbach, *The Sages, Their Concepts and Beliefs,* trans. I. Abrahams (Jerusalem: Magnes Press, 1979), vol. I, pp. 471–83.

[21] J. Licht, "An Analysis of the Treatment of the Two Spirits in DSD," in *Aspects of the Dead Sea Scrolls,* ed. C. Rabin and Y. Yadin (Scripta Hierosolymitana 4; Jerusalem: Magnes Press, 1958), pp. 88–100.

[22] Cf. H. Ringgren, *The Faith of Qumran: Theology of the Dead Sea Scrolls,* trans. E.T. Sanders (Philadelphia: Fortress Press, 1963), pp. 68–80.

[23] Cf. E.P. Sanders, *Paul and Palestinian Judaism, A Comparison of Patterns of Religion* (Philadelphia: Fortress Press, 1977), pp. 257–70; J. Duhaime, "Determinism," *Encyclopedia of the Dead Sea Scrolls,* vol. 1, pp. 194–8.

spirituality, would experience God's closeness in a variety of ways, and it is to them that we now turn.

VISITING THE TEMPLE

Much of the religious experience of the Jew in First and Second Temple times was connected with entering the Temple precincts. Visiting the Temple took place for the average Jew at festivals, sometimes but not always, and on special occasions, such as to give thanks or offer an expiatory offering.[24]

In the period of desert wandering, the camp of the children of Israel surrounded the Tabernacle. This geographical arrangement must have done much to foster the notion that the divine presence was truly dwelling (*ShKhN*) in the midst of the people (Exod. 29:42–46). The entire camp was arranged so that the most holy area was the Holy of Holies, in the middle, surrounded by the Tabernacle, then by the camp of the Levites, and then by the camp of the tribes of Israel, the outermost of these concentric areas. In fact, the purpose of the Exodus itself is not simply the entry into the Promised Land, but rather the intimacy with God which is provided by the Tabernacle and later, the Temple. "The endless rendezvous in the portable Temple is the teleological consummation of the history of redemption."[25]

When the First Temple was built, the architectural plan shifted from one of concentric squares to one of increasingly inner and more sanctified areas. This meant that the worshiper was "climbing a spiritual ladder" as he or she entered the Temple area.[26] One entered the Temple precincts and then proceeded through the gates into what was later termed the women's court, since women were allowed only this far. Further in, males could enter the small strip of the inner *azarah* called the "Court of the Israelites." The fact that

[24] On pilgrimage to the Jerusalem Temple, see S. Safrai, *Ha-Aliyah la-Regel bi-Yemei Bayit Sheni* (Tel Aviv: Am Hassefer, 1965), pp. 145–9.

[25] J.D. Levenson, "The Jerusalem Temple in Devotional and Visionary Experience," in *Jewish Spirituality,* vol. 1, p. 37.

[26] In the Second Temple the worshiper physically ascended while proceeding to areas of greater sanctity.

only priests entered further, and that access to the Holy of Holies was reserved for the high priest on Yom Kippur, heightened the sense of sanctity for the worshiper.[27]

This sense of sanctity was no doubt increased by the beauty and grandeur of the sanctuary as well as by the costumes of the *kohanim*. Descriptions of the high priest from several Second Temple period sources (*Ben Sira* 50:1–21, *Ant.* 15, 3, 3 (51–52); *War* 1, 22, 2 (437)) indicate that he was truly perceived, because of his appearance and his vestments, as if he were part of the divine retinue. His very appearance helped to foster the numinous experiences of those who saw him in the Temple.[28] All of this created the mood that the worshiper was truly in a holy place. That he or she actually experienced the feeling of closeness to the divine of a type not usually felt outside the sanctuary, can be inferred from a variety of biblical passages (Ps. 73:29, 145:18).

The importance of the Temple is as a vehicle for the meeting of God and man. From the Temple, blessings flow in reciprocal fashion, both from God to His people and from the people to God. Psalm 134 illustrates this reciprocal blessing as part of the liturgy of the Temple. Here we find, "Bless the Lord, all you servants of the Lord," and "May the Lord, maker of heaven and earth, bless you from Zion." The blessings flow from Zion, the capital of the spiritual world, and are received all over the world. God dwells in His heavenly palace and in His earthly Temple simultaneously (Ps. 11:4; 79:1).

If the Temple is the dwelling-place of God on earth, then it seems logical that it has to be a place fit for God to inhabit. Only if it is a place of purity and sanctity can God continue to abide there. Indeed, God's presence, and therefore His closeness to His people, was seen as conditional upon human obedience to the covenant (1 Kings 6:11–13; Ezek. 43:8–9). Thus, the neglect of *mizvot* and the

[27] Cf. L.H. Schiffman, "Architecture and Law: the Temple and its Courtyards in the Temple Scroll," in *From Ancient Israel to Modern Judaism: Intellect in Quest of Understanding, Essays in Honor of Marvin Fox*, ed. J. Neusner, E.S. Frerichs, and N.M. Sarna (BJS 159; Atlanta: Scholars Press, 1989), vol. 1, pp. 267–84.

[28] C.T.R. Haywood, *The Jewish Temple: A Non-biblical Sourcebook* (London and New York: Routledge, 1996), pp. 29–30, 34–5, 38–84.

breach of the covenant between God and humanity can result in the destruction of God's House. Psalm fifteen sets forth the entrance requirements for the Temple: "Lord, who may sojourn in Your Tent, who may dwell on Your holy mountain? He who lives without blame, who does what is right..." (vss. 1–2).

In this context the righteous visitor to the Temple longs "to see the face of God," an idiom which means to worship at the Temple (Deut. 16:16; Psalm 11:4–7).[29] In particular, this term seems to refer to a level of intimacy with God's presence which was available to the worshiper in the Temple. *Panim* here means "presence" in a variety of passages and to appear *lifne ha-Shem* or *et penei ha-Shem* (after the *nifal* of the root *R'H*) refers not only to the physical worshiper in God's Temple, particularly at pilgrimage festivals, but also to the attendant religious experience. It was the availability of this experience, often resulting in "joy" (on which see below), that led people to pray for the opportunity to spend time in God's holy House. The term *panim* here does not imply a physical appearance, and in any case, we exclude visionary appearances of God from this study as they properly belong to the domain of mysticism, not to the spirituality of the average worshiper.

That entry into the Temple stirred spiritual feelings in Second Temple times can be seen in *Letter of Aristeas* 99 where it is said that anyone who sees the Temple and its priests "will come to astonishment and indescribable wonder, and will be stirred in mind by the holy quality which pertains to every detail."[30] The author apparently saw the Temple service as a revelation on earth of the heavenly world.[31]

Temple service is, to some extent, also described in Ben Sira's well-known description of the high priest. While this text clearly shows the impression that the high priest himself made, it also gives

[29] Both Abraham and David had visionary experiences at the place where the future Temple would be located (Gen. 22:14; 2 Chron. 3:1; 2 Sam. 24:15–25). Cf. E.R. Wolfson, *Through a Speculum That Shines, Vision and Imagination in Medieval Jewish Mysticism* (Princeton: Princeton University Press, 1994), pp. 13–33.

[30] Trans. Haywood, *The Jewish Temple*, p. 30.

[31] Haywood, p. 37.

some information about the people's reaction to the ceremonies in the Temple. We read there (50:17) that all assembled prostrated themselves before God, that (vs. 19) all the people shouted with joy in prayer before God and (Hebrew text, vs. 20) received the priestly blessing, again prostrating themselves (vs. 21).[32] Clearly, the Temple service made a beautiful and inspiring impression on the Israelites who participated.

To Philo,[33] the Temple was representative of the entire universe. The specifics of its construction symbolized various aspects of the manner in which the soul was to dominate the body.[34] By entering the Temple one comes to appreciate the role of God as creator of the universe, the nature of the universe, and the manner in which the spiritual world must dominate the physical. The virtuous individual, freed from the passions, is symbolized by the Temple and its service, and the virtuous are, so to speak, a Temple unto themselves.[35] In essence, then, the Temple for Philo, when entered by the worshiper, taught through its physical form the quest for communion with God and the life of virtue that made this possible. Further, the greatness of the universe created by God was taught by the very design of each detail. The Temple, then, had as its purpose – even its architectural details – the inculcating of the highest of spiritual teachings.

SACRIFICE

Of course, the primary reason to visit the Temple was to offer a sacrifice. Sacrifice in biblical Israel may be primarily classified as several types: Some sacrifices function primarily as expiatory rites, intending to provide atonement (*kapparah*) for one who has transgressed, mostly unintentionally. Other sacrifices provide a sort of shared meal, in which the Deity joins the community or family in "partaking" of the offering. This second type of sacrifice has as its purpose establishing a close relationship with God. Other offer-

[32] The sacrificial service is also described in 45:6–22 (Hebrew).

[33] See Haywood, pp. 109–41.

[34] Haywood, pp. 120–7 regarding the furnishings of the Temple.

[35] Haywood, pp. 140–1.

ings provide praise of God or thanksgiving, whether in connection with communal, i.e. historical events, or individual good fortune or salvation.[36] These types of sacrifice, as well as the various ancillary offerings and additional acts performed in the Temple, were all highly spiritually meaningful to biblical Israel.

Expiatory rites are essentially sacrifices of substitution. A human being is aware of his or her transgression and expiates it by offering an animal whose life is taken and which is offered up as a substitute for the guilty party. In bringing such a sacrifice, and in reciting the required confessional formula over the animal,[37] the person is acutely conscious of his own failings and of the opportunity for a new start. The combination of repentance and a sort of transfer of his transgressor status to the animal (similar to the Yom Kippur ritual of Leviticus 16), provides the worshiper with a deeply religious feeling of having been granted forgiveness by God in His holy place, the Temple.

The *shelamim* offering provided the experience of a shared meal. This type of offering emphasizes communion with God, and the almost familial relationship of God with the one who offers the sacrifice and with his family who share in eating it together with him. Participation in such offerings served not only to provide a feast in the presence of God, but also inculcated a feeling of a personal relationship with the Deity in Whose House, the Temple, the shared meal occurred.

Participation in thanksgiving or festival sacrifices provided an opportunity to render to God thanks and appreciation for His bounties to humanity. Here the dominant human emotions were

---

[36] For a survey of the phenomenon of sacrifice in religious studies, see J. Henninger, "Sacrifice," in *Encyclopedia of Religion,* vol. 12, pp. 544–57. See also R. de Vaux, *Ancient Israel* (Grand Rapids, MI: Eerdmans, 1960), pp. 447–56; Y. Kaufmann, *Toledot ha-Emunah ha-Yisra'elit* (Jerusalem: Bialik Institute; Tel Aviv: Dvir, n.d.), vol. 1–3, pp. 560–74, who emphasizes the differences between the religious meaning of Israelite sacrifice and the magical and demonic basis of pagan sacrifice.

[37] On confession, see J. Milgrom, *Leviticus 1–16, A New Translation with Introduction and Commentary* (Anchor Bible 3: Garden City, NY: Doubleday, 1991), pp. 301–3.

gratitude for God's gifts and awe at His power to save, in the personal context as well as in the national history of Israel.

All in all, therefore, the sacrificial system inculcated the notion that God was a close, almost familial God, we might say an immanent God, but also One Who demanded obedience, and therefore expiation, when His law was violated. At the same time, His transcendence was manifest in the great deeds He had done on the stage of national history, and it was He Who had the power to grant the individual gifts for which thanksgiving offerings had to be rendered.

That these theological notions were inherent in the sacrificial system is evident. But can we be sure that in biblical times they were in the minds of the worshipers so that the act of sacrifice and participation in it was truly a spiritual experience? When we take into consideration the overall aspects of the religious significance of a visit to God's Temple, as well as the pomp and ceremony of the rituals performed there, we can see that worshipers must have truly had a feeling of God's presence there. But specific aspects of the rituals, like the laying on of hands (*semikhah*) and the recital of confessions, were intended to foster such feelings. We can be sure that the individual Jew would have felt the significance of his sacrifices and would have been drawn closer to God and His way of life by this experience.

For Philo, thanksgiving is one of the central purposes of the Temple service, which expresses the thanksgiving of the entire universe.[38] The universe as a Temple is somehow equivalent to the divine logos,[39] and correspondingly, the rational soul of each person functions as a Temple.[40] The Temple worship therefore symbolizes the unity of heaven and earth, with the high priest functioning as the unifier of the two realms, symbolizing the divine logos and the

[38] Hayward, p. 110.

[39] On Philo's theory of the *logos*, see Winston in *Jewish Spirituality*, vol. 1, pp. 201–11 and H.A. Wolfson, *Philo*, vol. 1 (Cambridge, MA: Harvard University, 1947), pp. 200–82.

[40] Hayward, p. 111.

rational human soul.[41] The sacrifices were intended to remove sin from the soul and control the passions, as well as to offer thanksgiving to God. The rituals teach that the soul must serve God completely, and purify itself of lusts and appetites so that the offerer will rise from earth to heaven and meditate on the one God and unite with Him.[42] Other offerings reassure the penitent that he is forgiven. The soul is purified by sacrifice and brings the person to self-knowledge as he comes into the divine presence.[43]

Thus, to Philo, the act of offering a sacrifice was itself an action which, by its very nature, purified and elevated the soul, if undertaken with an understanding of its symbolism. To him, spirituality consisted of an ascent of the soul in virtue, which led to an almost mystical union with God. This spiritual journey was effected, in his analysis of biblical symbolism, by participation in the sacrificial service.

PRAYER

Theoretically, there are a variety of ways in which to understand prayer, and, for that matter, various other rituals. One can imagine situations in which prayer takes place either out of obligation, fear, or just plain need. In such a situation, the worshiper might have no more emotional involvement in placing his or her requests before the Deity than he or she might have making similar requests of a human sovereign. Such prayer could not be seen as a spiritual experience. But Deuteronomy makes clear that the human relationship to God should be one of love,[44] and so it is reasonable to imagine a very different kind of prayer. In this situation, requests are not the only form of prayer, but thanksgiving plays an important role.

---

[41] On the symbolism of the priestly garments, see Hayward, pp. 114–6.

[42] Cf. Winston, pp. 211–5.

[43] Hayward, pp. 116–8; cf. Winston, pp. 216–7.

[44] Cf. W.L. Moran, "The Ancient Near Eastern Background of the Love of God in Deuteronomy," *Catholic Biblical Quarterly* 25 (1963): 77–87. Moran sees the fear of God as required by the command to love Him. Cf. also G.A. Anderson, *A Time to Mourn, A Time to Dance* (University Park, PA: Pennsylvania State University Press, 1991), pp. 9–10.

Furthermore, prayer of this kind presumes a different relationship of the worshiper to God and to the prayer experience.

In this approach, prayer, based as it is on the love of God, becomes a spiritual experience. The human being feels him or herself to be in a relationship with God which is fostered by the act of prayer, not to mention by the specific words he or she says. In prayers of thanksgiving, gratitude merges with request and with joy, and this kind of prayer produces a feeling of closeness to God and attendant spiritual fulfillment. This relationship with the divine can be understood as theurgic, as it is in Jewish mysticism; the individual seeks to attain a special feeling of one who sees him or herself communing with God as in some way, as it were, in the Holy of Holies.

Although many biblical prayers may be classified entirely as petitions, the second type, entailing a spiritual dimension, underlies much of the biblical prayer experience.

Sometimes it is associated with the act of sacrifice as in Ps. 54:8: "Let me offer up a willing sacrifice to You and greatly praise Your name, Lord." (Cf. also 27:6; 54:6; 116:7; and 141:2). In these instances there is no outpouring of sudden emotion; rather, there is a link between the praise of God and the offering of sacrifice. In fact, praise and sacrifice are both referred to as *avodah*, "worship." Praise, petition, and sacrifice are all presented together in the inauguration of Solomon's Temple (1 Kings 8), and praise of God is often located specifically in the Temple (Ps. 29:9; 84:5; 100:1; 134:1; 138:2).[45]

It is usual to divide prayer in the Bible into two types, structured and spontaneous.[46] It is often said that only spontaneous prayer can be spiritual, or truly a religious act in the full meaning of the

[45] J. Kugel, "Topics in the History of the Spirituality of the Psalms," in *Jewish Spirituality*, vol. 1, pp. 113–44. Kugel notes that the biblical texts which describe the sacrifices and the festival calendar never mention the role of praise, hymns, or psalms to accompany the sacrifices. These psalms were apparently more flexible and seen to be more tailor-made to the specific situation than the prescribed sacrificial offering.

[46] On prayer in the biblical and Second Temple periods, see S.C. Reif, *Judaism and Hebrew Prayer: New Perspectives on Jewish Liturgical History* (Cambridge: Cambridge University Press, 1993), pp. 22–52.

word. But in reality, biblical prayer comes in three varieties. In one, the prayer is totally spontaneous. In a second, standard formulae are adapted to the particular circumstances. In the third, the worshiper uses an already existing composition to express his or her prayers.[47] But when it comes to true religious meaning, in our view, these categories do not hold. No matter what the origin of the prayer texts, spontaneous, formulaic, or totally fixed, depending on the fundamental axiomatic attitudes brought to the prayer experience, it can be a fully mechanical experience or one of great spiritual meaning. Often the same prayers can be said in either way. But prayer in the Bible is clearly intended to foster a feeling of closeness to God beyond that normally experienced when not engaged in prayer.

That such an experience did, indeed, occur seems to be shown by the use of terms for joy which often appear in contexts of prayer in the Bible. It is true that various biblical passages discussing joy in a ritual context refer simply to a ritual act of rejoicing,[48] but such rituals are intended to produce precisely the type of experience we have been describing. Over and over the book of Psalms, certainly biblical Israel's greatest collection of individual, Levitical, and communal prayer, terms as "joy" the religious satisfaction – the normal mysticism – connected with the experience of prayer before God.[49]

A few examples of the use of "joy" to designate this spiritual satisfaction which results from prayer can be cited here. Psalm 16 is a prayer for protection. The author places his complete trust and faith in God, indicates that he will bless Him, and then declares, "Therefore my heart is happy and my being (*kavod*) has rejoiced." Ps. 104:34 declares, "I will rejoice in the Lord." Upon seeing the works of God, the righteous will rejoice in God and take refuge in Him (Ps. 64:11). The hearts of those who seek God will rejoice (Ps. 105:

[47] M. Greenberg, *Biblical Prose Prayer* (Berkeley: University of California Press, 1983). Cf. M. Greenberg, "On the Refinement of the Conception of Prayer in Hebrew Scriptures," in *Studies in the Bible and Jewish Thought* (Philadelphia: Jewish Publication Society, 1995), pp. 75–108.

[48] Anderson, pp. 37–45.

[49] We ignore here references to joy resulting from God's fulfillment of one's prayers, a material, rather than spiritual, joy.

3). The psalm exhorts listeners to seek God and His strength (*uzo*), really His presence, and to "seek His face," another term for the same, then to "remember His miracles and great deeds" (vss. 4–5). Clearly some kind of closeness to God and attendant religious experience are meant by rejoicing here. Similar is Ps. 69:33, referring to an occasion of thanksgiving and praise (vs. 31), which states, "The meek saw, let them rejoice, the seekers of God, and let their hearts come alive." Ps. 5:12 concludes its prayer, "Let all those who take refuge in You rejoice, let them sing eternally, and give them shelter so that those who love Your name may rejoice (*ve-yaaleẓu*) in You." "You, God, surround the righteous with Your favor like a shield (vs. 13)." Joy also comes with praise of the Lord in Ps. 32:11, 34:3, 86:4, 92:5, 97:11–12. Ps. 4:7–8 speaks of joy in the heart immediately after "the light of Your face, O Lord." Certainly, therefore, some sense of an experience of the numinous was associated with prayer in the Psalms. Further, the Psalms often accompanied sacrifice, and the ritual of sacrifice was also expected to provide such a spiritual feeling.

Prayer continued in this role into Second Temple times, but it was enlarged for a number of reasons. In general, throughout Second Temple times prayer was expanding in its role as a central institution of the Judaism of each individual, so that the full system of daily and festival prayers would be in place by the time of the Temple's destruction. But even earlier, in communities that separated themselves from the Temple, such as the Qumran sect that collected the Dead Sea Scrolls, prayer functioned as the primary vehicle for spiritual experience.[50]

The basic prayer times observed by the Qumran sect are presented in the Rule of the Community.[51] The text refers to prayers recited evening and morning (Rule of the Community 10:1–3), on the New Moon, and the festivals (10:3–8). In addition, we know that they

---

[50] L.H. Schiffman, *Reclaiming the Dead Sea Scrolls: The History of Judaism, the Background of Christianity, the Lost Library of Qumran* (Philadelphia and Jerusalem: Jewish Publication Society, 1994), pp. 289–301.

[51] See L.H. Schiffman, "The Dead Sea Scrolls and the Early History of Jewish Liturgy," in *The Synagogue in Late Antiquity*, ed. L.I. Levine (Philadelphia: American Schools of Oriental Research, 1987), pp. 33–48.

recited the *Shema* each evening and morning (10:10). Some of the liturgical expressions in the Rule of the Community parallel those of the *Shema* and the *Amidah*. Prayers for the festivals from caves 1 and 4, like the rabbinic liturgy, expressed the joy of the festivals and the wish that the exiles be gathered once more to the Land of Israel.[52] These prayers from the Qumran caves provide evidence that prayers were recited as a substitute for the sacrificial rites even before the Temple was destroyed.[53]

Further parallels exist between the Qumran materials and the rabbinic liturgy. A supplication remarkably like the *Taḥanun*, called Lament, was found in cave 4.[54] It emphasizes the destruction of the First Temple. A similar composition is the Words of the Luminaries, which reflects notions of sin, destruction as a punishment from God, the mercy that God shows, and prayer for repentance and purification from sin.[55] The supplications were designated for specific days of the week, including a version for the Sabbath, which avoided the mention of certain subjects about which it was inappropriate to speak on the Sabbath.[56]

For Philo and the Jews of Alexandria, physically separated as they were from Jerusalem and the Temple, prayer and the synagogue were central institutions already in the Second Temple period. For this reason, we should not be surprised that prayer is discussed extensively by Philo.[57] He saw prayers of thanksgiving as emanating from love of God and, therefore, as a higher form than prayers of petition, which were seen as based on fear.[58] Over and over he

---

[52] 4Q509 frag. 3 (M. Baillet, *Qumrân grotte 4, III (4Q482–5Q520)* (Discoveries in the Judaean Desert 7; Oxford: Clarendon Press, 1982), p. 186.

[53] B. Niẓan, *Qumran Prayer and Religious Poetry* (Leiden; New York: E.J. Brill, 1994), pp. 47–87.

[54] 4Q501, Baillet, pp. 79–80.

[55] 4Q504–506, Baillet, pp. 137–75. Cf. M.R. Lehmann, "Be'ur Ḥadash le-'Divrei ha-Me'orot' shel 4Q," *Masot u-Masa'ot* (Jerusalem: Mossad ha-Rav Kook, 1982), pp. 169–73.

[56] Niẓan, pp. 84–116.

[57] See D. Winston, "Philo and the Contemplative Life," in *Jewish Spirituality*, vol. 1, pp. 217–20.

[58] Cf. BT *Sotah* 31a.

speaks of the obligation to give thanks to God, as everything comes from Him and belongs to Him.

Petitionary prayer in Philo tends not to be the request of humans that God grant them material goods, but rather, these prayers aim at knowledge of God and spiritual perfection. Such prayers are really self-exhortations for spiritual growth, asserting that all spiritual achievement is really a gracious outflow from the divine. In this respect Philo seems to be following the model of the Greek philosophical tradition from which he appears to have derived the idea for such prayers.

To Philo, the highest form of prayer is contemplative or intellectual prayer. This kind of wordless prayer is part of the soul's journey to God and is unencumbered by any direct requests. It results in the cleaving of the soul to the "Alone Existent." In order to allow this cleaving, words need to be abandoned so that thought can cleave in absolute purity to God (*On Flight*, 92). The inadequacy of language is actually a Greek philosophical notion.[59] It is harnessed by Philo to conclude that the soul in contemplation of God is the highest form of prayer.

Indeed, for Philo, the soul's unification with God is the highest achievement possible. Scholars have debated whether this is a mystical, or only an intellectual, contemplative relationship.[60] But there can be no question that, for Philo, prayer was a mechanism to spiritual elevation and appreciation of the divine. For biblical, sectarian, and Hellenistic Judaism alike, prayer was seen as an experience of connecting with God. The ritual and cognitive aspects were crowned with the spiritual dimension of feeling a closeness to God not otherwise attainable.

RITUAL PURIFICATION

One particular area in which the spiritual dimension needs to be stressed is the process of ritual purification. The biblical purification

[59] Winston, p. 219.

[60] Winston, pp. 223–6, who sees Philo as a "theoretical mystic;" cf. E.R. Goodenough, *By Light, Light: The Mystic Gospel of Hellenistic Judaism* (New Haven: Yale University Press, 1935) who argues that Philo was in reality a mystic.

rites have been subject to different kinds of interpretations throughout the years, both traditional and modern. Some of these have seen purification in either mechanistic or magical ways, failing to understand the underlying dimension of spirituality. The various forms of defilement detailed in the Bible fall into two types. One can become defiled by experiencing or coming in contact with that which interrupted the normal life forces, such as death or bodily fluxes, or one can become impure by touching that which was sacred or consecrated in some way.

To be sure, some of these impurities are similar to taboos known in other societies, including some of the neighboring civilizations of the ancient Near East. But, these notions have been totally turned upside down in the Bible. What may have been taboo in other systems of thought are here occasions for emphasizing the consecration of people, objects, and places to God. Essentially, ritual purity and impurity for Judaism, already in the biblical period, is a way of taking occasions of transition – even of fear or of tragedy – and making them opportunities to emphasize God's intimate relation to the life of His people, as individuals and as a group.[61]

Purification rituals generally involved sacrifices and lustrations. Sacrifice is dealt with elsewhere in this paper. We will concentrate here on ritual immersion. Over and over the Bible commands "washing" (*KhBS*) or " bathing" (*RHẒ*) which was understood from earliest times to refer to ritual immersion, in which the entire body is submerged under the "waters of creation"[62] so as to allow the ritually impure individual to return to his or her naturally pure state. But these rituals have often been looked at by outsiders as if they were

[61] De Vaux, *Ancient Israel*, p. 460. For a review of theories put forth by modern biblical scholars to explain ritual impurity, see D.P. Wright, "Unclean and Clean (OT)," in *Anchor Bible Dictionary*, vol. 6, pp. 739–41. Wright stressed the non-demonic character of biblical purity laws (p. 739), following Kaufmann, *Toledot ha-Emunah ha-Yisre'elit*, vol. 1–3, pp. 539–45.

[62] The term *mikveh* for "pool" is used in Gen. 1:10 as a term for the waters that God had to gather together to create the dry land. The use of the term for "immersion pool" is clearly based on the relationship of immersion to the primeval waters of creation.

a mechanical ritual in which the feelings of the purificand played no part in the efficacy of the ritual. In other words, the specifically spiritual character of these rituals is often assumed to be lacking.

The proof of the meaningful spiritual character of biblical purification can be seen outside of the Torah's codes in the figurative references to purification rituals in the Prophets.[63] Several passages refer to bathing as an image for religious repentance (e.g., Is. 1:16), but some texts clearly are using images of hygienic bathing, as in Is. 4:4. Jer. 4:14 has the root *KhBS* referring to the purification of the heart. This same verb appears in Ps. 51:4, David's plea for repentance after the visit of Nathan the prophet. In vs. 4, the psalm explicitly associates ritual cleansing with repentance from sin. The mention in vs. 9 of hyssop and the root *ḤTA*, meaning "to purify," shows that the reference is to the red-heifer purification which is understood here as an experience of repentance and atonement. Vs. 12 asks for the creation of a pure heart (*lev ṭahor*) and the gift of God's spirit (*ruaḥ kodshekha*). Without such repentance, the expiation rites are useless.

Since the sprinkling of water played such a large role in the purification rituals, we should not be surprised to find that it is also understood as a process of repentance. Ezek. 36:25–28 speaks of the waters of purification, purifying by creating a new heart and a new spirit (*ruaḥ ḥadashah*). There the passage specifically tells us that God will implant his spirit (*ruaḥ*) in the midst of Israel, thereby causing the people to observe God's laws, live in the land of their fathers, and be His people as He is their God, an image of God and Israel in a close relationship. We take these passages not as reinterpretation intending to give meaning to mechanical rituals, but rather as an accurate reflection of how sophisticated and learned Jews in biblical times understood and taught that ritual purification was indeed an inner spiritual experience.

In Second Temple literature there is no question that there is an experiential and penitential side to the rituals of purification. Speaking of the "men of iniquity," whom the Dead Sea sectarians

[63] The passages are listed in Wright, p. 738.

wanted to avoid at all costs, the Rule of the Congregation (1QS 5:13–15)[64] states that such a person may not (or shall not) enter the waters of purification, the *mikveh*, as they will be unable to purify him unless he repents. Here the biblical idea has been taken further. If repentance is the purpose of ritual purification, an unrepentant sinner may as well not even undergo the ritual. For the sectarians, the *mizvah* of ritual purification required the *kavvanah* (intention) of moral and religious purification.

It is no doubt that for the same reason the sectarians developed prayers to be recited as part of the ritual of purification. Several prayers existed for the third and seventh days of ablutions for various impurities, and they were to be recited by the person undergoing purification. The text is very fragmentary, but survives in three manuscripts which do indeed appear to be the same text. It includes also specific halakhic instructions for the rites. Some prayers were intended to be recited before immersion, and others afterwards. Most prayers seem to have included the motifs of confession, forgiveness, and, finally, thanksgiving for being purified by God.[65] The Ritual of Purification reads: "and he shall bless and recite: Blessed are You, [O God of Israel, Who saved me from all] my transgressions and purified me from the nakedness of impurity...."[66] Another passage quotes a prayer to be recited after immersion: "Blessed are You, O God of Israel, for from that which issues from Your lips, the purification of all has been explained,[67] in order to separate from all impure people according to their guilt, so that they not be purified by the waters of washing."[68]

We take these prayers as expressing not a sectarian approach to purity, but rather a widespread understanding of the function of ritual purification as a religious experience in the Second Temple period. As these texts show, purification was to be accompanied by

[64] Cf. also 4Q414 (Ritual of Purification A) 2 ii 3, 4 line 8.

[65] E. Eshel, in J. Baumgarten, et al., *Qumran Cave 4, XXV: Halakhic* Texts (Discoveries in the Judaean Desert 35; Oxford: Clarendon Press, 1999), pp. 176–7.

[66] 4Q512 29–32 vii 6–8, M. Baillet, *Qumran Grotte 4, III*, p. 265.

[67] The Torah prescribes the specific regulations for purification.

[68] 4Q414 2 ii 3, 4 lines 5–8 (=4Q512 42–44 ii), Eshel, p. 141.

a process of repentance and personal redirection, and then, after its completion, by a feeling of emergence anew into the state of purity and, hence, connection with God. It is the spirit of the person that is purified and now able to renew and intensify its relation to God.

One particular aspect of Second Temple spirituality seems to have little real background in the biblical period, although it is based primarily on biblical laws. This is the widespread pattern of adopting the standards of Temple purity as requirements for the eating of meals (*ḥullin al ṭohorat ha-kodesh*). This phenomenon is best known from three separate sets of sources: the tannaitic descriptions of the *ḥaverim* (Mishnah *Demai* 2:2–3; Tosefta *Demai* 2:2–14),[69] Josephus's descriptions of the Essenes (*War* 2:137–142), and the Qumran regulations for the conduct of sectarian life (*Rule of the Community* 6:13–23).

That this pattern was in effect among such diverse religious elites, as well as among the Sadducean priesthood which had to observe these laws in connection with Temple offerings, is indicative of the central role such purity laws played in Second Temple times. For those practicing these rules out of a Temple context, the basic purpose was to elevate the eating of non-sacral food to an experience close, if not identical, to the eating of the priestly emoluments. While this appears to be a matter of ritual stringency (*ḥumrah*) at first glance, it is really an attempt to bring sanctity into the home, family, and community.

One of the inherent problems in a sacrificial system of Temple worship is its non-democratic nature. The "kingdom of priests and holy nation" (Exod. 19:6) is not provided with total access to the sancta reserved for the real priests. By imitating priestly purity in one's personal life, an act not required by the Torah, one extends that sanctity, and participates in it, and, in so doing, democratizes access to holiness. Such steps are clearly intended to increase spirituality – closeness to God and His holiness.

The groups that we mentioned have very similar rules for admission to their pure meals.[70] After progressing through initiation

[69] Cf. JT *Demai* 22d–23a; BT *Bekhorot* 30b–31a.

[70] Cf. C. Rabin, *Qumran Studies* (Scripta Judaica 2; Oxford: Clarendon Press,

rites, members are considered to be ritually pure, that is, maintaining the standards of priestly purity, and are admitted to the meals.[71] The feasts are not true sacred meals, in that the food eaten is never considered sacral, but the atmosphere of these meals mimics that of the eating of sacral food. For the Essenes, these meals may have served as substitutes for Temple ritual,[72] while for the Qumran sect, they were eaten in imitation of the messianic banquets in which they expected to participate, believing as they did that they were living on the verge of the *eschaton*.[73]

In the case of the Qumran sectarians, the purpose of establishing such purity rules and using them to define the limits of the community (the "true Israel") is directly stated. For them the entire community was a replacement for a Temple which they abjured, seeing it as defiled by the faulty halakhic views and practices of its priests and leaders. They described their own group as "an eternal planting, a holy Temple (lit. 'house') and as a council of the Holy of Holies for Aaron, true witnesses for justice, and the elect of [God's] will to atone for the land and to pay back the evildoers their deserved punishment" (1QS 8:5–7). For this reason they separated from the mainstream (line 13). Instead, they saw themselves as a "chamber of the Holy of Holies for Aaron...to offer a sweet savor and a Temple (lit. 'house') of perfect truth in Israel" (lines 8–9).

The *ḥaverim*, unlike the sectarians, did not see their group as representing a virtual Temple. However, we can assume that even though the *ḥaverim* participated in official Temple worship, they too would have agreed with the attempt to infuse the home and community with the holiness of the Temple, so that meals became quasi-sacrificial experiences. This process certainly represents

---

1957), pp. 1–21; S. Lieberman, "The Discipline in the So-Called Dead Sea Manual of Discipline," *JBL* 71 (1951): 199–206; reprinted in S. Lieberman, *Texts and Studies* (New York: Ktav, 1974), pp. 200–7.

[71] L.H. Schiffman, *Sectarian Law in the Dead Sea Scrolls* (Brown Judaic Studies 33; Chico, CA: Scholars Press, 1983), pp. 161–5.

[72] J.M. Baumgarten, *Studies in Qumran Law* (Leiden: E.J. Brill, 1977), pp. 39–74.

[73] Schiffman, *Sectarian Law*, pp. 191–210.

a spiritualization of normal life, and is an attempt, in some small measure, to bring God, the object of sacrificial worship, into the home and community.

CONCLUSION

Biblical Israel received and fostered an approach to its religion which understood that it was the soul that ultimately entered into the closest relationship with the divine. Through the performance of various rituals, visiting the Temple, offering sacrifices and prayers, and following the rules of ritual purification, individual Jews experienced the relationship of God and Israel in their own lives, feeling His presence in their sanctuary and community. In Second Temple times, a variety of developments took place which led to a strengthening of these approaches to spirituality, even as the concept of the soul became increasingly Hellenized in some segments of the Jewish community. As some groups withdrew from the Temple, and others seemed to prepare unknowingly for its eventual destruction, the spiritual aspects of prayer and the fulfillment of purity regulations outside of the Temple sphere became more and more significant. After the Temple was destroyed, Judaism would continue to develop approaches to spirituality which had taken shape originally during the Second Temple period.

3

Torah ve-Avodah: Prayer and Torah Study As Competing Values in the Time of Ḥazal

Yaakov Elman

The following essay will attempt to examine the way in which two of the major outlets for human spiritual yearnings were construed in the classic rabbinic era of Late Antiquity, as expressed in talmudic literature.[1] More particularly, it attempts – at least in part and as far as the talmudic texts allow us – to reconstruct classic rabbinic

[1] Thus we will exclude extra-talmudic material of all sorts, not limited to texts emanating from both the land of Israel and Babylonia, either from Jewish or non-Jewish sources, including inscriptions, magic bowls and magic texts, *heikhalot* literature, and the like.

spirituality in experiential terms, by examining specific incidents and testimonies about important rabbinic figures.[2]

This is no easy task. Generally speaking, rabbinic culture carries the general biblical reticence on such matters to a still higher degree. The confessional style which came so easily to Augustine and later Christian mystics finds few counterparts in Jewish writing as a whole (Jeremiah and the Psalmist, R. Yaakov Emden in the eighteenth century and, to an extent, R. Yosef Karo in the sixteenth, are among the few exceptions.) Certainly, this holds true for rabbinic literature. Fortunately, however, two of the greatest of the Babylonian *amoraim* are among those whose personal life is somewhat revealed. Abaye, himself, often speaks of his education (citing his foster-mother) or cases in which he changed his mind on certain existential issues. As for Rava, who occasionally echoes Abaye in this proclivity, all sorts of information about his personal life has been preserved in the *Bavli*, both from his own ruminations and from reports which seem to emanate from his family and/or close associates.[3] But even in regard to other, less well-documented talmudic lives, some revealing

[2] The use of anecdotal material is liable to the danger of shifting attributions (*amri lah, iteima*), variant details and the like (*ika de-amri*), or parallel sources may record these variants; in a number of cases, we have a direct reports of error such as (*ki ata…, hadar amar*), in Ula's correction of a report by R. Zeira in regard to R. Yishmael be-R. Yose: "It was not at the side of a palm tree but at the side of a pillar; it was not R. Yishmael be-R. Yose but R. Eleazar be-R. Yose; and it was not the *tefillah* of *Shabbat* on the eve of *Shabbat* but the *tefillah* of the end of the Shabbat on the Shabbat" (BT *Ber.* 27b). In the following, these matters are confirmed, when possible, by parallels in other rabbinic collections. In any case, an understanding of what the talmudic tradents *could* believe of *tannaim* and *amoraim* is as important in comprehending their view of rabbinic spirituality as is comprehending the reality. Nevertheless, it is our belief that talmudic statements may be used to gain an understanding of *Ḥazal*'s views in historical perspective; see Richard Kalmin, *Sages, Stories, Authors, and Editors in Rabbinic Babylonia* (Atlanta: Scholars Press, 1994), and my "How Should a Talmudic Intellectual History Be Written? A Response to David Kraemer's *Responses*," *Jewish Quarterly Review* 89 (1999): 361–86. However, not all sources are equal; see R.Y.Y. Weinberg, *Meḥkarim ba-Talmud*, (Berlin: Druk N. Kronenberg, 1936), pp. 171–9, and C. Hezser, *Form, Function, and Historical Significance of the Rabbinic Story in Yerushalmi Nezikin*, [Tübingen: J.C.B. Mohr (Paul Siebeck), 1993], esp. pp. 362–409.

[3] Some of this material was collected in my "Rava in Mahoza: Rabbinic Theology

statements and anecdotes about other sages, Rav and R. Yehudah, for example, are scattered through the vast discourse of that literature, and, when combined, provide us with the beginnings of a picture which coheres with later developments.

I will not attempt to proffer my own "definition" of the object of our study, at least at the outset. As James Kugel has said of *midrash*, "since [previous] studies have already not defined *midrash* in ample detail, there is little purpose in not defining it again here."[4] Still, it is self-evident that no investigation can be carried out without some working definition of the subject under study, at least for the purposes of the study. And so we will begin with some attempt at one. Let us then begin with the definition offered by the Orthodox Forum's president, and the President of Yeshiva University, Dr. Norman Lamm, in his recently published *The Shema: Spirituality and Law in Judaism.*[5]

> By "spirituality" I mean the intention we bring to our religious acts, the focusing of the mind and thoughts on the transcendent, the entire range of mindfulness – whether simple awareness of what we are doing, in contrast to rote performance, or elaborate mystical meditations – that spells a groping for the Source of all existence and the Giver of Torah.

Note that in defining spirituality in terms of the intention brought to "religious acts," Dr. Lamm has given the term a decidedly normative Jewish (or Muslim) cast, one which has a clear Hebrew referent, *kavvanah*, and refers primarily to the proper attitude and intention which should accompany the performance of *mizvot*, that

---

and Law in a Cosmopolitan Setting," Ninth Orthodox Forum, New York, March 29, 1998.

[4] In his delightful essay, "Two Introductions to Midrash," originally published in *Prooftexts* 3 (1983): 131–55, and reprinted in G. Hartman and S. Budick ed., *Midrash and Literature* (New Haven: Yale University Press, 1986), pp. 77–103.

[5] Philadelphia: Jewish Publication Society, 1998. The definition appears on p. 6.

is, "religious *acts*."[6] Still, it could be argued the even the most ritual-averse religions and sects (say, certain forms of Buddhism, Ethical Culture, or Unitarianism) have defined certain acts as "religious." The inadequacy of this equation of "spirituality" with *kavvanah* is clear from the next paragraph in which Dr. Lamm contrasts spirituality with law.

> Spirituality is subjective; the very fact of its inwardness implies a certain degree of anarchy; it is unfettered and self-directed, impulsive and spontaneous. In contrast, law is objective; it requires discipline, structure, obedience, order.... Spirituality alone begets antinomianism and chaos.... Without the body of the law, spirituality is a ghost."

The ideal is thus a fruitful symbiosis: "[But] such a simplistic dualism misses the point. The life of the spirit need not be chaotic and undisciplined.... In Judaism, each side – spirit and law – shows understanding for the other; we are not asked to choose one over the other, but to practice a proper balance...."[7] While admitting that this balance is difficult to achieve, and even more difficult to maintain, he asserts that, at least, in the recitation of the Shema "in its proper manner," "Judaism has accommodated both spirituality and law within its practice."[8]

Dr. Lamm's treatment is thus theological/typological and homiletical, but not particularly historical. How often *was* that "proper manner" of recitation achieved, one wonders? How did that achievement vary in time and place, and from individual to individual in any one time and place? And, most important, how was that manner achieved?

There is yet a broader issue to be addressed (though not necessarily here), and that is the relation of spirituality, here defined as

---

[6] This is true by and large even of the chapter by Robert Goldenberg, "Law and Spirit in Talmudic Religion," in *Jewish Spirituality*, ed. Arthur Green, vol. 1 (New York: Crossroad, 1986), pp. 232–52; see n. 9 below.

[7] *Ibid.*, p. 7.

[8] *Idem.*

roughly coterminous with the Hebrew *kavvanah*, with the more generally accepted understandings of the term as used in contemporary discourse. For by equating the two in this way, Jewish writers attempt to domesticate a term whose connotations still retain something of its original antinomian context. Indeed, the tension between the two may clearly be discerned in Dr. Lamm's treatment of it.[9] The following will however be restricted to the attitudes toward the two major modes of spiritual expression within talmudic sources, without directly considering this broader issue.

Such an approach carries risks and benefits. The risk is that we will miss some important aspect of rabbinic spirituality in not considering (except tangentially) such matters as pertain to the performance of the *mizvot* themselves (e.g., the question of לשמה, "for their own sake"). The benefit is that we will focus on those areas of Jewish life which are most congruent with the more general understanding of spirituality.[10]

The following outline will proceed in roughly chronological

---

[9] Indeed, even as interdenominational an enterprise as the two-volume *Jewish Spirituality: Vol. I: From the Bible Through the Middle Ages, Vol. II: From the Sixteenth-Century to the Present*, ed. by Arthur Green, (New York: Crossroads, 1986 and 1987), which constitutes Volumes 13 and 14 of the series, "World Spirituality: An Encyclopedic History of the Religious Quest," declines to define the term in any way which would elide the differences between various faiths. The following "definition" was used (Vol. I, p. xii):

> The series focuses on that inner dimension of the person called by certain traditions "the spirit." This spiritual core is the deepest center of the person. It is here that the person is open to the transcendent dimension; it is here that the person experiences ultimate reality. The series explores the discovery of this core, the dynamics of its development, and its journey to the ultimate goal. It deals with prayer, spiritual direction, the various maps of the spiritual journey, and the methods of advancement in the spiritual ascent.

[10] The history of Jewish prayer and that of the synagogue has attracted a large body of scholars over the last century, but "prayer" has, in the main, been construed textually, that is, the history of the liturgy, rather than the phenomenology of prayer *per se*. For that one must turn to halakhic, ḥasidic and pietistic works, which approach the subject from a non-historical point of view. They do not recognize any difference between prayer as practiced by *Ḥazal* and that of later eras. As a consequence, both of these vast literatures will be little cited in the following essay. More recently, archaeologists

order, from R. Ḥanina b. Dosa to R. Akiva, from R. Akiva to R. Shimon b. Yoḥai, his disciple, and to Rabbi Judah the Prince; from Rabbi Judah the Prince to R. Ḥiyya, his disciple; from his nephew, Rav, to R. Yehudah, his disciple, and to R. Hisda and R. Naḥman, who flourished in the next generation; from R. Yoḥanan, of the second generation of Israeli *amoraim* to R. Yiẓḥak and Ula; in Babylonia to Abaye and Rava in the fourth. As noted, we will concentrate on two areas which embody and facilitate rabbinic spirituality: prayer and Torah study; mystical study, to the extent that the latter is available for study, will not be examined at this juncture.

---

have had their say. Indeed, some 150 synagogues dating from the fourth and fifth centuries in the Land of Israel have been uncovered.

Among the highlights of this literature are, of course, Y.L. Elbogen's *Ha-Tefillah be-Yisrael be-Hitpatḥutah ha-Historit*, trans. Y. Amir and edited by Y. Heinemann (Tel Aviv: Devir, 1972); Y. Heinemann, *Ha-Tefillah bi-Tekufat ha-Tannaim ve-ha-Amoraim* (Jerusalem: Magnes, 1966); *idem.*, *Iyyunei Tefillah*, ed. A. Shinan (Jerusalem: Magnes, 1981), a collection of essays by Heinemann; S. Reif, *Judaism and Hebrew Prayer: New Perspectives on Jewish Liturgical History* (Cambridge: Cambridge University Press, 1995), and E. Fleischer's studies cited below in n. 13. See however Reif's critique of the views of Heinemann and Fleischer in Reif, pp. 119–20.

On the history of the synagogue in the time of *Ḥazal* ("Late Antiquity"), see *Ancient Synagogues: The State of Research*, ed. Joseph Gutmann (Chico, CA: Scholars Press, 1981); *Beit ha-Knesset bi-Tekufat ha-Mishnah ve-ha-Talmud: Leket Maamarim*, ed. Zev Safrai (Jerusalem: Merkaz Zalman Shazar, 1981); *The Synagogue in Late Antiquity*, ed. Lee I. Levine (Philadelphia: The American Schools of Oriental Research, 1987); see also the latter's "The Sage and the Synagogue in Late Antiquity: The Evidence of the Galilee," in Lee I. Levine, *The Galilee in Late Antiquity* (New York: Jewish Seminary of America, 1992), pp. 201–22; *idem.*, "The Nature and Origin of the Palestinian Synagogue Reconsidered," *Journal of Biblical Literature* 115 (1966): 425–48, and his *Judaism and Hellenism in Antiquity: Conflict or Confluence?* (Seattle: University of Washington Press, 1986), pp. 139–79; Dan Urman, "The House of Assembly and the House of Study: Are They One and the Same?," *Journal of Jewish Studies* 44 (1993): 236–57, and F. Huettenmeister, "*Bet ha-Knesset u-Veit Midrash ve-ha-Zikkah Beinei-hem*," *Kathedra* 18 (1981): 38–44.

A comprehensive bibliography may be found in the supplement to Kiryat Sefer 64 (1992–1993), *Reshimat Maamarim be-Inyenei Tefillah u-Mo'adim*, by Y. Tabory; the latter is also the editor of a recent collection of essays on prayer, Mi-Kumran 'ad Kahir: *Meḥkarim be-Toledot ha-Tefillah* (Jerusalem: Orḥot, 1999).

I

> Those who say that the commandment to pray is only rabbinic [in origin] have never seen the light. For while the text of the prayers and the requirement that they be recited thrice daily may be rabbinic, the essential concept and content [of the miẓvah to pray] are the foundation of the whole Torah: to know the Lord; to acknowledge His greatness and glory with perfect and serene knowledge and an understanding heart; to contemplate them to such an extent that the intellective soul is inspired to love the Name of the Lord, to cleave to Him and His Torah, and to crave His *miẓvot.*[11]

R. Shneur Zalman does not mention petitionary prayer directly, though acknowledgment of God's greatness is certainly preparatory to it. This omission is hardly accidental; ḥasidic thinkers often downplay the worth of such prayer, and try to direct the one praying to more God-centered concerns.[12] Indeed, recently Ezra Fleischer has pointed to the communal (or, rather, the nationalist) nature of *the* prayer *par excellence, Shemoneh Esreih.* Fleischer notes that even those few *berakhot* which seem to sound an individual note (those for sustenance and healing) are expressed in the plural.[13]

Having said all this, the reader will gain more insight into the topic of our essay from the halakhkic and pietistic literature alluded to above. I will cite just two, which have accompanied me in one form or another, for much of my life: Alexander Ziskind, *Yesod ve-Shoresh ha-Avodah*, corr. ed. (Jerusalem: Mekhon Harry Fischel, 1978), and R. David Abudarham ("the Avudram"), *Abudarham ha-Shalem*, corr. and expanded ed. (Jerusalem: Usha, 1963). The reader will learn more from these works on the nature of Jewish prayer than a bookcase of more historically minded studies – including the following.

[11] D.Z. Hillman, *Iggerot Baal ha-Tanya* (Jerusalem: 1953), p. 33f. The letter of R. Shneur Zalman of Liady was sent to R. Alexander Sender of Shklov; the translation is from Norman Lamm, *The Religious Thought of Ḥasidism: Text and Commentary* (New York: Yeshiva University Press, 1999), p. 185.

[12] See R. Menahem Mendel of Vitebsk, *Peri ha-Areẓ, Mikhtavim*, p. 57, in Lamm, *Ḥasidism*, p. 187f. "If you serve God in utter truth, you should have no desire or lust for anything except to do His will. How then do you come to pray and seek divine mercy for yourself, or others...?"

[13] See E. Fleischer, "*Tefillat Shemoneh Esreih – Iyyunim be-Ofyah, Sidrah, Tokhnah,*

This strain of self-abnegation is absent from personal testimonies regarding prayer. Indeed, among the most personal statements preserved in rabbinic literature on prayer are several which emphasize its petitionary aspect. In M *Berakhot* 5:5 and the accompanying *Yerushalmi* (41a) we have the following reports.

> מתני׳ המתפלל וטעה סימן רע לו ואם שליח ציבור הוא סימן רע לשולחיו מפני ששלוחו של אדם כמותו. אמרו עליו על רבי חנינא בן דוסא שהיה מתפלל על החולים ואומר זה חי וזה מת. אמרו לו מנין אתה יודע אמר להם אם שגורה תפילתי בפי יודע אני שהוא מקובל ואם לאו יודע אני שהוא מטורף: גמ׳...מעשה ברבן גמליאל שחלה בנו ושלח שני תלמידי חכמים אצל רחב״ד בעירו. אמר לון המתינו לי עד שאעלה לעלייה ועלה לעלייה וירד. אמר להו בטוח אני שנינוח בנו של ר״ג מחליו וסיימו באותה שעה תבע מהן מזון. אמר רבי שמואל בר נחמני אם כוונת את לבך בתפילה תהא מבושר שנשמעה תפילתך ומה טעם תכין לבם תקשיב אזניך אמר ריב״ל אם עשו שפתותיו של אדם תנובה יהא מבושר שנשמע תפילתו מה טעם בורא ניב שפתים שלום שלום לרחוק ולקרוב אמר ה׳ ורפאתיו:
>
> Mishnah: When one prays and makes a mistake it is a bad omen for him, and if he be the Reader for a congregation it is a bad omen for those who appointed him, because the representative of a person is like to himself. They related of R. Chanina ben Dosa that when he prayed on behalf of sick people he used to say, "This one will live," or "That one will die." They said to him, "Whence dost thou know?" He replied to them, "If my prayer be uttered fluently I know it is granted,

---

u-Maggamoteha," *Tarbiz* 62 (1993): 179–223, esp. pp. 178–88; see also his "*Le-Kadmoniyut Tefillot ha-Ḥovah be-Yisrael*," *Tarbiz* 59 (1990): 397–441, and Y. Tabory, "*Avodat Hashem shel Anshei ha-Maamad*," in Y. Tabory, ed., *Mi-Kumran ʿad Kahir*, pp. 145–69.

Much has been written on the date of the composition of the *Shemoneh Esreih*; see most recently S. Safrai, "*Ha-Hitkansut be-Vatei ha-Knesset bi-Yemei Moʿed be-Shabbatot u-vi-Yemot ha-Ḥol*," in Zev Safrai, *et. al.*, *Ḥikrei Ereẓ: Iyyunim be-Toldot Ereẓ Yisrael Mugashim le-Khvod Prof. Yehudah Feliks*, (Ramat Gan: Bar Ilan University Press, 1997), pp. 235–45, and the brief bibliographical reference in n. 50; see also U. Erlich, "*Le-Ḥeker Nusaḥah ha-Kadum shel Tefillat Shemoneh Esreih – Birkhat ha-Avodah*," in *Mi-Kumran ʿad Kahir*, Y. Tabory, ed., pp. 17–38.

> but if not, I know that it is rejected. Gemara: A story regarding Rabban Gamaliel, whose son was ill, and sent two scholars to R. Ḥanina b. Dosa in his city: [When he met them] he said to them: "Wait until I go up to the attic room." He went up to the attic room and descended. He said to them: "I am certain that [the condition of] the son of Rabban Gamaliel has improved."[Later] they estimated that at that moment he asked for food from [those attending him]. Said R. Samuel b. Naḥmani: If you have [properly] directed your heart in prayer, be assured that your prayer is heard. What reason [(=scriptural source) is there for this]? "Prepare their heart, let your ears listen" (Ps. 10:17). Said R. Joshua b. Levi: If a person's lips have produced fruit, he will be assured that his prayer will be heard. What reason [(=scriptural source) is there for this]? "Creator of the utterance of the lips, peace, peace to far and near, says God, and I have healed him" (Is 57:19).

And in M *Berakhot* 4:3:

> רבן גמליאל אומר, בכל יום מתפלל אדם שמונה עשרה. רבי יהושע אומר, מעין שמונה עשרה. רבי עקיבה אומר, אם שגורה תפלתו בפיו, יתפלל שמונה עשרה. ואם לאו, מעין שמונה עשרה.
>
> Rabban Gamliel says: A man should pray the Eighteen [Benedictions] every day. Rabbi Joshua says: The substance of the Eighteen. Rabbi Akivah says: If his prayer is fluent in his mouth he should pray the Eighteen, but if not, the substance of the Eighteen.

And, to provide some context for R. Akiva's view, let us not forget the arresting description of his private prayer as recorded in BT *Berakhot* 31a.

> תניא אמר רבי יהודה כך היה מנהגו של רבי עקיבא כשהיה מתפלל עם הצבור היה מקצר ועולה מפני טורח צבור וכשהיה מתפלל בינו לבין עצמו אדם מניחו בזוית זו ומוצאו בזוית אחרת וכל כך למה מפני כריעות והשתחויות:

> It has been taught: Rabbi Yehudah said: such was the custom of R. Akiva; when he prayed with the congregation, he used to cut it short and finish in order not to inconvenience the congregation, but when he prayed by himself, a man would leave him in one corner and find him later in another, on account of his many genuflexions and prostrations.

It is clear that the "balance" of which Dr. Lamm wrote has been a shifting one, and M *Berakhot* 4:3 seems situated at its very cusp, with a range of opinions which proceed from institutionalization to its opposite. It would be jejune to oppose spirituality and the "free-form" type of prayer which R. Akiva evidently both represented and exemplified, and deny it to Rabban Gamaliel's normative opinion. But Dr. Lamm's description of the dilemma faced by those who would either legislate the requirements for prayer on the one hand, or leave the fulfillment of the duty to pray to the feelings of the one offering the prayer on the other, reflects not only a legislative dilemma, but a personal one.

R. Akiva's solution is one which has undoubtedly been adopted by many. In public he restricted himself to what Max Kadushin called "normal mysticism";[14] in private he allowed his impulses more unfettered play. Note that the reason for this bifurcated approach lay in his responsibility to the community and its communal forms of prayer – a responsibility which took precedence over his own spiritual fulfillment. Unfortunately, R. Yehudah does not describe the circumstances under which R. Akiva prayed privately, or how often, but in describing the practice as "מנהגו" he implies that this was his ordinary course of behavior. Still, his opinion, as recorded in M *Berakhot* 4:3, still leaves a good deal of flexibility in the hands of the one offering prayer. R. Yehudah's description of R. Akiva's public behavior as מקצר ועולה (abridge and continue) does not necessarily imply that he would choose the מעין שבע (an abbreviated seven

[14] See Max Kadushin, *Organic Thinking: A Study in Rabbinic Thought* (New York: Bloch Publishing, repr. n.d.), pp. 237–40, and *idem.*, *Worship and Ethics: A Study in Rabbinic Judaism* (New York: Bloch Publishing, 1963), pp. 13–7, 167–8, 203–5.

[blessings]), or that the congregation would. But the opportunities for spontaneity for which his view allowed makes his own public practice – especially as compared to his private behavior – all the more striking.

R. Yehudah's explanation of R. Akiva's private practice, while couched in terms of physical gesture and time expended clearly points to another aspect of R. Akiva's prayer: the emphasis on self-abasement. This is clearly the prayer of the man who spoke of loving God with all one's might as implying that this applied "even if he takes your soul."[15]

The reports of R. Ḥanina b. Dosa exemplify a different mode of prayer, perhaps one comparable to R. Akiva's private custom, or perhaps one pertaining only to his petitionary prayers. It would be mistaken, however, to associate his behavior with the חסידים הראשונים (Early Pietists) described in M. *Berakhot* 5:1, which do not seem to relate to petitionary prayer exclusively, or perhaps not at all. One would expect that individual petitionary prayer would not require an admonition for כובד ראש (deep earnestness).

> משנה: אין עומדין להתפלל אלא מתוך כובד ראש. חסידים הראשונים היו שוהין שעה אחת ומתפללין כדי שיכוונו לבם לאביהם שבשמים אפילו המלך שואל בשלומו לא ישיבנו ואפילו נחש כרוך על עקבו לא יפסיק:
> Mishnah: One must not stand up to say the Amidah without deep earnestness. The early pietists used to wait for one hour and then pray in order to direct their minds to God. Should even the king greet one, he may not return the greeting to him. And if even a snake be curled round his heel he must not pause.

Indeed, the reports of R. Ḥanina b. Dosa and R. Akiva, and associated traditions seem to date from a different era, one in which the emphasis was put on unstructured, perhaps ecstatic, prayer. The Mishnah also seems somewhat disproportionately (from our perspective) concerned with laborers fitting their prayers

[15] BT *Ber.* 61b.

into their work environment, once again an instance of fulfilling one's obligatory prayers within a context which does not allow for institutionalized prayer, as in M *Berakhot* 2:4.

> האומנים קורין בראש האילן או בראש הנדבך מה שאין רשאין לעשות כן בתפילה:
>
> Craftsmen may recite the Shema on the top of a tree or on top of a course of stones, which they may not do when they say the *Amidah*.

Indeed, one reading of R. Eliezer's famous dictum regarding one who prays under obligation – אין תפלתו תחנונים (His prayer is not one of supplication.) – may be read either as pertaining to a context of fixed prayer, as do most commentators, or as a protest against Rabban Gamaliel's insistence of instituting the fixed daily *Shemoneh Esreih*[16] (M *Berakhot* 4:3–4):

> רבן גמליאל אומר, בכל יום מתפלל אדם שמונה עשרה. רבי יהושע אומר, מעין שמונה עשרה. רבי עקיבה אומר, אם שגורה תפלתו בפיו, יתפלל שמונה עשרה. ואם לאו, מעין שמונה עשרה. רבי אליעזר אומר, העושה תפלתו קבע, אין תפלתו תחנונים. רבי יהושע אומר, המהלך במקום סכנה, מתפלל תפלה קצרה. אומר, הושע השם את עמך את שארית ישראל, בכל פרשת העבור יהיו צרכיהם לפניך. ברוך אתה ה', שומע תפלה.
>
> Rabban Gamliel says: A man should pray the Eighteen [Benedictions] every day. Rabbi Joshua says: The substance of the Eighteen. Rabbi Akivah says: If his prayer is fluent in his mouth he should pray the Eighteen, but if not, the substance of the Eighteen. Rabbi Eliezer says: He that makes his prayer a fixed task, his prayer is no supplication. Rabbi Joshua says: He that journeys in a place of danger should pray a short prayer saying, "Save O Lord, the remnant of Israel; at their every crossroad let their needs come before thee. Blessed art thou, O Lord, that hearest prayer!"

[16] See *Melekhet Shelomo ad loc.*, in the name of R. Yehosef Ashkenazi.

In either case, however, *Ḥazal* express a very realistic view of the effects of fixed prayer: lack of spontaneity, sincerity and authenticity.[17] Note though that R. Eliezer does not employ the formula אין תפלתו תפלה (His prayer is not a prayer), but rather אין תפלתו תחנונים (His prayer is not one of supplication) – yet another mark of his realistic assessment of humanity's limited capacity for regular, recurrent, mandated yet heartfelt prayer.[18] Given its context, R. Eliezer's statement would seem to refer to *Shemoneh Esreih*, *tefillah par excellence*, and thus primarily to petitionary prayer. It is undeniable, however, that prayer as such must contain this element of תחנונים (supplication), an admission of the petitioner's creatureliness and need. Prayer without these characteristics is hardly worthy of the name. Or, as we noted above, in R. Shneur Zalman's formulation,

> the essential concept and content [of the miẓvah to pray] are the foundation of the whole Torah: to know the Lord; to acknowledge His greatness and glory with perfect and serene knowledge and an understanding heart; to contemplate them to such an extent that the intellective soul is inspired to love the Name of the Lord, to cleave to Him and His Torah, and to crave His *miẓvot*.[19]

It is inconceivable that the cavalier attitude that R. Shimon seems to display towards prayer was not tempered by something of this consideration (see p. 77 below). It may well be that he considered

---

[17] Note *Tiferet Israel*'s definition of want of תחנונים (supplication): תחנונים: ר"ל שחוטפה או שאינו אומרה להכנעה או שאינו מחדש בו דבר או שאינו מתפלל בנץ החמה "that is to say, that he 'snatches' it [= says it too quickly for proper intention], or does not recite it with proper submission, or he does not add something of his own, or he does not pray with the sunrise."

[18] In this respect, of course, institutionalized prayer is only one victim of the general problem of habituation. Humans are so constituted as to crave novelty and to adjust to almost any situation, good or bad. Human sensibility tends toward a status of mediocrity, which requires constant attention to resist.

[19] See above, pp. 6–7.

his Torah study as fulfilling some of the same purposes and yielding the same results. We will explore this further below.

As far as the matter of personalized petitionary prayer goes, it is clear from the very structure and formulation of one of the earliest of rabbinic prayers, *Shemoneh Esreih* (as indeed from the Book of Psalms), that personal petitionary prayer was perfectly acceptable to *Ḥazal*. So long as one expressed his or her dependency on God in prayer, it seems to have been perfectly acceptable to make both personal and communal requests for mundane needs – primarily health and sustenance. Nevertheless, the pronounced emphasis on national (the messianic redemption and associated events, protection from slanderers) and religious (repentance and forgiveness) needs is undeniable.

The personal aspect of prayer is perhaps most clearly expressed in the voluntary prayers offered by a number of (mostly) *amoraim*, and gathered together in BT *Ber.* 16b–17a and JT *Ber.* 33a.[20] Among them are several attributed to R. Yoḥanan, the great second-generation Israeli *amora*, and head of the Tiberian school, in both Talmuds.

> רבי יוחנן בתר דמסיים צלותיה אמר הכי יהי רצון מלפניך ה׳ אלהינו שתציץ בבשתנו ותביט ברעתנו ותתלבש ברחמיך ותתכסה בעזך ותתעטף בחסידותך ותתאזר בחנינותך ותבא לפניך מדת טובך וענותנותך.
>
> רבי יוחנן כי הוה מסיים ספרא דאיוב אמר הכי סוף אדם למות וסוף בהמה לשחיטה והכל למיתה הם עומדים. אשרי מי שגדל בתורה ועמלו בתורה ועושה נחת רוח ליוצרו וגדל בשם טוב ונפטר בשם טוב מן העולם ועליו אמר שלמה טוב שם משמן טוב ויום המות מיום הולדו.
>
> ר׳ יוחנן הוה מצלי יהי רצון מלפניך ה׳ אלהי ואלהי אבותי שתשכן בפוריינו אהבה ואחוה שלום וריעות ותצליח סופינו אחרית ותקוה ותרבה גבולנו בתלמידים ונשיש בחלקינו בג"ע ותקנינו לב טוב וחבר טוב ונשכים ונמצא ייחול לבבינו ותבא לפניך קורת נפשינו לטובה:
>
> R. Yoḥanan on concluding his prayer added the following: "May it be Thy will, O Lord our God, to look upon our shame,

[20] See Y. Heinemann, *Ha-Tefillah bi-Tekufat ha-Tannaim ve-ha-Amoraim*, pp. 108–20.

and behold our evil plight, and clothe Thyself in Thy mercies, and cover Thyself in Thy strength, and wrap Thyself in Thy lovingkindness, and gird Thyself with Thy graciousness, and may the attribute of Thy kindness and gentleness come before Thee!"

When R. Yoḥanan finished the Book of Job, he used to say the following: "The end of man is to die, and the end of a beast is to be slaughtered, and all are doomed to die. Happy he who was brought up in the Torah and whose labour was in the Torah and who has given pleasure to his Creator and who grew up with a good name and departed the world with a good name; and of him Solomon said: A good name is better than precious oil, and the day of death than the day of one's birth."[21]

R. Yoḥanan would pray [as follows]: "May it be [Your] will in Your Presence, O Lord my God, and God of my fathers, that You cause love and brotherhood, peace and friendship in our forums, that You provide purpose and hope for our end, You enlarge our boundary with disciples [that] we rejoice in our portion in the next world [lit., the Garden of Eden], and cause us to acquire a good heart, a good companion, that we rise early and find our heart's hope, and that our souls come before You for good."[22]

The personal and penitential nature of the additions transmitted by the *Bavli* is unmistakable, and go beyond the sentiments expressed by any version of the standard *Shemoneh Esreih* prayer for forgiveness.

---

[21] BT *Ber.* 16b.

[22] JT *Ber.* 33a; all references in this paper will refer to the standard Vilna edition of the *Yerushalmi* rather than the *editio princeps*. In the *Bavli* (BT *Ber.* 16b), the latter – with a few minor variations – is attributed to R. Eleazar, R. Yoḥanan's Babylonian disciple and successor.

רבי אלעזר בתר דמסיים צלותיה אמר הכי יהי רצון מלפניך ה׳ אלהינו שתשכן בפורינו אהבה ואחוה ושלום וריעות ותרבה גבולנו בתלמידים ותצליח סופנו אחרית ותקוה ותשים חלקנו בגן עדן ותקננו בחבר טוב ויצר טוב בעולמך ונשכים ונמצא יחול לבבנו ליראה את שמך ותבא לפניך קורת נפשנו לטובה.

The even darker note sounded by the prayer R. Yoḥanan composed on the occasion of completing the book of Job is entirely appropriate to that occasion. However, the prayer found in the *Yerushalmi* (which in the *Bavli* is attributed to R. Eleazar; see n. 23), expresses much broader and more personal sentiments, feelings which are mostly unexpressed in the standard versions – a request for household peace, personal and professional success, and the appropriate reward in the World to Come.

These occasional prayers may provide a hint of what R. Yoḥanan had in mind when he expressed the wish, recorded in both Talmuds, that "would that a man pray all the day long" (BT *Ber.* 21a = JT *Ber.* 1b, 34b and JT *Ber* 8a–b = JT *Shab.* 7a–b = JT *Hor.* 18a–b). In each of the *Yerushalmi*'s quotes, however, an additional comment is appended: למה שאין תפילה מפסדת (Why? Because no prayer causes loss.).[23]

This is a curious wish for R. Yoḥanan to express. After all, he sacrificed all his possessions in order to study Torah,[24] and indeed achieved great heights in Torah study. He is the most frequently-cited *amora* in both Talmuds – so much so that Maimonides in his introduction to the *Mishneh Torah* credited him with the redaction of the *Yerushalmi*. What would have become of his Torah scholarship

---

> R. Eleazar on concluding his prayer used to say the following: "May it be Thy will, O Lord our God, to cause to dwell in our lot love and brotherhood and peace and friendship, and mayest Thou make our borders rich in disciples and prosper our latter end with good prospect and hope, and set our portion in Paradise, and confirm us with a good companion and a good impulse in Thy world, and may we rise early and obtain the yearning of our heart to fear Thy name, and mayest Thou be pleased to grant the satisfaction of our desires!"

Since the *Bavli* attributes a different prayer to R. Yoḥanan, it is unlikely that this one was shared by both *amoraim*; it seems more likely that the *Bavli*'s tradition confused the teacher and his disciple.

[23] See Rashi in BT *Pes.* 54b s.v. והאמר ר׳ יוחנן: במסכת ברכות ואין בתפלה יתֵרה משום ברכה לבטלה, "But did not R. Yoḥanan say: in Tractate *Berakhot*, that excessive prayer does not [violate the prohibition] of a blessing [recited] in vain."

[24] See *Leviticus Rabbah* 30:1, ed. Margulies, pp. 688–90, and see his note on pp. 689–90.

had he spent his entire life in prayer? The context of this remark in JT *Ber.* 8a–b (= JT *Shab.* 7a–b and JT *Hor.* 18a) may provide a clue.

רבי יוחנן בשם רבי שמעון בן יוחי כגון אנו שעוסקים בתלמוד תורה אפילו לקרית שמע אין אנו מפסיקין. רבי יוחנן אמרה על גרמיה כגון אנו שאין אנו עסוקים בתלמוד תורה אפילו לתפלה אנו מפסיקין. דין כדעתיה ודין כדעתיה רבי יוחנן כדעתיה דאמר רבי יוחנן ולואי שיתפלל אדם כל היום למה שאין תפילה מפסדת רבי שמעון בן יוחאי כדעתיה דרשב״י אמר אלו הוינא קאים על טורא דסיני בשעתא דאתיהיבת תורה לישראל הוינא מתבעי קומי רחמנא דיתברי לבר נשא תרין פומין חד דהוי לעי באוריתא וחד דעבד ליה כל צורכיה. חזר ומר ומה אין חד הוא לית עלמא יכיל קאים ביה מן דילטוריא דיליה אילו הוו תרין עאכ״ו.

א״ר יוסי קומי רבי ירמיה אתיא דרבי יוחנן כרבי חנינא בן עקביא אומר כשם שמפסיקין לק״ש כך מפסיקין לתפילה ולתפילין ולשאר כל מצותיה של תורה. ולא מודה רשב״י שמפסיקין לעשות סוכה ולעשות לולב. ולית ליה לרשב״י הלמד על מנת לעשות ולא הלמד שלא לעשות שהלמד שלא לעשות נוח לו שלא נברא. וא״ר יוחנן הלמד שלא לעשות נוח לו אילו נהפכה שלייתו על פניו ולא יצא לעולם.

טעמיה דרשב״י [ח/ב] זה שינון וזה שינון ואין מבטל שינון מפני שינון.

והא תנינן הקורא מכאן ואילך לא הפסיד כאדם שהוא קורא בתורה. הא בעונתה חביבה מד״ת. היא היא.

א״ר יודן רשב״י ע״י שהיה תדיר בד״ת לפיכך אינה חביבה יותר מד״ת.

אמר רבי אבא מרי לא תנינן אלא כאדם שהוא קורא בתורה הא בעונתה כמשנה היא רשב״י כדעתיה דרשב״י אמר העוסק במקרא מידה ואינה מידה ורבנן עבדי מקרא כמשנה:

[…If they began, they do not interrupt, [but] they interrupt for the recitation of the *Shema* but do not interrupt for *Tefillah* (=*Shemoneh Esreih*)….] R. Yoḥanan said in the name of R. Shimon b. Yoḥai: [Those] such as we, who are occupied with Torah study [exclusively], we do not interrupt even for the recitation of the *Shema*. R. Yoḥanan said regarding himself: [Those] such as we who are not occupied with the study of Torah [as were previous generations] – we interrupt even for *Tefillah* (=*Shemoneh Esreih*). Each one follows his own view. R. Yoḥanan [follows] his own view, for R. Yoḥanan said: Would that a person would pray all day long. Why? Because no prayer causes lost.

R. Shimon b. Yoḥai [follows] his own view, for R. Shimon b. Yoḥai said: If I had stood at Mount Sinai at the time that the Torah was given to Israel, I would have requested of God that these people have two mouths created for them, one with which to study Torah and one with which he would perform all his [physical] needs. He [later] changed his mind, [and said]: Since with only one [mouth] the world can scarcely exist because of the informers, all the more so if there were two [mouths]!

Said R. Yosa before R. Jeremiah: [The view of R. Yoḥanan] is according to [that] of R. Ḥananiah b. Akiva, for it was taught: The writers of [Torah] scrolls, *tefillin* and *mezuzot* interrupt for the recitation of the *Shema* but not for *Tefillah*. R. Ḥananiah b. Akiva says: Just as they interrupt for the recitation of the Shema, so do they interrupt for *Tefillah*, [donning] *tefillin* and the other *miẓvot* of the Torah.

[But] does R. Shimon b. Yoḥai not admit that they interrupt in order to build a *sukkah* and do [the miẓvah] of *lulav*? And does R. Shimon b. Yoḥai not hold that one should study [in order to] perform [the *miẓvot*] and that one who studies not in order to do [the miẓvot] – it were better for him that he had not been created!

Said R. Yoḥanan: One who studies not in order to perform [the *miẓvot*], it were better for him that his afterbirth be turned over his face, and that he not be born! [However, in this case] the reason of R. Shimon b. Yoḥai is that each one (=Torah study and prayer) is [called] 'recitation' [in the Torah], and we do not cancel one recitation for the other recitation.

But have we not learned: One who reads [the *Shema*] from here onward (=the time of recitation) has not lost

> [thereby], [but has received his reward] as one who reads in the Torah [that is, as Torah study even if not as prayer]. Thus, in its [proper] time [as prayer] it is more beloved than words of Torah!
>
> Said R. Yudan: [As to] R. Shimon b. Yoḥai, since he was steadily [engaged] in words of Torah, therefore [recitation as prayer] is not more beloved to him than words of Torah.
>
> R. [A]bba Mari said: We learnt [this] only of one who reads [words of] Torah [not in its proper time], but [in its proper] time [prayer is] like Mishnah [study].
>
> [While] R. Shimon b. Yoḥai [goes] according to his own view. For R. Shimon b. Yoḥai says: [As to] one who occupies himself with Scripture – it is a trait which is not [the best] trait – but the Rabbis consider Scripture like Mishnah.

This *sugya*, only part of which we have excerpted, is richly laden with the themes which will occupy us for much of the following discussion: the question of whether prayer or Torah study ranks higher in Judaism's scale of values, how both relate to the practical observance of *miẓvot*, and how these relations change with respect to person and condition.

At base is R. Yoḥanan's drawing a radical distinction between his time and that of R. Shimon b. Yoḥai's.[25] While R. Yoḥanan may

[25] The same view is attributed to R. Yoḥanan in the *Bavli* as well; see BT *Shab.* 11a:

> מפסיקין לקריאת שמע: הא תנא ליה רישא אין מפסיקין סיפא אתאן לדברי תורה דתניא חברים שהיו עוסקין בתורה מפסיקין לקריאת שמע ואין מפסיקין לתפלה אמר רבי יוחנן לא שנו אלא כגון רבי שמעון בן יוחי וחביריו שתורתן אומנותן אבל כגון אנו מפסיקין לקריאת שמע ולתפלה והתניא כשם שאין מפסיקין לתפלה כך אין מפסיקין לקריאת שמע כי תני ההיא בעיבור שנה דאמר רב אדא בר אהבה וכן תנו סבי דהגרוניא אמר רבי אלעזר בר צדוק כשהיינו עוסקין בעיבור השנה ביבנה לא היינו מפסיקין לא לקריאת שמע ולא לתפלה:
>
> Yet if they began, they need not break off. One must break off for the reading of the *Shema* [but not for prayer]. But the first clause teaches, "They need not break off?" The second clause refers to study. For it was taught: If companions [scholars] are engaged in studying, they must break off for the reading of the *Shema*, but not for prayer. R.

have been viewed by his disciples[26] as the epitome of a life totally devoted to Torah,[27] he seems to have viewed himself in a different light, at least in comparison with R. Shimon b. Yoḥai.[28] R. Shimon b. Yoḥai represented the epitome of devotion to Torah learning to him, and only to such scholars was permission to continue their study through the time of the recitation of *Shema* granted; his own generation must interrupt their study even for *Shemoneh Esreih*.

But this is also linked to R. Shimon b. Yoḥai's view of the recitation of *Shema* as representing שינון, or *Talmud Torah*. Since it is (only) on a par with the general miẓvah of *Talmud Torah*, it is not necessary to interrupt one's study for the recital of the *Shema*. Since the *Shema* is clearly superior to *Shemoneh Esreih* in terms of obligation (the reasons given in the *Yerushalmi* are various; see JT *Ber.* 18a), that too is deferred. For R. Yoḥanan, however, his generation's deficiency in pursuing *Talmud Torah* is such that he and his contemporaries must interrupt their studies even for *Shemoneh Esreih*.

> Yoḥanan said: This was taught only of such as R. Shimon b. Yoḥai and his companions, whose study was their profession, but we must break off both for the reading of the *Shema* and for prayer. But it was taught: "Just as they do not break off for the service, so do they not break off for the reading of the *Shema*?" – That was taught in reference to the intercalation of the year. For R. Adda b. Ahabah said, and the Elders of Hagronia recited likewise: R. Eleazar b. Zadok said: When we were engaged in intercalating the year at Yavneh, we made no break for the reading of the *Shema* or prayer.

However, the *Bavli* does not specifically attribute the contrary view to R. Shimon b. Yoḥai, but merely cites him as an exemplary case.

[26] It should be recalled that, despite his well-known antipathy to Babylonians, his academy included a good number of them, thus testifying to his reputation in both the Land of Israel and in Babylonia.

[27] He is the most frequently cited *amora* in both *Bavli* and *Yerushalmi*; see *Leviticus Rabbah* 30:1 on his reflections on having sold his patrimony in order to devote himself to Torah study.

[28] R. Yoḥanan's views on the subject of "the devolution of the species" may have something to do with this. Many of the famous and oft-quoted statements relating

רבי יוחנן בשם רבי שמעון בן יוחי כגון אנו שעוסקים בתלמוד תורה אפילו לקרית שמע אין אנו מפסיקין. רבי יוחנן אמרה על גרמיה כגון אנו שאין אנו עסוקים בתלמוד תורה אפילו לתפלה אנו מפסיקין. דין כדעתיה ודין כדעתיה רבי יוחנן כדעתיה דאמר רבי יוחנן ולואי שיתפלל אדם כל היום למה שאין תפילה מפסדת.

טעמיה דרשב"י זה שינון וזה שינון ואין מבטל שינון מפני שינון.

והא תנינן הקורא מכאן ואילך לא הפסיד כאדם שהוא קורא בתורה.
הא בעונתה חביבה מד"ת. היא היא.

א"ר יודן רשב"י ע"י שהיה תדיר בד"ת לפיכך אינה חביבה יותר מד"ת.

אמר רבי אבא מרי לא תנינן אלא כאדם שהוא קורא בתורה הא בעונתה כמשנה היא רשב"י כדעתיה דרשב"י אמר העוסק במקרא מידה ואינה מידה ורבנן עבדי מקרא כמשנה:

R. Yoḥanan said in the name of R. Shimon b. Yoḥai: [Those] such as we, who are occupied with Torah study [exclusively], we do not interrupt even for the recitation of the *Shema*. R. Yoḥanan said regarding himself: [Those] such as we who are not occupied with the study of Torah [as were previous generations] – we interrupt even for *Tefillah* (= *Shemoneh Esreih*). Each one follows his own view. R. Yoḥanan [follows] his own view, for R. Yoḥanan said: Would that a person would pray all day long. Why? Because no prayer causes loss.

The reason of R. Shimon b. Yoḥai is that this is learning and that is learning, and one [form of] learning does not nullify another [form] of learning.

But did we not learn: One who recites [the recitation of the *Shema*] from here on does not lose [any merit thereby, but is regarded as] a person who reads [that passage] in the Torah? But then, in its proper time is it more beloved than words of Torah? [No,] it is the same.

Said R. Yudan: [As to] R. Shimon b. Yoḥai, since he was always engaged in words of Torah, [the recitation of the *Shema*] is not more beloved than words of Torah.

Said R. Abba Mari: Have we not learned: "But [rather, he is considered] as a person who reads [the passage] in the Torah – thus in its proper time it is [considered as important] as Mishnah? That is [the view] of R. Shimon b. Yoḥai but the rabbis [i.e., the majority view] make Bible [study] like Mishnah [study].

Yet another theme seems intertwined with this discussion. Since R. Shimon b. Yoḥai views the obligation to study מקרא (Bible) as clearly inferior to Talmud (JT *Ber.* 7b = JT *Shab.* 8b = JT *Hor.* 18b), even the recitation of *Shema* does not take precedence over Talmud study.

> טעמיה דרשב"י [ח/ב] זה שינון וזה שינון ואין מבטל שינון מפני שינון.
> והא תנינן הקורא מכאן ואילך לא הפסיד כאדם שהוא קורא בתורה. הא בעונתה חביבה מד"ת. היא היא.
> א"ר יודן רשב"י ע"י שהיה תדיר בד"ת לפיכך אינה חביבה יותר מד"ת.
> אמר רבי אבא מרי לא תנינן אלא כאדם שהוא קורא בתורה הא בעונתה כמשנה היא רשב"י כדעתיה דרשב"י אמר העוסק במקרא מידה ואינה מידה ורבנן עבדי מקרא כמשנה:
>
> [However, in this case] the reason of R. Shimon b. Yoḥai is that each one (= Torah study and prayer) is [called] 'recitation' [in the Torah], and we do not cancel one recitation for the other recitation.
>
> But have we not learned: One who reads [the *Shema*] from here onward (= the time of recitation) has not lost [thereby], [but has received his reward] as one who reads in the Torah [that is, as Torah study even if not as prayer]. Thus, in its [proper] time [as prayer] it is more beloved than words of Torah!
>
> Said R. Yudan: [As to] R. Shimon b. Yoḥai, since he was steadily [engaged] in words of Torah, therefore [recitation as prayer] is not more beloved to him than words of Torah.
>
> R. [A]bba Mari said: We learnt [this] only of one who reads [words of] Torah [not in its proper time], but [in its proper] time [prayer is] like Mishnah [study].

The view alluded to here is clearly that expressed more fully in a *baraita* cited in JT *Shab.* 79b, and better known (anonymously) in BT *Baba Meẓia* 33b.

> הדא אמרה שהמשנה קודמת למקרא. ודא מסייעא לההוא דתני ר"ש בן יוחי. דתני ר"ש בן יוחי העוסק במקרא מידה שאינה מידה. העוסק במשנה מידה שנוטלין ממנה שכר. העוסק בתלמוד אין לך מידה גדולה מזו.
> לעולם הוי רץ אחר המשנה יותר מן התלמוד.
> א"ר יוסי בי ר' בון הדא דאת אמר עד שלא שיקע בו ר' רוב משניות. אבל משיקע בו ר' רוב משניות לעולם הוי רץ אחר התלמוד יותר מן המשנה.
>
> They then said that the Mishneh has precedence over *Mikra* (Bible). And this supports that which R. Shimon b. Yoḥai taught. For R. Shimon b. Yoḥai taught, involvement in [the study of] *Mikra* (Bible) is a measure that is not a measure. One who is involved in [the study of] Mishneh, it is measure that they take from it reward. One who is involved in [the study of] Talmud, there is no measure greater than that.
>
> And one should always run after Mishneh more than Talmud.
>
> R. Yosi the son of R. Bun said: Now that which you said applies before Rabbi included most *mishnayot* [in his Mishnah], but that Rabbi has included most *mishnayot* in his Mishnah. One should always run after the Tamud more than the Mishneh.

The redactor of this *sugya* represents R. Shimon's view as a minority one. The "rabbis" give the recitation of *Shema* the status of, at least, the study of Mishnah. R. Shimon b. Yoḥai's view is thus clear. The recitation of *Shema*, and certainly *Shemoneh Esreih*, is not superior to *Talmud Torah* as manifested by "Talmud" study. However, other *miẓvot* have a different status, and they must be performed in any case, as the end of the *sugya* in each of its parallels states.

> ולא מודה רשב"י שמפסיקין לעשות סוכה ולעשות לולב. ולית ליה לרשב"י הלמד על מנת לעשות ולא הלמד שלא לעשות שהלמד שלא לעשות נוח לו שלא נברא.

וא"ר יוחנן הלמד שלא לעשות נוח לו אילו נהפכה שילייתו על
פניו ולא יצא לעולם. טעמיה דרשב"י זה שינון וזה שינון ואין מבטל שינון
מפני שינון

[But] does R. Shimon b. Yoḥai not admit that they interrupt
in order to build a *sukkah* and do [the *miẓvah*] of *lulav*? And
does R. Shimon b. Yoḥai not hold that one should study [in
order to] perform [the *miẓvot*] and that one who studies not
in order to do [the *miẓvot*], – it were better for him that he
had not been created!

 Said R. Yoḥanan: One who studies not in order to
perform [the *miẓvot*], it were better for him that his afterbirth
be turned over his face, and that he not be born! [However,
in this case] the reason of R. Shimon b., Yoḥai is that each
one (= Torah study and prayer) is [called] 'recitation' [in the
Torah], and we do not cancel one recitation for the other
recitation.

Still, the *sugya* does not clearly ground the view attributed
to R. Shimon b. Yoḥai in a statement directly linked to him. The
difficulty the redactor had may be gauged from the source he chose
to quote.

רבי שמעון בן יוחאי כדעתיה דרשב"י אמר אלו הוינא קאים על טורא דסיני
בשעתא דאתיהיבת תורה לישראל הוינא מתבעי קומי רחמנא דיתברי לבר
נשא תרין פומין חד דהוי לעי באוריתא וחד דעבד ליה כל צורכיה. חזר ומר
ומה אין חד הוא לית עלמא יכיל קאים ביה מן דילטוריא דיליה אילו הוו
תרין עאכ"ו.

R. Shimon b. Yoḥai [follows] his own view, for R. Shimon b.
Yoḥai said: If I had stood at Mount Sinai at the time that the
Torah was given to Israel, I would have requested of God that
these people have two mouths created for them, one with
which to study Torah and one with which he would perform
all his [physical] needs. He [later] changed his mind, [and
said]: Since with only one [mouth] the world can scarcely
exist because of the informers, all the more so if there were
two [mouths]!

R. Shimon's initial complaint does not relate to prayer in any direct way unless one assumes that the second mouth which would have been created for כל צורכיה (all of his needs) would have been used for prayer. However, his rueful reconsideration of his original statement – that since even the one mouth we have is used for informing on others, how much more evil would we do with two – relates to prayer even less. Rather, it undoubtedly reflects his experience as a fugitive from the Roman authorities. His reconsideration provides a framework for interpreting his original statement. Indeed, if the later redactional statement regarding the similarity of *Talmud Torah* to the recitation of *Shema* (since both are types of שינון) accurately reflects his view, he may have included prayer along with study as the proper use of the "first" mouth, and *not* left it for the "second" mouth. In any case, though, it is remarkable that R. Shimon is hardly represented in the *halakhot* of prayer,[29] though, of course, one's creativity or interest in the legal aspects of a particular area may not always correspond to one's personal predilections.[30] Indeed, the *Bavli* preserves at least one statement (BT *Berakhot* 7b–8a), attributed by R. Yoḥanan to R. Shimon b. Yoḥai,[31] which expresses the importance of communal prayer.[32]

---

to this theme are attributed to him; see especially his remarks on R. Oshaya and the stature of earlier generations in BT *Eruv.* 53a.

[29] Indeed, in the *Bavli* he is represented by two statements regarding the recitation of *Shema*, as we might well expect in light of the data presented above; see BT *Ber.* 8b and 14b, and one on the importance of praying with the community in BT *Ber.* 7b–8a (see immediately below). The contrast to his many (and striking) statements regarding the importance of Torah study is noteworthy; see BT. *Ber.* 5a, 7b, 35b, *Shab.* 138b, *Baba Kama* 17a, and see *Pes.* 112a.

[30] In addition, one could hardly portray R. Shimon as a "dry" legalist; his aggadic contribution is also sizeable. Indeed, this (Christian influenced?) stereotyped image is hardly true to reality. Even *baalei halakhah* may have rich interior lives of meditation and prayer.

[31] In *Tanḥuma Mikeẓ* 9 this view is attributed to R. Yose b. Halafta. Nevertheless, see *Dikdukei Soferim ad loc.*, n. *kaf*, where R.N.N. Rabinowitz notes that this statement is part of a collection of traditions reported by R. Yoḥanan in the name of R. Shimon b. Yoḥai.

[32] Though it may be argued that the wording indicates that the reference is to the

> ...דאמר רבי יוחנן משום רבי שמעון בן יוחי [ח/א] מאי דכתיב ואני תפלתי לך ה' עת רצון אימתי עת רצון בשעה שהצבור מתפללין
>
> For R. Yoḥanan said in the name of R. Shimon b. Yoḥai: What does it mean, "And I will pray to you, God in the time of desire." When is the 'time of desire'? At the hour that the community is praying.

Nevertheless, even if R. Shimon b. Yoḥai's view was not as lopsidedly in favor of study over prayer as represented by the redactor of this *sugya*, the view which the redactor expresses regarding the overwhelmingly greater importance of study over prayer clearly had echoes within the rabbinic community, though it is difficult to conceive of non-scholars holding such a view. In the *Bavli*, however, the view contrary to R. Yoḥanan's is not identified with R. Shimon b. Yoḥai's, perhaps, as we shall see, because in the *Bavli* (perhaps unlike that of the *Yerushalmi*?)[33] he is one of the proponents of the importance of communal prayer.[34]

Before turning to R. Yoḥanan and his view, however, we should consider for moment the result of such a policy. For, if prayer represents תחנונים, an expression of human need and dependence on the Creator, to some extent study represents a greater assertion of human reason and even (within certain spheres) the autonomy of human judgment. Can a life without recurrent and regular expression of human needs be conceived? As William James put it, "Prayer in [the wider sense as meaning every type of inward communion or

---

maintenance of communal *times* of prayer even when praying privately (even if we accept the reading of MS Munich: אין תפלתו של אדם נשמעת אלא בשעה שהצבור מתפללין "Prayer is not heard except at the time when the community is praying"), it is clear that R. Yiẓḥak did not understand the statement this way. The context of his conversation with R. Naḥman was to stress the importance of prayer *with* the community; see below, p. 38.

[33] See N. Lamm, *Torah Lishmah: Torah for Torah's Sake in the Works of Rabbi Ḥayyim of Volozhin and His Contemporaries* (New York: Yeshiva University Press, 1989), pp. 159–60.

[34] See above, and below in regard to the dialogue in BT *Ber.* 7b–8a between R. Yiẓḥak and R. Naḥman (p. 38).

conversation with the power recognized as divine] is the very soul and essence of religion." And, quoting the French theologian Auguste Sabatier, he adds that "prayer is religion in act; that is, prayer is real religion.... Religion is nothing if it be not the vital act by which the entire mind seeks to save itself by clinging to the principle from which it draws its life. This act is prayer..., the very movement itself of the soul, putting itself into a personal relation of contact with the mysterious power of which it feels the presence...."[35]

It is inconceivable that R. Shimon felt that Torah study could replace prayer, unless it partook of prayer's signal characteristics. The following *midrash*, quoted in R. Shimon's name in a number of places (Midrash Tehillim 19:17), squarely conjoins the two.

שגיאות מי יבין. תני ר׳ שמעון בן יוחי כמה גבורים הן הצדיקים, שהן יודעין לפתות את בוראם, ויודעין היאך לקלס, ראה דוד היאך מקלס את בוראו, התחיל לקלסו בשמים, שנאמר השמים מספרים כבוד אל, אמרו השמים שמא אתה צריך לכלום, מעשה ידיו מגיד הרקיע, אמר ליה הרקיע שמא אתה צריך לכלום, היה מזמר והולך, התחיל לקלס בתורה, שנאמר יראת ה׳ טהורה, אמר לו הקב״ה מה את בעי, אמר לו שגיאות מי יבין, שגיאותיו דעבדית קמך בעינא דתשרי לי, אמר ליה הא שרי לך והא שביק לך. גם מזדים חשוך עבדך. אלו הזדונות. אל ימשלו בי אז איתם. אלו תוקפי עבירות, כמה דאת אמר איתן מושבך (במדבר כד כא) . ונקיתי מפשע רב. מאותו עון רב, אמר ר׳ לוי אמר דוד רבש״ע אתה אלוה רב, ואנא חוביי רברבין, יאה לאלהא רבא למישבק חובין רברבין, שנאמר למען שמך ה׳ וסלחת לעוני כי רב הוא (תהלים כה יא). דבר אחר אל ימשלו בי אז איתם.

R. Shimon b. Yoḥai: How powerful are the righteous who know how to persuade their Creator and know how to praise! See how David praises his Creator. He begins by praising Him through His heaven: "The heavens declare God's glory, the firmament recounts the work of His hands" (Ps 19:2). – Are You then in need of anything? "The firmament recounts the work of His hands" – Are you then in need of anything? He

[35] James, p. 464. The quotation from Sabatier is from his *Esquisse d'une Philosophie de la Religion*, 2nd ed. (1897), pp. 24–6.

would continue to praise, [and] began to praise by the Torah, as Scripture states: "The fear of God is pure" (Ps 19:10) – Said the Holy One, blessed be He, to him: What do you want?

[David] said to Him: "Who can be aware of errors?" (Ps 19:13) – for the unwitting sins I have committed before You I wish that You forgive me.

He said to him: Behold, it is pardoned and forgiven.

"And from willful sins keep Your servant" (Ps 14) – these are the witting ones.

"Let them not dominate me" (Ps 19:14) – these are the severe sins, as one says: "Your abode is secure" (Num 24:21). "And clear me of great sin" (Ps 19:14) – of that sin [regarding Bathsheba].

R. Yoḥanan's view is less clear. Does his giving preference to prayer – *Shemoneh Esreih*, and certainly the recitation of *Shema* – stem from the inferior status of his generation in regard to the miẓvah of *Talmud Torah*, or because of prayer's intrinsic value ("Would that a person pray all day long")? If we are to judge from R. Yoḥanan's own behavior, it would seem to be the former, unless we are to interpret the wish to spend the day in prayer as referring to those who could not spend the day in study, but there is no indication of that.

The redactor who linked R. Yoḥanan's view regarding interrupting one's study for the recitation of *Shema* and *Shemoneh Esreih* seems to have taken this statement ("Would that….") as emphasizing the importance of prayer and indicating that it was not to be delayed by one's studies, once the hour had arrived (or was about to pass). It was not to be taken literally.

Again, just as in the case of R. Shimon b. Yoḥai, the view attributed to R. Yoḥanan by the redactor does not conform to the statement quoted in his name. For if we are to take it literally, R. Yoḥanan was urging a life of prayer on his interlocuters, rather than a life of study – the course he personally chose for himself and his disciples.

However, "would that a man pray all the day long" need not be taken as a recommendation. It could have been intended as a rueful remark regarding man's fallen state: we cannot devote ourselves entirely to devotional activities given the pressing needs of material existence. Or, less likely, "prayer" may be understood as a synecdoche for what the *Bavli* calls מִילֵּי דשמיא, religious concerns. In the final analysis, though, the redactor was correct in not taking R. Yoḥanan's statement at face value, given his own career as head of the Tiberias school and teacher of the largest cohort of all the amoraic authorities of any generation.[36]

Nevertheless, the redactors of both Talmuds took this statement as arguing for as much prayer as possible, at least in the absence of competing factors. Thus, as we have seen, when one is in doubt as to having prayed, the initial presumption is that R. Yoḥanan would hold that the prayer must be recited again. In BT *Pes.* 54b, where the question of *ne'ilah* on *Tish'ah Be-av* is raised, R. Yoḥanan is initially thought to be in favor, given this predisposition for maximum prayer. In the end, then, in both Talmuds, this apodictic statement of R. Yoḥanan's is interpreted as expressing a general predisposition in favor of a maximum of institutionalized prayer rather than a lifestyle devoted to it entirely – despite its literal meaning.

What might have been the antecedents of such a statement? Could it be that R. Yoḥanan was expressing – or transmitting – a view which he did not share, but which he certainly respected?

There are echoes of something approximating such a view in tannaitic sources. As Shlomo Na'eh has recently pointed out, M *Ber.* 5:5 and 4:3 seem to describe an ideal form of ecstatic prayer, where the prayer's efficacy can be judged by its fluency, אם שגרה בפיו.[37] It is difficult to imagine that such virtuosi of prayer as R. Neḥuniah b. Hakanah or Ḥoni ha-Me'aggel achieved the heights of prayerful intimacy with God without devoting major efforts to the task.

---

[36] Almost all the third-generation *amoraim* in the Land of Israel were his disciples, and that cohort is estimated as numbering 135. No amoraic generation, whether represented in the *Yerushalmi* or in the *Bavli*, comes close to matching this number. See the tables in Lee I. Levine *The Rabbinic Class of Roman Palestine in Late Antiquity* (Jerusalem: Yad Izhak Ben-Zvi, 1989), pp. 67–8.

[37] See Na'eh's article, "'*Boreh Niv Sefatayyim.*'" *Tarbiz* 62 (1994) pp. 185–218

Clearly, their spiritual life was one of prayerful devotion more than Torah study. Could R. Yoḥanan have had them in mind when he made his statement?

Perhaps his model was R. Akiva, who was a great scholar, but of whom it is reported that though when he prayed with a *minyan*, he would deliberately recite his prayers with dispatch

> וכשהיה מתפלל בינו לבין עצמו אדם מניחו בזוית זו ומוצאו בזוית אחרת וכל כך למה מפני כריעות והשתחויות:
>
> When he prayed with the congregation, he used to cut it short and finish in order not to inconvenience the congregation, but when he prayed by himself, a man would leave him in one corner and find him later in another, on account of his many genuflexions and prostrations.[38]

Indeed, were we to speculate further, we might connect R. Yoḥanan's statement with his own personal experience.

> אמר רבי יוחנן כל המאריך בתפלתו ומעיין בה סוף בא לידי כאב לב.
>
> If one draws out his prayer and expects therefore its fulfillment, he will in the end suffer vexation of heart.

and while the following statement – מאי תקנתיה? יעסוק בתורה (What is the solution? Study Torah.) – is redactional, it may nevertheless also mirror his experience. While we have no certain way of relating R. Yoḥanan's observation here with his wish that דאמר רבי יוחנן ולואי שיתפלל אדם כל היום למה שאין תפילה מפסדת, discussed above, we may speculate that one of the reasons R. Yoḥanan's statement remained within the realm of desirable practices which could not be realized ("would that they prayed all day") was simply that the end result of too much introspection was heartache and depression.

It would seem that the *Bavli* recognizes three degrees of in-

---

[38] BT *Ber.* 31a.

volvement in prayer: one is to pray at length (המאריך בתפלתו), another to cultivate the proper intention (כוונה), and, finally, to anticipate that it be answered to the degree of his sincerity and intention (מעיין בה).[39] The latter seems to have been the object of mixed emotions, as *Tosafot* note, with some sources promoting it as bringing great rewards in both worlds, and some pointing out its dangers.[40]

The resulting complex and to some extent perplexing evaluation of עבודה שבלב (worship of the heart) cannot be easily attributed to a disagreement on principle, since R. Yoḥanan, for one, is found on both sides of the issue. Given the perverse and contrary nature of humans beings, the psychological consequences of עיון תפלה are not always desirable, despite their spiritual benefits. Indeed, as noted, this may be one of the reasons that R. Yoḥanan's wish that people spend their entire day in prayer remained only that: a wistful sentiment impossible of being carried into practice, even apart from the practical difficulties.[41] Indeed, the *Bavli*'s suggestion (BT *Ber.* 32b): מאי תקנתיה? יעסוק בתורה may reflect R. Yoḥanan's own conclusion as carried out in his own choice of lifestyle.

II

If the redactional understanding of R. Shimon b. Yoḥai's view reflects an earlier attitude which had struck roots in the early amoraic period, that is, in the very first amoraic generation, it may help explain an otherwise troubling incident in Rav's life, one which is reported in the *Yerushalmi* though not in the *Bavli* (JT *Yom.* 7b).

---

[39] See Rashi BT *Ber.* 55a (top), s.v. מעיַן בה: אומר בלבו שתֵעשה בקשתו לפי שמתפלל בכוָנה. However, as R. Yaakov Ibn Ḥabib notes in his יעקב עיון (*ad loc.*, s.v. שלשה דברים, following *Tosafot*, *Ber.* 32b. s.v. כל המאריך), there are other sources which consider עיון תפלה as a positive practice (BT *Shab.* 127a, where according to R. Yoḥanan it brings reward in both worlds, and BT *Baba Batra* 164b, where Rav laments that most people are not innocent of neglecting this aspect of prayer every day). *Tosafot* conclude that there are two types of עיון תפלה, one (the positive one) which is identical with כוונה, and one as defined by Rashi.

[40] See previous note.

[41] This subject will be examined again below, section III.

אם היה חכם דורש ואם לאו תלמידי חכמים דורשין לפניו אם רגיל לקרות קורא ואם לאו קורין לפניו ובמה קורין לפניו באיוב ובעזרא ובדברי הימים זכריה בן קבוטל אומר פעמים הרבה קריתי לפניו בדניאל: כהנא שאל לרב מה ניתני קבוטר קבוטל והוה קאים מצלי וחוי ליה באצבעתיה צפר קבוטר:

It was taught: [In order to keep him awake, the high priest was read selections from] R. Zakhariah b. Kabutar said: At times I read to him from the book of Daniel, Job, Ezra and Chronicles.

...Kahana asked Rav: What do we learn [= what is the proper form of the patronym]? Kabutar? Kabutal?

[Rav] was standing and praying [*Shemoneh Esreih*] [and could not answer directly. Instead,] he showed him with his finger a *kabutar* bird [= a pigeon or dove].

Rav, founder of the Sura yeshiva and disciple, along with his uncle R. Ḥiyya, uncle of R. Judah the Prince, was standing in prayer and reciting the *Shemoneh Esreih*, and just at that moment his disciple [R.] Kahana was contemplating the *mishnah* in *Yoma* 1:6 in which one Zechariah b. Kabutar or Kabutal reported that he had often read from the book of Daniel on the night of Yom Kippur in order to keep the high priest awake. Kahana was in doubt about Zechariah's patronym: was it Kabutar or Kabutal? For some reason he could not wait for Rav to complete his prayer and asked him as to the correct form of the name. Rav, in turn, did not wait till the end of *Shemoneh Esreih* and indicated that the name was Kabutar.[42] According to E.S. Rosenthal, the meaning of the last sentence is: "He was standing and praying, and showed him a dove (*kabutar* in Middle Persian) with his

[42] While the general import of this incident is clear, the commentaries have differed considerably as to Rav's exact reaction. See E.S. Rosenthal, "Talmudica Iranica," in *Irano-Judaica: Studies Relating to Jewish Contacts with Persian Culture throughout the Ages*, ed. Shaul Shaked, pp. 38–134 (Hebrew section), esp. 48–50 and associated notes and appendix.

finger." Since both R. Kahana and Rav spoke (or at least understood) Middle Persian, the play on words was clear to both.[43]

The philological problem is, for us, less of a concern than the religious one. What could have been the status of prayer in the mind of R. Kahana and of Rav if both could interrupt Rav's prayer in order to clarify the exact pronunciation of Zechariah b. Kabutar's name?[44] Certainly this question was peripheral to the proper understanding of the *mishnah*. Were Rav and R. Kahana then of the opinion that the urgency and immediacy of *any* aspect of *Talmud Torah* superseded the sanctity and intention of prayer?

The *Bavli* preserves another story of Rav and R. Kahana which may shed light on the relations between them, and, if read correctly, may point us toward an understanding of Rav's position (BT *Ber.* 62a–b).

---

[43] It is intriguing to consider that this by-play was preserved in the *Yerushalmi* and not in the *Bavli*.

[44] See for example the report of Rav's behavior when visiting Geniva (BT *Ber.* 27a–b):

> רב איקלע לבי גניבא וצלי של שבת בערב שבת והוה מצלי רבי ירמיה בר אבא לאחוריה דרב וסיים רב ולא פסקיה לצלותיה דרבי ירמיה. שמע מינה תלת שמע מינה מתפלל אדם של שבת בערב שבת ושמע מינה מתפלל תלמיד אחורי רבו ושמע מינה אסור לעבור כנגד המתפללין. מסייע ליה לרבי יהושע בן לוי דאמר רבי יהושע בן לוי אסור לעבור כנגד המתפללין. איני והא רבי אמי ורבי אסי חלפי רבי אמי ורבי אסי חוץ לארבע אמות הוא דחלפי. ורבי ירמיה היכי עביד הכי והא אמר רב יהודה אמר רב לעולם אל יתפלל אדם לא כנגד רבו ולא אחורי רבו. שאני רבי ירמיה בר אבא דתלמיד חבר הוה.
>
> Rav was once at the house of Geniva and he said the Sabbath *Tefillah* on the eve of Sabbath, and R. Jeremiah b. Abba was praying behind Rav and Rav finished but did not interrupt the prayer of R. Jeremiah. Three things are to be learnt from this. One is that a man may say the Sabbath *Tefillah* on the eve of Sabbath. The second is that a disciple may pray behind his master. The third is that it is forbidden to pass in front of one praying. But is that so? Did not R. Ammi and R. Assi use to pass? R. Ammi and R. Assi used to pass outside a four cubit limit. But how could R. Jeremiah act thus, seeing that Rav Judah has said in the name of Rav: A man should never pray either next to this master or behind his master? R. Jeremiah b. Abba is different, because he was a disciple-colleague.

תניא אמר רבי עקיבא פעם אחת נכנסתי אחר רבי יהושע לבית הכסא ולמדתי ממנו שלשה דברים למדתי שאין נפנין מזרח ומערב אלא צפון ודרום ולמדתי שאין נפרעין מעומד אלא מיושב ולמדתי שאין מקנחין בימין אלא בשמאל. אמר ליה בן עזאי עד כאן העזת פניך ברבך אמר ליה תורה היא וללמוד אני צריך. תניא בן עזאי אומר פעם אחת נכנסתי אחר רבי עקיבא לבית הכסא ולמדתי ממנו שלשה דברים למדתי שאין נפנין מזרח ומערב אלא צפון ודרום ולמדתי שאין נפרעין מעומד אלא מיושב ולמדתי שאין מקנחין בימין אלא בשמאל. אמר לו רבי יהודה עד כאן העזת פניך ברבך אמר לו תורה היא וללמוד אני צריך. רב כהנא על גנא תותיה פורייה דרב. שמעיה דשח ושחק ועשה צרכיו אמר ליה דמי פומיה דאבא כדלא שריף תבשילא אמר ליה כהנא הכא את פוק דלאו אורח ארעא.

It has been taught: R. Akiva said: Once I went in after R. Joshua to a privy, and I learnt from him three things. I learnt that one does not sit east and west but north and south; I learnt that one evacuates not standing but sitting; and I learnt that it is proper to wipe with the left hand and not with the right. Said Ben Azzai to him: Did you dare to take such liberties with your master? He replied: It was a matter of Torah, and I am required to learn. It has been taught: Ben Azzai said: Once I went in after R. Akiva to a privy, and I learnt from him three things. I learnt that one does not evacuate east and west but north and south. I also learnt that one evacuates sitting and not standing. I also learnt it is proper to wipe with the left hand and not with the right. Said R. Judah to him: Did you dare to take such liberties with your master? He replied: It was a matter of Torah, and I am required to learn. R. Kahana once went in and hid under Rav's bed. He heard him chatting [with his wife] and joking and doing what he required. He said to him: One would think that Abba's mouth had never sipped the dish before! He said to him: Kahana, are you here? Go out, because it is inappropriate.

It could, of course, be argued that this want of tact, or even bumptiousness, is typical of R. Kahana. Indeed, it has been suggested that the story of R. Akiva dates from his early days as a rabbinic disciple.[45] However, it is worthy of note that while R. Akiva responds (to R. Yehudah, and not, it should be noted, to R. Yehoshua) with a *teshuvah niẓahat*, תורה היא וללמוד אני צריך (It is Torah and learn it I must!), Rav has no compunction in ordering R. Kahana out of the room, and telling him in no uncertain terms: לאו אורח ארעא (It is inappropriate)!

It may be that each of the three types of intrusions we have surveyed may prompt a different reaction. Following one's master into the outhouse is not quite the same thing as hiding under his bed under intimate circumstances, and neither is quite the same as interrupting during *Shemoneh Esreih*. Moreover, it may be that R. Akiva remained undetected, and only when he told R. Yehudah of his exploit was the objection raised. Had R. Yehoshua realized that he was not alone in the outhouse, he also would have sent R. Akiva packing.

However, the varied reactions to these intrusions are clearly not the point here; the redactor has gathered these stories together because of their common theme: תורה היא וללמוד אני צריך. One may well wonder why this "Torah" could not be taught descriptively in the schoolroom and not mimetically in the outhouse and the bedroom. The point is clear: neither R. Akiva nor R. Kahana allowed propriety to interfere with their passion for learning Torah. While R. Kahana may well have passed the bounds of proper behavior, Rav responds rather patiently, all things considered.[46]

Why was this? Certainly, part of his reaction must have been due to his fondness for R. Kahana, and his understanding of his underlying good intentions; there was no prurience in his burning desire to master all aspects of a Torah life. But I think that there is yet another factor: Rav's recognition that, indeed, תורה היא וללמוד אני צריך. If that is so, this may also have underlined his reaction to R. Kahana's query during the *Shemoneh Esreih*.

---

[45] See L. Finkelstein, *Akiva: Scholar, Saint and Martyr* (New York: Atheneum, 1970), p. 82.

[46] Note that Rava would not initiate marital relations when even a mosquito remained in the room; see BT *Niddah* 17a.

However, we must also take note of Rav's differing reactions in the two situations. While such comparisons are disagreeable, one must nevertheless ask why Rav sent R. Kahana out of the room in the one case while not forcing him to wait for an answer until he concluded his prayer in the other. Is צנעיות (modesty) then of greater import than קבלת פני השכינה (receiving the divine presence), as the *Midrash* would have it of the comparison between the latter and hospitality in regard to Abraham's running to greet the wandering Arabs while in communion with God in Genesis 18:1–3?[47] May we say that if the latter argument *a fortiori* is true, then all the more so in regard to *Talmud Torah*?

To do so would violate the distinction between *halakhah* and *aggadah*. Certainly, one may not interrupt his *Shemoneh Esreih* in order to invite guests into his home – even if he thereby loses his opportunity to fulfill the miẓvah of הכנסת אורחים (hospitality). And so, likewise, one might consider the matter of *Talmud Torah*. תפלה לחוד ותלמוד תורה לחוד (Prayer and the study of Torah are distinct). Each has its own requirements and duties. Indeed, generally speaking, *Talmud Torah* by its inclusive nature must *for that very reason* give way to other *miẓvot*, for were that not the case, no other *miẓvot* could be performed![48]

However, this is not to say that prayer was neglected. As we shall see, a momentary lapse in attention to prayer in order to foster *Talmud Torah* was most definitely an exception.

On the other hand, Rav was well aware of the difficulties in maintaining one's concentration in prayer (BT *Baba Batra* 164b).

> אמר רב עמרם אמר רב שלש עבירות אין אדם ניצול מהן בכל יום הרהור עבירה ועיון תפלה ולשון הרע.

---

[47] BT *Shev.* 35b, *Midrash Tehillim* 18:29.

[48] See BT *Meg.* 28b–29a, and the following *sugya*:

> ת"ר [כט/ב] מבטלין תלמוד תורה להוצאת המת ולהכנסת הכלה אמרו עליו על רבי יהודה ברבי אילעאי שהיה מבטל תלמוד תורה להוצאת המת ולהכנסת הכלה.
>
> Our Rabbis taught: We take time from the study of Torah to take out the dead and to accompany a bride. It was said about R. Yehudah bi-Rabbi Illay that he would take time from Torah study to take out the dead and to accompany a bride

> ...R. Amram said in the name of Rav: [There are] three transgressions which no man escapes for a single day: Sinful thought, calculation on [the results of] prayer, and tale-bearing.

In this appreciation, Rav was at one with both the tradition of his master and of his family (BT *Ber.* 13a–b).

> תנו רבנן שמע ישראל ה׳ אלהינו ה׳ אחד זו קריאת שמע של רבי יהודה הנשיא. אמר ליה רב לרבי חייא לא חזינא ליה לרבי דמקבל עליה מלכות שמים. אמר ליה בר פחתי בשעה שמעביר ידיו על פניו מקבל עליו עול מלכות שמים. חוזר וגומרה או אינו חוזר וגומרה בר קפרא אומר אינו חוזר וגומרה רבי שמעון ברבי אומר חוזר וגומרה. אמר ליה בר קפרא לרבי שמעון ברבי בשלמא לדידי דאמינא אינו חוזר וגומרה היינו דמהדר רבי אשמעתא דאית בה יציאת מצרים אלא לדידך דאמרת חוזר וגומרה למה ליה לאהדורי כדי להזכיר יציאת מצרים בזמנה.
>
> Our Rabbis taught: 'Hear, O Israel, the Lord our God, the Lord is one': this was R. Judah the Prince's recital of the Shema'. Rav said once to R. Ḥiyya: I do not see Rabbi accept upon himself the yoke of the kingdom of heaven. He replied to him: Son of Princes! In the moment when he passes his hand over his eyes, he accepts upon himself the yoke of the kingdom of heaven. Does he finish it afterwards or does he not finish it afterwards? Bar Kappara said: He does not finish it afterwards; R. Shimon son of Rabbi said, He does finish it afterwards. Said Bar Kappara to R. Shimon the son of Rabbi: On my view that he does not finish it afterwards, there is a good reason why Rabbi always is anxious to take a lesson in which there is mention of the exodus from Egypt. But on your view that he does finish it afterwards, why is he anxious to take such a lesson? – So as to mention the going forth from Egypt at the proper time.

This attitude toward כוונה seems to have been rooted in a thoroughly realistic assessment of the human power of concentration, at least in their own time. Indeed, some of the greatest of the early *amoraim* had no compunction in admitting their own failures in this regard, not excluding R. Ḥiyya, Rav's revered uncle (JT *Ber.* 17b).

...א"ר יוחנן קרא ומצא עצמו בלמען חזקה כוין.

ר' לא ר' יסא בשם ר' אחא רובא נתפלל ומצא עצמו בשומע תפילה חזקה כוין.

ר' ירמיה בשם ר' אלעזר נתפלל ולא כוין לבו אם יודע שהוא חוזר ומכוין את לבו יתפלל ואם לאו אל יתפלל.

א"ר חייא רובא אנא מן יומי לא כוונית אלא חד זמן בעי מכוונה והרהרית בלבי ואמרית מאן עליל קומי מלכא קדמי ארקבסה אי ריש גלותא.

שמואל אמר אנא מנית אפרוחיא.

רבי בון בר חייא אמר אנא מנית דימוסיא.

א"ר מתניה אנא מחזק טיבו לראשי דכד הוה מטי מודים הוא כרע מגרמיה:

Said R. Yoḥanan: [If] he recited [the Shema] and found himself [in the verse beginning] with *lema'an*, the presumption is that he had [the proper] intention [that is, of reciting it for the sake of a mizẓvah, and not merely mouthing secular words].

R. [I]lla, R. Yosa in the name of R. Aḥa Rabba: [If] he prayed and found himself [in the blessing of] *Shome'a Tefillah*, the presumption is that he had had [the proper] intention.

R. Jeremiah in the name of R. Eleazar: [If] he prayed but did not have any intention, and if he is certain that if he repeats [the prayer] he will have [the proper] intention, he should pray [again], but if not, he should not pray [again].

Said R. Ḥiyya the Great: I in all my days have only had proper intention once [when] I tried to have the [proper] intention and I thought in my heart and said [to myself]: Who is coming before me? The King is before me, a high official or the exilarch.

Samuel said: I counted chicks.

R. [A]bun b. Ḥiyya said: I counted bricks.

R. Mattaniah said: I am grateful to my head that when I reach the Modim [benediction] it bows of itself [by habit, without my intention].

Rav's uncle, the esteemed disciple of Rabbi Yehudah ha-Nasi, confessed that he had managed to have proper intention in prayer only once in his life, and his colleague Samuel noted that he counted young birds while praying, while R. Abun b. Ḥiyya counted rows of building stones.[49] However one interprets these statements, however, it is remarkable that R. Kahana interrupted Rav's prayer *ab initio* and quite consciously. In this case, it was not human frailty and lack of ability to maintain one's concentration for the duration of the *Shemoneh Esreih*.

Still, once he did interrupt, Rav responded. Could this have been because Rav's concentration, once impaired, could not easily be restored, as recorded in BT *Eruv.* 65a?

> אמר רב חייא בר אשי אמר רב כל שאין דעתו מיושבת עליו אל יתפלל. משום שנאמר בצר אל יורה. רבי חנינא ביומא דרתח לא מצלי. אמר בצר אל יורה כתיב.
>
> R. Ḥiyya b. Ashi citing Rav ruled: A person whose mind is not at ease must not pray, since it is said: 'He who is in distress shall give no decisions.' R. Ḥanina did not pray on a day when he was agitated. It is written, he said: 'He who is in distress shall give no decisions.'

Rav's personal predilection may be indicated by an interesting report, again one given quite matter-of-factly in the course of a halakhic discussion, of Rav's behavior during *ne'ilah*. The Yerushalmi preserves another report of Rav's practice of prayer, one which points in a different direction, at least as regards his recitation of *ne'ilah* (JT *Ber.* 31a).

---

[49] The *Rishonim* of course could not let this pass without comment. See *Perush mi-Baal ha-Ḥaredim ad loc.*, and *Tosafot R.H.* 16b s.v. ועיון; see also *Tosafot B.B.* 164b s.v. עיון, *Ber.* s.v. כל, *Shab.* 118b s.v. עיון. Among more recent writers, see R. Ẓadok ha-Kohen of Lublin, *Ẓidkat ha-Ẓaddik* (Bnei Brak: 1973/4), no. 209, who suggests that R. Ḥiyya's "I never had *kavvanah*" meant "I never had the need for it," since the *halakhah* mandating it was meant for those liable to lose it. "R. Ḥiyya, however, never experienced any other thought except the Presence of God…."

אימתי הוא נעילה רבנן דקיסרין אמרין איתפלגון רב ור׳ יוחנן רב אמר בנעילת שערי שמים ור"י אמר בנעילת שערי היכל אמר ר׳ יודן אנתורדיא מתני׳ מסייע לר"י בג׳ פרקים הכהנים נושאים את כפיהם ד׳ פעמים ביום בשחרית ובמוסף במנחה ובנעילת שערים בתעניות ובמעמדות וביה"כ אית לך מימר נעילת שערי שמים ביום אחוי דאימא דרב אדא הוה צייר גולתיה דרב בצומא רבא א"ל כד תיחמי שמשא בריש דיקלי תיהב לי גולתי דנצלי נעילת שערים מחלפא שיטתיה דרב תמן הוא אמר בנעילת שערי שמים וכא אמר בנעילת שערי היכל אמר רב מתנה על ידי דרב מאריך בצלותא סגין הוה מגיע לנעילת שערי שמים

When is [the time for] *ne'ilah*? The rabbis of Caesaria say: Rav and R. Yoḥanan disagreed. Rav said: When the gates of heaven are closed, and R. Yoḥanan said: When the gates of the Temple are closed.

Said R. Yudan Antordaya: Our mishnah supports R. Yoḥanan['s view]: Three times the priests recite the Priestly Blessing [and on Yom Kippur] four times during the day: during Shaḥarit, during Musaf, during Minḥah, and during the closing of the gates – during fasts and *ma'amadot* [= when the Israelites recite biblical verses accompanying the priestly service] and Yom Kippur.

[If so] you may say that [that this refers to] the closing of the gates of heaven during the day.

The brother of R. Aḥa's mother would place fringes on Rav's cloak on Yom Kippur.

He said to her: When you see the sun above the palms give me my cloak so that I can pray Neilah.

It would seem that Rav contradicts himself here; there he says: [this refers] to the closing of the gates of heaven, and here he says: the closing of the gates of the Temple?

Said R. Mattaniah: Since Rav prolonged his prayer greatly, he reached the [time of the] closing of the gates of heaven.

Of course, it is entirely possible that this report of his behavior at *ne'ilah* on Yom Kippur does not reflect his practice during the rest of the year. On the other hand, if it does, it may be that R. Kahana, knowing this, was unwilling to wait for Rav to complete his prayer, and asked him his question when he did.[50] However, this does not seem likely, given the respect due to his teacher. If he interrupted Rav's prayer, it is likely that he knew that this would not be held against him. Indeed, even his escapade under Rav's bed seems not to have been held against him, given the good relations between them even on the eve of his departure to the Land of Israel.[51] Thus, a line may be traced which links R. Shimon b. Yoḥai to Rabbi to Rav: טע־מיה דרשב"י [ח/ב] זה שינון וזה שינון ואין מבטל שינון מפני שינון. "([However, in this case] the reason of R. Shimon b. Yoḥai is that each one (= Torah study and prayer) is [called] 'recitation' [in the Torah], and we do not cancel one recitation for the other recitation.)"[52]

Still and all, the picture of Rav's attitude towards prayer would be lacking were we not to consider several other sources which point to his great concern for תפלה, as Y.S. Zuri pointed out in his biography of Rav (BT *Ber.* 12a).[53]

> אמר רבה בר חיננא סבא משמיה דרב כל שלא אמר אמת ויציב שחרית ואמת ואמונה ערבית לא יצא ידי חובתו שנאמר להגיד בבקר חסדך ואמונתך בלילות: ואמר רבה בר חיננא [סבא] משמיה דרב המתפלל כשהוא כורע כורע בברוך וכשהוא זוקף זוקף בשם. אמר שמואל מאי טעמא דרב דכתיב ה' זוקף כפופים. אמר ליה שמואל לחייא בר רב בר אוריאן תא ואימא לך מלתא מעלייתא דאמר אבוך הכי אמר אבוך כשהוא ורע כורע בברוך כשהוא זוקף זוקף בשם.
>
> Rava b. Ḥinena the elder said in the name of Rav: If one omits to say True and firm' in the morning and 'True and trustworthy' in the evening, he has not performed his

[50] R. Kahana's behavior in other situations testifies to his impatience and perhaps impetuosity; see D. Sperber," The Misfortunes of Rav Kahana: A Passage of Post-Talmudic Polemic," in D. Sperber, *Magic and Folklore in Rabbinic Literature* (Ramat Gan: Bar Ilan University Press, 1994), pp. 145–64.

[51] See BT *Baba Kama* 117a–b, and D. Sperber's article cited in previous note.

[52] JT *Ber.* 7b; see above.

[53] Y.S. Zuri, *Rav* (Jerusalem: 1985), pp. 258–60, though his description is not free of distortions and exaggerations.

obligation; for it is said, To declare Thy lovingkindness in the morning and Thy faithfulness in the night seasons.

Rava b. Ḥinena the elder also said in the name of Rav: In saying the Tefillah, when one bows, one should bow at [the word] 'Blessed' and when returning to the upright position one should return at [the mention of] the Divine Name. Samuel said: What is Rav's reason for this? – Because it is written: The Lord raiseth up them that are bowed down. An objection was raised from the verse, And was bowed before My name? – Is it written, 'At My name'? It is written, 'Before My Name'. Samuel said to Ḥiyya the son of Rav: O, Son of the Law, come and I will tell you a fine saying enunciated by your father. Thus said your father: When one bows, one should bow at 'Blessed', and when returning to the upright position, one should return at [the mention of] the Divine Name.

In this we may perhaps see a survival of the ecstatic prayer practiced by R. Akiva in private, as noted above.

Thus, aside from the halakhic aspects of Rav's response to R. Kahana, we must consider the experiential dimension as well. While both prayer and *Talmud Torah* may be considered activities which involve communion with God, the nature of the interaction is quite different. One is primarily an emotional experience – עבודה שבלב (worship of the heart), the other primarily intellectual. Moreover, in prayer one stands submissively, as a supplicant, as R. Shimon b. Shetaḥ said of Ḥoni ha-Me'aggel, as a "child before his father," while R. Shimon b. Shetaḥ himself described his own standing as that of a courtier.[54] Can one experience then be substituted for another? Indeed, R. Shimon b. Yoḥai's reference to the recitation of *Shema* in terms of שינון may not at all apply to prayer (JT *Ber.* 8a)!

תמן תנינן מפסיקין לקרית שמע ואין מפסיקין לתפילה.
אמר רבי אחא קרית שמע דבר תורה ותפילה אינה דבר תורה.
אמר רבי בא ק"ש זמנה קבוע ותפילה אין זמנה קבוע.

אמר רבי יוסי ק"ש אינה צריכה כוונה ותפילה צריכה כוונה.
אמר רבי מנא קשייתה קומי רבי יוסי ואפילו תימר קרית שמע אינה צריכה כוונה שלשה פסוקים הראשונים צריכין כוונה מן גו דאינון צבחר מיכוון:

There we learned: We interrupt for the recitation of the *Shema* and we do not interrput for Tefillah (= *Shemoneh Esreih*).

Said R. Aḥa: Recitation of the Shema is biblically ordained, while *Tefillah* is not biblically ordained.

Said R. [A]bba: The time of the recitation of the Shema is set while the time for Tefillah is not set [referring to Maariv, which at that time was not yet obligatory].

Said R. Yose: The recitation of the Shema does not need concentration while Tefillah does need such concentration?

Said R. Mana: I asked this question before R. Yose: Even if you say that the recitation of the Shema does not require concentration, the first three verses do require concentration? – Since they are limited, he can concentrate.

According to R. Yose, then, the very requirement that prayer requires inward intention relegates it to second place. Because of the stringent requirement of *kavvanah*, we do not require one to interrupt one's meal for its recital, even though one must interrupt it for the recitation of the *Shema*. After all, one may – following Rabbi, or other, more stringent prescriptions – fulfill the miẓvah of the recitation of *Shema* by concentrating on one verse, or the first paragraph. Prayer requires a much greater measure of *kavvanah*.

The clue to R. Shimon b. Yoḥai's understanding of the relationship between the two modes of spiritual communion may inhere in this fundamental difference: there is no need for the requirement of *kavvanah* for *Talmud Torah*. Without proper attention, *there is no Talmud Torah*. Of course, *kavvanah* has another, less rigorous, meaning, that of intending the act to be for the sake of Heaven, and without that there is no *miẓvah*. But that is not the level on which the

54 See BT *Ber.* 19a, *Tan.* 19a, 23a.

debate is being carried out in these texts. For it is ineluctably clear that R. Ḥiyya and the others who confessed to a lack of *kavvanah* did not, *ḥas ve-shalom*, intend this second meaning.[55]

III

It is perhaps a combination of these two considerations, the difficulty of *kavvanah* on the one hand, and the supreme value of *Talmud Torah*, on the other, which may account for yet another surprising report, that regarding R. Yehudah in BT *Rosh Ha-Shanah* 35a.

> אמר רבי אלעזר לעולם יסדיר אדם תפלתו ואחר כך יתפלל. אמר רבי אבא מסתברא מילתיה דרבי אלעזר בברכות של ראש השנה ושל יום הכפורים ושל פרקים אבל דכל השנה לא. איני והא רב יהודה מסדר צלותיה ומצלי שאני רב יהודה כיון דמתלתין יומין לתלתין יומין הוה מצלי, כפרקים דמי.
>
> ...R. Eleazar said: A man should always arrange (= review the wording) his prayer and then recite it. R. Abba said: The dictum of R. Eleazar appears to be well founded in respect of the blessings of New Year and the Day of Atonement and periodical [prayers] but not of the rest of the year. Is that so? Did not Rav Judah use always to prepare himself for his prayer before praying? – Rav Judah was exceptional; since he prayed only every thirty days, it was [to him] like a periodical [prayer].

Since R. Yehudah, founder and head of the Pumbedita yeshiva – and, be it noted, a disciple of Rav – recited *Shemoneh Esreih* only once in thirty days, he treated the ordinary prayer as though it were as unfamiliar as that of the High Holy Days, and thus requiring review before it was recited.

The *Bavli* does not attempt to explain R. Yehudah's practice. Was it his commitment to *Talmud Torah* which led to this relative neglect of prayer? That this may not have been the only consideration

---

[55] See N. Lamm, *Torah Lishmah*, pp. 141–147. The teaching regarding לא ימוש in BT *Men.* 99b is not relevant here.

is indicated by his insistence (albeit in the name of his teacher Shmuel) on the need for *ḥiddush* in prayer, no less than in study (BT *Ber.* 21a). Institutionalized, mandated prayer is here given a strongly personal cast.

> ואמר רב יהודה אמר שמואל התפלל ונכנס לבית הכנסת ומצא צבור שמתפללין אם יכול לחדש בה דבר יחזור ויתפלל ואם לאו אל יחזור ויתפלל
>
> Rav Judah further said in the name of Samuel: If a man had already said the *Tefillah* and went into a synagogue and found the congregation saying the *Tefillah*, if he can add something fresh, he should say the *Tefillah* again, but otherwise he should not say it again.

Of course, R. Yehudah does not define the nature or extent of the *ḥiddush*; however, given the general nature of the rule, which applies to all Jews, articulate or not, the requirement was probably minimal. Nevertheless, this *halakhah* is evidence of his awareness of the problem of maintaining a certain measure of freshness and spontaneity within the parameters of institutionalized prayer.

Again, R. Yehudah accepted his teacher Rav's insistence on the necessity for עיון תפלה: עיון תפלה תיתי לי שקיימתי (It comes to me because I fulfilled expectation in prayer; BT *Shab.* 127a). This statement both expresses his appreciation for the importance of concentration, on the one hand, and his acknowledgement of the difficulty of achieving it, on the other. Is it thus any wonder that he prayed only once in thirty days?

Indeed, the Talmud preserves a discussion which expresses the tension involved in balancing the demands of prayer with its dangers. Note that one statement in favor of devoting a large amount of time to prayer is that of R. Yehudah (BT *Ber.* 54b–55a, see also BT *Ber.* 32b).

> ואמר רב יהודה שלשה דברים [המאריך בהן] מאריכין ימיו ושנותיו של אדם המאריך בתפלתו והמאריך על שלחנו והמאריך בבית הכסא. והמאריך בתפלתו מעליותא היא והאמר רבי חייא בר אבא אמר רבי יוחנן כל המאריך

בתפלתו ומעיין בה סוף בא לידי כאב לב שנאמר תוחלת ממושכה מחלה לב. ואמר רבי יצחק שלשה דברים מזכירים עונותיו של אדם ואלו הן קיר נטוי ועיון תפלה ומוסר דין על חבירו לשמים הא לא קשיא הא דמעיין בה הא דלא מעיין בה. והיכי עביד דמפיש ברחמי.

Rav Judah said further: There are three things [the drawing out of which] prolongs a man's days and years; the drawing out of prayer, the drawing out of a meal, and the drawing out of [easing in] a privy. But is the drawing out of prayer a merit? Has not R. Ḥiyya b. Abba said in the name of R. Yoḥanan:

If one draws out his prayer and expects therefore its fulfillment, he will in the end suffer vexation of heart, as it says, 'Hope deferred maketh the heart sick. And R. Isaac also said: Three things cause a man's sins to be remembered [on high], namely, [passing under] a shaky wall, expectation of [the fulfillment of] prayer, and calling on heaven to punish his neighbour. – There is no contradiction; one statement speaks of a man who expects the fulfillment of his prayer, the other of one who does not count upon it. What then does he do? – He simply utters many supplications.

Note that these reports all involve the leading scholars, and, one presumes, role models, of their respective generations. Note also that these reports are given in a matter-of-fact way. There is no hint of disapproval or incredulity such as we find among the *Rishonim*. This, of course, does not mean that all their colleagues followed the same practices. Nor should we unthinkingly interpret all these practices as identical. Rav allowed interruptions in prayer, and R. Ḥiyya, Samuel, R. Abun b. Ḥiyya and R. Mana[56] confessed a certain laxity in maintaining concentration, and R. Yehudah of Pumbedita prayed once in thirty days. While all of these "practices" betoken a less than exemplary attitude to prayer (let alone, we should suppose, communal prayer), they are not alike. However, we may see all these

[56] Or R. Mataniah or R. Yoḥanan. Note that two of these variants involve leading scholars of their times.

anecdotes as representing a certain trend which harks back to the views of R. Shimon b. Yoḥai.

IV

With the coming of the third generation, the framework of the dispute over the importance of prayer *vis-à-vis* that of Talmud study changes its venue. Now the question is no longer one of prayer versus study, but rather the place of prayer, whether in the *beit ha-midrash* (study hall) or the *beit ha-knesset* (synagogue).

In a plangent anecdote in BT *Ber.* 7b–8a, R. Yiẓḥak reproves R. Naḥman for not coming to synagogue or praying with a *minyan*. It is not altogether clear from the dialogue whether this was his general practice, though it is not impossible that this construction may be put on it. Note that it is R. Shimon b. Yoḥai who here is represented as pressing the importance of praying with a congregation.

> ...אמר ליה רבי יצחק לרב נחמן מאי טעמא לא אתי מר לבי כנישתא לצלויי אמר ליה לא יכילנא אמר ליה לכנפי למר עשרה וליצלי אמר ליה טריחא לי מלתא ולימא ליה מר לשלוחא דצבורא בעידנא דמצלי צבורא ליתי ולודעיה למר אמר ליה מאי כולי האי אמר ליה דאמר רבי יוחנן משום רבי שמעון בן יוחי [ח/א] מאי דכתיב ואני תפלתי לך ה׳ עת רצון אימתי עת רצון בשעה שהצבור מתפללין
>
> R. Isaac said to R. Naḥman: Why does the Master not come to the synagogue in order to pray? – He said to him: I cannot. He asked him: Let the Master gather ten people and pray with them [in his house]? – He answered: It is too much of a trouble for me. [He then said]: Let the Master ask the messenger of the congregation to inform him of the time when the congregation prays? He answered: Why all this [trouble]? – He said to him: For R. Yoḥanan said in the name of R. Shimon b. Yoḥai:
>
> What is the meaning of the verse: But as for me, let my prayer be made unto Thee, O Lord, in an acceptable time? When is the time acceptable? When the congregation prays.

In another case, the neglect of synagogue attendance is directly linked to teachings brought from the Land of Israel (BT *Ber.* 8a).

> ...אמר ליה רבא לרפרם בר פפא לימא לן מר מהני מילי מעלייתא דאמרת משמיה דרב חסדא במילי דבי כנישתא אמר ליה הכי אמר רב חסדא מאי דכתיב אוהב ה׳ שערי ציון מכל משכנות יעקב אוהב ה׳ שערים המצויינים בהלכה יותר מבתי כנסיות ומבתי מדרשות והיינו דאמר רבי חייא בר אמי משמיה דעולא מיום שחרב בית המקדש אין לו להקדוש ברוך הוא בעולמו אלא ארבע אמות של הלכה בלבד ואמר אביי מריש הוה גריסנא בגו ביתא ומצלינא בבי כנישתא כיון דשמענא להא דאמר רבי חייא בר אמי משמיה דעולא מיום שחרב בית המקדש אין לו להקדוש ברוך הוא בעולמו אלא ארבע אמות של הלכה בלבד לא הוה מצלינא אלא היכא דגריסנא רבי אמי ורבי אסי אף על גב דהוו להו תליסר בי כנישתא בטבריא לא מצלו אלא ביני עמודי היכא דהוו גרסי:....
>
> Rava said to Rafram b. Papa: Let the master please tell us some of those fine things that you said in the name of R. Ḥisda on matters relating to the synagogue! – He replied: Thus said R. Ḥisda: What is the meaning of the verse: The Lord loveth the gates of Zion [*Ziyyon*] more than all the dwellings of Jacob? The Lord loves the gates that are distinguished [*mezuyyanim*] through *halakhah* more than the synagogues and houses of study. And this conforms with the following saying of R. Ḥiyya b. Ammi in the name of 'Ulla: Since the day that the Temple was destroyed, the Holy One, blessed be He, has nothing in this world but the four cubits of *halakhah* alone. So said also Abaye: At first I used to study in my house and pray in the synagogue. Since I heard the saying of R. Ḥiyya b. Ammi in the name of 'Ulla: 'Since the day that the Temple was destroyed, the Holy One, blessed be He, has nothing in His world but the four cubits of *halakhah* alone,' I pray only in the place where I study. R. Ammi and R. Assi, though they had thirteen synagogues in Tiberias, prayed only between the pillars where they used to study.

According to Rashi, R. Ḥisda's שערים המצויינים בהלכה are ציון ואסיפת צבור, presumably referring to halakhic gatherings such as a פרקא or the like. Thus, such meetings find more favor in God's eyes than בתי כנסיות or בתי מדרשות. Ordinarily, one would expect him to counterpose the latter two, as we find in BT *Meg.* 26b, where the one represents the life of prayer, and the other the life of Torah study.[57] In this case,

---

[57] It may be worthwhile quoting the passage as it appears in both Talmuds. First we will present an excerpt from the *Bavli* (BT *Meg.* 26b–27a), followed by the corresponding *Yerushalmi* (JT *Meg.* 23a).

<ואמר> [אמר] רב פפי משמיה דרב [דרבא] מבי כנישתא לבי רבנן שרי מבי רבנן לבי כנישתא אסיר. ורב פפא משמיה דרבא מתני איפכא אמר רב אחא כוותיה דרב פפי מסתברא דאמר רבי יהושע בן לוי בית הכנסת מותר לעשותו בית המדרש שמע מינה. דרש בר קפרא מאי דכתיב וישרף את בית ה׳ ואת בית המלך ואת כל בתי ירושלם ואת כל בית גדול שרף באש. בית ה׳ זה בית המקדש בית המלך אלו פלטרין של מלך ואת כל בתי ירושלם כמשמען ואת כל בית גדול שרף באש. רבי יוחנן ורבי יהושע בן לוי חד אמר מקום שמגדלין בו תורה וחד אמר מקום שמגדלין בו תפלה. מאן דאמר תורה דכתיב ה׳ חפץ למען צדקו יגדיל תורה ויאדיר. ומאן דאמר תפלה דכתיב ספרה נא הגדולות אשר עשה אלישע. ואלישע דעבד ברחמי הוא דעבד. תסתיים דרבי יהושע בן לוי הוא דאמר מקום שמגדלין בו תורה דאמר רבי יהושע בן לוי בית הכנסת מותר לעשותו בית המדרש שמע מינה:

מהו למכור בית הכנסת וליקח בית המדרש מילתיה דר׳ יהושע בן לוי אמרה שרי דא״ר יהושע בן לוי וישרף את בית ה׳ זה בית המקדש ואת בית המלך זה פלטין של צדקיהו ואת כל בתי ירושלים אלו ד׳ מאות ושמונים בתי כניסיות שהיו בירושלים דא״ר פינחס בשם ר׳ הושעיה ארבע מאות ושמונים בתי כניסיות היו בירושלם וכל אחת ואחת היה לה בית ספר ובית תלמוד בית ספר למקרא ובית תלמוד למשנה וכולהם עלה אספסיינוס ואת כל בית הגדול שרף באש זה מדרשו של רבן יוחנן בן זכיי ששם היו מתנין גדולותיו של הקב״ה כגון ספרה נא לי את כל הגדולות אשר עשה אלישע ר׳ שמואל בר נחמן בשם ר׳ יונתן הדא דאת אמר בבית הכנסת של יחיד אבל בבית הכנסת של רבים אסור אני אומר אחד מסוף העולם קנוי בו והא תני מעשה בר״א בי ר׳ צדוק שלקח בית הכנסת של אלכסנדריים ועשה בה צרכיו אלכסנדריים עשו אותה משל עצמן עד כדון כשבנייה לשם בית הכנסת בנייה לשם חצר והקדישה מהו נישמעינה מן הדא קונם לבית הזה שאיני נכנס ונעשה בית הכנסת הדא אמרה בנייה לשם חצר והקדישה קדשה אימתי קדשה מיד או בשעת התשמיש נישמעינה מן הדא העושה תיבה לשם ספר ומטפחות לשם ספר עד שלא נשתמש בהן הספר מותר להשתמש בהן הדיוט משנשתמש בהן הספר אסור להשתמש בהן הדיוט ומה אם אלו שנעשו לשם ספר אינן קדושות אלא בשעת התשמיש זו שבנייה לשם חצר לא כ״ש אלו שעשאן לשם חולין והקדישו מה הן כמה דאת אמר תמן בנייה לשם חצר והקדישה קדשה והכא עשאם לשם חולין והקדישן קדש כלי שרת מאימתי הם קדושין מיד או בשעת התשמיש אין תימר מיד ניחא אין תימר בשעת התשמיש כאחד הם קדושים ומתקדשין ניחא

R. Papi said in the name of Rava: To turn a synagogue into a college is permitted; to turn a college into a synagogue is forbidden. R. Papa, however, also reporting Rava, states the opposite. R. Aḥa said: The statement of R. Papi is the more probable, since R. Joshua b. Levi

however, *both* synagogues and study halls are contrasted – unfavorably – to halakhic gatherings.[58]

This teaching of R. Ḥisda, whose daughter married Rava *en secundas noches*, is presented within a *mise en scène* in which Rava asks one of R. Ḥisda's disciples for a report of one of the latter's teachings on synagogues. One would expect a teaching which would emphasize the *importance* of synagogues. Whether Rava knew of R. Ḥisda's rather dim view of non-halakhic gatherings is not clear. Moreover, his reaction to this surprising view is not recorded here. However, unlike Abaye, who takes to heart a similar (Palestinian) view expressed by 'Ulla, and changes his practice of praying in a synagogue to praying "where I learn," Rava is quoted in BT *Meg.* 29a as preaching on the importance of synagogues and study halls as places in which God dwells, and emphasizing this with a personal recollection, one exactly at odds with Abaye's in BT *Ber.* 8a. At first Rava would study at home and pray in the synagogue, but once he understood the purport of Ps. 90:1 he made a point of studying in the synagogue as well.

---

said: It is permissible to make a synagogue into a beth ha-midrash. This seems conclusive.

Bar Kappara gave the following exposition: What is the meaning of the verse, 'And he burnt the house of the Lord and the king's house and all the houses of Jerusalem even every great man's house burnt he with fire? 'The house of the Lord': this is the Temple. 'The king's house': this is the royal palace. 'All the houses of Jerusalem': literally. 'Even every great man's house burnt he with fire': R. Yoḥanan and R. Joshua b. Levi gave different interpretations of this. One said, it means the place where the Torah is magnified; the other, the place where prayer is magnified. The one who says Torah bases himself on the verse, The Lord was pleased, for his righteousness' sake to make the Torah great and glorious. The one who says prayer bases himself on the verse, Tell me, I pray thee, the great things that Elisha has done; and what Elisha did, he did by means of prayer. It may be presumed that it was R. Joshua b. Levi who said, 'the place where Torah is magnified,' since R. Joshua b. Levi said that a synagogue may be turned into a beth ha-midrash which is a clear indication.

[58] So most commentators; see Maharsha *ad loc.*, and most commentaries included in *Ein Yaakov*.

דרש רבא מאי דכתיב ה׳ מעון אתה היית לנו אלו בתי כנסיות ובתי מדרשות. אמר אביי מריש הואי גריסנא בביתא ומצלינא בבי כנשתא כיון דשמעית להא דקאמר דוד ה׳ אהבתי מעון ביתך הואי גריסנא בבי כנישתא.

Rava gave the following exposition: What is the meaning of the verse, 'Lord, thou hast been our dwelling [*ma'on*] place?' This refers to synagogues and houses of learning. Abaye said: Formerly I used to study at home and pray in the synagogue, but when I noticed the words of David, 'O Lord, I love the habitation [*me'on*] of thy house,' I began to study also in the synagogue.

There are several problems, both lower critical and interpretive, that this passage raises, however. First, there is the question of the author of the personal recollection in BT *Meg*. Such recollections on the part of both Rava and Abaye are cited elsewhere in the *Bavli*, though Abaye's are more numerous, and so there is no way to determine the attribution on the basis of personal style. The manuscripts, as well as text witnesses such as *Ein Yaakov* and *Yalkut Shimoni* have the reading "Rava."[59] The reading of the printed editions is "Abaye," presumably because of the apparent contradiction between Rava's sermon regarding the status of *both* synagogues and study halls as contrasted to the following statement which emphasizes the importance of synagogues alone.

On the other hand, in *Ber.* 8a Abaye is quoted as reflecting that he had originally prayed in the synagogue and studied at home. After hearing the statement of 'Ulla regarding the importance of halakhic study and its venue, he took pains to pray where he studied – presumably at home.[60] This would contradict the practice reported in *Meg.* 29a.

It is noteworthy that Rava's statement is prefixed with the verb דרש, implying here, as elsewhere, that it reflects Rava's public teaching as *mara de-atra* in Mahoza. Could he have been encouraging the Ma-

[59] See *Dikdukei Soferim ad loc.*, n. *dalet*.

[60] Note the reading of MS Munich: בתאי, "my house." It is clear that Abaye refers to studying and praying at home, and not in the study hall. The question of where study took place in Babylonia in this period, and the size and character of the

hozans to be more attentive to their synagogue prayers? Nevertheless, it is undeniable that here, as in many other areas, Rava's opinion prefigured the direction that future developments would take.[61]

Quite apart from these considerations is the question of why Abaye accepted 'Ulla's statement without taking into account other statements which emphasize the importance of synagogue prayer and denigrate the practice of praying privately.[62]

> רבי נתן אומר מנין שאין הקדוש ברוך הוא מואס בתפלתן של רבים שנאמר הן אל כביר ולא ימאס וכתיב פדה בשלום נפשי מקרב לי וגו׳. אמר הקדוש ברוך הוא כל העוסק בתורה ובגמילות חסדים ומתפלל עם הצבור מעלה אני עליו כאילו פדאני לי ולבני מבין אומות העולם. אמר ריש לקיש כל מי שיש לו בית הכנסת בעירו ואינו נכנס שם להתפלל נקרא שכן רע שנאמר כה אמר ה׳ על כל שכני הרעים הנוגעים בנחלה אשר הנחלתי את עמי את ישראל ולא עוד אלא שגורם גלות לו ולבניו שנאמר הנני נותשם מעל אדמתם ואת בית יהודה אתוש מתוכם. אמרו ליה לרבי יוחנן איכא סבי בבבל. תמה ואמר למען ירבו ימיכם וימי בניכם על האדמה כתיב אבל בחוצה לארץ לא כיון דאמרי ליה מקדמי ומחשכי לבי כנישתא אמר היינו דאהני להו. כדאמר רבי יהושע בן לוי לבניה קדימו וחשיכו ועיילו לבי כנישתא כי היכי דתורכו חיי. אמר רבי אחא ברבי חנינא מאי קרא אשרי אדם שומע לי לשקד על דלתותי יום יום לשמור מזוזת פתחי וכתיב בתריה כי מוצאי מצא חיים.

amoraic schools, while a matter of dispute, is gradually becoming resolved in favor of such a reading. For the basic lines of dispute, see David M. Goodblatt, *Rabbinic Instruction in Sasanian Babylonia* (Leiden: E.J. Brill, 1975), and his "*Hitpatḥuyot Ḥadashot be-Ḥeker Yeshivot Bavel*," in *Zion* 46 (1981): 15–38; for an alternate view, see Y. Gafni, "'*Yeshiva*' *u-'Metivta*'," *Zion* 43 (1978): 12–37, his "*He'arot le-Maamaro shel D. Goodblatt*," *Zion* 46 (1981): 52–6, and his *Yehudei Bavel bi-Tekufat ha-Talmud: Ḥayyei ha-Ḥevra ve-ha-Ruaḥ* (Jerusalem: Merkaz Zalman Shazar, 1990), esp. pp. 177–236.

Among other relevant articles, see David Goodblatt, "Local Traditions in the Babylonian Talmud," *Hebrew Union College Annual* 48 (1977): 187–217, and Y. Gafni, "*Ḥibburim Nestoriyanim ke-Makor le-Toledot Yeshivot Bavel*," *Tarbiz* 51 (1982): 567–76, and, most recently, J.L. Rubenstein, *Talmudic Stories: Narrative Art, Composition, and Culture* (Baltimore: Johns Hopkins University Press, 1999), pp. 21–2, 270–2.

[61] See my "Rava in Mahoza: Rabbinic Theology and Law in a Cosmpolitan Setting," Ninth Orthodox Forum, New York, March 29, 1998.

[62] Indeed, now located on the very same *daf* of the *Bavli*, *Ber.* 8a.

> R. Nathan says: How do we know that the Holy One, blessed be He, does not despise the prayer of the congregation? For it is said: 'Behold, God despiseth not the mighty.' And it is further written: 'He hath redeemed my soul in peace so that none came nigh me, etc.' The Holy One, blessed be He, says: If a man occupies himself with the study of the Torah and with works of charity and prays with the congregation, I account it to him as if he had redeemed Me and My children from among the nations of the world.
>
> Resh Lakish said: Whosoever has a synagogue in his town and does not go there in order to pray, is called an evil neighbor. For it is said: 'Thus saith the Lord, as for all My evil neighbors, that touch the inheritance which I have caused My people Israel to inherit. And more than that, he brings exile upon himself and his children. For it is said: 'Behold, I will pluck them up from off their land, and will pluck up the house of Judah from among them.'
>
> When they told R. Yoḥanan that there were old men in Babylon, he showed astonishment and said: Why, it is written: That your days may be multiplied, and the days of your children, upon the land; but not outside the land [of Israel]! When they told him that they came early to the synagogue and left it late, he said: That is what helps them. Even as R. Joshua b. Levi said to his children: Come early to the synagogue and leave it late that you may live long. R. Aḥa son of R. Ḥanina says: Which verse [may be quoted in support of this]? Happy is the man that hearkeneth to Me, watching daily at My gates, waiting at the posts of My doors, after which it is written: For whoso findeth me findeth life.

Indeed, on the one hand, R. Natan's statement seems tailor-made for Abaye's own life-style, given his reputation for both learning and *gemilut ḥasadim*, and, on the other, Resh Lakish's denigration of those who do not pray in a synagogue, coupled with the threat of exile for his descendants, should, one imagines, have offset 'Ulla's tradition. It is difficult to avoid the conclusion that these teachings had not yet reached Babylonia. Additional proof for this contention is to be found in the fact that Rava grounds his own (reverse) decision to return to synagogue prayer not on these teachings, but his own understanding of Ps. 90:1. Still, though he quotes that verse, his position mirrors that of R. Yoḥanan and the sages of the Land of Israel, a phenomenon that has long been noted.[63]

On the whole, the *Bavli*'s statements emphasizing the importance of Torah study far outnumber its statements regarding synagogue prayers, which, on the whole, stem from the Land of Israel, as the citations from *Ber.* 8a (and others not cited here) demonstrate.[64] Indeed, even when presenting a tradition recommending the latter, it may undercut the teaching in not-so-subtle ways, as in BT *Ber.* 6a.

> תניא אבא בנימין אומר אין תפלה של אדם נשמעת אלא בבית הכנסת שנאמר לשמוע אל הרנה ואל התפלה במקום רנה שם תהא תפלה. אמר רבין בר רב אדא אמר רבי יצחק מנין שהקדוש ברוך הוא מצוי בבית הכנסת שנאמר אלהים נצב בעדת אל ומנין לעשרה שמתפללין ששכינה עמהם שנאמר אלהים נצב בעדת אל ומנין לשלשה שיושבין בדין ששכינה עמהם שנאמר בקרב אלהים ישפוט ומנין לשנים שיושבין ועוסקין בתורה ששכינה עמהם שנאמר אז נדברו יראי ה׳ איש אל רעהו ויקשב ה׳ וגו׳. מאי ולחושבי שמו אמר רב אשי חשב אדם לעשות מצוה ונאנס ולא עשאה מעלה עליו הכתוב כאילו עשאה. ומנין שאפילו אחד שיושב ועוסק בתורה ששכינה עמו שנאמר בכל המקום אשר אזכיר את שמי אבוא אליך וברכתיך. וכי מאחר דאפילו חד תרי מבעיא תרי מכתבן מלייהו בספר הזכרונות חד לא מכתבן מליה בספר הזכרונות. וכי מאחר דאפילו תרי תלתא מבעיא מהו

---

[63] See Zvi Dor, *Torat Ereẓ Yisrael be-Vavel* (Tel Aviv: Devir, 1971), and see my "*Rava ve-ha-Ḥeker ha-Areẓyisreli be-Midrash Halakhah*," in *Ba-Golah u-Vatefuẓot*, eds. Y. Gafni and L.H. Schiffman (Jerusalem (forthcoming)) and "*Derashot shel Kefilot Mikra'iyot be-Ereẓ Yisrael u-ve-Vavel*," *Sidra* (forthcoming).

[64] Of course, so does 'Ulla's reverse sentiment. Among the other voices from the Land of Israel heard expressing the same view are those of R. Yoḥanan and R. Yose beR. Ḥanina (BT *Ber.* 7b–8a). Whether this difference of viewpoints between the two Torah centers is linked to the different views and practices regarding rabbinic interaction with other classes of society which characterize the rabbinic elites of Babylonia and the Land of Israel is difficult to say at this distance. See Richard Kalmin, *The Sage in*

דתימא דינא שלמא בעלמא הוא ולא אתיא שכינה קמשמע לן דדינא נמי היינו תורה. וכי מאחר דאפילו תלתא עשרה מבעיא עשרה קדמה שכינה ואתיא תלתא עד דיתבי:

It has been taught: Abba Benjamin says: A man's prayer is heard [by God] only in the synagogue. For it is said: 'To hearken unto the song and to the prayer.' The prayer is to be recited where there is song. Rabin b. R. Adda says in the name of R. Isaac: How do you know that the Holy One, blessed be He, is to be found in the synagogue? For it is said: 'God standeth in the congregation of God.' And how do you know that if ten people pray together the Divine presence is with them? For it is said: 'God standeth in the congregation of God.' And how do you know that if three are sitting as a court of judges the Divine Presence is with them? For it is said: 'In the midst of the judges He judgeth.' And how do you know that if two are sitting and studying the Torah together the Divine Presence is with them? For it is said: 'Then they that feared the Lord spoke one with another; and the Lord hearkened and heard, and a book of remembrance was written before Him, for them that feared the Lord and that thought upon His name.' (What does it mean: 'And that thought upon His name'? – R. Ashi says: If a man thought to fulfill a commandment and he did not do it, because he was prevented by force or accident, then the Scripture credits it to him as if he had performed it.) And how do you know that even if one man sits and studies the Torah the Divine Presence is with him? For it is said: 'In every place where I cause My name to be mentioned I will come unto thee and bless thee.' Now, since [the Divine presence is] even with one man, why is it necessary to mention two? – The words of two are written down in the book of remembrance, the words of one are not written down in the book of remembrance. Since this is the case with two, why mention three? – I might think [the dispensing of] justice is only for making peace, and the Divine Presence does not come [to participate]. Therefore he teaches us that justice also is Torah. Since it is the case with three, why mention ten? – To

> [a gathering of] ten the Divine Presence comes first, to three, it comes only after they sit down.

Note that while Abba Binyamin's statement *limits* efficacious prayer to the synagogue, R. Yiẓḥak's discourse opens with a proof that the *Shekhinah* dwells in a synagogue[65] – a somewhat surprising turn of thought. One might have thought that such a fundamental doctrine was not in need of proof. Nevertheless, since the rabbinic tendency to seek Scriptural proof-texts is omnipresent, we may assume that this idea was not really in doubt. However, the exclusivity argued for the synagogue by Abba Binyamin, and the place of the synagogue as the location of the Divine Presence is immediately undermined by the widening circles of R. Yiẓḥak's teaching. The *Shekhinah* is to be found not only in the synagogue, but also among any ten who gather for prayer. Not only that, but it is present among judges, and even between two who study – or even one who studies alone.[66]

The following *sugya* (BT *Baba Batra* 25a) proceeds along the same lines.

> דאריב״ל בואו ונחזיק טובה לאבותינו שהודיעו מקום תפלה דכתיב וצבא השמים לך משתחוים. מתקיף לה רב אחא בר יעקב ודלמא כעבד שנוטל פרס מרבו וחוזר לאחוריו ומשתחוה קשיא. ורבי אושעיא סבר שכינה בכל מקום דאמר רבי אושעיא מאי דכתיב אתה הוא ה׳ לבדך אתה עשית את השמים וגו׳ שלוחיך לא כשלוחי בשר ודם שלוחי בשר ודם ממקום שמשתלחים לשם מחזירים שליחותן אבל שלוחיך למקום שמשתלחין משם מחזירין שליחותן שנאמר התשלח ברקים וילכו ויאמרו לך הננו יבואו ויאמרו לא נאמר אלא וילכו ויאמרו מלמד שהשכינה בכל מקום. ואף רבי ישמעאל

Jewish Society of Late Antiquity (London and New York: Routledge, 1999), but the parallel is suggestive.

[65] It should be noted that R. Yiẓḥak is reported to have remonstrated with R. Naḥman on the latter's neglect of communal prayer; see p. 38 above.

[66] What *Ḥazal* in their reticence do not provide us with is a description of being in "the presence of the *Shekhinah*," the experience of "to gaze upon the beauty of the Lord" (Ps. 27:4). See *Yesod ve-Shoresh ha-Avodah, Shaar* 1, chap. 3; note also that by and large the author's sources are biblical and Zoharic.

סבר שכינה בכל מקום דתנא דבי רבי ישמעאל מנין ששכינה בכל מקום שנאמר הנה המלאך הדובר בי יוצא ומלאך אחר יוצא לקראתו אחריו לא נאמר אלא לקראתו מלמד ששכינה בכל מקום. ואף רב ששת סבר שכינה בכל מקום דאמר ליה רב ששת לשמעיה לכל רוחתא אוקמן לבר ממזרח ולאו משום דלית ביה שכינה אלא משום דמורו בה מיני. ורבי אבהו אמר שכינה במערב דאמר רבי אבהו מאי אוריה אויר יה.

For so said Joshua b. Levi: Let us be grateful to our ancestors for showing us the place of prayer, as it is written, 'And the host of heaven worshippeth thee.' R. Aḥa bar Jacob strongly demurred to this [interpretation]. Perhaps, he said, [the sun and moon bow down to the east], like a servant who has received a gratuity from his master and retires backwards, bowing as he goes. This [indeed] is a difficulty. R. Oshaia expressed the opinion that the *Shekhinah* is in every place. For R. Oshaia said: What is the meaning of the verse, 'Thou art the Lord, even thou alone; thou hast made heaven, the heaven of heavens, etc.'? Thy messengers are not like the messengers of flesh and blood. Messengers of flesh and blood report themselves [after performing their office] to the place from which they have been sent, but thy messengers report themselves to the place to which they are sent, as it says. 'Canst thou send forth lightnings that they may go and say to thee, here we are.' It does not say, 'that they may come and say', but 'that they may go and say', which shows that the *Shekhinah* is in all places. R. Ishmael also held that the *Shekhinah* is in all places, since R. Ishmael taught: From where do we know that the *Shekhinah* is in all places? – Because it says. 'And behold, the angel that talked with me went forth, and another angel went out to meet him.' It does not say, 'went out after him,' but 'went out to meet him.' This shows that the *Shekhinah* is in all places. R. Shesheth also held that the *Shekhinah* is in all places, because [when desiring to pray] he used to say to his attendant: Set me facing any way except the east. And this was not because the *Shekhinah* is not there, but because the Minim prescribe turning to the east. R. Abbahu, however, said that the *Shekhinah* is in the west; for so said R. Abbahu:

What is the meaning of '*Uryah*'? It is equivalent to *avir Yah* [air of God].

Contrast the following (from BT *Sotah* 49a and BT *Tamid* 32b, respectively) to Abba Binyamin's teaching.

אמר רבי יהודה בריה דרבי חייא כל ת"ח העוסק בתורה מתוך הדחק תפלתו נשמעת שנאמר כי עם בציון ישב בירושלים בכה לא תבכה חנון יחנך לקול זעקך כשמעתו ענך וכתיב בתריה ונתן ה' לכם לחם צר ומים לחץ. רבי אבהו אומר משביעין אותו מזיו שכינה שנאמר "והיו עיניך רואות את מוריך. רבי אחא בר חנינא אמר אף אין הפרגוד ננעל בפניו שנאמר "ולא יכנף עוד מוריך:

תנא רבי חייא כל העוסק בתורה בלילה שכינה כנגדו שנאמר קומי רוני בלילה לראש אשמורות שפכי כמים לבך נכח פני ה'.

R. Judah, son of R. Ḥiyya said: Any disciple of the Sages who occupies himself with Torah in poverty will have his prayer heard; as it is stated: 'For the people shall dwell in Zion at Jerusalem; thou shalt weep no more; He will surely be gracious unto thee at the voice of thy cry; when He shall hear, He will answer thee,' and it continues, 'And the Lord will give you bread in adversity and water in affliction.' R. Abbahu said: They also satisfy him from the lustre of the *Shekhinah*, as it is stated: 'Thine eyes shall see thy Teacher.' R. Aḥa b. Ḥanina said: Neither is the veil drawn before him, as it is said: 'Thy teacher shall no more be hidden.'

R. Ḥiyya taught: If one studies the Torah at night, the Divine presence faces him, as it says, 'Arise, cry out in the night, at the beginning of the watches; pour out thy heart like water before the face of the Lord.'

Indeed, in most cases rabbinic teachings regarding the presence or absence of the *Shekhinah* are closely linked to the *performance* of *mizvot* other than תפילה. While many passages may be cited, the following, classic statement of the doctrine of *imitatio Dei* may serve to represent them all (BT *Sot.* 14a).

ואמר רבי חמא ברבי חנינא מאי דכתיב אחרי ה׳ אלהיכם תלכו וכי אפשר לו לאדם להלך אחר שכינה והלא כבר נאמר כי ה׳ אלהיך אש אוכלה הוא אלא להלך אחר מדותיו של הקדוש ברוך הוא מה הוא מלביש ערומים דכתיב ויעש ה׳ אלהים לאדם ולאשתו כתנות עור וילבישם אף אתה הלבש ערומים הקדוש ברוך הוא ביקר חולים דכתיב וירא אליו ה׳ באלוני ממרא אף אתה בקר חולים הקדוש ברוך הוא ניחם אבלים דכתיב ויהי אחרי מות אברהם ויברך אלהים את יצחק בנו אף אתה נחם אבלים הקדוש ברוך הוא קבר מתים דכתיב ויקבר אותו בגיא אף אתה קבור מתים:

R. Ḥama son of R. Ḥanina further said: What means the text: 'Ye shall walk after the Lord your God?' Is it, then, possible for a human being to walk after the *Shekhinah*; for has it not been said: 'For the Lord thy God is a devouring fire?' But [the meaning is] to walk after the attributes of the Holy One, blessed be He. As He clothes the naked, for it is written: 'And the Lord God made for Adam and for his wife coats of skin, and clothed them, so do thou also clothe the naked.' The Holy One, blessed be He, visited the sick, for it is written: 'And the Lord appeared unto him by the oaks of Mamre,' so do thou also visit the sick. The Holy One, blessed be He, comforted mourners, for it is written: 'And it came to pass after the death of Abraham, that God blessed Isaac his son,' so do thou also comfort mourners. The Holy one, blessed be He, buried the dead, for it is written: 'And He buried him in the valley,' so do thou also bury the dead.

In the end, of course, the logical conclusion was drawn: God too prays (BT *Ber.* 7a) and God too dons *tefillin* (BT *Ber.* 6a–b):

אמר רבי יוחנן משום רבי יוסי מנין שהקדוש ברוך הוא מתפלל שנאמר והביאותים אל הר קדשי ושמחתים בבית תפלתי תפלתם לא נאמר אלא תפלתי מכאן שהקדוש ברוך הוא מתפלל. מאי מצלי אמר רב זוטרא בר טוביה אמר רב יהי רצון מלפני שיכבשו רחמי את כעסי ויגולו רחמי על מדותי ואתנהג עם בני במדת רחמים ואכנס להם לפנים משורת הדין.

אמר רבי אבין בר רב אדא אמר רבי יצחק מנין שהקדוש ברוך הוא מניח תפילין שנאמר נשבע ה׳ בימינו ובזרוע עוזו בימינו זו תורה שנאמר מימינו אש דת למו ובזרוע עזו אלו תפילין שנאמר ה׳ עוז לעמו יתן. אמר

ליה רב נחמן בר יצחק לרב חייא בר אבין הני תפילין דמרי עלמא מה כתיב בהו אמר ליה ומי כעמך ישראל גוי אחד בארץ. ומי משתבח קודשא בריך הוא בשבחייהו דישראל אין דכתיב את ה׳ האמרת היום <וכתיב> וה׳ האמירך היום. אמר להם הקדוש ברוך הוא לישראל אתם עשיתוני חטיבה אחת בעולם ואני אעשה אתכם חטיבה אחת בעולם אתם עשיתוני חטיבה אחת בעולם שנאמר שמע ישראל ה׳ אלהינו ה׳ אחד. ואני אעשה אתכם חטיבה אחת בעולם שנאמר ומי כעמך ישראל גוי אחד בארץ. אמר ליה רב אחא בריה דרבא לרב אשי תינח בחד ביתא בשאר בתי מאי אמר ליה כי מי גוי גדול ומי גוי גדול אשריך ישראל או הנסה אלהים ולתתך עליון. אי הכי נפישי להו טובי בתי אלא כי מי גוי גדול ומי גוי גדול דדמיין להדדי בחד ביתא אשריך ישראל ומי כעמך ישראל בחד ביתא או הנסה אלהים בחד ביתא ולתתך עליון בחד ביתא וכולהו כתיבי באדרעיה:

R. Yoḥanan says in the name of R. Jose: How do we know that the Holy One, blessed be He, says prayers? Because it says: 'Even them will I bring to My holy mountain and make them joyful in My house of prayer.' It is not said, 'their prayer,' but 'My prayer'; hence [you learn] that the Holy One, blessed be He, says prayers. What does He pray? – R. Zutra b. Tobi said in the name of Rav: 'May it be My will that My mercy may suppress My anger, and that My mercy may prevail over My [other] attributes, so that I may deal with My children in the attribute of mercy and, on their behalf, stop short of the limit of strict justice.'

R. Abin son of R. Ada in the name of R. Isaac says [further]: How do you know that the Holy One, blessed be He, puts on tefillin? For it is said: 'The Lord hath sworn by His right hand, and by the arm of His strength.' 'By His right hand:' this is the Torah; for it is said: 'At His right hand was a fiery law unto them. 'And by the arm of his strength:' this is the tefillin; as it is said: 'The Lord will give strength unto His people.' And how do you know that the tefillin are a strength to Israel? For it is written: 'And all the peoples of the earth shall see that the name of the Lord is called upon thee, and they shall be afraid of thee,' and it has been taught: R. Eliezer the Great says: This refers to the tefillin of the head.

> R. Naḥman b. Isaac said to R. Ḥiyya b. Abin: What is written in the tefillin of the Lord of the Universe? – He replied to him: 'And who is like Thy people Israel, a nation one in the earth?' Does, then, the Holy One, blessed be He, sing the praises of Israel? – Yes, for it is written: 'Thou hast avouched the Lord this day…and the Lord hath avouched thee this day. The Holy One, blessed be He, said to Israel: You have made me a unique entity in the world, and I shall make you a unique entity in the world.' 'You have made me a unique entity in the world,' as it is said: 'Hear, O Israel, the Lord our God, the Lord is one.' 'And I shall make you a unique entity in the world,' as it is said: 'And who is like Thy people Israel, a nation one in the earth.' R. Aha b. Rava said to R. Ashi: This accounts for one case, what about the other compartments [of the tefillin]? – He replied to him: [They contain the following verses]: 'For what great nation is there, etc.; And what great nation is there, etc.; Happy art thou, O Israel, etc.; Or hath God assayed, etc.; and To make thee high above all nations. 'If so, there would be too many compartments? – Hence [you must say]:' For what great nation is there, and And what great nation is there, which are similar, are in one case; 'Happy art thou, O Israel,' and 'Who is like Thy people, in one case; 'Or hath God assayed,' in one case; and 'To make thee high,' in one case. And all these verses are written on [the tefillin of] His arm.[67]

It is of course hardly surprising that halakhic literature should in general emphasize the overwhelming importance of Torah study, and that masters of *halakhah* should be pictured in their primary social role rather than in their personal experiences of standing before their Maker. However, some inkling of the attitude with

[67] See Maharal, *Be'er ha-Golah*, Be'er Revi'i, for the theological problem that this prayer raises; see however R. Ẓadok ha-Kohen of Lublin, *Ẓidkat ha-Ẓaddik*, no. 212. This doctrine was applied across the board; see R. Yonatan Eibeshuetz, *Tiferet Yehonatan ad* Lev. 1:1, p. 79, s.v. *adam*.

which they stood in prayer may be garnered from the discussion in BT *Ber.* 30b.

משנה אין עומדין להתפלל אלא מתוך כובד ראש חסידים הראשונים היו שוהין שעה אחת ומתפללין כדי שיכוונו לבם לאביהם שבשמים אפילו המלך שואל בשלומו לא ישיבנו ואפילו נחש כרוך על עקבו לא יפסיק:

גמרא מנא הני מילי אמר רבי אלעזר דאמר קרא והיא מרת נפש ממאי דילמא חנה שאני דהות מרירא לבא טובא אלא אמר רבי יוסי ברבי חנינא מהכא ואני ברב חסדך אבא ביתך אשתחוה אל היכל קדשך ביראתך ממאי דילמא דוד שאני דהוה מצער נפשיה ברחמי טובא אלא אמר רבי יהושע בן לוי מהכא השתחוו לה׳ בהדרת קדש אל תקרי בהדרת אלא בחרדת ממאי דילמא לעולם אימא לך הדרת ממש כי הא דרב יהודה הוה מציין נפשיה והדר מצלי אלא אמר רב נחמן בר יצחק מהכא עבדו את ה׳ ביראה וגילו ברעדה מאי וגילו ברעדה אמר רב אדא בר מתנא אמר רבה במקום גילה שם תהא רעדה....

Mishnah: One should not stand up to say tefillah save in a reverent frame of mind. The pious men of old men of used to wait an hour before praying in order that they might concentrate their thoughts upon their father in heaven. Even if a king greets him [while praying] he should not answer him. Even if a snake is wound round his heel he should not break off.

Gemara: What is the [Scriptural] source of this rule? – R. Eleazar said: Scripture says, 'And she was in bitterness of soul.' But how can you learn from this? Perhaps Hannah was different because she was exceptionally bitter at heart! Rather, said R. Jose son of R. Ḥanina: We learn it from here: 'But as for me, in the abundance of Thy lovingkindness will I come into Thy house, I will bow down toward Thy holy temple in the fear of Thee.' But how can we learn from this? Perhaps David was different, because he was exceptionally self-tormenting in prayer! Rather, said R. Joshua b. Levi, it is from here: 'Worship the Lord in the beauty of holiness.' Read not ḥadrath [beauty] but ḥerdath [trembling]. But how can you learn from here? Perhaps I can after all say that the word '*ḥadrath*' is to be taken literally, after the manner of Rav Judah,

> who used to dress himself up before he prayed! Rather, said R. Naḥman b. Isaac: We learn it from here: 'Serve the Lord with fear and rejoice with trembling.' What is meant by 'rejoice with trembling'? – R. Adda b. Mattena said in the name of Rav: In the place where there is rejoicing there should also be trembling.

Nevertheless, even here, this verse is employed elsewhere in the *Bavli* to describe the experience of *mattan Torah* (BT *Yom.* 4a–b and *Zeb.* 116a).

> וישכן כבוד ה׳ מראש חודש ויכסהו הענן להר ויקרא אל משה רבי מתיא בן חרש אומר לא בא הכתוב אלא לאיים עליו כדי שתהא תורה ניתנת באימה ברתת ובזיע שנאמר עבדו את ה׳ ביראה וגילו ברעדה. מאי וגילו ברעדה אמר רב אדא בר מתנה אמר רב במקום גילה שם תהא רעדה. ר״א המודעי אומר מתן תורה שמע [ובא] שכשניתנה תורה לישראל היה קולו הולך מסוף העולם ועד סופו וכל [מלכי] עובדי כוכבים אחזתן רעדה בהיכליהן ואמרו שירה שנאמר ובהיכלו כולו אומר כבוד.
>
> 'And the glory of the Lord abode' from the beginning of the [third] month, and the cloud *va-yekasehu* [covered it], i.e., the mountain, then 'He called unto Moses on the seventh day.' Moses and all Israel were standing there, but the purpose of Scripture was to honor Moses. R. Nathan says: The purpose of Scripture was that he [Moses] might be purged of all food and drink in his bowels so as to make him equal to the ministering angels. R. Mattiah b. Ḥeresh says, The purpose of Scripture here was to inspire him with awe, so that the Torah be given with awe, with dread, with trembling, as it is said: 'Serve the Lord with fear and rejoice with trembling.' What is the meaning of 'And rejoice with trembling'? – R. Adda b. Mattena says in the name of Rav: Where there will be joy, there shall be trembling.
>
> R. Eleazar of Modim said: He heard of the giving of the Torah and came. For when the Torah was given to Israel the sound thereof travelled from one end of the earth to the other, and all the heathen kings were seized with trembling

> in their palaces, and they uttered song, as it is said, 'And in his place all say: "Glory".'

We can but conclude that the masters of *halakhah* saw in Torah study and prayer a seamless web of devotion to God. In the end one's submission to God's *halakhah* converts an intellectual activity into an emotional and spiritual one – and also a joyous one. Note that the same verse, גילו ברעדה (rejoice in trembling), and the *memra* of R. Ada b. Mattanah in the name of Rav, is employed both in connection with the experience of prayer *and* that of *mattan Torah*. Whatever the original context of Rav's statement, whether intended in relation to prayer or learning, the redactors of the *sugyot* in BT *Ber.* 30b, *Yom.* 4a–b, and *Zeb.* 116a, taken in the aggregate, yield the result just noted: the same dictum is employed to describe both experiences.

Or, as we noted above, in the name of R. Natan:

> רבי נתן אומר אמר הקדוש ברוך הוא כל העוסק בתורה ובגמילות חסדים ומתפלל עם הצבור מעלה אני עליו כאילו פדאני לי ולבני מבין אומות העולם.
>
> Rabbi Nathan said: The Holy One, blessed be He, says: 'If a man occupies himself with the study of the Torah and with works of charity and prays with the congregation, I account it to him as if he had redeemed Me and My children from among the nations of the world.'

Nevertheless, it must be admitted that our examination of the sources has not succeeded in penetrating to the experience behind the halakhic descriptions; rabbinic reticence, coupled perhaps with the intrinsic difficulty in describing the ineffable experience itself have, in the end, left us with a paucity of material. The combination of joy and trembling, alluded to in the sources just cited, must be intuited, reconstructed and reenacted in the life of each one of us in his or her life of learning and prayer, and on that note our historical survey is concluded.

Section three

Spirituality Across Intellectual History – Medieval and Modern Period

4

Dwelling with Kabbalah: Meditation, Ritual, and Study

Alan Brill

The English word mysticism has its origins in the word mystery. Jewish mysticism may be understood similarly as a process of opening oneself up to the mystery of the Torah. It is a means to cultivate a sense of the wondrous powers of Torah, thereby initiating one into the presence of God: "Open my eyes that I may see wonders out of your Torah" (Psalms 119:18). Naḥmanides uses this verse to explain that the Torah is greater than is apparent from an ordinary empiricist perspective; it transcends the natural realm to reveal the divine powers. The same verse is invoked in the *Zohar* to indicate that Torah is not an ordinary document but a subtle secret pointing to an alternate divine reality. One reaches this mystical Torah by accepting the existence of these higher realms and then dwelling within them.[1] My working definition of the Kabbalah is the knowledge of this higher realm. One becomes a kabbalist in order to experience the wonders of Torah, to attain an experience of God, and to view reality as infused with the divine.[2] This paper will discuss the definition of spirituality and then apply this definition to the halakhic realms of prayer, *miẓvot*, and study.

How does this spiritual Torah of Kabbalah relate to the halakhic realms of prayer, *miẓvot*, and study? Sociologists (Wade Clark Roof and Robert Wuthnow)[3] describe the contemporary return to spirituality as being undertaken by a "generation of seekers." They present contemporary spirituality as a novel phenomenon, as a journeying to create something new. In contrast to that sociological perspective, this paper will assume that one can dwell within the traditional kabbalistic spirituality, and that one who is engaged in a quest for spirituality need not seek new models. The traditional texts offer resources and possibilities for spirituality beyond the currently available approaches. The most significant conflict presented by the return to kabbalistic spirituality is not between Kabbalah and *halakhah*, but rather between piety and modernity. Modern Jewry has generally turned a blind eye to traditional spiritual approaches. We need to reawaken the ability to dwell in the kabbalistic wondrous, while at the same time acknowledging the differences between the Kabbalah and modern perspectives.

SPIRITUALITY

If Kabbalah presents the hidden reality, then what is the relationship of this reality to spirituality as it is currently understood? I would like to start by defining my terms. A working definition useful for the Kabbalah is the following statement by Bouyer who, in his

[1] "Torat Hashem Temimah" in *Kitvei Ramban* ed. C. Chavel (Jerusalem: Mossad ha-Rav Kook, 1963), vol. 1, p. 142; *Zohar* (Jerusalem: Mossad ha-Rav Kook, 1944), 3:152a.

[2] Moses Cordovero, *Or Neerav* (Jerusalem, 1965).

[3] Wade Clark Roof, et al. *A Generation of Seekers: The Spiritual Journeys of the Baby Boom Generation* (San Francisco: Harper San Francisco, 1993); Robert Wuthnow, *After Heaven: Spirituality in America Since the 1950's* (Berkeley: University of California, 1998).

introduction to his multi-volume work on spirituality, discusses the work of his predecessors, especially the great project of Pourrat.

Pourrat in the first of his four volumes on Christian spirituality distinguishes spirituality or "spiritual theology" not only from "dogmatic theology which teaches what must be believed," but also from moral theology which, according to him, teaches only "what must be done or avoided so as not to sin mortally or venially." "Spirituality," on the contrary, includes "ascetic theology" which has "as its object the exercises to which every Christian who aspires to perfection must devote himself," together with "mystical theology" which is concerned with "extraordinary states...such as the mystical union and its secondary manifestations...."[4] While Bouyer's categories have been formulated for his particular denominational purposes, from this short citation I would like to select five basic themes of spirituality.

First, spirituality is not the study of philosophy, dogma, or theology in the abstract. Rather, it is the effect of the divine on religious consciousness. Spirituality is concerned with the doctrine's experiential or performance elements. For example, the study of Maimonidean philosophy is not the same as a study of Maimonides on prayer, ritual performance, spiritual direction, or mystical development. Even a theological analysis of Maimonidean prayer is not the same as the spiritual question of how to perform Maimonidean prayer, or the consciousness that such prayer seeks to evoke. Similarly, study of the language of the Kabbalah is not spirituality if it limits itself to a history of ideas and does not include religious psychology. Most academic studies of the Kabbalah are restricted to describing its theosophy, devoid of implications for ritual and prayer.

Within the academy, Moshe Idel's writings offer a corrective to earlier scholarship by attempting to catalog the mystical experi-

---

[4] Louis Bouyer, *A History of Christian Spirituality: Volume One: The Spirituality of The New Testament and the Fathers* (New York: Desclee Company, 1963), p. vii, citing P. Pourrat, *Christian Spirituality* (London: Burns, Oates, and Washbourne, 1922), p. v.

ences and techniques of the Kabbalalists.[5] While Idel's history of ideas do address the experiential aspects of Kabbalah, in his writings the spiritual still remains elusive because he does not attend to the psychology of the texts. Idel warns against the reductionist tendencies of psychological analysis and emphasizes the impossibility of reconstructing psychology.[6] His sobering caveats have been heeded by many of the scholars in the field. Nevertheless, Idel himself admits:

> If the approach proposed here to see Kabbalah far more in terms of experiential phenomena than has been previously done is correct, then psychology, as an invaluable tool, must gradually be integrated into further study of this kind of mysticism.[7]

Current trends in the academic study of mysticism understand mysticism as a psychological universal. A contemporary position associated with Robert Forman assumes that mysticism is not a universal philosophy, but an innate psychological capacity for mystical experience, which is influenced by particular cultures and religions.[8] The main theorist in the field, Ken Wilber, explains that this innate human capacity is achieved through a fixed pattern of growth in which ordinary perceptions lead to a transpersonal sense of oneness

[5] In a recent interview Idel stated, similar to James, that the Kabbalah is based on experience and that the theology is accidental. Mysticism is the experience, and the Aristotelian, Platonic, and Hermetic languages are cultural constructs. *She'elot al Elohim: Dialogim*, eds. Yizhar Hes, Elazar Shturm (Or Yehudah: Hed Arẓi, 1998), pp. 131–46.

[6] "Any reconstruction is mostly an approximation based more on the presuppositions and tendencies of the scholar than on recombination of the authentic components of the original experience." Moshe Idel, *Kabbalah: New Perspectives* (New Haven: Yale University Press, 1988), pp. 35–6.

[7] Idel, *Kabbalah: New Perspectives*, p. 25.

[8] "The transformative efficacy of practices like meditation lies in the stripping away of learned cultural and linguistic categories to expose an underlying 'innate capacity' for experiencing mystical 'pure consciousness.' This state of 'pure consciousness'

with the divine, then to symbolic thinking. From there, the inner capacity culminates in reaching the Absolute.[9]

Yet, there is no free-form mysticism. In a lived context, the dogma and practices of a given religion always inform the process of developing this innate capacity. In the case of Judaism, it is the *halakhah* which informs Jewish spirituality. While Kabbalah reverberates with psychological universals, the kabbalistic experience is based on Jewish theology and *halakhah* and cannot be separated from them. There is no abstract feeling of spirituality that is not a lived sense of the theological structure of the divine attributes and of the extensive discussions concerning those attributes that are found in Jewish mystical and philosophical texts. In spirituality "the reference to God is not only explicit but immediate."[10] These theoretical discussions map the interdivine structures perceived in the religious experience and can be used to chart the spiritual journey.

Ethics

The second point made by Bouyer in the introduction to his work

---

is cross-culturally and historically stable. Forman argues, in other words, that mystical experiences of pure consciousness, made possible by transformative processes like meditation, transcend historical and cultural differences and are in some way 'innate.'" Diane Jonte-Pace, "The Swami and the Rorschach" in *The Innate Capacity*, ed. Robert Forman (New York: Oxford University Press, 1998), p. 137.

Her own research shows the convergence of Rorshachs of meditators from a variety of traditions despite their cultural categories. James H. Austin's *Zen and the Brain: Towards an Understanding of Meditation and Consciousness* (Cambridge: M.I.T. Press, 1998) provides an excellent presentation of the innate capacity for mystical experience from the perspective of neurology (including cognitive psychology), explaining that meditation and mystical experience occur along specific habituated neural pathways.

[9] Ken Wilber, *Eye to Eye: The Quest for the New Paradigm* (Boston: Shambala, 1990). Wilber presents hierarchical levels of spiritual experience, offering a more nuanced perspective than Forman whose focus is on the moment of pure consciousness. An approach similar to Wilber's was offered by the psychologist Erich Neumann in *The Mystic Vision* (Papers from the Eranos Yearbooks, 6; Princeton: Princeton University Press, 1968); *idem*, *The Origins and History of Consciousness* (Princeton, NJ: Princeton University Press, 1970).

[10] Bouyer, p. v.

on spirituality is that even though the mystic's ethical path reflects his spiritual experience, spirituality is not to be confused with ethics. Spirituality is the lived consciousness of the divine; spiritual ethics are the applications of the divine imperative to life. While a discussion of the relationship of ethics to mysticism is beyond the scope of this paper, the difference between ethics and mysticism is apparent in a quick survey of crucial kabbalistic thinkers. If we use Naḥmanides as a case in point, something of a distinction can be drawn between his mystical doctrines and his ethical sensitivity. The imperative to do "the good and the right" and to seek the "will of the creator" is his ethical doctrine, while "you shall cleave unto Him" characterizes his mysticism. Naḥmanides' ethics and his spirituality are of course very much related, but their processes and goals are quite different.[11]

By comparison, in the *Zohar*, divine character traits are translated into ritualism through the modeling of human behavior on the divine structure and the acceptance of the reward for good behavior in the form of divine blessing or plenitude.[12] In the Kabbalah of Moses Cordovero, the diffusion of divine goodness in all things is emphasized. The Cordoveran tradition tends towards a monistic ethic of love in which one sees the divine even in the lowliest gnat. Naḥmanides and others, in contrast to Cordovero, accentuate the transcendent nature of the divine, tending towards an ascetic dualism.

Ascetic Theology

The discussion of ethics brings us to our third point, that beyond ethics there is a practical discipline designed to prepare one to relate

[11] We would do well to lay to rest the ignorant old canard that mysticism is non-ethical. However, it should be acknowledged that social planning or any other modern social and political topic is not the concern of Kabbalah. The field of inquiry of Kabbalah is God more than it is Jewish peoplehood. See William Wainwright, *Mysticism: A Study of its Nature, Cognitive Value, and Moral Implications* (Madison: University of Wisconsin Press, 1981).

[12] Demonology is not its major ethical approach. This paper does not develop a kabbalistic ethic and such an ethic needs its own discussion.

to the influx of the holy. The analysis of this discipline is sometimes called ascetic theology. To return to the case of Naḥmanides, it is imperative to "be holy" – *kedoshim*. According to Nachmanides this state of holiness is attained through the reduction of physical experience, the rejection of sexuality, and the development of a spiritual body. Naḥmanides considers the ascetic lives of Elijah and Enoch as paradigms of piety. In his spiritual writings, writing from the standpoint of a pietist, he advocates the need to avoid this-worldly pleasure and sexuality, yet he does not permit this ascetic stance to influence his halakhic decisions.[13]

Traditional pietistic works, such as the anonymous *Iggeret ha-Kodesh*, Cordovero's *Tomer Devorah*, or Elijah DeVidas's *Reshit Ḥokhmah* are usually read only for their moralistic content. In fact, they provide direction on a range of ascetic theological practices including the control of mind and body, the channeling of emotions, and healing. The field of kabbalistic *mussar* has not been extensively studied in the academy, but it is there that one finds the most extensive descriptions of the spiritual path. For example, scholars, even in the new *Encyclopedia of Religion*, do not generally discuss the awe and fear of God central to any traditional pietistic approach. Ascetic behavior takes many forms: mortification of the flesh, control of the passions, mild limitations on food and sleep, the imaging of pain and the experience of death for God's sake, extensive *mikveh* use, and the elimination of negative character traits. Moderns seek the discipline of asceticism but not the dualism or the mortification that accompanies it. (There are still today some who seek the pain, deprivation, and asceticism in mysticism. While the efforts of this small constituency are noble and important, this is not the concern of our paper.) Traditional ascetic paths are now packaged in attractive forms as meditation and activities that promote well-being. Ascetic

---

[13] On directives beyond the *halakhah* see Leviticus 19:2, 23:36; Deut. 6:18, Exod. 20:8, 32:13. On Naḥmanides' ascetic transformation of the body see Jonathan Feldman, "The Power of the Soul Over the Body: Corporeal Transformation and Attitudes Towards the Body in the Thought of Naḥmanides" (Unpublished Dissertation N.Y.U., 1999).

practices are returning, but with an avoidance of the language of body/soul dualism.

One of the basic texts of early Kabbalah describes, as a prerequisite for advanced work, the need for meditation in order to still the emotions and attain equanimity.

> A sage once came to one of the Meditators (*Mitbodedim*) and asked that he be accepted into their society.
>
> The other replied, "My son, blessed are you to God. Your intentions are good. But tell me, have you attained equanimity or not?"
>
> The sage said, "Master, explain your words."
>
> The Meditator said, "If one man is praising you and another is insulting you, are the two equal in your eyes or not?"
>
> He replied, "No, my master. I have pleasure from those who praise me and pain from those who degrade me. But I do not take revenge or bear a grudge."
>
> The other said, "Go in peace my son. You have not attained equanimity.... You are not prepared for your thoughts to bond on high, that you should come and meditate (*hitboded*). Go and increase the humbleness of your heart, and learn to treat everything equally until you have become tranquil (*hishtavut*). Only then will you be able to meditate."[14]

The ascetic texts emphasize the necessity of engaging in psychological self-scrutiny and analyzing one's personality traits in preparation for transcending the self in kabbalistic practice. They also take for granted that mindfulness and the ability to transcend ordinary concerns are a prerequisite for a serious form of mystical experience.

---

[14] Aryeh Kaplan, *Mediation and the Kabbalah* (York Beach, ME: Samuel Weiser, 1982), p. 143.

Extra-ordinary and monastic

Bouyer's fourth point is that spirituality is extra-ordinary, experienced beyond ordinary life. The term spirituality originally was used to describe the activities of the clergy. However, in seventeenth-century France, the term was used reproachfully with regard to mystics and their separation from material life. From there, Samuel Johnson was influenced already by 1755 to use the word to refer to "pure acts of the soul." Later the term took on positive connotations, and became a designation for the cultivated inner life, especially one focused on prayerful piety. Following the suppression of the monastic orders during the French Revolution, their restoration in both charter and ideology during the post-Revolutionary period sought to recapture the best of monastic spirituality and to revive it, through extensive publishing projects, for a nineteenth century audience.[15] Parenthetically, the writings of Franz Joseph Molitor, one of those known for the revival of spirituality, were influential in Gershom Scholem's decision to study Kabbalah. These nineteenth-century reprints of spiritual volumes made possible comparative studies across the various works. No longer was it necessary to choose a monastery and accept the traditional set of doctrines. Now, one scrutinized the differences between the Benedictine, Carmelite, Franciscan, Jesuit, and Dominican orders, and other spiritualities. Each order was understood now as a discrete path, with its own approach to inner spiritual work and a distinct spiritual dynamic. As spirituality became accessible to the educated general public, spiritual works were read and applied to the lives of ordinary clerics, not just monks.

A similar phenomenon occurred in Judaism. Originally, Jewish spirituality was monastic in its elitism, otherworldliness, and the extreme demands made of its practitioners. Jewish mystics lived lives that were equivalent to those of monks; they were married and had leadership roles, but they were nonetheless monks. A recent author termed R. Akiva "a married monk" to describe the twenty-four year leave that he took from his wife in order to teach

[15] Louis Bouyer, p. xxiv.

his students.[16] While we know little about the social structures according to which the early Kabbalists lived, in particular those of the circle responsible for the authorship of the *Zohar*, we do know of the otherworldliness of the Safed mystics, the Ḥasidic rebbes, and the Vilna Gaon. The early modern period brought the monastic culture to a broader public through the printing press, the prestige enjoyed by Safedian kabbalists, lay devotions, and by popular movements such as Ḥasidism, but the practice of spirituality as such remained otherworldly and limited to the few.

Following the advent of modernity, much of Jewry discarded the experiential traditions, including Kabbalah. Instead, Jewish philosophy and *halakhah* were read by nineteenth-century readers as abstract texts in an Enlightenment spirit. Traditional Jewish metaphysical understandings of God, prophecy, providence, and eschatology were transformed by modern scholarship from a Platonic encounter with the infinite divine, to a limiting negative knowledge or a supernatural theism. The world of the Vilna Gaon, R. Yonatan Eibeschutz, and the Ḥatam Sofer was still connected to the traditional monastic, elite, meditative, magical, and God-infused world,[17]

[16] On the literary ideal of R. Akiva as a married monk see Daniel Boyarin, *Carnal Israel: Reading Sex in Talmudic Culture* (Berkeley: University of California Press, 1993). On R. Akiva and mysticism see C.R.A. Murray-Jones, "Paradise Revisited," HTR, 86:3 (1993): 265–292; Dalia Hoshen, "*Torat ha-Ẓimzum u-Mishnat R. Akiva: Kabbalah u-Midrash*," *Daat*, 34 (1995): 34–40; idem, "*Torat ha-Yissurim be-Tefisat ha-Elohut shel R. Akiva*," *Daat*, 27 (1991): 3–33; Alon Goshen-Gottstein, "Four Entered Paradise Revisited," HTR, 88:1 (1995): 69–133. The former two authors consider the attribution of mysticism to R. Akiva credible, while the latter does not.

[17] It would be helpful is we had quantitative data for different decades, populations, and topics within this breakdown of tradition, instead of generalizations and impressionistic accounts. Rather than broad discussions concerning the influence of the Enlightenment, we need studies of the incremental changes in the observance of *miẓvot*, belief in the supernatural, and the decline in the acceptance of the spiritual. For some models based on the de-christianization of French peasants in the sixteenth-nineteenth centuries, see Gabriel Le Bras, *Introduction à la practique religieuse en France* (Paris: PUF, 1942); Michel Vovelle, *Piété baroque et dechristianisation en Provence au XVIII siècle* (Paris: Editions du C.T.H.S., 1997) *Idem*, *Les metamorphoses de la fête en Provence de 1750–1820* (Paris: Aubier/Flammarion, 1976); *idem*, *Mourir autrefois: attitudes collectives devant la mort aux XVIIe*

whereas Orthodoxy, in all its modern forms, rejected these beliefs and practices, including kabbalistic spirituality, as obsolete.[18]

Orthodoxy's break with traditional elite spirituality is reflected in many documents, including Neẓiv's famous essay entitled "Right and Left."[19] The essay was a response to the Maḥzikei ha-Dat of Belz, who had presented Judaism as consisting of a left, a center, and a right; corresponding to sinners, average observers of the commandments, and saints. Neẓiv rejected this tripartite analysis. First, he excluded sinners from his analysis of the community since all Jews are required to keep *miẓvot*.[20] Then he proceeded to explain away the saints as phenomena of the past – most people are not on that level anymore. He focuses on the distinction between the average people in the center and those on the right who have a mystical love of God, seek illumination, and separate themselves from the world. He presents a Maimonidean distinction between two types of love of God. The first is the love of God available through self-sacrifice and the sanctification of God's name, which is available to all Jews (*Hilkhot Yesodei ha-Torah* 5:7). The second love of God is achieved through developing a continuous sense of His grandeur (*Hilkhot Yesodei ha-Torah* 2:1). A person who has achieved the second level of love of God cleaves to the divine in thought and strives for divine inspiration (*ruaḥ ha-kodesh*) and mystical illumination. Neẓiv comments, based on Maimonides' description, it is understood that "not everyone is worthy to reach this."

Neẓiv, unlike Maimonides, finds fault in an isolationist spirituality that lacks social involvement. In a creative rereading of Ḥatam Sofer, he comments that only Moshe was able to cleave to God and to

---

et XVIIIe siècles (Paris: Gallimard, 1974); Jean Delumeau, *Catholicism between Luther and Voltaire* (London: Burns and Oates, 1977).

[18] We must also move beyond the nineteenth-century rhetoric that the East is spiritual and Judaism is this-worldly.

[19] R. Naftali Zevi Yehudah Berlin (Neẓiv), *Meshiv Davar* (Warsaw, 1894), 1:44.

[20] In contrast to Neẓiv's assumption that all Jews are to keep the *halakhah*, Maḥzikei ha-Dat's approach might be the more traditional answer in terms of what was expected from the laity. The change of the status of the laity deserves a separate study.

show leadership simultaneously. All others, according to his reading, including Abraham, were aloof when cleaving to God, and able to show leadership only after descending to deal with other people.[21] Like many late nineteenth century theologians, Neẓiv limits mysticism to a feeling that is only felt "in the alone," and asserts that the social world remains non-mystical or even anti-mystical.[22] Furthermore, he views contemplative piety as dependent on and supererogatory to the learning in the *Beit Midrash*, as the learning ensures that piety remains within halakhic parameters. *Miẓvot* are portrayed not as acts of Safedian style, which, when performed properly, are able to raise one to mystical rapture, lead one to illumination, and affect the cosmos. Rather, *miẓvot*, for Neẓiv, are a step down to the social realm from the plane of mystical vision. Similarly, Neẓiv's vision of society includes no mention of Safedian concepts of mystical leadership or its monistic ethic of love. Neẓiv comments that "someone who separates himself to serve God in isolation, whose mind is immersed in the love of God…nevertheless is warned to stop his cleaving to God in order to perform the *miẓvah* in the proper time." In contrast, Neẓiv glorifies the center as always capable of great devotion to Torah, prayer, *miẓvot*, and communal service. Therefore, according to Neẓiv, those in the center are not mediocre but may attain the status of piety (*ḥasidut*); they are the pious ones described in the Bible and *Gemara*.

The far-reaching changes associated with modernity had their effect even on those of Neẓiv's contemporaries who were still on the elite path, having taken what Habermas called "a leap into foreign history," and becoming alienated from their own traditions. I find particularly vivid the account of this process of alienation from the

---

[21] On Maimonides and solitude see Guide III.51 (Pines 621); Harry Blumberg, "Alfarabi, Ibn Bajja, and Maimonides on the Governance of the Solitude: Sources and Influences," *Sinai* 78 (1976): 135–45. Notice how far Neẓiv's position is from Maimonides' contemplative one.

[22] Neẓiv, *Meshiv Davar* 52. For one of the most influential anti-mysticism theologians, whose influence extended into Karl Barth's Neo-Orthodoxy, see, Albrecht Ritschl, *The Christain Doctrine of Justification and Reconciliation*, English translation H.R. Macintosh and A.B. Macauly (Edinburgh: T&T Clark, 1902).

tradition in *The Sins of My Youth* by the *Haskalah* writer Moses Leib Lillienblum:

> On *Rosh ha-Shanah* in 1861, I was filled with religious ecstasy. Wherever I was, wherever I went, I concentrated on the Tetragrammaton. The two days of *Rosh ha-Shanah* and the Sabbath of Return I was in this frenzy. On the fourth day, a frightening idea suddenly floated into my consciousness: "Who can prove there is a God?"[23]

Lillienblum continues his story describing how he accepted the entire Enlightenment program including its invalidation of all traditional Judaism. He lost his faith, piety, and observance. Even his meditative practice and ability to achieve high religious levels could not withstand the challenge of modernity. His Enlightenment philosophy did not allow him to accept his own experience as valid. Nevertheless, his autobiography provides valuable evidence as to how recently these kabbalistic techniques were still part of the accepted tradition. Ultimately, his heresy left him removed from the entire rabbinic world. Yet, four years later, he remained nostalgic for his lost ecstasy:

> When I recited the prayer *u-ve-khen ten paḥdekha*, proclaiming man's recognition of God's sovereignty, the song of unity, which most deeply touches the heart of everyone who loves God, I was immediately affected. To those who do not know what this is like, I can tell them that it is like embracing one's beloved.[24]

Lillienblum, like so many others, rejected meditative practice as worthless to the modern Jew who can no longer believe in spiritual entities. Lillienblum's experience is instructive: not only for

---

[23] Cited in Lucy Dawidowiẓ, *The Golden Tradition: Jewish Life and Thought in Eastern Europe* (Boston: Beacon, 1968), p. 122.
[24] *Ibid*, p. 126.

nonbelievers but also for those who remained within the fold despite modernity, spirituality was pushed aside and prayer was transformed from a meditative and theurgic act into a communal one.

Ordinary Life

Let us proceed to our fifth point, derived from Bouyer, concerning spirituality: the applicability of these doctrines to modernity. Is it only in the extraordinary life that one may find spirituality? While the historian of Jewish spirituality studies the works of the religious virtuosi of past centuries for scholarly purposes, the spiritual seeker reads these texts in order to integrate their teachings into a religious life. Just as the elitist and esoteric teachings of Maimonides who wrote for those who were training for the true knowledge of God, and not for the vulgar masses, have been adapted for modern needs, so too the Kabbalah needs adaptation and popularization. Even those of us who look to our tradition as the locus of spirituality must appreciate that there is no naïve sameness with the past that can overcome the historical distance and otherness. The theological question which then arises is what aspects of traditional Jewish mysticism can be integrated into the life of the spiritually sensitive Jew?

For a new definition of spirituality, we turn to a recent book series that consists of reprints of many earlier spiritual texts, called *The Classics of Western Spirituality*, and their companion volumes, the *World Spirituality* series. The series' general editor, Ewert Cousins, set forth as a guiding principle that the study of spirituality remain distinct from philosophy of religion or history of religion. Cousins used the following as his working hypothesis.

> The Series focuses on the inner dimension of the person called by certain traditions "the spirit." This spiritual core is the deepest center of the person. It is here that the person is open to the transcendental dimension; it is here that the person experiences ultimate reality. The series explores the discovery of this core, the dynamics of its development, and its journey to the ultimate goal. It deals with prayer, spiritual

> direction, the various maps of the spiritual journey, and the methods of advancement in the spiritual sense.[25]

This approach to spirituality looks at the texts through a modern lens by correlating their medieval cosmologies with the transpersonal psychological aspects of the person, namely his 'core'; this is the part of him that is capable of experiencing the ultimate reality. Rather than leaving these peak experiences as romantic flight, disjointed from the world of rational discourse, a contemporary approach to spirituality points toward a way to cultivate these experiences by providing a map of the journey. While this approach may perhaps downgrade mysticism to a psychology of spirituality, this modernizing trend does not flatten out the experience and maintains its contours.

My definition of Jewish spirituality encompasses the traditional categories of love and fear of God, trust in God, holiness, and knowledge of God found in the traditional kabbalistic *mussar* literature. It is these traditional kabbalistic definitions of spirituality which can serve as our guide to achieve an experience of the ultimate reality. In order to overcome the modern non-spiritual definitions of these terms, it is important to carefully translate their mystical meanings into a modern mystical idiom.

Amidst the contemporary return to tradition and search for a religious path, "spirituality" has become a catch-phrase for all existential commitments and quests for meaning. The new Jewish spirituality that has been created is free from the historically tangible, objective, and articulated kabbalistic traditions, and instead constitutes a subjective appropriation of these traditions. In contrast, the approach which we are suggesting here retains the classic definition that one becomes a Kabbalist in order to experience the wonders of Torah, to attain an experience of God, and to view reality as infused

---

[25] Ewert Cousins, "General Editor's Introduction to the Series" in *World Spirituality: Christian Spirituality: Origins to the Twelfth Century,* eds. Bernard McGinn and John Meyendorff (New York: Crossroads, 1985), p. xiii.

with the divine.[26] Kabbalistic spirituality is a circumscribed realm; it does not encompass all that ennobles humanity, all transcendent quests, and all inwardness. Nor does it address the crisis of not having a presence of God in one's life. As a means to address these modern needs the spiritual approach Cousins presented in his introduction to *World Spirituality* is the best alternative.

The vagueness with which the term spirituality has been misused in a contemporary context, exacerbated by the widespread skepticism towards organized religion that has become increasingly prevalent in the last few decades, has caused people to look for a religious practice without dogma, and 'spirituality' became the odd term of choice for what everyone was now seeking, an anemic term, spirituality devoid of clarity. Spirituality is not simply a balm to ease the pain of conflict with the times, or an apologetic instrument with which to reach out to the marginally affiliated. It is not to be identified with neo-Ḥasidism, limited to the enthused homiletics of '*tisch* Torah,' or confused with the search for a spiritual essence outside of traditional forms. Spirituality is not the creation of new categories from the unusable shards of the past or from the sterility of academic philology. And certainly Kabbalah is not to be identified with the irrational and the absurd.[27] Jewish spirituality needs to be developed from within the corpus of traditional Jewish mystical and ethical texts that provide instruction in the cultivation of the soul.

Enthusiasm, including song, dance, and the many outreach techniques that excite the emotions (generally called *hitlahavut*, or *ruḥaniut*), should not be confused with kabbalistic spirituality.[28]

---

[26] Cordovero, *Or Neerav* (Jerusalem, 1965).

[27] Prior ages more attuned to spiritual differences were willing to label many lay devotions as forbidden, even as *ov ve-yidoni*. See the current work of R. Yaakov Moshe Hillel, *Kuntres Tamim Tihyeh ha-Shalem*, third edition (Jerusalem: Ahavat Shalom, 1995), the first edition was abridged and translated as *Faith and Folly: The Occult in Torah Perspective* (Spring Valley, NY: Feldheim, 1990). The book was written against the contemporary turn to magic and fortune telling among Israeli rabbis. Traditional Jewish idolatry and folly is still idolatry and folly.

[28] *Ḥasidut* has become (under thte influence of Perez̧, Dubnow, and others) a word to describe all the folkways, customs, *yiddishkeit*, and *heimishe* practices of the common people, and has little to do with the actual doctrines of *Ḥasidut*. The

Spirituality, rather than being the affective high of inflaming the heart, is the slow development of this psychological core by means of traditional techniques.[29] Enthusiasm is not a mystical experience of the divine, but rather an emotional expression of self.[30] Originally a derogatory term for false religious emotion or deluded claims of divine communication, enthusiasm is known for its antinomian, trans-denominational, sectarian, and anarchistic elements. Enthusiasts in many religions are renowned for their blasphemous state-

---

rabbinic and Ḥasidic elite tended to remove themselves from the values of the people. While common Ḥasidic householders did enthusiastically drink on Purim, in Poland, the elite did not. Ḥasidic texts include stern warnings concerning the evils of drinking, see R. Elimelekh of Lizhensk, *Hanhagot Adam*, no. 18. Since the late nineteen-eighties, Modern Orthodox neo-Ḥasidism has become associated with drinking and going to pubs. In my opinion, this equation is a result of several factors: (1) The death of Shlomo Carlebach and the replacement of his ecstatic spirituality with the creation of a 'Shlomo Lite' that is basically entertainment. (2) The influence of contemporary Breslov that teaches the importance of primal emotions and getting beyond the intellect. (3) The use of Alcoholics Anonymous doctrines as spirituality within the Orthodox world. (4) Our bringing in various "Chasidic" bands into our day schools and calling it "*ruaḥ*", "spirituality" or "*Chasidus*" (rather than teaching them real *Chasidus*) and then not understanding that our students will, as a consequence, find the same brand of "spirituality" in pop music.

[29] This paper takes issue with the widespread neo-Ḥasidic approach within modern Orthodoxy of identifying spirituality with the outpouring of the heart. On the Ḥasidic position itself, see R. Joseph I. Schneersohn, *Bikkur Chicago* (Brooklyn: Oẓar Hach⊠asidim Lubaviẓ, 1944), p. 21ff., who presents a Ḥasidic approach for the modern city worker in which the unquenchable burning of the heart of an ordinary Jew is greater than that of the rabbinic scholar. R. Ḥayyim of Volozhin, in his *Nefesh ha-Ḥayyim*, unnumbered section between sections 3 and 4, already rejected the foolishness of thinking that enthusiasm of the heart alone is the standard of piety. Kabbalistic spirituality is like Torah study: it takes years of application and diligence.

[30] Ḥasidic tradition itself differentiates between different types of experiences and considers enthusiasm induced by nigun, song or alcohol to be a lower experience, "a hearing from afar" compared to a self-generated inner fire of contemplation that transforms the person. See Dov Baer of Lubavitch, *On Ecstasy*, trans. Louis Jacobs (Chappaqua: Rossel Books, 1963). On the role of the emotional enthusiasm generated by music within religion, the best discussion remains Al-Ghazali's discussion of *sama* in *Ihya Ulam al-Din*, or *The Alchemy of Happiness*. Al-Ghazali accepts the enthusiasm of music against those who limit religion to a sense of transcendence, but values mystical use over emotional use.

ments in which they identify themselves with God. The expression of enthusiasm in an ordinary religious context remains safe, provided that one is not reaching for the hidden reality. However, once one sets one's attention on the mysterious realm, then spirituality without the relinquishing of selfhood has always been – and still is – dangerous. The turn to kabbalistic metaphysics without the requisite meditative awe of self-abnegation leads to a mistaken identification of the self with divine metaphysics and revelation. When the eighteenth-century writers warned against enthusiasts, they were well aware of this hazard.[31]

If Ramḥal (1707–1747) wrote that in his age so-called piety was limited to fools who fail to understand the meaning of true piety and squander their effort on needless activities, then all the more so in this impious century.[32] Several social critics (Neil Postman, Wendy Kaminer) have labeled the nineteen-nineties as one of the most superstitious decades of the century. Tragically, pseudo-Kabbalah has been swept up in this trend.[33]

RENEWAL

Although, there is a great renewal of interest now in Kabbalah, *Ḥasidut*, Safed piety, Jewish meditation, and the reading of pietistic

[31] The classic work is Ronald Knox, *Enthusiasm: A Chapter in the History of Religion with Special Reference to the Seventeenth and Eighteenth Centuries* (Oxford: Oxford University Press, 1950). In antiquity, the term enthusiasm referred to those participating in Dionysus rituals that, "had the god within." In modern centuries it was used to refer to those deluding themselves. On Ḥasidism as enthusiasm (*schwarmer*) and superstition (*aberglauben*) see Naḥman Krokhmal, *Moreh Nevukhei ha-Zeman* (Berlin: L. Lamm, 1924), chap. 1.

[32] One example of the modern trend toward accepting kabbalistic practices in a totemistic way is the increased popularity of the annual festivities in Meron. Most participants do not know that R. Yosef Karo rejected the practice as halakhically and kabbalistically questionable lay piety. Meir Benayahu, "Devotional Practices of the Kabbalists of Safed in Meron" (Hebrew), in *Sefer Ẓefat* (Jerusalem: Makhon Ben Ẓvi, 1962), pp. 1–40.

[33] Wendy Kaminer, *Sleeping with Extra-Terrestrials: The Rise of Irrationalism and the Perils of Piety* (New York: Pantheon Books, 1999); Neil Postman, *Building a Bridge to the Eighteenth Century* (New York: Alfred A. Knopf, 1999).

works, their traditional practice in fact has never completely disappeared. The fifth and sixth Lubavitcher Rebbes continued the *Ḥabad* meditative tradition and expected their followers to meditate, in addition to the fixed daily prayers, for at least an hour and a half a day. Some of these followers were still teaching meditation in the nineteen-forties, and many older Ḥabad Ḥasidim in the nineteen-seventies and even in the early nineteen-eighties were still practicing this tradition. However, the seventh Rebbe was modern, "scientific," and this-worldly, and he transformed a devotional Ḥasidism into an outreach movement. Meditation was downplayed, and many of the writings of the earlier Rebbes were not reprinted. Is the restoration of the meditative tradition, and the reprinting of the earlier devotional works to be considered neo-Ḥasidism? A new movement? Or a restoration of earlier traditions, continuously practiced, but temporarily eclipsed? The restoration of these activities involves transformations necessary to accommodate modern sensibilities but, unlike the New Age varieties, the practices that emerge have not been created *ex nihilo*. Meditation is an ancient practice, requiring living models as well as appropriate texts. The new generation currently involved in meditation brings to bear different values in different circumstances. Similar statements apply in the practice of the kabbalistic tradition of Rabbi Yehudah Ashlag which, under leadership of his grandson, Rabbi Baruch, returned to meditation, as well as to the Vilna Gaon tradition of meditation found in the writings of Rabbi Sherayah Deblinsky of Ponovezh and popularized by Yehiel Bar-Lev. The practice of meditation skipped two generations and took a new direction, but it is not a new creation.[34] During most of the present century, meditative practices have been eclipsed by the concerns of modernity. Nevertheless, in Jerusalem currently, there exist at least ten *minyanim* that use Lurianic intentions (*kavvanot*).

---

[34] There is a contemporary three-volume set of meditation techniques produced anonymously within the Ḥasidic community, showing how widespread is this revival. See *Sheva Einayim* (Jerusalem, 1995). Many of the comments here also apply to the teachings of R. Moshe Shapiro in Israel and R. Moshe Wolfson in Brooklyn.

Meditation

Kabbalistic practices have deep roots in the halakhic tradition, and can still be practiced in the modern world. Ultimately, to dwell in kabbalistic spirituality, we need a broad reorientation to the mystical. As a start, we will consider that today a serious Orthodox kabbalistic path would include immersion in at least the three halakhic realms of prayer, *miẓvot*, and study. Many topics need to be addressed in order to develop a modern Kabbalah in all of its fullness. These include: images of God, God language, mystical psychology, dreams, the soul, afterlife, health and healing, science and the natural order, and magic.

Jewish Meditation is popular because it can offer a direct experience of the divine to a broad cross-section of Jews, from yeshiva high school and college-age students, to mature *baalei batim*, and the elderly. It is self-validating and brings immediate changes to one's life. In fact, traditional texts have a broad and complex program of Jewish spiritual praxis that extends far beyond simple meditation exercises. The pious person is expected to visualize God's name continuously, sense His providence constantly, respond to the inner meaning of the Sabbath and holidays, and before prayer, to visualize that he is standing before the divine.[35] It involves a hierarchical ladder of internal states. In its initial stages, it provides a tether to still the mind and calm the emotions.[36] This enhances intention both in the ordinary

[35] Gershom Scholem, "The Concept Of Kavvanah in the Early Kabbalah," in *Studies in Jewish Thought*, ed. Alfred Jospe (Detroit: Wayne State University Press, 1981); Moshe Idel, "R. Isaac Sagi Nahor's Mystical Intention of the *Shemoneh Esreh*," in *Massuot: Studies in Kabbalistic Literature and Jewish Philosophy in Memory of Prof. Ephraim Gottlieb*, eds. M. Oron and A. Goldreich (Jerusalem: Bialik Institute, 1994), pp. 25–52; Moshe Idel, "Kabbalistic Prayer in Provence," in *Tarbiz* 62:2 (Jan.–March 1993); Moshe Idel, "Kabbalistic Prayers and Colors" in *Approaches to Judaism in Medieval Times*, vol. 3, ed. David Blumenthal (Chico, CA: Scholars Press, 1984–1987), pp. 17–28; Moshe Idel, "Ḥitbodedut As Concentration" in *Jewish Spirituality*, vol. 1, ed. Arthur Green; R. Shalom Dov Baer Schneersohn, *Tract on Prayer* (Brooklyn: Kehot Publication Society, 1992); Aryeh Kaplan, *Meditation and the Kabbalah* (York Beach, ME: Samuel Weiser, 1982); Mark Verman, *The History and Varieties of Jewish Meditation* (Northvale, NJ: Jason Aronson, 1996).

[36] When I teach meditation, the first sessions are on how to sit properly, relax the

practice of prayer and in the continuous focus on God's presence. In its higher stages, it leads to equanimity, freedom from emotional entrapment, a control of the mind's processes and an overall sense of wholeness and balance. The next level is the development of an internal life in which one plays out contemplative dramas in order to enter the divine hierarchy. The highest levels involve the bringing of an influx of the divine into the world.

Meditation has particular halakhic relevance when utilized as a means to pray with intention. Many medieval legal commentators, especially those influenced by philosophy or pietism, assume that prayer requires intention on the part of the devotee.[37] Therefore, one of the first goals of Jewish meditative practice is to learn to still the mind and, before one sits down to pray, to bring about a consciousness of God's glory. Some of these practices are explained in the corpus of halakhic literature. However, for a more detailed and fuller spectrum of kabbalistic prayer techniques, ranging from the fairly simple focusing of one's mind on God's glory and light *(kavod)*, to Cordovero's visualizations of the divine names, to the complex Lurianic *kavvanot*, it is necessary to refer to kabbalistic works.

An example of a method of increasing intentionality during prayer that is significant for a halakhic community is R. Ḥayyim of Volozhin's method as described in his *Nefesh ha-Ḥayyim*. R. Ḥayyim divides the performance of worship into several distinct elements: stillness, emotions, and visualization. The first element involves the contemplative practice of turning one's mind from its ordinary

---

body, and tether one's busy mind. Next there follows an instruction on letting go of distractions by allowing them to gently flow away. Even these basic exercises require months of practice before one can perform them properly, and I suggest that my students take their early steps in meditation outside of formal prayer. At the second level, students try various techniques of Jewish meditation and develop the needed internal mental framework for actually using these methods.

[37] For example see Tur's paraphrase of the *Talmidei Rabbenu Yonah*, Yaakov ben Asher, *Arbaah Turim: Oraḥ Ḥayyim, siman* 98: "Arouse your concentration and remove all disturbing thoughts from your mind, so that when you pray, your thoughts will be pure.... Pious men of deeds used to meditate and concentrate in prayer until they divested themselves of the physical. They attained a spiritual strength almost on par with prophecy."

business with matters of the world, to the meaning of the words, to allowing those words to complete and deeply affect the heart. This requires one to wait before prayer in order to still the mind and then fill it with prayerful content. Distracting thoughts in prayer are avoided by training the mind to attain this stillness.[38]

The second element in R. Ḥayyim's method of prayer-readiness is the turning of the object of one's emotions from worldly desires to the Holy One, blessed be He. The worshipper turns a loving gaze upon the divine and receives pleasure from the words of the prayers. R. Ḥayyim of Volozhin models this practice on the custom of the early pious ones, *ha-Ḥasidim ha-Rishonim*, who sat for an hour before prayer in order to attain an ecstatic taking leave of their senses, as explained by the students of R. Yonah in their commentary on Tractate *Berakhot*. Finally, he exhorts his readers to use R. Yosef Karo's technique of visualizing the words of prayer. He calls it "a tried and tested method" for stilling the mind, acquiring purity of thought, and bringing down blessing. From R. Ḥayyim's statement that this method has been proven to be effective, it is clear that he is not writing merely in the abstract, but that he actually practiced these techniques. This visualization of the letters as a means to provide purity of mind seems to function on two levels simultaneously: it tethers the mind to allow the requisite stillness and it brings down blessing from above. After passing through the emotional, contemplative, and imaginative prerequisite states, the process culminates in the use of kabbalistic intentions (*kavvanot*).

In addition to these preparatory meditations, Naḥmanides and his school, the *Zohar*, R. Moses de Leon, R. Joseph Gikkatilla, and R. Moses Cordovero all describe meditations on divine lights and names in a variety of spatial configurations which allow for an ascent into the higher realms of divinity. Initially, they envision a lower level of divinity, immanent and embodied in this world, receiving its light from above, similar to light shining into a prism. A higher

[38] Nefesh ha-Ḥayyim (Vilna, 1859) 2:1, p. 47. The method was distilled into a small tract by his student R. Zundel of Salant. See Eliezer Rivlin, *Sefer ha-Ẓaddik R. Yosef Zundl mi-Salant* (Jerusalem, 1927).

light is bestowed on it from a higher realm of God's manifestation and power. Finally, they image an infinite realm of brilliant shining light that is the source of all light, energy, and power. One reaches the infinite realm through slow ascent by creating and following a spatial map of the divine. To successfully work with this map, one must develop, over time, clarity, breadth, and depth of vision and provide oneself with psychological safety nets. Only then can one bind oneself in emotion, will, and intellect to this transcendent infinite vision. Afterwards, one slowly descends and brings the infinite light down into the lower lights, letting this light grow and give energy. Finally, the light cascades into the lower level of divinity – the prism, as it were – then into the mind of the devotee, and finally into his body. One has to make certain that it is channeled slowly and safely to avoid being overwhelmed. Kabbalists used this meditation during prayer, ascending before the silent *Amidah*.[39] There are many variants of this meditation using a candle flame, regions of different colored lights, divine names, *sefirot*, or various parts of the soul. Each provides a ladder of psychic development, which parallels the gradual entrance into God's manifestation.

In the study and pursuit of spirituality, the central concerns of meditation are identifying the mental states of consciousness in which one finds oneself during those activities. One notices the different mental processes of the various forms of meditation which include intellectual contemplation, visualizations, stillness exercises, imagination meditations, loving-kindness meditations, focused meditations, free-form meditations within daily life, and meditations reserved for prayer. Furthermore, serious study needs to address the questions of the spiritual practices of meditation. How to still the mind, attain focus and concentration, and relax the body? How does one focus on the mental icon, in the mind's eye or in the imagination? Is there a mental screen, as it were, on which one envisions the divine? Are there particular bodily

[39] In contrast, Lurianic Kabbalists focus on restoring a single configuration of the divine, with many discrete intentions, before the start of the *Shema* and then again at the start of the *Amidah*.

sensations associated with the encounter; or is the experience one of synesthesia? Is the process active or passive, one of habituation, or de-automatization, one with a single focus or with two foci?

Aryeh Kaplan wrote great introductions to the world of Jewish meditation, but he was negligent in omitting the most primary preparatory stages of meditation from his works. A reader of Kaplan's works who does not possess these rudimentary meditational tools risks entering the meditative realm with an excess of self-concern. Basic exercises in visualization techniques are necessary in order to commence meditation without the distraction of thoughts and emotions. These initial exercises also provide a release of tension and emotions in order to prevent anxiety, depression, and other forms of psychic harm which might otherwise arise from the practice of these techniques. If one were to use the advanced techniques in Kaplan's books without preparation, one runs the risk of burning up in self-effacement or self-delusion. R. Ḥayyim Vital had a terrible reaction the first time R. Isaac Luria gave him a *yiḥud* to perform. It is necessary to confront one's emotions, pains, and past traumas before beginning to practice advanced kabbalistic techniques. The expertise required in order to block pain and fend off distracting thoughts, or to use the Ḥasidic technique of raising distractions to their source, is a slow and gradual process. The objective of these techniques is ultimately to enable prayer as meditation, as an encounter with an awareness of the divine, and as an outpouring of the self.

Miẓvot

Formerly, Neoplatonic writers downplayed the role of external ritual; Bahye's *Ḥovot ha-Levavot* is paradigmatic of this tendency. In opposition to this emphasis on internal piety, the Kabbalah stresses ritual performance, including the importance of the proper recitation and enunciation of words. The importance of *miẓvot* is amplified through this integration of body and mind, especially when combined with correlated requirements in ascetic theology. Rituals invoke a sense of awe in the participation within the timeless divine.[40] By provid-

[40] Another more psychological approach is the re-sanctification and ritualization

ing cosmic reasons why one must have three meals on the Sabbath, say one hundred blessings a day, and be exacting in the minutiae of the *halakhah*, the Kabbalah heightened rabbinic requirements in an almost obsessive manner.

In the thirteenth century, Kabbalists developed traditions concerned with a theology and set of practices in which cosmic effects are produced through the performance of *mizvot*. There are several kabbalistic approaches to ritual,[41] among them the idea of ritual as participation in a cosmic drama, or as an entering into sacred time in order to capture the ontic status of the liturgical calendar. Mystical ritual provides an entrance through the boundaries and heterogeneity of sacred time and space. This realm is one of cosmic drama and visionary antecedent to the performance itself. The ritual and its ocular prerequisites create an experience that is qualitatively different from ordinary life. Transformative experiences can occur when human actions are considered a portal to the realm of the divine.

Sometimes, ritualization provides a sense of participation in the divine through parallel modeling – creating harmonies between the worlds in the form of a "just as" (*kegavna*) parallel of the higher world. Ritual becomes sacramental. At other times, ritual acts to provide a sense of blessing. The effect of ritual in bringing down blessing in the form of influx from above (*shefa*) is described in the *Shaarei Oraḥ*.

The thirteenth-century emphasis on ritual was developed further in the spiritually charged community of sixteenth-century Safed. Safed mystics applied the teachings of the *Zohar* to their own systems

---

of everyday life. Eating, work, and leisure are to be sanctified beyond the general framework provided by the observance of *mizvot*.

[41] I am pointing out approaches to the performance of ritual here rather than cataloging the myriad of different kabbalistic explanations of the *mizvot*. For explanations of the commandments, see Isaiah Tishby, *Wisdom of the Zohar* (Oxford and New York: Littman Library, 1989), pp. 867–1323; Moshe Idel, *Kabbalah: New Perspectives*, pp. xiii–v; Charles Mopsik, *Les grands textes de la kabbalah: les rites qui font dieu* (Paris: Verdier, 1993); Elliott R. Wolfson, "Mystical Rationalization of the Commandments in Sefer ha-Rimon," HUCA 59 (1988): 217–51.

of ritual practice. Cordovero discusses the importance of focused awareness during ritual. According to him, all of one's intentionality while performing *miẓvot* brings *ruḥaniut* (quanta of spiritual blessing) from the realm of the divine. In his *Reshit Ḥokhmah*, R. Elijah DeVidas, of the Cordoveran school, presents this process of bringing down *ruḥaniut* as a journey, a cyclical but differentiated spiritual path. R. Yosef Karo, also a member of this school, is a prime exemplar of one who achieved mastery in the areas of both *halakhah* and Kabbalah. His spirituality, methods of visualization, and the combination of *halakhah* and Kabbalah which he represented, served as a model for mitnaggedic piety.[42]

An entirely different approach is that of the Lurianic drama in which one identifies oneself with the High Priest in order to rectify the sin of Adam. Luria postulates a cosmic fall of man as a consequence of the Sin of Adam and the need for theurgy, unifications (*yiḥudim*), and universal reincarnation to restore a lost harmony. In a theurgic modeling of the Temple structure, one eats on a four-legged table, with twelve loaves for *ḥallot*, and closes one's eyes to avoid gazing on the *shekhinah*. One also binds oneself to the dead, engages in *yiḥudim* for illumination, and performs many preparatory immersions in a *mikveh*.

In the literature of nineteenth-century Polish Ḥasidism *miẓvot* are considered to have been fulfilled properly only when their performance is accompanied by total mental concentration. One does not perform the *miẓvah* until one is able to have complete intent of the holiness specific to the particular *miẓvah*. The intentionality found in Polish Ḥasidism is revelatory of the sacredness of the *miẓvah*.

In contrast to these kabbalistic approaches, the early modern Polish *Aḥaronim* (c. 1630–1800) seem to have a mixed canon without clear lines of demarcation between works of law, custom, piety, and Kabbalah. Many of their readings of Kabbalah suffer from misplaced

---

[42] R.J.Z. Werblowsky, *Joseph Karo: Lawyer and Mystic* (Philadelphia: Jewish Publication Society, 1977), pp. 158–61, 311–2.

concreteness and a weakness in their exteriorization. They should be judged as early modern, and not as kabbalistic, phenomena. An example of this tendency which troubles many of my contemporaries is the transformation of the *Zohar*'s panegyric on the beauty of the daily recitation of the chapter from the Mishnah on the Temple incense offering into a fearful early modern debate on the dangers of missing out a word in the recitation. This kind of error of omission was considered to be as dangerous as leaving out one of the ingredients from the offering which was punishable by death.[43]

Similarly, myth, folklore, and lay devotions should not automatically be associated with the Kabbalah. The citation by early modern halakhic authorities of the custom to refrain from eating nuts on *Rosh ha-Shanah*, or for women not to taste of the *havdalah* wine, are indigenous Ashkenazic customs that were only later associated with Castilian demonology.[44] Just as a weak halakhic comment in an eighteenth-century devotional *siddur* is not to be confused with sophisticated halakhic thinking, so too, these kabbalistic-style comments should not be confused with rigorous kabbalistic thought. For example, the recitation of *le-Shem Yiḥud* became a magical act intended to serve as a shortened exteriorized substitute for the requisite hours of daily Lurianic intentions. According to the Kabbalists one should either perform the meditations of the Lurianic path in all their extensive detail, or not at all. Although in earlier centuries these methods of recitation and externalization served the purpose of popularizing kabbalistic ideas, in our age in which far more people possess a highly developed sense of self, a yearning for personal

---

[43] The formalistic stringencies of Polish seventeenth-eighteenth century Jewish culture, many of them based on externalization, demonization, recitation, and magic for personal benefit, are a widespread early modern phenomena and are not intrinsic to the Kabbalah. Cf. Jacob Katz, *Tradition and Crisis: Jewish Society at the End of the Middle Ages*, translated by Bernard Dov Cooperman (New York: New York University Press, 1993), pp. 190–4.

[44] For example, according to R. Isaiah Horowitz, *Shenei Luḥot ha-Berit, Masekhet Shabbat*, women should not taste of the *havdalah* wine because women are identified with Lilith. This is in contrast to the Spanish and Safed traditions of Kabbalah, in which women are not identified with the demonic.

authenticity, and the ability to engage in serious intellectual study, these contracted versions are far less beneficial.[45]

Scholarly and spiritual readings of Kabbalah also differ on questions of heresy, and concerning their normative and halakhic status. It is instructive to remember that Rashba issued sharp warnings against using Abraham Abulafia's methods of meditation and those of other lay mystics such as the prophet of Avila. While it is true that Cordovero and others did indeed cite whole paragraphs from Abulafia's texts, they took care to integrate his ideas into a rabbinic system. When Idel comments that anomic practices were integrated into nomic systems, it should be taken as more than a passing scholarly observation. The integration of a text into a nomic context alters its meaning, just as Maimonides changes the meaning of Al-Farabi's ideas when he cites his works.[46] A different and difficult case for the halakhic community is that of Ḥayyim Vital whose integration of Kabbalah and *halakhah* that is taken by many as paradigmatic of the Kabbalah is for at least three reasons problematic.[47] (1) He situates kabbalistic practice in the world of emanation (*aẓilut*), hierarchically above rabbinic Judaism. (2) He uses kabbalistic explanations to generate *halakhah*. (3) He downgrades rationality as a guide to Judaism in favor of revelation and intuition. While R. Ḥayyim's approach was acceptable to many Lurianic practitioners because it values Kabbalah

[45] On the history of the recitation of *le-Shem Yiḥud* from its origins as a medieval devotional formula before *miẓvot*, to a short substitute for Lurianic intentions, see Moshe Halamish, *Ha-Kabbalah bi-Tfillah, be-Halakhah, u-ve-Minhag* (Ramat Gan: Bar Ilan Press, 2000), pp. 45–105.

[46] Moshe Idel, *Kabbalah: New Perspectives*, pp. xv–vii. On Rashba's rejection of Abulafia see *Responsa of R. Shlomo ben Avraham ben Adret*, ed. Ḥayyim Dimotrovsky (Jerusalem: Mossad ha-Rav Kook, 1990), Responsa 34, p. 101.

[47] *Tikkunei Zohar* 28; R. Hayim Vital's *Introduction to the Shaar ha-Hakdamot* (also printed as the introduction to the *Eẓ Ḥayyim*) presents a distinction between the enclothed *halakhah* and the inner light of the Kabbalah. Scholem used Ḥayyim Vital in order to read the *Tikkunei Zohar* as implying an anarchistic heterodox transvaluation through the Kabbalah of the written Torah; see Gershom Scholem, *On the Kabbalah and its Symbolism* (New York: Schocken, 1969), pp. 66–86. By comparison, R. Ẓadok uses the same *Tikkunei Zohar* passage to develop a halakhic approach to these texts. For him, the written Torah is enclothed and limited while the Oral Law, consisting of both *halakhah* and Kabbalah, is liberating.

over *halakhah*, it would not be suitable for an halakhic approach to spirituality. The Vilna Gaon expressed similar reservations concerning R. Ḥayyim's understanding of Lurianic Kabbalah. He affirmed that Luria could not override the Talmud, the *Zohar*, or the intellect, therefore the Gaon was criticized by others of for rejecting Lurianic Kabbalah, even though he uses the Lurianic corpus extensively as a commentary on the *Zohar.*[48]

Study: From Philosophy to Kabbalah to Torah

Kabbalah, rather than being a form of subversive spirituality resting on the shards of rationalism, or a type of mythopoesis favored by those seeking to amplify the imaginative element in Judaism through an emphasis on Kabbalah, Midrash and literature, is the study of a canon of texts concerning the divine throne and divine names combined with a real celestial hierarchy. The study of the Kabbalah includes exegesis that deals with events in higher realms adding deeper meaning to *miẓvot* and Torah. While much of this scheme is not translatable into modern categories, the basic frameworks need at least to be acknowledged. It must lead to a partial knowledge of God, a sense of the celestial hierarchy, and the development of positive language about God.

Those who exclude Kabbalah from the canon of Judaism or those who advocate finding the imaginative element outside of

[48] For an example of the followers of Luria appealing to an authority, both textual and charismatic, higher than the halakhic tradition, see Yaakov Gartner, "The Influence of the Ari on the Custom of Wearing Two Pair of Tefillin," *Daat* 28 (1992): 51–64 (Hebrew). The Ḥatam Sofer and the Vilna Gaon offer models of accepting Kabbalah without it overriding *halakhah*. Compare Ḥabad, which accepts the charismatic cult around the memory of Luria and therefore has to deal with these problems of the Vital tradition. See Moshe Dober Rivkin, *Kuntres Ashkavta de-Rebbi* (Brooklyn, 1976). Contemporary spiritual practitioners would also be troubled by the magic and necromancy found in Vital. An opposite case, not without some irony, is that of Nathan of Gaza's ideas. Both *Sefardim* and *Mitnaggedim* use them as interpretations of particulars within Safed Kabbalah. When Luzzatto wrote that he uses Sabbatean Kabbalah but he is not a Sabbatean, he should be taken at his word. His statement is reflective of the tradition of the selective use of Sabbatean writings.

Judaism would do well to read the recriminations of Rashba, Rama, Maharasha, and Gra, all of whom castigate those who seek to limit the tradition to *halakhah* and ignore the Kabbalah.[49] The early Kabbalists themselves pointed out that Kabbalah is part of the Oral tradition, hence the name "received tradition" (*kabbalah*), the tradition. According to the aforementioned halakhic authorities, one cannot select only those parts of the tradition that one likes. Furthermore, to limit Judaism to *halakhah* is to ignore the gamut of literary and pietistic works produced within Jewish culture that describes religious experience. R. Akiva's journey to paradise in the *Heikhalot* and the spiritual descriptions found in the *Zohar*, Karo, Cordovero, Vital, Komarno, R. Naḥman, Rav Kook, or even those of the Vilna Gaon, rival anything in the Christian writings.

Reinhold Niebuhr comments on the hubris of those modernists who reduced the Christian trinity to a matter of culture, a Neoplatonic

[49] The descriptions of religious experience in Rav Soloveitchik's writings, including *u-Vikashtem mi-Sham*, are generally of a William James, this-worldly, variety, in which mysticism consists of deep feeling in prayer, emotionalism, powerful dreams, acceptance of transcendence within one's life, or redemptive sacrificial acts. They are all experiences that come on without preparation, training, meditation, or a clear divine object. Rav Soloveitchik offers *halakhah* as a means of articulation, control, and deepening of these experiences. However, neither William James nor Rav Soloveitchik recognizes anything similar to the halakhic tradition of figures like R. Yosef Karo. R. Karo explicitly states that beyond *halakhah* is Kabbalah, and that neither the *halakhah* nor natural human emotions are sufficient to relate to God. R. Karo's own practice consisted of the following: (1) one should cultivate continuous consciousness of Torah in one's mind in order to have a sense of Unity of Being. (2) One should cultivate this unity of thought even in one's dream states. (3) One should pray using Cordovero's kabbalistic intentions, meaning that prayer is not just an outpouring of the soul (as in James or neo-Ḥasidism) but it is a trained ascent through the celestial realms, throne rooms, and then up to the *Ein Sof.* (4) One who is on a sufficiently elevated level should recite *mishnayot* in order to have the spirit of the *Mishnah* or various *tannaim* come to visit him. (5) R. Karo himself did *yiḥudim* using the secrets of the divine name and the secret of the Chariot Vision. (6) *Miẓvot* affect the *sefirot* in order to bring down blessing. Halakhic authorities did not expect to find spirituality within *halakhah*. One can find a similar range of spiritual practices that transcend the *halakhah* in the thought of other halakhic figures.

vestige to be replaced in the modern era, rather than assuming that the trinity constitutes the believer's efforts to formulate the religious experience. Similarly, Naḥmanides' and Cordovero's mystical attempts to express their religious experience mediated through biblical and rabbinic texts cannot be dismissed as cultural vestiges. Recontextualized in their original context, the *sefirot* do not become a special problem of arbitrary symbolism and structures. Moderns find medieval symbolism, especially cosmology, numerology, and angelology, difficult to appreciate, and so these symbols have fallen into disuse. But is the number symbolism and cosmology of the *Zohar* any more arbitrary or medieval than those of Ibn Ezra? Just as Yehudah ha-Levi and Maimonides have been re-read in a Modern Orthodox context without their attendant medieval worldviews, so too medieval features of Kabbalah need not be seen as an obstacle to our acceptance of the Kabbalah as an authentic understanding of Judaism.

In the twelfth and thirteenth centuries, there was an intellectual commitment to the study of the Platonic cosmology contained in both Neoplatonic and Platonic-Aristotelian thought. Eventually, this was succeeded by the acceptance of a kabbalistic realm that lay beyond the philosophical. R. David Kimhi's biblical commentary contains a Platonic reading of Maimonides, in which he discusses such topics as attaining knowledge of the *kavod*, how creation leads to knowledge of the sacred, the importance of the soul, and the role of angels in the cosmic chain. Neoplatonic Maimonideanism works well in high school education. Those topics can be smoothly integrated into the study of *Navi*, and may lead to discussions of meditation, the divine *kavod*, and the service of God through contemplative knowledge. However, by the time students reach college age, there tends to be an implicit bifurcation between the secular sciences and Torah, and spirituality must be added artificially to the realm of philosophy. Many students who are interested in metaphysics travel the same route as Gikkatilla, from the *Guide of the Perplexed* to eventually arrive at an acceptance of an objective divine realm. Other students become attracted to the panentheism of Cordovero, still others find their place in the responsibility of R. Ḥayyim of Volozhin's chain of Being.[50]

The textbooks used mostly widely on college campuses to teach Kabbalah are those authored by Gershom Scholem. But Scholem's presentation of Jewish mysticism is far from a spiritual reading of the Kabbalah. Many students, having read Scholem, associate the Kabbalah only with the doctrine of the *sefirot*, a thirteenth-century cluster concept that is an attempt to make sense out of the plethora of referents to God in *Tanakh*, rabbinic literature, and Neoplatonism, and the *merkavah*, magical, and angelic traditions. In the Bible, God is referred to as warrior, bride, king, as the ancient of days, as crashing waves, dew, and ice. In the rabbinic and midrashic traditions, God appears as *shekhinah* and *gevurah*, as being enclothed in his *tiferet*, crowned, wearing *tefillin*, moving from His seat of judgment to His seat of mercy, and as incomplete until His name becomes complete. The medieval tradition offers us awe of the grandeur of God as presented in Ibn Gabirol's *Keter Malkhut*, and the love of the divine manifestation as an *anthropos* in Ashkenaz's *Shir ha-Kavod*. In thirteenth century Kabbalah these references are treated as a holistic cluster concept. They are understood as hypostases of the divine in a variety of forms – a tree, a macrocosm of the human body, or a cosmological chart.

Yet, neither this rich forest of symbols, nor Gershom Scholem's presentation of Jewish mysticism is the message of the Kabbalah in its entirety. Although Scholem wrote that there is no such thing as "the doctrine of the Kabbalists," nevertheless, he limited his studies mostly to the sefirotic realms. There are many kabbalistic texts – mystical, meditative, ethical, devotional, philosophic, or contemplative works – which are not specifically theosophic. And

[50] This dualism reflects the majority of later Kabbalists, such as Cordovero, who place Kabbalah above philosophy, while medieval Kabbalists tend to identify Kabbalah with the natural order and philosophy. See Yosef Ben-Shlomo, *The Mystical Theology of Moses Cordovero* (Jerusalem: Bialik Press, 1986), pp. 32–5 (Hebrew). Cordovero uses philosophy dogmatically as metaphysical scaffolding, or as cultural background. While avoiding philosophy, he nevertheless does not negate the autonomy of philosophy.

those texts that are concerned with theosophy present many images of the divine other than *sefirot*, such as names of God, angels, lights, celestial realms, and the divine in the form of a human figure. Even the classic work by R. Yosef Gikkatilla, *Shaarei Oraḥ*, is as much about the divine Name, a spiritualized body, and meditation, as it is about the *sefirot*.[51]

The genealogies of texts that are so important in the philological study of the Kabbalah are far less significant for those who study these texts as part of a spiritual practice. Just as the philological study of Maimonides focuses on Alfarabi and Geonic fragments while studies of Maimonides' spirituality use a different canon, so too in spiritually oriented study of the Kabbalah, historically significant works are not necessarily of greatest importance. The most central works of Jewish spirituality are not the *Heikhalot* texts, the *Bahir*, Castilian works, or Sabbatian texts. The Castilian texts are certainly antecedents of the *Zohar*, but the role they play in exegesis or in the spiritual usage of the text is minimal.[52] The *Zohar* itself is important because it became a canonical work used for spiritual purposes in later centuries. A spiritual text must readily be applicable for pietistic purposes. For example, *Heikhalot* spirituality, which was alive until the nineteenth century, refers to the *Heikhalot* of the *Zohar* rather than the less spiritually accessible *Heikhalot* of the rabbinic period. Gikkatilla's *Shaarei Oraḥ*, a bestseller in its own day and ever since, stands in marked contrast to the Hebrew writings of Moses de Leon, which were unread in his time and are today read only by scholars. The basic texts for a spiritual reading of the Kabbalah include the *Zohar, Tikkunei Zohar,* Naḥmanides, Gikkatilla, Recanati, Cordovero and his students, and Ḥayyim of Volozhin.[53]

---

[51] Moshe Idel, "Defining Kabbalah: The Kabbalah of the Divine Names" in *Mystics of the Book: Themes, Topics, and Typologies* ed. R.A. Herrera (New York: Lang, 1993), pp. 97–122; Moshe Idel, Introduction to R. Joseph Gikatilla, *Gates of Light*, trans. Avi Weinstein (Sacred Literature Trust Series; San Francisco: Harper, 1993), p. xxviii.

[52] I do not want to overly simplify the issue because R. Moshe de Leon's *sodot* of the commandments were cited in later centuries.

[53] Those students returning from study in Israel are inclined to read later theological works including those by Maharal, Ramḥal, and R. Eliashiv's *Leshem Shevo*

Cordovero's voluminous corpus is so widely read because it includes a synthetic reading of the *Zohar* and other kabbalistic schools, and integrates them with rabbinic and philosophic material. Notwithstanding Cordovero's lack of theosophic innovation or of a radical turn on the system worthy of scholarly attention, his mild synthesis was read and used extensively by most Kabbalists from the sixteenth century up to and including today. Concerning his integrated formulation of the Kabbalah, Cordovero quotes Maimonides' requirement to know God (even though Maimonides was not a Kabbalist), explaining that Kabbalah is the fullest version of that knowledge. In order to study Kabbalah he states that one should be twenty years old, possessed of a rabbinic education, including the ability to learn in depth (*be-iyyun*), observant, and of sound character.[54] Cordovero lays out a path that enables one to read Kabbalah as a resource for theology, meditative prayer, ritual creativity, and for the purpose of the psychological internalization of a kabbalistic worldview. Cordovero's reading of Kabbalah sustains an integrated approach to spiritual development because it is founded on a broad and firm basis of *halakhah*, *minhag*, and philosophy.

In addition to the earlier models of studying the Platonic divine

---

ve-Aḥlamah. However, I find that Yeshiva University students do not relate well to *Tikkunei Zohar* with its highly specific letter and shape visualizations.

[54] Even though Kabbalah should not be studied before the age of twenty, the process of "softening of the soul" by introducing spirituality, meditation, and snippets from Kabbalah should be initiated far earlier, already in the eighth grade. From this age until the age of twenty the students' souls are prepared through a variety of spiritual works that do not involve explicit discussions of theosophy. The reading list should include the famous non-sefirotic passages of the *Zohar* "How to Look at Torah" or "Guests in the Sukkah," discussions of Naḥmanides' *sod*, the beginning of the third section of Yehudah ha-Levi's *Kuzari* on visualizing during prayer, discussions of the soul and afterlife from Cordovero, selections from Luzzatto, and Maimonides' *Guide* III.51. The writings of R. Kalonymus Kalman Shapira of Piaseczna including his *Ḥovot ha-Talmidim*, and *Hakhsharat ha-Avreikhim* are replete with suggestions for introducing spirituality to high school students based on his own experience educating adolescents. By the time students reach my university class, they are approximately twenty years old, have spent at least one year in Israel, have the requisite background in *Gemara* and *halakhah*, and are committed to observance.

hierarchy and of studying Kabbalah, some mystics used halakhic study as a means of achieving *deveikut*. Moshe Idel points out that R. Yosef Karo was able to have nightly mystical encounters because his meditative method was based upon his daily study of Torah and not on extra-ordinary techniques. Similarly, Polish Ḥasidut used ordinary *Beit Midrash* learning as a path to mystical experience.[55] In Poland, Ḥasidism took an intellectual turn and created the *Ḥasid-Lamdan* who sought to cleave to God by means of studying Torah in purity and holiness. The *Ḥasid-Lamdan* is devoted to Talmud and *halakhah*, but not to Kabbalah, and finds his piety in Talmud study itself. The approach is best typified by the son-in-law of Rabbi Menahem Mendel of Koẓk, Rabbi Avraham Borenstein, who, in his introduction to his book *Eglei Tal* on the laws of the Sabbath, understands the continuous study of Torah as a means by which to cleave to God. The learning is to be done in purity and holiness, in order to maximize the effect on the individual. God's grandeur can be experienced as a mental presence, asserts R. Borenstein, and behind all the varied manifestations of the modern world, one can find consciously the hidden will of the divine. Torah study cultivates the requisite feeling of awe before the divine; the rabbinic tradition becomes a dwelling for a mystical life.[56]

Finally, dwelling reaches its peak in a psychological sense of indwelling and a feeling of oneness. Only when one accepts the hierarchal structure of reality and avoids enthusiasm in one's study of Kabbalah can theologies of indwelling safely be navigated. An example of this sense of indwelling that can be found even in Torah study is typical of the thought of R. Ẓadok ha-Kohen of Lublin, who develops the rabbinic exhortation to learn for its own sake (*Torah li-shmah*) into a mystical psychology. According to R. Ẓadok, one studies the Torah for its own sake with a passion for the divine so that "by means of desire man is a receptacle for the indwelling of God in the midst of the heart."[57] This ardent study continues until God recognizes the student as "my dove, my beloved," (Song of

[55] On R. Ẓadok, see Alan Brill, *Thinking God: The Mysticism of Rabbi Zadok Ha-Kohen of Lublin* (New York: Yeshiva University Press, 2002).

[56] Introduction to *Eglei Tal* (Pietrkov, 1905, reprinted with corrections 1931).

[57] *Ẓidkat ha-Ẓaddik*, sec. 251.

Songs 5:2). The Midrash reads the word "beloved" (*tammati*) as twin (*te'omati*), showing that the relation between man and God is one of lovers twinned in union. R. Ẓadok extends the meaning of the verse "my dove my twin" to express that the bond of love is so intense that man, by means of his passionate knowledge, makes himself the veritable twin of God.[58]

[58] *Ibid.*

5

Models of Spirituality in Medieval Jewish Philosophy

Daniel J. Lasker

Medieval Jewish philosophers did not have a specific concept of human spirituality in the modern sense of the term, although they did distinguish between the physical and the non-physical, or spiritual, aspects of existence. God was the ultimate non-physical being, having neither a body nor any physical properties.[1] Other non-physical

[1] See, for instance, Maimonides' formulation in the third of his thirteen principles of Judaism in his *Commentary on the Mishnah*, Introduction to Chapter Ḥelek (Sanhedrin, chapter 10); the Arabic text can be found in Israel Friedlaender, *Selections from the Arabic Writings of Maimonides* (Leiden: E.J. Brill, 1951), pp. 28–9; a medieval Hebrew translation is available in *Hakdamot le-Feirush ha-Mishnah*, ed. by M.D. Rabinowitz (Jerusalem: Mossad ha-Rav Kook, 1961), pp. 137–8. Cf. also Yosef Kafih, *Mishnah im Peirush Rabbeinu Moshe ben Maimon*, vol. 4 (Jerusalem: Mossad ha-Rav Kook, 1964), p. 211. A convenient English translation can be found in Menachem Kellner, *Dogma in Medieval Jewish Thought* (Oxford: Littman Library, 1986), pp. 11–12.

entities in the world were the separate intellects (assumed to be the angels of Jewish tradition)[2] and certain aspects of the human soul. Since the Jewish philosophers shared the Greek assumption that the non-physical is preferable to the physical, even when it is less accessible to intelligent discourse, they devoted much attention to these spiritual entities. If we wish, therefore, to appreciate the concept of spirituality in medieval Jewish philosophy, we must look at these discussions. More specifically, we should examine the discussions where the philosophers expounded upon the incorporeal human soul and its properties, including its intellectual aspects, to the exclusion of the physical properties of the body. When the philosophers attempted to understand the relation of the soul to ultimate reality which they also considered to be an incorporeal reality, they were dealing with what we might call the spiritual. As a result, our best chance of understanding the medieval philosophers' views of spirituality is by analyzing their descriptions of the religious and intellectual life (and afterlife) of the human soul.[3]

It would appear that in their discussions of the soul, the medieval Jewish philosophers offered two models of personal spirituality. The first can be called the intellectualist model, wherein spirituality is considered to be purely intellectual, and the highest personal level of existence, whether in this life or after death, is the contemplation of the intelligibles and the denial of all physicality. Other properties of the soul are secondary to the intellect in this world and non-existent in the next. The more radical philosophers thought that the goal of

---

[2] See Maimonides, *The Guide of the Perplexed*, trans. by Shlomo Pines (Chicago and London: University of Chicago Press, 1963) (below, *Guide*), 2.6, pp. 261–5.

[3] For instance, whereas Maimonides referred to the "soulful" world (*al-ʿālam al-nafsānī*) in his "Introduction to Chapter Ḥelek", the medieval Hebrew translator called it the spiritual world (*ha-olam ha-ruḥani*); see the Arabic text in Israel Friedlaender, *Selections*, p. 18; the Hebrew text in *Hakdamot*, p. 125. Yosef Kafih translated the term as *ha-olam ha-nafshi*; see *Mishnah*, p. 204.

There are additional medieval references to "spirits," but these probably had to do more with residual idolatrous beliefs in *pneumata* rather than with spirituality; for Judah Halevi's often negative view of the "spirits," see Shlomo Pines, "*Al ha-Munaḥ 'Ruḥaniyyot' u-Mekorotav ve-al Mishnato shel Rabbi Yehudah Halevi*," *Tarbiz* 56:4 (Tamuz–Elul, 1988): 511–40.

human spirituality was the assimilation of the human intellect into a more universal intellect, most notably what the Aristotelian philosophers called the Agent Intellect. In contrast, the second model could be called a holistic one, wherein all, or many of, the facilities of the soul can take part in the spiritual quest, and individuals maintain their separate identities, both in this world and in the world to come. Not surprisingly, intellectual spirituality is the religious goal advocated by the Aristotelians such as Maimonides (1138–1204) and Gersonides (1288–1344); holistic spirituality is the domain of the anti-Aristotelians such as Judah Halevi (d. 1141) and Ḥasdai Crescas (1340–1410/11).[4] A brief survey of the positions of these four major thinkers concerning the spiritual quest will serve to highlight the two models of spirituality just mentioned. A full discussion would have to take into account not only the summaries below but also the views of the many medieval Jewish philosophers who dealt with these issues in their writings.

*

For Judah Halevi the prophet was the prototype of the spiritual person who had achieved the highest level. The prophet's inner eye was able to see phenomena, which were not sensed by the normal person, and to understand their true meaning.[5] The prophet, however, was not the only person to achieve spirituality. The attainment of proph-

[4] This distinction apparently has its origin in Islamic philosophy, with Alfarabi as the representative of the intellectualist model and Avicenna as the representative of a more holistic model; see Herbert Davidson, "Alfarabi and Avicenna on the Active Intellect," *Viator* 3 (1972): 109–78; Dov Schwartz, "Avicenna and Maimonides on Immortality: A Comparative Study," in R.L. Nettler, ed., *Modern Perspectives on Muslim Jewish Relations* (Luxembourg: Harwood Academic Publishers, 1995), pp. 185–97. See also Gabriella Berzin, "The Concept of Happiness in the Teachings of Maimonides and Rabbi Chasdai Crescas," Masters Thesis, Ben-Gurion University of the Negev, 1998 (Hebrew), pp. 18–33. I would like to thank Ms. Berzin, and another student of mine, Ehud Krinis, for their comments on this paper.

[5] Judah Halevi, *Kitāb al-Radd wa-' l-Dalīl fī 'l-Dīn al-Dhalīl (al-Kitāb al-Khazarī)*, ed. by David H. Baneth, prepared for publication by Haggai Ben-Shammai (Jerusalem: Magnes Press, 1977) (below, *Khazarī*), 4:3, p. 155. The mystical background of Halevi's view of spiritual sight is discussed in Elliot R. Wolfson, "Merkavah Traditions in Philosophical Garb; Judah Halevi Reconsidered," *PAAJR* 57 (1991): 179–242.

ecy by the select few had advantages also for those who were in the presence of the prophet. Thus, Halevi wrote in *Kuzari* 1:103:

> The sons of Jacob were all the chosen (*ṣafwa/segulah*) and the core (*lubūb/lev*), distinguished from other people by their Godly qualities, as if making them into a separate species and a separate angelic substance. All of them sought the level of prophecy, and most of them succeeded in reaching it. He[6] who did not reach that level tried to approach it by means of pious acts, sanctification, purification and encountering the prophets. Know that when he who encounters the prophet hears his divine words, he experiences spiritualization (*rūḥānīyya*), being distinguished from his genus by means of the purity of his soul, the desire for those levels, and the attachment to meekness and purity.[7] This was for them the manifest proof and the clear and convincing sign of reward in the hereafter, in which one desires that the human soul becomes divine, separated from its senses, envisioning the upper world, enjoying the vision of the angelic light and hearing the divine speech.[8]

[6] The medievals generally thought in terms of male spirituality only, even though some were willing to admit that women can also achieve intellectual perfection; see, e.g., Abraham Melamed, "Maimonides on Women: Formless Matter or Potential Prophet?" in Alfred L. Ivry, *et al.*, eds., *Perspectives on Jewish Thought and Mysticism: Dedicated to the Memory of Alexander Altmann* (Amsterdam: Harwood Academic Publishers, 1998), pp. 99–134. The use of the male pronoun here reflects medieval assumptions.

[7] Cf. Saadia Gaon, *Kitāb al-Amānāt wal-'Itiqādāt (Sefer ha-Emunot ve-ha-De'ot)*, 3:5, ed. by Yosef Kafih (New York: Sura Institute, 1970), p. 127; trans., Saadia Gaon, *The Book of Beliefs and Opinions*, trans. by Samuel Rosenblatt (New Haven: Yale University Press, 1948), p. 151. Yosef Kafih, *Sefer ha-Kuzari le-Rabbeinu Yehudah Halevi zaẓa"l* (Kiryat Ono: Mekhon ha-Rambam, 1997), p. 35, n. 88, expresses surprise at Halevi's statement given the biblical descriptions of the mistreatment of the prophets at the hands of those to whom they were sent.

[8] *Khazarī*, p. 35. English translations of the *Kuzari* are generally my own, although Hartwig Hirschfeld, translator, *The Kuzari* (New York: Schocken Books, 1964), will be consulted. Comparison will also be made to the Hebrew translations of Judah

In this life, the ultimate spiritual experience is prophecy, an experience which encompasses the prophet's soul, not just his intellect. Furthermore, a person in the presence of the prophet also undergoes a spiritual experience. After death, when the human soul becomes separated from its senses, and spirituality is easier to attain, there are still sensual aspects to human spirituality, such as the vision of the angelic light and the hearing of divine speech.

Spirituality is not restricted to the prophets and to those in their presence. At the beginning of book three of the *Kuzari*, Halevi described the devout worshipper of God (*al-muta'abbid*). This person is one who does good deeds inside society, not one who separates himself from other humans. "Rather, he loves this world and the length of days, since by means [of this world] he can acquire the next world, and the more good he does, the higher will his level be in the next world."[9] Whereas in the past certain individuals, such as philosophers like Socrates, or some of the prophets in the land of Israel, may have benefited from isolating themselves from others, this is no longer the case. Religions which advocate asceticism as a means of achieving spirituality mislead their believers, since, according to Halevi, spirituality in our day and age is a function of the whole person, even his physical parts, and not just some of his qualities. The pursuit of spirituality requires full participation in society.

Halevi then turns to a discussion of the good person (*al-khair*).[10] This person is one who controls his physical and spiritual (*nafsāniyya*) powers, allocating to each its due. Unsurprisingly, the

Ibn Tibbon (Hartwig Hirschfeld, ed., *Das Buch al-Chazarī des Abū-l-Hasan Jehuda Hallewi* [Leipzig: Otto Schulze, 1887; reprinted Israel, 1970]), Yehudah Even-Shmuel (*Sefer ha-Kosari shel Rabbi Yehudah Halevi* [Tel Aviv: Dvir, 1972]) and Yosef Kafih (*Sefer ha-Kuzari*). Another description of the prophet's becoming almost angelic by receiving "another spirit" (*ruaḥ aḥeret*, in the Judaeo-Arabic text) can be found in 4:15, *Khazarī*, p. 168. For general reviews of the Islamic background of Halevi's spirituality, see Diana N. Lobel, *Between Mysticism and Philosophy: Sufi Language of Religious Experience in Judah ha-Levi's Kuzari* (Albany: State University of New York Press, 1995); Shlomo Pines, "Shi'ite Terms and Conceptions in Judah Halevi's Kuzari," *Jerusalem Studies in Arabic and Islam* 2 (1980): 165–251.

[9] *Khazarī*, p. 90.

[10] *Kuzari*, 3:2–22; *Khazarī*, pp. 91–112. Judah ibn Tibbon translated *al-khair* as *he-*

best way to live a life of physical and mental equilibrium is to observe the commandments of the Torah, worshipping God through joy. The commandments are for the soul what food is for the body:

> The good person never acts or speaks or thinks without believing that he is in the presence of eyes which see him and take note of him, rewarding him and punishing him, calling him to account for all his words and deeds which were not correct. He walks and sits as one who is afraid and humble, sometimes ashamed of his actions, just as he is glad and rejoices and is proud of himself when he has done a good deed.[11]

Perhaps the best example of Halevi's stress on holistic spirituality is his distinction between the two names of God, the Tetragrammaton (God's personal name as per *Kuzari* 4:1 and the God of Abraham) and *Elohim* (a generic name of God and the God of Aristotle).

> One craves for [the Tetragrammaton] with a craving of taste and perception (*dhaukan wa-mushāhadah*),[12] whereas one inclines towards *Elohim* through syllogistic reasoning (*qiyāsan*). The taste leads one who has sensed Him (*adrakihi*) to give up their lives out of love for Him and to die for him. Syllogistic reasoning, however, makes honoring Him obligatory only when there is no harm in it or no suffering.[13]

ḥasid (the pious). Unfortunately, he translated two other terms (*fāḍil* and *walīy*) with the same Hebrew word, confusing future readers who had only the Hebrew text in front of them. Even-Shmuel also did not distinguish between the terms; Kafih was not consistent, although generally *al-khair* is translated by *ha-tov*. Charles Touati in his French translation, Juda Hallevi, *Le Kuzari: Apologie de la religion méprisée*, trad. par Charles Touati (Louvain-Paris: Peeters, 1994), renders *walīy* as *intime*; *khair* as *l'homme pieux*, and *fāḍil* as *l'homme éminent*.

[11] *Kuzari*, 3:11; *Khazarī*, p. 98. Obviously this short summary does not do justice to the full discussion in the first half of *Kuzari*, book three.

[12] See Lobel, *Mysticism*, pp. 89–102.

[13] *Khazarī*, 4:16, pp. 168–9.

The intellect alone, with its syllogistic reasoning, will not lead to true spirituality, since only the senses, taste and perception, bring one to the highest levels of love and devotion to God. In this context, Halevi quoted the Psalmist (34:9): "Taste and see (*ta'amu u-re'u*) that the Lord is good."

From the few examples adduced here, especially the last one, it is obvious that for Halevi, human spirituality is a function of more than the intellectual capacities. The whole person, body and soul, is mobilized in pursuit of the good life, a life which is characterized by observance of the commandments which brings about religious spirituality. Although there will be no body in the world to come, the spiritual enjoyment achieved through prophecy in this world will serve as a model for the soul's pleasure in the hereafter.[14]

*

Judah Halevi's adoption of a holistic approach to human spirituality can be seen not only in the models of spirituality just now recorded from his work, but also in his explicit rejection of the intellectualist model. The *Kuzari* provides a detailed description of intellectual spirituality, presenting it as the view of the Aristotelian philosopher. Responding to the Khazarian king's dream in which the king was told that his intentions were good but his actions were unacceptable, the philosopher ignored the king's dream by responding that one's religious activities are irrelevant for achieving perfection. Instead, people prepare themselves to become perfect by studying and education, until they can connect with the Agent Intellect in a continuous connection, such that the perfect person actually becomes the Agent Intellect. That person's limbs will be used only at the appropriate times and in the appropriate manner, as if he himself were the limbs of the Agent Intellect, not of the individual's passive, material intellect. This is the final and highest degree, which can be achieved by the perfect person whose soul has become purified from any doubt

[14] More details concerning Halevi's view of the afterlife can be found in my "Judah Halevi on Eschatology and Messianism," to be published in the *Proceedings of the Ninth Conference of the Society for Judaeo-Arabic Studies* (forthcoming).

and who conceives the sciences in truth. At this point, the perfect person is like an angel, for the Agent Intellect is on the lowest rank of the angels, and he has no worry that his personal intellect will be corrupted, since both the Agent Intellect itself is incorruptible and also the intellects of all the perfect people are united with the Agent Intellect.[15]

The extreme Aristotelian view of the denial of individual immortality after death, described in the *Kuzari* apparently on the basis of the doctrines of the Muslim philosopher Abu Bakr Ibn Bajja,[16] was generally not explicitly adopted by Jewish thinkers. Undoubtedly, they were sensitive to the problematics of such a doctrine for traditional belief. Nevertheless, the Aristotelian model was followed in the assumption that spirituality is a function solely of intellectual accomplishments. Maimonides, for instance, stated in his *Commentary on the Mishnah* that the pleasure of the soul after death is purely intellectual, a pleasure which cannot be fully understood in this world, although it is a goal before death as well as after. Although Maimonides did not accept Halevi's holistic view of spirituality, the two of them did agree that the ultimate realization of the spiritual quest is only after death:

> Just as the blind person cannot conceive the reality of colors; and the deaf person cannot conceive the hearing of voices, and the eunuch cannot conceive the desire for intercourse, so, too, bodies cannot conceive the pleasures of the soul. Just as fish do not know the element of fire, since their existence is in the element which is the opposite [of fire], so, too, the pleasure of the spiritual world is not known in the physical world. We have no other pleasures than the pleasures of the body, namely the senses' conception of food, drink, and intercourse. We consider anything other than these as if it did not

[15] *Khazarī*, pp. 4–5. For the background of this view of conjunction with the Agent Intellect, see, e.g., Herbert Davidson, "The Active Intellect in the Cuzari and Hallevi's Theory of Causality," *REJ* 131 (1973): 351–96.
[16] Pines, "Shi'ite Terms," pp. 210–7.

> exist, not recognizing it and not conceiving it at the beginning of thought, but only after great research. This is proper since we are in the physical world; therefore, we can conceive only the temporary, lower pleasures. The pleasures of the soul, however, are continuous and uninterrupted. There is neither relationship nor any similarity whatsoever between these [pleasures] and the bodily pleasures. It would be unseemly for us, believers in the Torah, or for the metaphysicians among the philosophers, to say that the angels, the stars and the spheres have no pleasure. In truth, they have great pleasure in that which they know intellectually about the Creator, may He be exalted and blessed, thereby being in great continuous pleasure. They have no physical pleasure and no concept of it, since they do not have senses as we do in order to conceive that which we conceive. Similarly, we, also, to the extent to which part of us will become purified and will reach that level after death, it will not conceive the physical pleasures and will have no desire for them.[17]

Maimonides continued his discussion of these two pleasures by emphasizing the superiority of intellectual pleasure over physical pleasure, even in this world. If this is so now, in the physical world, how much more will it be true in the spiritual world (*al-ʿālam al-nafsānī/ha-olam ha-ruḥani*; Kafih: *ha-olam ha-nafshi*), namely the world to come where the souls have intellectual knowledge of the Creator, just as in this world they are able to have some intellectual knowledge of the upper physical realms and more.[18]

A similar description of afterworldly spiritual bliss is provided by Maimonides in his *Mishneh Torah* ("Laws of Repentance," chapter

[17] Maimonides, *Commentary on the Mishnah*, Introduction to Chapter Ḥelek, Arabic pp. 15–7; Hebrew, pp. 123–4 (Kafih ed., pp. 203–4).

The Arabic term for both physical and spiritual/intellectual pleasure here is *ladhdha*, which usually means physical pleasure; for Maimonides' use of this term, see Berzin, "Happiness."

[18] See note 3.

eight). Life in the world to come is the great good which is intended (*ha-tovah ha-ẓefunah*)[19] for the righteous, a life which is not accompanied by death and a good which is not accompanied by evil. In this world, there is neither body nor corporeality, but only the souls of the righteous who are like the ministering angels;[20] there is neither eating nor drinking nor any other physical activity; rather the souls of the righteous "enjoy the splendor of God's presence" (*nehenin mi-ziv ha-shekhina*):

> For they will know and acquire knowledge of the essence of the Holy One Blessed be He, that which they cannot know while they are in the dark and lowly body. The soul (*nefesh*) described thereby is not the spirit (*neshama*) which needs a body, but the form of the soul which is knowledge (*ha-dei'ah*) which has been achieved from the Creator to the extent of its power, conceiving the separate intelligibles (*ha-dei'ot ha-nifradot*) and the rest of His actions.[21]

Echoing his discussion in the *Commentary on the Mishnah*, Maimonides remarked that no one can fully understand pure spirituality in this corporeal world; only in the world to come, the world of pure intellect, will true human good be attained.

For Maimonides, then, spirituality is achieved by the intellect and not by the physical properties of the soul, such as taste and sight. It should be noted, however, that this type of spirituality is available solely for the intellectual elite; most people's souls share

[19] Maimonides used the Hebrew term *tovah* (Arabic: *sa'adah*) rather than *ta'anug* which represents the Arabic *ladhdha*, the term used in the *Commentary on the Mishnah*. See Berzin, "Happiness," pp. 62–71. For a comparison of Maimonides' views of the afterlife in *Hilkhot Teshuva* with his other writings, see Adiel Kadari, "Thought and Halakhah in Maimonides' Laws of Repentance," Ben-Gurion University diss., 2000 (Hebrew), chapter 8.

[20] Since Maimonides understood the angels as separate intellects (*Guide*, 2.6), the souls of the righteous are then similar to the separate intellects.

[21] *Mishneh Torah, Hilkhot Teshuvah*, 8:2–3. The "knowledge" which remains after death is obviously a reference to the acquired intellect; see below, note 28.

the fate of *karet* (excision), in which the soul completely disappears after death.[22] Yet, Maimonides did not clearly offer the radical view of annihilation of personal identity through assimilation into the Agent Intellect, the view attributed to the philosopher in Judah Halevi's *Kuzari*, and to Abu Bakr ibn Bajja by Maimonides himself.[23] Perhaps since such a view would have been harmful for the masses, Maimonides refrained from explicitly discussing the afterlife altogether in his *Guide of the Perplexed*.[24]

*

Gersonides shared Maimonides' view that human spirituality is a function of the intellect and not of any of the physical aspects of the soul. Thus, for instance, immortality of the soul is a natural result of intellectual achievement, and the greater the achievement, namely, the greater the approximation of the knowledge held by the Agent Intellect, the greater the pleasure in the hereafter.

Gersonides outlined the intellectualist position at the very

---

[22] *Ibid.*, 8:1, 5. Maimonides also explained the concept of *karet* in the Introduction to Chapter Ḥelek (although in *Hilkhot Teshuvah* 3:6, Maimonides indicated that certain very evil people will suffer eternal punishment). At the end of his Commentary to Tractate Makkot (3:17; Kafih edition, p. 247), however, Maimonides stated that anyone who performs one of the 613 commandments in the correct manner and out of love will merit life in the world to come. The great number of commandments were commanded so as to assure that a Jew will observe correctly at least one of them and, thereby, guarantee his immortality.

Shlomo Pines has argued that according to Maimonides' esoteric doctrine, no one can attain intellectual perfection, and, therefore, there is no afterlife, even for the intellectually accomplished; see "The Limitation of Human Knowledge, according to Al-Farabi, Ibn Bajja and Maimonides," in Isadore Twersky, ed., *Medieval Jewish History and Literature*, vol. 1 (Cambridge, MA: Harvard University Press, 1979), pp. 82–109. Other students of Maimonides have rejected Pines' conclusion, maintaining instead that Maimonides, indeed, believed that the intellectually perfect do merit an afterlife; cf. Alexander Altmann, "Maimonides on the Intellect and the Scope of Metaphysics," in *Von der mittelalterlichen zur modernen Aufklärung* (Tübingen: Mohr, 1987), pp. 60–128.

[23] *Guide* 1.74.7, p. 219; cf. also "Translator's Introduction," pp. ciii–iv.

[24] See Howard Kreisel, *Maimonides' Political Thought* (Albany: State University of New York Press, 1999), pp. 141–3.

beginning of his *Wars of the Lord* as a preamble to his discussion of the nature of the intellect (1:1):

> Since the intellect is the most fitting of all the parts of the soul for immortality – the other parts are obviously perishable together with the corruption of the body because they use a bodily organ in the exercise of their functions – it is necessary that we inquire into the essence of the human intellect before we investigate whether it is immortal or not, and whether if it is immortal, in what way it is immortal. For human immortality and human happiness are accidental qualities (*masigim*) of the intellect, and it is not proper to investigate the accidents of a substance before we know the essence of it.[25]

Gersonides then proceeded with an analysis of the nature of the human intellect, an analysis which takes up the greater part of Book One of his *Wars of the Lord*, concluding that the immortal part of humans is the "acquired intellect." Without discussing the details of Gersonides' views, it is noteworthy that Gersonides believed in individual immortality, in which each person's intellect enjoys the afterlife to the extent that it had been developed during the person's life, and not in the collective immortality of the acquired intelligibles. He also maintained that this afterworldly experience is available to many more people than Maimonides thought, since almost any intellectual cognition is sufficient to achieve an acquired intellect, an intellect which rejoices in the knowledge that it has achieved. That joy, experienced by the intellect, is a feature of both this world and the next, but, as might be expected, only after death does the intellect reach its highest level of pleasure:

[25] Levi ben Gerson, *Sefer Milḥamot ha-Shem* (Riva di Trento, 1560) (below, *Milḥamot*), p. 4a; translation, Levi ben Gershom (Gersonides), *The Wars of the Lord*, trans. by Seymour Feldman, vol. 1 (Philadelphia: Jewish Publication Society of America, 1984) (below, *Wars*), p. 109.

> If the unity of knowledge approximates the unity of knowledge of the Agent Intellect, then the possessor of that knowledge has attained a greater level of perfection, and the joy (*simḥah*) and pleasure (*ta'anug*) in his knowledge is greater. Differences are found such that the pleasure enjoyed by one man in his knowledge is not the same as the pleasure enjoyed by another in his knowledge.... It is also important to realize that each man who has attained this perfection enjoys the happiness resulting from his knowledge after death. We have some idea of this pleasure (*areivut*) from the pleasure that we derive from the little knowledge we now possess which subdues the animal part of our soul [so that] the intellect is isolated in its activity. This pleasure is not comparable to other pleasures (*areivuyyot*) and has no relation to them at all. All the more so will this pleasure be greater after death; for then all the knowledge that we have acquired in life will be continuously contemplated and all things in our minds will be apprehended simultaneously, since after death the obstacle that prevents this [kind of cognition], i.e., matter, will have disappeared. For, since the soul is a unit, the intellect is prevented from apprehending [simultaneously] when it (the soul) employs another of its faculties.... After death, however, it will apprehend all the knowledge that it has acquired during life simultaneously.[26]

For Gersonides, the spiritual quest is clearly an intellectual one, and the greater the attainment of intellectual perfection, the higher the level of spirituality in this world and the next. Other facilities of the soul can only interfere with this intellectual spirituality.

*

The purely intellectualist vision of Jewish spirituality, as advocated by Maimonides and Gersonides, was subjected to a trenchant criti-

[26] *Milḥamot ha-Shem*, 1:13, p. 16a; *Wars*, pp. 224–5.

cism by Ḥasdai Crescas. Generally protesting the Aristotelization of Jewish thought, Crescas attempted to disprove the basic assumptions of Jewish Aristotelianism. Thus, Crescas refuted Maimonides' proofs of the existence of God, based upon twenty-six propositions of Aristotelian physics, by demonstrating the logical untenability of those propositions.[27] Similarly, Maimonides' and Gersonides' view that the afterlife is reserved for the acquired intellect,[28] and thus human spiritual perfection is purely intellectual, was the object of Crescas' critical arguments.[29]

What seems to have bothered Crescas most about the Aristotelian view of intellectual perfection was that it made observance of the commandments of the Torah apparently irrelevant. As we have seen, Judah Halevi claimed that humans can achieve spiritual perfection only by observing God's commandments, but the philosopher in the *Kuzari* had clearly expressed the position that God could not care less what rituals one performed. Although neither Maimonides nor Gersonides advocated abandoning the commandments, and both were observant Jews, Aristotelianism's opponents understood philosophy as undermining Jewish observance.[30] As we have seen, Maimonides' and Gersonides' discussions concerning the pleasure of the intellect make no explicit reference to the need to observe the commandments of the Torah to help achieve that pleasure. Certainly, if one's afterworldly success is a function of his intellectual perfection, what benefit would accrue to the intellect by observing rituals pertaining to the corporeal body?

---

[27] See Harry A. Wolfson, *Crescas' Critique of Aristotle* (Cambridge, MA: Harvard University Press, 1929); see now also, Warren Zev Harvey, *Physics and Metaphysics in Ḥasdai Crescas* (Amsterdam: J.C. Gieben, 1998).

[28] Although Maimonides does not specifically use the term "acquired intellect" in this context, it would seem that attributing this concept to him is not inappropriate. He does use it in *Guide* 1.72, p. 193; cf. Kreisel, *Political Thought*, pp. 136–50.

[29] Crescas' criticism of the intellectualist view of the perfection is the subject of Warren (Zev) Harvey, "Ḥasdai Crescas's Critique of the Theory of the Acquired Intellect," Columbia University diss., 1973; see also Berzin, "Happiness."

[30] This was one of the major accusations in the Maimonidean controversy; see, e.g., Joseph Sarachek, *Faith and Reason: The Conflict over the Rationalism of Maimonides* (Williamsport, PA, The Bayard Press, 1935).

There is another aspect of Crescas' critique of Aristotelianism. Writing in the wake of the anti-Jewish riots of 1391, in which his only son was killed, and the vigorous Christian campaign to convert Iberia's Jews, Crescas was well aware that a purely philosophical Judaism might appear stark and uninviting in comparison with Christianity's emphasis on love of God and divine grace. It was important, then, for Crescas to produce a model of human spirituality which could compete with both Jewish Aristotelianism and Christian emotionalism.

Crescas' model of spirituality is based on divine love, both God's love for the Jews as well as Jewish love of God as expressed, among other ways, by observing the commandments. Thus, Crescas was able to argue that Judaism was a religion of love (contra the Christians), in which observing the Torah played a role in human spirituality (contra the Aristotelians). Before presenting his alternate view, however, Crescas outlined the philosophical opinion:

> Eternal happiness (*haẓlaḥah*) is the apprehension of the acquired intelligibles; the more concepts one apprehends the greater in quality the happiness, and all the more so when the concepts are more precious *per se*. And it is also agreed among them, that each of those who attain happiness will rejoice and delight (*yismaḥ ve-yitaʿneg*) after death in that which he has apprehended. Now, they estimated the degree of this [pleasure] on the basis of the pleasure (*areivut*) which we attain in our lifetime in our apprehending the intelligibles, and, how much more so must it be after death, as we shall intellectually cognize them simultaneously, continuously.[31]

Crescas considered the advocates of this view to be heretical (*horesim ha-torah ve-ʿokerim shoreshei ha-kabbalah*), since they ostensibly denied the efficacy of observing the commandments. It is well-known, argued Crescas, that "according to the plurality of

[31] Ḥasdai Crescas, *Or ha-Shem*, ed. by Shlomo Fisher (Jerusalem: Sifrei Ramot, 1970), 2:6:1, p. 233; trans. based on Harvey, "Critique," pp. 426–7.

merits and sins shall be the delight and misery of the souls [after death]."[32] If the commandments are solely a preliminary step in attaining the intelligibles, there is no intrinsic advantage in performing those commandments.

Furthermore, Crescas argued that having conceptual knowledge of the intelligibles is not in itself pleasurable. What is pleasurable is the intellectual pursuit, not necessarily having knowledge of the intelligibles in actuality.

> The pleasure (*areivut*) which is found in them in our lifetime is due to the attainment of the yearned-for thing. For inasmuch as man has the potential of attaining the intelligibles, and he yearns for them, and inasmuch as yearning is none else but the excitement of the will to attain the yearned-for object, the will having been demonstrated to be other than intellectual cognition, then when that yearned-for apprehension is *in actu* which beforehand had been *in potentia*, there is found a great pleasure.[33]

According to the philosophers, therefore, after death, when all cognition is *in actu*, there will no longer be a transition from potentiality to actuality and no yearning, since, at that point, the intellect has no will. For Crescas, such a situation cannot provide the soul with pleasure. The intellectualist model of spirituality is, hence, insufficient, even in its own terms.

Crescas' own theory of what can be considered spirituality can be seen in his discussion of the afterlife of the soul. After recalling his rebuttal of the philosophical position, Crescas outlined his doctrine:

> Now, therefore, what ought to be said in affirmation of the survival of the soul is that, once it has been established in the

---

[32] *Or ha-Shem*, 2:6:1, p. 234; trans., p. 431.

[33] *Ibid.*, p. 246; trans., p. 465.

> definition of the soul that it is an intellectual substance, not containing within it causes of corruption;[34] then, when the soul becomes perfected in conjunction and love (*ba-kesher ve-ha-ahava*), by means of what it apprehends (*ma she-tasig*) of the Law and of the wonders of the Lord, may He be blessed, it should remain in its perfection and in a strong conjunction and in the shining forth of unremitting light, owing to the removal of the obstacle which darkens its intrinsic reality, which [obstacle] is matter...and since man is compounded of a material part and of an essential spiritual (*ruḥani*) part, which is an overflow from an overflowing intellectual substance, be that overflowing agent an angel or something else, it is fitting and necessary that that spiritual part not undergo corruption, just as it is clear with regard to the material part, that it returns to its simple components to the four elements.[35]

For Crescas, spirituality is achieved by love and not by intellection alone, and it is the individual soul with will, not an acquired intellect, which survives death.

*

At first glance, there seems to be a strict dichotomy between the intellectualist and holistic views of spirituality. A closer look, however, indicates that perhaps the distinction between the two models is not as absolute as it appears initially. Thus, although those who maintained intellectualist spirituality did not see observance of the commandments as an intrinsic part of that spirituality, or the afterlife as a reward for observing the commandments, nevertheless they emphasized the importance of the commandments as a step towards achieving spirituality, at least for Jews. Furthermore, intellectualist

[34] Crescas' definition of the soul may have been influenced by the Catalan thinker Bernat Metge; see Zev Harvey, "*R. Ḥasdai Crescas u-Bernat Metge al ha-Nefesh*," *Jerusalem Studies in Jewish Thought* 5 (1986): 141–54.

[35] *Or ha-Shem*, 3:1:2:2, p. 322, trans., pp. 489–90.

spirituality can also have the emotional element of love; and the holistic view has an intellectual component. Both look to the afterlife as the time when true spirituality can be attained.[36]

Let us analyze, for instance, Maimonides' prescription for attaining spirituality which is presented near the end of the *Guide of the Perplexed* (3.51). First, Maimonides employed a controversial analogy between attaining closeness to God and entering the presence of a king sitting in his palace, in which those who have intellectual perfection enter into the palace, whereas those with only traditional rabbinic learning are kept outside.[37] Then, Maimonides offered advice to his readers as to how to attain intellectual perfection:

> We have already made clear to you that that intellect which overflows from Him, may He be exalted, toward us is the bond between us and Him. You have a choice: if you wish to strengthen and to fortify this bond, you can do so; if, however, you wish gradually to make it weaker and feebler until you cut it, you can also do that.[38]

How does one strengthen one's intellectual bond with God? One should start with making every effort always to be thinking about God. The purpose of worship, such as reading the Torah,

---

[36] In addition, the Maimonidean view of the prophet shares the holistic view that spirituality is a function of more than just the intellect, since the prophet uses both his intellect and his imagination. Nevertheless, the use of the imagination is more for the purpose of disseminating the prophetic message than for achieving personal spirituality.

[37] Maimonides, *Guide*, pp. 618–21. According to the late fifteenth-century commentator on the *Guide*, Shem Tov ben Joseph Ibn Shem Tov, many rabbinic sages opined that this analogy was not actually Maimonides', and if it were, it should at a minimum be hidden, but preferably burned; cf. also Menachem Kellner, *Maimonides on Human Perfection* (Atlanta: Scholars Press, 1990), pp. 13–39; David Shatz, "Worship, Corporeality, and Human Perfection: A Reading of *Guide of the Perplexed*, III.51–54," in *The Thought of Moses Maimonides*, Ira Robinson, *et al.*, eds. (Lewiston: The Edwin Mellon Press, 1990), pp. 77–129.

[38] *Guide*, p. 621.

prayer and the performance of other commandments, is to bring the worshippers closer to God by excluding thoughts of this world from their minds. Thus, people should not just pray with their lips at the same as they are thinking about business, or read the Torah as they are considering building a new house. Even when performing a commandment whose fulfillment merely requires the use of one's limbs, their thoughts should be towards God.

Maimonides suggested a practical regimen for attaining this goal. When saying the *Shema*, people should empty their minds of everything else and not be content (as the law allows) with having the proper intention for only the first verse of *Shema*. Similarly, when reciting the *Shemoneh Esreih* prayer, one should not be content with the proper intention for only the first benediction.

> When this has been carried out correctly and has been practiced consistently for years, cause your soul, whenever you read or listen to the Torah, to be constantly directed – the whole of you and your thought – toward reflection on what you are listening to or reading. When this too has been practiced consistently for a certain time, cause your soul to be in such a way that your thought is always quite free of distraction and gives heed to all that you are reading of the other discourses of the prophets and even when you read all the benedictions, so that you aim at meditating on what you are uttering and at considering its meaning.[39]

Once one has achieved this discipline, it is permitted occasionally to think of worldly matters, such as maintaining one's household and dealing with one's wife and children.

> When, however, you are alone with yourself and no one else is there and while you lie awake upon your bed, you should take great care during these precious times not to set your thought to work on anything other than that intellectual wor-

[39] *Ibid.*, p. 622.

> ship consisting in nearness to God and being in His presence in that true reality that I have made known to you and not by way of affections of the imagination. In my opinion this end can be achieved by those of the men of knowledge who have rendered their souls worthy of it by training of this kind.[40]

This regimen of constantly thinking about God, even when performing physical acts or when in conversation with other people, was the level of Moses and the Patriarchs, whose goal in life was to bring into being a religious community who would know and worship God by spreading the notion of God's unity, "and to guide people to love Him, may He be exalted."[41]

What is the nature of this love of God? Maimonides continued by offering a model of divine providence in which the person who is constantly thinking about God cannot be harmed; only when one's thoughts are diverted from God is His providence removed from the individual. As proof for this theory, Maimonides offered Psalm 91, the "Song on Mishaps." This psalm describes the protection offered to the worshipper of God, whether from illness or from human evil, such as war. The reason for this protection is cited in the psalm (v. 14): "Because he has set his passionate love (*ḥashak*) upon Me, therefore I will deliver him; I will set him on high, because he has known my Name." As Maimonides understood the verse, the individual is protected from all evil because he has "known Me and then passionately loved Me." This "passionate love" (*'ishq*) is an excess of love, so that there remains no thought other than those directed towards the beloved:

> The philosophers have already explained that the bodily faculties impede in youth the attainment of most of the moral virtues, and all the more that of pure thought, which is achieved through the perfection of the intelligibles that lead to passionate love (*'ishq*) of Him, may He be exalted. For

---

[40] *Ibid.*, p. 623.

[41] *Ibid.*, p. 624.

> it is impossible that it should be achieved while the bodily humors are in effervescence. Yet in the measure in which the faculties of the body are weakened and the fire of the desires is quenched, the intellect is strengthened, its lights achieve a wider extension, its apprehension is purified, and it rejoices in what it apprehends. The result is that when a perfect man is stricken with years and approaches death, this apprehension increases very powerfully, joy over this apprehension and a great love (*'ishq*) for the object of apprehension become stronger, until the soul is separated from the body at that moment in this state of pleasure (*ladhdha*).... After having reached this condition of enduring permanence, that intellect remains in one and same state, the impediment that sometimes screened him off having been removed. And he will remain permanently in that state of intense pleasure (*al-ladhdha al-'aẓīmah*), which does not belong to the genus of bodily pleasures, as we have explained in our compilations and as others have explained before us.[42]

From these passages, it would appear that human spirituality extends beyond mere intellectual pleasure and reaches a form of passionate love, albeit an intellectualist passionate love, one in which bodily faculties are completely negated.[43] Furthermore, although the observance of the commandments is not sufficient for intellectual spirituality, the prescribed regimen to achieve such spirituality is by observing the commandments and not solely by contemplating

---

[42] *Ibid.*, pp. 627–8. As noted before, Maimonides used the term *ladhdha* to describe the pleasure of the intellect in his *Commentary on the Mishnah*, and cf. Berzin, "Happiness."

[43] Similar to the description of the philosopher in *Kuzari* 1:1; see Shatz, "Worship," n. 47 (citing Barry Kogan).

Warren Zev Harvey argues that Maimonides' view of loving God by striving to achieve more and more knowledge about Him is very similar to Crescas' belief that joy is found in acquiring knowledge, not necessarily in having that knowledge; see Harvey, "Crescas versus Maimonides on Knowledge and Pleasure," in *A Straight Path: Studies in Medieval Philosophy and Culture: Essays in Honor of Arthur Hyman*, Ruth Link-Salinger, *et al.*, eds., (Washington, DC: The Catholic University of America Press,

upon God and the world. The Jewish search for spirituality begins with the punctilious observance of the commandments as a means of drawing close to God and ends with a passionate love which some might even understand as a mystical relationship with God.[44]

Turning back to Crescas, we see that although his concept of spirituality is a function of the whole soul, especially the will, and his emphasis is on love and not intellectual achievement, still, the place of the intellect in his system is not insignificant. The soul, after all, is defined as "an intellectual substance, not containing within it causes of corruption." Furthermore, the soul survives after death when it "becomes perfected in conjunction and love (*ba-kesher ve-ha-ahava*), by means of what it apprehends (*mah she-tasig*) of the Law and of the wonders of the Lord, may He be blessed," namely, perfection of conjunction and love is a function of one's intellectual knowledge of God.[45] Since the soul is a substance which contains an intellectual capacity, "it is possible, indeed necessary, for it to have pleasure (*areivut*) in its intellection."[46] Afterworldly perfection can be enjoyed because that which interferes with human knowledge, namely matter, will no longer be present.[47]

Both Maimonides and Crescas, though employing different ways of expressing ultimate felicity, or what we might call ultimate spirituality, blurred the distinction between absolute intellectual perfection and love of God. Neither was an anti-rationalist who denied the intellectual component of spirituality; both can be considered philosophers for whom use of the intellect is crucial for

---

1988), pp. 113–23. In this article, Harvey also stresses the aspect of will in Crescas' theory of the survival of the soul after death.

[44] This is the view of David Blumenthal, "Maimonides: Prayer, Worship and Mysticism," in Roland Goetschel, ed., *Prière, mystique et Judaïsme* (Paris: Presses Universitaires de France, 1987), pp. 89–106; cf. also *idem*, "Maimonides' Intellectualist Mysticism and the Superiority of the Prophecy of Moses," in *Approaches to Judaism in Medieval Times*, vol. 1, David Blumenthal ed., (Chico, CA: Scholars Press, 1984), pp. 27–51.

[45] See above, n. 35.

[46] *Or ha-Shem*, 2:6:1, p. 247; trans., p. 465.

[47] *Ibid.*, 3:1:2:2, p. 322; trans., pp. 489–90.

human perfection. For Maimonides, observance of the Torah leads to knowledge of God, which in turn leads to love of God. For Crescas, observance of the commandments and love of God are themselves the essence of spirituality, but neither is sufficient without knowledge of God. Both believed that one's spiritual accomplishments, whether they be fully intellectual or both intellectual and emotional, survive death. Thus, although Maimonides stressed the intellect, and Crescas stressed the will and its love of God, the differences between them were not as momentous as might at first be imagined.

Both the intellectual and holistic models of medieval spirituality used a vocabulary which is foreign to ours: separate intellects, acquired intellect, intellectual substances. Similarly, the modern notion that spirituality somehow is dependent solely upon the emotions without a rational component was not shared by our medieval predecessors. Nevertheless, perhaps the medieval beliefs can serve as a model of Jewish spirituality today: a spirituality which is anchored in the observance of the Torah and which reaches its highest expression by means of the intellect, not by its rejection.

Section four

Spirituality and the Arts

6

Spirituality and the Art of the Ancient Synagogue[1]

Steven Fine

In 1952, Cornell University opened an "interfaith chapel" on its Ithaca, New York campus. The chapel was established in Cornell's Anabel Taylor Hall after "long and protracted" discussions regarding the furnishing and decoration of the chapel among the various religious groups that were to conduct religious services there. Among the most interesting features of the chapel as it was constructed was a "3-sided revolving altar." One side of the "altar" (a term, like "chapel," drawn from the vocabulary of Christian sacred architecture) bore a cross, a second side was left undecorated, and the third side bore

[1] This paper is dedicated to my first "rebbe," Mr. Yearl E. Schwartz of San Diego, with thanks. Many thanks to participants in the Orthodox Forum for comments that enriched this paper. I particularly thank Rabbi Norman Lamm, Professor Daniel Lasker, and Professor Vivian Mann. The discussion of ancient synagogues in this article is based upon material that I discussed more extensively in my *Art and Judaism During the Greco Roman Period: A New Jewish Archaeology* (Cambridge: Cambridge University Press, forthcoming).

more intricate Jewish iconography.[2] The Cornell chapel was part of a growing trend in post-war America, giving expression in stone, glass and wood to the newly-developing American religious triumvirate of Protestantism, Catholicism, and Judaism.[3] Among those consulted in the course of the "long and protracted" discussions was Rabbi Joseph B. Soloveitchik.

In his highly critical response, dated December 6, 1950, Rabbi Soloveitchik stressed his concern that if the chapel were to come about, then students might "later be inclined to introduce a church-synagogue center into their own communities."[4] Interfaith chapels did indeed develop in American communities during the post-war years, albeit rarely.[5] In his response, Rabbi Soloveitchik did not discuss in a detailed manner the nature of Christianity. There is no discussion of idolatry, syncretism *(shituf),* or any of the classical categories of the Jewish-Christian relationship.[6] There is not even any mention of *kedushat beit ha-knesset,* synagogue holiness! Rabbi Soloveitchik dispenses with this discussion by stating that "Halachic

---

[2] E-mails from Robert Johnson, 28 June 2000 and Morris Goldfarb on 4 July 2000.

[3] The classic statement of this ideology is W. Herberg's *Protestant, Catholic, Jew: An Essay In American Religious Sociology* (Garden City, NY: Anchor Books, 1960).

[4] Letter on the Cornell interfaith chapel, p. 3. Many thanks to Rabbi Dov Berkowitz for making this responsum available to me in the course of his seminar on Art and Judaism at the Pardes Institute for Jewish Studies, Jerusalem, in 1981. I also thank the anonymous recipient of this private communication from Rabbi Soloveitichik and Rabbi Morris Goldfarb, formerly of Cornell University, for his help in contacting the recipient and for providing vital information about the chapel.

[5] A fine example of the interfaith chapel approach, and of the ideology that spawned it, is the planned community of Columbia, Maryland (with ground breaking in 1966). According to the community web site, Columbia has "4 Interfaith Centers, where denominations share common worship facilities (plus a fifth center planned in River Hill)." See: www.columbia-md.com/columbiaindex.html. Rabbi Soloveitchik ascribes the possible development of local inter-faith chapels to the "almost neurotic fear of anti-Semitism" among American Jews. While this was certainly an important factor, the issues relating to the development of such chapels were considerably more complex than he allows for here.

[6] On these categories, see: Jacob Katz, *Exclusiveness And Tolerance: Studies In Jewish-Gentile Relations In Medieval And Modern Times* (Westport, CT: Greenwood Press, 1980).

formalism and syllogism will not suffice to solve it [the question at hand]. Central historical realities with their deep seated philosophical meaning must be taken into account."[7] These categories, which clearly would place Christianity in a negative light, were best unstated in post-war America. In a telling statement, Rabbi Soloveitchik writes that "I am firmly convinced that it is our privilege and duty, as Jews and Americans, to oppose the Christianization of the synagogue either in its architectural form or in the mode of worship as it would be the privilege and duty of a good Christian to object to the Judaization of the Church."[8] Rabbi Soloveitchik dealt in depth with Jewish aesthetics of synagogue construction and decoration, and to differentiate the categories that he develops from Christian art and architecture. His analysis encompasses biblical sources, the writings of Philo and Josephus, and rabbinic literature medieval and early modern halakhists.

In his analysis, Rabbi Soloveitchik distinguishes between rabbinic and medieval attitudes toward synagogue art:[9]

> In regard to the synagogue, we do not find in the Halachic literature (with the exception of a single passage of the Mekhilta quoted by Rashi, Exodus 20:20) a specific prohibition against paintings or any other design representing the human figure. On the contrary, our sages were more tolerant toward the display of human images in the synagogue than at home.

[7] Letter on the Cornell interfaith chapel, p. 1.

[8] Letter on the Cornell interfaith chapel, p. 4. Rabbi Soloveitchik's approach to Christianity in this responsum was later stated in a prescriptive manner in his "Confrontation," *Tradition* 16:2 (1964): 21–9: "It is self-evident that the confrontation of two faith communities is possible only if it is accomplished by clear assurance that both parties will enjoy equal rights and full religious freedom. We shall resent any attempt on the part of the community of the many to engage us in a peculiar encounter in which our confronter will command us to take a position beneath him while placing himself not alongside of but above us" (p. 21). In 1964 Rabbi Soloveitchik was concerned that in Jewish-Christian "debate" concerning "matters of faith," "one of the confronters will be impelled to avail himself of the language of the opponent" (p. 24). In our case he is similarly concerned with loss of Jewish individuality in the physical prayer environment.

[9] Letter on the Cornell interfaith chapel, p. 2.

> In the tractates Rosh Hashana (24) and Avoda Zara (43) we find that the statue of the king was displayed in a Babylonian synagogue and nevertheless, Rav, Samuel, and Levi did not refrain from worshipping there, though they would have objected to the exhibition of the effigy in a private home. The reason for the distinction between synagogue and home is that while in the synagogue no one would suspect the community of having the statue for a religious purpose, such suspicion would be warranted concerning a private home. In the course of time, however, tradition has reversed its attitude. While pictures were not banned from Jewish homes as I have mentioned, the synagogue had excluded any image of man from its decorative motives. Moreover, many Halachic scholars insisted upon utmost simplicity of the synagogue, and disapproved of elaborate ornaments in general. Maimonides, for instance, objected to murals and mosaics which would confront the worshipper during his devotional mediation because they might serve as a distraction. An even stronger dislike was shown towards figured subjects such as animals. Rabbi Eliakim of Cologne ordered his congregation to remove from the synagogue a carpet which had animal designs woven on it. Likewise, we know of a controversy concerning the display of the lion of Judah above the ark that raged in the sixteenth century and in which Rabbi Moses Di'Tirani, Rabbi Mayer of Padua, and Rabbi Joseph Karo were involved. There were many synagogues that did not tolerate panels representing animals. Yet again the practice was more liberal and all figures with the exception of the human form were introduced as architectural designs for the synagogue. As to the anthropomorphic symbols, there is almost unanimity of disapproval (the fact that some excavations disclose such motives is irrelevant to us. The tradition as such has rejected them).

The art that is the subject of this inquiry began to appear during the latter part of the fourth century, and continued through the eighth century. It roughly dates after the Palestinian *Amoraim* and before the onset of the Medieval period. This period in late antiquity witnessed first the Christianization and then the Islamicization of Jewish Palestine. Both the leniencies suggested by Rabbi Soloveitchik and the later stringencies that he observes may be seen in the archaeological record, though a chronological distinction does not exhaust the complexity of the situation on the ground. From the latter fourth through the sixth centuries, communities throughout the land of Israel widely embraced the visual arts of their day, while other nearby synagogue communities rejected them. During the seventh and eighth centuries numerous communities came to discard the visual arts of their ancestors, some even altering synagogue art that their ancestors had found to be acceptable.[10] In a sense, the move toward aniconicism was anticipated by Rabbi Soloveitchik's comment that "the fact that some excavations disclose such motives is irrelevant to us. The tradition as such has rejected them."[11]

For the purposes of this essay, I will focus upon a group of synagogues that once bore carpet mosaics. In particular, the fourth century synagogue of Hammath Tiberias B, the fifth century synagogue of Sepphoris, and the sixth century synagogues of Na'aran and Beth Alpha. These mosaics form a definite group, bearing very similar iconography. In fact, this regional type is unique in ancient Jewish artistic production. In cities of the Diaspora no specific Jewish iconography may be found in floor mosaics, synagogue mosaics being representative of local techniques and having no relationship with one another. In the land of Israel, on the other hand, such a regional type existed over a three hundred year period. For Jews, of course, simple continuity is a form of spirituality, and this fact should not be overlooked. What unifies these floors is that each bears the image of a zodiac wheel in the center, and a Torah shrine on the

---

[10] In a series of studies I have dealt with the "spirituality" of the synagogue, focussing upon the sanctity of the synagogue. See in particular my *This Holy Place: On the Sanctity of the Synagogue During the Greco-Roman Period* (Notre Dame, IN: University of Notre Dame Press, 1997).

[11] Letter on the Cornell interfaith chapel, p. 2.

floor immediately before the podium (in Na'aran and Beth Alpha, the apse) where an actual Torah shrine stood.[12]

The use of mosaics within synagogues was typical of public places during the Byzantine period. This was not a distinctly "Jewish" art form by any means. In fact, there is little in the actual iconography, or, for that matter, in the architecture and furnishings of the buildings, that is uniquely "Jewish." These are buildings of their time and place. They do not reflect a Jewish national art, or a unique architectural legacy. As in later periods, the architecture of the synagogue was part and parcel of the world in which Jews lived – in this case the Greco-Roman world. Yet it is not difficult to apprehend the "spirituality" of the synagogues under discussion, and by extension the "spirituality" implicit in the art of other synagogues in Palestine during late antiquity. Though virtually every element has parallels, and often roots, in the Christian art of late antiquity, once these elements entered the synagogue, to quote Byzantinist Thomas Mathews, "Together with the ritual that they (the buildings) contained, they constitute a single symbolic matrix."[13] In our case a single Jewish "symbolic matrix."

The focal point of the synagogue, and hence of the spirituality of the synagogue, was the Torah. When one entered one of our synagogues, it was natural to look across a long nave to a Torah shrine. The shrine was undoubtedly flanked by seven branched *menorot.*[14]

[12] The most recent discussion of these materials is to be found in L.I. Levine, *The Ancient Synagogue: The First Thousand Years* (New Haven: Yale University Press, 1999).

[13] T.F. Mathews, *Byzantium From Antiquity to the Renaissance* (New York: Abrams, 1998), p. 97. For fuller discussions, see my "Art and the Liturgical Context of the Sepphoris Synagogue Mosaic," in *Galilee: Confluence of Cultures: Proceedings of the Second International Conference on the Galilee,* ed. E.M. Meyers (Winona Lake, IN: Eisenbrauns, 1999), pp. 227–37; *idem,* my "On the Liturgical Interpretation of Ancient Synagogues in the Land of Israel," in *Jewish Cultural Life of Late Antiquity in its Byzantine-Christian Context,* ed. L.I. Levine, (forthcoming) (Hebrew) and *Art and Judaism during the Greco-Roman Period.*

[14] The presence of seven-branched *menorot* is an issue of some halakhic interest, owing to a tradition that appears in the BT *Rosh ha-Shanah* 24a–b (= *Avodah Zarah* 43a, *Menaḥot* 28b. See *Midrash ha-Gadol* to Exodus 20:20):

This is the image that emerges from the Torah shrine panels in our mosaics. A large shrine, crowned with an aedicula, in some cases with a lamp suspended from its apex, stood at the focal point of the synagogue. In fact, all of the elements of such a Torah compound have been discovered.[15] An aedicula topped with rampart lions, with a suspension hole at its apex for a lamp, was uncovered in the synagogue of Nabratein in the Upper Galilee. This shrine is especially similar to the shrine illustrated at Beth Alpha. Cloths like those that hang before the shrine, called a *vilon* or *parokhta* (reminiscent of the biblical *parokhet*),[16] are well known from extant Coptic textiles and images in non-Jewish contexts.[17] *Menorot* like the flanking *menorot* illustrated were discovered at Hammath Tiberias A, and more recently at Maon in the Mt. Hebron region. Even sculptured lions like those illustrated flanking the Beth Alpha ark were found at Chorazin and Baram. In short, what is illustrated is, to a large extent, what actually stood in the synagogue. Seven-branched *menorot* blazed on either side of a cabinet that by the third century was already being associated with the Ark of the Covenant, and was called an *arona*.[18] These lamps not only reflected a connection between the *mikdash me'at* ("small temple" or "lesser holiness") and the Temple. They served to focus the eye of the visitor on the Torah shrine. The lamp suspended from the Torah shrine would have provided an additional spotlight for the true focal point of the synagogue, the Torah. All of these lights together served an important practical function: they provided the light necessary for the reading of Scripture in other-

---

> Our Rabbis taught: No one may make a building (*bayit)* in the form of the shrine (*hekhal),* an exedra in place of the entrance hall (*ulam*), a courtyard (*ḥaẓer*) in place of the court (*azarah*), a table in place of the table (of the bread of the Presence), a *menorah* in place of the *menorah*, but one may make (a *menorah*) with five, six or eight (branches). Even of other metals (you shall not make a *menorah*).

See my discussion of this issue in *This Holy Place*, pp. 46–49.

[15] See my "Art and the Liturgical Context" for a full discussion.

[16] E.g. JT *Meg.* 3:1, 73d; JT *Yoma* 7:1, 44b; JT *Meg.* 4:5, 75b; JT *Sot.* 8:6, 22a.

[17] See examples presented by A. Stauffer, ed., *Textiles of Late Antiquity* (New York: Metropolitan Museum of Art, 1995), esp. pp. 8, 10, 14, 24, and 43.

[18] *This Holy Place*, p. 80.

wise dark (and in the winter, cold) halls. When later traditions bless those who provide *ner le-ma'or,*[19] they reflected a true need of the synagogue and a real opportunity for participation in synagogue life that is difficult to appreciate for us who live in a world changed forever by Mr. Edison. The brilliance of light at the focal point of the synagogue must have been quite striking, bringing to my mind (though apparently not to the mind of any preserved ancient interpreter) the adage in *Proverbs* (6:23): *Ki ner mizvah, ve-torah or*, "For the commandment is a lamp and Torah is light."

Scholars have long asked why, if the furnishings illustrated actually existed, it was necessary to illustrate them on the floor. The answer is a simple one. The ark panels of our mosaics are reflections of the Torah shrine and *menorot* of the synagogue. Christians used the same technique within churches, paralleling the ritual furnishings of the church in its wall and floor decorations. They serve the same function that a reflecting pool does (and did) before a major public building: these reflections add dignity to the Shrine, and to the Torah within it. The mosaicist at Na'aran went a step further. Below the image of the Torah shrine the artist set the image of Daniel in the Lion's Den. Daniel's hands are raised in a gesture known as an orans position in Christian art, and as *nesiat kappayim*, the "raising of hands," in biblical and rabbinic sources. Elsewhere in this mosaic we find additional figures, male and female, assuming this position. This image of Daniel is not unique. It appears on a basalt member that was most likely a Torah shrine base from the Golan, and once appeared in the synagogue mosaic at Susiya in Mt. Hebron. In fact, the orans position seems to have been a common Jewish prayer stance during the Byzantine period.[20] It is my suggestion that

[19] "Lamp for illumination." *Seder Avodat Yisrael*, ed. Z. Baer (Jerusalem: Schocken, 1937), p. 230; A. Yaari, "The *mi-Shebeirakh* Prayers: History and Texts," *Kirjath Sepher* 33, nos. 1–2 (1957–1958): 118–30, 233–51 (Hebrew).

[20] G. Alon, *Studies in Jewish History* (Israel: ha-Kibbutz Hame'uchad, 1967), pp. 181–4, Hebrew; Y. Deviri, *Light in the Sayings and Aphorisms of the Sages*, (Holon: the author, 1976), pp. 112–15 (Hebrew); E. Zimmer, *Society and its Customs: Studies in the History and Metamorphosis of Jewish Customs* (Ramat Gan: Bar Ilan University Press, 1996), pp. 78–88 (Hebrew); D. Sperber, *The Customs of Israel* (Jerusalem: Mossad ha-Rav Kook, 1994), vol. 3, pp. 88–91 (Hebrew).

"Daniel" was placed before the ark so as to reflect another important feature of synagogue furnishing: the *sheliaḥ ẓibbur* (prayer leader) who stood before the ark, in the technical language of the period, *over lifne ha-tevah.*[21] In a sense, the flesh and blood *sheliaḥ ẓibbur* fills the ritual space between the three dimensional ark, and the two dimensional representation of the same ark. The actual image of Daniel, drawn from Christian art, was placed in a position in our mosaic that reflects an essential element of Jewish spirituality. Like the *sheliaḥ ẓibbur,* Daniel directs his prayers toward the ark, and through it, towards the Holy City of Jerusalem. Daniel here is illustrated fulfilling Daniel 6:10, where Daniel "went to his house where he had windows in his upper chamber open toward Jerusalem...."[22] Closing the loop, this text was taken by the Sages to be the biblical warrant for our own alignment toward Jerusalem in prayer.[23] The use of biblical characters to presage and reflect contemporary practice is well known in rabbinic sources, as well as in Christian sources.[24]

Another important feature of many of our synagogues was the

---

[21] "Pass before the [Torah] chest." See the relevant bibliography cited by Z. Weiss, "The Location of the Sheliaḥ Ẓibbur during Prayer," *Cathedra* 55 (1990): 9–21 (Hebrew). To this, add: J. Hoffman, "The Ancient Torah Service in Light of the Realia of the Talmudic Era," *Conservative Judaism* 42:2 (1989–90): 42–44; Yaakov Elman, "Babylonian Baraitot in the Tosefta and the 'Dialectology' of Middle Hebrew," *AJS Review* 16 (1991): 23; D. Rosenthal, "Palestinian Traditions and their Transmission to Babylonia," *Cathedra* 92 (1999): 25–27, and especially note 140 (Hebrew).

[22] Revised Standard Version.

[23] Tosefta *Berakhot* 3:6.

[24] The art of late antique churches often reflects this type of projection. So, for example, in the wall mosaics of San Vitale in Ravenna we find that:

> All four scenes allude to the eucharist sacrifice. To make this significance plain, an altar is depicted between Abel and Melchizedek, on which are placed a chalice and two loaves of bread, identical in shape with that which Melchizedek offers and also with the eucharistic bread which the church used during the sixth century. The altar motif appears again in the opposite mosaic: Isaac is shown kneeling upon the altar, and even the table behind which the three angels are seated resembles the simple wooden altar of Christian antiquity. The three round cakes which Sarah has placed before the heavenly messengers are marked with the sign of the cross and recall again the eucharistic hosts of that time (O.G. von Simson, *Sacred Fortress: Byzantine Art*

presence of biblical scenes. At Na'aran and Susiya, Daniel appears. At Gaza, David the harpist; at Gerasa, Noah's ark; at Meroth a lamb lying with a lion; and at Beth Alpha *akeidat Yiẓḥak*, the "Binding of Isaac." At Sepphoris we have an absolute medley of images, ranging from the annunciation to Abraham that Sarah would give birth, to *akeidat Yiẓḥak* and finally Aaron before the Tabernacle, the table for showbread, first fruits, and assorted sacrifices. Again, all of these images are, in one way or another, associated with Christian art, and have distinct parallels in Christian art. Unique to the Binding of Isaac scene at Sepphoris is the image of Abraham's and Isaac's shoes left at the base of Mt. Moriah. This theme is known from later Christian illustrations.[25] This detail is unknown, however, in Jewish art or literature. Nowhere do we hear in midrashic literature of God ordering Abraham to "remove your shoes, for the place where you are standing is holy." Whether the source of this detail was Christian, or whether, by one of those circuitous paths of relationship by which Jewish sources made their way to Christian audiences, its origin was Jewish, this detail reflects a notion that the Sages and others attending synagogue in antiquity would have well understood. A hint of the need for clean feet within synagogue contexts may be found in *Genesis Rabbah* 42. In this text clean feet are clearly described as a virtue for one who was entering the synagogue. According to this tradition, when Abraham and his men chased after the kings to rescue Lot in far-away Dan, miraculously, "their feet did not become dusty (*lo nitabku ragleihen*). Rather, they were like he who walks from his home to the synagogue."[26] The necessity of removing shoes before going up to the Temple Mount appears in *Mishnah*

---

and Statecraft in Ravenna (Princeton: Princeton University Press, 1987), p. 25; Mathews, *Byzantium*, p. 103).

The art of the church, so influential in so many ways upon the art of the synagogue, provides a reasonable parallel for interpreting Daniel at Naaran. Daniel in our synagogue, like Melchizedek at San Vitale, is a legitimization and projection of contemporary practice into the eternal present.

[25] Z. Weiss and E. Netzer, *Promise and Redemption: A Synagogue Mosaic from Sepphoris* (Jerusalem: Israel Museum, 1996), pp. 30–1.

[26] *Genesis Rabbah* 42, ed. J. Theodor and Ch. Albeck (Jerusalem: Wahrmann, 1965), p. 419, and the parallels cited there.

Berakhot, chapter nine, and the requirement of removing shoes (and washing feet) before entering synagogues is well documented.[27] In a Genizah document, titled *Hilkhot Ereẓ Israel* by its editor, this is stated explicitly:[28]

> And so the Sages said: One shall not enter the Temple Mount with his staff and shoes" (M. *Berakhot* 9:5).
>
> Though by our sins the Temple Mount is not ours, we do have the *mikdash me'at*, and we are obligated to behave [towards it] in sanctity and awe. For it is written: "My Temple, fear" (*Lev*. 19:30, 26:2).
>
> Therefore the ancients decreed in all synagogue courtyards that lavers of living water for the sanctification of the hands and feet [be set up].
>
> If there was a delicate or sick person, unable to remove [his shoes], and he was careful as he walked [not to dirty them], he is not forced to remove [his shoes]....

This passage suggests that piety towards the synagogue, and particularly ritual ablution of the feet and entry to the synagogue barefooted, was taken over from the Temple to the *mikdash me'at*. The notion that ritual purity was necessary for entrance into synagogues first appears in post-Amoraic literature.[29] An interesting parallel to our text is the liturgy of Anan son of David (c. eighth century), who, on the model of the Temple, decreed that worshippers wash their hands and feet before entering synagogues associated with what became known as Karaism.[30] A washing installation (*gorna*) in

[27] This Holy Place, pp. 82–3.

[28] *Hilkhot Ereẓ-Israel min ha-Geniza*, ed. M. Margoliot, ed. I. Ta-Shma (Jerusalem: Mossad ha-Rav Kook, 1973), pp. 131–2.

[29] Cf. Z. Safrai, "From Synagogue to Little Temple," in *Proceedings of the Tenth World Congress in Jewish Studies*, Division B, (Jerusalem: World Union for Jewish Studies, 1990), pp. 150–51. See Levine, "From Community Center to Small Temple: The Furnishings and Interior Design of Ancient Synagogues," *Cathedra* 60 (1991): 40–41.

[30] J. Mann, "Anan's Liturgy and His Half-Yearly Cycle for Reading the Law," *Journal of Jewish Lore and Philosophy* 1:1–4 (1919): 344, n. 26 (Hebrew). Al-Qumisi informs

the synagogue compound (forecourt?) is evidenced as early as the *Yerushalmi.*[31] Evidence of ritual ablution is found in synagogue ruins from the Byzantine period. A particularly well-preserved washing installation was discovered in the narthex of the last stage of the Ein Gedi synagogue.[32] By placing the images of shoes near the entrance to the synagogue, the artist, inadvertently or not, suggests that just as Abraham and Isaac removed their shoes prior to ascending the Temple Mount, so too are shoes to be removed before entering the synagogue. Cues of this sort are known from non-Jewish mosaics, my favorite being a mosaic from Pompeii that shows a dog on a leash, with the inscription "beware of the dog." [33]

The images of the Temple service at Sepphoris are particularly exciting, since they are the only such images extant from ancient synagogues. While a few lists of the priestly courses, the *mishmarot,* have been uncovered, here we find images that truly reflect Jewish conceptions.[34] To choose a single detail: on the basket of *bikkurim,* birds appear on either side of the basket. This is not an unusual convention in Byzantine period art, appearing, for example, in Ravenna. What is unusual is that the doves are suspended upside down from their sides. This fits nicely with a early tradition (*baraita*) in *Yerushalmi Bikkurim* 3:4 (65d) that suggests that the birds were

---

us that by analogy to the Temple, Rabbanites would not enter synag33ogues in a state of impurity [M. Zucker, *Rav Saadya Gaon's Translation of the Torah* (New York: Jewish Theological Seminary, 1959), p. 171, n. 666 (Hebrew)].

[31] JT *Meg.* 3:3, 74a. On ablution of hands and feet before prayer, see N. Wieder, "Islamic Influences on the Hebrew Cults," *Melilah* 2 (1946): 43 (Hebrew).

[32] D. Barag, Y. Porat, and E. Netzer, "The Synagogue at En-Gedi," in *Ancient Synagogues Revealed,* ed. L.I. Levine (Jerusalem: Israel Exploration Society, 1981), p. 117; On other washing installations in Palestinian synagogues, see Levine, "From Community Center to Small Temple," pp. 39–41 and n. 26 (Hebrew).

[33] For Byzantine period examples, see E. Kitzinger, "The Threshold of the Holy Shrine: Observations on the Floor Mosaics at Antioch and Bethlehem," in *Kyriakon: Festschrift Johannes Quasten,* eds. P. Granfield, J.A. Jungmann (Muenster: Aschendorff, 1970), pp. 139–67.

[34] M. Avi-Yonah, "The Caesarea Inscription of the Twenty-Four Priestly Courses," *Ereẓ-Israel* 7 (1964): 24–28 (Hebrew); H. Eshel, "A Fragmentary Inscription of the Priestly Courses?" *Tarbiz* 61:1 (1991): 59–161 (Hebrew), has shown that an inscription from Kissufim is not a fragment of a *mishmarot* plaque.

suspended "outside" the baskets in order to maintain the cleanliness of the first fruits.[35] Our image of the *bikkurim* goes a step further: it seems that the birds are suspended upside down to ensure that the first fruits remain unsoiled. Similarly, the image of Aaron before the Tabernacle is not unusual. Such imagery is well known from the Greco-Roman world, where priests before altars are a common motif. I would argue that the shape of the top of the horned altar, a kind of rhombus, visually parallels the image of the ark with which it is aligned, and the three dimensional ark of the synagogue towering above. When the *sheliaḥ ẓibbur* stood to lead the community in prayer, he would have essentially stood, *de facto,* in the position of Aaron. This would be particularly meaningful on the festivals, and even more so at *musaf Yom ha-Kippurim*, when the prayer leader, in any event, takes the role of the High Priest in the Temple. This re-living and revitalization of the priestly service is well reflected in *piyyut* literature, a tradition that continues to our own day.[36] Aaron at Sepphoris is dressed, as far as we can tell, in clothing that well suits the Byzantine period, just as the youths are in the Binding of Isaac panel, and as Abraham and Isaac must have been. In a real sense, the *sheliaḥ ẓibbur* looked like Aaron, and Aaron looked like him.

The central register of each of our mosaics is decorated with a zodiac wheel, flanked on each corner by personifications of the four seasons. That these panels appeared over a three hundred year period is particularly exciting. In fact, the changes that took place over this period reflect the spiritual paths of differing, and in two cases, changing, Jewish communities. The earliest zodiac panel exists in the synagogue of Hammath Tiberias B. The quality of this mosaic is particularly fine. At the center of this mosaic is the image of the sun god Helios, in full regalia, riding through the heavens on

[35] This observation was made to me in personal correspondence by Stuart Miller shortly after the discovery of the mosaic. Cf. Weiss and Netzer, *Promise and Redemption*, p. 24.

[36] M. Swartz, "Sage, Priest and Poet: Typologies of Religious Leadership in the Ancient Synagogue," in *Jews, Christians and Polytheists in the Ancient Synagogue: Cultural Interaction During the Greco-Roman Period*, ed. S. Fine (London: Routledge, 1999), p. 109.

his quadriga. In his hand is a staff and a globe. The image of Libra is also particularly interesting. Libra is a nude, uncircumcised male. The quality of the mosaic, and the detail of non-circumcision, led the excavator to suggest that the floor was laid by non-Jews. All that these details prove, however, is that the pattern was followed rigorously by the artisans, and that the local community found no fault in them. The image of a zodiac panel was in no way distinctly Jewish, though it seems that Jews in Palestine showed a particular preference for it.[37] Early on scholars recognized that this panel does not reflect strictly rabbinic norms. After all, in *Mishnah Avodah Zarah* 3:1 the Sages specifically forbid any image, *ẓelem*, "that has in its hand a staff or a bird or a globe (*kadur*)," and circumcision is a basic identifying feature of Jews, while public nudity was not. The dedicatory inscriptions set in the mosaic provide an answer to this mystery. All the individuals mentioned in the inscriptions bear Greek names. Not a single one has a Hebrew or Aramaic name. Twice a particular individual is mentioned, "Severos the student of the illustrious Patriarch." Joseph Baumgarten was the first to recognize that this was a synagogue belonging to strongly Hellenized and urban members of the Patriarchal community. By the fourth century a rather wide schism had developed between the Sages and the Patriarch, and literary sources suggest that the Patriarchal circle was taking on the mores of the Roman urban elite.[38] It is not that they had relinquished their Jewish identity. These folks built this synagogue, with its large Torah shrine and mosaic Torah shrine panel. Like other Jews, they called their synagogue an *atra kedisha* or *hagios topos* – a "holy place." If the synagogue inscriptions are any

[37] See R. Hachlili, "The Zodiac in Ancient Jewish Art: Representation and Significance," *Bulletin of the American Schools for Oriental Research* 228 (1977): 62–77; G. Foerster, "The Zodiac Wheel in Ancient Synagogues and Its Iconographic Sources," *Ereẓ-Israel* 18 (1985): 380–91 (Hebrew). See also the zodiac mosaic from the Aegean island of Astypalaia at http://astypalaia.com/astypalaia-frame.htm.

[38] J.M. Baumgarten, "Art in the Synagogue: Some Talmudic Views," *Judaism* 6 (1970), reprinted in my *Jews, Christians, and Polytheists in the Ancient Synagogue: Cultural Interaction During the Greco-Roman Period* (London: Routledge, 1999), p. 80; L.I. Levine, *The Rabbinic Class of Roman Palestine* (Jerusalem: Ben Zvi Institute, 1989), p. 183.

hint, their prayers used terminology well known in rabbinic sources, and they valued the Hebrew language, labeling each element of the zodiac in Hebrew (even if some inscriptions were written as mirror images). The zodiac itself is not so much of a problem, as references to the zodiac are common in rabbinic thought. Long ago Michael Avi-Yonah suggested that the zodiac represents the Jewish months, and he is certainly correct.[39] The presence of Helios, however, shows just how far the spirituality of this community was from rabbinic norms. Some Jews even ascribed to Helios magical power, as is suggested in a Greek prayer, transcribed into Hebrew script, that appears in a document from the Cairo Genizah.[40] When Rabbi Abun, "did not object" to the use of mosaics by Jews,[41] and Rabbi Abahu was willing to prostrate himself on mosaic without any qualms of violating Levitcus 26:1,[42] they surely could not have imagined mosaics with pagan images and nudity![43] If the floor of the synagogue is any indication, the "spiritual" life of this community was clearly different from the thought-world of our Sages – though apparently only in degree and not in its totality. It was urban and sophisticated, in the provincial Roman sense. These Jews must have developed ways of explaining, or simply not noticing, Helios and the naked Libra. Nudity too was a costume in the Roman world! The local Jewish aristocracy must have been responsible for the sculpture that was covered up at the death of Nahum *ish kodesh kodeshim,* who had never looked upon

[39] M. Avi-Yonah, *Art in Ancient Palestine: Selected Essays,* ed. H. and Y. Tsafrir (Jerusalem: Magnes, 1981), pp. 396–7. See my expanded discussion on this issue in *Art and Judaism During the Greco-Roman Period.*

[40] Opinions regarding Helios are summarized by Levine, *The Rabbinic Class*, pp. 178–9; M. Margaliot's introduction to *Sefer ha-Razim* (Tel Aviv: Yediot Aharonot, 1966), pp. 12–16 (Hebrew). See now S.S. Miller, "'Epigraphical' Rabbis, Helios, and Psalm 19: Were the Synagogues of Archaeology and the Synagogues of the Sages One and the Same?" *JQR* 94,1 2004) 27-76.

[41] JT *Avodah Zarah* 3:3, 42d, as preserved in a Cairo Genizah fragment published by J.N. Epstein, "Additional Fragments of the Jerushalmi," *Tarbiz* 3:1 (1931): 20 (Hebrew).

[42] JT *Avodah Zarah* 4:1, 43d; Gerald Blidstein, "Prostration and Mosaics in Talmudic Law," *Bulletin of the Institute of Jewish Studies* 2 (1974): 33–7.

[43] See M. Satlow, "Jewish Constructions of Nakedness in Late Antiquity," *Journal of Biblical Literature* (1997).

such images in his life.[44] As in all Roman cities, one would imagine that nudity was an essential element of these sculptures. Amoraic literature reports that Rabbi Yehuda ha-Nasi was called *Rabbenu ha-Kadosh,* because "he never looked at his circumcision, all the days of his life."[45] The Jews of Hammath Tiberias, by contrast, looked upon the uncircumcised every time they entered their synagogue. The rabbinic warning to stay away "from the synagogues of the *amei ha-areẓ*"[46] was a judgment that the Sages well may have applied to the Jews who built this synagogue.

The zodiac wheel at Sepphoris reflects a more "rabbinic feel" than we find at Hammath Tiberias. Helios is gone, his image replaced with a sun disk. No nudity appears.[47] Rather, together with the signs of the zodiac, we find personifications of the Hebrew months. In essence, the possibly objectionable imagery has been cleaned up. As in Hammath Tiberias, all labels are in Hebrew. This is the case in most labels in synagogue mosaics. While dedicatory inscriptions are in Aramaic and Greek, labels for biblical scenes and the zodiac are in Hebrew. This reflects a distinctly Jewish form of spirituality that was essential to the Judaization of each of these scenes when they were carried over from the church context to the synagogue. The "holy tongue," the "language of the holy house," was a fundamental element of synagogue spirituality. Not always fully understood, translated into Aramaic and sometimes Greek in simultaneous translation, Hebrew was taken to be God's vernacular.[48]

The zodiac wheels at the sixth-century synagogue of Beth Alpha and Na'aran are more like Hammath Tiberias B than Sepphoris. In fact, the case may be made that the plan of Hammath Tiberias B mosaic stands in a direct line of tradition with the Beth Alpha mosaic. By the sixth century, however, paganism was dead in this part

[44] JT *Meg.* 1:11, 72b; JT *Sanh.* 10:5, 29c; JT *Avod. Zar.* 3:1, 42c; BT *Pesahim* 104a, BT *Avod. Zar.* 50a; *Eccl. Rab.* 9:10.

[45] BT *Shab.* 118b.

[46] M. *Avot* 3:10.

[47] Though the image of Gemini is incomplete, and so this point cannot be fully supported.

[48] See *This Holy Place*, pp. 15–16, and the bibliography there.

of the world, and even orthodox churches and monasteries were decorated with images of gods and goddesses. The zodiac, however, was an integral part both of midrashic literature and of the liturgy of the synagogue.[49]

Still, why were these particular images chosen for synagogue decoration? The pairing of the ark panel and the zodiac was set already during the fourth century, and was followed later by the addition of biblical themes. I think that they were chosen in the first instance because they were available. Jews borrowed imagery from the general culture and Judaized it. Of all the options available, these were chosen. This is clearly the case in the Gaza region, where the self-same imagery appears in Christian and Jewish mosaics, laid by the same "school of Gaza."[50] The only difference is the presence of a menorah or a cross before the apse of the building. Once the decision to lay a mosaic was made, the communities at Sepphoris, Beth Alpha, and Na'aran needed only to choose from a pattern "book" (which we might imagine, for the sake of argument, had been Judaized long before) what other scenes to incorporate. These were communal decisions, undoubtedly made by some sort of committee, or perhaps by the donors who financed each panel (and, at Sepphoris, have their names inscribed *in situ*).

The themes of the mosaics blended well with the liturgy of the synagogue. The interpretation of Scripture was essential to this liturgy, from the homily to the Aramaic paraphrase to the artful *kedushta*. The rich "literature of the Synagogue," as Joseph Heinemann and Jakob Petuchowski have called it, ranges from homiletic

[49] See the sources cited by M. Klein, "Palestinian Targum and Synagogue Mosaics," *Immanuel* 11 (1980): 33–45; J. Yahalom, "The Zodiac Wheel in Early Piyyut in Ereẓ-Israel," *Jerusalem Studies in Hebrew Literature* 9 (1986): 313–22 (Hebrew); "Piyyut as Poetry," in *The Synagogue in Late Antiquity*, ed. L.I. Levine (Philadelphia: American Schools for Oriental Research, 1987), pp. 111–26; Shinan, "Synagogues in the Land of Israel,": 146–52.

[50] M. Avi-Yonah, *Art in Ancient Palestine: Selected Essays,* ed. H. and Y. Tsafrir (Jerusalem: Magnes, 1981), pp. 389–92; A. Ovadiah, "The Mosaic Workshop of Gaza in Christian Antiquity," in *Ancient Synagogues: Historical Analysis and Archaeological Discovery*, ed. D. Urman and P.V.M. Flesher (Leiden: E.J. Brill, 1995), vol. 2, pp. 367–72.

midrashic collections to liturgical texts to the Aramaic paraphrases of Scripture, the *targumim.*[51] What unites all of these literatures is not only their apparent synagogue context, but their focus upon the biblical text. While it is useful to draw parallels from throughout the rabbinic corpus in interpreting individual images, this practice creates a kind of textual free-for-all when one attempts to construct a global interpretation. Fortunately, the large number of extant *piyyutim* (from the Greek *poietas*), provides a kind of control. Written by individuals, these poems can be roughly dated. The *piyyutim* differ markedly from the midrashic collections, with their long and often difficult redactional histories and their unclear *Sitz im Leben,* and the *targumim,* which were also the works of numerous hands. Reading through one poet's corpus of work, one can observe how a single Jew in late antiquity Palestine formulated and reformulated tradition within the synagogues of his day. The best example for our purposes is Yannai the Paytan, a sixth century poet. Z.M. Rabbinowitz, editor of Yannai's corpus, assembled 165 poems from the Cairo Genizah that were to be recited on the Sabbath according to the so-called triennial cycle, and another fifteen or so for special days.[52] The striking fact is that all the issues that appear in our mosaics are dealt with by Yannai. Themes that appear in the Sepphoris mosaic, including the binding of Isaac, Aaron in the Tabernacle, the table for the showbread, the first fruits, the menorah, and the zodiac all appear.[53] By reading how this author understands these subjects, it is possible to construct a picture of how one Jew who could well have

[51] J. Heinemann and J.J. Petuchowski, *The Literature of the Synagogue,* (New York: Bloch, 1975). See A. Shinan's survey of this literature "Synagogues in the Land of Israel: The Literature of the Ancient Synagogue and Synagogue Archaeology," in *Sacred Realm: The Emergence of the Synagogue in the Ancient World,* (New York: Yeshiva University Museum and Oxford University Press, 1996), pp. 130–52.

[52] *The Liturgical Poetry of Rabbi Yannai*, ed. Z.M. Rabinovitz (Jerusalem: Bialik Institute, 1985–1987); S. Lieberman, "Hazanut Yannai," *Sinai* 4 (1939): 221–50 (Hebrew); M. Zulay, "Rabban shel ha-Paytanim," in *Eretz Israel and its Poetry,* ed. E. Hazan (Jerusalem: Magnes, 1995), pp. 85–94 (Hebrew).

[53] For example, see *The Liturgical Poetry of Rabbi Yannai*, first fruits: vol. 2, pp. 175–82, menorah: vol. 1, pp. 340–345; zodiac 1, pp. 83–9; vol. 2, p. 242.

visited the Sepphoris synagogue understood the themes that were set in stone by the mosaicist.

I will cite here one poem by Yannai that within just a few lines utilizes many of the themes represented on the Sepphoris floor. The poem was recited on *Rosh ha-Shanah*. This extended poem, like most of Yannai's poetry, reflects upon the liturgical themes of the day as it poetically embellishes the themes of the central *tefillah* prayer that it celebrates. While I am in no way suggesting that this particular poem influenced the floor, it is my contention that the selection and arrangement of themes to decorate the Sepphoris mosaic and the selection and arrangement of themes by the liturgical poet are both reflections of how Jews constructed the synagogue environment through image and word at nearly the same time. The literary and the visual artists each assembled similar building blocks in constructing their own unique presentation for a synagogue setting. The section of Yannai's poem that concerns us translates as follows:[54]

> Then the *shofar* will be blown for the Complete [One]//
> The hope that the complete (shofar blasts) be recieved like peace offerings (shelamim).
>
> Hence any *shofar* that has a crack//
> Is not fit, for it interrupts the sounding.
>
> Come forth with a broken soul and not with a broken horn//
> With a broken heart and not with a broken *shofar*.
>
> Lovers drawn after Him (God), and, like the girdle, cleave//
> They will sound a long *shofar* that has no adhesions.
>
> For from the ram come the horns//
> To remember the merit of the ram stuck by its horns [at the binding of Isaac].

[54] *The Liturgical Poetry of Rabbi Yannai*, vol. 2, p. 204.

Sound, O sons of God/ Sound to the God of gods//
Who covers over and removes/from them all sins.

A time of concealment when the moon is concealed/
To conceal sins well, just as the moon [is concealed].

The sun, how can it bear witness [to the new month] alone?/
When one witness is not enough [for a court] to inflict the death penalty?

The [heavenly] array of the seventh month, its constellation is Libra/
For sin and righteousness God will lay upon the scales.

His hand will remove sin and we will proclaim the day with the *shofar*/
To the scale of utter righteousness He will incline.

We see here that the themes of the *shofar*, the binding of Isaac, the sun, moon and astronomical symbols are among the building blocks for Yannai's *Rosh ha-Shanah* liturgy. Elsewhere in his corpus, Yannai weaves these themes and many others together in different ways, depending upon the reading for the day and the festival context. It is important to note, however, that the binding of Isaac, representing the doctrine of "merits of the ancestors,"[55] the zodiac, representing both the heavens and the Jewish solar-lunar calendar, and the sacrificial system, are extremely common throughout Yannai's corpus, due to their centrality within the *tefillah* prayer upon which our author artistically expands. Yannai, reflecting upon the Scriptural readings of *Rosh ha-Shanah*, upon the ceremonies of that day, and upon the calendrical cycle, brought together imagery that gives texture to his liturgical creation. That all of this imagery ap-

[55] Solomon Schechter, *Aspects of Rabbinic Theology* (New York: Macmillan, 1909), pp. 170–98; G.F. Moore, *Judaism in the First Centuries of the Common Era* (Cambridge: Harvard University Press, 1927–1930), vol. 1, pp. 538–46.

pears in our floor is no accident. These themes were central to Jewish liturgical life during this period. At other seasons Yannai stresses other subjects, many of which are expressed in our synagogue mosaics. The Menorah, for example, is the subject of Yannai's Hanukkah and liturgical poems for *parshat be-ha'alotekha*. On *Tisha be-Av* the Tabernacle/Temple is dealt with differently than on *Sukkot,* and on and on. One might even conjecture that on various occasions the synagogue was furnished differently. We know that this was the case in contemporary churches, and among Jews in Geonic Babylonia.[56] Why should this not have been the case in Jewish Palestine? As we dress the synagogue in white for the *Yamim ha-Nora'im*, and in flowers for *Shavuot*, perhaps ancient Jews had their own distinctive ways of decorating their synagogues throughout the year. The various elements of the synagogue, the visual, the textual, and the human actors, were as so many molecules, interacting with one another in different ways at different seasons and in different contexts. The art and the liturgy of the synagogue are cut from a single cloth, reflecting differing, but always interwoven, aspects of the spirituality of the synagogue in Byzantine Palestine.

Not all late antique Jews considered the art of our ancient synagogues to be conducive to their spiritual needs. We have suggested, for example, that the Sages would likely not have been pleased with the decorations of the fourth-century Hammath Tiberias synagogue mosaic. Apparently Jews in the same locale during the sixth century were not either. When they rebuilt and enlarged their synagogue, the later builders made no effort to reuse or copy their earlier mosaics. They laid a floor of simple patterns and built right through the zodiac mosaic. At Khirbet Susiya, in the Mt. Hebron area, a zodiac and an image of Daniel were replaced with a simple geometric pattern of tesserae. Images of animals on the synagogue's *bima* screens were removed. There are many other examples. The Jews of Na'aran carefully removed the human and most animal images that appeared in their mosaic. The Jews of Ein Gedi included the zodiac in the

[56] A. Yaari, *The History of the Festival of Simḥat Torah* (Jerusalem: Mossad ha-Rav Kook, 1964), p. 215 (Hebrew); J. Wilkinson, *Egeria's Travels to the Holy Land* (Jerusalem: Ariel and Warminster: Aris & Phillips, 1981), pp. 82–4.

decoration of their synagogue, but only in the form of a list; and the Jews of Jericho, only a few kilometers from Na'aran, laid a floor with images of a stylized geometric Torah that included only images of a shrine and a *menorah*.[58] I could list many other examples of aniconic or iconoclastic behavior, and, in fact, have done so elsewhere.[59] The point here is that during the Byzantine and early Islamic periods there were Jewish communities who found the kind of imagery that we have discussed to be fundamentally contrary to their own sense of spirituality. As Nahum *ish kodesh kodashim* never looked on a pagan image on a coin, these Jews tried not to either – at least not within their synagogues.

What influenced this transformation? Goodenough and Avi-Yonah attributed it to the rising power of those big-bad-iconophobic-rabbis. Avi-Yonah's disappointment, as well as his own anti-rabbinism, is palpable when he writes that:[60]

> The figurative efflorescence of Jewish Art, which began in the third century, did not last beyond the sixth. As the times became more difficult and the Byzantine laws directed against

---

[57] M. Dothan, *Hammath Tiberias: Late Synagogues* (Jerusalem: Israel Exploration Society, 2000)

[58] J. Sussman, "A Halakhic Inscription from the Beth-Shean Valley," *Tarbiz* 43 (1973–74): 88–158, 44 (1974–75), pp. 193–5 (Hebrew).

[59] "Iconoclasm and the Art of Late Antique Palestinian Synagogues," In *From Dura to Sepphoris: Studies in Jewish Art and Society in Late Antiquity*, ed. L.I. Levine and Z. Weiss, Journal of Roman Archaeology Supplementary Series (1999) 182-93.

[60] M. Avi-Yonah, *Oriental Art in Roman Palestine* (Rome: Centro di Studi Semitici of the Istituto di Studi del Vicino Oriente, 1961), p. 42, reprinted *Art in Ancient Palestine*, p. 159. See the secularized Christian statement of this as related to iconoclasm in E.R. Goodenough, *Jewish Symbols in the Greco-Roman Period* (New York: Pantheon, 1953), vol. 2, pp. 256–7. Regarding iconoclasm at Na'aran, Goodenough states: "again, we might suppose that the 'different type' of Judaism was rabbinic, halakhic Judaism at last coming to dominate Jewish standards and conceptions, at last becoming normative." On Goodenough's understanding of the rabbinic sages, see: M. Smith, "Goodenough's Jewish Symbols in Retrospect," *Journal of Biblical Literature* 86 (1967): 53–68; *Fine Art and Judaism During the Greco Roman Period, part I.*

> the Jews more oppressive, aniconic orthodoxy resumed its sway, even before similar trends prevailed in Islam and in the iconoclastic tendency at Byzantium.... The old fear of the human image returned again, as in Hellenistic times....

In effect, this interpretation is the other side of the coin from Rabbi Soloveitchik's comment that "[T]he tradition as such has rejected them (that is, figurative mosaics)." What is clear is that the Jews who chose against visual images during the Byzantine period clearly were choosing a path that veered away from the artistic traditions that we have seen thus far. Were they responding to the Christian veneration of images? When an Aramaic-speaking poet wrote against Christian images of Jesus "painted on wood," he certainly reflects an abhorrence for such images.[61] Still, there is a great distance between an image set in two dimensions in a mosaic or carved in low relief on a lintel and the Christian cult of the saints. The rise of Islam was significant for Jewish aniconicism and iconoclasm. From the first, Islam eschewed images within religious settings. Islamic aesthetics must have been particularly influential among Jews. The Moslem rulers of Palestine were greeted positively by Palestinian Jews, and Islam was not subjected to the level of scorn that Jews felt (and continued to feel) toward Christianity.[62] Jewish wariness of idolatrous imagery proved to be an asset for Jews living in a Muslim society. In

---

[61] Nailed on the wood [the cross, *kis*]
And my image in the church [*ba-Merkoles*]
Is painted on wood [*kis*]

M. Sokoloff and J. Yahalom, *Jewish Palestinian Aramaic Poetry from Late Antiquity: Critical Edition with Introduction and Commentary* (Jerusalem: Israel Academy of Sciences and Humanities, 1999), p. 217 (Hebrew).

[62] See R. Wilken, *The Land Called Holy: Palestine in Christian History and Thought* (New Haven: Yale University Press, 1992), pp. 216–32, and my "Non-Jews in the Synagogues of Palestine," pp. 231–41, and the bibliography cited there. On relations between Jews, Christians, and Moslems on the subject of Christian images, see G.R.D. King, "Islam, Iconoclasm and the Declaration of Doctrine," *Bulletin of the School of Oriental and African Studies* 48:2 (1985): 275–7; S.H. Griffith, *Theodore Abu Qurrah, A Treatise on the Veneration of the Holy Icons* (Leuven: Peeters, 1997), esp. pp. 6–7.

a sense, it gave the Jews "one up" on the Christians and the appearance of being closer in attitude to the Moslems in this multi-cultural, though increasingly Islamic, culture. The intrinsic ambivalence of rabbinic tradition toward images certainly provided ready ground for this shift, leading to the iconographic transformation of synagogue floors. We might assume that Palestinian Jews would have had no particular interest in continuing to use a now *passé* art form. Jews simply adopted and adapted the aesthetics of the new colonial power. According to this scenario, the close of antiquity and the rise of Islam reinforced a less figurative sensibility than had existed in Jewish thought in the Land of Israel throughout the Greco-Roman period. Jewish attitudes reflect the transition from a visual vocabulary to a less figurative approach, that some (though not all) Jewish communities found to their liking in the Byzantine Holy Land. In the end, the most significant non-Jewish influences were clearly the artistic and religious mores of Islamic Palestine.

In this paper I have suggested that the art of ancient synagogues was part-and-parcel of the period as a whole, and that Jews were essentially consumers of Byzantine and early Islamic artistic forms. In taking on and Judaizing the art of this period, Jews created an art that was uniquely Jewish. "Spirituality" may be found in synagogue art at the point that it intersects with the liturgy of the ancient synagogue. If the life of the synagogue was the play, then the synagogue building was the set. The set developed with the changing attitudes of the community, and with the aesthetics of each community and succeeding era. In eschewing and often removing the selfsame imagery, communities made a very different Jewish choice, a move toward a less figurative iconography that has been a defining feature of much (though certainly not all) synagogue art from the early Islamic period to our own. This transition generally sits well with Rabbi Soloveitchik's notion that Judaism holds "an unequivocal iconoclastic attitude...toward the display of human images in houses of worship."[63]

[63] Letter on the Cornell interfaith chapel, p. 2. Although Rav Soloveitchik, like many contemporary scholars, uses the word "iconclastic" broadly to describe both material *and* spiritual non-figurarive representation.

7

Spirituality and Jewish Ceremonial Art

Vivian B. Mann

INTRODUCTION

The relationship of Jewish ceremonial art to spirituality was a question considered in rabbinic literature, sometimes directly and, at other times, by inference. Various factors affected rabbinic views of the role of ceremonial art in promoting spirituality: the developmental history of Judaica; the age in which the rabbinic decisor lived; and even the culture of which he was a part. As a result of these variables, opinions ranged from the view that works of art interfered with spirituality to the opinion that art could serve as an agent of spiritual inspiration.

THE HISTORY OF JUDAICA

Not all the Judaica that we know and use today existed in the past. Certain types of Judaic objects have always been necessary for the practice of Judaism and are discussed in the Mishnah (first-second centuries) and the Talmud (third–sixth centuries), for example, a cup or goblet for the recitation of blessings over wine, a common ceremony in Jewish life. Yet, none of the texts outlining the requirements for the cup describe its form or decoration (e.g., BT *Berakhot* 51a), and no ancient vessel has been found that was designated by inscription or imagery as having been made exclusively for the sanctification over wine.[1] Other types of Judaica that are ubiquitous today were unknown in antiquity, for example, a lamp with eight lights designated for use on Hanukkah, although branched synagogue *menorot* did exist.[2] The earliest extant Hanukkah lamp dates only to the twelfth century (fig. 1) as does the earliest mention of a container used to hold the spices for *havdalah*, the ceremony that marks the conclusion of Sabbaths and festivals.[3] A somewhat amusing responsum of Maimonides considers the case of an inebriated cantor who caused the finials to fall from the staves of a Torah scroll,[4] one of the first citations of Torah finials as objects independent of the staves, aside from records found in the Cairo Genizah. The inventory of the Babylonian synagogue in Fostat of 1095 includes the first mention of copper *tikim*, rigid cylindrical cases for the Torah scroll.[5] By the twelfth century, then, other forms of ceremonial art had appeared in addition to those known from the Mishnah and the Talmud.

In the late Middle Ages and the modern period, many new types of Judaica were created. For example, silver Torah shields did not exist during the lifetime of R. Israel ben Petaḥiah Isserlein who died in 1460. He described plaques placed on the scrolls as utilitar-

[1] Rachel Hachlili, *Ancient Jewish Art and Archaeology in the Land of Israel* (Leiden, New York and Copenhagen: E.J. Brill, 1988), p. 238.

[2] Hachlili, op. cit., pp. 238–241; figs. 54 a–b and 57.

[3] B. Narkiss, "Un objet de culte: la lampe de Hanuka," in *Art et archéologie des Juifs en France médiévale*, ed. Bernhard Blumenkranz (Toulouse: Edouard Privat, 1980), pp. 200–1; Isaac ben Moses of Vienna wrote that his teacher, Rabbi Ephraim of Regensburg (1110–75), stored spices in a glass container for use in the *havdalah* ceremony (*She'elot u-Teshuvot Or Zaru'a*, vol. II, [Zitomir, 1862], no. 92).

[4] Maimonides, *Teshuvot ha-Rambam*, vol. II, ed. Jehoshua Blau (Jerusalem: Meikiẓei Nirdamim, 1960), no. 165.

[5] Shlomo Dov Goiten, *"Beit ha-Keneset ve-Ẓiyudo lefi Kitvei ha-Genizah," Ereẓ Israel* 7 (1964): 81–97.

fig. 1

ian devices that indicated the lection to which the scroll was turned, but that did not add to the beauty of the Torah.[6] But, as a result of the exploration of the Americas at the end of the fifteenth century, the European supply of silver increased, resulting in the creation of new types of tableware and display plates, and their availability to a broader population. These innovative works in silver sometimes inspired new forms of Judaica, like the Torah shield, which answered a long-standing need for an appropriate means of identifying which Torah is to be used for a specific service (fig. 2). Only seventy years after Rabbi Isserlein's death, in 1530, Antonius Margarita described silver Torah shields in his *Die Ganz jüdisch Glaub*.[7] Silver created for guilds likewise stimulated the commissioning of similar objects for *ḥevrot*, the Jewish societies devoted to the same social welfare functions similar to those of Christian guilds. Burial Society beakers are one example.

In the eighteenth century, the expansion of European Jewish

[6] Israel ben Petaḥiah Isserlein, *Terumat ha-Deshen*, no. 225.

[7] Antonius Margarita, *Die Gantz jüdisch Glaub* (Augsburg, 1530), pp. 267–8.

fig. 2

communities and the resulting need for ceremonial objects for new synagogues joined the general desire for silver *objets de luxe*. The result was another creative period in the history of ceremonial art with new types created and much experimentation with the decoration and iconography of existing types. During the last two centuries, the increased affluence of the Jewish community, coupled with new and cheaper mechanical means of production, have led to the creation of ceremonial art without any halakhic imperative, e.g. silver plates for *maẓot*, the unleavened bread eaten on Passover.

To conclude: the corpus of Jewish ceremonial art has evolved over time. Innovative forms and decoration often became the subject of halakhic discussion when rabbinic authorities were questioned on the appropriateness of new Judaica: its form, decoration, or its medium. Interestingly, their responsa on ceremonial art are largely all post-facto; they result from the creation of a work commissioned or made by a donor that is subsequently questioned by another member of the community.[8]

SPIRITUALITY AND ART: THE NEGATIVE VIEW

An oft-quoted responsum of Maimonides discusses art in liturgical spaces in the context of the need to concentrate during prayer,[9] a subject treated more fully in his code of Jewish law, the Mishneh Torah.[10] The text of the responsum paraphrases a discussion in the Babylonian Talmud, *Berakhot* 5b:

> From what do we learn that nothing should project between a worshipper and the wall (*shelo yehei davar ḥoẓeẓ beino ve-ḥa-kir)*? It is said, "and Hezekiah turned his face to the wall [and prayed to the Lord. (Is. 38:2)].

The questioner in the responsum addressed to Maimonides sought to know what constitutes a forbidden projection between worshipper and wall, and for what reason is it forbidden? He asked:

> Is a Torah curtain and objects like it included in the ban? Is the Torah curtain to which we direct ourselves during prayer, which incorporates images that do not project and these [images] are at the sides [of the curtain], or the covers placed on walls of the house to beautify them, forbidden?

---

[8] The exceptions are questions on the architecture of synagogues (e.g. Ezekiel Landau, *Responsa Noda bi-Yehuda*, vol. 1: no. 18 and vol. 2: no. 16). Probably, the relatively high cost of building acted as a deterrent to commissioning without rabbinic approval.

[9] Maimonides, *Teshuvot ha-Rambam,* II, no. 215. This translation as well as other cited in this paper are from Vivian B. Mann, *Jewish Texts on the Visual Arts* (Cambridge: Cambridge University Press, 2000).

[10] *Ibid.*, Mishneh Torah, *Hilkhot Tefillah* 4:15–18.

Maimonides answered:

> [It is not a matter of a prohibition, but] of what is preferable. Coming close to the wall allows for concentration. The Torah curtain doesn't prevent concentration, but cupboards, boxes, sacks and household utensils, or similar things confuse one's concentration. Turning toward images during prayer, even those that do not project, distracts us into looking at them and our *kavvanah,* or concentration, is lost. Our practice is to avert our eyes if we happen to pray opposite a fabric or a wall with drawings on it.

In this responsum on the disruption of *kavvanah* – the rabbinic equivalent to spirituality – Maimonides differentiated between figured textiles hung in a home for aesthetic reasons and a Torah curtain incorporating imaged textiles. One reason for his distinction between the two may have been their compositions. Presumably, the textile or mural in the home was composed entirely of images, while only the less significant portions of the curtain bore images, i.e. the sides of the composition. There is no description of its center. A review of fabrics that date to Maimonides' lifetime found in Fostat reveals that the decorated examples were woven with floral designs or fauna; they lack human images.[11] A further hint as to the appearance of the textiles hung in the home comes from a quotation of the same responsum by Joseph Karo:

Maimonides was asked:

> What constitutes [a barrier] between oneself and the wall [during prayer]; why is one restrained from praying in front of such a barrier; and is the fine wool screen that is hung on the wall of a house for beauty, which contains non-projecting images, included in this prohibition or not?[12]

---

[11] See for, example, Clive Rogers, ed., *Early Islamic Textiles* (Brighton: Rogers & Podmore, 1983), Pls. IV, VIII, IX, figs. 28–9.

[12] Joseph Karo, *Responsa Avkat Rokhel* (Jerusalem, 1959), no. 66.

In the first text, Maimonides' responsum, the questioner mentioned covers on the walls of homes placed there for aesthetic appreciation. Maimonides stated that the problem was with both walls painted with murals and imaged textiles hung in the home. Karo's text, however, cites only the "fine wool screen that is hung on the walls of a house for beauty." He could have been referring to woven textiles[13] or to knotted pile rugs; an Islamic art form with a long history whose earliest documentation comes from the Cairo Genizah.[14] Maimonides' responsum was cited by later respondents as proof that both art and ceremonial objects with images might prevent the achievement of a level of spirituality by interfering with concentration. In a famous case, Eliakim ben Joseph of Mainz (b. ca. 1170) objected to the presence of stained glass with depictions of snakes and lion in the synagogue of Cologne.[15]

> They drew images of lions and snakes in the windows, a custom which the early sages were not accustomed to [do] in all the places of their exile.... You may not say: Because permission was given to make images for the Temple, I can do so in the synagogues and study halls...even though we learn that images are permitted, except for the image of man. The forms of the sun and the moon and the dragon are prohibited because they are cult images, as is the serpent.... It is also [prohibited] because one who is praying is commanded that there should not be anything interposed between him and the wall. Moreover, when one bows during [the recitation of] his blessings, it would appear as if he bows to those images....

---

[13] Decorated textiles dated to the 12th and 13th centuries have been recovered from Muslim graves in Egypt (Paul Schulze, *Alte Stoffe* [Berlin: Richard Carl Schmidt & Co., 1920], pp. 19–21, fig. 10).

[14] Richard Ettinghausen, "The Early History, Use and Iconography of the Prayer Rug," in *Prayer Rugs*, exhibition catalogue (Washington: The Textile Museum, 1974–5), p. 15.

[15] Isaac ben Moses of Vienna, *Or Zaru'a* (Jerusalem: Aaron Freimann, 1887), *Avodah Zarah*, par. 203; Isaac Farkas Kahan, *Meḥkarim be-Sifrut ha-Teshuvot* (Jerusalem: Mossad ha-Rav Kook, 1960), pp. 352–3.

The images of lions and dragons in Romanesque stained glass had no liturgical purpose, nor did contemporary Christian writers consider them to have symbolic value.[16] They were considered decorative forms derived from the general vocabulary of stained glass workshops that furnished windows for the twenty-eight new churches built in Cologne during the twelfth century, and for the existing ecclesiastical foundations that were remodeled in the same period.[17] It is unlikely that the Jewish community with its one synagogue could have supported its own stained glass atelier. Rather, the community must have patronized an existing workshop, choosing what appeared to be its least offensive subjects. Scenes from the Hebrew Bible predominated in the first narrative glass in German churches during the first half of the twelfth century (e.g. fig. 3). Nevertheless, Rabbi Eliakim objected to their presence in the synagogue for four reasons: there was no halakhic precedent for their incorporation into a Jewish house of worship; the dragon was an idolatrous image; an observer might construe that worshippers were praying to images in the glass; and finally, the stained glass interfered with the attainment of the spiritual state of *kavvanah*.

Rabbi Eliakim's responsum on stained glass was published in a volume by his slightly younger contemporary, Isaac ben Moses of Vienna (ca. 1180-ca. 1250), who added the following short text at the end of Rabbi Eliakim's words:

> And I remember that when I…was a youth in Meissen, they used to draw birds and trees in the synagogue, and I determined that it is forbidden to do so from what we learned: "One [should not] stop his study and say, 'How beautiful is that tree!'" (Mishnah, *Avot* 3:7). Consequently, it appears to me that he who pays attention to a beautiful tree does not concentrate on his study and interrupts it. All the more so during prayer, which requires greater concentration;

[16] Creighton Gilbert, "A Statement of Aesthetic Attitude around 1230," *Hebrew University Studies in Literature and the Arts* 13:2 (1985): 140–2, 151.

[17] Werner Schafke, *Kölns romanische Kirchen: Architektur, Ausstattung, Geschichte*, 2nd ed. (Cologne: Dumont Buchverlag, 1985), p. 17.

fig. 3

one cannot concentrate as required when he looks at trees drawn on the wall.

One of the earliest extant examples of synagogue frescoes of birds and leafy branches is on the corbels of the ribs in the Pinkas Synagogue, Prague, rebuilt between 1520 and 1535.[18] The large expanses of glass windows in twentieth-century suburban synagogues, made possible by modern technology, suggests renewed attention to the talmudic prooftext cited by Rabbi Isaac, "One [should not] stop his study and say how beautiful is that tree!" Although often

[18] These frescoes were photographed by the author, but have not been published. On the history of the synagogue see Hana Volavková, *The Pinkas Synagogue*, trans. Greta Hort (Prague: Státní židovské museum v Praze, 1955).

of clear glass, modern synagogue windows may introduce the same problem of distraction as the decorations cited above.

Another, slightly later, responsum of Rabbi Meir of Rothenburg (1215–1293) discusses a ceremonial object of venerable age and precedent, but one that had been newly decorated with images. Illuminated Hebrew Bibles and festival prayer books of large size appeared in the middle of the thirteenth century, probably in imitation of contemporary Latin manuscripts and in response to the secularization of scriptoria, which previously had been located solely in monasteries and convents. These new artistic genres led to the question of their permissibility in the following question posed to Rabbi Meir of Rothenburg.[19] Rabbi Meir begins by repeating the question of his respondent:

> You asked concerning the forms of animals and birds that are in prayer books, and are surprised that I do not object to them, since it has been taught: "You shall not make yourself a sculptured image" (Ex. 20:4) even of animals and fowl, nor an engraving. One might say, you may make a two-dimensional representation. Therefore, Scripture states you shall not make any likeness: even of cattle, animals, birds, fish, grasshoppers, and even images of water animals.

He then answered,

> It seems to me they are not acting properly, since when they look at these forms, they do not concentrate [during their prayers] on their Father who is in heaven. However, there is no prohibition in this case because of [idolatry].... There is no substance at all to pictures that are made merely from paints. We are suspicious [of idolatry] only with a projecting relief seal, but not with an intaglio, and certainly not with an image that does not project and is not sunken, but is merely painted....

[19] Meir of Rothenburg, *Responsa Maharam of Rothenburg* (Jerusalem: Bet Mishmar Sefarim "Yahadut", 1986), no. 56.

These examples should suffice to show that during the Middle Ages, the presence of art in a liturgical space or embodied in a ceremonial object was deemed by some rabbis to interfere with the achievement of *kavvanah*, the spiritual state necessary for prayer. The tone of their responsa is often negative, as the rabbis sought to establish limits to the works of art used in places of worship.

The medium of the artwork situated in a place of prayer was another key consideration in rabbinic discussions of appropriateness. For example, many texts articulate a reluctance to fabricate Torah mantles, binders, and curtains from secondhand textiles. Previously worn textiles, generally fine silks, were highly valued, as few could afford these very expensive cloths when they were new. Jewish involvement in the textile trade during the Middle Ages and later is well known. The prohibition against reused textiles sometimes resulted from a ruler's acknowledgment of the religious imperative to avoid the biblical prohibition against wearing a garment composed of both linen and wool (Deut. 22:11), or because ecclesiastical textiles were used as pawns in moneylending. Rabbi Meir of Rothenburg was one of the first decisors to rule on their use:[20]

> Maharam[21] forbids using the fabric from a vestment that a priest wears when he enters the house of idolatry to fashion an article used for fulfilling a commandment.... However, the textile may be used for purposes other than the fulfillment of a commandment. [And further:] Although priestly ornaments are permitted for everyday use, it is improper to use them to adorn a prayer shawl. Such ornaments have come from a place of filth; let them return to a place of filth.

It is impossible to know how widely Rabbi Meir's restrictions were observed. There are instances of similar fabrics used both for ecclesiastical garments and Torah mantles and if there are no seams to indicate prior use, then it is impossible to say that one was made

[20] Meir of Rothenburg, *Responsa Maharam*, vol. II, *Pesakim u-Minhagim*, ed. I.Z. Kahan (Jerusalem: Mossad ha-Rav Kook, 1960), nos. 123–5.

[21] Maharam is an acronym for Rabbi Meir's name.

from a secondhand textile rather than both having been made from new fabrics.[22] But there are some clear cases of the Jewish reuse of church vestments as synagogue textiles. A specialty of one Bohemian nunnery in the eighteenth century was the embroidery of naturalistic flowers and leaves on silk in the style of earlier Dutch still-life paintings. These textiles were made into church vestments and donated to Santa Maria in Loretto, Prague, and to Austrian monasteries.[23] Two Torah mantles now in the Jewish Museum, Prague, are composed of small pieces of the nuns' embroidery, skillfully patched to preserve their original patterns (fig. 4).[24]

ART THAT CONTRIBUTES TO SPIRITUALITY

The most frequently cited passage on the need to fashion beautiful ceremonial art begins "*Zeh E-li ve-anvehu*" (This is my Lord and I will exalt Him. Ex. 15:2). The Babylonian Talmud (Sabbath 133b) comments,

> Adorn yourself before Him through the commandments. Make a beautiful *sukkah*, and a beautiful *lulav*, and a beautiful *shofar*, beautiful *ẓiẓit*, a beautiful Torah scroll in which to write His name with beautiful ink and penmanship by a trained scribe, and bind it with fine silks.

This passage is so often cited in discussions of Jewish ceremonial art as to have become a catch-all explanation for the development of new forms and decoration when, in reality, those developments depend in part on historical and art historical circumstances. The inadequacy of "This is my Lord and I will exalt Him" as the sole

---

[22] For an example of the use of the same cloth for both Jewish and Christian liturgical textiles, see D. Altshuler, ed., *The Precious Legacy: Judaica Treasures from the Czechoslovak State Collections* (New York: Summit Books, 1983), cat. no. 21, fig. 67 and Milena Zeminová, *Barokni Textilie* (Prague: Uměleckoprúmyslového muzea v Praze, 1974), nos. 62–3.

[23] Zeminová, nos. 48 and 78.

[24] Altshuler, *The Precious Legacy*, cat. no. 24, fig. 110; J. Doležal and E. Vesely, *Památky pražkého ghetta* (Prague: Olympia, 1969), no. 138.

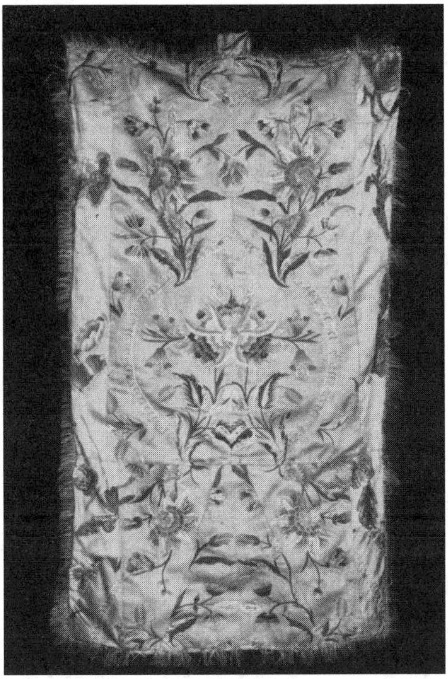

fig. 4

stimulus for the creation of Judaica may be deduced from an analysis of the artistic categories to which the cited ceremonial objects belong. The *shofar* (ram's horn), the *lulav*, and the silk binder or mantle for the Torah scroll are all preexisting objects that are modified or finished (in the case of the *shofar* and the coverings) or arranged as a compound object (in the case of the *lulav*). In art historical parlance, they are "found objects," typologically the same the same as similar works created of mundane objects in the oeuvres of Marcel Duchamp and Picasso. The writing of a Torah scroll is subject to such precise rules as to allow little room for creativity, except in the excellence of the script. Never decorated, the Torah scroll is above all a text, rather than a work of art. We are left to consider the *sukkah* and *ẓiẓit*. The *sukkah* is a structure used only eight days of the year as a site for ceremonial meals, study, entertaining, and sleeping during the holiday of Tabernacles. Even when its constituent building components remain in a fixed arrangement, the decoration of the *sukkah* may vary from year to year as old wall hangings wear out and new ones are acquired. The decorated *sukkah* could be considered the setting for what is termed today "performance art," a temporary environment enlivened by the activities that take place within.

The only object cited above that might qualify as art in the sense of a work created by a trained artist or artisan is the *ẓiẓit*, a term that refers either to the knotted fringes at the corner of a rectangular garment, or to a garment with such fringes. Its wearing is mandated in the Bible (Deut. 22: 12). A garment with fringes may vary in material or color according to the traditions of the Jewish community in which it was made or the whim of its wearer, although the manner of knotting the fringes is prescribed by Jewish law. If the cloth to which the fringes are attached is handwoven or embroidered, the garment could qualify as a work of art (e.g. fig. 5). No other type of art is mentioned in the passage "*Zeh E-li ve-anvehu,*" despite the fact that the rabbis of the Talmud must have been familiar with art created for the Tabernacle and the Temple from their description in biblical texts. To gain another view of a positive relationship between art and spirituality in Judaism, one must turn to later texts, to the responsa.

A key shift in the halakhic attitude toward decoration in the synagogue appears in the responsum of Joseph Karo cited above, which was written before his death in 1575:[25]

> One cannot argue from Maimonides' words... [that one should not hang a Torah curtain with figures on it], because he had said that it is not proper that figured textiles should create a barrier between one and the wall. It is the custom throughout the Diaspora to hang figured and embroidered Torah curtains, and no one has been concerned about diminished concentration on prayer as a result. Honoring the Torah [by placing an attractive curtain on the ark] is given precedence, and one praying before such a curtain can avert his eyes in order not to gaze at the figures. In any case, people do not concentrate properly on their prayers today....

[25] See above, n. 12.

fig. 5

The earliest extant Torah curtains with complex compositions and iconography date from Joseph Karo's lifetime. One is a knotted pile carpet created by an Egyptian artist working either in Egypt or Padua ca. 1550, and the other is an embroidered ark curtain made by Solomon Perlsticker and his wife in Prague in 1547 and refurbished by their son and daughter-in-law in 1592.[26] The appearance of complex compositions and iconographical elements on these Torah curtains contrasts to the unembellished appearance of curtains depicted in medieval Hebrew manuscripts.[27] This development is probably due to the spread of printed books with their decorated titles pages and illustrations. Karo rejected the opinion that decorated curtains in-

[26] The State Jewish Museum in Prague, *Synagogical Textiles* (Prague: State Jewish Museum, 1984), p. 18.

[27] For example, see Annette Weber, "Ark and Curtain: Monuments for a Jewish Nation in Exile," *Jewish Art* 23–4 (1997/1998): 92, figs. 3 and 5.

terfered with concentration on prayer, and instead viewed them as contributing to the honor of the Torah and as enhancing the spiritual atmosphere of the synagogue.

A positive statement on the role of media in contributing to the spiritual atmosphere of the synagogue appears in a responsum authored by the Ashkenazi rabbi, Yair Ḥayyim Bacharach (1638–1672):[28]

> QUESTION: A congregation had a silver lamp, called a *lampe*, which hung before the Torah ark. It was stolen, and the congregation is unable to gather sufficient donations to purchase another silver lamp. Some of the congregants wish to replace the stolen lamp with a brass one, which is called *mess[ing]*, while others wish to prevent this, saying that hanging a brass lamp in the synagogue [similar to those] found in homes infringes on the "dignity" of the community.
>
> ANSWER: If the lamp is large and has many nozzles [for wicks] and its brass is gilt so that it is an unusually attractive type found only in the homes of the nobility and the extremely wealthy, then clearly the law sides with the donors.... If it is a more modest lamp of the type found in homes, it still seems appropriate.... When [the congregants] become wealthier, they can replace the brass lamp with a silver one, as was recorded in regard to the menorah in the Temple....

On the other hand, an individual who wishes to donate an expensive lamp requires the congregation's consent, as does a society within the city [offering a donation].... The community should, therefore, grant permission for a lamp to be donated to the synagogue only if it is proper and respectable, and "fit to honor the synagogue...."

[28] Yair Ḥayyim Bacharach, *Ḥavvot Ya'ir* (Frankfurt am Main: Johannes Wust, 1699), no. 68.

> It seems to me, however, that in the case of a synagogue menorah owned by the congregation whose branches are broken, or of a synagogue lamp with similar damage that would be demeaning for a homeowner to keep, then it is a dishonor for the congregation [to retain such lamps].

Rabbi Bacharach made three important points related to the aesthetics of the synagogue: 1) *prima facie*, a more expensive material like silver is preferable; 2) the composition and the condition of the ceremonial object are important factors in judging whether or not a work is "fit to honor the synagogue," i.e. to contribute to the spiritual atmosphere of the synagogue; 3) Judaica for the synagogue must meet the community's aesthetic standards. That a community could hold commonly accepted standards of aesthetics is also an assumption underlying a sixteenth-century decision by Rabbi David ibn abi Zimra of Cairo concerning the distribution of ceremonial objects between an established congregation and a breakaway group.[29] After reviewing various criteria that might have been applicable to dividing the art, he stated:

> In the present case, however, none of these factors [regarding the donation of the works] is present.... Therefore, the donations of ceremonial objects were made with the implicit consent of the whole congregation, [and] because of that, it seems to me that the two congregations should use ritual objects on alternating weeks. If the works may be appropriately divided, for example, if there are two Torah crowns and two pairs of finials, each congregation should use one. *If one work is more beautiful than the other, they should be shared in alternating use.*[30]

There are also many references in rabbinic literature to beauty

---

[29] David ibn abi Zimra, *Shu"t ha-Radbaz*, pt. 8 (Warsaw: Aaron Walden, 1882), no. 170.

[30] Italics mine.

as the imperative factor in the creation of ceremonial objects, as in this passage from Maimonides' Mishneh Torah:[31]

> One acts towards a kosher Torah scroll with additional holiness and great honor. [And after enumerating all the objects necessary for the reading of the Torah he concludes] and the silver and gold finials, and the like, *that are made for the beauty of the Torah scroll*, are instruments of holiness.

CONCLUSION

Figurative art in the home could interfere with spirituality, since art attracts attention by virtue of what David Freedberg has termed "The Power of Images."[32] It is, therefore, better to pray at home opposite a blank wall. Art in the synagogue, in a public place, may also distract the worshipper if it appears in an inappropriate object like the cantor's prayer book, or in inappropriate forms or media. Nevertheless, the rabbis saw that art could contribute to spirituality. This is apparent in the citations of beauty as an objective halakhic criterion, and in the many references to works made solely for the sake of beauty. Rabbinic literature reflects what Umberto Eco has written about the Middle Ages: "...intelligible beauty was in the medieval experience a moral and psychological *reality*."[33]

The most explicit passage on the power of art to inspire spirituality is in Profiat Duran's *Ma'aseh Efod*:[34]

> Study should always be in beautiful books, pleasant for their beauty and the splendor of their scripts and parchments, with

[31] Maimonides, Mishneh Torah, *Hilkhot Sefer Torah*, 10:4. (Italics mine.)
[32] David Freedberg, *The Power of Images: Studies in the History and Theories of Response* (Chicago and London: University of Chicago Press, 1991).
[33] Umberto Eco, *Art and Beauty in the Middle Ages* (New Haven and London: Yale University Press, 1986), p. 5.
[34] Profiat Duran, *Sefer Ma'aseh Efod* (Vienna: Yomtov Friedlander and Jacob Hakohen, 1891), p. 19. In Spain, Bibles were referred to as a *mikdash me'at* or *mikdashiah*, a lesser sanctuary, in imitation of the Temple in Jerusalem referred to in Hebrew as the *beit ha-mikdash*.

elegant ornament and covers. And the places for study would be desirable; the study halls beautifully built so that people's love and desire for study will increase. Memory will also improve since contemplation and study occur amidst beautifully developed forms and beautiful drawings, with the result that the soul will expand and be encouraged and strengthen its powers.... It is also obligatory and appropriate to enhance the books of God and to direct oneself to their beauty, splendor, and loveliness. Just as God wished to adorn the place of His Sanctuary with gold, silver, and precious stones, so is this appropriate in His holy books, especially for the book that is "His Sanctuary [the Bible]."

Figures

1. Hanukkah Lamp, Lyons, twelfth century, stone (Paris, Klagsbald Collection).
2. Torah Shield, Johann Michael Schüler, Frankfurt-am-Main, ca. 1720, silver (New York, The Jewish Museum, Gift of Dr. Harry G. Friedman, F740).
3. Moses and the Burning Bush with a self-portrait of Gerlachus, the artist, Middle Rhine, ca. 1150–1160, stained glass (after *Meisterwerke mittelalterlicher Glasmalerei*, fig. 4).
4. Torah Mantle, Prague, eighteenth century, silk: embroidered with silk and metallic threads (Prague, židovské Muzeum, 32.105).
5. *Ẓiẓit*, Gallipoli, nineteenth century, silk *batiste*: embroidered with silver thread washed with gold; wool fringes (New York, Yeshiva University Museum, Gift of Mr. and Mrs. Naḥman Yoḥai, 77.157).

Section five

Spirituality in Education

8

Teaching Spirituality in Day Schools and Yeshiva High Schools

Moshe Sokolow

The man of faith is 'insanely' committed to and 'madly' in love with God.

The Rav[1]

BACKGROUND AND OUTLINE

This paper will deal with the form that curriculum and instruction for spirituality may take. For this purpose, I have adopted the Orthodox Forum's definition of spirituality as a blend of, and balance between, a relationship with God and halakhic observance.

I shall first raise six points about the educational process in general and then relate them, individually, to spirituality. In

[1] Joseph B. Soloveitchik: *The Lonely Man of Faith*, (Northdale, NJ: Jason Aronson, 1997), pp. 61–2.

conclusion, I will present a model lesson, which will illustrate some of the proposed theoretical points.

1. Mission and Vision
2. Commonplaces and Eccentricities of the Curriculum
3. Tuition: The Virtues, Vices, & Vicissitudes of Teaching
4. תכונות הנפש: Soul-based Learning: Spiritual Intelligence and the Learner
5. Service Learning: Spirituality in the "Flesh"
6. Spirituality and Community
7. A Sample Lesson

PROLOGUE

The universal maxim, "If it ain't broke, don't fix it," has an obverse: "If everyone is fixing it, it must be broke." What is "broke" in the contemporary Jewish education of the spirit? Is the problem that we are teaching spirituality improperly, insufficiently, or that we aren't teaching it at all? Is the solution, then, more spirituality, better spirituality, or just any spirituality?

We have a lot to be grateful for in contemporary Jewish education. New day schools are opening and the existing ones keep growing. Many of our classrooms are cyber-ready (and some of our teachers, too), and any day now Bar Ilan University will release a CD-ROM making the totality of Torah accessible from every personal computer. Most teachers earn a living wage, receive life insurance and health benefits, and are eligible for pension programs. Administrators, increasingly, earn six-figure salaries. Tuition is high by nearly any standard (Dalton and Choate are still more expensive), but such enterprising projects as George Hanus's day school scholarship endowment and the experience of the SAMIS Foundation in Seattle (subsidizing day school tuition) offer a promise of relief just over the horizon.

Our children now regularly supplement their elementary and secondary education with a year – or even two – in Israel. They attend prestigious colleges and universities and are accepted to the leading graduate and professional schools. In ever-increasing numbers, they are joining the ranks of business as both financial technicians and entrepreneurs with a significant concomitant increase in their contributions – of both human and financial resources – to charitable Jewish institutions and causes.

And could a litany of our accomplishments be complete without reference to our many acts of personal and communal ḥesed? We may be underrepresented in the kiruv movement, worldwide, but we are the rov minyan and rov binyan of such noteworthy enterprises as Yachad and Camp HASC.

And what of politics? We may have lost the eminence we once had in the Conference of Presidents, but have we not become a force to be reckoned with, a potential spoiler, in Israeli and Middle Eastern politics? Are our voices not heard, even solicited, by the movers and shakers on the domestic scene? Was not Senator Lieberman a voice – our voice – of conscience crying out in a wilderness of crass immorality and lewdness?

*

Why, in the face of these accomplishments, is there such breast-beating over spirituality? It is because we are educating a generation of children who lack the time-honored traditional trappings of spiritual values or concern.

Disgruntled elementary school students bemoan their fate as their parents plan yet *another* trip to Israel for the summer. Middle school students compete over Bar and Bat Miẓvah celebrations for which the term lavish is ineffectual. Ambivalence over parental authority, ever an outward hallmark of adolescence, has deteriorated into frequent disregard for all heteronomous authority whether parental, pedagogic, or rabbinic. Parents who suffer their children's disobedience toward themselves, and sometimes even abet their disobedience towards others – e.g. teachers, now look up in abject surprise when those children turn out to have no fear of God.

Self-centeredness, marked by insensitivity towards the needs and feelings of others, is on constant display in school, at home and in the public thoroughfare. And, sad to say, the latent culture of alcohol and drugs has pierced the veil of communal denial and is putting "*talmidim* at risk" center stage.

Finally, if I may be permitted a modicum of universalism in an otherwise highly particularistic presentation: What are the students and graduates of our day schools contributing towards eradicating the evils of slavery, poverty, war, racism, sexism, inequality, and hunger that regularly plague our planet – inhabited, as it happens to be, by creatures created in a *ẓelem E-lohim* fundamentally no different from our own? And if they do not actively search for a cure for these ills, do they, at least, bemoan them?

Paradoxically, failure to do so can be attributed to the kind of education we most often take for granted and tend to regard as exemplary, rather than unwholesome.

> This refusal to take responsibility and hence to grieve and mourn for the pain we as a community have inflicted represents … the limitations of an education grounded primarily in critical rationality, study, and the exchange and analysis of information.[2]

As enunciated by Rav Kalonymus Kalman Shapira, the main principle of ḥasidic teaching is:

> …that a person must not consider it sufficient that he has firmly placed his intellect into the service of God. A connection made with the intellect alone is not a lasting connection. A person can subject his whole intellect to spiritual searching and can come to know with complete clarity of mind that he must serve only God in his every single thought, word, or action. And yet his heart and his whole body may still be very far away from this reality.[3]

As eager as we are to pull onto and speed ahead on the

[2] David E. Purpel, "Moral Outrage and Education," in *Education, Information, and Transformation,* ed. Jeffrey Kane (Upper Saddle River, NJ: Prentice Hall, 1999), p. 69.

[3] Kalonymus Shapira, *A Student's Obligation,* trans. Micha Odenheimer (Northvale, NJ: Jason Aronson, 1991), p. 17.

information superhighway; as much as we delight in extolling the virtue of the "computer smarts" our children obtain; as convinced as we are that the key to their professional and economic success lies in technological sophistication, there is a danger that we are shortchanging them spiritually in the process.

> Although new technologies offer previously unimagined power and information, they may also deflect our consideration of the larger questions of who we are, what we are doing, and why.... The argument does not follow that teaching children to meet the requirements of the technological future in any way serves their educational interests. They might be far better served, practically and soulfully, by teaching them to approach the world with wonder and a sense of reverence, even though such dispositions may seem cognitively superfluous....[4]

Or, as Abraham Joshua Heschel wrote:

> Mankind will not perish from want of information, but only for want of appreciation.[5]

The problem seems to be that people who recognize the importance of the mind, and even of the body, do not grant the same recognition to the spirit. Howard Gardner, explorer of Multiple Intelligences, ruefully acknowledges his own shortcomings in this regard, stating:

> Many people, including me, do not grant the same ontological status to the transcendent or the spiritual as we do, say, to the mathematical or the musical... The vast majority of scholars in the cognitive and biological sciences turn away from ques-

[4] Kane, p. 208.

[5] Abraham Joshua Heschel, *God in Search of Man* (New York: Harper and Row, 1955), p. 46.

tions of a spiritual nature, hence consigning this realm chiefly to the true believers and to the quacks.[6]

Being, as we believe we are, true believers, who yet value the "cognitive and biological sciences," we are obliged to challenge Gardner's assertion. This we shall do in Part Two, as we explore the "cognitive" and "affective" dimensions of the curriculum. First, however, a word about the role that spirituality assumes – or fails to assume – in our day schools' visions.

PART ONE: THE "VISION" THING

A school's vision (alternatively, its philosophy, mission, or goal statement) is its reply to the perennial questions of מאין באת ולאן אתה הולך (whence and whither)? It reflects a school's educational philosophy and indicates what courses of study, programs, and activities it plans to conduct in order to educate its students. Among the issues addressed in such statements are:

- What was the school designed to do?
- Is there a distinct body of knowledge that all students must acquire in order to be considered culturally literate?
- Are children blank slates to be written upon, lumps of clay to be molded, wild animals to be tamed, or unique spirits to be nurtured?
- How do you define the role of teachers: subject matter experts, facilitators of learning, disciplinarians, pseudo-parents, part-time counselors, educational leaders or followers of state mandates?
- Who owns schools? Who is accountable to whom and for what? Do schools have "clients?" Are students and their parents the clients, are the students the products of schools, or are the stu-

[6] Gardner in Kane, p. 118. In *Frames of Mind: The Theory of Multiple Intelligences* (New York: Basic Books, 1983), Gardner substantially changed the concept of intelligence, expanding it to include diverse abilities. Initially he spoke of seven intelligences: verbal-linguistic, logical-mathematical, spatial, bodily-kinesthetic, musical, interpersonal and intrapersonal. He has since added two others: naturalistic and spiritual.

dents workers who are being managed by teachers to produce knowledge?[7]

I have examined several mission statements in search of the role that spirituality plays in day school education. While laying no claim to comprehensiveness (I merely visited some school web sites), I found the verbatim term "spiritual" in only one school's philosophy (Hebrew Academy of the Five Towns and Rockaway). It reads as follows:

> It is the role of both the teacher and parent to cooperate, to guide, and assist in the development of the whole child, academically, intellectually, emotionally, spiritually, and socially.

The school defines the spiritual component in terms of the following objectives:

> To develop sound moral principles and enthusiasm within the context of an Orthodox Jewish life; to motivate our students
> - to learn and love Torah
> - to observe rituals and *miẓvot*
> - to be charitable and respectful

On the other hand, another school (Netivot HaTorah, Toronto), equally "committed to addressing the needs of the whole child," itemizes those needs as: "social, emotional, physical, and intellectual," clearly, if inadvertently, omitting the spiritual.

A second school (Maayanot Yeshiva High School for Girls, Teaneck, New Jersey), while not actually using the "S" word, cites as its first objective:

---

[7] Frank Siccone, *The Power to Lead* (Boston: Allyn and Bacon, 1997), p. 2. On the ostensible distinction between "mission," "vision," and "goal" statements, see John Hoyle, et. al., *Skills for Successful 21st Century School Leaders* (Arlington, VA: American Association of School Administrators, 1998), pp. 2, 38.

To foster the development of a Torah personality
- whose life decisions are guided by the values and traditions of a halakhically committed community
- who strives to build a personal relationship with God through fulfillment of miẓvot, study, and reflection
- who is committed to acting with integrity, compassion, and respect in her relationships with people
- whose general conduct is informed by *ahavat Hashem* and *yirat shamayim*

Several additional schools utilize what may be called "euphemisms" for spirituality, such as:

- an appreciation of the wonder of the world He created (Torah Academy of Bergen County, Teaneck, New Jersey);
- to achieve the love of God and humankind and be imbued with the joy found in these relationships (Fuchs Bet Sefer Mizrachi, Cleveland, Ohio);
- promote *ahavat Hashem*....and allegiance to halakha (Kushner Yeshiva High School, Livingston, New Jersey).

If yeshiva day schools indeed aspire to inspire their students – even if only by inference – how do they prepare appropriate courses of study for that objective? That is the function of curriculum development.

PART TWO: THE CURRICULUM OF SPIRITUALITY: COGNITION AND AFFECT

> And if you shall ask, How shall the fear of God bring a person to this high level of achieving eternal life – after all it seems more worthy that intellectual comprehension will do this – Solomon in Ecclesiastes has already explained this and said that only fear of God is the cause of immortality....
>
> R. Yosef Albo: *Sefer ha-Ikkarim* 3:7

It has been customary, if not *de rigeur*, these past forty plus years to address educational concerns on two fronts: the "cognitive" and the "affective." The former designates what the student is supposed to know, the latter, what the students is supposed to become. To the extent that we are well served by these designations and distinctions (as they create, for example, a pedagogical *lingua franca*), we would be advised to delineate our quest for an education of the spirit in these common terms. In the specific case of spirituality, the terminological vocabulary of the "affect" is equal to the task. The following taxonomy of affective goals for *limudei kodesh* cites behaviors and attitudes that are consistent with the definitions of spirituality that are implicit in such day school mission statements as we perused at the end of Part One.

The student will:

1.31 believe in the Creator of the universe and its Conductor, Who selected the nation of Israel, gave them His Torah, selected the land of Israel and gave it to His nation.

1.32 wish to order his lifestyle according to the Torah

1.33 aspire to worship God wholeheartedly

1.331 observe *miẓvot* regularly

1.332 observe *miẓvot* elegantly

1.333 be prepared, at all times, to correct his behavior and examine his ideas, in light of the Torah

1.334 attempt to achieve the fear and love of God, and the love of all His creatures, and the love of Israel

1.34 wish to engage in Torah study regularly

1.35 attempt to reveal the Torah's outlook on social and natural phenomena, and relate to them according to that outlook

1.36 attempt to fulfill his obligations in defense of the State, and in the preservation of its existence and complexion in the spirit of the Torah.[8]

---

[8] Ministry of Education of The State of Israel, The National-Religious Stream, *The Affective Goals of Teaching Bible* (undated; my translation).

It is in the realm of the "cognitive," however, that enumerating the goals of spirituality falters. Such taxonomical terms as: knowledge, comprehension, application, analysis, synthesis, and evaluation are seemingly inimical to a concept that comes with no specific set of subject-matter baggage. It is possible, indeed, that spirituality is only behavioral-attitudinal and has no cognitive dimension. So, it appears, is the opinion of Howard Gardner who, in discussing a possible "spiritual intelligence," defines it as:

> Primarily emotional or affective in character…and hence, again, ruled as beyond the confines of a cognitive investigation.[9]

*

I would like to propose that there *is* a cognitive side to spirituality. Moreover, I would argue that it is precisely this cognitive aspect that will allow us, subsequently, to map a spiritual curriculum and locate its coordinates among the normative cognitive goals of Jewish and general studies disciplines. The validation of this proposal requires the prior stipulation of two premises.

First we will postulate that the relationship to the divine that we wish to cultivate in man is manifest in his exercise of free will to transform his fate into his destiny.

> "היכולת לצאת מתחומי מגבלות הקיום הנתונות לו, ולבחור בנתיבים אחרים."[10]

Second, we will postulate that this relationship to the divine is informed by the application of reason and intelligence to Torah and *halakhah*.

> "כי לא נתנה התורה לאשר אין דעת בו. והמלאך בין אדם ובין אלהיו הוא שכלו."[11]

---

[9] Gardner in Kane, p. 121.

[10] Adin Steinzaltz, pp. 87–88., י"ג עלי השושנה (ירושלים, תשנ"ח)

[11] Abraham Ibn Ezra ר' אברהם אבן עזרא, הקדמה לפירוש התורה, הדרך השלישית

These postulates accepted, education for spirituality means developing the capacity for informed choice. [In the Sample Lesson, we will illustrate this capacity by means of *Parshanut ha-Mikra*.]

Curriculum Development: Method and Meaning

Joseph Schwab, late professor of education at the University of Chicago, proposed a model of curriculum development based upon the recognition of five "commonplaces" – fixtures that control and mediate the formal educational enterprise. They are: the learner, the teacher, the subject matter, the milieu, and curriculum making.[12] The curricular specialist, who negotiates the needs and desires of each constituency and prevents any single commonplace from monopolizing the discussion and the development, conducts the deliberations.

In day-school terms, a deliberation over a curriculum for spirituality would involve:

- An educational psychologist (a.k.a. a learning specialist), representing the student, to comment on modalities of learning;
- A master teacher, to advise on available instructional methods;
- A member of the school's board of education, to advocate for parental and communal interests;
- A participant in this Forum, to provide enlightenment and direction on the textual and thematic substance of spirituality.

While Schwab's construct informs the essence of curriculum deliberation, Ralph Tyler,[13] guides its practical operation. Tyler would have us chart, sequentially, our aims or objectives, our means of implementation and, finally, the process of assessment by which we can evaluate our success. An idiosyncratically Orthodox problem with Tyler's model, however, is our penchant to define our objectives

---

[12] Joseph Schwab, *Science, Curriculum and Liberal Education* (Chicago, 1978), p. 365

[13] Ralph Tyler, *Basic Principles of Curriculum and Instruction* (Chicago: University of Chicago Press, 1949).

in textual terms, rather than the standard "cognitive" and "affective" goals of Bloom's "Taxonomy." Ask a fourth-grade day school teacher for his curriculum and he invariably answers: "ספר שמות" and "ספר יהושע".

The Paideia Proposal

The *Paideia* group, headed by Mortimer Adler, creator and editor-in-chief of the *Encyclopedia Britannica*, advanced an alternative model of curriculum development. Advocating a revamping of public education, the group devised its own curricular structure – one intrinsically more compatible with traditional day-school education. According to the *Paideia* model, one stipulates the "organized knowledge" to be acquired, the "intellectual skills" of acquisition and analysis, and the "enlarged understanding of ideas and values" to be derived from the application of those skills to that body of knowledge.[14]

Applying the *Paideia* corollary to Schwab, a curriculum deliberation on education for spirituality within day schools would encourage the commonplaces (as delineated just above) to direct their remarks to:

- Which subject matter already part of the traditional curriculum offers the greatest potential for spiritual development?
- Which learning skills have to be cultivated and refined to make that subject matter accessible and malleable?
- What are the spiritual values that the students should discover, deliberate and internalize in the course of their encounter with these texts and themes?

The actual deliberations – led by the experienced curriculum designer – and the ongoing follow-up – led by the head of school and master teachers – will provide the optimal situation in which the desirable values of spirituality can be infused into the traditional curriculum.

---

[14] Mortimer Adler: *The Paideia Proposal: An Educational Manifesto* (New York: Macmillan, 1982).

PART THREE: TUITION; THE VIRTUES, VICES, AND VICISSITUDES OF TEACHING

The crucible in which every curriculum is tested is the classroom and the watchman who can open or seal the portals of education before every change and innovation is the teacher. Masterful teaching has rescued many a flawed curriculum from disaster, and poor pedagogy has consigned more than one great idea to oblivion.

What qualifies teaching as adequate, and what distinguishes teaching as great? The answer – cast in terms borrowed from last year's Forum on the "Brisker" method – is that teaching melds the גברא and the חפצא, the persona and the subject matter. Neither consummate pedagogy nor academic expertise is complete without the other (although opinions differ sharply on which, alone, is preferable).

Teacher training tries to accommodate both these virtues by combining formal education in the subject matter area with training and practice in pedagogy and methodology. In traditional disciplines, the prescription is readily filled. A B.A. in English, plus credits in education or certification from a teachers' college will equal a licensed English teacher. Continuing teacher education (or in-service training) will contribute to the teacher's remaining current in the field and aware of changing or developing standards of assessment and qualification.

Beyond Adequacy

A licensed English teacher need not be a published novelist, need never have written an original short story, nor composed original verse. A licensed English teacher need not even speak English as a mother tongue. A licensed English teacher certainly need not embody any – let alone all – of the qualities and characteristics esteemed in English literature. Hardened cynics, even misanthropes, can teach romantic verse (albeit, perhaps, not well).

On the other hand, identification with one's subject matter is one way of cutting the exceptional teachers from the pack. A teacher of French who has never visited France, a teacher of music who attends no concerts, a teacher of Talmud who has no personal סדר

קבוע, may be adequate. A civics teacher who volunteers in an election campaign, an art teacher who frequents galleries, and a תנ"ך teacher who subscribes to *B.A.R.* (and *Megadim*, of course), have the potential for mastery. Their personal interest in the subjects they teach and their passion for their disciplines communicate themselves to their students, who are charged and inspired by their example.

Training to Teach Spirituality

What are the personal and professional prerequisites for the adequate teaching of spirituality (or is "adequate spirituality" an oxymoron)? Can one train to be a teacher of spirituality?

The theory of teacher training best suited for the preparation of teachers of spirituality is that of Lee Shulman, president of the Carnegie Foundation for the Advancement of Teaching.[15] Rather than undertaking two independent (consecutive or simultaneous) preparations, one each in subject matter and pedagogy, he has advocated a synthesis of the two, which he has called: "Pedagogic Content Knowledge." In this construct, aspiring teachers study aspects of the disciplines they plan to teach that have been selected because they allow for a presentation and discussion that exemplify and facilitate their classroom implementation.

In other words, we have to teach teachers as we want them to teach their students. If our ultimate goal is to have students derive spiritual values through their analysis of classical texts, then we have to insure that their teachers are capable both of analyzing those texts and extrapolating those values as well as presenting that analysis in a pedagogically proven format likely to produce comparable results in their students.

A Dialogue between Teacher Trainers

The key to successful training and successful teaching is reflection. The training of our teachers of spirituality (alternatively: our teachers of Jewish and general studies who will inculcate spiritual values in

15 See, inter, alia., Lee Shulman, "Knowledge and Teaching: Foundations of the New Reform," *Harvard Educational Review* 57:1 (February, 1987).

their students) will include their participation in a dialogue on the balance we seek to achieve between the spiritual experience and halakhic observance.

To facilitate this dialogue, we shall expose them to several of the operative definitions we have encountered among those modern and contemporary writers who have addressed the relationship between spirituality and *halakhah*: Aryeh Kaplan, Yeshayahu Leibowitz, Abraham Joshua Heschel and Joseph Soloveitchik. To provide an educational *nafka-minah*, we shall relate their comments to the use of *taamei ha-mizvot* as a pedagogical foil for the study and stimulus of *halakhah* based upon a definitive pedagogical statement on this issue by Moshe Ahrend.

Aryeh Kaplan:

> The main benefit of the commandments is mainly in the realm of the spiritual. Observance of the commandments is ultimately the means through which a person brings himself close to God. As such, they are like nourishment to the soul. They strengthen man's soul, and at the same time, fortify him spiritually.[16]

EDUCATIONAL IMPLICATIONS/APPLICATIONS

Mizvot can become spiritually fortifying only as automatic responses, not as considered responses. Discussions of *taamei ha-mizvot*, then, should either be eliminated or, at least, postponed until their performance is ingrained to the point of habit.

After the level of spiritual fortification is reached, students can be instructed in the rationales of *mizvot* (Kaplan: "a great many mundane benefits") for the purpose of either reinforcement or as a *kiruv* tool to broach *mizvot* to those who are not on a comparable spiritual level.

---

[16] Aryeh Kaplan, *Love and the Commandments* (1973), 11.

Yeshayahu Leibowitz:

> The first mark of the religion of *halakhah* is its realism. It perceives man as he is in reality and confronts him with this reality – with the actual conditions of his existence rather than the "vision" of another existence.... It precludes the possibility of man shirking his duties by entertaining illusions of attaining a higher level of being.... Halakhic religion has no flair for the episodic excursions from the routine of everyday life, for the evanescent moments of solemnity.... [T]he *miẓvot* require observance out of a sense of duty and discipline, not ecstatic enthusiasm or fervor, which may embellish one's life but do not tell how to conduct it.[17]

EDUCATIONAL IMPLICATIONS/APPLICATIONS

While Kaplan sees *miẓvot* in the service of spirituality, Leibowitz sees them as divine dictates whose main – if not exclusive – purpose lies in their performance. Although they disagree on whether *miẓvot* lie above or below the spiritual horizon (Leibowitz: "The fundamental and endearing elements of human existence are in life's prose, not in its poetry"), Leibowitz would agree to the postponement or elimination of discussions on *taamei ha-miẓvot* because faith is a value decision and cannot be reached as a logical conclusion.

Abraham Joshua Heschel:

> It is not only important what a person does; it is *equally* and even more important what a person *is*. Spiritually speaking, what he does is a minimum of what he is. Deeds are outpourings, they are not the essence of the self. Deeds reflect or refine but they remain functions. They are not the substance of the inner life. Hence it is the inner life that is the problem for us, Jewish educators, and particularly the inner life of the Jewish

---

[17] Yeshayahu Leibowitz, *Judaism, Human Values and the Jewish State* (Cambridge, MA: Harvard University Press, 1992), pp. 12–3.

> child. On the other hand, we must never forget that in Judaism we answer God's will in deeds. God asks for the heart, but the heart is often a lonely voice in the market place of living, oppressed with uncertainty in its own twilight. God asks for faith and the heart is not sure of its faith. It is good, therefore, that there is a dawn of decision for the night of the heart, deeds to objectify faith, definite forms to verify belief.[18]

EDUCATIONAL IMPLICATIONS/APPLICATIONS

Just as a book cannot be told from its cover, a student's spirituality cannot be judged entirely by his performance of *mizvot.* On the other hand, a claim to spirituality must rest on a minimum standard of observance. In Heschel's scheme, *taamei ha-mizvot* have the status of *le-khathilah* since they serve as a fulcrum for the translation of spiritual desire into objective religious reality.

Joseph B. Soloveitchik:

> Most of all I learned [from my mother] that Judaism expresses itself not only in formal compliance with the law but also in a living experience. She taught me that there is a flavor, a scent, warmth to *mizvot.* I learned from her the most important thing in life – to feel the presence of the Almighty and the gentle pressure of His hand resting on my frail shoulders. Without her teachings, which quite often were transmitted to me in silence, I would have grown up a soulless being, dry and insensitive.[19]

EDUCATIONAL IMPLICATIONS/APPLICATIONS

Taamei ha-mizvot, to the Rav, seek to apprise us and to repeatedly remind us, that behind every commandment is a benign commander whose instructions are intended to draw us nearer to Him and

---

[18] Abraham Joshua Heschel: *The Insecurity of Freedom* (New York: Jewish Publication Society, 1966), p. 232.

[19] Joseph B. Soloveitchik, "A Tribute to the Rebbetzin of Talne," *Tradition* 17:2 (1978), 76–7.

cement our relationship. The pedagogical conclusion to draw from the Rav's reminiscence is the importance of teachers as role models – a point to which we shall next pay minute attention.

Moshe Ahrend:

> Above all else it is vital that we project the *miẓvot* of the Torah as *miẓvot* of God and emphasize their legal and heteronomic character. They are neither rituals nor customs nor traditions; they are laws that the Supreme Legislator has imposed upon us, commanded us to observe, and by which He has sanctified us. Our obligation towards them does not depend either upon our consent or our comprehension, and we are commanded to fulfil them, not to analyze or internalize them. Moreover, even when we "comprehend" a *miẓvah*, its intentions and reasons, or we believe we comprehend it, this comprehension has no "legal" status and we are forbidden to draw halakhic conclusions from what appears to us to be the source or objective of a *miẓvah*....
>
> *Miẓvot* are a symmetrical mesh of transcendent instructions that come to weave a tapestry of *kedushah*, which has the capacity to elevate man precisely at the time when he is caught in the maelstrom of profane life and subjected to desires and passions that threaten to cause him to deteriorate and be demolished.[20]

In advocating restraint in the use of *taamei ha-miẓvot*, Ahrend cautions us not to exaggerate the importance of reason as though there actually were a sufficient answer to each and every question our students might pose. If everything were susceptible to rational analysis, he asks, what would be the purview of faith? His advice:

---

[20] Moshe Ahrend, *"Taamei ha-Miẓvot*: Their Essence and their Place in Religious Education," *Itturim* (Jerusalem: 1986): 81–3 (my translation). Reprinted in Ahrend, *Ḥinukh Yehudi be-Ḥevrah Petuḥah* (Ramat Gan: Bar Ilan University Press, 1995).

make *mizvot* "reasonable" by means of *Midrash* and *Aggadah*, which conform to the students' levels of understanding, rather than philosophy, which often just increases their perplexity.

The Teacher as Role Model

Teaching for spirituality imposes certain prerequisites on both personality and pedagogy. Here is what Heschel advocated:

> What we need more than anything else is not *textbooks* but *textpeople*. It is the personality of the teacher which is the text that the pupils read; the text that they will never forget. The modern teacher, while not wearing a snowy beard, is a link in the chain of a tradition. He is the intermediary between the past and the present as well. Yet he is also the creator of the future of our people. He must teach the pupils to evaluate the past in order to clarify their future.[21]

The Rav put it this way when describing one of the dominant spiritual influences in his life – his *melamed*:

> However, besides teaching the *yeled zekunim* discipline, the *av zaken* teaches him something else – the romance of *yahadut*. He teaches the child how to experience and feel *yahadut*. *Yahadut* is not only discipline. Yes, we start with that, to discipline the child on all levels, on the physical level, on the social level, on the emotional level, and on the intellectual level. Above all, he teaches the child how to experience *yahadut*, how to feel *yahadut*. That is what my *melamed* taught me.[22]

The point has not been lost on contemporary educators either:

---

[21] Heschel, *Insecurity*, p. 237.

[22] Joseph B. Soloveitchik, "The Future of Jewish Education in America," May 28, 1975. Cited from Aaron Rakeffet: *The Rav* (Northvale, NJ: Jason Aronson, 1999), vol. II, p. 178.

> Soulful education, because it does not remain within the confines of logical empirical science, depends on living people. Its lessons cannot be found in books, computer programs, or floppy disks; they are not reducible to information that in some way can be processed.[23]

PART FOUR: תכונות הנפש "SOUL-BASED" LEARNING: SPIRITUAL INTELLIGENCE AND THE LEARNER

Children, we constantly hear, have no need and nary an opportunity today to use their imaginations. Radio replaced storytelling but, at least, left something to be depicted by the mind's eye. Television and video have curtailed, if not eliminated, the need for imagination. The images they generate that have taken over our consciousnesses are not of our choosing and, often, are antithetical to the values we want to inculcate. Most egregious – for this context – is that they ceaselessly hawk the crassest materialism.

It would appear, then, that a strategy to counter the materialistic urge would involve the retrofitting of the imagination through a technique called "Guided Imagery" – "eduspeak" for visualization – that can activate the spiritual potential within a student.

> Guided imagery is simply picturing an object or a set of events in the mind's eye.... One way is to have students close their eyes and imagine a story as it is being read or told. This can be done in language arts or even history as students can see themselves as people in a certain historical period or event. In science, students can also visualize activities, such as the water cycle, after they have studied the cycle. By visualizing becoming the water and going through evaporation and condensation, the students connect their inner life with abstract subject matter.
>
> One of the most creative ways of using guided imagery is to have students visualize a set of events (e.g., going underwater or into space) and then write stories about what they

[23] Kane, p. 208.

> saw. They can also draw pictures. Many visualizations use symbols from nature, such as the sun, mountains, and water, to help in the process of personal integration and nourishment of the soul.[24]

Another technique used successfully to nourish the soul is keeping a journal – already part of the curriculum of some schools that employ whole language instruction. Students can be instructed, or encouraged, to keep daily journals in which they record their most private feelings and desires. From these diaries, they can subsequently withdraw ideas and material for compositions and essays. There has even been an experiment with recording dreams for discussion. Students who participated in this experiment credited it with enhancing their creativity.

The Arts would seem to offer the greatest potential for inculcating spirituality, yet they have traditionally been the poor relatives – if not actually the orphans – of the day school curriculum. Music, drama, and the visual and plastic arts can contribute to the development of the soul.

Experiential Learning and the Child

The educational philosophy of John Dewey and Ralph Tyler stressed the importance of integrating learning experiences into the curriculum to provide a framework for learning. These educators, as well as Piaget, Coleman, and Kolb, have long urged teachers to teach through experiences. Dewey maintained that learning is a by-product of social activities and that all curricula must be generated out of social situations, based on organized principles, but founded on the twin pillars of the capacity of the child and the demands of the environment. Tyler, too, maintained it is what the student does that he learns, not what the teacher does.

[24] John P. Miller: "Education and the Soul," in *Education, Information, and Transformation*, ed. Jeffrey Kane, p. 215.

The Romance of *Yahadut*

The Rav, too, understood the value of experiential learning, describing it as the transmission of cultural experience from the preceding generation to the succeeding one:

> A Jew is not only supposed to know what *yahadut* stands for and to have knowledge of *yahadut*; he is also called upon to experience *yahadut*, to live it, and somehow to engage in a romance with the Almighty. Knowing about *yahadut* is not enough; it is a norm to be implemented and experienced. It is to be lived and enjoyed. It is a great drama which the *yeled zekunim* must act out after observing the *av zaken*.
>
> Studying the *Torah she-baal peh*, the Oral Tradition, and complying with its precepts are the greatest pleasures a person can have. It is an exciting and romantic adventure. It is the most cleansing and purging experience a human being can experience. The *av zaken* teaches the *yeled zekunim* how to live and feel *yahadut*.[25]

PART FIVE: SERVICE LEARNING; SPIRITUALITY IN THE FLESH

David Elkind, has written,

> Young people believe that by expressing a value they are working toward its realization.... If it is not realized once it [has been] expressed, then it must be someone else's fault. And that someone else usually happens to be the corrupt adults over thirty. It is only when young people engage in meaningful work that they begin to differentiate between the expression of an ideal and the hard work necessary to bring it to fruition.[26]

[25] Soloveitchik, pp. 177–8.

[26] David Elkind, *All Grown Up and No Place To Go: Teenagers in Crisis* (Reading, MA: Addison-Wesley, 1984), p. 41.

To be effective, spiritual values have to be internalized. To internalize a value, one first has to experience it. The lessons of spirituality have to be practiced. If, as we postulate, the minimum of spirituality is the deferment of material gratification and the abnegation of self, then the way to achieve practice and experience in spiritual values is through the performance of gratuitous acts of loving-kindness – what the jargon currently calls "service learning."

To properly inculcate spirituality, we have to chart a course of both study and practice that will accompany students throughout twelve years of formal schooling, exposing them to spiritual ideas and values via the formal curriculum and through co- and extra-curricular activities. From early childhood through high school, students have to experience and practice sacrifice as the most basic step on the road to spirituality. If their supreme value is money, they have to make financial sacrifice; if it is time, they have to preoccupy themselves; if it is freedom, they must submit to the will of another; and if it is self, they must relinquish their own satisfaction.

This can be accomplished via the type of activities known in our schools as *ḥesed* projects: from performing in old age homes, to visiting the hospitalized and homebound, to donating new and used clothing, to preparing and serving meals for the homeless and the indigent, to providing tutoring for those with learning disabilities and companionship to those with special needs. These are but a sampling of what our students need to do on a regular and ongoing basis – all without thinking that it has to be "fun."

Won't this experience be superficial? Won't the spirituality it produces be only skin-deep? David Elkind's advice cited above is confirmed by the folk wisdom enshrined in the *Sefer ha-Ḥinukh*: "כי אחרי הפעולות נמשכים הלבבות" (actions impact on attitudes; *passim*).

Won't these activities "steal" time away from studies? Yes, they will; but it is justifiable, even necessary. R. Aharon Lichtenstein, in an address to the Educators Council of America some 15 years ago, told the following story that transpired shortly after his *aliyah*. He observed several *Ḥareidi* youngsters discussing whether – according to the *Gemara* in *Pesahim* – a secular Jew whose car was stuck was entitled to their help.

> I wrote a letter to the Rav at that time and I told him of the incident. I ended with the comment: Children of that age in our camp would not have known the *Gemara*. But they would have helped him. The feeling which I had then was: Why, *Ribbono shel Olam*, must this be our choice? Can't we find children who are going to help him and know the *Gemara*? Do we have to choose? I hope not; I believe not. If forced to choose, however, I would have no doubts where my loyalties lie; I prefer that they know less *Gemara*, but help him.[27]

Effects of Service Learning on Youth

The effects of service learning on our students go well beyond basic training for spirituality. Based on twenty years of teaching community service in the classroom and a review of research in the field, Conrad and Hedin (1989) hypothesized that well-designed community service programs would have a positive effect on youth in the following areas:[28]

PERSONAL GROWTH AND DEVELOPMENT

- Self-esteem
- Personal efficacy (sense of worth and competence)
- Ego and moral development
- Exploration of new roles, identities, and interests
- Willingness to take risks, accept new challenges

[27] Aharon Lichtenstein: " Developing a Torah Personality," lecture 24; Yeshivat Har Etzion Israel Koschitzky Virtual Beit Midrash (http://www.etzion.org.il).

[28] The following examples are drawn from Conrad and Hedin, *High School Community Service: A Review of Research and Programs* (Washington DC: December, 1989). Additional material on service learning can be obtained from the National Center on Effective Secondary Schools, U.S. Department of Education, Office of Educational Research and Improvement, and the Wisconsin Center for Education Research, School of Education, University of Wisconsin-Madison.

- Revised and reinforced values and beliefs
- Taking responsibility for, accepting consequences of own actions

INTELLECTUAL DEVELOPMENT AND ACADEMIC LEARNING

- Basic academic skills (expressing ideas, reading, calculating)
- Higher-level thinking skills (open-mindedness, problem solving, critical thinking)
- Content and skills directly related to service experiences
- Skills in learning from experience (to observe, ask questions, apply knowledge)
- Motivation to learn and retention of knowledge
- Insight, judgment, understanding – the nuances that can't be explained in a book or lecture but are often the most important things of all to know

SOCIAL GROWTH AND DEVELOPMENT

- Social responsibility, concern for the welfare of others
- Political efficacy
- Civic participation
- Knowledge and exploration of service-related careers
- Understanding and appreciation of, and ability to relate to, people from a wider range of backgrounds and life situations

PART SIX: SPIRITUALITY AND COMMUNITY; IT TAKES TWO (AT LEAST) TO SPIRITUALIZE

There are dangers in spirituality. Unregulated spirituality can deteriorate into a self-centered free-for-all that finds its realization on Tibetan mountaintops and its fulfillment in "kosher" sex. The wide proliferation of *faux* Kabbalah testifies to both the popular thirst for spiritual enlightenment as well as how easy it is to slake that thirst without providing real nourishment to the soul.

From *The Jerusalem Post* (2/20/2000) comes the following description of "The Living Waters Weekend," a "Jewish Renewal Retreat" offered to congregants by co-rabbis Philip and Shoni Labowitz of Temple Adath Or in Ft. Lauderdale, Florida:

> Optional sunrise walk and meditation. Musical workshop service at the ocean. Guided conscious eating at breakfast. Water exercises for body toning. Yoga with Kabbalah. Outdoor games, time for massage. Sacred gathering for men and women. Poetry readings and music. *Havdalah* ritual on the beach. Sunrise co-ed *mikvah* ritual in the ocean. Breakfast celebration with new affirmation. Kabbalistic meditation. Sacred sharing ceremony.

A greater, if more subtle danger lies in the extreme individuation of the spiritual experience. As Charles Liebman has cautioned (in that very *Jerusalem Post* article):

> Spiritualist Judaism is a serious problem because it releases Jews from obligations which devolve from the organized Jewish discipline, and consequently weakens their commitment to collectives, such as the Jewish people.

He cites the quest for spiritual Judaism as an example of a shift from "ethnic Judaism" that values community and solidarity, to "privatized religion" that emphasizes personal fulfillment. He charges: "Spirituality is not the answer to the Jewish problem in America; it is the problem."

I am confident that Professor Liebman would concur that spirituality is dangerous when it substitutes for religion, not when it complements it. Setting aside, momentarily, the question of whether there exists spirituality entirely free of formal religion, we can still discuss the role in the educational process of the existential quest to which we referred earlier in citing the observations of Howard Gardner. In the words of another educator:

> We need to shake off the narrow notion that "spiritual" questions are always about angels or ethers or must include the word *God*. Spiritual questions are the kind that we, and our students, ask every day of our lives as we yearn to connect with the largeness of life:

- Does my life have meaning and purpose?
- Do I have gifts that the world wants and needs?
- Whom and what can I trust?
- How can I rise above my fears?
- How do I deal with suffering, my own and that of my family and friends?
- How does one maintain hope?
- What about death?[29]

The questions we hear our students ask are: "Is this on the test?" or: "Will there be extra credit?" but the existential questions are the ones that, at moments at which their egos are caught off guard, pierce their veils of indifference and apathy, and utter, through clenched teeth, a cry of anxiety or despair.

Spirituality in a Community of Service

To teach spirituality successfully, the children cannot be the only ones participating. If we do not promote a collective spiritual ethic, we will be spinning our spiritual wheels in a futile exercise. Our schools need to become the focal point of spiritual communities in which teachers reinforce the formal lessons delivered in the classrooms during after-school activities, rabbis validate them in the synagogue, neighbors in the market and the workplace, and parents, at home, incessantly.

Without this support system, we will be creating spiritual schoolchildren whose experience with spirituality – like their experiences with a goodly portion of our curricula – is limited to the *dalet amot* of the *beit ha-medrash* and is not readily transferable to "real life."

In this respect, it is somewhat akin to *tefillah*. No matter how many times we teach the relevant *simanim* in the *Mishnah Berurah*; how frequently, or successfully, we emphasize the prohibitions against conversation during *tefillah*; how much time we allocate

[29] Parker J. Palmer, "Evoking the Spirit in Public Education," *Educational Leadership* 56:4 (1998–1999): 6–8.

to meditation before and concentration during *tefillah*, one visit to a run-of-the-mill *Shabbat* service in a run-of-the-mill Orthodox synagogue will undo whatever spiritual good the school may have accomplished.

The quandary of materialism, too, demands redress. As the Rav noted in a 1968 address to the R.C.A.:

> The problem with the American Jew is that he is not sensitive to Torah values. He must understand that human happiness does not depend upon comfort. The American Jew follows a philosophy which equates religion with making Jewish life more comfortable and convenient. It enables the Jew to have more pleasure in life. This de-emphasizes Judaism's spiritual values. What the rabbi should do is somehow expose the Jew to proper Torah Judaism. This cannot be accomplished by preaching and sermonizing. Many times, as I know from my own experience, they accomplish precisely the opposite.[30]

PART SEVEN: A SAMPLE LESSON EXTRAPOLATING "WONDER" FROM THE MUNDANE

How does one create a school culture that nurtures wonder at creation, love of God and mankind, and allegiance to *halakhah* – separately, let alone simultaneously? In a 1969 address to students at Y.U., the Rav gave us an example drawn from his personal experience:

I remember that I was grown up when I went to Danzig. I saw the [Baltic] sea for the first time, and it made a tremendous impression upon me. From afar, it looked like a blue forest. I was used to forests from Russia. When I drew closer and saw that it was the sea, I was overwhelmed. I made the benediction of "Blessed be He who wrought creation," which is recited when "one sees mountains, hills, seas, rivers, and deserts." This blessing came from the depths of my heart. It was one of the greatest religious experiences I have ever had.[31]

---

[30] Rakeffet, vol. II, p. 18.

[31] *Ibid.*, 164.

Through a personal narrative, the Rav has pointed to a simple, yet effective way to transform the mundane and material into the sublime and spiritual: a *berakhah*. The drawback to utilizing his anecdote as a paradigm, however, is the implicit requirement that the recitation of the *berakhah* be preceded by a relatively extraordinary experience. The argument could be made that such an event could trigger a spiritual reaction all by itself, rendering the *berakhah* superfluous. Can we provide comparable stimulation for even a blasé student who will never greet nature with a sense of wonder? Can we "inspire" routine experiences and activities with the same spiritual significance?

Abraham Joshua Heschel – in an essay on "Jewish Education" that calls, explicitly, for "a survey of its spiritual aspects" – advises us on just how this can be done:

> At all religious schools, pupils are taught the benediction to be said before drinking a beverage. It is taught as a custom, as a practice. But how many teachers attempt to convey the grand mastery and spiritual profundity contained in these three Hebrew words – "Everything came into being by His word"? It is unfair and unfortunate that we ignore, or fail to communicate the spiritual substance of our tradition.[32]

By following Heschel's advice and the Rav's example; by inviting God's presence into every nook and cranny of our lives – from a glass of water to the great sea – we can aspire to regain for Him the primacy He seems to have recently surrendered.

Educating for Informed Choice

In discussing the "cognitive" dimension of spirituality (see above, Part Two), I postulated that the relationship to the divine that we wish to cultivate is manifest in the exercise of free will and the capacity for informed choice. The subject we have chosen to illustrate the education for informed choice is *Parshanut ha-Mikra*. We have

---

[32] Heschel, *Insecurity*, p. 234.

chosen it because it is the area we know most thoroughly, as well as the curricular area present in all schools throughout the greatest part of a student's primary and secondary education. The specific text we have chosen consists of the commentaries of Rashi and Rashbam to Yaakov's dream (*Bereishit* 28:10 ff.). The methodological point we shall try to make is that *Parshanut* (and, similarly, every subject in *limudei kodesh*) can be utilized to inculcate and promote the capacity for informed choice. The pedagogical point we shall try to make is that spirituality can be found wherever we wish to give it entry.

A participant in an Internet exchange for Jewish educators ("LookJed") concerning "Spirituality in Teaching" offered the following prescription for spiritual validation:

> A good way to test yourself is to examine: do you always tend to find the same message (or small group of messages) in all texts or does each *sugya* present something (at least somewhat) new? Does the *Gemara*, in your reading, come out fashioned in your image, or do you (at least sometimes) come out of the *sugya* with new spiritual insights – and sometimes at the expense of long-cherished presuppositions? Differently put – in a conflict between you and the text (do these conflicts ever arise), does one side or the other always win?

The test for spirituality in teaching (who tends to win, the text or the reader?) is utilized to great pedagogical effect by Uriel Simon in an essay that focuses on the role of *Tanakh* and *Parshanut ha-Mikra* in religious education:

> The *pashtan*, attentively listening to the text and striving for objectivity, is bewildered at what he sees as the confident subjectivism of the *darshan*. He is inclined to thrust at him the words of Rabbi Ishmael to his colleague Rabbi Eliezer: "You are saying to Scripture, 'Be silent while I make a *derash!*'" The *darshan*, on the other hand, seeking to give voice to the verses out of an intimate relationship with them, fears that there is nothing in the *pashtan's* objectivism but spiritual indiffer-

> ence and lack of creativity. He would incline to identify with the response uttered by Rabbi Eliezer: "You are a mountain palm!" (whose fruit is so meager that it may not be brought as *bikkurim*).
>
> Yet, woe to the *pashtan* who completely effaces himself before the text, and woe to the *darshan* who completely silences it. The former would deplete his *peshat* interpretations of all living meaning, and the latter would drain his *derashot* of their status as an interpretation of Scripture....
>
> It is the glory of *peshat* interpreters that they shun arbitrary interpretation and stand guard against pressing spiritual demands which are apt to twist the line of truth. But this is also their weak point: they insist on the truth at the price of diminishing their message. The *darshan* may never rest content with merely interpreting the words of the text; he must dare to make it speak out. When he does it well, he becomes a partner in the creative process. "Even that which a veteran student will one day teach in the presence of his rabbi has already been said to Moses at Sinai."[33]

For the reasons outlined by Simon, "the fact that Rashi's commentary has earned him preeminence among Torah interpreters attests to the great educational and spiritual significance that generations of Jews have attached to the *derashot* that became the possession of all thanks to their inclusion in his commentary."[34] Moreover, he adds, "whoever compares the Torah commentary of Rashi...to the exclusively *peshat* commentaries of Rashbam and Rabbi Abraham ibn Ezra, senses at once the contrast between the abundance of thought and feeling in the former over against the dry mundaneness of the latter."[35]

I should like to challenge that assertion and offer, in its stead, the proposition that spirituality is, to paraphrase the Kotzker (and,

---

[33] Uriel Simon, "The Religious Significance of the *Peshat*," *Tradition* 23:2 (1988): 41–2.

[34] *Ibid*: 45.

[35] *Ibid*: 44.

obviously, Heschel), "the attempt to let God in, particularly where there is some question about whether He belongs." The verse that exemplifies this quest is, "אכן יש א-לוהים במקום הזה ואנכי לא ידעתי" and the exegetical disagreement between Rashi and Rashbam over the interpretation of Yaakov's dream, the context in which it appears, is the substance of the lesson I choose to present.

The Synopsis, According to Each *Parshan*

According to Rashi's aggadic interpretation, Yaakov, who had already reached Haran, was on his way back to Yerushalayim (to pray there) when God brought *Har ha-Moriah* to intercept him at Luz. In order to constrain him to remain overnight, God caused the sun to set prematurely. Yaakov collected several stones, which he placed about his head and went to sleep. In his dream – during which God compressed the entire Land of Israel beneath him – he saw angels first ascending, and then descending, a ladder. When he awoke, he discovered that God had fused the several stones together into one.

According to Rashbam, however, Yaakov, on his way to Haran, stopped at an anonymous site outside Luz when he ran out of daylight for travelling. There he went to sleep on only as much ground as his body occupied. In his dream he saw angels going up and down a ladder in no particular sequence and when he awoke the single stone he had placed beneath his head was still there.

The respective interpretations of these two *parshanim* are as different as can be. Rashi sees every element in the narrative framework of the dream as a supernatural contrivance designed to stick Yaakov in that holy place at that designated time. Rashbam, on the other hand, sees only the casual, even random, meandering of a man who gets stuck at a place not of his own choosing, where he cautiously beds down for the night. With respect to the dream itself, Rashi sees it as beginning with the sequential changing of the heavenly guard, continuing with the compression of the land on which he slept, and culminating in the fusion of the selected stones. Rashbam denies absolute sequence, and, hence, significance, to the movements of the angels, and declines to accommodate either the compression of the earth or the fusion of the sundry stones.[36]

The Pedagogic and Exegetical Reconciliation

These two interpretations illustrate two diametrically opposite treatments of a Biblical narrative. On the one hand, they belong to two eminently, and almost equally, respected authorities and, as such, should be given equal consideration and regarded as equally valid. On the other hand, however, our students usually demand that all differences be resolved in favor of one interpretation or the other.

Our pedagogic challenge is to persuade them that:

(a) Their differences are the result of distinct methods of interpretation;

(b) As long as each is consistent with its own method it is as valid as the other;

(c) In spite of their mutual validity, teachers and students, alike, are entitled to express a preference for one over the other;

(d) Such preference should not be arbitrary, but should be argued on the basis of linguistic, literary, or thematic merit.

The normative methodological and pedagogical conclusion would be that Rashi's interpretation, as usual, is suffused with spiritual significance whereas that of Rashbam is, as usual, so matter-of-fact as to be devoid of spiritual import. In fact, the opposite here is true. Consider: the challenge of religious education is NOT to recognize God when you encounter moving mountains, unnatural sunsets, and stones that fuse together. The challenge is to recognize the divine in the ordinary; the spiritual in the mundane.

Rashi would have God hit Yaakov *Avinu* over the head, as it

---

[36] This constitutes an excellent exercise for advanced students. Have them: (a) read the commentaries of Rashi and Rashbam; (b) paint a composite picture of the narrative according to each one; (c) and then draw the appropriate conclusions regarding their respective treatments of the text.

were, in an attempt to coerce him into spiritual recognition whereas Rashbam would have that sublime realization dawn upon him, gradually, as he moves from one scene and verse to the next. I submit that Rashbam's interpretation offers the greater grist for the mill of spirituality precisely because it depicts Yaakov as an "Everyman," rather than a "Superman."

Like Yaakov, our students must be challenged and equipped to see spirituality rather than superficiality.

CONCLUSION

We have endeavored to present a holistic educational strategy for teaching spirituality in day schools and yeshiva high schools. Beginning with the role spirituality plays in the articulation of a day school's vision, we moved to the curriculum development process, to the characteristics of teaching and teacher training and then, to assumptions that we may make about the process of learning spirituality.

Having dealt with the formal, structural aspects, we moved to the substantive ones. First, we presented a suggestion for a service learning project to promote the experiential dimension of spirituality and recommended that it be allocated a communal, participatory component as well. The dangers of spirituality were noted, with the suggestion that it not be divorced from the normative, collective Jewish religious experience, by increasing and reinforcing interaction with parents and community.

Finally, we provided a sample lesson based upon a reasonably standard piece of Jewish Studies material, focusing on the exegesis of Yaakov's dream. In it, we utilized several of the principles we earlier advocated, particularly the presentation of spirituality as education for informed choice.

We close with a particularly felicitous description by Leon Roth of the interpretive process. It encapsulates what we have been trying to say:

> It is ultimately the determining of an ideal of life, the establishing of a preference among possible ends. It is the ordering

> of types of action in an ascending and descending scale of better and worse, an ordering that shapes the kind of life we choose to live.... Interpretation thus becomes the gateway to life, and in this wide sense is synonymous with education.[37]

[37] Leon Roth, "Some Reflections on the Interpretation of Scripture," in *The Montefiore Lectures* (London: 1956), pp. 20–1.

9

Orthodoxy and the Search for Spirituality in Jewish Adult Education

by Erica S. Brown

Within the entire Jewish community, adult education is blossoming. Synagogues and local *kollelim*, women's organizations, and schools host weekly, if not daily, offerings for adults.[1] In the Orthodox community, adult education programs often assume of their students a solid grounding in sacred texts and a commitment to *Talmud Torah* in general. Such programs and individual classes are not necessarily presenting new forms of study to adults; they usually provide a place for the continuation of an education cultivated decades earlier. Within this plethora of educational opportunities, there is room for

[1] For more discussion of the Jewish "renaissance" in adult Jewish study, see my article, "The Federation as an Educational Catalyst," *Journal of Jewish Communal Service* 75:4 (1999): 202–9.

some questions about what it is that educators are trying to achieve in such settings and what it is that students are accomplishing. Can we continue the process of Torah education, as if from childhood, without acknowledging the developmental changes that take place within adults? How does life experience impinge on the acquisition of knowledge for adults? How should our work be informed by pedagogy and the literature on adult education? Each of these is an important and valuable question, but an investigation of even one of these issues would exceed the limited focus of this paper. Our specific interest is in the role of spirituality in Jewish adult education in the Orthodox community, and our central question is, are adults more interested in information and skill acquisition, or in inspiration and in the relevance of their studies to their lives? Are they getting both? The commitment to *Talmud Torah* exhibited in the Orthodox community is so strong that educators and rabbis might assume that along with it is a concomitant regard for spiritual development. This article aims to demonstrate that the existence of such a commitment cannot be assumed, and, furthermore, will suggest that in order to enhance the spiritual dimension in adult education within the Orthodox community, educators must be attentive to three central concerns: 1) the content of the material which they are teaching, 2) the assumptions that adults make about the material which they are studying, and 3) the impact of non-intellectual endeavors on spiritual development. Preliminary to all of this is a discussion on the hazards of "spirituality" and a working definition of spirituality that implies more than an amorphous religious feeling.

SPIRITUALITY: DANGERS AND DEFINITIONS

You have just been invited to a "Jewish Women's Spirituality and Creativity Conference" where you have been asked to bring your own drum and beat spiritual tunes with a group leader in honor of the biblical heroine, Miriam. There, you will "recapture the sounds of our heritage" because, "women in the ancient Jewish world were great drummers." Alternatively, you might choose the pottery workshop where "participants will carve and mold a piece of clay into a creative expression of the One Who Breathes Us." Don't forget a smock, we're reminded. On the Jewish Renewal circuit, you might attend a *Shabbaton* advertised this way: "Sunrise walk with a musical service at the ocean. Guided conscious eating at breakfast. Water exercises for body toning. Yoga with Kabbalah.... Sunset barbecue with folk dancing. *Havdalah* ritual on the beach. Kabbalistic meditation...sunrise co-ed *mikvah* ritual in the ocean."[2] These are not fabricated advertisements, but direct quotes from brochures that represent a growing trend in Jewish adult education to teach "spirituality" experientially. Spirituality in these settings is cultivated through personal and artistic expression with only a minimally Jewish framework. We immediately understand why the Orthodox community today approaches the arena of spirituality with caution and often with disdain. In the spirit of "*Am ha-areẓ ḥasid*," traditional Jewish spirituality is pursued through intensive study, an emphasis on *kavvanah* in prayer,[3] and in the performance of commandments. In the Jewish mystical tradition, spirituality is pursued through the achievement of *deveikut*.[4] In contrast, Jewish education in some segments of the Jewish community, often but not always, demands little knowledge or intensive commitment; feelings often replace

---

[2] From a description of a "Living Waters Weekend" of the Jewish Renewal movement, as seen in Charles Liebman, "When Judaism Gets Personal," *The Forward*, 4 June 1999.

[3] The role of *kavvanah* in prayer and whether its emphasis was within normative Jewish practice receives an interesting treatment in Louis Jacob's *Ḥasidic Prayer* (New York: Schocken Books, 1973).

[4] Moshe Halbertal cites Rabbi Joseph Karo's equation of *deveikut* with the scholarly study of Torah in his discussion of the loss of intellectual meaning when the study of Torah is manipulated for contemplative purposes in *The People of the Book: Canon, Meaning and Authority* (Cambridge, MA: Harvard University Press, 1997), p. 123. In *Maggid Meisharim* (Amsterdam, 1708), R. Karo states, "Be careful not to interrupt the *dibbuk* [*deveikut*] between you and your Creator...for the study of Torah strengthens the communion and grace is infused into him from heaven to strengthen communion further." For more on techniques to achieve *deveikut* and its relationship to Torah study within *Ḥasidut*, see Moshe Idel, *Ḥasidism: Between Ecstasy and Magic* (New York: SUNY Press, 1995), pp. 171–88. In a non-mystical context, Rabbi Joseph Soloveitchik equated the study of Torah with an act of prayer in his collection of essays, *Shiurim le-Zekher Avi Mori*, vol. II "*Be-inyan Birkhat Ha-Torah*," (Jerusalem, 1985), pp. 1–16, especially pp. 7–8.

rigorous analysis. Make-your-own midrash as part of the search for self has sometimes supplanted the study of rabbinic midrash in search of the meaning of Judaism.

This new age Jewish spirituality has been called into question by the sociologist Charles Liebman, who sees in this quest for a personal spiritual life-style a decline in long term observance, commitment, and concern for the collective good:

> Understood in terms of personal meaning, Jewishness becomes – even for Jews – an acquired taste, a take-it-or-leave it affair. Moreover, experience-based religiosity has no intrinsic justification for exclusion or boundaries; it necessarily includes all who are partner to the inspirational moment.[5]

SPIRITUAL "FEELINGS" AND THE ROLE OF THE TEACHER

In this age of new-wave religion, Orthodox Jews should rightly approach the word "spirituality" with hesitation. If its meaning is entrenched in "feel good" forms of expression without implying long-term commitment, knowledge, or self-sacrifice, it is to be shunned.[6] The methods by which greater spiritual living are to be achieved must also be called into question. Spiritual seeking in other

[5] Charles S. Liebman, "Post-War American Jewry: From Ethnic to Privatized Judaism," in *Secularism, Spirituality, and the Future of American Jewry*, ed. Elliot Abrams and David G. Dalin (Washington, DC: Ethics and Public Policy Center, 1999), p. 13.

[6] For how such trends have been making an impact on Orthodoxy, see Rabbi Aharon Lichtenstein, "Take Rav Soloveitchik at Full Depth," *The Forward*, 12 March 1999. There Rabbi Lichtenstein writes,

> Shallowness…is the Achilles' Heel of modern Orthodoxy. As such, it elicited some of the Rav's sharpest critiques of religious modernism. Flaccid prayer, lukewarm commitment to learning, approximate observance, tepid experience – anything that reflected comfortable mediocrity in the quality of acculturated American Judaism, he deplored and sought to ennoble. This is not to suggest that he regarded the anti-modernists as his ideal. He had high standards of spirituality and few met them fully. But with respect to this particular failing, I believe it is fair to state that, both intellectually and emotionally, he

traditions, in contradistinction to Judaism, often hinges upon the spiritual "master," mentor, or teacher. Although the teacher or *rebbe* is revered in Jewish tradition, it is not in the same fashion as the regard given to the charismatic leader in Eastern religions. In his discussion of the nature of the Hebrew prophet, Michael Fishbane, makes an important comparison between the spiritual teacher in Eastern religions and the Hebrew prophet:

> In Eastern religions...one dominant pattern of the spiritual teacher is that of an exemplary master who provides a model of salvific action...the path of wisdom is not a universal revelation but a personal realization of the truth of reality. Accordingly, although a few spiritual virtuosos may in fact choose to emulate their teacher's way – the way he points to but does not prescribe – they do not and cannot imitate it, since every individual's path to illumination is necessarily unique. In contrast, the classical Hebrew prophet is the recipient of supernatural divine stipulations that prescriptively instruct the entire nation of Israel in its path of obligation...the ancient Israelite prophet is not a perfected spiritual master who has transcended the illusions of temptation or the temptations of his ego. He is rather a person who is deeply

---

> regarded it as afflicting the modern community more than others. His ideological commitment to the cardinal concerns of Modern Orthodoxy – an integrated view of life, the value of general culture and the significance of the State of Israel – and his genuine pride in some of its accomplishments – did not prevent him from demanding that it hold a mirror to its face and probe for intensity and depth."

While Rabbi Lichtenstein is not suggesting here that modern Orthodox Jews are drawn to innovative practices but have difficulty achieving depth within traditional observance, the waning of religious intensity within tradition often leads to innovations to create the missing sense of depth. Another article deals more with the specific problems Liebman addresses: see Nathan Diament, "The Age of Oprah-Orthodoxy" *The Jewish Week*, 27 November 1998, where Diament claims, perhaps somewhat harshly, that for the modern Orthodox, "Rabbinic authority can be questioned when it seems to clash with 'personal moral sensibilities'...almost any aspect of secular culture may be embraced if it provides the individual 'with personal or spiritual insight.'"

> aware of his covenantal Lord, and one for whom a radical spiritual encounter has inspired an acute consciousness of the necessity to avoid sin and heed the stipulations of God's autonomous will.[7]

Even the Hebrew prophet, the emissary of God's will, is not regarded as a spiritual master or model but as a mediator in the covenantal relationship between God and man. The prophet does not seek a unique and individual path to God but engourages observance of and fidelity to the commandments. Fishbane's distinction is particularly relevant today since the appeal of Eastern religion is pervasive and has even led to a new type of spiritual seeker, the "Jew-Bu" or Jewish Buddhist, the combination of East-West, that is largely more East than West.[8] In Eastern religions it is the attraction of a charismatic teacher rather than a set of laws and ethics that becomes the focus for the spiritual seeker.

It is important to distinguish between personal, creative forms of expression or spiritual charisma with minimal Jewish content, and more rigorous scholarship of spirituality within general and Jewish literature. In *The Idea of the Holy*, Rudolph Otto argued that concepts in a religious vocabulary did not defy comprehension or analysis. Otto, in his own words, claimed that "The 'irrational' is today a favorite theme of all who are too lazy to think or too ready to evade the arduous duty of clarifying their ideas and grounding their convictions on a basis of coherent thought."[9] In that spirit, Otto undertook, "a serious attempt to analyze all the more exactly, the *feeling* which remains where the *concept* fails."[10] Otto acknowledged that, on one level, such religious feelings elude or defy conceptual

[7] Michael Fishbane, "Biblical Prophecy as a Religious Phenomenon," in *Jewish Spirituality: From the Bible through the Middle Ages*, ed. Arthur Green (New York: Crossroad, 1986), p. 70.

[8] For a good illustration of this dilemma, see "Jewish Buddhists, Buddhist Jews," pp. 128–46 and "JUBUS in America," pp. 147–57 in Rodger Kamenez̨, *The Jew in the Lotus* (San Francisco: Harper San Francisco, 1994).

[9] Rudolph Otto, *The Idea of the Holy* (London: Oxford University Press, 1958), p. xxi.

[10] *Ibid.*

analysis. Nevertheless, he tried to give the ineffable a language. William James, who also undertook a study of religion's attractions, made a similar claim:

> All our attitudes, moral, practical or emotional, as well as religious, are due to the 'objects' of our consciousness, the things we believe to exist, whether really or ideally, along with ourselves. Such objects may be present to our senses or they may be present only to our thought. In either case they elicit from us a *reaction*; and the reaction due to things of thought is notoriously in many cases as strong as that due to sensible presences. It may be even stronger.[11]

Rather than feelings, James terms them "reactions" to the objects of our consciousness. They are not less real than 'sensible presences' and may elicit reactions that are even stronger than reactions to normal sense perceptions. The philosopher Robert Nozick offers us an insight into what such a 'reaction' might be:

> Faith's particular route to belief is the following. There is an encounter with something very real – an actual person, a person in a story, a part of nature, a book or work of art, a part of one's being – and this thing has extraordinary qualities that intimate the divine by being forms of qualities that the divine itself would have: these extraordinary qualities touch you deeply, opening your heart so that you feel in contact with a special manifestation of the divine, in that it has some form of divine qualities to a very great extent.[12]

Once Otto, James, and other scholars of religion turned their attention to the *mysterium tremendum* and created a basic vocabulary with which to discuss spirituality, we have fewer excuses for not

[11] William James, "The Reality of the Unseen," *The Varieties of Religious Experience* (New York: New American Library, 1958), p. 58.
[12] Robert Nozick, *The Examined Life: Philosophical Meditations* (New York: Simon and Schuster, 1989), p. 51.

being able to put inexplicable feelings into words. Our concern is to put their language of spirituality into a uniquely Jewish context and to package it for Jewish education. How do we communicate these "extraordinary qualities that intimate the divine" into a curriculum for Jewish adult education? What do our own sources say about spirituality?

Rabbinic literature is replete with the concern for an added dimension of worship, something beyond perfunctory observance, something which we might term "spiritual" in nature.[13] R. Bahya ibn Pakuda writes movingly in the introduction to his *Ḥovot ha-Levavot* of the importance of emphasizing the way both the mind and heart contribute to the performance of *miẓvot*. He addresses the concern that along with the performance of commandments that affect the body, there will be a waning of concern for the soul's development. This concern for additional spiritual or ethical conduct was addressed throughout the generations: Kabbalah,[14] the writings of the *Ḥasidei Ashkenaz,*[15] and the literature of the *Mussar* Movement are but a few examples.[16] Supererogation is beautifully expressed in the words of R. Isaiah Horowitz, the *Shelah*:

---

[13] For more on supererogation, see Rabbi Aaron Lichtenstein, "Does Jewish Tradition Recognize an Ethic Independent on Halakha?" in *Contemporary Jewish Ethics*, ed. Menachem Marc Kellner (New York: Sanhedrin Press, 1978), pp. 102–23, particularly pp. 115–6.

[14] See Gershom Scholem's introduction to *Major Trends in Jewish Mysticism* (New York: Schocken Books, 1946) with attention to the needs that Kabbalah sought to address and Moshe Idel, *Kabbalah: New Perspectives* (New Haven: Yale University Press, 1988). For the impact of this on curricular issues, see Moshe Halbertal, *People of the Book: Canon, Meaning and Authority,* "Kabbalists and Talmudic Curriculum," pp. 119–24.

[15] For more on the educational aspects of this group, see Ephraim Kanarfogel, "Educational Theory and Practice in the Teachings of the German Pietists," *Jewish Education and Society in the High Middle Ages*; Haym Soloveitchik, "Three Themes in *Sefer Ḥasidim*" *AJS Review* 1 (1976); Y. Baer, "*Ha-Megammah ha-Dati ha-Ḥevratit shel Sefer Ḥasidim* in *Zion* 3 (1937): 10–4; I. Ta-Shma, "*Miẓvat Talmud Torah ki-Ve'ayah Hevratit Datit be-Sefer H⊠asidim,*" *Bar-Ilan* 14–5 (1977): 98–112; and Ivan Marcus, *Piety and Society: The Jewish Pietists of Medieval Germany* (Leiden: Brill, 1981).

[16] For more on the Mussar Movement as a response to the need for increased spiri-

> Fear the Lord your God and serve Him with the kind of service a faithful servant gives. Serve him by day and by night, at all times, in every hour, every moment, every period. Serve him with speech, with thought, and with the hidden thoughts of the heart. Serve Him as if His worship were always new and fresh and serve Him with a heart on fire.... Serve the Lord with all your heart and pour out your heart like water in God's presence. Be as far as possible from the performance of the precepts in a routine manner without the heart being in them.... Every command should appear to you as if you had only been given it recently, today or yesterday.[17]

At the heart of all of these spiritual movements, and what makes them distinct from Otto's or James' assessment of religion, is that they all have commandment performance and study at their core. Traditionally, Jewish spirituality was never severed from the observance of *miẓvot*, as we are seeing today. Any discussion of superagatory behavior in traditional texts assumed the performance of *miẓvot*. *Kavvana* or acting *"lifnim mi-shurat ha-din"*[18] was seen as a way to inform or enhance *miẓvot*, but not to replace them.

In establishing some guidelines for spiritual searching within Orthodoxy, we have tried to demonstrate that the path is not an essentially individual or charismatic one but one of joint participation in the covenant as it is expressed in commandment performance. Jewish spirituality may be, at times, an accretion to the commandments, but it cannot demand a depletion or negation of them. Rather, the object of the religious experience that James describes is sought by an observant Jew through a profound

---

tuality, see Immanuel Etkes, "The Founding of the Mussar Movement: Historical Background," *Rabbi Israel Salanter and the Mussar Movement: Seeking the Torah of Truth* (Philadelphia: Jewish Publication Society, 1993), pp. 117–174 and Lester Eckman, "The Mussar Movement's Relationship to the Enlightenment," *The History of the Mussar Movement, 1840–1945* (New York: Shengold, 1975), pp. 25–48.

[17] R. Isaiah Horowitz, Shenei Luḥot ha-Berit, IV, "*Asarah Hillulim*."

[18] See Maimonides *Hilkhot Dei'ot,* chapter 1, and in particular law 5, and Aharon Lichtenstein, "Does Jewish Tradition Recognize an Ethic Independent of Halakha?," pp. 105–15.

understanding and performance of the commandments and through prayer and study. While some forms of spiritual seeking should be rejected by Orthodoxy, a search for spirituality that is grounded in Jewish practice and study, an appreciation of the wonder and mystery of the universe, and a desire for ethical interpersonal relationships, should be actively encouraged in adult education settings.

RELIGION AND FAITH

At this juncture it is important to consider yet another distinction by the scholar of comparative religion, Wilfred Cantwell Smith. Smith makes a distinction between religion and faith. Religion, in Smith's definition, is essentially about "cumulative traditions," a combination of traditional texts – scholarly and liturgical, symbols, rites, ethics, music, and dance. Faith is the response engendered by the performance or participation in these rituals. According to Smith, faith is more personal than religion and serves as a "reaction" to cumulative tradition. Both religion and faith require the other, but the two are not coterminous.[19] The reaction of faith to cumulative tradition brings these traditions meaning and increased vitality in their repeated performance. Smith uses the term "faith" in a universalistic way, free from religious associations. His analysis is both too simplistic and too individualistic for wholesale acceptance by an observant Jew. However, Smith's attempt to distinguish between actions and reactions is important and his distinctions can prove helpful in thinking about adult education in the Orthodox Jewish community. We are blessed with such rich "cumulative traditions" that simply mastering them and understanding the texts and rituals we observe would take a lifetime of study. However, our preoccupation with texts and commandments sometimes leads us to neglect the development of faith as a response to the world of cumulative traditions that we occupy. To return to a question asked earlier: does our emphasis on information and skill acquisition provide room

[19] Wilfred Cantwell Smith, *The Meaning and End of Religion* (New York: Macmillan, 1963), chapters six and seven.

for inspiration in the classroom? Are we teaching about actions or encouraging "reactions"?

The answer to that question depends on where your classroom is and who you seek as a teacher, but more often than not, the answer is "no." With only forty-five minutes to cover the *daf* each morning at the break of dawn, there is little time to discuss the impact of the text on the adult learner. A weekly class held at a local synagogue does not allow the teacher enough time to cover the subject, let alone to take time out to discuss its meaning. In addition, most instructors have expertise only in the material studied and may not feel equipped to take the material beyond the realm of skill acquisition. Even if they were to have the time and inclination, if a teacher said, "Let's talk about how our study of *ḥumash* has contributed to your "hunger for wonder,"[20] the student might wonder only why you failed to cover all of the *Rashis* on the *perek*. We have become so accustomed to a diet of consistent learning styles and content that a sudden switch of orientation might not meet the student's expectations. Little would be gained. I vividly recall leaving a classroom where a teacher had attempted some such spiritual meandering to overhear a student complain that the class was not one on which she could have made a "*birkat ha-Torah.*" If adult students are more concerned with information and the mastery of the material through skill acquisition than spiritual development or the personal relevance of the material, should we, the instructors, be concerned with promoting the spiritual dimension of the learning experience?

RESEARCH ON ADULT EDUCATION

To address this question, we will have to digress briefly from the topic to look at the academic literature on adult education. Currently, the literature on adult education tends largely to be student, rather than subject, centered.[21] The objective in much of this literature is

[20] This expression was used by Theodore Roszak, "On the Contemporary Hunger for Wonder," in *The Pushcart Prize VI: Best of the Small Press – 1980/81*, ed. Bill Henderson (New York: Avon Books, 1981).

[21] For example, see Jack Mezirow, *Transformative Dimensions of Adult Learning* (San Francisco: Jossey-Bass, 1991), particularly chapters 2 and 4; Mark Tennant,

to develop more critical forms of reflection[22] and to develop character, rather than to encourage the mastery of a particular body of information.[23] In such a scheme, relevancy would most likely be valued over information. Although this is a largely oversimplified view of the resaerch on pedagogy for adults, I think that it explains why much of this literature is not making a greater impact on teaching methods within the Orthodox community.[24] Our educational system has, for thousands of years, promoted the mastery of text as its primary goal and mastery of person as an ancillary benefit. There is an unstated assumption that learning the material alone will promote spiritual growth. Learning is also subject based rather than student-centered.[25] It is not that we do not care about the student's

Psychology and Adult Learning (New York: Routledge, 1997); Robin Usher, Ian Bryant, and Rennie Johnston, *Adult Education and the Postmodern Challenge: Learning Beyond the Limits* (New York: Routledge, 1997); and Joe E. Heimlich and Emmalou Norland, *Developing Teaching Style in Adult Education* (San Francisco: Jossey-Bass, 1994).

[22] Stephen Brookfield has been a major proponent of the development of critical thinking as a goal of adult education. See his book, *Developing Critical Thinkers: Challenging Adults to Explore Alternative Ways of Thinking and Acting* (San Francisco: Jossey-Bass, 1987), with particular attention to part one and his article, "The Development of Critical Reflection in Adulthood: Foundations of a Theory of Adult Learning," *New Education* 13:1 (1991): 39–48.

[23] Even in the sphere of religion, the tendency in education often leans toward reflection rather than mastery of material or skill acquisition. For a good example of this, see Cate Siejk, "Learning to Love the Questions: Religious Education in an Age of Unbelief," *Journal of Religious Education* 94:2 (1999): 155–71 and Mary Boys, *Educating in Faith: Maps and Visions* (San Francisco: Harper and Row, 1989). Although these are not oriented to adults specifically, the ideas promoted could certainly be applied to an adult audience.

[24] The same could also be said about the orientation of educational literature on the role of the teacher. Kimberly Patton wrote an article about the influence of the teacher in the academic teaching of religion and arrived at the conclusion that as much as the teacher wished to distance himself or herself from the material, the student still made an association between the information and the teacher beyond pure academic interest, "'Stumbling Along Between the Immensities': Reflections on Teaching in the Study of Religion," *Journal of the American Academy of Religion* 65:4 (1997): 831–50.

[25] In Gary Fenstermacher and Jonas Soltis' book, *Approaches to Teaching*, third edition (New York: Teachers College Press, 1998), the authors present three approaches

religious growth in this picture, but it is presumed that personal growth comes on its own as a result of intensive study. Whether or not this educational leaning has always been productive is not the issue here; we must be concerned with our reality and the educational landscape as it is currently. That is why I believe that Orthodox Jewish adults are not predominantly interested in spiritual development in their learning. Information and skill acquisition largely represented the core of their education in day schools. They have become habituated to study in a way which achieves very limited educational objectives.

The separation of information and inspiration as teaching goals is quite artificial from a traditional Jewish point of view. We have always assumed that the material itself will be spiritually transformative; we would never consider that learning even the most technical details of the most arcane body of Jewish knowledge would be free from inspiration. However, as stated in the introduction to this paper, we may be assuming too much. As early as day school, we make assumptions that students can create a meaningful framework for the Jewish studies that they have learned. We rarely articulate the connection between text and meaning because we automatically assume that there is one. This may be true for the instructor. It is not always true for the student. In particular, much of Jewish studies is intended for the sophisticated intellectual mind that might naturally make such connections. Can we assume this to be true for the non-intellectual adults in our midst who may not be coming to our classes? Perhaps we have erroneously assumed that the information

to teaching: what they term the executive approach, the therapist approach, and the liberationist approach. The executive approach is most akin to the type of learning encouraged within traditional Orthodox circles where the teacher is not a facilitator but is regarded as the top in a hierarchy of learning and is charged with dispensing information. This is in contrast to the therapist approach where the teacher tries to draw out the student in a more individualistic style of teaching. The authors are critical of both approaches but perhaps have not credited the executive approach enough. On the other hand, their simple typologies are instructive in challenging approaches that are too narrow and fail to include different teaching styles and goals.

we impart will be automatically framed in a religiously relevant context by our students so that we need not articulate it.

Barry Holtz addresses the process of reading and self-definition and identify. He articulates how to "listen to the voice behind the text."[26] Once I realized that this gap between text and life existed for many of my non-affiliated or non-observant students, I began to wonder if it was also true for my Orthodox students. They would rarely question the commitment of a biblical character or criticize a sacred text, but they were not always able to articulate easily or effortlessly move from text to life. The same pre-texts and contexts that I had to enunciate before learning texts with one group, I began to do routinely, albeit differently, with all of my students. I have come to believe that, without this spiritual framework or the injection of meaning into textual orientation, (as artificial a bifurcation as that may sound to the reader), students will lose their motivation for life-long learning and fail to see the depth and profundity that underlies their commitment to Judaism.

REACHING OUT, GROWING UP

Up until this point, we have described the student in such a class as having benefited from a day school education and possibly a university background in Jewish studies. We have also assumed Jewish observance. But, perhaps again, we have assumed too much. Opening our eyes to the student population in our adult classrooms will probably reveal that the same individuals consistently attend classes; this pool of interest may represent a very small percentage of the total population within a synagogue or community setting. Where are the rest of the potential life-long students?

Robert Wuthnow, author of *Growing Up Religious: Christians and Jews and Their Journeys of Faith*, might help us answer this question. Wuthnow describes some of the most trying aspects of a

[26] Barry Holtz, *Finding Our Way: Jewish Texts and the Lives We Lead Today* (New York: Schocken Books, 1990), pp. 3–14. Holtz also addresses this issue in his introduction to *Back to the Sources: Reading the Classic Jewish Texts* entitled, "On Reading Jewish Texts" (New York: Simon and Schuster, 1984), pp. 11–29.

strong religious commitment. Although he is not addressing himself to Orthodox Jews, his words resonate nonetheless:

> How do people who grew up religious move from the taken-for-granted world in which they had been raised to a more deliberate, intentional approach to faith? Many people, of course, do not make this move at all. People from the most intensely religious homes sometimes lose interest in their spirituality, either from sheer boredom or because they found such upbringing oppressive. Others continue on, perhaps claiming to believe what they always did and even attesting to the centrality of faith to their lives, yet doing little as adults to deepen their spirituality.[27]

We recognize the faces behind Wuthnow's words in our communities and in our own families. They are the day school graduates who tired of the routine, who sought newness in their university studies or professional lives, who think of their Judaism as a fine way to raise children but lacking in the sophistication and depth necessary to reach them as adults. Their religious beliefs did not grow with them; they grew out of them. Even those who maintain observance, according to Wuthnow, can fall into this category. Since their current practices are the same as those they observed as children, they have learned to associate them with childhood and childishness. They continue to practice, but are often motivated not by spiritual depth, but by the fear that not observing them will either result in punishment or in a loss of family attachments. Alternatively, they may see value in the lifestyle generally but not feel personally inspired.

Wuthnow's central thesis is that in order to sustain the religious commitment of one's youth an individual must undergo his or her own spiritual search. It is critical that religion be not only an anchor from childhood but a compass for the future. We can only come to

[27] Robert Wuthnow, *Growing Up Religious: Christians and Jews and Their Journeys of Faith* (Boston: Beacon Press, 1999), p. 162.

this conclusion on our own. It is not only a legacy; it is also a pursuit. In describing adults who grew up with religion and either returned to it or still maintain their level of observance, Wuthnow concludes,

> Although the specific practices may vary, the common dimension is that people start to take responsibility for their own spiritual development and thus begin to acquire personal knowledge and skill that goes beyond what they have learned simply by being a member of a congregation.[28]

Wuthnow believes that "growing up spiritually" involves not only a personal investment in and a sense of ownership of one's religion but also an acknowledgment of how religious practices, "develop in conjunction with changing social relationships." He believes that, "childhood spirituality is rooted in authority relationships with one's parent and with God."[29] As our social world matures, so does our need for the maturation of religion in order to continue spiritual development. Part of this process is the move away from a fear of authority in religion to a loving relationship with God, moving away from the "should do" in religion to the "want to do." Self-motivation from love, rather than guilt from desire, rather than authority helped people find a spiritual path within their own respective faiths. In addition to this change, the web of social connections created by religious communities is also strengthened and matures. Instead of taking from one's congregation or institution, adult spirituality is based on giving back and becoming more selflessly involved. Wuthnow concluded from his interviews that adults who were raised religious and stayed or returned to their traditions all did so not by increased religious behavior, but by making their religion more personally compelling.

> For those who continue on a significant spiritual journey as adults, the pattern we observe repeatedly in our interviews is

[28] Wuthnow, pp. 167–8.
[29] Wuthnow, p. 175.

> one of gaining distance from religious organizations through a process of discovering a more personalized style of faith. Gaining distance does not mean that people necessarily quit participating in religious organizations but they expect to receive less from these organizations, often become willing to *give* more of themselves in service to these and other organizations, and learn more effectively how to communicate with God in their personal lives.[30]

How might this study make an impact on Jewish adult education? It might challenge practices we currently regard as spiritually edifying. For some, increased spirituality comes in doing more – learning more, adding to the litany of prayers or becoming more stringent in one's observance. The spiritual pursuit results in added or heightened commandment performance or in the observance of *ḥumrot,* religious stringencies.[31] This, however, probably does not address the spiritual conundrum; it is not always a matter of doing more: It may be a matter of thinking more about that which we already do. Adult education can play a critical role in helping adults create a personal path of meaning by turning material that they learned as children into more sophisticated religious concepts. It can also point the way to recognizing how social relationships affect religious growth as we move from childhood models based on authority, to more equal and participatory roles in our communities. How can we accomplish this? On the most rudimentary level, it is a matter of the presentation of the material that educators choose to teach.

CONSIDERATION OF CONTENT

Arguments about the content of Jewish learning are centuries old. We find that, historically, whenever there was a strong push for a heavily Talmudic diet, there also was a corresponding pull back towards the study of topics that are less intellectually casuistic and more morally

[30] Wuthnow, p. 167.

[31] Sara Epstein-Weinstein, "The Permissibility of Self-Imposed Religious Stringency," in *Piety and Fanaticism* (Northvale, NJ: Jason Aaronson, 1997), pp. 23–63.

or religiously compelling. The argument over the study of Bible, not in preference, but in addition, to Talmud, was often the platform upon which this battle was waged.[32] A visit back into the curricular world of the sixteenth century might be instructive. According to one scholar at that time, the goal of spiritual perfection was not at issue; the question was which discipline maximized the chances of spiritual attainment:

> The issues in the heated dialogue or rather trialogue between Talmudists, philosophers, and kabbalists are the attainment of spirituality, the deepening of ideological sensitivity, religious vitality, and understanding – the interlocking of "du-

[32] The argument over content played out most fascinatingly in the discussion of the merits and disadvantages of engaging in *pilpul*. This debate came to its acme in the sixteenth century. Simha Assaf's compendium of writings on this issue in *Toledot ha-Ḥinukh* provides a good starting point for the debate. R. Handel Manoah ben Shmaryahu (d. 1612), a Polish student of the Maharshal, wrote a commentary on *Ḥovot ha-Levavot* advising students to stay away from intellectual Talmud exercises because they distanced an individual from the Torah and were a means of vanity without utility, (Assaf, pp. 48–9). The Maharal (p. 47) and R. Ephraim Lunshitz (1550–1619) took the same view: "The students can see how corrupt these mental exercises are…they do this only for self-aggrandizement," p. 63. Jacob Horowitz (d. 1622), the brother of the *Shelah,* was also a staunch advocate of Bible studies and was concerned that not only were *yeshivot* neglectful of the obligation to study Bible, they were also lacking in the spiritual wisdom it provided. See Shnayer Z. Leiman, "From the Pages of Tradition: R. Jacob Horowitz on the Study of Scripture," *Tradition* 27:1 (1992): 68–70. For more general information of the study of *pilpul*, see Moshe Shulvass, *Jewish Culture in Eastern Europe: the Classical Period* (New York: Ktav, 1975), pp. 25–30. For the treatment of this issue in the medieval period, see *Tosafot* to BT *Sanhedrin* 24a, s.v. "*Belulah*," BT *Kiddushin* 30a, s.v. "*Lo ẓerikha*," and BT *Avodah Zara* 19b, s.v. "*Yeshallesh*," and Ephraim Kanarfogel, *Jewish Education and Society in the High Middle Ages* (Detroit: Wayne State University Press, 1992), pp. 79–90. For a comparison between Sephardic and Ashkenazic treatments of Bible in the medieval period, see Frank Talmage, "Keep Your Sons from Scripture: The Bible in Medieval Jewish Scholarship and Spirituality" in *Understanding Scripture: Explorations of Jewish and Christian Traditions of Interpretation*, Clemens Thoma and Michael Wyschogrod, eds. (New York: Paulist Press, 1989), pp.81–101; Ephraim Kanarfogel, "On the Role of Bible Study in Medieval Ashkenaz" in *The Frank Talmage Memorial,* vol. 1, ed. Barry Walfish (Haifa: Haifa University Press, 1993), p. 154; Haym Soloveitchik, "Three Themes in *Sefer Ḥasidim*," in *AJS Review*,

> ties of the limb" with "duties of the heart." The key term in the vocabulary of spirituality and religiosity is perfection (*sheleimut* or *hashlamat ha-nefesh*). Within the framework of accepted views or on the basis of shared traditional premises, the debate revolves around how these disciplines interact, which is superior and which is subordinate and which is most conducive to *sheleimut*.... The curricular aspect is the practical expression while the phenomenological aspect is the theoretical motive.[33]

"*Sheleimut*" or religious perfection was the universally agreed goal; scholars argued about the means. Spiritual attainment was not always seen as a matter of content but rather as a matter of intent. Multiple disciplines ("within the framework of accepted views") could provide the map for the achievement of "*sheleimut*." If adult education today in the Orthodox world provided only one map of spirituality, it would severely curtail the inclusion of people whose spiritual avenues come through the rigorous study of a *blatt gemara* or those who find themselves moved by a Ḥasidic tale. Historical debates are relevant today in their concern for intentioned study. *Talmud Torah* was informed by the concern that it contributed to one's "ideological sensitivity." Some might conclude that the only way to achieve this "*sheleimut*" is through teaching subjects like *mussar* or selected passages from *Tanakh* and Talmud which directly deal with personal growth. But, with added flexibility, we might be more expansive. Any subject of Jewish study may help create *sheleimut* if certain assumptions are made about the reasons that we study.

1 (1976): 339; and Mordechai Breuer, "*Minu Beneikhem min ha-Higgayon*," in *Mikhtam le-David: Sefer Zikkaron ha-Rav David Ochs*, ed. Yiẓḥak Gilat and Eliezer Stern (Ramat Gan: Bar Ilan University Press, 1978), pp. 242–64.

[33] Isadore Twersky, "Talmudists, Philosophers, Kabbalists: The Quest for Spirituality in the Sixteenth Century," in *Jewish Thought in the Sixteenth Century*, ed. Bernard Dov Cooperman (Cambridge, MA: Harvard University Press, 1983), p. 440. See also Halbertal, "Strong Canonicity and Shared Discourse," in *People of the Book*, pp. 124–8.

RE-READING RELIGION

Like religion, reading is taught at a young age, and we assume it need not be taught again. The sophisticated process of analysis involved in adult reading, however, forces us to rethink what it means to read as an adult.[34] Much of the reading we did as children was not by choice and took place in a school environment where we had to master material and were held accountable for it. Most adults who read do so in a completely different context. They read for pleasure, insight, or information. If a book fails to stimulate them or provide the information they seek, they have the liberty to close it. While this description may sound pedestrian, it is exactly the dilemma that the adult educator faces. Adults have many demands on their time, and most adults who study devote only a fraction of their time to Jewish studies. There is no accountability in a class for adults; they do not have to be there if they are bored, and there is no incentive for attending, other than personal gain. In addition, there are so many familial and fiscal responsibilities which adults shoulder that there are often more compelling or immediate reasons not to be present in a class than to attend it. Culturally, there is an ever-widening emphasis on leisure and physical fitness that competes with adult students for time.[35] Can we assume that the *mizvah* of *Talmud Torah* alone will bring adults into the classroom? For some, yes, but for most the answer is no. Adult educators need to supply reasons why their students should come back into the classroom.[36]

---

[34] An excellent study on the complexity of the reading endeavor is presented by Paul Ricoeur in *From Text to Action: Essays in Hermeneutics*, II, trans. Kathleen Blamey and John Thompson (Evanston, IL: Northwestern University Press, 1991) and Geoffrey Hartman, "The Work of Reading," in *Criticism in the Wilderness: The Study of Literature Today* (New Haven: Yale University Press), pp. 161–88.

[35] See Norman Lamm's analysis in "A Jewish Ethic of Leisure," *Faith and Doubt: Studies in Traditional Jewish Thought* (New York: Ktav, 1986), pp. 187–211 and Erica Brown, "Jewish Adult Education: Creating an Educational Democracy," *Ten Daat: A Journal of Jewish Education* 9:1 (1996): 63–77.

[36] One way to stimulate some discussion on the contribution of study to personal development is to introduce students to texts, articles and books that discuss this issue directly. I often recommend Barry Holtz's introductory chapter "On Reading Jewish Texts" from *Back to the Sources: Reading the Classic Jewish Texts* (New York:

Here, a distinction drawn by E.D. Hirsch may enlighten our discussion. Hirsch distinguishes between the concepts of significance and meaning. Meaning, he claims, is "fixed and immutable;" in contrast, "significance is open to change."[37] A text's meaning, Hirsch argues, is fixed on one level, since without rootedness it would merely "float on the tides of preference."[38] However, the reader will assign to a text significance based upon personal proclivities and subjective tastes. In the Orthodox community, texts are always meaningful as transmitters of tradition; their significance, however, is not always discussed. One might view the role of the instructor in an adult education classroom as lending significance to a text that is already meaningful to their students. One way to do this is to suggest that lifelong Jewish education will contribute to *sheleimut*, a more developed and coherent sense of faith and spiritual sensitivity. Teachers can promote this by ensuring that subjects are taught with a preamble and a "de-briefing," or with contexts and pretexts. The preamble can assume many forms; it might be a short *tefillah* to begin the session, a personal anecdote, or an inspiring story. It might be a reminder given throughout the class of the beauty of the material or its profundity.[39]

Simon and Schuster, 1984), pp. 11–29. Even individuals who have had a life-long commitment to *Talmud Torah* have difficulty articulating why they study and what they "get out" of learning. Exposing students to the formulations of others is a good way to get students thinking and debating about their personal investment in Jewish texts.

[37] E.D. Hirsch, "Meaning and Significance Reinterpreted," *Critical Inquiry* (December, 1984): 202. Hirsch first presented this distinction in *Validity in Interpretation* (New Haven: Yale University Press, 1967), p. 4, but revisited and further refined it in this paper.

[38] Hirsch, p. 203.

[39] In a study I conducted about the spiritual development of women in adult Jewish education "An Intimate Spectator: Jewish Women Reflect on Adult Study," I found, much to my surprise, that several women commented that Jewish study for them was not a spiritual experience and in some cases actually diminished their spirituality because of its critical nature. Often, teachers contribute to this irony by being analytical or critical without moderating or tempering their discussion by articulating the inherent beauty of the text or the endeavor. The results of this research are published in the journal *Religious Education* 98:1 (2003).

It might consist of a sentence of reflection when the information has already been covered.[40]

These small "injections of meaning" should not be underestimated as a pedagogic tool. Israel Scheffler promoted what he termed "cognitive emotions" as an outcome of education. His claim is that cognition and emotion are not "hostile worlds apart," and that when emotions are in the service of cognition, both the emotional and the intellectual realms work in confluence for true and deep understanding.[41] If we were to substitute in his dichotomy the words "spiritual" and "intellectual," we might arrive at the same conclusion. Intellectual mastery combined with spiritual depth should be the goal of an adult education encounter. Naturally, some instructors will gravitate towards a more direct form of spiritual explication by choosing a subject replete with obvious religious significance. I do not believe, however, that this is always necessary or even desirable. It often creates self-righteousness or guilt-inducing lessons that may not compel the student to return to class. Instead, imagine a class as a walk through an art gallery and the observation of a painting. The teacher comments on the history and significance of the work and then, in a brief sentence, points out the use of light or shadow. That brief encounter will force the student to look at the painting in a radically different way. The teacher is not forcing understanding, but guiding the student's vision. It is this need to show students the light and shadows of the material that lends vision and depth to study. When the messages are religious in nature, it will help infuse the information with inspiration and relevancy. If Orthodox adults are accustomed to receiving information and skill-acquisition in learning, then we need to continue those valuable patterns already

[40] Stephen Brookfield recommends that adults keep learning journals to help them become more reflective, "Grounded Teaching in Learning" in *Facilitating Adult Learning: A Transactional Process,* ed. Michael Galbraith (Malabar, FL: Kreiger Publishing Company, 1991), pp. 37–9. However, as Brookfield himself admits, this practice can become cumbersome and tedious and become counterproductive.

[41] Israel Scheffler, "In Praise of the Cognitive Emotions," *Inquiries: Philosophical Studies of Language, Science and Learning* (Indianapolis: Hackett Publishing Company, 1986), pp. 347–62.

established. These small "injections of meaning" help frame the information with inspiration.

NON-INTELLECTUAL FORMS OF SPIRITUALITY

In his article, "Preparing Children for Spirituality," Lawrence Scheindlin posits that in order to make children receptive to matters of the spirit, one must focus on five aspects of education: 1) help children value their inner lives, 2) engage children's curiosity and their early experiences of wonder, 3) assist children in articulating feelings, 4) develop children's aesthetic sensitivity, and 5) develop interpersonal sensitivity.[42] In the early years, encouraging children to respond to their experiences with wonder will help them recognize and feel the impact of a spiritual encounter. Scheindlin writes that, "[t]he senses of awe, mystery, and wonder are, obviously, complex emotional responses to a complex universe. Understanding these emotions is elusive to us – adults and religious educators. However, since spiritual awe (*yirat shamayim*) is a complex emotional experience, it must be preceded by simpler emotions from the same family of feelings."[43] Scheindlin's recommendation for the education of children is no less important for adults, particularly those adults who may not have benefited from these guidelines as children. Injecting meaning and inspiration in an adult classroom is difficult if there is little readiness for spirituality to begin with. The sense of awe and mystery that Scheindlin encourages is harder to achieve as an adult, when the world and its wonders may not be so new. It is then that we may have to travel farther or walk deeper into the woods.

In *Stages of Faith: The Psychology of Human Development and the Quest for Meaning,* James Fowler discusses adult faith development through an imagined dialogue between Erikson, Piaget, and Kohlberg.[44] Building his research upon the work of others, he creates six stages of faith, the last being the "universal ethical principle"

---

[42] Lawrence Scheindlin, "Preparing Children for Spirituality," *Journal of Religious Education* 94:2 (Spring, 1999): 191–2.

[43] Scheindlin, p. 194.

[44] James W. Fowler, *Stages of Faith: The Psychology of Human Development and the Quest for Meaning* (San Francisco: HarperSanFrancisco, 1995), pp. 78–85.

stage of faith. Stages four and five have to do with the performance of rules, laws, and societal adjustments. Educating adults for the sixth stage requires an ability to see past law and rules or simple social-contract theory, to universal truths. Jewish spiritual development does not culminate in universality, but it does need to see beyond rules and laws alone and place value on meaning and complex social interactions within a religious context. The problem that most concerns Fowler is adult stagnation: moving through the stages, getting caught in one stage, and never growing beyond it. Important future research on Jewish faith development might need to take Fowler's stages and contrast them to an imagined set of Jewish "stages." Nevertheless, Fowler's concern with stagnation should be adopted as our own. Adults also need to move in stages of spiritual development. The *berakhot* we learned as children need to take on additional significance for us as adults now that we sustain our own families. The *tefillot* we learned as children have to grow in meaning as we bring to them decades of life experience. Shabbat and holiday observance, rituals we may have observed for a lifetime, must become more significant anchors in our lives now that we work the rest of the week. All of these non-intellectual, experiential aspects of religion require cultivation outside of the classroom, if we are to highlight inspirational moments within the classroom.

IN CONCLUSION

In the first chapter of the Laws of Idol Worship, Maimonides describes the eclipse of monotheism, the rise of idol worship and the spiritual seeking of Abraham who recaptured the belief in one God. Maimonides' portrait of Abraham, based on observations from the Midrash and Talmud, describes a search that began at age three. From this age onward, Abraham contemplated the universe until he arrived at the notion of God thirty-seven years later. Not until the prime of his adulthood did Abraham find what he was searching for. We know from Genesis 12 that Abraham did not receive his mission until he was seventy-five years old. Only then was he to go to Canaan and establish a nation. The process of self-discovery, that led to action, took seventy-two years. The struggle of faith continued for Abraham well into his hundredth year. At no point did his contemplation end; rather it continually intensified. Using Abraham as our guide, perhaps we can help adults walk in the footsteps of the patriarch and show them that adulthood is the beginning, and not the end, of faith and character formation.

[45] The author would like to express her gratitude to Dr. Jacob Meskin and Dr. Harvey Shapiro for their insights in shaping this paper.

Section six

Spirituality and Prayer

10

Maimonides on Prayer

Arthur Hyman

Maimonides discusses prayer in all of his major writings: the *Commentary on the Mishnah*, *Sefer ha-Miẓvot*, *Mishneh Torah*, and *The Guide of the Perplexed*. Perhaps the clearest view of Maimonides' perception of prayer emerges from two statements in his *Sefer ha-Miẓvot*. In the fifth positive commandment of this work he first comments on the halakhic status of prayer making it a specific instance of the general obligation to worship God. He writes:

> The fifth [positive] commandment is to serve God and [this commandment] has been repeatedly stated [in the Bible].... And even though this is one of the general commandments (*me-ha-ẓivuyyim ha-kollelim*), ...it has a particular instantiation, namely the commandment to pray. This is clear from the comment of the *Sifrei* – "To serve Him" – this refers to prayer.[1]

[1] *Sefer ha-Miẓvot*, Positive Commandment 5 [Arabic and modern Hebrew: ed. and trans. Joseph Kafah (Jerusalem: Mossad ha-Rav Kook, 1971), pp. 60–1; medieval

For Maimonides, then, prayer is, first of all, a halakhic obligation. However, as we shall see, this obligation also includes his understanding of the origin of prayer and its historic development.

A second aspect of Maimonides' conception emerges from the third [positive] commandment in his *Sefer ha-Miẓvot*, discussing the halakhic obligation to love God (*ha-ahavah ha-meḥuyyevet*). Love, it is generally held, must be spontaneous and cannot be commanded, but Maimonides recognizes that love can also be a matter of [religious] obligation. This love comes about when one reflects on God [which is the first positive commandment], which in turn leads to pleasure, and ultimately results in the obligatory love of God. Maimonides writes:

> We have explained to you that through reflection [on God] (*hitbonenut*) you will attain pleasure (*hanaah*), and this will be followed by obligatory love (*ha-ahavah ha-meḥuyyevet*).[2]

Combining, then, these two statements, we find that to understand Maimonides' conception of prayer we must consider its halakhic status, its affective (emotional) status, its intellectual status, and, finally, its relation to the love of God. It is to these four topics that this paper is devoted.

In describing the halakhic origin of prayer Maimonides differs from other decisors. Speaking for these, Ramban, in his commentary on Maimonides' fifth [positive] commandment in the *Sefer ha-Miẓvot*, holds that the obligation to pray is rabbinic, while according to Maimonides the general obligation to pray is biblical.[3] Since this obligation is a positive commandment not subject to any

---

Hebrew: trans. Mosheh Ibn Tibbon, ed. Hayim Heller (Jerusalem: Mossad ha-Rav Kook, 1946), p. 36; English: trans. Ch. B. Chavel (London: Soncino Press, 1967), p. 8]. For a recent discussion of Maimonides' account of prayer, see Ehud Benor, *Worship of the Heart: A Study in Maimonides' Philosophy of Religion* (Albany, NY: SUNY Press, 1995).

[2] *Sefer ha-Miẓvot*, Positive Commandment 3 (Arabic and modern Hebrew: 59; medieval Hebrew: 35–6; English: 3–4).

[3] *Hasagot Ramban* on *Sefer ha-Miẓvot*, Positive Commandment 5 (Jerusalem – Benei Berak: 1955), p. 210.

time constraints (*mizvat aseh she-lo ha-zeman gerama*), it is also incumbent on women.[4]

In *Mishneh Torah, Hilkhot Tefillah*, 1:1 Maimonides further describes the nature of biblically ordained prayer. It must be uttered every day, but the number of prayers, their form, and their time are left to each individual's desires, needs, and abilities.[5] Those who are articulate will pray many times a day; those less gifted will pray only once daily.[6] While the biblically ordained prayer is spontaneous, it should still have three parts – all of which reappear when prayer is formalized. It should express praise of God, go on to the requests for the fulfillment of one's needs, and conclude with thanks to God for the benefits that He has bestowed on us.[7] It should be noted that biblically ordained prayer, while spontaneous, still has a halakhic structure: recognition of God, man's dependence on God for fulfillment of his needs, and gratitude to God for providing for these needs. All this is in accordance with Maimonides' conviction that whatever the intellectual and emotive content of prayer, even spontaneous prayer requires some form of halakhic structure. Finally, Maimonides adds, wherever human beings pray they should turn in the direction of the Temple.[8] This emphasizes the inner connection between prayer and sacrifices, a notion that takes on a more central role when prayer is formalized. Maimonides concludes this phase of the discussion by pointing out that this was the nature of prayer from the time of Moses to that of Ezra.[9]

With the Babylonian exile, which resulted in a confusion of tongues, the situation began to change. People no longer spoke

---

[4] *Mishneh Torah, Hilkhot Tefillah*, 1:2. The text is cited from the standard edition (Warsaw), but reference is also made to the edition and English translation contained in Moses Hyamson, ed. and trans. *Mishneh Torah, Sefer Ahavah* (Jerusalem: Boys Town, 1965), 98a. In Hyamson's edition the text is based on an Oxford manuscript in which the numbering of the *halakhot* differs in some cases from that of the standard edition.

[5] *Mishneh Torah, Hilkhot Tefillah*, 1:1 (Hyamson: 98a).

[6] *Mishneh Torah, Hilkhot Tefillah*, 1:3 (Hyamson: 98b).

[7] *Mishneh Torah, Hilkhot Tefillah*, 1:2 (Hyamson, 98b).

[8] *Mishneh Torah, Hilkhot Tefillah*, 1:3 (Hyamson: 98b).

[9] *Mishneh Torah, Hilkhot Tefillah*, 1:3 (Hyamson: 98b).

Hebrew and they lost the ability to utter spontaneous prayer in that language. Consequently, Ezra and his court ordained formal prayer with formal prayer times. The *Shemoneh Esreih* they now ordained contained the same three-fold structure as spontaneous prayer – the first three benedictions devoted to the praise of God, the middle twelve requests for the fulfillment of one's needs, and the last three expressing thanks to God.[10] Prayer's relation to sacrifices is once again emphasized by patterning the times of prayer after the times of sacrifices – *shaḥarit* corresponding to the morning *korban tamid* and *minḥah* corresponding to the afternoon *korban tamid. Arvit*, which had no corresponding time for sacrifices, paralleled the time when the members of the animal offered as the afternoon sacrifice were burned. The relation of prayer to sacrifice is emphasized further by *musaf* on days on which the *korban musaf* was offered. Since there was no sacrifice corresponding to *arvit*, the recitation of this prayer is only *reshut;* but still, it became *ḥovah* since all of Israel accepted it as *tefillat ḥovah.*[11]

The connection of prayer and sacrifices also has a negative effect. While voluntary prayer (*tefillat nedavah*) is permitted, such prayer could only be individual not communal, since the community could not offer a voluntary sacrifice (*korban nedavah*).[12] From all this it seems to follow that the formal prayer that we now possess is inferior to spontaneous prayer. One might wonder whether Maimonides would advocate a return to spontaneous, biblical prayer when the time of the exile is ended and the Jews once again will have their own land and a common language.

Another aspect of Maimonides' discussion of prayer requires our attention, namely the use of prayer to propagate true ideas and to combat false ones. Embodied in *birkat ha-minim*, this practice goes back to rabbinic times. When the number of unbelievers (*epikursim)* who tried to turn the Israelites away from God increased, Rabban

---

[10] *Mishneh Torah, Hilkhot Tefillah,* 1:4 (Hyamson: 98b).
[11] *Mishneh Torah, Hilkhot Tefillah,* 1:5–6 (Hyamson: 98b–99a).
[12] *Mishneh Torah, Hilkhot Tefillah,* 1:10 (Hyamson: 99a).

Gamliel and his court added this blessing to the *Shemoneh Esreih*. In this blessing God is asked to destroy the unbelievers.[13]

Two other instances manifest prayer as an instrument for the propagation of ideas. Citing the Mishnah, Maimonides, in *Mishneh Torah, Hilkhot Tefillah*, 9:4 and 7,[14] holds that someone who, in reciting the public prayer, utters the term "*modim*" twice should be removed and prevented from continuing the public recitation of the *Shemoneh Esreih*. While the *Mishnah* generally provided for the correction of verbal mistakes or slips of the tongue in prayer, in this case it does not. For, in the case of someone who says "*modim*" twice it is not clear whether this was only a slip of the tongue or an attempt to propagate the dualistic notion that there are two deities. Similarly, someone should not add in the prayer of supplication (*taḥanunim*) "He (God) who has mercy on the bird's nest (*kan ẓippor*) [ordaining] not to take the mother with her offspring and not to kill the mother with her offspring on the same day, may He have mercy on us." For these commandments are divine decrees (*gezerot ha-katuv*) not expressions of mercy. It is in this context that Maimonides ordains that one should not add, in the *Shemoneh Esreih*, new attributes describing God in addition to those sanctioned by tradition. He writes:

> Likewise one should not multiply the attributes describing God (*kinuyyim*) saying God who is great, valiant, awe-inspiring, strong, vigorous, and mighty, for human beings do not have the power to express all the praises of God. A person should only say those attributes that were spoken by Moses, of blessed memory.[15]

This statement, based on a story about Rabbi Ḥanina, which appears in *Mishneh Torah* in support of the halakhic obligation not to increase divine attributes in prayer, appears also in *The Guide of the Perplexed* as the centerpiece of Maimonides' philosophic interpretation of

[13] *Mishneh Torah, Hilkhot Tefillah*, 2:1 (Hyamson: 99a).

[14] *Mishneh Torah, Hilkhot Tefillah*, 9:4 and 7 (Hyamson: 108a).

[15] *Mishneh Torah, Hilkhot Tefillah*, 9:7 (Hyamson: 108a).

prayer. It is one of the examples showing the conflation of halakhic and philosophic ideas in the thought of Maimonides.

It becomes clear from several *halakhot* that the laws of prayer take into account human shortcomings and needs. For example, someone carrying a load may pass by a synagogue without participating in communal prayer, someone praying with the congregation should not prolong his prayer unduly, and a laborer engaged in work on top of a tree does not have to descend in order to pray.[16]

Intention (*kavvanah*) is one of the central requirements of prayer, so much so that one may not pray without it. In fact, *kavvanah* is one of the five factors that prevent one (*me'akvin*) from praying even if the time for prayer has arrived.[17] Even more strongly Maimonides ordains that prayer without *kavvanah* is not prayer and must be repeated. One may not pray if his mind is confused or his heart is troubled and one may wait three days until one's mind and heart are at rest.[18] But what is *kavvanah*? Maimonides, in *Mishneh Torah, Hilkhot Tefillah*, 4:15[19] defines:

> *Kavvanat ha-lev* occurs when a person removes [from his mind] all [worldly] thoughts and considers himself as if he were standing in the presence of the *shekhinah*.

To attain this state, one must rest a while before reciting the prayer and one must rest a while after reciting it. In fact, the pious of earlier times prepared themselves for prayer an hour before reciting it, prayed for an hour, and then spent another hour resting after completing their prayer. It is this notion that is probably closest to the modern notion of spirituality, that is, a meditative state in which one is aware of the presence of God. It must, however, be emphasized that this is only one aspect of prayer; the other part being its halakhic obligation and its halakhic structure.

In his *Guide of the Perplexed*, Maimonides discusses prayer in

---

[16] *Mishneh Torah, Hilkhot Tefillah*, 6:1–2 (Hyamson: 104a–b).
[17] *Mishneh Torah, Hilkhot Tefillah*, 4:1 (Hyamson: 101b).
[18] *Mishneh Torah, Hilkhot Tefillah*, 4:15 (Hyamson: 102b).
[19] *Mishneh Torah, Hilkhot Tefillah*, 4:16 (Hyamson: 102b).

two contexts: in his description of the reasons for the commandments (*taamei ha-miẓvot*) and, more philosophically, in his interpretation of divine attributes. His discussion among the reasons for the commandments is rather brief because, as he states in *Guide* 3.44,[20] prayer has "manifest reasons and evident causes." To present them at length is not of help because "it would be nothing but repetition." Prayer, Maimonides points out, is included in those commandments that are mentioned in *Mishneh Torah* in *Sefer Ahavah* (The Book of Love) whose purpose is constant commemoration of God, the love of Him and the fear of Him, the obligatory observance of the commandments in general, and the bringing about of such belief concerning Him, may He be exalted, as is necessary of everyone professing the law.

It should be noted that in the *Guide* Maimonides emphasizes the cognitive function of prayer – instilling correct beliefs – and its role in fostering the love of God.

Maimonides' most philosophic discussion of prayer occurs in the first part of the *Guide* in chapters devoted to his theory of divine attributes. There he proposes the thesis that anthropomorphic and, to a lesser extent, anthropopathic attributes predicated of God must be interpreted in such a way that they yield non-anthropomorphic and non-anthropopathic meanings. As a first step, applicable to ordinary people and the philosophic elite alike, Maimonides shows exegetically that even in the Bible, such terms have non-anthropomorphic and non-anthropopathic meanings. This even the philosophically unsophisticated masses must understand. But, for the philosophically trained, the matter is more complicated, for they must understand such attributes according to the canons of language and logic.

By way of preliminary observation, it should be noted that, absolutely speaking, Maimonides takes a rather dim view of the ability of human language to convey significant truths about God

---

[20] *The Guide of the Perplexed*, 3.44 [medieval Hebrew: trans. Samuel Ibn Tibbon, ed. Yehudah Even Shemuel (Jerusalem: Mossad ha-Rav Kook, 1981) p. 534; English: trans. Shlomo Pines (Chicago: Chicago University Press, 1963), p. 574.

and he prefers silent contemplation to linguistic expression. He writes in *Guide* 1.57[21]:

> These subtle notions (divine attributes) that very clearly elude the minds cannot be considered through the instrumentality of the customary words, which are the greatest among the causes leading unto error. For the bounds of expression in all languages are very narrow indeed, so that we cannot represent this notion to ourselves except through a certain looseness of expression.

Even more explicitly, he writes in *Guide* 1.59[22]:

> The most apt phrase concerning this subject is the dictum occurring in the Psalms (65:2) 'Silence is praise to Thee', which interpreted signifies: silence with regard to You is praise.... Accordingly, silence and limiting oneself to the apprehensions of the intellect are more appropriate – just as the perfect ones have enjoined us when they say (Ps. 4:5): 'Commune with your own heart upon your bed, and be still, Selah.'

While, then, silent contemplation of God seems to be Maimonides' ideal goal, still, human beings are halakhically commanded to pray to Him. Maimonides still has to explain how human language can signify correctly in speaking about God.

Maimonides' exposition is guided by two principles: (1) language about God must signify literally and in accordance with the customary usage, and (2) since God is one, attributes forming predicates of propositions describing Him must not introduce any multiplicity in Him.

For Maimonides is was axiomatic that God is "one," but what does the proposition "God is one" mean? Its common meaning is that God is unique, that is, there is no other being like Him. This

[21] *The Guide of the Perplexed*, 1.57 (medieval Hebrew: p. 113; English: pp. 132–3).
[22] *The Guide of the Perplexed*, 1.59 (medieval Hebrew: p. 119; English: pp. 139–40).

is what the masses seem to mean. But for philosophers this is not enough, for a being can be unique and still be composite. If, then, God is one, he must not only be unique but also simple, that is non-composite. That God possesses no physical composition is clear from his incorporeality, but, in addition, he must lack ontological composition. It is this proposition that governs Maimonides' discussion of divine attributes. He writes in *Guide* 1.51[23]:

> For there is no oneness at all except in believing that there is one simple essence in which there is no complexity or multiplication of notions, but one notion only; so that from whatever angle you regard it and from whatever point of view you consider it, you will find that it is one, not divided in any way and by any cause into two notions; and you will not find therein any multiplicity either in the thing as it is outside the mind or as it is in the mind.

Attributes that form the predicates of propositions are divided into two kinds: essential and accidental. Essential attributes are those the denial of which entails the denial of the existence of their subject. For example, if in the proposition "Socrates is living" the predicate "living" is denied, the existence of Socrates is denied thereby. Accidental attributes, by contrast, are those the denial of which does not entail the denial of the existence of their subject. If, for example, in the proposition "this table is brown" the predicate "brown" is denied, the existence of the table is not denied thereby. For it may be the case that the table is brown at the present time, but it remains the same table even it is painted green at a future time.

It was generally admitted by medieval philosophers that accidental attributes introduce ontological multiplicity in the subject of which they are predicated, but they differed concerning essential

[23] *The Guide of the Perplexed,* 1.51 (medieval Hebrew: p. 96; English: p. 113). For a fuller discussion of Maimonides' opinion concerning the religious use of language, see my article "Maimonides on Religious Language," in *Perspectives on Maimonides: Philosophical and Historical Studies,* ed. Joel Kraemer (Oxford: Littman Library, 1991), pp. 175–91.

attributes. There were those who maintained, Gersonides among the Jews, that essential attributes are explicative, that is, they explain the meaning of the subject; hence they do not introduce any ontological multiplicity. According to this view essential attributes can be predicated of God affirmatively, though it still must be shown how they differ between their application to God and to His creatures. For Gersonides, for example, essential attributes such as wise and powerful, have positive signification even though they are applied to God according to priority, but to human beings, according to posteriority.[24] It would appear that this opinion is closer to our understanding of how the language of prayer functions. For, while we are aware that God's attributes differ from ours, still, there is a commonality of meaning.

Others, including Maimonides, maintain that essential attributes predicated of God are expansive, that is, they introduce ontological multiplicity in the subject. He writes in *Guide* 1.57[25]:

> It is known that existence [and one may add, other essential attributes], is an accident attaching to what exists. For this reason, it is something that is superadded to the quiddity [essence] of what exists.

Having maintained that neither accidental nor essential attributes can be predicated of God affirmatively, Maimonides now has to show how propositions containing these attributes must be interpreted as propositions that say something significant about God, yet do so without applying to Him attributes that signify affirmatively.

Accidental attributes predicated of God, Maimonides affirms, must be understood as attributes of action.[26] For the case of human beings such attributes must meet two conditions: someone possess-

---

[24] Levi ben Gershom, *The Wars of the Lord*, 3.3 [Hebrew: (Leipzig: 1866) pp. 132–7; English: trans. Seymour Feldman (Philadelphia: Jewish Publication Society, 1987) pp. 107–15).

[25] *The Guide of the Perplexed*, 1.57 (medieval Hebrew: p. 112; English: p. 132).

[26] *The Guide of the Perplexed*, 1.52 (medieval Hebrew: p. 101; English: pp. 118–9).

ing them must (1) have a certain disposition, either habits or affects, and (2) must perform or be able to perform habitually actions of a certain kind. Since dispositions introduce ontological multiplicity into the subject to which they belong, they cannot be predicated of God at all. It only remains that accidental attributes must be understood as referring to God's actions. While the knowledge of God's actions is more limited than the knowledge of dispositions and actions together, knowledge of God's actions has the advantage that it preserves the simplicity of God.

Having shown that accidental attributes predicated of God must be interpreted as attributes of action, Maimonides might have gone on to maintain that essential attributes should be understood as attributes of action as well. However, he never seems to have considered this possibility. He might also have held that essential attributes can be understood as metaphors, but he rejected this possibility as well.[27] For besides introducing multiplicity into God, metaphors require that there be some likeness between God and creatures, and this, according to Maimonides, cannot be. (Differing from Maimonides, Gersonides later on picks up on this option.) The only option that remains is that such terms signify by way of complete equivocation, or, more precisely, by way of negation (*shelilah*) or negation of privation (*shelilat ha-he'ader*).

When Maimonides describes in general fashion how essential attributes predicated of God are to be understood, he maintains that they must be understood as negations. But, speaking more technically in *Guide* 1.58, he states that they must be understood as negations of privations. H.A. Wolfson has shown[28] that in the tradition that reached Maimonides, privations were of two kinds: (1) the absence of a property (or habit) that can naturally be there, and (2) the absence of a property (or habit) that can never be there. An example of the former is "the man is blind," and an example of

---

[27] *The Guide of the Perplexed*, 1.56 (medieval Hebrew: pp. 111–12; English: pp. 130–1).

[28] H.A. Wolfson, "Maimonides on Negative Attributes," in *Studies in the History of Philosophy and Religion*, vol. 2 (Cambridge, MA: Harvard University Press, 1977), pp. 195–230.

the latter is "the wall is not seeing." Privations of the second kind exclude the subject of which they are predicated from a certain class of beings or properties. Since God can never have any properties or habits that are affirmatively predicated of him, the privations that are negated of Him must be of the second kind. Hence, the proposition "God is wise" must be understood as "God is not ignorant," that is, it must be understood as excluding God from the class of ignorant beings.

But does negative languages applied to God provide any knowledge of Him? Maimonides concedes that affirmative attributes provide a more adequate account of the essence and attributes of that which they describe, but as the following example illustrates, negative attributes provide some knowledge as well. Suppose that someone knows that a ship exists, but does not know the object to which this term applies. Let us now imagine that someone finds out that the ship is not an accident, another that it is not a mineral, a third that it is not a plant, and so forth. As the negations are multiplied one comes closer and closer to knowing what a ship is, though he will never know in positive fashion the essence of a ship. "It is clear," writes Maimonides in *Guide* 1:60,[29] "that the last individual [in the example] has nearly achieved by means of these negative attributes the representation of the ship as it is." From all this it follows that we can say something significant about God's essential attributes without assigning to them positive signification.

One question remains. If essential attributes are understood as negations, would it not be sufficient to affirm generally that God is unlike any of His creatures? In that case, however, it would follow, as Maimonides states in *Guide* 1.59,[30] that "Moses our Master and Solomon [the wisest of men] did not apprehend anything different from what a single individual from among the pupils apprehends." This, however, is not the case. For, just as each additional affirmative attribute increases our knowledge of that which is described, so

[29] *The Guide of the Perplexed*, 1.60 (medieval Hebrew: pp. 122–5; English: pp. 143–7).

[30] *The Guide of the Perplexed*, 1.59 (medieval Hebrew: pp. 117–8; English: pp. 137–8).

each additional negative attribute "particularizes" God more and more. Moreover, it is not enough to deny certain attributes to God; a trained philosopher must know by apodictic, that is, demonstrative proof, why a given attribute is to be denied. The acquisition of this knowledge requires ability, time, and training.

While the terms discussed so far are attributes predicated of God, there is one term, the Tetragrammaton, which signifies what He is. Indicating God's essence, this term has no association with any term applied to creatures. "This name," writes Maimonides in *Guide* 1.61,[31] "gives a clear and unequivocal indication of God's essence." Maimonides' theory of how proper names signify requires further study.

What are the implications of Maimonides' rigorous conception of human language for its use in prayer? Is it not the case that someone who prays means something more in saying that God is one and living than that He is not many and not dead? Would one not expect, as Gersonides does later on, that language about God signifies positively in some fashion? Ever the purist, Maimonides would reply that positive predication introduces multiplicity into God and this is to be avoided at all cost. It is better to say little about God and to say it correctly than to say much and mislead. It is in this context that, in *Guide* 1.59,[32] he inveighs against "poets and preachers," and he approvingly cites once more the story of Rabbi Haninah, which in *Mishneh Torah* he had used for the halakhic prohibition that it is not permissible to add descriptions of God to those uttered by Moses and confirmed by the Men of the Great Assembly.

Maimonides describes the love of God to which prayer (and the observance of other commandments) leads in *Mishneh Torah, Laws of Repentance*, Chapter Ten.[33] It is an unselfish love, that is, a love not based on the expectation of reward or fear of punishment. Maimonides defines it as:

---

[31] *The Guide of the Perplexed*, 1.61 (medieval Hebrew: pp. 125–6; English: pp. 147–8).

[32] *The Guide of the Perplexed*, 1.59 (medieval Hebrew: pp. 119–22; English: pp. 140–3).

[33] *Mishneh Torah, Hilkhot Teshuvah*, 10:3 (Hyamson: 92b).

> to love God with a great and exceeding love so strong that one's soul should be knit up with the love of God and one should be continually enraptured by it, like a lovesick person, whose mind is never free from his passion for a particular woman, the thought of her filling his heart at all times, when sitting down or rising up when he is eating or drinking. Even more intense should be the love of God in the hearts of those who love him. And this love should continually possess them, even as He commanded us (*she-ẓivanu*) '[to love God] with all your heart, with all your soul and with all your possessions'.

Once again we hear of love that is commanded. What is striking in this description is that the love of God is compared to physical, human love. This suggests that this love has an affective, that is, emotional, dimension. Maimonides' understanding that *Shir ha-Shirim* is totally devoted to a description of this love further supports this interpretation.

But this is not a full account. For in *Hilkhot Teshuvah* 10:6[34] he adds:

> One only loves God with the knowledge with which one knows Him. According to the knowledge will be the love. If [the knowledge of God] is little, so will be the love of Him.

Having traced Maimonides' complex discussion in his halakhic and in his philosophic writing, we may now ask what is the result of the discussion and how is it related to the topic of our session. I must confess that while I have a reasonably clear perception of Maimonides' halakhic and philosophic views, I have a less clear understanding of what is meant by "spirituality." I have searched books and encyclopedias with little success. There were instructions of all kinds, religious and secular, how to acquire a state of spirituality, but I could not find any clear definition of what that state is. Let us then take as a working definition that spirituality is an existential

[34] *Mishneh Torah, Hilkhot Teshuvah*, 10:6 (Hyamson: 93a).

state (of detachment) achieved through some instrumentality, such as recitation, singing, reflection, or even prayer. While this may form part of Maimonides' discussion of prayer, it is by no means its major part nor is it its goal.

As Maimonides sees it, prayer is a many-layered activity involving the whole human personality. It is one that is applicable to both ordinary people and the intellectual elite alike, though for the elite it may pose issues that do not exist for ordinary folk. For a Jew, prayer is, first of all, a mandated halakhic obligation. Even spontaneous biblically ordained prayer, which defines man's relation to God, requires that it be recited once a day. In its structure it must contain praise of God, recognition that God answers our requests, and gratitude to Him for providing for us. Prayer is connected to sacrifices thereby emphasizing a ritual counterpart to prayer. Prayer takes account of the vicissitudes of human life by making room for situations in which prayer has to be limited or cannot be offered at all.

In a more spiritual vein, prayer requires *kavvanah*, that is, an act of concentration. A prayer uttered without *kavvanah* is not a valid prayer and must be repeated. While it is halakhically prohibited to increase attributes predicated of God; those with philosophical training must understand the reason for this prohibition. Thus, in his *Guide* Maimonides sets down a theory of language, according to which accidental attributes must be understood as attributes of action, while essential attributes must be understood as negations of privation. While Maimonides has a rather dim view of the ability of human language to provide an adequate description of God and ultimately prefers silent contemplation, this does not remove the obligation to pray from the intellectual elite. And finally, prayer, similar to the observance of the other *miẓvot*, leads to the love of God which, for Maimonides, seems to be a combination of an emotive and an intellectual state. Prayer, then, has some affinity to today's concern with spirituality, but it is a good deal more. It does not require separation from this world nor does it require denial of the importance of the human body. In its nature it is a structured activity addressed to body and soul alike.

11

Liturgical Innovation and Spirituality: Trends and Trendiness

Judith Bleich

For I know that Thou wilt not be appeased by a plethora of words nor wilt Thou be found by the breath of the lips, but only by a broken spirit, trembling soul and softened heart.... Deliver me from the troubles, distresses and evils of this world..., both those that are known to me and those that are hidden from me, which separate me from Thee and drive me away from Thy service.

R. BAḤYA BEN JOSEPH IBN PAKUDA, "BAKASHAH," APPENDED TO ḤOVOT HA-LEVAVOT

I. INTRODUCTION

Prayer – involving, as it does, the paradoxical attempt of a finite being to approach the *Ein-Sof* and to enter into communication with a transcendent God – is fraught with theological tension. The difficulties facing the worshiper have been recognized from time immemorial. Small wonder, then, that the Psalmist's plea, "Oh Lord open my lips that my mouth may declare Your praise" (Psalms 51:17), acknowledging the need for assistance in facilitating prayer, was incorporated by the Sages as a prefatory petition[1] to be recited before approaching God in the *Amidah* prayer.[2] The Deity to whom prayer is addressed must be beseeched not only to answer prayer but even to enable prayer itself to become a possibility. The Talmud relates that *ḥasidim ha-rishonim*, the pious men of ancient times, were wont to spend an hour in preparation before engaging in prayer and another hour in meditation thereafter.[3]

Foremost medieval Jewish philosophers and theologians stressed the perils and dangers of careless prayer. Explicit and emphatic are the oft-cited admonitions of Maimonides[4] and Ibn Ezra[5] in their respective explications of the verse in Ecclesiastes 5:1, "Be not rash with your mouth, and let not your heart be hasty to utter one thing before God: for God is in heaven and you upon earth; therefore let your words be few." Closer to our own era, within the devotional movements of more modern times, ḥasidic teachers[6] and exponents of *Mussar*[7] alike dwelt upon the obstacles that must be overcome in finding suitable modes of prayer.

If a significant period of time elapses during which one is un-

---

[1] BT *Berakhot* 4b and 9b.

[2] The *Amidah* or *Shemoneh Esreih* (Eighteen Benedictions) is referred to in the Talmud as *Tefillah* because it is the quintessential prayer.

[3] BT *Berakhot* 32b.

[4] *Guide of the Perplexed*, I.59.

[5] Commentary on Eccles. 5:1.

[6] See, for example, sources cited in Norman Lamm, "Worship, Service of God," in *The Religious Thought of Ḥasidism: Text and Commentary* (Hoboken, NJ: Yeshiva University Press, 1999), chap. 6, pp. 175–218, especially pp. 197–8, the translation of a passage of R. Levi Yiẓḥak of Berdichev, *Kedushat Levi*, *Va-etḥanan*, s.v. *o yevu'ar*, that concludes, "Hence there are two aspects to prayer: the prayer itself, and a prayer for the ability to pray [properly]."

[7] See the earlier text, much beloved of devotees of the *Mussar* movement, R. Moshe Ḥayyim Luzzatto, *Mesillat Yesharim*, chap. 17, on preparation for prayer, concentration and avoidance of distraction. See also R. Israel Salanter, *Or Yisra'el*, no. 28 and R. Yiẓḥak Blaser, *Netivot Or* published with *Or Yisra'el* (London: 1951), p. 121;

able to pray in a meaningful manner, "there accumulate in one's heart numerous stumbling blocks that produce an inner heaviness of the spirit" writes Rav Kook. Only when the gift of prayer is restored do the barriers disappear, but they do not disappear "all at once; it is a gradual process."[8] The difficulties encountered in expressing oneself in prayer, the obstructions – psychological and religious, personal and social – that virtually everyone experiences at one time or another, need not be belabored. A popular Ḥabad ḥasidic melody set to Yiddish lyrics gives voice to this commonly experienced frustration: "*Essen esst zikh un trinken trinkt zikh; der khisoren iz nor vos es davent zikh nit.*" Essentially untranslatable, a paraphrase would be: "Eat, it's easy for us to eat; and drink, it's easy for us to drink; the problem is that it's just not at all easy for us to *daven*."[9]

Yet when a contemporary writer states that "Religious worship is a particularly acute problem for the modern individual"[10] the statement does not reflect the hubris of a modern writer who is convinced that present-day man faces novel predicaments and who is unaware that in seeking meaningful modalities of prayer moderns are engaged in reinventing the wheel. Commencing with the period of the Enlightenment, traditional religion has been confronted with unprecedented challenges. Contemporary Western culture, predominantly secular in nature, has created an environment in which religious worship does indeed pose a "particularly acute problem." If in earlier ages the worshiper was frustrated by the daunting task of summoning emotional fortitude and of finding the appropriate words to address an awesome God, the modernist is all too often paralyzed by the notion of addressing prayer to a

---

Dov Katz, *Tenu'at ha-Mussar*, second ed. (Tel Aviv: A. Zioni, 1944), II, 302; and R. Simchah Zisel Ziff, *Ḥokhmah u-Mussar* (New York: 1958), pp. 65, 215–16.

[8] *Olat Re'iyah*, (Jerusalem: Mossad ha-Rav Kook, 1963), I:11.

[9] See *Sefer ha-Niggunim*, ed. Samuel Zalmanov (Brooklyn: Hevrat Nihoah, 1949), pp. 57 and 97. R. Shalom Ber Butman relates that the late *Lubavitcher Rebbe*, Rabbi Menachem Mendel Schneerson, who inveighed against wasting time in sleep, was wont to sing this stanza with a slight variation, "*Essen esst zikh un shlofen shloft zikh* (Eat, it's easy for us to eat; and sleep, it's easy for us to sleep").

[10] Chava Weissler, "Making *Davening* Meaningful," YIVO *Annual* 19 (1990): 255.

Deity with regard to whose existence, power or concern he or she is deeply conflicted.

Presently, at the dawn of a new millennium, increasingly large numbers of people, feeling themselves alienated and desolate in an atomized, technological universe, are endeavoring to find meaningfulness and purpose in their lives. In a secular culture devoid of a religious infrastructure this quest often expresses itself in a vague and inchoate affirmation of spiritual values. Those who find conventional religious belief difficult to accept are attracted to a form of "secular spiritualism"[11] akin to the teachings promoted by the Dalai Lama who purports to find some benefit in religion yet also asserts, "But even without a religious belief we can also manage. In some cases we manage even better."[12]

Within the Jewish community as well, the hunger of the soul that underlies the search for spirituality has motivated many who heretofore were distant from Judaism to engage in a renewed encounter with their tradition. Unfortunately, far too often, those seekers find themselves in a New Age type of environment in which their encounter is with an amorphous syncretistic Judaism. Thus, a recent news item reports that a participant in a "Jewish Renewal" retreat described as "Living Waters…a spiritual health spa program grounded in ancient kabbalistic teachings" avowed that the recital of the *Ave Maria* at the retreat's Sabbath services was "one of the most moving experiences of the week."[13]

The early minor liturgical innovations and the subsequent trajectory of the nineteenth-century Reform movement as well as the return swing of the pendulum in the latter part of the twentieth century are well known. What is sometimes overlooked or forgotten is the rhetoric that urged implementation of those reforms in the name of spirituality and enhancement of religion. An analysis of

[11] Richard Bernstein, "Critic's Notebook," *New York Times*, 7 Oct. 1999, p. A2.

[12] Tenzin Gyatso, the Dalai Lama, and Howard C. Cutler, *The Art of Happiness: A Handbook for Living* (New York: Riverhead, 1998), p. 306. See also *idem*, *Ethics for the New Millennium* (New York: Riverhead, 1999).

[13] *The Jerusalem Report*, 2 Aug. 1999, p. 38. Cf. Gary Rosenblatt, "Spirituality (Whatever That Means) Is on the Rise," *The Jewish Week*, 14 Jan. 2000, p. 7.

those phenomena is particularly valuable for the light it casts on the ambiguous and amorphous meanings that attach themselves to the concept of "spirituality" and on the extent to which such meanings are influenced by, and reflective of, regnant cultural trends in society at large.

II. MOTIVATIONS

The earliest stirrings of Reform centered on improvement of the worship service. The changes advocated involved matters extrinsic to the liturgy, i.e., matters of aesthetics and comportment (the three D's: design, dignity and decorum), as well as the language and content of the prayers themselves. From the outset, complex motivations, both assimilationist and religious in nature, were expressed candidly. Thus it was easy for opponents to point an accusatory finger. Yet the total picture is much more subtle; a skein of contradictory considerations must be unraveled.

Ostensibly, the failings and flaws of then existing synagogal practices were the impetus for innovation. But a closer look at even the very earliest formulations of the concerns of the innovators reveals a mixture of motivations, viz., a desire – quite possibly sincere – for enhanced spirituality and devotion combined with an equally strong desire – quite obviously sincere – for the acceptance and regard of non-Jewish neighbors.

Perception of the teachings and religious observances of Judaism as outmoded and primitive was rooted in the currents of antisemitism that permeated intellectual circles of the era. During the eighteenth century, the "century of Voltaire," France developed an intelligentsia that unabashedly expressed pronounced anti-Jewish sentiments. By the end of the century their influence had spread throughout Europe. In Germany, Immanuel Kant's hostility to Judaism and his characterizations of the Jewish religion as obsolete and lacking in morality was representative of the thinking of his time. The only possibility for social rehabilitation of the Jews, according to Kant, lay in their rejection of unedifying rites and acceptance of "purified" religious concepts. Nor was Kant's younger friend and sometime student, Johann Gottfried von Herder, commonly regarded as a liberal and philosemite, incapable of expressing anti-Jewish comments. Herder disparaged what he termed "pharasaism" and disdained halakhic distinctions as ponderous hairsplitting.[14] Deprecatory attitudes such as these were internalized by acculturated Jewish intellectuals in their desperate quest for acceptance in a society that had always rejected them as alien.

The imperative for change in divine worship was vigorously articulated by the forerunners and pioneers of the Reform movement, Israel Jacobson and David Friedlander. Jacobson, whose status as the father of Reform Judaism was acknowledged in the dedication of the *Hamburg Temple Prayerbook* (1819), was the president of the Westphalian Consistory. In 1810 Jacobson founded a synagogue in Seesen that he named the Temple of Jacob. The edifice was adorned with a belfry, the *bimah* was removed from its central position, and prayer was accompanied by the music of an organ. In an address delivered at the Temple's inaugural ceremony, Jacobson declaimed with a rhetorical flourish:

> What I had in mind when I first thought about building this temple was *your* religious education, my Israelite brothers, *your* customs, *your* worship, etc. Be it far from me that I should have any secret intention to undermine the pillars of your faith.... You know my faithful adherence to the faith of my fathers.... [But] Who would dare to deny that our service is sickly because of many useless things, that in part it has degenerated into a thoughtless recitation of prayers and formulae, that it kills devotion more than encourages it.... On

[14] The ambiguities and ambivalences surrounding Emancipation in France are depicted in Arthur Hertzberg, *The French Enlightenment and the Jews* (New York and London: Columbia University Press and Philadelphia: Jewish Publication Society, 1968). An excellent portrayal of the German climate of thought is found in Paul Lawrence Rose, *German Question/Jewish Question: Revolutionary Antisemitism from Kant to Wagner* (Princeton, NJ: Princeton University Press, 1992); see especially, pp. 90–132.

> all sides, enlightenment opens up new areas for development. Why should we alone remain behind?[15]

But, after stressing the importance of restoring spiritually degenerated services to religious purity, Jacobson did not hesitate to mention a further consideration and admitted:

> Let us be honest, my brothers. Our ritual is still weighted down with religious customs which must be rightfully offensive to reason as well as to our Christian friends.[16]

In 1786 David Friedlander published his *Gebete der Juden auf das ganze Jahr,* a translation of the liturgy into German but printed in Hebrew characters because German Jews had not yet acquired facility in the reading of German. Dedicated by Friedlander to his mother and mother-in-law, the work was intended for the edification of Jewish women whose ignorance of Hebrew was taken for granted.[17] The text of this prayerbook and its brief preface extolling the merits of prayer reflect no intimation of dissatisfaction with the liturgy. But not long thereafter, in his infamous proposal to Probst Teller for a conditional merging of Judaism and Christianity, Friedlander's muddled mixture of spiritual concern and denigration of the traditional liturgy is evident in his description of the *siddur:*

> From century to century these prayers became more numerous and worse and worse, the conceptions more mystical,

[15] W. Gunther Plaut, *The Rise of Reform Judaism: A Sourcebook of its European Origins* (New York: World Union for Progressive Judaism, 1963), p. 29.

[16] *Ibid.*, p. 30.

[17] Early Reform writings are striking in their commendable attentiveness to the religious needs of women. A cursory glance at the history of the nineteenth-century German Jewish community reveals the presence of a cadre of educated and sophisticated women, the Salon Jewesses, who played a prominent role in German society, but were only marginally involved in the Jewish community and many of whom intermarried. A lacuna in the education and religious experience of Jewish women is unmistakable.

> muddied with the principles of Kabbalah which were in direct contradiction to the genuine spirit of Judaism…. The larger portion of our nation understands nothing of these prayers and that is a happy circumstance, because in this way these prayers will have neither good nor bad effect on the sentiment of the worshipers.[18]

In these remarks Friedlander did not limit himself to a veiled critique of the content of the liturgy; his comments include a series of unsubstantiated slurs. The formulas of the prayers composed in Hebrew, Friedlander claimed, reveal "the weakness of an aging language." The prayers, even those of thanksgiving for divine beneficence and including the benedictions recited under the wedding canopy, he characterized as "without exception" resounding with "the plaintive cry of slaves who pine for redemption." In a sweeping statement filled with innuendo, he expressed the canard that, "finally, the language in which these prayers are expressed offends not only the ear, but also mocks at all logic and grammar."[19]

A marginally more temperate tone pervades Friedlander's detailed 1812 proposals for the "reformation" of Jewish worship services and educational institutions. The focus of this document is on "devotion and elevation of the soul to God." Hebrew prayers in their traditional form, he avers, are a barrier to sincere worship. To pray in a language one does not comprehend is off-putting. But for one who does understand the language the problem is even graver because the prayers, as constituted, stand "in sharpest contrast to his convictions, his aspirations and his hopes."[20] Friedlander further bemoans the substitution of quantity for quality, the dissonance be-

[18] *Sendschreiben an seine Hochwürdigen, Herrn Oberconsistorialrat und Probst Teller zu Berlin, von einigen Hausvätern jüdischer Religion* (Berlin: 1799), pp. 34–5. This tract has been republished in an offset edition and with a Hebrew translation (Jerusalem: Zalman Shazar Center, 1975).

[19] *Loc. cit.*

[20] Jakob J. Petuchowski, *Prayerbook Reform in Europe: The Liturgy of European Liberal and Reform Judaism* (New York: World Union for Progressive Judaism, 1968), p. 132.

tween the content of the prayers and the reality of the needs of the times as well as the absence of musical accompaniment as a result of which circumstances "the knowledgeable man of religion" who seeks edification must perforce abandon the synagogue.[21]

Although it was never explicitly stated, imitation of Protestant worship was an implicit objective. A telling anecdote illustrates this fact. Josef Johlson[22] compiled one of the earliest books of hymns in the vernacular for use in a synagogue. That work, entitled *Gesangbuch für Israeliten* (Frankfurt-am-Main, 1816), attained a measure of popularity. The vast majority of these songs were taken verbatim from Protestant hymnals save that Johlson substituted the words "Lord" or "my Refuge" for each mention of the name "Jesus." Only after the book was printed was it discovered that, inadvertently, in one such occurrence the substitution had not been made. As a result, it was necessary for an entire signature of the book to be removed and replaced. This publishing mishap piquantly underscores the Christological orientation of the innovators.[23]

The few rabbinic figures who responded affirmatively to the early innovations were also influenced by a variety of factors and considerations ranging from opportunism, accomodationism, naivete and desire for containment to genuine conviction and empathy. The somewhat quixotic approach of Aaron Chorin in his early writ-

---

[21] *Ibid.*, p. 133.

[22] A teacher of religion at the Frankfurt Philanthropin school, Johlson, under the *nom de plume* Bar Amithai, later published a pamphlet, *Über die Beschneidung in historischer und dogmatischer Hinsicht* (Frankfurt am-Main: 1843), in which he recommended abolition of circumcision and substitution of another ceremony. Johlson prepared a rubric for such a ceremony prospectively termed "The Sanctification of the Eighth Day" and designed as an egalitarian ritual suitable for both male and female infants. See Michael A. Meyer, *Response to Modernity: A History of the Reform Movement in Judaism* (New York and Oxford: Oxford University Press, 1988), pp. 123 and 423, n. 86.

[23] See Heinrich Zirndorf, *Isaak Markus Jost und seine Freunde: Ein Beitrag zur Kulturgeschichte der Gegenwart* (Cincinnati: Block Publishing Co., 1886), pp. 161–2. Zirndorf adds that the historian Jost remarked, perhaps in jest, that an unemended copy of the Christological version should have been kept intact because, as a collector's item, it would one day command a handsome price.

ings in support of liturgical reform[24] reveals a complexity of intent. Deep concern for the esteem of non-Jewish fellow citizens is demonstrated in his *Davar be-Ito*[25] both in the extensive discussions of the status of non-Jews in the first portion of each section of that work[26] and in his pointed remarks regarding disruptive and indecorous services that he regarded as a disgrace in the eyes of the nations.[27] But it is an entirely different motif that is pervasive throughout this brief work. Chorin argues that a conciliatory and moderate approach is essential in order to stem the loss of vast numbers of Jews who have become entirely disenchanted with Judaism. Contemporary Jews find existing religious services outmoded and alien. Aesthetically attractive public worship is the most effective way to arouse the alienated to renewed reverence of God and even "to observe the commandments."[28] Castigating the negativity of rabbis serving the established community, Chorin contrasts their forbidding stance with the midrashic portrayal of the spiritual leadership of Moses and David, both of whom are depicted as loving shepherds who nurtured their flocks with compassion and concern for the distinctiveness of

[24] Chorin's views evolved over the years from an initial moderate support of innovation to a marked break with accepted halakhic practice. For biographical data on Chorin see Leopold Löw, "Aron Chorin: Eine biographische Skizze," in *Gesammelte Schriften*, ed. Immanuel Löw (Szegedin: 1890), vol. II, pp. 251–420 and Moshe Pelli, "The Ideological and Legal Struggle of Rabbi Aaron Chorin for Religious Reform in Judaism," (Hebrew), *Hebrew Union College Annual* 39 (1968): Hebrew Section 63–79.

[25] Chorin's first defense of synagogue reform was his responsum included in *Nogah ha-Ẓedek* (Dessau: 1818) sanctioning the practices of the Berlin Beer Temple. In response to the attacks on him in *Eileh Divrei ha-Berit* (Altona: 1819), he published *Davar be-Ito* (Vienna: 1820). This slim book is presented in a curious format. It is comprised of three sections: A Hebrew section; a similar but not identical German section in Gothic characters entitled *Ein Wort zu seiner Zeit: Über die Nächstenliebe und den Gottesdienst*; and the identical German section in Hebrew characters. The German-language section is sharper and more condemnatory in tone than the Hebrew one. Citation in this paper will be either to the Hebrew or to the German sections as identified by their respective titles.

[26] "Nächstenliebe, *Ein Wort*, pp. 5–27 and "Shaar Torah," *Davar be-Ito*, pp. 5–22.

[27] *Davar be-Ito*, p. 43.

[28] *Ibid.*, pp. 26–7.

each and every one of their charges. The Midrash portrays David as taking pains to give sheep of different ages food appropriate to their needs and describes how Moses followed a small kid that strayed from its flock in search of water, picked it up and carried it in his arms.[29] Those models should illustrate for us, Chorin contends, that one must exercise wisdom and understanding in guiding each individual Jew in accordance with his needs and talents and must lovingly mentor the weak and frail who flee the flock "bearing them on one's shoulder to green pastures – to the paths of faith, that they not be utterly cast aside from the paths of life."[30]

Chorin's later writings, however, emphasize not so much the need to attract the disaffected as the quest to enhance devotion. During the last weeks of his life he wrote to a conference of Hungarian rabbis in Paks:

> I need not tell you that of all the external institutions the public service demands our immediate and undivided attention. He who is faithful to his God, and is earnestly concerned for the welfare of his religion, must exert himself to rescue our service from the ruin into which it has fallen and to give it once again that inspiring form which is worthy of a pious and devout worship of the one true God. For it is not only the excrescences of dark ages which cover it with disgrace, but thoughtlessness, lack of taste, absence of devotion, and caprice have disfigured its noble outlines."[31]

Reform reconceptualization of Judaism, it has been quite correctly noted,[32] was an attempt to recast Judaism in the cultural

[29] *Ibid.*, pp. 47–8, citing *Midrash Rabbah, Shemot* 2.

[30] *Davar be-Ito*, p. 48.

[31] Cited in David Philipson, *The Reform Movement in Judaism*, revised ed. (New York: Ktav, 1967), p. 442, n. 112.

[32] See Meyer, *Reponse*, pp. 17–18. In stating that, like early Lutheranism, Judaism paid little attention to the subjective religious state of the individual and regarded observance of the commandments "as an end in itself, not the means to any other," Meyer, in common with Reform thinkers of the nineteenth century, overlooks classical Jewish sources.

and theological mold of the host country. In the seventeenth and eighteenth centuries the center of gravity in Protestantism moved from a God-centered faith to a focus on the individual's subjective religious conscience. The concepts of *Glückseligkeit* (spiritual contentment) and *Erbauung* (edification) became much vaunted religious goals. Following those Christian trends, Reform innovators favored retention of customs and rituals that they perceived to be spiritually uplifting and proposed innovations that they thought would enhance religious experience.

In doing so they remained blissfully unaware of classic sources of Jewish teaching and failed to seek guidance in the vast corpus of Jewish ethical literature. The classic early-day work *Sefer ha-Ḥinnukh* unambiguously finds moral edification to be the primary goal of particular *miẓvot*. According to *Sefer ha-Ḥinnukh*, the multiplicity of commandments is intended as a form of behavior modification designed to habituate man to the path of virtue. *Sefer ha-Ḥinnukh*'s philosophy of *miẓvot* is exemplified in a number of emblematic statements that serve as a motto for the entire work:

> Know that a man is influenced in accordance with his actions. His heart and all his thoughts are always [drawn] after his deeds in which he is occupied, whether [they are] good or bad.... For after one's acts is the heart drawn....
>
> The omnipresent God wished to make Israel meritorious; therefore He gave them...a multitude of *miẓvot*...that all our preoccupation should be with them.... For by good actions we are acted upon to become good....[33]
>
> ...For the physical self becomes cleansed through [its] actions. As good actions are multiplied and as they are continued with great perseverance, the thoughts of the heart become purified, cleansed and refined.[34]

[33] *Sefer ha-Ḥinnukh* ascribed to R. Aaron ha-Levi of Barcelona, trans. Charles Wengrov (Jerusalem and New York: Feldheim Publishers, 1991) vol. 1, no. 16, pp. 119–21.

[34] *Ibid.*, vol. 1, no. 95, pp. 359.

Centuries later, R. Moshe Ḥayyim Luzzatto expressed similar concepts in nomenclature paralleling the language of *Erbauung* and *Glückseligkeit*. Central to his thought is his description of man's goal in life as attainment of perfection through attachment to God by means of the *miẓvot*.[35]

The term *Glückseligkeit*, or spiritual contentment, lends itself to a wide variety of interpretations, some worldly, others somewhat otherworldly. Nevertheless, as used in theological writings, the term clearly connotes a state of spiritual well-being. The distinction between worldly success (*haẓlaḥah*) and serenity of spirit (*osher*) is emphasized in the much later comments of R. Meir Leibush Malbim in his explication of the spiritual contentment the Psalmist ascribes to the righteous.[36]

A major contribution of R. Samson Raphael Hirsch in *Ḥoreb* was precisely his analysis of *miẓvot* in a manner that stressed their ethical moment. He made use of the vocabulary and conceptual framework of the day in demonstrating the manner in which *miẓvot* further the goals regarded by Reform thinkers as paramount. The *miẓvot* that Reform regarded as superfluous R. Hirsch found to be invaluable in promoting the selfsame spirituality that the innovators found so significant. He faulted Reform ideologues for failing to appreciate the richness of their heritage and for not mining its treasures. It is this fundamental assessment that underlies R. Hirsch's sharp critique of the Reform movement.

Although many rabbinic authorities indiscriminately branded all innovators as rebels and sinners whose goal was simply to ease the burden of religious observance, some realized that the picture was not monochromatic. R. Samson Raphael Hirsch disarmingly chose to seize upon the positive motivations of the innovators even while deploring their actions. Regarding those who proposed innovations for the sake of promoting spiritual improvement he counseled, "Re-

---

[35] *Derekh ha-Shem*, (Amsterdam: 1896), chaps. 3–4.

[36] Psalms 1:1. Cf. R. Samson Raphael Hirsch, *The Nineteen Letters*, trans. Karin Paritzky (Jerusalem and New York: Feldheim, 1995), second letter, pp. 14–5, for R. Hirsch's rejection of happiness in the conventional sense as the ultimate goal of mankind.

spect all of them, for they sense a shortcoming; they desire the good as they conceive it."[37] It was a tragedy, he maintained, that their good intentions had led to deleterious results. That occurred, he asserted, because exponents of Reform responded to the spiritual challenge of the time in a shallow and superficial manner. These individuals were satisfied, claimed R. Hirsch, with an "uncomprehended Judaism and merely to revise the outward forms of one misunderstood part of it, the Divine service and [to] remodel it according to the sentimentalities of the age"[38] rather than seeking to intensify efforts to invigorate a Judaism "intellectually comprehended and vigorously implemented."[39]

In turning our attention to specific liturgical innovations with regard to language, music, aesthetics, decorum, duration of services, recitation of *piyyut* (litugical poetry) and fundamentals of belief, it is instructive to take cognizance of rabbinic discussions of those issues in order to appreciate the extent to which traditionalists did or did not relate to the concerns expressed by Reform writers.

III. LANGUAGE

The second[40] formal prayerbook incorporating liturgical reforms, *Die deutsche Synagoge*, edited by Eduard Kley and C.S. Günsburg, clearly articulated the ardor with which the constituency to whom it was addressed embraced the German language. While the editors acknowledge a lingering fealty to Hebrew ("Holy is the language in which God once gave the Law to our fathers") based on a reverence for past history ("...a memorial...a sweet echo...and venerable it will remain for everyone who still reveres the past"), they were unabashed in their passionate expression of sentiment for the German language, proclaiming:

---

[37] *Ibid.*, seventeenth letter, p. 243.

[38] *Loc. cit.*

[39] *Ibid.*, p. 242.

[40] *Gebete am Sabbath Morgens und an den beiden Neujahrs-Tagen*, the earliest Reform prayerbook published anonymously, probably in 1815, without indication of city or year of publication, consists of a number of sections that originally appeared separately and were subsequently bound together. As early as 1815, Jacobson

> But seven times more holy unto us is the language which belongs to the present and to the soil whence we have sprung forth...the language in which a mother greets her new-born child...the language which unites us with our fellow men... the language, finally, in which our philanthropic and just king speaks to us, in which he proclaims his law to us....[41]

The ensuing controversy over the language of prayer can be properly appreciated only in light of extravagant rhetoric such as this and the ideology it betrays. At issue were not the bare bones of halakhic rulings regarding the legitimacy of prayer in the vernacular but the much more profound questions of motivation and of fundamental loyalty to, and appreciation of, the sancta of Judaism.

Promotion of prayer in the vernacular was a primary issue in the agenda of worship reform. While yet in Westphalia, Israel Jacobson solicited halakhic opinions in an endeavor to validate the contemplated change. The responses of R. Samuel Eiger of Brunswick, a cousin of the famed R. Akiva Eiger, deploring the proposal[42] and of the Westphalian Consistory's own R. Menahem Mendel Steinhardt endorsing hymns in the vernacular and alluding to the permissibility of vernacular prayer in general,[43] were but the first salvos in what was to become a pitched battle.

---

sent copies of those prayers and of German hymns from a songbook issued in Cassel (1810 and revised in 1816) to a government minister. See Meyer, *Response to Modernity*, p. 49 and p. 406, n. 145.

[41] From the preface to *Die deutsche Synagoge*, vol. 1 (Berlin: 1817), cited in Petuchowski, *Prayerbook Reform*, p. 135. The same year that this prayerbook was published, the first French Jewish periodical, *L'Israélite Français*, advocated the introduction of French language prayers. However, in France, unlike in Germany, substitution of the vernacular for Hebrew, as espoused by radicals, did not gain popular acceptance. See Phyllis Cohen Albert, "Nonorthodox Attitudes in French Judaism," in *Essays in Modern Jewish History*, ed. Frances Malino and Phyllis Cohen Albert (Rutherford: Fairleigh Dickinson University Press, 1982), pp. 123–4 and 132.

[42] R. Samuel Eiger's letter to Jacobson is published in B.H. Auerbach, *Geschichte der Israelitischen Gemeinde Halberstadt* (Halberstadt: 1866), pp. 219–221.

[43] *Divrei Igeret* (Rödelheim: 1812), p. 10a.

Turning the question on its head, Aaron Chorin noted that the proper question to be posed is not whether one may pray in the vernacular but whether one may pray in Hebrew, a language understood by "barely three out of ten." Chorin suggested the existence of an absolute requirement that prayer services be conducted in the vernacular in order to be understood by all.[44] Conceding that Hebrew, no less so than any other language, is subsumed in the dispensation "A person may pray in any language in which he desires" and that, in addition, Hebrew carries with it the distinction of history and tradition as well as the encomium "holy tongue," Chorin concludes that, nevertheless, it is preferable that a person pray in the language he understands as recommended by *Magen Avraham, Oraḥ Ḥayyim* 104:4. Since *Magen Avraham*'s ruling applies to an individual rather than to the community, Chorin commends as sagacious the decision of the innovators who reached a compromise in maintaining Hebrew as the language used by the cantor in chanting major obligatory prayers while introducing German in other parts of the liturgy.[45]

Chorin's final comment on the language of prayer illustrates the manner in which people who viewed themselves as the cultural vanguard and in tune with the *Zeitgeist* were yet limited and constrained by the very notions that they deemed to be enlightened and liberal. Chorin concludes his call for enhanced, aesthetically pleasing worship services with the observation that women must not be excluded from the benefits of communal prayer for gone are the barbaric ages in which women were viewed as an inferior species. "But," he asks, "in which language are such services to be conducted? Surely not solely in Hebrew, of which women do not have the vaguest notion and which has no appeal whatsoever to their spirit *(die ihr Gemüth in gar keiner Beziehung anspricht)*."[46] *Tempora mutantur et nos mutamur in eis!*

Chorin's initial moderate stance was soon abandoned. As is well known, extensive discussions regarding the use of Hebrew in reli-

[44] *Ein Wort*, p. 38.
[45] *Ibid.*, pp. 39–40.
[46] *Ein Wort*, p. 47.

gious services took place at the second Reform rabbinical conference in Frankfurt in 1845. The delegates determined that Jewish law did not require use of Hebrew as the language of prayer. A subsequent vote of 15 to 13, affirming that retention of Hebrew in public services was not necessary on other grounds, led Zecharias Frankel to leave the conference and part company with the Reform movement. Insistence on preservation of Hebrew as the language of liturgy was a defining feature of Frankel's positive historical Judaism, an ideology that was later to be institutionalized in this country as Conservative Judaism. Frankel contended that the Hebrew language was integral to the essence of Judaism and still vibrantly alive in the emotions of Jews even if their knowledge of the language was deficient.[47]

At the Frankfurt conference, Abraham Adler, Joseph Kahn, Abraham Geiger and David Einhorn made unequivocal statements endorsing prayer in the vernacular. Adler urged his colleagues to avoid sentimentality in the search for truth, to recognize that no language is sacred and instead to acknowledge that it is the content of language rather than the words that convey sanctity. Prayer in Hebrew, he contended, offered by those who do not understand the language, encourages lip service and hypocrisy. Moreover, he argued, the Hebrew language is meager and inadequate as a medium for prayer since it is lacking in vocabulary and nuances of expression and "In any case, it is dead because it does not live within the people."[48] Kahn similarly claimed that there is "no pure religious impulse" inherent in a language. Although he conceded that some Hebrew must be retained provisionally, Kahn asserted that under ideal circumstances services should be conducted entirely in German.[49] Geiger confessed that, as far as he personally was concerned, prayer in German aroused him to deeper devotion than did Hebrew prayer for it is in German that "All our deepest feelings and sentiments, all

---

[47] See Meyer, *Response*, pp. 88 and 137, and Philipson, *Reform Movement*, pp. 165–6 and 189–93.

[48] *Protokolle und Aklenstücke der zweiten Rabbiner-Versammlung* (Frankfurt-am-Main, 1845), p. 45.

[49] *Ibid.*, p. 41.

our highest thoughts, receive their expression."[50] Hebrew must be viewed as a dead language, argued David Einhorn, and, assuredly, smiting the rock of a dead language will not produce living waters with which to quench people's thirst.[51] Accordingly, for Einhorn, there is no doubt that Hebrew

> is not the organ with which to express the feelings of the people. Aforetimes, prayer was only a cry of pain; a scarcely intelligible expression sufficed for this; but now people need a prayer that shall express thoughts, feelings and sentiments; this is possible only through the mother tongue.[52]

It is evident from these comments that Reform abandonment of Hebrew was not motivated purely by concern for enhancement of devotion in prayer but was motivated equally by an announced desire to deemphasize nationalistic aspirations. Joseph Maier did indeed acknowledge the "nationalistic" value inherent in the phenomenon of Jews in different lands sharing a common language of prayer but asserted that any such benefit could be achieved by restricting use of Hebrew to a few brief prayers such as the *Shema* and *Kedushah* and to some Torah readings. "Anything else," he added "I consider detrimental."[53] Jacob Auerbach more candidly asserted that the fundamental question to be addressed was "the relationship of the national to the religious element." The question, he declared, is no longer what is desirable but what is necessary "to accomplish our mission." In that respect, "History has decided; centuries lie between the national and the religious elements.... The purely religious element is the flower of Judaism."[54] Nevertheless, Auerbach

---

[50] *Ibid.*, pp. 32–3. Cf. the contention of J. Jolowicz, *ibid.*, p. 38, *contra* Z. Frankel, that "*vox populi*" and "*salus publica*" militate for German and against Hebrew since the vast majority of the populace "think and feel in German" and have therefore turned their backs on synagogues that employ Hebrew as the language of prayer.

[51] *Ibid.*, p. 49.

[52] *Ibid.*, p. 27.

[53] *Ibid.*, p. 39.

[54] *Ibid.*, p. 46.

contended, Jewish history mandates continued study of Hebrew as the language of Scripture and of the sources upon which the liturgy is based. However, he asserted, the language of devotional prayer at its core must be the vernacular.[55]

One of the few congregations to give concrete expression to this extreme viewpoint was the Berlin *Genossenschaft für Reform im Judenthum* (Association for the Reform of Judaism) whose published prayerbook eliminated almost all vestiges of Hebrew. Their prayerbook reflected the firm conviction of members of the Association that liturgy must employ only a living language whose mode of thought and expression was familiar to the worshiper.[56] Similarly, a radical group, Friends of Reform, located in Worms stated forthrightly: "We must no longer pray in a dead language when word and sound of our German mother tongue are to us both understandable and attractive. These alone, therefore, are suited to lift us up to our Creator."[57]

Remarkable is the fact that proponents of Reform in Germany differed from their counterparts in other countries in the nature of their espousal of vernacular prayer. Thus, for example, in the United States, the members of the Charleston congregation who joined Isaac Harby in 1824 in petitioning for worship innovation and prayer in the vernacular[58] and, at a later date, Isaac M. Wise, in advocating the rendition of selected prayers in English,[59] presented a straightforward case based on the need to understand the content

[55] *Ibid.*, p. 47. One of the dissenting votes at the Conference was that of Leopold Schott of Randegg who underscored the significance of educating youth in the Hebrew language by citing Maimonides, *Commentary on the Mishnah*, *Avot* 2:1. Maimonides categorizes the study of Hebrew language as an example of an "easy *mizvah*." In response, Gotthold Salomon countered that Maimonides "is not an unimpeachable authority (*keine unumstössliche Authorität*)." See *ibid.*, pp. 49–50.
[56] Plaut, *Rise*, p. 59.
[57] *Ibid.*, p. 62.
[58] See the memorandum submitted to the Adjunta of Congregation Beth Elohim, in Charleston published in *A Documentary History of the Jews of the U.S. 1654–1875*, ed. Morris U. Schappes, third ed. (New York: Schocken Books, 1975), pp. 172–3.
[59] James G. Heller, *I.M. Wise: His Life, Work and Thought* (New York: Union of American Hebrew Congregations, 1965), pp. 393, 395, and 566.

of the liturgy. In contrast, the German writers exhibited an exaggerated veneration of German and gave voice to an often mean-spirited denigration of the Hebrew language.[60]

From the outset, rabbinical scholars were keenly aware of the implications of decisions regarding the language of prayer both for the individual and for the community *qua* community. It was precisely the *spiritual* aspect of this question rather than its halakhic parameters that was emphasized by authoritative rabbinic spokesmen.

With regard to some areas of dispute it may be the case that nuances of the Reform proposals were not fully appreciated by rabbinic figures because of the culture gap that existed between those rabbis and their more worldly coreligionists. However, rabbinic leaders demonstrated in their responses that, with regard to the question of use of Hebrew as the language of prayer, they were not at all unaware of issues that went far beyond technicalities of *halakhah*. They realized that preservation of the Hebrew language was intimately linked to the unity of the Jewish people and the preservation of the Torah.

---

[60] It is noteworthy that in the opinion of the radical exponent of Reform, David Einhorn, the triumph of Reform ideology was contingent upon preservation of the German language. Accordingly, he advocated that American-born youngsters be taught German so that they might become familiar with the German philosophical background of the Reform movement. See Kaufmann Kohler, "David Einhorn, the Uncompromising Champion of Reform Judaism," *Central Conference of American Rabbis Yearbook* 19 (1909): 255. In light of his attitude toward Hebrew it is instructive to note Einhorn's assertion: "If you sever from Reform the German spirit – or what amounts to the same thing – the German language, you will have torn it from its native soil and the lovely flower will wilt." See *Dr. David Einhorn's Ausgewählte Predigten und Reden*, ed. Kaufmann Kohler (New York: Steiger, 1880), p. 90.

Passionate espousal of the German language remained a characteristic feature of German Jews well into the twentieth century. There is an excellent literary portrayal of this phenomenon in Nathan Shaham's masterful novel, *The Rosendorf Quartet*, translated from Hebrew into English by Dalya Bilu (New York: Grove Press, 1991). Shaham's fictional protagonist, the German writer Egon Lowenthal, who finds himself in misery as an expatriate in Palestine of the 1930s ("I am a German writer who thinks in German, writes in German, and loves and hates in German" [p. 270]; "I am full of longing for Germany. Lines of German poetry buzz in my head, and in my heart

Although R. Samuel Eiger's responsum dwelt on the pivotal role of Hebrew as a spiritual bond for Jews the world over[61] and R. Akiva Eiger's pronouncement was predicated upon halakhic minutiae, R. Akiva Eiger was aware, no less so than his cousin, of the assimilatory motives of the innovators, of their desire to curry favor in the eyes of the nations[62] and of their "shaming our pure and beautiful language."[63]

The several contributions of R. Moses Sofer, *Ḥatam Sofer*, to the anti-Reform tract *Eileh Divrei ha-Berit* were the subject of much satiric comment on the part of early partisans of Reform who asserted that his rulings on vernacular prayer were contrary to talmudic law and the general tenor of his comments was abstruse and mystical, naïve and superstitious.[64] There is, however, no naiveté at all evident in *Ḥatam Sofer's* response to the suggestion of Aaron Chorin that the *Pesukei de-Zimra* (Verses of Song) be recited in the vernacular and Hebrew preserved only for recitation of the *Shema* and the *Amidah*. *Ḥatam Sofer* concedes that, with regard to recitation of the *Pesukei de-Zimra* in the vernacular, "I, too, would say that it is not such a terrible thing." However, he pointedly questions Chorin's ultimate agenda. If most congregants are able to master some Hebrew there is no need to make specious distinctions and therefore, he queries,

is only a deep pain" [p. 278]; "there is no music sweeter to my ear than the sound of the German language" [p. 325]), expresses a view of Hebrew fully consistent with that of members of the early Reform movement when he derides his Zionist friends as "People who are content with a vocabulary of three hundred words" (p. 270) and who "speak an artificial language" (p. 281) and describes Hebrew as "a dead language which all of the flogging in the world will not revive" (p. 318).

61 Auerbach, *Geschichte*, pp. 219–21.

62 This responsum is published in L. Wreschner, "Rabbi Akiba Eiger's Leben und Wirken," in *Jahrbuch der Jüdisch-Literarischen Gesellschaft*, vol. 3 (1905), pp. 75–7 and in *Likkut Teshuvot ve-Ḥiddushim mi-Rabbi Akiva Eiger* (Bnei Brak: 1968), pp. 11–3.

63 *Eileh Divrei ha-Berit*, pp. 27–8.

64 See, for example, Meyer Israel Bresselau, *Ḥerev Nokemet Nekom Berit* (Hamburg: 1819), p. 15; Chorin, *Davar be-Ito*, pp. 46–7 and *Ein Wort*, pp. 43–4; and David Caro, *Berit Emet* (Dessan: 1820), p. 52.

why does Chorin "not direct them to study the holy tongue? After all, they do study the languages of the nations."[65]

An unwillingness to veer from the traditional use of Hebrew in statutory prayer does not necessarily imply that rabbinic authorities were insensitive to the advantages of self-expression in a language in which an individual is fully conversant. One of the most intransigent halakhic discussions regarding acceptability of prayer in the vernacular is that of R. Abraham Lowenstamm of Emden.[66] Yet even R. Lowenstamm explicitly adds that, following recitation of the statutory prayers, every individual should feel free to address personal prayer, thanksgiving or supplication as moved by one's spirit in any form one chooses. In offering such private prayer one should take pains that one's language be both pure and clear as befits supplication addressed to a monarch and "Of course, a prayer or thanksgiving such as this must necessarily be said in the language one understands and not in a language one does not understand, even if it is in the holy tongue."[67]

The importance of fluency and understanding in prayer was particularly well appreciated by the ḥasidic teacher, R. Naḥman of Bratslav. Although he cannot be described as a representative of mainstream rabbinic or even ḥasidic thought, R. Naḥman's teachings are much revered in Orthodox circles. R. Naḥman urged his followers to address supplications to the Almighty daily in the language in which they were accustomed to speak. Especially when the "channels of prayer" are clogged or blocked, asserted R. Naḥman, there is a need to use one's native language in order to burst the dam. R. Naḥman extolled the virtue of solitude and recommended

---

[65] *Eleh Divrei ha-Berit*, p. 38. Jakob J. Petuchowski, *Understanding Jewish Prayer* (New York: Ktav, 1952), p. 52, concedes that the hidden agenda of Reform exponents is evidenced by the fact that they did not make any attempt to encourage adult study of Hebrew; their obvious intent was to propagate an ideology that would divorce Judaism from its nationalistic foundations.

[66] *Ẓeror ha-Ḥayyim* (Amsterdam: 1820), "*Lashon Esh*," pp. 28a–35b and "*Safah Nokhriyah*," pp. 42a–53b. The second edition of *Ẓeror ha-Ḥayyim* (Ujhely: 1868), with different pagination, has been reproduced in an offset edition (Brooklyn: 1992).

[67] *Ẓeror ha-Ḥayyim*, p. 52b.

seclusion in a room or a field for a designated period of time for the purpose of engaging in solitary communion the more readily to attain singleminded devotion in service of God. R. Naḥman explicitly advised:

> This prayer and conversation should be in the vernacular, Yiddish,[68] since you may find it difficult to express yourself fully in the Holy Tongue (Hebrew). Furthermore, since we do not customarily speak Hebrew, your words would not come from the heart. But Yiddish, our spoken language and the one in which we converse, more readily engages the emotions, for the heart is more attracted to Yiddish. In Yiddish we are able to talk freely and open our hearts and tell God everything, whether remorse and repentance for the past, or supplications for the privilege of coming closer to Him freely from now on, or the like, each of us according to his own level. Try carefully to make this a habit, and set aside a special time for this purpose every day....
>
> ...Even if you occasionally fumble for words and can barely open your mouth to talk to Him, that in itself is [still] very good, because at least you have prepared yourself and are standing before Him, desiring and yearning to speak even if you cannot. Moreover, the very fact that you are unable to do so should become a subject of your discussion and prayer. This in itself should lead you to cry and plead before God that you are so far removed from Him that you cannot even talk to Him, and then to seek favor by appealing to His compassion and mercy to enable you to open your mouth so that you can speak freely before Him.
>
> Know that many great and famous *ẓaddikim* relate that they reached their [high] state only by virtue of this

[68] The Hebrew text reads "*bi-leshon ashkenaz* (*be-medinatenu*)," i.e., in the German language (in our country). The reference is obviously to Yiddish. See "*Or Zoreaḥ*," p. 4, published as an addendum to *Ḥayyei Moharan* (Brooklyn: Moriah Offset, 1974), where, in discussing R. Naḥman's advocacy of personal prayer in the vernacular, the term "*prost Yiddish*," i.e., simple Yiddish, is employed.

> practice. The wise will understand from this how important such practice is and how it rises to the very highest levels. It is something that everyone, great or small, can benefit from, for everyone is able to do this and reach great heights through it.[69]

Doubtless as a result of their distrust of the motives of protagonists of Reform, rabbinic respondents who addressed the issue of prayer in the vernacular tended, at times, to overstate their opposition. A prime example is the *Ẓeror ha-Ḥayyim* of R. Abraham Lowenstamm of Emden. R. Lowenstamm's monograph stands out as the most systematic discussion of the halakhic questions raised by the innovations of the Hamburg Temple. However, although his halakhic analyses are comprehensive and his principal theses are cogent, his analogies and justifications are, at times, weak. Thus, in emphatic rulings confirming the necessity of retaining Hebrew as the language of prayer, R. Lowenstamm declares that accurate translation into Western European languages is not at all feasible with the result that it is entirely impossible to fulfill one's obligation with regard to prayer by reciting the *Amidah* in the vernacular.[70] Other authorities are careful to note that one who cannot read Hebrew but prays in the language he understands fulfills his duty.[71]

Addressing the question of alteration of the text of statutory

[69] *Likkutei Moharan, Tinyana*, no. 25 (New York: 1958), p. 301. The translation is taken from Lamm, *Ḥasidism*, pp. 198–199. See also *Ḥayyei Moharan*, vol. II, "*Shivḥei Moharan, maalat ha-hitboddedut*," nos. 3–4, p. 45, in which it is reported that R. Naḥman saw merit in utter simplicity in personal supplication, in the manner of a child turning to a parent or a person approaching a friend, and that he asserted that if one is but able to utter the words "*Ribbono shel Olam*" as a plea, that alone is beneficial. Cf. R. Yonatan Eibeschutz, *Yaarot Devash* (Lemberg: 1863), pt. 2, p. 4a, who recommends recitation of a private confession or *viduy* in the vernacular.

[70] *Ẓeror ha-Ḥayyim*, pp. 49a–b.

[71] See, for example, R. Samson Raphael Hirsch, *Ḥoreb: A Philosophy of Jewish Laws and Observances*, trans. Isidor Grunfeld, fourth ed. (New York, London, & Jerusalem: Soncino Press, 1981), no. 688, pp. 544 and 547, who carefully stipulates that a person may pray in the vernacular only "as long as he faithfully mentions all the essential parts of prescribed forms of prayer." See his comments on the *Shema* and the Torah reading. *Ḥoreb* is noteworthy for the precision and meticulousness with

blessings and prayers, R. Lowenstamm focuses particularly on the contention of the innovators that their motive for change was the desire to increase devotion and spirituality and on their claim that if the wording of prayers and blessings were to be in closer consonance with the usage of the time, prayer would become more meaningful to contemporary worshipers and the atmosphere of the services would be enhanced. R. Lowenstamm stresses that the precise wording of prayer was meticulously chosen by inspired sages whose intent was to find the vocabulary most perfectly attuned to spiritual requests. Those saintly teachers plumbed the wondrous secrets and mysteries of the metaphysical world, knew exactly how to relate them to human concerns, and understood how best to find intelligible language to describe an unknowable God. Later generations, lacking comparable wisdom, must rely on, and be guided by, those saintly and inspired sages.[72]

R. Lowenstamm then offers a much more dubious argument in suggesting that the matter may be understood by analogies to two separate situations. A physician prescribes various medicines and serums for a patient. Bystanders lacking medical sophistication, who neither know the properties of the medicaments nor appreciate the nature of the disease, should hesitate to tamper with the physician's prescriptions even if, for whatever reason, those prescriptions are not to their liking. Or, to take a different example, a commoner finding himself a stranger at the royal court would do well to follow the protocol and instructions of the king's trusted courtiers. Aware of the obvious counterarguments, R. Lowenstamm seeks to deflect them. He admits that the selfsame examples may be employed to demonstrate the very opposite conclusion. Medicine has changed over the centuries and remedies that were once deemed beneficial are no longer in vogue. Changes have occurred in royal courts as well; in modern times rulers eschew pomp and ceremony and have adopted a far less formal mode of conduct in interaction with their subjects. In a rather feeble rebuttal, R. Lowenstamm avers that physi-

---

which halakhic rulings are formulated. Cf. R. Ẓevi Hirsch Chajes, *Minḥat Kena'ot* in *Kol Sifrei Maharaẓ Ḥayes*, vol. 2 (Jerusalem: Divrei Hakhamim, 1958), pp. 983–4.

[72] *Ẓeror ha-Ḥayyim*, "*Siftei Yeshenim*," p. 20b.

cal illnesses rather than medications have changed, whereas with regard to maladies of the soul such change has not occurred. With regard to the second analogy, he declares that one cannot possibly compare temporal kings who, as human beings, are prone to change, to the King of Kings before whom our conduct must always reflect an unchanging standard of reverence and awe.[73] Of course, in offering that final debater's point, R. Lowenstamm vitiates his own analogy. If there can be no comparison between human monarchs and the Deity in terms of present-day conduct, the analogy may be equally flawed with regard to comportment of a bygone era.

R. Ẓevi Hirsch Chajes, known as *Maharaẓ Ḥayes*, presents a detailed discussion of various technical halakhic questions with regard to prayer in the vernacular and adds the comment that, by eschewing Hebrew, Reform leaders sinned greatly in sundering the firm bond that exists among Jews dispersed to all corners of the world

> who are yet united and intertwined with one another through the medium of the Hebrew language that is understood by them since they pray in it. This alone remains to us as a portion from all the precious things that we had in days of yore. And now these villains come to rob us of even this ornament so that there will not remain with us anything at all that can testify to the magnitude of the holiness of our people. The danger threatens that with this conduct the entire Torah will also be forgotten even from those few who yet occupy themselves with it.[74]

Maharaẓ Ḥayes points to an important historical precedent in the conduct of Jews at the time of Ezra. The exiles who returned from Babylon had become habituated to the language of their host country and in a relatively brief period of time had forgotten Torah and *miẓvot* to the point that they were no longer familiar even with

[73] *Ibid.*, pp. 20b–21a.

[74] *Minḥat Kena'ot*, p. 984, note.

the manner of celebrating the festivals and the sanctity of the Day of Atonement. Ezra sought to restore the Torah to its glory and it was precisely for that reason that Ezra introduced the weekday public reading of the Torah and, together with the Men of the Great Assembly, established a uniform liturgy. It was in this manner that Ezra assured the continuity of the Torah:

> This is the principal cause that has sustained our ancestors and us so that the Torah is yet our portion in all its details. Those...who call themselves Reformers wish to uproot everything. From this alone [the abandonment of Hebrew] it is evident that their entire aim is to erase from us anything that has a connection to our holy Torah in order that we may join and make common cause with the nations in whose midst we dwell. If their spirit were loyal to the people of Israel and its God, as they constantly dare to claim in their deception...they would not dream of a ruinous matter such as this.[75]

R. Chajes emphasizes that the preservation of Torah is inextricably bound with preservation of the holy tongue. Citing the talmudic comment, BT *Megillah* 10b, "'and I will cut off from Babylon the name and remnant' (Isaiah 14:22) – This is the writing and the language," *Maharaẓ Ḥayes* concludes, "If the populace will become accustomed to pray in the language of the country in which they live, then in a short time there will be forgotten from us the writing and the language in which the Torah is written. And the Torah, what will become of it?"[76]

In one of the most inspiring passages of *Ḥoreb*,[77] R. Samson Raphael Hirsch, advancing beyond the technical halakhic issues posed by the question of prayer in the vernacular, addresses the broader dimensions of the problem and its fundamental significance for the

[75] *Loc. cit.*
[76] *Loc. cit.*
[77] *Ḥoreb*, no. 688, pp. 544–7.

"spirituality" of the Jewish people. R. Hirsch's trenchant remarks reflect three fundamental points:

1. Familiarity with Hebrew is a primary educational goal. It is the first and earliest duty of a father to assure that his child become familiar with the Hebrew language of prayer. For the community, this is a *sine qua non* for preservation of its heritage.
2. Many authorities had pointed out that translation, by its very nature, must be inexact and that nuances of expression cannot be preserved. Therefore prayer in the vernacular leads to a loss of the benefit of the mysteries and the "*tikkunim*" (mystical effects) incorporated by the Sages in their prayers. R. Hirsch incisively points out that even more is at stake. The Hebrew liturgy constitutes the repository of Israel's collective religious-national thought. There is no adequate translation that is able to capture all the nuances of this world of thought and aspiration. Supplantation of Hebrew by any other language, he argues, may lead to introduction of concepts alien to Judaism into divine worship with the result that foreign ideology may gain credence and even acquire an undeserved aura of sanctity.
3. Individuals have obligations to the community. Prayer in the vernacular thwarts the educational goals of the Sages and removes a principal bulwark against assimilation. In contrast, prayer in Hebrew on the part of each individual leads to the fulfillment of communal educational goals and to spiritual elevation of the community. Abandonment of Hebrew by the community, writes Hirsch, would "tend to drag down to our own level that which should raise us."[78]

In encouraging the community to be steadfast in their loyalty to the Hebrew language in prayer, R. Hirsch stresses the role of a community *qua* community and affirms his faith in the future:

[78] *Ibid.*, p. 546.

> A community is not in truth as a single individual. The individual may and should consider his specific circumstances; he may and should use the means which are to hand as a help in his weakness. A community, however, has to consider the future generations in everything that it does, for a community is eternal and can always be rejuvenated. A community as a community is never incapable of fulfilling its task. When the older ones cannot do it, then the younger generation enters into the ranks of the community, and in twenty years or so the general body can be rejuvenated and strengthened, the younger generation achieving that which the older one did not attain. The community carries all the sanctities of Israel for the future generations. It must therefore beware of undermining what is by no means the least important pillar of the community – namely, *Avodah*, which is communal prayer in the holy tongue."[79]

In a complete *volte face*, at the present time, virtually all Reform spokesmen repudiate the negative attitude of classical Reform vis-a-vis Hebrew. Poignant is the fact the arguments they now proffer echo precisely those of Orthodox rabbis of a century and a half ago.[80]

The trend toward reversal was already clearly evident in the 1970s in the writings of the historian of Reform liturgy, Jakob Petuchowski. Petuchowski writes appreciatively of the genius of the Hebrew language in conveying a wide variety of meaning in a few words with the result that, for the Hebraist, prayer provides a rich spiritual and intellectual experience. Petuchowski adds that even

---

[79] *Loc. cit.*

[80] Before reintroduction of Hebrew had gained popularity in Reform circles, Solomon B. Freehof authored an elementary text, *In the House of the Lord: Our Worship and our Prayer Book* (New York: Union of American Hebrew Congregations, 1951), for use in supplementary religious schools. In moving words (pp. 140–143), Freehof presents precisely the argument of R. Samuel Eiger for retention of Hebrew as the bond joining Jews into a common fraternity. However, Freehof takes it for granted that English will also be used extensively during the services.

for those who do not understand the language, prayer in Hebrew affords a glimpse of what they readily perceive to be a holy language, a language that conveys an intimation of transcendence.[81] Writing from a post-Auschwiẓ perspective, Petuchowski endorses prayer in the vernacular only as a transient arrangement dictated by necessity while cautioning that vernacular prayer "must never become an ideology."[82]

More recently, an outspoken critic of Mordecai Kaplan's prayer-book revisions, Alan W. Miller of Manhattan's Society for the Advancement of Judaism, asserts bluntly, "The entire effort by Jews to reshape the classical Jewish liturgy since the nineteenth century has been, in my considered judgment, a huge mistake."[83] Recognizing that a radical change in our understanding of language has taken place, Miller observes:

> For the Jew to pray in English – as opposed to study or to teach in English – is to incorporate automatically the value system of that language into his worship. If we have learned anything from modern linguistics it is that no language is transparent. All language is ideological...as Marshall McLuhan would say: "The medium is the message....[84]
>
> ...We must go back, in all humility...to the sources.... To pray as a Jew is to talk as a Jew. Without a thorough grounding in that language [Hebrew], prayer may evoke or edify, but it will bear no relationship to the past, present or future of a viable ongoing Jewish people.[85]

---

[81] Petuchowski, *Understanding Jewish Prayer*, pp. 47–8.

[82] *Ibid.*, pp. 53–4.

[83] Alan W. Miller, "The Limits of Change in Judaism: Reshaping Prayer," *Conservative Judaism* 41:2 (Winter, 1988–89): 27.

[84] *Loc. cit.*

[85] *Ibid.*, p. 28. The most recent call for revitalization of Reform worship services was issued by Eric H. Yoffie, president of the Union of American Hebrew Congregations (UAHC) at the sixty-fifth General Assembly of UAHC, in his presidential sermon, "Realizing God's Promise: Reform Judaism in the 21st Century" (New York: UAHC, Dec. 18, 1999). Yoffie advocates "a new Reform revolution" (p. 2) that emphasizes the primacy of Hebrew and the promotion of a vigorous program of adult Hebrew

IV. MUSIC

The power of music in arousing the religious spirit has always been acknowledged in Judaism. Prayer was frequently accompanied by song ("to hearken unto the song and the prayer," I Kings 8:28) and the Temple service incorporated elaborate musical components. Speaking of the prophet Elisha, Scripture tells us that music was a catalyst for the prophetic spirit: "*Ve-hayah ke-nagen ha-menagen va-tehi alav yad Hashem* – And it came to pass when the minstrel played, the hand of the Lord came upon him" (II Kings 3:15). In the striking ḥasidic interpretation of R. Dov Ber of Mezritch this passage is rendered: "When the music and the minstrel became a unitary whole [i.e., when the music, *ke-nagen*, became the minstrel, *ha-menagen*], then the hand of the Lord came upon him." When musician and music fuse, inspiration is present.[86]

Nonetheless, there are forms of music that are inherently inappropriate in a synagogue. In Germany the dispute over the use of the organ in the synagogue became the defining issue dividing traditionalists and the Reform elements. Introduction of the organ at services in Seesen and later in Berlin, Hamburg and Budapest was one of the earliest Reform innovations and was followed in subsequent decades in many cities in Germany, Hungary, Austria, England and the United States. Eventually, the growth and spread of Reform could be marked by the rising number of "organ synagogues," of which there were more than thirty in the United States by 1868[87] and one hundred and thirty in Germany by the early twentieth century.[88]

---

literacy. Yoffie states that Hebrew, as the sacred language of Jews, is "part of the fabric and texture of Judaism, vibrating with the ideas and values of our people" and that "absence of Hebrew knowledge is an obstacle to heartfelt prayer" (p. 4). Missing from this positive statement is acknowledgment of the steadfastness of the Orthodox community that preserved Hebrew prayer so that, in R. Hirsch's words, "the general body can be rejuvenated and strengthened."

[86] See Aaron Marcus, *He-Ḥasidut*, translated into Hebrew from German by M. Schonfeld (Tel Aviv: Neẓah, 1954), p. 84.

[87] Meyer, *Response*, p. 251.

[88] *Ibid.*, p. 184.

The halakhic question is threefold: is instrumental music permissible at worship services; if yes, is it permissible to make use of the instrument on the Sabbath; and, finally, may the instrument be played by a Jew on the Sabbath? With regard to use of the organ an additional question arises, namely, since this instrument is characteristically used in church services, is its use in the synagogue proscribed as a distinctively gentile practice prohibited by Leviticus 18:3? A host of halakhic authorities ruled against use of the organ at any time and against use of any musical instrument on the Sabbath, even when played by a non-Jew.[89]

Initially, Reform sympathizers permitted the use of the organ on Sabbath but only if played by a non-Jew.[90] In his *Davar be-Ito*, Chorin expounds on the effect of music in enhancing worship and promoting spirituality. Reiterating his previously expressed decision[91] permitting use of the organ, Chorin disdainfully dismisses R. Mordechai Benet's assertion that instrumental music accompanying prayer does not constitute fulfillment of a *mizvah*.[92] Even someone

[89] The earliest discussions are found in *Eileh Divrei ha-Berit*, pp. 1, 5, 18, 23, 25, 28–31, 50, 61, 76, 81 and 85; *She'elot u-Teshuvot Ḥatam Sofer*, vol. 6, nos. 84, 86 and 89; and *Ẓeror ha-Ḥayyim*, "Kol ha-Shir," pp. 1A–6B. R. Chajes, in a subsequent discussion, *Minḥat Kena'ot*, pp. 988–990, is unequivocal in ruling that it is forbidden to utilize the services of a non-Jew to play the instrument on Sabbath. R. Chajes deemed employment of a non-Jew for that purpose not only to be halakhically prohibited but also unseemly in that "it is not befitting for a non-Jew to take part in a service that is not in accordance with his belief." Cf. R. Abraham Sutro, "Be-Mah she-Hidshu ha-Mithadshim be-Inyanei Beit ha-Knesset," *Shomer Ziyyon ha-Ne'eman*, 144 (5 Shevat, 5613): 287 and 217 (4 Shevat, 5616): 433. A later treatment of this issue is included in R. David Zevi Hoffman, *Melamed le-Ho'il*, part 1, no. 16; see also R. Yehiel Yaakov Weinberg, *Seridei Eish* (Jerusalem: Mossad ha-Rav Kook, 1962), vol. 2, no. 154. Jerusalem: Mossad ha-Rav Kook, 1962), vol. 2, no. 154; and R. Abraham Isaac ha-Kohen Kook, *Oraḥ Mishpat* (Jerusalem: Mossad ha-Rav Kook, 1985), pp. 49–50. The discussion of Akiva Zimmermann, *Sha'arei Ron: Ha-Ḥazzanut be-Sifrut Ha-She'elot u-Teshuvot ve-ha-Halakhah* (Tel Aviv: Bronyahad, 1992), pp. 21–46, focuses on the dispute over use of organs in Hungarian synagogues. See also Abraham Berliner, *Ketavim Nivḥarim* (Jerusalem: Mossad ha-Rav Kook, 1963), I: 173-187.

[90] *Nogah ha-Ẓedek*, pp. 3–28.

[91] *Ibid.*, p. 21.

[92] *Eleh Divrei ha-Berit*, p. 15.

"who understands but a little of the wisdom of the ways of the soul," writes Chorin, "must admit that the sound of an instrument has the power and force to dominate the powers of the soul, whether for joy or sadness, or whether also to give thanks, to pray and sing the kindnesses and praises of God."[93] Not only is instrumental music as an accompaniment to prayer absolutely permissible, Chorin avers, but it will serve as a means of enticing many of those who have abandoned the synagogue to return. In the German section of this work, Chorin makes the sweeping statement that whatever enhances the religious spirit is not halakhically forbidden and music obviously arouses religious consciousness. Moreover, he declares, the assertion that a Christian religious practice may be proscribed on the basis of Leviticus 18:3 is not to be countenanced since that prohibition applies only to pagan ceremonies. In acid tones Chorin disparages the rabbinic establishment that disputes those views, is not open to rational argument, and, by means of ban, bell, book, and candle, exercises unchallenged tyranny over the community.[94]

Delegates to the Second Reform Rabbinical Conference in Frankfurt unanimously affirmed that the organ "may and should be played by a Jew on the Sabbath."[95] During the discussion concerning the organ that took place at the Frankfurt Conference, Samuel Holdheim expressed the conviction that the contemporary synagogue with its devotional inwardness is of a loftier character than the sacrificial services it replaces. If the sacrificial service involved no desecration of the Sabbath, then certainly, argued Holdheim, instrumental music accompanying present-day services involves no desecration of the Sabbath.[96]

---

[93] *Davar be-Ito*, p. 47.

[94] *Ein Wort*, pp. 42–4.

[95] *Protokolle*, p. 151.

[96] *Ibid.*, p. 150. Declaring that the organ "may and should" be played on Sabbath by a Jew, Holdheim stated: "Activity that serves for such enhancement of divine worship cannot at all be biblically proscribed. We have virtually unanimously removed from our prayers the plea for return to Jerusalem and the reinstituting of the sacrificial cult and have thereby clearly stated that our houses of worship are equal to the Temple in Jerusalem...that our divine worship, with its inwardness, is higher than the sacrificial cult, replaces it and renders it superfluous for all future time."

Proponents of the organ argued heatedly – if not very convincingly – that this instrument alone has the potential to transform the quality of worship services. Delivering a lengthy report on the question of the organ to the Frankfurt Conference on behalf of the commission on liturgy, Leopold Stein ascribed well-nigh wondrous attributes to the instrument. It might be inadvisable, he averred, to introduce the organ into the not-yet-reconstituted worship services. Yet,

> introduction of the organ in the synagogue, even though it is not advisable [at present], is still *necessary*. For no service needs elevation as much as ours, during which somnolence and nonchalance are predominant. There is no more exalting means of encouraging devotion than the music which issues from that...grand instrument.[97]

That emphasis on the putative role of the organ bordered on the absurd may be seen from the detailed record of the Conference proceedings. At the conclusion of the extensive report of the commission on liturgy, Jospeh Maier stated categorically that "without an organ an impressive and dignified divine service is impossible" and, consequently, "the commission has deemed [use of] of the organ in the synagogue not only permissible but *dringend nothwendig* (urgently necessary)."[98]

In the United States Isaac Mayer Wise introduced an organ in his temple in Cincinnati in 1855. Admitting that several years earlier such a step would have been considered "heretical," Wise

---

Holdheim's statement, uttered with perfect aplomb, did not meet with any protest on the part of his colleagues at the Conference. Although present-day Reform leaders express an attachment to the Land of Israel, these sentiments have never been accompanied by affirmation of the role of the Temple. Consequently, there is a painful incongruity in current vociferous Reform demands for unimpeded access to worship at the *Kotel* for formal Reform services.

[97] *Protokolle*, p. 328.

[98] *Ibid.*, p. 316.

championed the organ as a "Jewish instrument" commonly used in synagogues in Germany.[99] Contending that it was particularly suited for the expression of religious emotion, Wise termed the pipe-organ "the sublimest instrument of the world.... It is not so much a single instrument as a multitude of them, dwelling together – a cathedral of sounds within a cathedral of service."[100]

These encomia notwithstanding, use of the organ continued to engender heated controversy even in Reform circles.[101] Many individuals continued to express discomfort with an obvious emulation of church practice.[102] Among protagonists of Reform, the more conservative admitted openly that the organ's Christian associations were undeniable. Isaak Noa Mannheimer stated forthrightly:

---

[99] *The American Israelite* 1:45 (18 May 1855): 356.

[100] *The American Israelite* 5:49 (10 June 1859): 389. For a report on opposition to introduction of the organ in the United States see I. Harold Sharfman, *The First Rabbi: Origins of Conflict Between Orthodox and Reform* (n.p.: Joseph Simon, Pangloss Press, 1988), pp. 379–388. Sharfman, p. 383, cites (without source) the retort of Julius Eckman, spiritual leader of Temple Emanuel of San Francisco, when asked whether a Jew may play the organ on the Sabbath: "Fifty years hence our successors will wonder more at the question than at the reply." Ironically, Eckman's prophecy has been fulfilled but hardly in the manner that he anticipated.

[101] See the bibliographic references in Philipson, *Reform Movement*, p. 436, n. 95. See also Phyllis Cohen Albert, *The Modernization of French Jewry: Consistory and Community in the Nineteenth Century* (Hanover, NH: Brandeis University Press, 1977), pp. 264 and 290, for brief references to the situation in France where introduction of the organ continued to arouse opposition although it was endorsed by many delegates to the 1856 Paris rabbinical conference convened by Grand Rabbi Salomon Ullmann. In the United States controversy over introduction of the organ led to a court battle in Charleston in 1844. That incident involved a struggle over even more fundamental changes; the organ was simply emblematic of the underlying friction. See Allan Tarshish, "The Charleston Organ Case," *American Jewish Historical Quarterly* 54:4 (June, 1965): 411–49.

[102] Use of a guitar as an instrumental accompaniment has become the practice in a number of present-day Reform congregations. Restrictions pertaining to use of a musical instrument on the Sabbath apply to the guitar no less so than to other instruments. However, as a religiously neutral artifact of popular culture not identified with church services, the halakhic odium associated with use of the organ does not extend to the guitar.

> I would never figure on an organ, even if all outward objections against it were to cease. I admit that the sound of the organ, like the sound of bells, has become too much a characteristic of the Christian church, and it is, therefore, offensive to the Jew. Honestly, in the five years since I have become unaccustomed to the sound of the organ, it would no longer quite suit my own feelings.[103]

In a moving reflection on prayer, Rabbi Joseph B. Soloveitchik notes that overemphasis on an external aesthetic is alien to the mood of the synagogue and that organ music is not only halakhically objectionable but that it conjures a spirit foreign to the traditional "worship of the heart":

> From a musical viewpoint the forms developed by the generations lack perfect structure. The Jewish melodic formula is often marked by the absence of strict form, and by sudden leaps and bounds. One who seeks harmonies and euphonies in the tunes of Jewish prayer is destined to disappointment. What can be found is stychic eruption of feeling.... Unlike the Church, Jewish Synagogues never developed architecture or decorative means with which to enchant man, to anesthetize him into a supernatural mood. They never created the illusion of standing before God when the heart seeks Him not, when the heart is, in fact, hard as stone, cruel and cynical. Our Synagogues were never in the dominion of half-darkness; the clear light of the sun was never hidden by narrow stained-glass windows. There never echoed the rich, polyphonic strains of the organ, and the song of the mixed choir, hidden from the eyes of worshippers, in order to create a mysterious, unworldly, mood. They never tried to extract the Jew from reality, to introduce him to spirits. To the contrary: they always demanded that prayer be continuous to life and that in

[103] Cited in Plaut, *Rise*, p. 44.

> it man confess the truth. For this reason the Catholic-style dramatization of prayer is so utterly alien to our religious sense, therefore the great opposition of Halakhah to so-called modernization of prayer services which erases the uniquely original in "worship of the heart."[104]

Once welcomed as the hallmark of Reform innovation, the organ has lost its popular appeal. In Great Britain, the West London Synagogue and Manchester's Park Place Synagogue both installed organs in 1858.[105] In recent years, however, an increasing number of Britain's Reform synagogues have abandoned the instrument. In a brief journalistic survey of attitudes in the British Reform movement, Simon Rocker cites reactions such as "...we prefer congregational singing. Our performances may be less polished but they are more *heimeshe*;" "[with an organ] the congregation was quite passive.... [Without an organ], there is now more participation and people feel less inhibited." Respondents admitted quite candidly "...I have always associated organs with churches.... I'd much rather hear the beautiful voices than an electric whine;" "I suppose it (the organ) has an association with the Church of England;" and "I would say that the congregation is split fifty–fifty in favor and against. The young don't want it. They feel it is anachronistic, untraditional, and doesn't reflect anything Jewish."

Ironically, several British Reform temples have discarded the organ during most services, but retain it for the High Holy Days. A number of clergymen point out that young people, and particularly those who have attended services in Israel without an organ, have a strong preference against use of the instrument. Rodney Mariner, minister of the Belsize Square Reform Synagogue in North-West London, comments on a tension in the congregation over whether or not the instrument enhances services and reports that a growing

---

[104] "Jews at Prayer," in *Shiurei ha-Rav: A Conspectus of the Public Lectures of Rabbi Joseph B. Soloveitchik*, ed. Joseph Epstein (New York: Hamevaser, 1974), pp. 27–8.

[105] Anne J. Kershen and Jonathan A. Romain, *Tradition and Change: A History of Reform Jews in Britain, 1840–1995* (London: Vallentine Mitchell, 1995), p. 66; and Meyer, *Response*, p. 177.

number of congregants are in favor of its abandonment. However, adds Mariner (without a trace of irony), "their voice is not loud enough to wipe away 150 years of tradition, but it is loud enough to be listened to seriously."[106] Although he was not prepared to take so radical a step as to forego the organ entirely, Mariner deemed the organ too intrusive for use during the Yom Kippur services in their entirety. He therefore reserved the instrument for the end of the day, thereby "creating a climax to a day of prayer."

A report of the experiences of the Bournemouth Reform Synagogue is instructive. While they have not phased out use of the instrument altogether, the congregation now offers a once a month "organless" Sabbath morning service. That innovation is the result of a series of events that, Rocker writes, "you might say was an act of God." One winter, on a number of occasions, the organist was homebound because of the snow and unable to participate in the services. After their initial panic, the members of the choir found that the organ-less service was to their liking. The synagogue's minister, David Soetendorp, anticipates dispensing with the organ in the course of time but states that, for the moment, "I wouldn't want to force a revolt. I'm a believer in evolution."[107]

Evolution is apparent in attitudes toward music in the Reform movement in the United States as well. In a groundbreaking address in which he urged Reform Judaism to proclaim a new revolution and reclaim synagogue worship as the movement's foremost concern, Eric Yoffie, president of the Union of American Hebrew Congregations, singled out the role of music as the key to ritual transformation. But, bemoaning the fact that Reform congregants "have lost our voices" and that Reform worship has become "a spectator sport," the music Yoffie seeks to enhance is primarily vocal, not instrumental. He anticipates a spiritual renewal that may be engendered by means

[106] The musical tradition of that Reform temple encompasses many of the works of the nineteenth-century German composer Louis Lewandowski set for organ music.

[107] Simon Rocker, "Instrumental Break," *The Jewish Chronicle* (London), 3 October 1997, p. 29.

of music that is "vibrant, spiritual and community-building" if "the congregation finds its voice."[108]

Apart from the controversy over instrumental music, as early as the mid-eighteenth century, there was considerable discussion in rabbinic writings of the role, whether positive or negative, of song and the precentor.[109] R. Yaakov Emden is censurious in the extreme of cantors of his day whose comportment detracted from public worship.[110] At a later date *Maharaẓ Hayes* wrote approvingly of some of the improvements in decorum and the conduct of services in the *Chorshulen*, but inveighed against those locales where innovators instituted halakhically proscribed mixed choirs.[111]

Melody and the role of the prayer leader as a spiritual force are the subjects of a luminous discourse by R. Naḥman of Bratslav. R. Naḥman emphasizes the need to judge one's fellow compassionately and to perceive the good qualities that are present even in the apparently wicked, (and in oneself as well, if for no other reason than that it serves to keep depression at bay!). That concept he finds reflected in the simple meaning of the Psalmist's words "For yet [*od*] a little while and the wicked shall not be; you shall diligently consider his place and it shall not be" (Psalms 37:10): "For yet a little while" – if one spends but a little time ferreting out good qualities in others, "the wicked shall not be" – it will turn out that the wicked

---

108 Yoffie, "Realizing," p. 3.

109 While a certain musical *nusaḥ* (melody or mode) is traditional, there is latitude in *halakhah* for musical innovation. See Lippmann Bodoff, "Innovation in Synagogue Music," *Tradition* 23:4 (Summer, 1988): 90–101. Apart from questions of *halakhah*, the type of music that is welcomed in the synagogue, or the extent to which it is shunned, deemed inspiring or deemed inappropriate, is often influenced by external cultural trends. Thus some forms of music may be inherently inappropriate because they are overly distracting or are associated with profane matters or with other religions. Cf. *Ḥoreb*, no. 689, p. 549. On changing cantorial styles see also R. Baruch ha-Levi Epstein, *Mekor Barukh*, pt. 2, chap. 2, sec. 5 (New York: M.P. Press, 1954), vol. II, pp. 1047–9 and 1048, note.

110 *Siddur Amudei Shamayim* (Altona: 1745), p. 27a; *She'ilat Yaaveẓ*, I, no. 61; and *Mor u-Keẓi'ah* 53. Cf. The centuries-earlier criticism of R. Asher b. Yehiel, *She'eilot u-Teshuvot ha-Rosh, kelal revi'i*, no. 22.

111 *Minḥat Kena'ot*, pp. 990–993. The *Chorshulen* were Orthodox synagogues that featured male choirs and promoted decorous and aesthetically pleasing services.

are not really wicked after all. A prayer leader is the *shaliaḥ ẓibur*, the messenger and agent of the congregation. As such, R. Naḥman points out, the prayer leader should be a person who is capable of representing the entire community and of discerning the positive qualities, i.e., the "good notes," of every worshiper. The prayer leader is charged with taking the "good notes" of each and every person and combining them into a melody[112] and only "one who has this noble talent...who judges everyone charitably, who finds their noble qualities and forms melodies from them...is fit to be the cantor and *shaliaḥ ẓibur* to stand in prayer before the lectern."[113]

Noteworthy in the context of the ongoing Orthodox-Reform debate over music in the synagogue is a remark found in the commentary to the prayerbook *Iyun Tefillah* of R. Jacob Zevi Mecklenburg, an articulate antagonist of Reform. The book of Psalms closes with a song calling upon an orchestra of musical instruments to join in a crescendo of praise. In the final verse the Psalmist calls out, "Let all souls [*kol ha-neshamah*] praise God, Hallelujah" (Psalms 150:6). *Iyun Tefillah* renders the verse: "Above all should the soul praise God, Hallelujah." Interpreting the word "*kol*" as connoting completeness and perfection, *Iyun Tefillah* explains the psalm as follows: after enumerating the various musical instruments with which praise is offered to God, the Psalmist employs the expression "*kol ha-neshamah*" to indicate that "superior in perfection" to instrumental music is the praise offered by the human soul.[114]

[112] In a play on words, R. Naḥman adds, in typical ḥasidic homiletic fashion, that in the Psalmist's exclamation, "While I exist [*be-odi*] will I praise the Lord" (Ps. 146:2), the word "*be-odi*" may be rendered as "with '*od*,'" i.e., "I will praise the Lord in prayer with the concept of '*od*' which occurs in 'yet but [*od*] a little while and the wicked shall not be,'" meaning that prayer shall be offered with an eye to the good qualities that negate the wickedness of those on whose behalf prayer is offered.

[113] *Likutei Moharan*, I, no. 282. Regarding cantors and melody see also *ibid.*, nos. 3 and 54.

[114] *Iyun Tefillah, Siddur Derekh Ḥayyim im Iyun Tefillah* (Tel Aviv: Sinai, 1954), p. 80. *Iyun Tefillah* observes that the vocalization of the consonant with a *ḥolam* rather than with a *kamaẓ* supports this interpretation. Cf. Redak, Psalms, *ad loc.*, who comments on the phrase *kol ha-neshamah* [rendering the phrase as if it read *al ha-kol, ha-neshamah*]: "Above all the praises is the praise of the soul and that is

V. DECORUM

Mirabile dictu, there was one matter pertaining to the synagogue regarding which Orthodox and Reform partisans were in agreement: that worship services ought not be marred by unseemly conduct was undisputed; that the synagogue was deficient in this respect was undeniable. The foibles of human nature are such that lapses in decorum at prayer services have been a persistent problem over the ages.[115] But the period immediately prior to the emergence of the Reform movement was a time during which the problem was particularly acute.

From the latter part of the seventeenth through the eighteenth centuries a general deterioration in religious sensibility took place. That deterioration was reflected in patterns of worship. In some of the smaller towns laxity in attendance at weekday prayer services became commonplace and communal attempts to remedy the situation by means of coercive regulations or by imposition of fines were unsuccessful.[116] Rabbinic writings of that period are replete with reports of chatter and gossip that profaned the solemnity of Sabbath

---

contemplation and knowledge of the works of the Lord, may He be blessed, as far as is in the power of the soul while it is yet in the body."

[115] On the ubiquitous nature of the problem see Moshe Halamish, "*Siḥat Ḥullin be-Vet ha-Knesset: Meẓi'ut u-Maavak*," in *Mil'et*, vol. II (Tel Aviv: 1984), pp. 225–51. The problem is common and ongoing and has been the subject of many essays and stories. See, for example, Chava Willig Levy, "Why There Was No Gabbai at the Regency Theater," *Jewish Action* 55:1 (Fall, 1994): 88 and Wallace Greene, "'In the King's Presence: Teaching for *Tefillah*: A Communal Responsibility," *Ten Daat* 12 (Summer, 1999): 60–70. A characteristic anecdote relates of the wealthy mogul who left instructions with a clerk that he not be disturbed in the synagogue on the Day of Atonement unless a certain stock, in which he had a considerable investment, reached the figure of twenty-five. Summoned to the vestibule to receive the news, he responded, "You are late. Inside they quoted twenty-seven a half hour ago."

[116] Azriel Shohat, *Im Ḥilufei Tekufot: Reshit ha-Haskalah be-Yahadut Germaniyah* (Jerusalem: Bialik Institute, 1960), pp. 144–5. Shohat, *loc. cit.*, cites the wry witticism of R. Aryeh Leib Epstein of Königsburg who remarked that the synagogue is desolate, visited only occasionally as if it were a sick person. It has become the custom to visit the synagogue (*le-vaker heikhalo*) in a manner similar to that which the *Shulḥan Arukh* prescribes for visiting the sick (*le-vaker ha-ḥoli*). Close relatives and friends visit the patient immediately and the more distant visit only

and festival services and of how the synagogue had become an arena for rowdy fights and altercations.[117] R. Yaakov Emden testified that "all the news and vain pursuits of the world are known and heard in the synagogue. There is even frivolity and levity, as if it were a gathering place for idlers."[118] If Reform writers were ashamed of the impression such services made on their non-Jewish neighbors, R. Emden was no less forthright in noting that in comparison to the worship service of their Christian compatriots Jewish performance was disgracefully deficient.[119]

Almost a decade before the founding of the Hamburg Temple, Moses Mendelssohn of Hamburg (not to be confused with Moses Mendelssohn of Berlin),[120] a moderate Enlightenment figure and author of *Pnei Tevel* (Amsterdam, 1872), wrote scathingly of the utter disorder prevalent in the traditional synagogue, of the fracas and rowdiness commonly found there, and of the boisterous conversation typical of a fish market.[121] It was this sorry state of affairs that later prompted him to praise the aesthetic improvements in the worship service introduced by the founders of the Hamburg Temple.

---

after three days; those close to God, i.e., the scholars and the pious, enter immediately while those more distant attend only after three days have elapsed, i.e., on Mondays and Thursdays.

[117] *Ibid.*, p. 146 and *Halamish*, "*Siḥat Ḥullin*," pp. 229–30.

[118] *Siddur Amudei Shamayim*, p. 27a.

[119] *Ibid.*, p. 26b. A much earlier work, the late twelfth-century figure, R. Judah he-Ḥasid, *Sefer Ḥasidim*, ed. Judah Wistinezky (Berlin: Mekiẓei Nirdamim, 1891), no. 1589, p. 389, bemoans the fact that Jews suffer by comparison to non-Jews in terms of comportment at religious services and *ibid.*, no. 224, p. 78, warns that synagogues in which Jews behave frivolously are fated to fall into gentile hands.

[120] "Moses Mendelssohn of Hamburg" is the name chosen for himself by Moses (1781–1867) son of Mendel Frankfurter (1742–1823), R. Samson Raphael Hirsch's paternal grandfather. Although Moses Frankfurter's writings include a biting, satirical denunciation of obscurantists and fanatical opponents of Enlightenment, he was clearly opposed to any actions that would undermine allegiance to rabbinic Judaism.

[121] See Noah Rosenbloom, "*Ha-Yahadut ha-Mesoratit ve-ha-Reformah kefi she-hen Mishtakefot be-'Pnei Tevel' le-Mendelson*," *Sixth World Congress of Jewish Studies* (Jerusalem: 1977), vol. 3, pp. 454–5. Halamish, "*Siḥat Ḥullin*," p. 242, no. 101, errs (possibly confusing Mendelssohn of Hamburg with Mendelssohn of Berlin) in assuming this to be a portrayal of a Reform worship service.

In the course of time he was, however, disappointed by the orientation of the Temple leadership and their substantive changes in the liturgy. Ultimately, he concluded that those efforts had not produced the desired result of enhancing religious devotion. Although the Hamburg Temple did not formally abrogate weekday prayer, it was not open during the week; certainly the Hamburg Temple was not seen as encouraging weekday prayer. To the author of *Pnei Tevel*, it appeared that the Sabbath worshipers at the Temple gradually decreased in number and that only on the High Holy Days did the Temple membership turn out in full force. Despite this disappointment, he harbored the hope that the example set by the Hamburg Temple would serve as a spur to the communal leadership and prompt them to institute long overdue improvements in synagogue services.[122]

In this respect the Reform critique was indeed salutary. Traditionalists were prompted to ask themselves: If so many of their coreligionists were attracted to the new-style services, was it simply because they presented a less demanding form of ritual; was it solely because of the prevalent assimilatory trend; or was it because these services were satisfying a deeply-felt need? A recognition that the desire for liturgical change was to be attributed to deficiencies in the services of the traditional synagogue was intimated by R. Eliezer of Triesch in the aftermath of the establishment of the Hamburg Temple.

---

[122] Rosenbloom, "*Ha-Yahadut ha-Mesoratit*," pp. 459–60. Others concurred in the assessment that the Hamburg Temple proved to be uninspiring. Of the Temple's spiritual leaders Moses Moser remarked in a letter to Immanuel Wolf-Wohlwill that one could learn more from a stuffed rabbi in a zoological museum than from a live Temple preacher. See Adolf Strodtmann, *H. Heine's Leben und Werke*, third ed. (Hamburg: Hoffmann and Campe, 1884), vol. 1, 326. Cf. Ismar Elbogen, *Jewish Liturgy: A Comprehensive History*, translated from German into English by Raymond P. Scheindlin (Philadelphia and Jerusalem: Jewish Publication Society, 1993), p. 306, who errs in attributing this comment to Leopold Zunz. A selection of the engaging Moser correspondence liberally cited in Strodtmann's work has since been published by Albert H. Friedlander, "The Wohlwill-Moser Correspondence," *Leo Baeck Institute Year Book* 11 (1966): 262–299. For the comment regarding the Temple preachers, see p. 271 and p. 297 for the original German. I thank Professor Michael A. Meyer for this latter reference.

In his second contribution to *Eileh Divrei ha-Berit* he urged his colleagues in Hamburg to examine the nature of their own services and to strive to make synagogue worship more edifying. He found poetic justice and even punishment "measure for measure" in the fact that the inroads and successes of Reform were precisely in the areas in which the Orthodox were remiss:

> It is well known that the punishments of the Creator, blessed be He, are measure for measure. Since our many sins have brought it upon us that this breach occurs in matters of the synagogue and prayer we must presume that, heaven forfend, you have not appropriately honored the holy synagogue that is in your noble community. Therefore this trouble has come upon you that they seek to desanctify and profane it entirely, heaven forfend. Indeed, because of our manifold sins, it has become accepted as permissible in several congregations (and, in particular, in provinces of Germany, according to reports) to engage in idle conversation in the synagogue. Great is this stumbling block and at times people even come to shouting and quarreling and that constitutes a grievous sin.[123]

Not content to limit himself to negative self-criticism, R. Eliezer of Triesch exhorted the rabbis and spiritual leaders of the generation to adopt a positive agenda, to institute seminars and lectures devoted to strengthening interpersonal relationships and ethical conduct and to reach out with patience and gentleness, with "a soft expression and intelligent ethical reproof," even to those with whom they had religious disagreements.[124]

Even more explicit was the *mea culpa* in R. Chajes' *Minḥat Kena'ot*. R. Chajes blamed a passive and apathetic Orthodox rabbinate for the spiritual malaise of their congregations. By contrast, he noted, synagogues that had introduced reforms were gaining in numbers because the innovators were concentrating their energies

[123] *Eileh Divrei ha-Berit*, pp. 94–5.
[124] *Ibid.*, pp. 95–6.

on attracting a following. The clergy were talented speakers who understood the temper of the times and, above all, were to be commended for expending time on a great deal of "activity and work for the congregation."[125] Writers such as R. Eliezer of Triesch and R. Chajes demonstrate a growing recognition among the Orthodox that the success of Reform institutions was related to lacunae in the existing traditionalist establishment and that efforts must be made to transform the atmosphere of the synagogue, albeit in an halakhic manner, to effect the desired results.

The decision of a number of Orthodox rabbis to officiate in clerical robes was an emulation of a Reform practice perceived by the laity as enhancing the dignity of services. Although disdained by many decisors as a practice that bordered on or actually infringed upon the prohibition of Leviticus 18:3, this innovation was nonetheless adopted by highly respected authorities. Among the prominent rabbinic figures who wore clerical robes were Rabbi Samson Raphael Hirsch[126] and the venerable halakhic scholar Rabbi Seligmann Baer Bamberger. Reportedly, Rabbi Bamberger defended this innovation as a reluctant concession to the liberal sectors of the Wurzburg community made in the hope of preventing more serious infractions of Jewish law.[127]

A much more pervasive manifestation of Reform influence

---

[125] p. 1019.

[126] Isaac Heinemann, "Samson Raphael Hirsch: The Formative Years of the Leader of Modern Orthodoxy," *Historia Judaica* 13 (1951): 46-47.

[127] Shnayer Z. Leiman, "Rabbi Joseph Carlebach–Wuerzburg and Jerusalem: A Conversation between Rabbi Seligmann Baer Bamberger and Rabbi Shmuel Salant," *Tradition* 28:2 (Winter, 1994): 60. Regarding clerical robes see also Shnayer Z. Leiman, "Rabbinic Openness to General Culture in the Early Modern Period in Western and Central Europe," *Judaism's Encounter with Other Cultures: Rejection or Integration?* ed. Jacob J. Schacter (Northvale, NJ and Jerusalem: Jason Aronson, 1997), p. 170, n. 56 as well as this writer's forthcoming "Orthodox Innovations Prompted by Reform Influence." In the course of time, clerical robes became normative in some Orthodox circles. In present-day England the by-laws of the (Orthodox) United Synagogue stipulate that canonicals are obligatory attire for clergy when officiating at services but the regulation is more honored in the breach than the observance. Currently, imposition of this dress code upon guest rabbis officiating at weddings in synagogues still adhering to the practice has become a

upon the traditional synagogue was the introduction of sermons in the vernacular. Ḥakham Isaac Bernays[128] and Rabbi Jacob Ettlinger[129] were the earliest Orthodox rabbis of note to preach in German. At first this development was vigorously opposed, particularly by Hungarian rabbinic authorities,[130] but, gradually, in most countries the vernacular sermon became an accepted feature of Orthodox services.[131]

The positive influence of Reform innovations on decorum in Orthodox synagogues is reflected in the formal synagogue statutes and regulations of the day. In 1810, the Westphalian Consistory over which Israel Jacobson presided, published a *Synagogenordnung* (Synagogue Order), an official pronouncement, roughly equivalent to contemporary by-laws, designed to promote order and decorum.[132] In the ensuing decades similar regulations were adopted by many communities in Germany. Those statutes, which frequently were accompanied by a government imprimatur, were binding upon all synagogues within the community, including the Orthodox. When, as was usually the case, those regulations provided for liturgical

---

source of contention. See Ruth Rothenberg, "New Rabbis' Distress Over Need to Dress to Impress," *The Jewish Chronicle* (London), 20 November 1998, p. 19.

[128] See Eduard Duckesz, "Zur Biographie des Chacham Isaak Bernays," *Jahrbuch der Jüdisch-Literarischen Gesellschaft*, vol. 5 (1907), pp. 298–307.

[129] Rabbi Ettlinger's sermons in German date from the very beginning of his rabbinic career. See, for example, *Rede gehalten zur Feuer des höchsten Namensfestes Seiner königlichen Hoheit des Grossherzogs Ludwig von Baden* (Carlsruhe: 1824) and Jacob Aron Ettlinger, Elias Willstätter and Benjamin Dispeckter, *Predigten, gehalten in den Synagogen zu Karlsruhe und Bühl von den Rabbinats-Kandidaten* (Carlsruhe: 1824).

[130] See R. Moses Sofer, *Teshuvot Ḥatam Sofer, Ḥoshen Mishpat*, no. 197; R. Akiva Joseph Schlesinger, *Lev ha-Ivri* (Jerusalem: 1904), part 1, pp. 19a–21b; R. Hillel Lichtenstein, *Teshuvot Bet Hillel* (Satmar: 1908), nos. 34, 35 and 39; "*Die Beschlüsse der Rabbiner-Versammlung zu Mihalowiẓ*," *Israelit* 7:32 (August 8, 1866), p. 521; and R. Moses Schick, *Teshuvot Maharam Shik, Oraḥ Ḥayyim*, nos. 70 and 311.

[131] By the mid-twentieth century Rabbi Yehiel Yaakov Weinberg, *Seridei Eish*, vol. 2, no. 149, p. 364, was unequivocal in ruling that, in his day, when the masses were fluent only in the vernacular, there could no longer be any legitimate halakhic objection to delivery of sermons in the language of the country.

[132] The document was published independently (Kassel: 1810) and also in *Sulamith* 3:1 (1810): 366–80.

reforms as well and were governmentally enforced they became a further source of communal factionalism. However, improvement of decorum in itself was viewed as a *desideratum* by traditionalists.

Most interesting is the fact that R. Hirsch's separatist *Israelitische Religionsgesellschaft* in Frankfurt-am-Main promulgated a *Synagogenordnung* upon the dedication of its own building in 1853 and a revised version in 1874, both of which were patterned upon prototypes enacted by Reform communities.[133] In formulating the detailed and strict rules of conduct enshrined in this code, R. Hirsch was responding to the concern for decorous and dignified behavior in the synagogue but, at the same time, he was meticulous with regard to halakhic practices. Accordingly, the *Synagogenordnung* stipulated a head covering and *tallit* for men and abstention from wearing leather shoes on the ninth of Av and *Yom Kippur*. However, removal of shoes by *kohanim* prior to recitation of the priestly blessing was permitted only in a designated room. Reacting to similar efforts to enact rules and statutes to enhance decorum, R. Chajes writes it is "clear as the sun" that promulgation of ordinances for that purpose is permissible provided that such ordinances do not encroach upon laws prescribed by the *Shulḥan Arukh*.[134]

Notice should be taken of the Copernican revolution that has taken place with regard to what is considered appropriate synagogue behavior. In the early days of the movement for synagogue reform, Aaron Chorin wrote disparagingly of the "unbecoming swaying and reeling back and forth" and of prayer uttered in a loud, shrill voice and urged that services be purged of such disruptiveness.[135]

---

[133] See Petuchowski, *Prayerbook Reform*, pp. 123–124 and Robert Liberles, *Religious Conflict in Social Context: The Resurgence of Orthodox Judaism in Frankfurt-am-Main 1838–1877* (Westport, CT: Greenwood Press, 1985), pp. 140–142. For similar regulations enacted by the consistories in France cf. Albert Cohen, *Modernization of French Jewry*, pp. 190–1.

[134] *Minḥat Kena'ot*, p. 993, note.

[135] Ein Wort, p. 34. Cf. Karla Goldman, *Beyond the Synagogue Gallery: Finding a Place for Women in American Judaism* (Cambridge: Harvard University Press, 2000), who notes nineteenth-century American Jews' discomfort with "the embarrassing disorder of traditional Jewish worship" characterized by "chaotic behavior and swaying movements" (p. 81). For sources describing the positive effects

Subsequently adopted synagogue regulations uniformly required the worshiper to behave in a seemly manner and to refrain from unnecessary bodily motion. Even in calling individuals to the reading of the Torah there was an attempt to eliminate the coming and going of synagogue officials and to reduce the number of individuals required to leave their pews. In contrast, contemporary Reform writers celebrate the value of movement and dance in conjunction with worship.[136] Admiration for staid churchly decorum has been replaced by appreciation of ḥasidic warmth and exuberance.

VI. AESTHETICS

In keeping with the desire to present an appealing religious service, new emphasis was also placed upon beautifying the synagogue building. The considerations that prompted aesthetic enhancement were purportedly spiritual. However, two innovations in synagogue design introduced by Israel Jacobson in the Seesen Temple in 1810, namely, removal of the *bimah* (also known as *almemor* or *teivah*), the raised platform from which the Torah is read, from the center of the synagogue to the front of the synagogue in proximity to the Ark creating a visual effect similar to that of the church nave leading to the altar and, in more obvious emulation of church edifices, erection of a belfry were changes that bespoke a desire to imitate man rather than to draw close to God.

In an intriguing analysis of differing cultural modes of expressing the quest for the numinous in prayer, Professor Lawrence Hoffman suggests that classical Reform's emphasis on imposing ar-

---

of swaying in prayer see Bernard M. Casper, *Talks on Jewish Prayer* (Jerusalem: World Zionist Organization Department for Torah Education and Culture in the Diaspora, 1958), pp. 27–8 and Abraham Kon, *Prayer* (London, Jerusalem, and New York: The Soncino Press, 1971), pp. 38–9. Cf. the satiric comments of Norman Lebrecht, "The Reason Why All Our Shuls Are Swaying," *The Jewish Chronicle* (London), July 13, 2001, p. 27.

[136] See, for example, Michael Swartz, "Models for New Prayer," *Response* 13:1–2 (Fall, Winter, 1982): 35 and Arthur Waskow, "Theater, Midrash, and Prayer," *ibid.*: 133 and 136–7; and, more recently, Joseph A. Levine, *Rise and Be Seated: The Ups and Downs of Worship* (Northvale, NJ: Jason Aronson, 2000), pp. 64–5 and 167–8.

chitecture, dignified and decorous services and use of the sonorous organ reflect an approach to the holy in which the transcendent Deity is perceived as awesome, lofty, and distant. This rationalistic approach, Professor Hoffman suggests, was shared by European Protestants and early partisans of Reform.[137] The suggestion that the imposing cathedrals, organs, and dignified services of Protestants mirrored this theological perspective of man's relationship to God is cogent. It is, however, questionable whether the motivation of Reform innovators was the product of a similar theological perspective or simply a desire to emulate Christian neighbors.

In defense of the early exponents of Reform it must be stated that the two matters may have been interrelated. A form of self-denigration born of what was perceived as "orientalism"[138] or primitivism in Judaism was clearly operative. They further presumed that what they perceived as a more advanced Western Protestant cultural aesthetic was worthy of emulation as a means of achieving a higher spirituality as well. In stark contrast is the view of R. Yaakov Emden that the key to prayer is an individual's appropriate appreciation and understanding of his own self-worth both as a human being and as a Jew. In forceful and unambivalent language Rabbi Emden encourages and exhorts the worshiper to develop feelings of self-confidence and self-assurance. Since prayer can be not only a source of personal benefit but also a matter of cosmic significance, R. Emden emphasizes the import of the worshiper's awareness of the awesome power, and hence the concomitant responsibility, he has as a praying individual: "Let it not be light in his eyes that he is created in the [divine] image and form and that the root of his soul is connected with the supernal world.... If he utters a holy and

[137] Lawrence A. Hoffman, *Beyond the Text: A Holistic Approach to Liturgy* (Bloomington and Indianapolis: Indian University Press, 1987), pp. 151–62.

[138] See Kaufmann Kohler, *Jewish Theology: Systematically and Historically Considered*, augmented ed. (New York: Ktav, 1968), pp. 470–3. See also Kohler on the Bar Miẓvah ceremony and the head covering as "a survival of orientalism," cited in W. Gunther Plaut, *The Growth of Reform Judaism* (New York: World Union for Progressive Judaism, 1965), p. 312.

pure utterance there is inherent in it the power to create effects in the loftiest heavens."[139] Confidence in the power of human prayer, writes Rabbi Emden, should be coupled with particular pride and assurance in one's status as a Jew for "Should we not take pride in this, a great, wondrous, pride of which there is none greater?"[140]

Rabbinic authorities had no problem with the general desire to enhance the beauty of synagogue buildings. However, the bell tower and location of the *bimah* did pose halakhic questions. Summoning worshipers to prayer by means of a bell was considered to be a Christological practice forbidden by Leviticus 18:3.[141] The belfry was so obviously borrowed from Christianity that it never became popular.[142] The more equivocal issue was the location of the *bimah*. Removal of the *bimah* from its central position was advocated by leading Reform spokesmen, including Aub, Geiger, Hess, Herxheimer, Samuel Hirsch, Holdheim, Hamburger, Kahn, Mannheimer, Maier, Philippson, Schwab, and L. Stein.[143]

Although in Germany introduction of the organ was the defining issue in Reform-Orthodox controversies, in Hungary location of the *bimah* became elevated to a question of ideology that became symbolic of the entire struggle for and against Reform. It was in connection with his unequivocal ruling on the impermissibility of shifting the *bimah* from its central position that *Ḥatam Sofer* applied his oft-quoted aphorism "*ḥadash asur min ha-Torah* – innovation,[144] i.e.,

---

[139] *Siddur Amudei Shamayim*, p. 5a.

[140] *Ibid.*, p. 18b.

[141] *Minḥat Kena'ot*, p. 991, note.

[142] The only other German synagogue to feature a bell tower was that in Buchau built in 1839. See Meyer, *Response*, p. 404, n. 115. Cf. also Michael A. Meyer, "Christian Influence on Early German Reform Judaism," *Studies in Jewish Bibliography, History and Literature in Honor of I. Edward Kiev* (New York: Ktav, 1971), ed. Charles Berlin, pp. 292–3.

[143] Kaufmann Kohler, "Almemar or Almemor" and A.W. Brunner, "Almemar or Almemor, Architecturally Considered," *Jewish Encyclopedia* (New York: 1906), vol. I, p. 431 and Leopold Löw, *Gesammelte Schriften* (Szegeden: 1899), IV, pp. 93–107.

[144] Use of the term "*ḥadash*" (new) is a pun based upon the term's denotation of "new" grain that is forbidden as food until an offering from the newly harvested produce is brought on the second day of Passover as prescribed by Leviticus 23:14.

departure from accepted practice, is forbidden by the Torah"[145] – a remark that became a slogan of the traditionalists.

In actuality, this halakhic ruling is the subject of considerable dispute. The halakhic basis for placing the *bimah* in the center of the synagogue is to be found in three rulings of Maimonides' *Mishneh Torah: Hilkhot Tefillah* 11:3; *Hilkhot Ḥagigah* 3:4; and *Hilkhot Lulav* 7:23. While R. Moses Isserles (Rema), *Oraḥ Ḥayyim* 150:5, maintains that the *bimah* should be placed in a central position, R. Joseph Karo rules otherwise in his commentary on Maimonides' *Mishneh Torah, Kesef Mishnah, Hilkhot Tefillah* 11:3. He notes that in some places the *bimah* was erected at the western side of the synagogue, "...for its location in the center is not mandatory; everything depends on the place and the time." Accordingly, many authorities viewed placement of the *bimah* in the center of the synagogue as recommendatory rather than mandatory while others ruled that the *bimah* must be centrally located and considered displacement of the *bimah* to be the thin end of the wedge of Reform.[146]

The attitude, generally adopted by Orthodoxy today, is best reflected in two responsa authored by R. Moses Feinstein.[147] R. Feinstein rules that, in building a synagogue structure, the *bimah* should be placed in the center but that failure to position the *bimah* in the center does not invalidate a synagogue as a place of prayer. In a comment placing the issue in historical perspective, Rabbi Feinstein adds that the stringent attitude ascribed to certain Hungarian rabbinic authorities who forbade prayer in a synagogue in which the *bimah* was not located in the center was based on a "*horaat shaah*," an *ad*

---

[145] *She'eilot u-Teshuvot Ḥatam Sofer, Oraḥ Ḥayyim*, no. 28. Cf. R. Jacob Ettlinger, *Abhandlungen und Reden* (Schildberg: 1899), pp. 7–10, on the symbolism of the central *bimah*.

[146] See Immanuel Jakobovits, *Jewish Law Faces Modern Problems* (New York: 1965), pp. 43–46. See also *Minḥat Kena'ot*, p. 992, note. Among the prominent halakhists who prohibit removal of the *bimah* from its central position are R. Abraham Samuel Benjamin Schreiber, *She'eilot u-Teshuvot Ketav Sofer, Oraḥ Ḥayyim*, no. 19; R. Yehudah Asad, *She'elot u-Teshuvot Mahari Asad, Oraḥ Ḥayyim*, no. 50; and R. Naftali Ẓevi Yehudah Berlin, *She'eilot u-Teshuvot Meshiv Davar*, vol. I, no. 15.

[147] *Iggerot Mosheh, Oraḥ Ḥayyim*, vol. II (New York: 1963), nos. 41 and 42.

hoc temporary ruling, as a means of stemming the tide of Reform.[148] The *bimah* controversy is an instance in which a comparatively minor halakhic matter assumed exaggerated significance and, as a focal point of ideological controversy, became the banner around which the opposing forces arrayed themselves.

A far more grave halakhic infraction is involved in removal of the *meḥiẓah* or barrier separating the men's and women's sections of the synagogue. If, as noted, use of the organ was the defining issue in Germany and location of the *bimah* the central point of dispute in Hungary, it was in the United States that the question of *meḥiẓah* became the *cause célèbre*. The reason for this is not that the gravity of the matter was insufficiently recognized in European countries but that the vast majority of European synagogues, including the Reform and Liberal, did maintain some form of separation of the sexes until well into the twentieth-century. It was in the United States that family pews were first introduced by Isaac Mayer Wise in Albany in 1851 and it was in the United States that mixed seating took root. Wise had long favored elimination of the separate seating of women in a balcony but the actual institution of mixed pews came about fortuitously when Wise's Reform congregation Anshe Emeth purchased a church building that already had family pews and Wise retained them.[149] A contemporary commentator observed that introduction of family pews in Germany would have been "a gross anomaly." Following the model of German churches in which separate seating was the norm, German Reform synagogues continued to maintain separate seating even when the *meḥiẓah* was abandoned.[150] In the United States, with the spread of mixed seating

[148] Cf. an illuminating comment on this issue in Naphtali Carlebach, *Joseph Carlebach and His Generation* (New York: The Joseph Carlebach Memorial Foundation, 1959), pp. 225–230. For further elaboration see also Leiman, "Rabbi Joseph Carlebach–Wuerzburg and Jerusalem: A Conversation between Rabbi Seligmann Baer Bamberger and Rabbi Shmuel Salant," pp. 58–63.

[149] Heller, *Isaac M. Wise*, pp. 160 and 213–4.

[150] See Meyer, *Response*, p. 426, note 107. Jonathan D. Sarna, "The Debate Over Mixed Seating in the American Synagogue," in *The American Synagogue*, ed. Jack Wertheimer (Hanover and London: Brandeis University Press and University Press of New England, 1987), p. 364, reports that as late as the early twentieth century

to Conservative synagogues as well, the *meḥiẓah* became the visible demarcation between Orthodoxy and other denominations.[151] In terms of synagogue design, removal of the *meḥiẓah* is the single most significant Reform departure from Jewish law. That change acquires greater significance when it is realized that it was introduced primarily for ideological, rather than aesthetic, reasons.

With regard to questions of synagogue structure and aesthetics in general, R. Chajes' comments on communal priorities are instructive. R. Chajes deems the expenditure of vast sums of money on an imposing edifice rather than on education or care of the needy to be misguided. Indeed, on one occasion he advised a small congregation to pawn the synagogue lamps in order to raise funds to enable individuals to avoid army service. The physical and spiritual welfare of the community, including support of hospitals, the freeing of captives, assistance to the poor, and establishing institutions for religious education as well as for professional training, he emphasizes, all take precedence over synagogue beautification.[152]

Thus, issues of synagogue design and structure also reflect a system of values. That even aesthetic perception is influenced by one's ideological perspective is evident from a brief passage in Howard Morley Sachar's *The Course of Modern Jewish History*. In discussing synagogues established in the New World, Sachar notes:

> The variety of functions performed by the synagogue was not always apparent to the outsider. Thus, a Christian traveler who visited Newport's synagogue once commented with sublime misunderstanding: "It will be extremely elegant when completed, but the outside is totally spoiled by a school

---

the Hamburg Temple, bastion of German Reform, refused a one million mark donation because the gift was conditioned upon introduction of mixed seating of men and women.

[151] *Ibid.*, pp. 380 and 386. For a discussion of the halakhic issues, including responsa in Hebrew and in English translation, see *The Sanctity of the Synagogue*, ed. Baruch Litvin (New York: Spero Foundation, 1959).

[152] *Minḥat Kena'ot*, p. 991.

> which the Jews [would] have annexed to it for the education of their children."[153]

That comment eloquently illustrates the influence of ideology upon the aesthetic perception of both the author and the individual he cites.

It is noteworthy that some twentieth-century writers have found the nineteenth-century Reform aesthetic a deterrent to religious spirituality. One of the criticisms of the overall tenor of Reform services centers upon a perception of the temple as a place of worship set apart and unconnected to a vital, living Judaism. One keen twentieth-century critic, Professor Eliezer Berkovits, has pointed to the nomenclature associated with temple worship. Words such as sanctuary, chapel, chants, altar, and holy ark are seen as illustrative of religious services that require consecrated props and take place in an artificial, synthetic atmosphere. In contrast to the functionality of the old-fashioned *shul* with its *tashmishei kedushah*, *shulḥan,* central *bimah,* and *aron ha-kodesh*, the temple artifacts, claims Berkovits, its clericalism and its overly solemn dignity reflect an emphasis on an external aesthetic that may hide a religious vacuum. Berkovits remarks that, ironically, the temple architecture, although new and expensive, has rarely resulted in inspired artistry, whereas old synagogues, often simple in design, have become more venerable with increasing age. The ritualism and clericalism of classical Reform worship may be an appropriate style, comments Berkovits, for individuals whose renewed interest in the synagogue is motivated by a desire for conformity or by other sociological and psychological considerations but has little to do with genuine religiosity; rather, it is worship directed to a god shaped in man's own image.[154]

---

[153] New York: Dell Publishing Co., 1963, p. 164.

[154] See Eliezer Berkovits, "From the Temple to Synagogue and Back," *Judaism* 8:4 (Fall, 1959): 303–311; reprinted in Jakob J. Petuchowski, *Understanding Jewish Prayer* (New York: Ktav, 1972), pp. 138–51. It is, of course, the constant use to which the old synagogue testifies that is the source of the veneration it evokes. Cf. the comments of Leon Wieseltier, *Kaddish* (New York: Alfred A. Knopf, 1998), p. 5: "There are stains in the velvet. In places it is threadbare. This is an exquisite erosion. It is not

VII. DURATION OF SERVICES

As early as 1796, when the Amsterdam break-away congregation Adath Jeschurun introduced a number of moderate reforms, a major objective of the young intellectuals at its helm was removal of what were viewed as distracting and unnecessary additions to the prayer ritual.[155] Virtually all early Reform spokesmen who focused on liturgical issues advocated streamlining services. Enhancement of worship would be achieved, they believed, if the length of prayer services were to be shortened in order to command the unflagging attention of congregants.[156]

The negative effects of unnecessarily prolonged services are acknowledged by all. In a famous passage included in the introduction to his *siddur*, R. Yaakov Emden cites in the name of "early scholars" the adage "Prayer without *kavvanah* (concentration and intentionality) is as a body without a soul."[157] Proceeding to delineate the obstacles to devotion and singlemindedness in prayer, R. Emden points to the stultifying effect of habit and the deadening quality of ritual (which he terms elsewhere as *"seremoniyah be-laaz"*)[158] performed in a mechanical manner *(miẓvot anashim mi-lumadah)*.[159] If it transpires that "the formula of prayer becomes almost a matter of habit in the constant use of one formula, the *kavvanah* evaporates in its habituation." The net effect of repetition is to heap rote upon

neglect that thins these instruments. Quite the contrary. The more threadbare, the better. The thinner, the thicker."

155 Meyer, *Response*, p. 26; Jaap Meijer, *Moeder in Israel: Een Geschiedenis van het Amsterdamse Asjkenazische Jodendom* (Haarlem: 1964), pp. 56–57; and Isaac Maarsen, "*Maamar Or ha-Emet*," *Oẓar ha-Ḥayyim*, vol. 9 (1933), pp. 110–20.

156 See, for example, Plaut, *Rise*, pp. 49, 155 and 181. See also Albert Cohen, "Nonorthodox Attitudes in French Judaism," pp. 131 and 133. Cf. Geoffrey Alderman, *Modern British Jewry* (Oxford: Clarendon Press, 1992), p. 35 and Todd M. Endelman, *The Jews of Georgian England 1714–1830: Tradition and Change in a Liberal Society* (Philadelphia: Jewish Publication Society, 1979), p. 162.

157 *Siddur Amudei Shamayim*, p. 4b. The saying is found in Abarbanel, *Naḥalat Avot* 2:17 and *idem*, *Mashmi'a Yeshuah* 12:1.

158 *Siddur Amudei Shamayim*, p. 411a.

159 Isaiah 29:13, lit.: "taught by the precept of men," idiomatically connotes performance of a precept in a mechanical manner.

rote and for the prayer to become so familiar "that the soul is not excited by it."[160]

R. Emden also recognized length of prayer services as a factor influencing devotion. Bemoaning the distressing "scandalous" proliferation of novel petitionary prayers and *teḥinot*, R. Emden notes that were an individual to recite all of those prayers he would have no remaining time for study or gainful employment. He adds that, if with regard to prayer in general there is a cautionary recommendation "Better a little with *kavvanah*,"[161] all the more so does this admonition apply to the verbose additions instituted in latter days whose drawbacks far outweigh their positive effects, whose harm is greater than their benefit, and with respect to which silence is preferable. Prudent communal policy with regard to such petitions, R. Emden advises, is selectivity and brevity.[162] His contemporary, R. Yonatan Eybeschuẓ, similarly remarks of those who continually mumble an overabundance of supplicatory prayers that, "Without *kavvanah*, any addition is a diminution."[163]

The concept of *tirḥa de-ẓibura* or burdening the congregation[164] has definite halakhic implications. Obviously, however, from the halakhic standpoint, there are set parameters and limits to what may legitimately be abridged. In Reform congregations that do not feel bound by *halakhah* and the requirements of basic statutory prayer and Torah reading, the question of what constitutes a reasonable shortening of the service remains open. Reform clergy tended to differ in their opinion of what constituted an adequate service. Of more than passing interest is a resolution adopted by the Touro Synagogue of New Orleans in June 1889 requiring that the Sabbath morning ritual be abbreviated to last no longer than one hour, including the sermon.[165]

---

[160] *Siddur Amudei Shamayim*, p. 5a.

[161] *Tur Shulḥan Arukh, Oraḥ Ḥayyim* 1 and *Shulḥan Arukh, Oraḥ Ḥayyim* 1:4.

[162] *Siddur Amudei Shamayim*, pp. 2b–3a.

[163] *Ye'arot Devash*, pt. 1, p. 8a.

[164] See "*Tirḥa de-Ẓibura*," *Encyclopedia Talmudit*, vol. 20, pp. 662–78.

[165] Leo A. Bergman, *A History of the Touro Synagogue, New Orleans* (Private pub., n.d.), p. 5.

In this context, it may be apposite to take note of a differing perspective based on an individual idiosyncratic reaction but offering a penetrating observation regarding the atmosphere and environment that foster spiritual responses. Milton Himmelfarb, in a personal memoir describing his own experiences during the time when he attended synagogue on a regular basis to recite *Kaddish* in memory of his father, describes the difficulty he experienced in keeping repeated obligatory prayer from becoming routine and perfunctory. He comments:

> But to make the service short will not help us much. I have felt most untouched and unmoved in short services, Reform or near-Reform Conservative or Reconstructionist; and my neighbors have seemed to me equally untouched and unmoved. In fact, lengths have certain advantages. In a way a long service is like a long poem. You do not want unrelieved concentration and tightness in a long poem; they would be intolerable. Length requires *longueurs*. A good long poem is an alternation of high moments and moments less high, of concentration and relaxation. In our synagogue, the heights may not be very high, but the long service does provide some ascent and descent. The short service tends to be of a piece, dull and tepid.[166]

VIII. *PIYYUTIM*

As noted, the desire to improve decorum and even to shorten the duration of services was heartily endorsed by traditionalists as well. Nor were the innovators on halakhic quicksand in their efforts to eliminate the *piyyutim* or liturgical poetry. However, once the theological battle had been joined on other fronts, any suggestion the innovators made was viewed with suspicion and trepidation.

The debate over recitation of *piyyut*, and particularly over its inclusion in the statutory blessings of the *Shema* and *Amidah*, dates

[166] "Going to Shul," *Commentary* 41:4 (April, 1966): 68–69; reprinted in Petuchowski, *Understanding Jewish Prayer*, p. 159.

as far back as geonic times.[167] R. Abraham Ibn Ezra's caustic critique of the *piyyutim* of R. Eleazar ha-Kalir[168] and the negative view of Maimonides[169] are well known and widely cited. Over the ensuing centuries recitation of *piyyut* had notable champions as well as fierce detractors. Among latter-day scholars, R. Elijah of Vilna eliminated most inserted *piyyut*[170] whereas R. Eleazar Fleckles was a staunch proponent of retention of all traditional *piyyutim*.[171] R. Fleckles' championship of *piyyut* is not yet tinged by the first glimmerings of the acrimonious battles over prayerbook revision.

Those intent on trimming the services focused on accretions to statutory prayer and consequently, quite naturally, on the *piyyutim*. Their suggestions were usually sweeping in nature. Chorin, who urged "cleansing" the liturgy and removal of *piyyut*, writes:

> Only a few words concerning the second category of prayers (*yoẓerot, keroveẓ* and *piyyutim*). In the whole Talmud there is not one relevant passage concerning the nonsense of these prayers (if they deserve that appellation at all). They were generally written much later, at the time of the darkest per-

---

[167] See the exhaustive and meticulous discussion in Ruth Langer, *To Worship God Properly: Tensions Between Liturgical Custom and Halakhah in Judaism* (Cincinnati: Hebrew Union College Press, 1998), pp. 110–87.

[168] Commentary on the Bible, Eccles. 5:1.

[169] *Teshuvot ha-Rambam*, vol. II, ed. Joshua Blau (Jerusalem: Mekiẓei Nirdamim, 1960), nos. 180, 207 and 254. See also Langer, *Worship*, p. 153, notes 167 and 168. Cf. also Maimonides, *Guide*, I.59.

[170] Exceptions allowed by R. Elijah of Vilna during the *Amidah* include the *piyyutim* of the High Holy Days and the prayers for rain and dew. He also recited the *piyyutim* of festivals and the four special pre-Passover Sabbaths but only after completion of the *Amidah*. See *Maaseh Rav*, secs. 127, 163 and 205. *Maaseh Rav* was compiled by R. Yissakhar Ber of Vilna and first published in Zolkiew, 1808. The edition of *Maaseh Rav* published in Jerusalem, 1987 by Merkaz Ha-Sefer incorporates anthologized comments and suggests a halakhic rationale for the practice adopted by the Gaon of Vilna; see pp. 191–2.

[171] *Teshuvah me-Ahavah*, I, nos. 1 and 90. The arguments of R. Eleazar Fleckles are based to a significant extent upon the earlier responsum of R. Ya'ir Ḥayyim Bachrach (d. 1702), *Teshuvot Ḥavot Ya'ir* (Lemberg: 1896), no. 238.

> secutions. They bear the mark of the extreme suppression of the human spirit.[172]

It is in light of such remarks that one must read the pronouncements of authoritative rabbinic figures of the time. For example, in R. Akiva Eiger's defense of the *piyyutim* of Kalir, he takes strong exception to Ibn Ezra's criticisms and endorses absolute faithfulness to the time-hallowed Ashkenazi tradition. His forceful remarks are, however, made in the context of a broader denunciation of liturgical innovations and a plea for steadfast following "in the footsteps of our fathers."[173]

Even those halakhists who did not favor retention of *piyyut* were now wary of deletion that might be misinterpreted. R. Ẓevi Hirsch Chajes favored eliminating *piyyutim* and noted approvingly that many congregations in Poland and Russia had done so. Yet he counseled that matters be allowed to take their natural course, that rabbis should issue no rulings on the subject and should avoid any publicity lest the untutored become confused and fail to distinguish between mere folkways and usages of no halakhic significance and those customs and practices that have the force of law.[174]

A completely different assessment is found in the writings of Rabbis Abraham Lowenstamm and Samson Raphael Hirsch who

[172] *Ein Wort*, p. 36. Cf. the remarks of Joseph Maier in the preface to his 1861 Stuttgart Prayerbook in which he advocated "total removal" of *piyyutim*: "Science has given the verdict on those additions. They have in part, artistic and, in part, scientific or historical value, but none as far as devotion and edification are concerned...they were to a certain extent a substitute for the sermon. But, since to the joy and refreshment of every truly pious spirit, the sermon has returned to the House of God, the *piyyutim* have completely lost any value. Lest they continue to interfere with the dignified recitation of the prayers, and disturb devotion, their total removal has become a holy duty." Cited in Petuchowski, *Prayerbook Reform*, p. 161.

[173] *Iggerot Soferim*, ed. Salomon Schreiber (Vienna and Budapest: Joseph Schlesinger, 1933), pt. 1, no. 35, pp. 48–9.

[174] Chajes, *Minḥat Kena'ot*, p. 992 and *idem*, *Darkei Hora'ah*, chaps. 6 and 7, in *Kol Sifrei*, I, 238–242. Cf. the quite different response of R. Yosef Stern, *Sefer Zekher Yehosef, Oraḥ Ḥayyim* 19:3–4, who concluded that *piyyut* must be retained lest its abolition be the thin wedge leading to further, unacceptable innovation.

both sought to portray *piyyut* as a positive element in the liturgy. R. Lowenstamm points to the then recently published felicitous translation and commentary of Heidenheim[175] that render even abstruse and verbally complex poems more readily understandable. Aware of current sensibilities and that the *piyyutim* are "not desirable in our eyes in accordance with the changed responses of this era with regard to aesthetics,"[176] R. Lowenstamm argued that nonetheless the *piyyutim* continue to arouse intense religious emotion even among those who deem them to possess neither stylistic elegance nor linguistic beauty. R. Lowenstamm decries the vagaries of popular taste and notes that fashion trends soon become outdated while classics are timeless. Of attractive new literary creations that sway the masses he writes, "At the first instance of their novelty they delight those who see them; yet after they have been recited two or three times, the ear becomes attuned to them and very quickly does their glory fade. But a moment and they are forgotten."[177] In contradistinction, he avers, the *piyyutim*, composed in antiquity, despite their linguistic failings and the absence of a grace of idiom or felicity of language, are yet dear to the populace and stir the spirit, "drawing us closer to our Father in Heaven, whether because of the holiness embedded in them or because of the greatness and nobility of their composers…time does not affect them."[178]

A more impassioned defense of *piyyutim* is offered by R. Samson Raphael Hirsch. Responding to the charge that in an era of enlightenment and emancipation it was no longer edifying to recite

[175] Wolf Heidenheim (1757–1832), an exegete and grammarian, established a press at Rödelheim where he published critical editions of the *siddur* and *maḥzor* that are justly acclaimed for their meticulously corrected texts, scholarly commentaries, and accurate translations.

[176] *Ẓeror ha-Ḥayyim*, "Bi-Yeshishim Ḥokhmah," p. 37b.

[177] *Loc. cit.* A similar argument ("Their worship will quickly become habitual and insipid.") is presented by Solomon Jehuda Leib Rappoport, *Tokhahat Megulah* (Frankfurt-am-Main: 1845), a pamphlet written in response to the Frankfurt Rabbinical Conference, cited in Paul R. Mendes-Flohr and Jehuda Reinharz, *The Jew in the Modern World: A Documentary History* (New York and Oxford: Oxford University Press, 1980), p. 172.

[178] *Ẓeror ha-Ḥayyim*, "Bi-Yeshishim Ḥokhmah," p. 37b.

poetry that spoke of oppression and persecution, R. Hirsch turns the tables and tauntingly poses the question: Is Judaism more secure now or does it face more even pernicious dangers than previously? In the period of the Crusades when many of the *piyyutim* were composed, Jews were threatened physically, but at that time were there ritual slaughterers who themselves violated the dietary code, butchers who profaned the Sabbath or Jewish schools that fostered abrogation of Jewish law? If the *piyyut* recited between *Pesaḥ* and *Shavu'ot* recalls the physical massacres of our ancestors then, suggests R. Hirsch, it may be appropriate to find in it a resonant plaint regarding spiritual degeneration in an era "in which rabbis among us publicly conferred about how – in a respectable manner – Torah and mitzvoth could be buried."[179] R. Hirsch's more trenchant question – one that cannot fail to elicit a shiver in any post-Holocaust reader who recalls that Germany is the venue of this discussion – is "Has such an era of brightness come to Israel everywhere among the nations that these prayers of lament no longer have a place in the synagogue?"[180]

Spirituality is enhanced, R. Hirsch contends, by arousing intimate empathetic feelings joining Jews into a community of destiny spanning the generations. The crucial mistake, he argues, is to assume that less is always better. It is the error of "Jewish 'Reform' enthroned in robe and hat...declaring war on *piyyutim* and *yoẓerot*" to assume "The prescription for creating devotion? Delete prayers!"[181] Rather, asserts R. Hirsch, acknowledging struggles and sorrows of

---

[179] *The Collected Writings*, English translation, I (New York and Jerusalem: Philipp Feldheim, Inc., 1984), p. 138.

[180] *Ibid.*, p. 133.

[181] *Ibid.*, p. 132. Cf. Petuchowski, *Prayerbook Reform.*, p. 30, who comments on *piyyut* as an expression of *kavvanah* and cites the remarks of Gustav Gottheil, a lone Reform champion of *piyyut*, delivered at the 1869 Israelite Synod in Leipzig: "I fully recognize the rights of the present to change the prayer, but I believe that the religious consciousness of other times also has the right to find expression in our prayers. I do not believe that our time, with its cold rational direction, is especially suitable to create warm, heart-stirring prayers. And for these I would rather go back to the warmer religious sentiment of antiquity, and let it supply us with such prayers. Therefore, I must speak out against the generally condemnatory judgment against *piyyutim*."

the past, remembering the sweat and blood, sacrifice and exertions endured to preserve Torah in centuries of "outer and inner *galut*" will create bonds of solidarity and bring to life models of faith.[182]

It would be an error to conclude that the contention of Rabbis Lowenstamm and Hirsch that *piyyutim* evoke strong emotional responses merely reflects the apologetics of anti-Reform writing of the nineteenth century. In a lecture on the sanctity of the Day of Atonement, the prominent twentieth-century rabbinic figure, R. Joseph B. Soloveitchik, acknowledged, "I must admit that my philosophy of *Yahadus* is the product, not of my talmudic studies or of my philosophical training, but of my childhood *Yom Kippur* memories and reminiscences."[183] He then proceeded to relate:

> It is quite strange that the *Piyutim* recited on *Yom Kippur* played a significant role in the formation of my religious personality. My father and grandfather taught me the beauty and grandeur of *Yom Kippur*. For them the *Maḥzor* was not just a prayer book. It was more than that. It was a book of knowledge. I do not know whether modern linguists would subscribe to the philological excursions made by my father and me in the *Maḥzor*. They might consider them obsolete. Regardless of the philology, however, the essence of the liturgy, with its lofty *Aggadic* and *Halachic* aspects, became suddenly inspirational and experiential. All of the *Halachic* and *Aggadic* teachings which I absorbed as a young child have remained with me until this day.[184]

---

[182] *Collected Writings*, 1, 138. R. Hirsch denigrated the pedantic academic study of Jewish history and literature then in vogue that he saw as breeding religious sterility. He was particularly unimpressed by scholarly interest in *piyyut*. "The true heirs" of Jewish prophets and poets who will they be, R. Hirsch asked rhetorically, "those who repeated their prayers but forgot their names, or those who forget their prayers and remember their names?" See *ibid.*, p. 343.

[183] Transcript of an Elul, 1974 lecture, published in *Sefer Nora'ot ha-Rav*, ed. B. David Schreiber, vol. 13 (New York: 2000), p. 96.

[184] *Loc. cit.*

IX. SPIRITUALITY: CLAIMS AND ASSESSMENT

Grandiose claims were made for the spiritual and religious impact of the liturgical innovations. The editors of the second edition of the Hamburg Prayerbook (1842) praised their prayerbook for restoring "simplicity" and "dignity" to synagogue services and asserted that, as a result, "the religious sense has been revived" among many individuals for whom religion had lost its sanctity.[185] That very same year the West London Synagogue published the first edition of the *Forms of Prayer Used in the West London Synagogue of British Jews.* The editors of that prayerbook similarly claimed that they had rendered the service more dignified and intelligible by expunging sections of the liturgy that "are deficient in devotional tendency" and linguistic expressions that are "the offspring of feelings produced by oppression, and which are universally admitted to be foreign in the heart of every true Israelite of our day."[186] So, too, laymen in Metz, eager to emulate the Hamburg model in order to "restore dignity" and avoid "oblivion, apathy, and indifference" prevalent at worship services, introduced modifications in synagogue practice and sought to abolish "superannuated ceremonies, practices which choke the sublimity of our teaching and are entirely at odds with today's customs and habits."[187] Others called for renunciation of "antiquated customs" in order "to give our religion a worthier form" and for the removal of practices that have "degraded and dishonored it in the eyes of thinking men."[188]

Few of the liturgical innovators would have concurred entirely with the radical statement of the Frankfurt Friends of Reform declaring that the "practical commands, the observance of which constitutes the bulk of present-day Judaism, ... [these] external form[s] are for the most part without significance – yes, even unworthy of pure religion."[189] Be that as it may, there is more than a whiff of smugness and sanctimoniousness in these writers' conviction that their "nec-

---

[185] Petuchowski, *Prayerbook Reform*, p. 138.

[186] *Ibid.*, p. 140.

[187] Plaut, *Rise*, p. 45.

[188] *Ibid.*, p. 51.

[189] *Loc. cit.*

essary" changes in synagogue practice are all salutary and edifying and in the frequently recurring phrases "the genuine spirit of Jewish religiosity,"[190] "true religiosity,"[191] or "pure divine worship service"[192] that dot the writings of protagonists of the new prayerbooks.

To many of those individuals the "genuine Jewish spirit" and "the spirit of true religiosity"[193] were congruent with what were the dominant cultural and philosophical perspectives of the time. Unabashedly, they proclaimed that it is "the religious spirit of the present to which Judaism owes its reawakening and revitalization"[194] and naively they placed their faith in "the trumpet sound of our time."[195] Only through discarding the "husk" of antiquated ritual did they believe they would gain access to "the treasure of the kernel" and bring Judaism into harmony with what they perceived as "the genius of the modern era."[196]

The *Zeitgeist* beckoned and many were caught up in its allure. Little wonder then that the ritual and religious practices of Judaism seemed "encrusted with moldering medieval ceremonies." Above all, they feared being considered backward or culturally inferior by their Western confreres and declared candidly: "Is this possible at a time when everything blossoms and decks itself with the fresh apparel of the new age; is our faith alone to declare itself absolutely incompatible with the new age? No! No! say we."[197]

The desire to be *au courant* by accepting current modes of thought as well as a longing to be considered worthy citizens led to modifications in the content of the prayers, particularly with regard to expressions of chosenness, prayer for ingathering of exiles and references to a personal messiah. Particularistic prayers were deemed to be narrow and selfishly ethnocentric; universalist prayers were

---

[190] *Ibid.*, p. 39.
[191] *Ibid.*, pp. 39 and 60.
[192] *Ibid.*, p. 42.
[193] *Ibid.*, p. 60.
[194] *Ibid.*, p. 59.
[195] *Ibid.*, p. 57.
[196] *Ibid.*, pp. 59–60.
[197] *Ibid.*, p. 62.

regarded as emblematic of a higher spiritual sensibility. The editors of the Berlin Reform Prayerbook (1848) articulated the new philosophy quite clearly:

> For a noble, truthful pious soul, the thought of the Father of all mankind is more stirring than that of a God of Israel. The image of God, imprinted upon every human being as a covenant-sign of divine love, has more poetry than the chosenness of Israel. The general love of a neighbor and brother, deeply imbedded in every man, has more attraction than a particular ceremonial law.[198]

Similarly, the *Reform-Freunde* in Worms declared in all honesty that they could no longer pay lip service to prayers for a return to Palestine "while at the same time our strongest bonds tie our souls to the German Fatherland whose fate is inextricably interwoven with ours – for what is dear and precious to us is embraced by her." They could no longer mourn the destruction of the Temple "for another fatherland had been ours for many years, one that has become most precious to all of us." To remember the historic fate of the destruction of the Temple does serve a purpose, "but why should we pretend a sorrow which no longer touches our hearts?" Rather, they conceded their inability to lament a historical event "in which we see the loving hand of God." In a spirit of enthusiasm and ardor, they sought to banish "untruth" from their service, to jettison "dead ballast" and to build a new temple in which a "fresh and free wind blows to animate our ambitious youth."[199]

Other writers accentuated the changing "religious needs of the times" that prompted a liturgical revision designed for "promotion of edification."[200] Taking note of the frequent references to the concept of "edification" (*Erbauung*) as the goal and purpose of religious services, contemporary scholars have observed that the term was used in association with religious worship by German Protestant

[198] *Ibid.*, p. 59.
[199] *Ibid.*, pp. 61–2.
[200] Petuchowski, *Prayerbook Reform*, pp. 143–4.

Pietists.[201] Thus, both German patriotism and Protestant theology exerted considerable influence on the ideological stance that early exponents of Reform equated with "the spirit of true religiosity."

The lofty rhetoric of the ideologues did not always appeal to the rank and file. There was a deep-seated traditionalism in many a simple German Jew, even those no longer punctilious in observance of *miẓvot*, that restrained them from embracing extreme innovation in synagogue services.

Abraham Geiger has been described as the most influential Reform Jewish liturgist of the nineteenth century. Adaptations of his *Israelitisches Gebetbuch* (1854) constitute the foundation of the more traditional prayerbook of Manuel Joel (1872) and the more radical text of Vogelstein (1894) and traces of his work are to be found in the *Einheitsgebetbuch* of German Liberal Jews (1929), edited by Seligmann, Elbogen, and Vogelstein, as well as in the United States in the second edition of Szold's *Avodath Yisrael* (1871) prayerbook as revised by Jastrow and Hochheimer.[202] The popularity of his liturgy may be attributed to the fact that, in practice, Geiger diverged sharply from his own very radical liturgical theory.

Geiger argued that Hebrew is no longer a live language, that Israel lives only as a community of faith, not as a people, that Amalek has become an irrelevancy and that no hope is to be associated with Jerusalem. Yet, in practice, when he published his own *siddur* in Breslau, he retained a basically Hebrew service and did not consistently revise the prayerbook to conform to his own radical theories. He had been scornful of the editors of the second edition of the Hamburg prayerbook because of their timidity but, in his own enterprise, he did not incorporate the changes (e.g., removal of *tal*

[201] See Alexander Altmann, "The New Style of Jewish Preaching," in *Studies in Nineteenth-Century Jewish Intellectual History*, ed. Alexander Altmann (Cambridge, MA: Harvard University Press, 1964), pp. 87 ff. See also *supra*, note 32 and accompanying text.

[202] Jakob J. Petuchowski, "Abraham Geiger, the Reform Jewish Liturgist," in *New Perspectives on Abraham Geiger*, ed. Jakob J. Petuchowski (New York: HUC Press, 1975), pp. 42–4.

and *geshem* prayers) that he had criticized the Hamburg editors for failing to implement.[203]

Whether, as his admirers have argued, the gap between Geiger's *Weltanschauung* and his practice is to be understood in a positive light, i.e., as an expression of his sincere desire to work within the framework of a total community rather than from a limited denominational platform,[204] or whether this divergence between theory and practice should be seen as a reflection of opportunism and an absence of integrity is debatable. What is apparent is that Geiger's decision that it was desirable to opt for "accommodation of the religious needs of a large segment of the present generation"[205] lies behind the secret of his popularity as a Reform liturgist. It is the instinctive reactions of *amkha*, the common folk, who retain a Jewish spark, that oft times preserve us from the follies of misguided leaders and prophets.

When innovations were introduced, to what extent did they

---

[203] *Ibid.*, pp. 47–8.

[204] *Ibid.*, pp. 48–52. See also Geiger's own comments on the distinction between theorists and practitioners and the constraints upon a rabbi functioning within a communal framework in *Abraham Geiger and Liberal Judaism: The Challenge of the Nineteenth Century*, ed. Max Wiener, trans. Ernst J. Schlochauer (Cincinnati: HUC Press, 1981), pp. 275–82.

Noting Petuchowski's discussion of the discrepancy between Geiger's theory and practice, Ken Koltun-Fromm, "Historical Memory in Abraham Geiger's Account of Modern Jewish Identity," *Jewish Social Studies*, The New Series, vol. 7, no. 1 (Fall, 2000), p. 116, suggests that "it is better to jettison talk of a theory/practice distinction and instead focus on how Geiger integrated significant theoretical claims about identity into practical discussions about Jewish liturgy." Koltun-Fromm's own analysis, in the opinion of this writer, is hardly compelling. He does, however, demonstrate that Geiger "blurred the historical memory" (p. 123) and that "For Geiger, Wissenschaft was neither a scientific nor an objective study of a past. It was a motivated retrieval of that past conditioned by modern concerns about identity" (p. 110). That Geiger's historical and liturgical writings did not always present a "scientific" and "objective study" of the past but rather "a constructed collection of meaningful memories that fashion a usable past for decidedly modern concerns" (p. 110) is an important acknowledgement. That foremost practitioners of the Wissenschaft des Judentums were not necessarily scientific or academic in their approach to liturgy has not been sufficiently recognized.

[205] *Protokolle*, p. 70.

lead to fulfillment of the lofty aspirations of the liturgists, i.e., to "edification" and to "true religiosity"? In order to answer this query a brief survey of reactions of Reform writers themselves is in order. Several of those discussions were offered decades later and bring a historical perspective to an analysis of the issues.

In the preface to the 1855 Mannheim prayerbook, M. Präger, the editor, conceded that while cities such as Mannheim required compilation of a text suited to their heterogeneity, liturgical innovation in general had splintered the greater community. Reform prayer modalities were so diverse and numerous that one might "indignantly proclaim with the Prophet, '*ki mispar arekha hayu elohekha*' (Jer. 11:13)[206] – as many prayerbooks as there are cities!"[207] The issue of liturgical uniformity dominated the agenda of three regional Reform rabbinical conferences held in Southern Germany in the 1850s. Conference delegates were caught on the horns of a dilemma, since the quest for creativity conflicted with the quest for unity and, in addition, local communities jealously sought to preserve their autonomy.[208] Because of those impediments, German Reform did not succeed in publishing a commonly accepted uniform prayerbook until the publication of the *Einheitsgebetbuch* in 1929.[209]

In the United States, a common Reform liturgy was adopted somewhat earlier. The earliest edition of the *Union Prayer Book* (*UPB*) was published in 1892, was revised by a committee and published as a prayerbook for the High Holy Days in 1894 and for Sabbaths, festivals and weekdays in 1895.[210] However, Reform clergy acknowledged that, even after successive further revisions, the *UPB* never became

[206] Lit.: "For according to the number of your cities are your gods."

[207] Cited in Petuchowski, *Prayerbook Reform*, pp. 152–3.

[208] Robert Liberles, "The Rabbinical Conferences of the 1850's and the Quest for Li9urgical Unity," *Modern Judaism* 3:1 (October, 1983): 312 and 315.

[209] *Gebetbuch für das ganze Jahr*, ed. Ceasar Seligmann, Ismar Elbogen, and Hermann Vogelstein. 2 vols. (Frankfurt-am-Main: 1924).

[210] Meyer, *Response*, p. 279. On Isaac Mayer Wise's persistent efforts for the adoption of a uniform Reform liturgy and the conflict between proponents of the respective prayerbooks of Wise and Einhorn see *ibid.*, pp. 258–9 and James G. Heller, *Isaac M. Wise: His Life, Work and Thought* (New York: UAHC, 1965), pp. 302–6 and 476.

a charmed medium capable of wafting souls heavenward. In 1928, Samuel S. Cohon, in a blistering critique of the infelicity of many English passages, of the "prosy homilies and stereotyped phrases,"[211] objected more fundamentally that the UPB did not faithfully or consistently reflect Reform theology.[212] Petitionary prayers to the Deity were replaced by vague meditations on ethical themes that conveyed the impression that they were "especially written for a people composed of retired philanthropists and amateur social workers."[213] In addition, Cohon bemoaned the manner in which congregations utilized the prayerbook, i.e., he regarded absence of congregational participation as a reflection of a loss of a desire to pray.[214]

Although Israel Bettan, writing a year later, disputed Cohon's suggested emendations because he feared a further denuding of the prayers of their poetry and emotional resonance in favor of a dry literalism, he fully concurred in the negative evaluation of the text of the ***UPB***, particularly of passages that read like sociological discourses and of those that cast a negative light on longings for a return to Zion or depicted the dispersion as a sign of blessed privilege. Far from arousing fervor, "the cure effected by early Reform gave rise to a new malady," Bettan charged, turning worshipers into passive participants, mere "weary auditors" and "languid spectators" and in consequence "our services have been immeasurably weakened."[215]

When growing frustration with the UPB led a number of Reform congregations to experiment with alternative texts, the results were no more inspiring. Reporting on a detailed analysis and study of thirty-three congregations' Rosh Hashanah evening services,

---

[211] "The Theology of the Union Prayer Book," in *Reform Judaism: A Historical Perspective*, ed. Joseph L. Blau (New York: Ktav, 1973), p. 281.

[212] *Ibid.*, pp. 265–81.

[213] *Ibid.*, p. 262, note 5.

[214] *Ibid.*, p. 283.

[215] Israel Bettan, "The Function of the Prayer Book," in *Reform Judaism*, ed. Blau, pp. 289 and 295–6. See the much later article of Lawrence A. Hoffman, "The Language of Survival in American Reform Liturgy," CCAR *Journal* 24:3 (Summer, 1977): 87–106, for a critique of the UPB's failure to express an effective message of Jewish particularism.

Daniel Jeremy Silver portrays the UPB liturgy as inadequate to their needs, decrying its propensity for "the vague and the high-flown," its failure to provide a "richness of ideas" and the fact that the meditations are usually devoid of specific Jewish elements. However, he admits that the substitute liturgies prepared by some congregations offered similarly "overblown language" and he confesses, "I am afraid that high-flown vagueness has a fatal fascination for our movement." Noting that 90% of the Hebrew portion of the service is recited or chanted by the rabbi, cantor, or choir, he observes that this enables "the worshiper, like an opera goer, to enjoy the mood without thinking about the libretto."[216] Discussing substitutions introduced into the High Holy Day liturgy, Silver characterizes one rewritten service as "an enthusiastic, if sometimes incoherent, blend of Buber's *Tales of Rabbi Naḥman* and classical Reform's social gospel."[217] Silver notes that, in general, the new prayers were vague and the "combination of fuzzy piety and fuzzy language sometimes boggled the imagination."[218]

More recent assessments of Reform liturgy have noted the contradictory tendencies of recovery and reconstruction evident in several new prayerbooks. On the one hand, these prayerbooks reflect an attempt to recover traditional texts and to incorporate more Hebrew and, on the other hand, they exhibit a significant degree of self-censorship and radical innovation, particularly as a response to feminist agitation for a liturgy that is entirely gender free.[219] The

---

[216] "Do We Say What We Mean? Do We Mean What We Say?" CCAR *Journal* 24:3 (Summer, 1977): 133–4.

[217] *Ibid.*, p. 128.

[218] *Ibid.*, p. 126. Of even felicitous creative prayers Eugene Borowitz, *Liberal Judaism* (New York: Union of American Hebrew Congregations, 1984), p. 439, writes: "Seeking to reuse a creative service which once moved us greatly, we are regularly disappointed. Few things we write retain their ability to inspire us. Fewer still can bear a community's repetition week after week after week." On the use of non-halakhic forms in prayers composed in post-talmudic times and on the limited success of innovative and creative prayers in Orthodox circles as well, cf. the brief comments of Joseph Tabory, "The Conflict of *Halakhah* and Prayer," *Tradition* 25:1 (Fall, 1989): 22–3.

[219] Arnold Jacob Wolf, "The New Liturgies," *Judaism* 46:2 (Spring, 1997): 235.

desperate attempt to be simultaneously more traditional and more modern has produced prayerbooks that one reviewer describes as "not very rigorous theologically" and "not very inspiring."[220]

Continuing dissatisfaction within the Reform rabbinate with the UPB led to the adoption of a new prayerbook, *Shaarei Tefillah – Gates of Prayer*, in 1975. This prayerbook offers several alternative liturgies, as many as ten separately themed Sabbath eve services and six different Sabbath morning services, ranging from the traditional to the radical. One of the proffered services omits any reference to God. The editors aimed for richness and diversity but many readers found the series of alternative options bewildering.[221] In response, the Reform movement is now preparing a new prayerbook to be issued by 2005 and to be published on CD-ROM as well as in the usual format so that users can create their own services. The two female co-editors, Judith Abrams and Elyse Frishman, hope to please traditionalist elements and to develop a more unified approach to synagogue worship but have not yet determined how to respond to the feminist critique of traditional prayer language. As the editors themselves indicate, their concern is that "we don't want to have a book that will feel dated in five years."[222]

The return to the traditional Hebrew texts demonstrates a significant phenomenon. Creative texts fail to be as spiritually elevating as anticipated while, in the final analysis, the spare wording of the Sages, is recognized as meaningful and moving. Rabbinic authorities emphasized that the words of the *Amidah* composed by the Men of the Great Assembly are ideal for prayer because each letter and syllable contains profound *kavvanot*. In the words of R. Yonatan

---

220 *Ibid.*, p. 242.

221 *Ibid.*, p. 240.

222 JTA *Daily News Bulletin*, 23 December 1999, p. 4. A concern for datedness is certainly not misplaced. Milton Himmelfarb, *The Jews of Modernity* (New York: Basic Books, 1973), p. 357, remarks: "Well, if you make revisions every twenty or thirty years, you run the risk of being irrelevant much of the time…[T]here is nothing so dead as the newspaper from the day before yesterday. The twentieth Psalm speaks of chariots and horses, which no army has used for some time now. Would it be more relevant if it spoke of tanks and planes? Chariots and horses make the point quite well."

Eybeschutz: "Every jot and tittle has within it mysteries of the Torah, secrets of the holy *Merkavah* [Chariot], and combinations of Names from the supernal worlds, that open up the gates and are efficacious and rise up higher than the highest to the Guardian."[223] But, quite apart from their mystical properties, the words of the ancient prayers are endowed with an unusual literary quality. The *Zohar* states: "Woe unto that person who says that the Torah has come to teach us mere stories or the words of an ordinary person for, if so, we could compose in our time a Torah from the words of an ordinary person even more beautiful than all these.... Rather, all words of the Torah are transcendent words and transcendent mysteries."[224] Yet who would deny that the Torah is indeed "the greatest story ever told" and that the stories alone are matchless? In like manner, the prayers of the Sages, immutably preserved on account of their transcendent sanctity, are, at the same time, incomparable in their pure literary power.

A glance at an entirely different, alternative type of liturgical innovation further highlights the drawbacks of classical Reform worship while at the same time it focuses our attention on what may well be the most vexing aspect of the entire Reform liturgical enterprise.

As noted, early liturgical innovators were influenced heavily by the style and manner of worship of nineteenth-century Protestantism. Quite different intellectual currents may be discerned in the *Ḥavurah* movement of the 1960s. Critical of the establishment and steeped in the counterculture, the founders of the *havurot* distanced themselves from the formality of mainstream institutions they looked upon as "sterile, hierarchical, divorced from Jewish tradition, and *lacking in spirituality*."[225] The emphasis in *Ḥavurah* movement services is on intimacy, warmth, egalitarianism and participatoriness.

---

[223] *Ya'erot Devash*, pt. 1, p. 8a.

[224] *Zohar, Behaalotkha*, 152a, cited by R. Yitẓchak Arama, *Akeidat Yiẓḥak*, introduction to the Book of Ruth. *Akeidat Yiẓḥak* cites this comment of the *Zohar* precisely because the Book of Ruth is acknowledged to be an exceptional literary masterpiece.

[225] Weissler, "Making Davening Meaningful," p. 257, emphasis added.

Typically, *Ḥavurah* worship takes place in a small room, the seating arrangement is circular, dress is highly informal and services are led by various members. Although many of the prayers are recited in Hebrew with traditional *nusaḥ*, there is much room for creative interpretations and interpolations. In an analysis of one particular *ḥavurah*, Chava Weissler quite accurately focuses on the crucial importance of the social and interpersonal element in those services whose success is gauged to a large extent by the interaction of leader and followers and by participants' responses to one another. Another characteristic element of *Ḥavurah* services is the reframing or reinterpretation of the prayers as a strategy for coping with what is perceived to be a "problematic liturgy."[226] Weissler points out that each week the role of the leader is to present a current and novel interpretation. The message conveyed is that meaning is fleeting and interpretation must continually be constructed anew.

This practice underscores the difficulty members experience in affirming the words of the liturgy. The *ḥavurah* thus reflects the members' "attraction to tradition and the ambivalence regarding it"[227] and makes "doubt and ambivalence as axiomatic a part of worship as faith once was."[228] Reflecting upon the specific circular seating arrangements and the manner in which sacredness is experienced by *ḥavurah* members through "sacralization of the interpersonal," Weissler concludes her remarks with the statement: "God is approached through human relationships; God is perhaps what happens across the circle."[229]

Weissler's comments lead us to the central, fundamental issue liturgical innovation forces us to confront, an issue beside which all other issues pale into insignificance: the question of the core beliefs and doctrines of Judaism.

---

[226] *Ibid.*, p. 270.

[227] *Ibid.*, p. 276.

[228] *Ibid.*, p. 279.

[229] *Loc. cit.*

X. FUNDAMENTAL BELIEFS

Probably no single work has had a greater impact on the average Jew over the course of millennia than the prayerbook. Jews to whom philosophical works were closed tomes, for whom the Talmud and *Shulḥan Arukh* were far too difficult, were thoroughly familiar with the words of the *siddur*. From these prayers simple Jews gleaned an awareness of, and an appreciation for, the fundamentals of faith. Belief in the messiah, in bodily resurrection, in the veracity of the prophets, and a yearning for Zion were thrice daily reinforced in the course of prayer; *meḥayeh ha-meitim, et ẓemaḥ David avdekha bi-m'heirah taẓmiaḥ, shuvekha le-Ẓiyyon* were familiar and tangible beliefs. The Jew who cleaved to his *siddur* was a Jew whose conceptual framework was rooted in the thought-world of the Sages that the liturgy mirrored. In describing the role of the synagogue in molding a religious personality, R. Hirsch points to the common usage of the term "*shul*" for synagogue and remarks, "We call our houses of worship '*Schulen*' [the German word for schools] and that is what they are meant to be: schools for adults, for those who have entered the mainstream of life."[230]

Let there be no mistake. The paramount concern of the nineteenth-century rabbinic authorities who were adamant opponents of liturgical innovation was the correctly perceived challenge to faith. The pages of *Eileh Divrei ha-Berit* contain many an argument regarding halakhic minutiae but the constant refrain is a fear and trembling in the face of erosion of "*ikkarei ha-dat*" or fundamentals of faith.[231] Similarly, two months after publication of the second edition of the Hamburg Temple Prayerbook, on October 16, 1841, when Ḥakham Isaac Bernays responded with a "*Modaah*," a public notice, declaring the prayerbook unfit for use in fulfillment of one's religious obligations, it was the ideological issue that was paramount. Three words appear in large, bold characters: Redemption, Messiah,

---

[230] R. Samson Raphael Hirsch, *Neunzehn Briefe über Judentum* (Berlin: Welt-Verlag, 1919), fourteenth letter, pp. 79–80; cf. *idem*, *The Collected Writings*, I, 193.

[231] See pp. iv, ix, 6, 12–3, 17, 22, 24, 27–8, 54–7, 67, and 90–1.

Resurrection.[232] The theological concern underlying Ḥakham Bernays' response to the Hamburg Temple *siddur* was clearly aroused by the renewed assault on those cardinal doctrines reflected in its liturgical emendations.

R. Chajes, sorely conflicted over an appropriate response to the Reform movement, writes that its blatant rejection of fundamental beliefs ultimately precluded compromise. As long as minor modification of synagogue custom was at issue and innovators paid at least lip service to the teachings of the Sages, there had existed a possibility for containment and the hope of finding a *modus vivendi* through the art of gentle persuasion. Even at the outset, he admits, rabbinic authorities "recognized that they [Reform leaders] had acted with deceit and intended to uproot everything," but with Reform renunciation of the basic doctrines of Judaism there was no longer even a possibility of accommodation.[233]

Earlier, Chorin argued that the rabbis' exaggerated prohibitions extending even to permissible matters would in the long run lead to a blurring of boundaries and transgression of the forbidden. Rather than multiplying prohibitions as a hedge against sin, he argued, the rabbis should have ruled in accordance with "the need of the time, the place and the generation."[234] Had they adopted a conciliatory posture, Chorin maintained, and, at the same time, in a non-strident manner correctly objected to the initial changes in the Hamburg Prayerbook with regard to ingathering of the exiles, their influence would have been salutary.[235]

A similar hypothesis was advanced a century later by Ismar Elbogen. Elbogen's history of the liturgy culminates in a survey of the liturgical controversies of the modern period in which he states that, rather than adopting a hostile position, had the rabbis "taken charge

---

232 *Theologische Gutachten über das Gebetbuch nach dem gebrauche des Neuen Israelitischen Tempelvereins in Hamburg* (Hamburg: 1842), p. 14.

233 *Minḥat Kena'ot*, p. 1007.

234 *Davar be-Ito*, pp. 57–8.

235 *Ibid.*, pp. 49–50.

of the new movement...who knows what the eventual development of German Jewry would have been?"[236]

An opposing view was espoused by R. Chajes who does not otherwise hesitate, when he deems it justified to do so, to take the rabbinic establishment to task. Addressing the contention that rabbis should be lenient in order to keep within the fold those whom either the blandishments or the pressures of modern life were distancing from religious observance, R. Chajes differentiates between a permissible temporary leniency (*horaat shaah*) and an impermissible permanent abrogation of the law. The matter is moot, he notes, because the innovators followed a different path entirely. It was not necessary for them to tamper with references to basic beliefs such as resurrection or the messiah in order to ease the burden of ritual observance. Nor had such beliefs stood in the way of attainment of civil rights. Indeed, in an aside, R. Chajes points out that, contrary to what might have been anticipated, in Germany, the seat of greatest Reform agitation, there was renewed prejudice and anti-Semitism whereas in France, Holland, and Belgium, where innovation was not widespread, Jews enjoyed equal rights and privileges.[237]

Foresight or hindsight? Would different tactics have altered the cataclysmic process? Could Niagara Falls be reversed by gentle persuasion? Whether or not their tactics were the wisest, whether or not their rhetoric was more harmful than helpful, one thing is clear: the foremost rabbinic authorities, the *gedolei horaah*, were not naïve. On the contrary, it was individuals such as the Italian rabbis who were initially sympathetic to the innovators and, in *Or Nogah* and *Nogah ha-Ẓedek*, lent their imprimatur to changes that appeared innocuous, who failed to recognize the dimensions of the hazard.

At the very heart of the endeavors of those engaged in the earliest experiments in worship reform was an attempt to alter the wording of the prayers to conform to the mindset and belief system of the majority of their enlightened coreligionists. To those individuals, the most troubling references in the prayerbook were the

[236] *Jewish Liturgy*, p. 304.

[237] *Minḥat Kenaʾot*, pp. 1021 and 1027.

petitions for rebuilding the Temple[238] and reinstitution of the sacrificial order. Later, other fundamental beliefs were also assailed. The concept of a personal messiah and the Davidic monarchy, prayers for return to Jerusalem and the ingathering of the exiles, mention of bodily resurrection, blessings that acknowledged a distinction between Jews and non-Jews[239] and between men and women as well as particularistic prayers that emphasized the chosenness of Israel aroused unease among many of their constituents. Leaders of the Reform movement argued that to give expression in prayer to doctrines that were contrary to their convictions was hypocritical and damaging to the spirituality to which divine service should aspire. The imagery and wording of some prayers was also viewed as problematic. References to angels were attacked by some as archaic and anachronistic and defended by others as merely poetic and fanciful embellishments.[240]

Conservative liturgists' alterations of the *siddur* were not as numerous or as blatant as those of Reform editors, but they too introduced changes that touched on matters of belief. Comfortable with

---

238 Many temples prominently display a large seven-branched menorah. It has been conjectured that Reform congregations consciously introduced the seven-branched menorah into their sanctuaries because this artifact is identified with the Temple that stood in Jerusalem. The subliminal message of a seven-branched menorah in a modern-day temple is that there is no longer a desire to rebuild the Temple in messianic times; the Temple has been supplanted by sanctuaries in the diaspora. See Joseph Gutmann, "A Note on the Temple Menorah," in *No Graven Images: Studies in Art and the Hebrew Bible*, ed. Joseph Gutmann (New York: Ktav, 1971), p. 38.

239 John D. Rayner, "Ideologically Motivated Emendations in Anglo-Jewish Liturgy," *Noblesse Oblige: Essays in Honor of David Kessler* OBE, ed. Alan D. Crown (London and Portland, OR: Valentine Mitchell, 1998), pp. 117–21, suggests that Reform practice influenced British Orthodox liturgists with regard to references to non-Jews. The examples Rayner cites, taken from (British) United Synagogue prayerbooks, are an emendation of the first stanza of the *Ma'oz Ẓur* hymn and changes in the Prayer for the Royal Family. Far from supporting Rayner's thesis, these examples actually demonstrate the opposite. Both changes are minor in nature and occur in non-statutory prayers. If indeed they reflect Reform influence, the influence was quite trivial.

240 See, for example, Elbogen, *Jewish Liturgy*, p. 326; Cohon, "Theology," pp. 267–9; and Bettan, "Function," pp. 285–7 and 294–5.

references to sacrifices in times gone by but maintaining that reinstitution of the sacrificial order "cannot be made to serve our modern outlook,"[241] the editors of the Conservative 1946 *Sabbath and Festival Prayer Book* modified the *Tikkanta Shabbat* and *Mipnei Ḥata'einu* prayers by altering the tense of the verbs employed. Their approach to the fundamental doctrine of resurrection was more oblique. In a manner similar to that of editors of the Hamburg Temple Prayerbook who retained the Hebrew word "*go'el*" (redeemer) but translated it into German as "*Erlösung*" (redemption)[242] in order to avoid reference to a personal messiah in the vernacular, the Conservative editors retained the Hebrew "*meḥayeh ha-meitim*" (who revives the dead) but rendered it in English as "who calls the dead to everlasting life." That ambiguous translation, they explicitly suggested, would be satisfactory to both liberals and traditionalists.[243] Moving from prevarication to a more definitive but still not quite honest formulation, the 1972 Conservative Prayer Book retains "*meḥayei ha-meitim*" but translates the phrase as "Master of life and death."[244]

Ironically, in the latter part of the twentieth century, even as the Reform movement has veered back toward reintroduction of more traditional prayers, to an appreciation of the Hebrew language and even (in muted form) to an acknowledgement of Zion and Jerusalem in prayer, deviation in the area of doctrine has become, if anything, more marked.

Prayer in essence is a petition, plea, meditation or praise that presupposes the presence of a Supreme Being; it constitutes a dialogue, an address or appeal to God. Even those commentators who emphasize the meditative aspects of prayer in interpreting the term *le-hitpalel* as a reflexive verb connoting self-judgment,

---

241 *Sabbath and Festival Prayer Book* (n.p.: Rabbinical Assembly of America and United Synagogue of America, 1946), p. ix.

242 *Ordnung der öffentlichen Andacht für die Sabbath-und Festtage des ganzen Jahres. Nach dem Gebrauche des Neuen-Tempel-Vereins in Hamburg* (Hamburg: 1819), p. 44.

243 *Sabbath and Festival Prayer Book* (1946), p. viii.

244 *Maḥzor for Rosh Hashanah and Yom Kippur: A Prayer Book for the Days of Awe*, ed. Jules Harlow (New York: The Rabbinical Assembly, 1972), p. 31.

recognize that the enterprise of prayer involves a perception of the individual standing before God at the moment of meditation.

Although the nineteenth-century innovators discarded the particularistic and nationalistic elements of the prayerbook, they were comfortable with conventional monotheistic beliefs and experienced no embarrassment in directing prayer to a Supreme Being. Prayers and meditations composed by classical Reform writers are unambiguously addressed to "Our father in heaven" and "merciful God." But it is precisely a belief in God, and especially in an all-powerful Almighty God whose providential guardianship is manifest and who is "nigh unto all them that call upon Him" (Psalms 145:18) that, today, is troubling to many of the laity and clergy of the Reform movement. In their denial of a personal God and the election of Israel,[245] Reconstructionists parallel the radical exponents of Reform, while devotees of Jewish Humanism opt for a genre of humanistic, nontheistic prayer.

[245] In the United States one of the most highly dramatized encounters involving changes in synagogue liturgy occurred at the time of the publication of Mordecai Kaplan's *Sabbath Prayer Book* (New York: Jewish Reconstructionist Foundation, 1945) in which the blessing "who has chosen us from among all the peoples" was changed to "who has drawn us (nigh) to His service" (pp. 10 and 160). This innovation aroused vociferous protest from many sectors of the community with one Orthodox rabbinical group excommunicating Kaplan and a public burning of the prayerbook. See Mel Scult, *Judaism Faces the Twentieth Century: A Biography of Mordecai M. Kaplan* (Detroit: Wayne State University Press, 1993), pp. 341, 344 and 360–1 as well as Jeffrey S. Gurock and Jacob J. Schacter, *A Modern Heretic and a Traditional Community: Mordecai M. Kaplan, Orthodoxy, and American Judaism* (New York: Columbia University Press, 1996), pp. 140–1 and p. 206, note 14. It is noteworthy that a number of Kaplan's prominent colleagues on the faculty of the Jewish Theological Seminary, Louis Ginzberg, Saul Lieberman and Alexander Marx, distanced themselves from Kaplan's prayerbook. See "*Giluy Daat*," in *Ha-Do'ar* 24:39 (Oct. 5, 1945), pp. 904–905. In 1945 an emendation rejecting chosenness could hardly be characterized as having been made in response to a cultural trend; Kaplan was making a forthright statement entirely consistent with his theology. David Novak, "Mordecai Kaplan's Rejection of Election," *Modern Judaism* 15:1 (February, 1995): 1–19, cogently points out that Kaplan's rejection of the election of Israel flows directly from his radical theology. To continue to pay lip service to the doctrine would have been dishonest and "whatever faults Kaplan may have had, hypocrisy was not one of them" (*ibid.*, p. 2).

In non-religious Israeli circles there is a new interest in study of the sources of Jewish thought and law but, for the moment, the turn toward study of the sources is far removed from traditional Jewish belief. There, too, a number of individuals have articulated a desire for a new *siddur* that expresses the sentiments of secular Jews[246] and for development of festival rituals "from which the Lord has been erased."[247]

Moreover, quite apart from issues involving belief in God and the efficacy of approaching God in prayer, a new and grave problem with regard to the wording of the liturgy has emerged in recent decades. The desire of many in the Reform movement to develop a prayer service that is completely gender neutral has led to a thorough revision of the basic elements of the blessings and prayers. These sweeping changes cannot be viewed as mere technical adaptations or semantic alterations.[248] A work such as Marcia Falk's *The Book of Blessings: New Jewish Prayers for Daily Life, the Sabbath, and the New Moon Festival* illustrates the extent to which much current feminist

[246] See Yael Tamir, "*Mahapekha u-Masoret*," *Anu ha-Yehudim ha-Ḥilonim*, ed. Dedi Zucker (Tel Aviv: Yedi'ot Aharonot, 1999), pp. 182–3.

[247] Dedi Zucker, "*Ha-Ẓabar Ḥayyav la-Lekhet*," *ibid*., p. 189.

[248] See, for example, a critique of the *siddur's* "unrelievedly masculine language," stereotyping the role of women and reflecting a male perspective in Annette Daum, "Language and Liturgy," in *Daughters of the King: Women and the Synagogue*, ed. Susan Grossman and Rivka Haut (Philadelphia, New York, and Jerusalem: Jewish Publication Society, 1992), pp. 183–202. Daum surveys Conservative and Reform liturgies designed to include feminist imagery and women's experiences and use of language to describe God utilizing both masculine and feminine terminology. See *ibid*., pp. 197–8, for how (in what one may characterize as the spirit of the Yiddish translator who presented Shakespeare "*vertaytsht un verbessert* – translated and improved") efforts to incorporate gender-neutral language encompass biblical verses as well so that, for example, Lev. 19:17 is translated "You shall not hate your brother or sister in your heart." Daum describes the process of revision as "slow and inconsistent," but "irreversible" (*ibid*., p. 199). See also Ellen Umansky, "(Re)Imaging the Divine," *Response* 13:1–2 (Fall-Winter, 1982): 110–19, who states that she is not suggesting rewriting the Bible and Talmud to make their ideas more consonant with contemporary ones but maintains that the *siddur* must be adjusted to reflect present notions lest "increasing numbers of men and women may find themselves forced to choose between membership in the Jewish community and communion with God" (*ibid*., p. 119).

liturgy celebrates a radical theology in which God is viewed, not as a transcendent Other, but as immanent in creation and inseparable from human empowerment.[249] Falk expresses fealty to Hebrew as "the heart of the heart of my work"[250] and there is moving poetry in her writing. But her newly-coined liturgical formulas, "*Nevarekh et eyn ha-ḥayyim*" which she renders as "Let us bless the source of life" and "*Nevarekh et maayan ḥayyeinu*" which she renders as "Let us bless the flow of life," are not simply innovative prayer texts; they constitute a theological statement.[251]

Thus we find ourselves at the cusp of the twenty-first century, almost two hundred years after the advent of the movement for liturgical change, confronting a Reform liturgy that has turned almost 180 degrees with regard to some respects but that, in another respect, is further removed from the classical prayer service of Judaism than at any previous time.

The appeal of familiar ritual has long been recognized.[252] Current eagerness on the part of segments of the liberal constituency to embrace a greater amount of religious ceremonial has been attributed to several factors: an increased identification with the Jewish people and concomitant waning of embarrassment with distinctive rites; a quest for spirituality in Judaism rather than mere ethnicity; and a holistic approach to life that prompts adoption of practices that appeal to emotion rather than to rational cognition alone. There

---

[249] Boston: Beacon Press, 1999. See especially the discussion pp. 417–23. See also Marcia Falk, "What About God?" *Moment* 10: 3 (March, 1985): 32–6.

[250] *The Book of Blessings*, p. xviii.

[251] For these blessing formulas see, for example, *ibid.*, pp. 18–19 and pp. 368–9. Noteworthy and characteristic are Falk's *Aleinu*, pp. 288–9, in praise of the beauty of the world and human power to heal and repair and her blessing for the New Moon, pp. 344–5, that is converted from a prayer that God renew the lunar cycle to a paean to the new moon that renews itself. Even a laudatory reviewer of Falk's work, Eric L. Friedland, "A Women's Prayer Book for All?" CCAR *Journal*, 49:1 (Winter 2002), comments critically on the "vaguely pantheistic" tone in which "more often than not, no God is addressed at all" (111).

[252] See, for example, Petuchowski, *Understanding Jewish Prayer*, pp. 37–9; Borowitz, *Liberal Judaism*, pp. 410–40; and the interesting personal remarks of Morris Raphael Cohen, "Religion," in *The Faith of Secular Jews*, ed. Saul L. Goodman (New York: Ktav, 1976), p. 163.

is also a newly-found recognition of the value of regulation and discipline and the sense, as Eugene Borowitz puts it colloquially, that "God deserves and our community requires rules."[253] The openness to Jewish ritual in general[254] finds particular expression in synagogue life and liturgical practice because of a renewed interest in observance of Sabbath and festivals including their distinctive prayers.

This welcome development should not, however, obscure the philosophical chasm that continues to divide liberal worship from that of halakhic Judaism. Borowitz, in his admittedly warm and appreciative endorsement of *mizvah* observance, hastens to reassure his readers that the words "who has sanctified us by divine commandments and commanded us to…" need not be taken in so literal a sense that they must fear being obligated by "the entire repertoire of Jewish ceremonial."[255] The essence of the liberal approach inheres in the commitment to personal autonomy and to the freedom to choose to accept or to desist from accepting specific observances.[256]

---

253 *Liberal Judaism*, p. 431.

254 I am indebted to Dr. Joel Wolowelsky for a telling example of the changing attitude toward ritual in the Reform movement. *The Union Haggadah: Home Service for the Passover* (n.p.: CCAR, 1923), p. 141, refers to "the quaint ceremony of 'b'dikas hometz – searching for leaven,' still observed by orthodox Jews." Fifty years later, *A Passover Haggadah* (n.p.: CCAR, 1974), p. 14, describes the search for leaven in a different manner entirely, portrays the ritual as "a dramatic and even compelling experience, particularly for children" and includes the Hebrew text of the blessing for disposal of *hamez*.

255 *Liberal Judaism*, p. 410.

256 *Ibid.*, p. 411. Cf. the news report of reactions to the new worship initiative announced at the 1999 biennial UAHC convention. According to the JTA *Daily News Bulletin*, 21 December 1999, p. 2, the response was positive as long as individuals felt that the new ideas were "encouraged, and not required." As one conventioneer phrased it, the changes "don't bother me, as long as there is a choice." Cf. Frederic A. Doppelt and David Polish, *A Guide for Reform Jews*, rev. and augmented ed. (New York: Ktav, 1973), p. 9: "For what determines whether a custom, ceremony or symbol is either Orthodox or Reform is not its observance or non-observance; it is rather the right to change it when necessary, to drop it when no longer meaningful, and to innovate when desirable." On the conflict between exercise of autonomy and attempts to establish standards of conduct see Dana E. Kaplan, "Reform Jewish Theology and the Sociology of Liberal Religion in America: The Platforms as Response to the Perception of Socioreligious Crisis," *Modern Judaism* 20:1 (February,

In his autobiography, Irving Howe describes how he watched, "at first with hostility and then with bemusement," his intellectual acquaintances seeking a way back to religion. A lifelong skeptic and professed non-believer, he writes that he himself found the temples to be inauthentic and uninspiring and their formless spirituality non-compelling. To him, the American Jewish community appeared to contain "little genuine faith, little serious observance, little searching toward belief. The temples grew in size and there was much busywork and eloquence, but God seldom figured as a dominant presence." But surely for religious belief, asserts Howe, there must be "more than fragile epiphanies;" there must be "a persuasion of strength."[257] In this Howe is, of course, correct. It is with R. Judah ben Tema's charge to be "strong as a lion" in divine service[258] that both *Tur* and *Shulḥan Arukh* introduce the laws of *Oraḥ Ḥayyim.*

Judaism is a demanding faith, a praxis and, *pace* Mendelssohn, a universe of belief. Judaism is not a religion without peoplehood, nor a peoplehood without religion, and certainly not a religion without God. Far from a fuzziness, the path to spirituality in Judaism is structured and limned with prescriptive detail. The table of contents and the orderly progression of Rabbenu Baḥya's classic *Ḥovot ha-Levavot* and R. Moshe Ḥayyim Luzzatto's *Mesilat Yesharim* illustrate the regimen and discipline these authorities posit as essential in the quest for spiritual attainment.

There are no simplistic answers to the struggles of faith. To some, belief comes easier than to others. R. Hirsch's perceptive comment that the *shul* is our school for adults points to the truism that, to the extent that belief can be taught, the liturgy and the synagogue are designed to instruct and to inculcate fundamentals of belief. Ideally, the *shul* becomes a crucible of faith.

Of the making of creative prayerbooks there may be no end. But

---

2000): 71–2. Cf. Simon Rocker, "Growing Through the Open Door," *The Jewish Chronicle* (London), May 24, 2002, p. 26.

[257] *A Margin of Hope: An Intellectual Autobiography* (San Diego, New York and London: Harcourt Brace Jovanovich, 1982), pp. 278–9.

[258] *Avot* 5:23.

whether these hundreds of works have engendered more profound or genuine prayer is open to question. Ultimately, the experience of spirituality in prayer is contingent upon faith. A trenchant folk explication of a difficult stanza in the *"Ve-Khol Maaminim"* prayer of the High Holy Day liturgy conveys this concept. According to that interpretation, the phrase *"Ha-vadai shemo ken tehilato"*[259] should be understood as meaning: "To the extent that one is certain of His name, to that extent can one praise Him." Such an understanding expresses the notion that, when the reality of God is taken as a certainty, man's prayers flow; when certainty of God is absent, prayer comes haltingly at best.[260]

Over the centuries, Jews consistently manifested an unwavering, bedrock faith and welcomed prayer as a haven, a comfort and a fountain of inspiration. As Jews we have a propensity for faith; we have a legacy if we but claim it. For *maamanim benei maamanim*, prayer, even if difficult, is always possible and spirituality in prayer, even if at times elusive, is attainable.

XI. ADDENDUM

OF WOMEN AND PRAYER: A PERSONAL REFLECTION[261]

As the vehicle for communication between man and God, prayer is at one and the same time both the medium of supplication for human needs ("A prayer of the afflicted when he is overwhelmed, and pours out his complaint before the Lord," Ps. 102:1) and the expression of human yearning for knowledge of, and the experience of closeness to (*deveikut*), the divine ("As the hart pants after the water brooks, so pants my soul after You, oh God. My soul thirsts for God, for the living God: when shall I come and appear before God?" Ps. 42:

[259] Lit.: "Whose name is certainty, so is His praise." The four-letter name of God transcends time and connotes necessity or "certainty" of existence.

[260] For this interpretation I am indebted to Louis I. Rabinowiẓ, *Sabbath Light* (Johannesburg: Fieldhill Pub. Co., 1958), p. 3.

[261] In keeping with the theme of the Conference, the Orthodox Forum Steering Committee has encouraged presenters to include personal reflections in their papers.

2–3). It is those dual aspects of prayer that are incorporated in the structure of the quintessential *tefillah*, i.e., the *Shemoneh Esreih*, in the supplications that are preceded and followed by blessings of praise and thanksgiving respectively.

If there are aspects of human life that lose luster or vigor with the passage of years, there are counterbalancing areas in which appreciation and sensitivity become more keen. I doubt whether youngsters are as aware of the healing balm of *Shabbat* as are people of mature years. Surely, *Shabbat* is a spiritual treasure whose "light and joy" is appreciated increasingly as one grows older. So, too, with prayer. It is only with the unfolding of time that one comes to perceive more fully its focal role in our lives.

As the body ages, as one becomes more sharply aware and keenly conscious of physical frailty and of one's utter, total dependence on the *Ribbon Olamim*, one's prayers assume a more urgent and pressing form. With the passage of time, for many, there also come the blessings – and the worries – of an expanding personal and familial universe. Prayers for parents and spouse are augmented by prayers for children and, as the circle of dear ones expands, for children's children, for friends and their children and grandchildren. Of the well known Yiddish jokester Hershele Ostropoler it was related that he prayed with utmost brevity. "What do I have to pray for?" said he. "I have but a wife and a goat, so my prayer is over very quickly: Wife, goat; goat, wife. What more need I say?" With the fullness of years and the blessings of families, our prayers expand.

But, with the passage of years, the overpowering urge to reach beyond the confines of the mundane grows as well. One experiences much more intensely the need to find meaningfulness in one's existence, the need to cleave to the Ineffable, the need to find an expression for the longings of the soul. And so it is that *tefillah* in both its manifestations assumes an even greater importance.

But how approach an awesome, majestic God? We Jews have always felt an intimacy with God even in our reverence.

My sainted grandfather, of blessed memory, in his frail old age, was wont to eat his evening meal at a late hour and to fall into a doze during the Grace after Meals. Inexplicably, he would almost invariably break off his loud recitation of the Grace immediately prior to "*Raḥem na*" (have mercy) and, after several moments of slumber, he would arouse himself and continue at the exact point at which the recitation was interrupted. He would then add his one interpolation in Yiddish: "*Raḥem na, heiliger Bashefer, darbarmdiger Gott*!" (Have mercy, Holy Creator, merciful God).

We approach the *Ribbono shel Olam* in prayer as the all-merciful God upon whose infinite loving kindness and boundless compassion we are dependent and to whose graciousness we appeal. In praying for the recovery of a person suffering from sickness it is customary to identify the person in prayer by means of that individual's matronym (in contrast to prayers for the repose of the soul of the deceased and other liturgical use of a person's name in which the patronym is employed). Several reasons for this practice have been advanced, some quite cogent, some arcane.[262] Perhaps yet another reason may be suggested for this age-old custom.

Prayer is offered for the very life of a person afflicted with illness. In almost every situation, there is an individual whose emotional involvement with the patient is particularly intense, namely, the patient's mother, whose heart and soul is concentrated on the well-being of her child. The Psalmist tells us, "*Lev nishbar ve-nidkeh Elokim lo tivzeh* – A broken and contrite heart, O Lord, Thou wilt not disdain" (51:19). As the *Kotzker* long ago is said to have remarked:

---

[262] A primary source for the practice is a comment of the *Zohar*. The *Zohar* points to the phrase in Psalms uttered by King David, "*ve-hoshia' le-ven amatekha* – and grant salvation to the son of your maidservant" (Psalms 86:16), as a paradigm for prayer and notes that the Psalmist invokes the maternal-filial relationship in his appeal. A petition for heavenly largesse, the *Zohar* adds, must be punctiliously accurate. When the mother's name is employed there can be no doubt that the individual has been correctly identified whereas paternal identity is not beyond question. See *Zohar* 84a, *Lekh Lekha*, s.v. *va-yelekh le-masa'av*. See also R. Yehudah Leib Zirelson, *She'elot u-Teshuvot Gevul Yehudah* (Pietrkow: 1906), *Oraḥ Ḥayyim*, no. 2 and R. Ovadiah Yosef, *Yabia Omer*, II (Jerusalem, 1955), no. 11. Other authorities advance more abstruse reasons for the practice. See reasons and sources cited by Josef Lewy, *Minhag Yisra'el Torah*, vol. 1, rev. ed. (Brooklyn: Fink Graphics, 1990), no. 139, p. 185.

There is nothing as whole as a broken heart.[263] Little wonder then that prayers directed to the Throne of Mercy on behalf of a sick person are offered in nomenclature that by allusion invokes the supplications of two "whole" broken hearts, of both child and mother.

The prayer that serves as the core of the liturgy, the *Amidah*, is modeled on the prayer of Hannah. Basic characteristics of the *Amidah* are ascribed to actions of Hannah. While Hannah was "*medabberet al libbah* (speaking in her heart), only her lips moved but her voice was not heard" (1 Sam. 1:13) as she "poured out her soul before the Lord" (1 Sam. 1:18). The words of Hannah, uttered in "great anguish and distress" (1 Sam. 1:15), constitute the paradigm for prayer. The Talmud derives many attributes of prayer from her heartfelt petition: to pray with concentration, with lips moving, in a low voice, and not in a state of inebriation. The Sages further teach that the power of sincere petition may be learned from the Almighty's answer to Hannah's plea, that the appellation "Lord of Hosts" was first addressed to God by Hannah[264] and that the nine blessings recited in the Rosh Hashanah liturgy correspond to the nine times she invoked the name of God in her prayer (1 Sam. 2:1–10).[265]

One may wonder why the Sages modeled the most fundamental of all prayers on that of Hannah. The most obvious reason is that the prayer of Hannah represents an instance of prayer that is demonstrably genuine, one that all would concede without cavil to be a prayer of sincerity, of intensity and of truth.

In the introduction to his commentary on the *siddur*, R. Yaakov Emden discusses the characteristics of genuine prayer. One aspect of genuine prayer, he maintains, is the element of *ḥiddush*, of novelty, rather than rote mouthing of words. Another hallmark of genuine

---

[263] See R. Yiẓḥak Mirsky, *Hegyonei Halakhah be-Inyenei Shabbat u-Mo'adim* (Jerusalem: Mossad ha-Rav Kook, 1989), p. 152.

[264] BT *Berakhot* 31a-b; BT *Yoma* 73a; and JT *Berakhot* 4:1 and 9:1.

[265] BT *Berakhot* 29a. Cf. the discussion of Leila L. Bronner, "Hannah's Prayer: Rabbinic Ambivalence," *Shofar* 17:2 (Winter 1999): 36–48. Unfortunately, the writer's polemic against rabbinic law prompts her to view the matter through a distorted prism, erroneously to find a willful rabbinic suppression of women and to discover ambivalence where there is none.

prayer is prayer that contains a petition for something greatly desired and requested of the Almighty in full recognition that the Deity has the power to respond to that request.[266] Moreover, the prayer of the afflicted arouses God's mercy[267] and prayer that is accompanied by tears assuredly evidences proper devotion. Thus, claims R. Yaakov Emden, "prayer with a tearful eye is desirable and well received for it emanates from the depths of the heart and therefore unto the uppermost heavens does it reach."[268] The prayer of Hannah quite obviously fulfills those criteria.

It is self-evident that models such as Hannah's prayer or Rachel's tears ("A voice is heard in Ramah, lamentation and bitter weeping, Rachel weeping for her children…refusing to be comforted," Jer. 31:14) are emblematic of a woman's deep longing for children and of a woman's depth of care and concern for children in this life – and even thereafter.[269] Such heartfelt prayer may be uttered by any person. Yet, all but the most doctrinaire advocate of absolute gender neutrality would concede that this type of openly emotional prayer is more often characteristic of women.

Dr. Haym Soloveitchik concludes his frequently cited, intriguing article, "Rupture and Reconstruction: The Transformation of Contemporary Orthodoxy,"[270] with a reflection concerning contemporary Orthodox society that he bases upon "personal experience."[271] He suggests that religious Jews who find that they have lost the ability to feel the intimacy of the divine presence now seek this presence

[266] *Siddur Amudei Shamayim*, p. 5a. Cf. R. Judah Loeb b. Bezalal, Maharal of Prague, *Netivot Olam*, *Netiv ha-Avodah*, chap. 3, who maintains that prayer is the ultimate form of adoration of the Deity because it presupposes recognition of God's absolute mastery over the universe and man's complete dependence upon, and inability to survive without, God.

[267] *Siddur Amudei Shamayim*, p. 411a.

[268] *Ibid.*, p. 5a. Cf. BT *Berakhot* 32b, "R. Eleazar also said: From the day on which the Temple was destroyed the gates of prayer have been closed…but though the gates of prayer are closed the gates of weeping are not closed."

[269] *Bereshit Rabbah* 82:11 and *Eichah Rabbah, petiḥah*, 24. Cf. Rashi, Genesis 48:7 and Redak, Jeremiah 31:14.

[270] *Tradition* 28:4 (Summer, 1994): 64–130.

[271] *Ibid.*, pp. 98ff.

in fulfilling the exacting demands of divine commandments. Dr. Soloveitchik describes his own experiences at High Holy Day services in a variety of different venues in both *ḥareidi* and non-*ḥareidi* communities over a period of thirty-five years and how he has found those services wanting by comparison to those he attended years ago in the company of ordinary lay people in Boston. What he has found missing has been a sense of fear, the presence of courtroom tears and an intimation of immediacy of judgment.

May I humbly offer a somewhat different conclusion based upon a somewhat different "personal experience." Apart from hypocrites and pietistic show-offs (of whom every society has its quota), I doubt if those who seek exactness in observance of *miẓvot* do so unless they experience the immediacy of *yirat shamayim* and *yirat ha-din*. The youngsters who are assiduous in *miẓvah* observance, who seek out every stringency based upon *halakhah*, who worry about the precise size of a *ke-zayit*, who use the largest *kiddush* cup, who investigate the pedigree of an *etrog*, who will not stray from a stricture of *Mishnah Berurah*, may or may not at times be misguided. But, excluding those engaged in holier-than-thou grandstanding, they *are* motivated by fear of Heaven and the awareness of the reality of the divine presence that hovers over their lives. It is the fear of invoking divine displeasure and the joy of fulfilling the divine will, both prompted by "the touch of His presence,"[272] that fuel their zeal.

I teach in a building located on Lexington Avenue and 30th Street. When I arrive early in the morning, I walk past groups of young women heading up Lexington Avenue toward 35th Street and the Stern College campus. Invariably, one or another of those young ladies has her face so deeply buried in a small *siddur* that I am concerned for her physical safety as she dashes to school while concentrating on the *shaḥarit* prayer. My classmates in Stern College for Women's pioneering class were fine women all, but I do not recall this type of *davening*. When I enter the Touro College Women's Division some minutes later there are always young women in a

[272] Cf. *Ibid.*, p. 103.

corner of the library or in the student lounge busily completing the *shaḥarit* prayer. Again, I do not recall similar devoutness from my earliest years of teaching.

For the past thirty-five years I have spent the High Holy Days among ordinary lay people at services probably not so very different from the Boston congregation of Dr. Soloveitchik's youth. The level of observance and knowledgeability of those congregants varies greatly. But they bring an earnestness and sincerity to prayer, keep small talk to a commendable minimum, follow the *sheliaḥ ẓibur* to the best of their ability, and become, on those Days of Awe, welded into a community of prayer of which it is an honor to be a part. Moreover, during this period, I have been privileged to travel quite extensively throughout the United States, Canada, Israel and to many cities in Europe, and to have attended worship services in a variety of different venues in *ḥareidi* and non-*ḥareidi* communities.

From Lakewood to Bobov, from Yeshivat Rabbenu Yitzchak Elchanan to Mir, including the *beit midrash* on the Bar Ilan campus, I have observed serious and devout *davening* and a distinct sense of awe in every yeshivah *beit midrash*. For the most part, with the notable exception of synagogues in Moscow and Berlin,[273] I have found worship services in synagogues as well to be both edifying and moving. To be sure, the loud crying and sighing I associate with European, Yiddish-speaking worshipers of my childhood is no longer common. But that manner of expression involved an edge of theatricality and/or hysteria that was part of the European mode whereas our own age has adopted a cooler demeanor. What has impressed me most of all is the fact that during this period the quality of *davening* at the synagogues I have attended has improved noticeably and consistently. Yes, there are still congregations in which there is more conversation during *tefillah* than there should be. Yet, if anything, I have found that, over the years, there has been

[273] Services in Moscow in the 1970s and 1980s were noisy social occasions. The synagogue served as a social and political meeting place and religious services were but incidental in nature and a distraction. The synagogue in Berlin suffers from the transplantation there of individuals who come with the Moscow-type experience and mentality.

a decided change for the better in halakhic observance in many of these synagogues.[274] The sense of immediacy and intimacy in prayer is quite palpable and those who come to pray do so with concentration and genuine devotion.

If I have found Dr. Soloveitchik's observation to be so different from my own, I do have a plausible explanation for the discrepancy. Perhaps it *is* different on the other side of the *meḥiẓah*. On the women's side, there is so much prayer with a tearful eye that "emanates from the depths of the heart and therefore unto the uppermost heavens does it reach."

But, there is a vast abyss between personal petition, serious and intense as it may be, and *hishtapkhut ha-nefesh*, the outpouring of the soul, of which Rav Kook writes, "Prayer actualizes and brings into light and perfect life that which is concealed in the deepest recesses of the soul."[275] And there is a vast abyss between personal petition, serious and intense as it may be, and the awareness of a responsibility for, and the interdependence of, fellow Jews that translates into the essence of communal prayer, an entreaty and beseeching for mercy on behalf of the pain and the anguish, the loss and the severedness, of each and every person in *klal Yisra'el*. How far we are from such prayer! There goes out to all of us, men and women alike, the imperative to bestir ourselves from the trivialities and the superficialities, the partisan and the divisive, and to heed the call of the ship-master, "What meanest thou, O sleeper? Arise, call upon thy God – *Mah lekha nirdam? Kum kera el Elokekha*!"[276]

---

[274] Years ago I would be somewhat nervous whenever my husband was accorded an *aliyah* at a synagogue away from home. More often than was comfortable, he would find a flaw in the script of sufficient gravity to disqualify the *Sefer Torah* and necessitate the removal of a second scroll from the Ark. In those days, synagogues were negligent in maintenance of Torah scrolls and the run-of-the-mill Torah reader was neither sufficiently learned nor sufficiently attentive to identify an error. The situation has changed dramatically. Younger rabbis tend to be more knowledgeable and conscientious, younger Torah readers are more meticulous, and synagogue officials have learned to be more sensitive to the need to assure the *kashrut* of Torah scrolls.

[275] *Olat Re'iyah*, I, 12.

[276] Jonah 1:6.

12

Spiritual Experience for Ḥasidic Youths and Girls in Pre-Holocaust Europe – A Confluence of Tradition and Modernity

Naftali Loewenthal

The eastern European Jewish community prior to the Holocaust was in a state of crisis as regards traditional Jewish values and observance. Secularization was widespread and increasing. This led a number of religious leaders to make an attempt to provide unusually intense levels of spiritual inspiration for Jewish youth, both males and females. These attempts sometimes crossed borders of normative, accepted traditional practice.

This is not unique to Ḥasidism: the Novaredok *Mussar* movement provides a non-Ḥasidic example of the same process.[1] However from its inception Ḥasidism had attempted to introduce overt spiritual practices into Jewish society, despite various forms of opposition. Hence this paper focuses on the theme of Ḥasidic prayer, meditation and spiritual experience particularly as seen in the first half of the twentieth century, relating to both males and females.

A number of instances will be considered. For males, we will outline the contemplation systems of Ḥabad and of Rabbi Kalonymus Kalman, the Piaseczner Rebbe (d. 1942). For females, we will examine some spiritual aspects of the pre-war *Beit Yaakov* movement, and a unique meditation system which was written by the sixth Lubavitcher Rebbe for a member of the Ḥabad girls' group in Riga. There will be some discussion of the way, in these examples, borders of previously 'accepted' orthodox practice were redrawn.

ḤASIDIC SYSTEMS OF CONTEMPLATION

Eastern-European Jewry, from the sixteenth to the twentieth centuries, saw the rise of a number of contemplation and meditation systems. The Lurianic *kavvanot*, originating in sixteenth century Safed, provided detailed information on kabbalistic concepts to bear in mind during one's prayer; at first these were available only in manuscript, then in the second half of the eighteenth century there were a number of editions of prayerbooks containing them.[2]

Of a rather different nature, a number of contemplation systems and approaches to prayer were produced by the ḥasidic movement.[3] Rabbi Yisrael Baal Shem Tov (1698–1760), the central figure of early Ḥasidism, emphasized the theme of *deveikut*, 'cleaving to God'. This is relevant in all aspects of life, at least for the *Ẓaddik*, but particularly in prayer and Torah study. An outline of this technique is provided

[1] See David E. Fishman, "Musar and Modernity: the Case of Novaredok," *Modern Judaism* 8:1 (1988): 41–64.

[2] Such as Zolkiev, 1744 and 1781; Koretz, 1782, 1785, 1794; Lvov: 1788. *Shaar ha-Kavvanot* was first printed in Salonika, 1852.

[3] See Rivka Schatz-Uffenheimer, *Ḥasidism as Mysticism: Quietistic Elements in Eighteenth Century Ḥasidic Thought*, trans. J. Chipman (Princeton: Princeton University Press, 1993); L. Jacobs, *Ḥasidic Prayer* (London: Routledge, 1972).

in the famous letter which the Baal Shem Tov wrote to his brother-in-law, R. Gershon of Kuty.

> During your prayer and study, in every single word, have the intention to achieve 'unification' there. For in every single letter there are worlds, and souls and Godliness, which rise and join and unify one with the other. Then the letters join and unify together and become a word. They achieve a true unity with God. You should include your own soul with them at every step....[4]

The idea of "having the intention to achieve 'unification'" led to the controversial practice of reciting a formula to this effect: *le-shem yiḥud kudsha berikh hu u-shekhinteh* ("for the sake of the Unification of the Holy One with His *Shekhinah*") before carrying out any *miẓvah*, including prayer.[5] Yet beyond the recitation is the idea that apart from the halakhic imperative to pray, a spiritual transformation of existence was taking place on account of one's prayer. The divine realm of the *sefirot* suffers from disunity, on account of exile; the Holy One, may He be blessed, the 'male' aspect of the Divine, is separate from the *Shekhinah*, the 'female' aspect. Through prayer, Torah study and the *miẓvot* these two aspects could be unified, achieving a mini form of redemption.

A form of the *le-shem yiḥud* formula found in ḥasidic prayer-books presents the goal as that of unifying the two halves of the Divine Name: *Yud* and *Heh*, the Holy One, should be joined with *Vav* and *Heh*, His *Shekhinah*.[6] One practice may have been to visual-

---

[4] R. Yaakov Yosef of Polonoye, *Ben Porat Yosef* (Koretz: 1781; New York: 1954, photog. reprint of Piotrikov: 1884), p. 128a. For the most recent and comprehensive discussion of this letter, see Moshe Rosman, *Founder of Ḥasidism: A Quest for the Historical Baal Shem Tov* (Berkeley: University of California Press, 1996), pp. 97–113.

[5] See L. Jacobs, *Ḥasidic Prayer*, pp. 140–53. Reciting this formula was condemned by Rabbi Yeḥezkel Landau (1713–93), in his *Noda bi-Yehudah* (Zolkiew, 1823), *Yoreh De'ah*, no. 93.

[6] In R. Shneur Zalman's *Seder Tefilot mi-Kol ha-Shanah* (Kopyst, 1816; Brooklyn: Kehot, 1965), fol. 39b before *barukh she-amar*.

ize these letters of the Divine Name, another to conceptualize the unity among the *sefirot*. Yet the statement by the Baal Shem Tov that within each letter there is "Godliness" leads to a rather different form of spiritual experience, described boldly by his disciple Rabbi Yakov Yosef of Polonnoye (d. 1784):

> The idea of *deveikut* to [God] may He be blessed is that by means of the letters of Torah and prayer, one makes one's thoughts and inwardness cleave to the inwardness and the spirituality which is within the letters, as is expressed esoterically by the verse 'let him kiss me with the kisses of his mouth' (Cant. 1:2), a *deveikut* of spirit to spirit…and when one prolongs reciting a word it is *deveikut*, that one does not want to separate from that word.[7]

In the next generation, Rabbi Dov Ber, the Maggid of Mezeritch (d. 1772), taught a form of mystical experience based on the concept of self-abnegation. In this state, the ego of the person dissolves. His speech is felt as an expression of the World of Speech, the Divine attribute *malkhut*; his thought expresses the World of Thought, the attribute *binah*.[8] A system of such mystical intensity may be considered suitable primarily for charismatic leaders, rather than followers.[9] By contrast, in the third generation of the movement, R. Dov Ber's disciple, Rabbi Shneur Zalman of Liadi (1745–1812), the founder of the Ḥabad school of Ḥasidism, taught a number of less

[7] *Keter Shem Tov* (Brooklyn: Kehot, 1977), p. 7, no. 44, based on R. Yaakov Yosef's *Ben Porat Yosef*, p. 59d, and see also his *Toledot Yaakov Yosef* (KoretZ, 1780), p. 132a.

[8] See Schatz-Uffenheimer, *Ḥasidism as Mysticism*, ch. 7.

[9] Another controversial aspect of his teaching, which originated with the Baal Shem Tov, was the concept of 'elevation' of foreign thoughts in prayer. If a stray thought enters the person's mind he can elevate it to its source by perceiving its spiritual root. For example, if it is a thought of love, it originates with the *sefirah* of *ḥesed* (Kindness). By the third generation of the movement it was widely felt that this practice was not suitable for the ḥasidic follower. See R. Shneur Zalman's *Tanya* (Slavuta, 1796; Brooklyn: Kehot, 1982), 1:28, fol. 35a.

intense systems of contemplation which he expected his followers to utilize in their prayer. In his work *Likkutei Amarim*, generally known as *Tanya*, he presented several alternative approaches to contemplation, such as what he called the "long way" and the "short way."[10] These comprise longer and shorter varieties of contemplative technique. The second section of the same work, *Shaar ha-Yiḥud ve-ha-Emunah*, functions as a manual providing material on which to base one's thoughts during a specific form of contemplation, focusing on the divine nature of existence. The first chapter describes a stream of divine energy in the form of Hebrew letters which is the true essence of all Creation. These letters flow from the "Ten Utterances" which originally brought the universe into being, and which now too continuously provide the force which keeps it in existence. Everything, even a stone, has a spiritual dimension, and the Hebrew word for any object is the key to that inner level of its reality. In practice, this means that the contemplative who follows R. Shneur Zalman's system perceives the world around him as an expression of the divine. An anecdote depicts R. Shneur Zalman as recounting what he was thinking about during prayer: "that this *shtender* (lectern) is Godliness."

This perception has different phases, such as the "Upper Unity" in which one perceives that 'all is God', meaning that there is *only* God, associated with the first line of the *Shema*. The words "God is One" are explained as meaning not that there is One God, but that there is *only* God – nothing else exists. Another phase is termed the 'Lower Unity', in which one perceives that there *is* a world, but it is an expression of God: "God is all." This theme is expounded in terms of the second line of the *Shema*, *"barukh shem…."*[11]

[10] The title page of R. Shneur Zalman's *Likkutei Amarim, Tanya* uses the terms 'long' and 'short', referring to various contemplative techniques described in the book. The 'short' path aims swiftly to awaken the 'hidden love' within the person, while the 'long path' consists of deliberate (and usually lengthy) contemplation, arousing feelings of love and fear of the divine, or a profound sense of self-abnegation. See M. Hallamish, *Netiv La-Tanya* (Tel Aviv: Papyros, 1987), pp. 277–94.

[11] See *Tanya, Shaar ha-Yiḥud ve-ha-Emunah*, ch. 7.

The second generation of Ḥabad was particularly rich in its exploration of and argument about issues relating to contemplative prayer. There is discussion of approaching contemplation in a general or a detailed way.[12] These mean, respectively, either an inspiring but general and relatively brief pondering on the divine nature of existence, or a detailed, step-by-step exploration of the spiritual succession of worlds and *sefirot* described in kabbalistic texts. This is similar to, but not identical with, the distinction between short and long contemplative approaches to prayer made in the *Tanya*.

Rabbi Dov Ber (1773–1827), the second leader of Ḥabad known as the *Mitteler Rebbe*, wrote tracts which provide material for these kinds of contemplation, as did his rival, Rabbi Aaron of Starroselye (d. 1828).[13] In this literature there are questions about the different goals to be achieved through contemplation – whether *bitul*, mystical self-abnegation, or heartfelt emotional ecstasy, and critical discussions about whether one's intense emotional experiences in prayer are really genuine. R. Dov Ber comments that the contemplative praying loudly with great enthusiasm may well get angry if someone else tells him to keep quiet, indicating the shallowness of his spiritual experience.[14] Rabbi Aaron countered that the person who rejects the path of spiritual enthusiasm is likely to remain attached to material desires.[15]

How did these contemplative practices fit with the synagogue

[12] See R. Dov Ber's *Shaar ha-Yiḥud*, the second part of *Ner Miẓvah ve-Torah Or* (Brooklyn: Kehot, 1974), p. 4b.

[13] See L. Jacobs, *Seeker of Unity: The Life and Works of Aaron of Starroselje* (London: Valentine Mitchell, 1966); *idem.*, (trans.), Dobh Ber, *Tract on Ecstasy* (London: Valentine Mitchell, 1963); Rachel Elior, *The Theory of Divinity in the Second Generation of Ḥabad* (Hebrew), (Jerusalem: Magnes Press, 1982); *idem.*, *The Paradoxical Ascent to God: The Kabbalistic Theosophy of Ḥabad Ḥasidism* (New York: SUNY, 1993); Naftali Loewenthal, *Communicating the Infinite: The Emergence of the Ḥabad School* (Chicago: University of Chicago Press, 1990).

[14] R. Dov Ber, *Shaar ha-Emunah* reprinted in *Ner Miẓvah ve-Torah Or* (Brooklyn: Kehot, 1974), ch. 48, fol. 88a. See also in the same volume, *Shaar ha-Yiḥud*, ch. 54, fol. 40b.

[15] Rabbi Aaron Halevi Horowitz of Staroselye, *Shaarei ha-Avodah* (Shklov, 1821; Jerusalem, 1970), *Shaar ha-Tefilah*, fol. 68b.

service? It seems that in the case of R. Shneur Zalman, the goal was a lengthy weekday morning service for the entire *minyan* which was geared to the requirements of the contemplatives. Thus he ordered his followers to ensure that the weekday morning service should proceed at a slow pace, "an hour and a half," considerably longer than most synagogues today, with no talking at all during the prayers.[16] At the same time, he gave permission to certain individuals to pray apart from the *minyan*.[17]

It is likely – but not certain – that this was the pattern followed by the followers of Rabbi Aaron of Starroselye: enthusiastic ecstasy would combine with the exigencies of prayer in a *minyan*, although certain individuals may have prayed alone. In the case of R. Dov Ber's followers the question is more acute. His path of intensive and lengthy meditative thought, which in some cases almost approached a trance-like state of immobility, beyond consciousness of one's surroundings, must have completely transcended the synagogue service.

We do not know how this problem was dealt with in R. Dov Ber's life-time. However, early in the twentieth century, when there was a revival of intensive contemplative prayer in Ḥabad, the compromise reached was that the contemplative would attend the synagogue service but would then stay on alone afterwards. The practice of contemplative prayer led also to structural refinements of the synagogue. The typical Ḥabad synagogue would include an extra room, adjoining the main synagogue hall, where contemplatives could pray at their own pace, not disturbing and not disturbed by others.[18]

What was the nature of this revival? Here we come to the crux of our discussion. Under the pressure of the secularizing

---

[16] See *Tanya*, fols. 103a, 137b–138a, 161b–163a. For discussion of R. Shneur Zalman's directives concerning prayer see I. Etkes, "Rabbi Shneur Zalman of Liadi as a Ḥasidic Leader" (Hebrew), Jubilee Volume of *Zion* 50 (1986): 347–9, and N. Loewenthal, *Communicating the Infinite* (n. 13 above), pp. 110–2.

[17] See the 'Liozna Regulations' in S.B. Levine, ed., *Iggerot Kodesh Admor ha-Zaken, Admor ha-Emẓa'i, Admor ha-Ẓemah Ẓedek* (Brooklyn: Kehot, 1980), p.105.

[18] See Haim Lieberman, *Ohel Raḥel*, vol. 2 (Brooklyn, 1980), pp. 354–9.

force of modernity, some Jewish leaders felt an urgent need for an intensification of spirituality. In the first decades of the twentieth century this led to radical steps in a number of different areas, including the development of *Beit Yaakov* and also other movements outside Ḥasidism such as Novaredok.

This radicalism developed despite the fact that in an earlier move to counter modernity, the mid-nineteenth century had seen the emergence of Hungarian ultra-Orthodoxy. Following the lead of the Ḥatam Sofer, this emphasised that *ḥadash assur min ha-Torah*, all innovations are to be eschewed, especially in matters relating to the synagogue. To a considerable extent this set the tone for the ḥasidic movement as a whole. Despite this, the quest for spirituality as the route to the survival of Orthodoxy led to a number of developments which were novel or even unprecedented.

The first of these was the establishment by Rabbi Shalom Dovber Schneersohn (1860–1920), the fifth Lubavitcher Rebbe, of the Tomkhei Temimim Yeshivah in 1897. This Yeshivah, in the townlet of Lubavitch, was distinguished by making the overtly mystical teachings of Ḥabad an integral part of the curriculum, in addition to study of Talmud, the main fare in other Eastern European *yeshivot* of the time, although some of these also included study of *mussar*.[19] Unusually lengthy and intense contemplative prayer was encouraged among the students of *Tomkhei Temimim*. R. Shalom Dovber compiled a number of works providing guidance for this spiritual practice, chief of which was *Kuntres ha-Tefillah*, distributed among the students of the Yeshivah and members of the community in mimeographed copies in 1900.[20]

[19] This was sometimes a controversial addition to the curriculum. See Ben Zion Dinur, *Be-Olam she-Shaka'* (Jerusalem: Mossad Bialik, 1958), pp.70–1 for an account of the Telshe Yeshiva around 1897–1898, when there was a strike of the students protesting against an attempt to make *mussar* study compulsory. See also Shaul Stampfer, *The Lithuanian Yeshivah* (Hebrew), (Jerusalem: Zalman Shazar Center, 1995), p. 233.

[20] It was printed in Vilna, 1924 and reprinted several times since (Brooklyn: Kehot, 1942, 1956, 1988) and there is an English translation, *Tract on Prayer*, trans. Y.E. Danziger (Brooklyn: Kehot, 1992). Another tract by R. Shalom Dovber relating to prayer is *Kuntres ha-Avodah* (Brooklyn: Kehot, 1946).

R. Shalom Dovber made clear in a letter from around the same year that he saw his Yeshivah as counteracting the secularizing tendencies of the time, which had crept into other, unnamed yeshivot. Their students, he claimed "are beardless, mocking the words of the Sages and especially of the *Zohar* and kabbalistic works, and are inclined to be permissive in matters of Jewish law."[21] His ideal for the Tomkhei Temimim students emerging from his yeshivah was that they would not only study Torah but also be noted for "service of God in the heart, which is prayer, in love and in fear"[22] – a hint at the emphasis on contemplative prayer in the Lubavitch Yeshivah.

This emphasis continued throughout the lifetime of R. Shalom Dovber's successor, Rabbi Yosef Yiẓḥak (1880–1950), as is attested by the tenor of his teachings in Otwock, Poland, where the main Lubavitch Yeshiva was situated during the 1930s, and also in Brooklyn, where he moved in 1940. The republication of *Kuntres ha-Tefilah* in Brooklyn in 1942 likewise attests to the concern to transport Ḥabad contemplative prayer techniques to the United States.

RABBI KALONYMOS KALMAN SHAPIRA

Another ḥasidic Rebbe who was concerned to intensify spiritual experience among the youth was Rabbi Kalonymos Kalman Shapira (1889–1942) of Piaseczno, author of the posthumously published *Aish Kodesh.*[23] His father-in-law Rabbi Yerahmiel Moshe was the grandson of the famous Kozhniẓer Maggid (1736–1814), and was Admor in Kozhniẓ. When his father-in-law passed away in 1909, R. Kalonymous Kalman took his position as *Rebbe* in Kozhniẓ, but in 1913 was persuaded to take up residence in Piaseczno, near Warsaw, where he conducted a ḥasidic 'court'. In 1923 he founded of one of the largest ḥasidic yeshivot in Warsaw, *Daat Moshe*, and in 1932 he published his famous work *Ḥovat ha-Talmidim*. This provides an

[21] R. Shalom Dovber, *Iggerot Kodesh*, vol. 1 (Brooklyn: Kehot, 1982), pp. 212–3.

[22] *Ibid.*

[23] Published in Jerusalem, 1960. See Nehemia Polen, *The Holy Fire, the Teachings of Rabbi Kalonymus Kalman Shapira, the Rebbe of the Warsaw Ghetto* (Northvale, NJ: Jason Aronson, 1994).

inspiring spiritual guide for Yeshivah students, including the outlines of some basic mystical concepts.

In the introduction to this work the author expresses his discontent with the separatist Orthodox approach which was prevalent in Poland, in which the heads of the *Yeshivot* would focus on the few who remained faithful to committed Orthodoxy, and, he claimed, give up hope for those who did not:

> Our heart mourns and our hair stands on end when we see how the younger generation have become impious and uncontrolled, Heaven protect us. They have no faith, no fear [of God], no Torah. They hate God and those Jews who serve Him. The principals and heads of the *yeshivot* who are completely immersed in their academies, with only the best students before their eyes, take comfort by saying 'it is true there are now many who are not observant, but nonetheless the Jewish people are not destitute, there are some first class scholars with excellent knowledge of Torah and true faith in God.' However, let them just stretch their heads out of the narrow enclave of their *yeshivot*! They will see the great mass who are not observant, Heaven protect us.... The Houses of Study which were filled with Torah scholars are now empty, and in their place are groups and clubs with goals of heresy and loathing of Torah.... Even the workers and the businessmen who previously, even if they were not Torah scholars, were nonetheless faithful Jews, have now joined with the youth in impiety, slipping into destruction.... Can we really be satisfied with just the handful of students who remain in our *yeshivot*? Are they the whole Jewish people?[24]

His remedy for this situation was to attempt to intensify the spiritual goals of those who were still studying in the *yeshivot*. Previously, writes Rabbi Shapira, ḥasidic practices such as the quest for

[24] Rabbi Kalonymus Kalman Shapira, *Kuntres Ḥovat ha-Talmidim* (Warsaw, 1932; Tel Aviv, n.d.), fol. 4a–b.

enthusiasm and ecstasy were considered appropriate only for older people, not for youths studying in *yeshivah*. Now, however, the need of the time indicates that younger people too should be taught to strive for these goals. Even if the enthusiasm is superficial, compared with that of the mature *ḥasid*, it is valuable. For, if the enthusiasm of the young is not drawn toward a sacred purpose, it will become focused on other, worthless, things.[25]

Defending this approach, R. Shapira argues that in Talmudic study too it is obvious that the young boy studying *Gemara* and *Tosafot* does not understand it to the same depth as does an adult. Nonetheless the boy is taught Talmud so that later he will become a scholar. In the same way, the youth who is taught ḥasidic ideas and practices will later become a true *ḥasid*.[26]

Ḥovat ha-Talmidim includes some material derived from kabbalistic sources.[27] In addition, the publication concludes with three essays aimed at "older students and young married men." The first presents some basic concepts from kabbalistic teaching, including the spiritual nature of the soul, the theme of *ẓimẓum* (the spiritual concealment or 'contraction' of Godliness, enabling the world to come into being), and the divine *sefirot*. The second gives guidance for an intensive, enthusiastic, and ecstatic approach to prayer and melody, while the third presents a mystical approach to Shabbat. In these essays the author repeatedly expresses concern about the question of study of kabbalistic material, but defends his decision to encourage it.[28]

Ḥovat ha-Talmidim was the only one of Rabbi Kalonymus Kalman's works to be published in his lifetime. *Hakhsharat ha-Avreikhim*, a work he left in manuscript, indicates that R. Kalonymus Kalman also taught a number of systems of contemplation or meditation to his disciples.[29]

---

[25] *Ḥovat ha-Talmidim*, fol. 7a–b.

[26] *Ibid.*

[27] See ch. 10.

[28] See, for example, fols. 59a, 81a.

[29] This was published in Jerusalem: 1966. See N. Polen, *Holy Fire*, pp. 4–5. See also L. Jacobs, *Ḥasidic Prayer*, p. 33.

One method he taught was that of visualization. For example, while in prayer, one should picture oneself as standing in the Temple, a method based on a passage by the early ḥasidic master (and ancestor of R. Kalonymus Kalman) R. Elimelekh of Lizhensk (d. 1786).[30] R. Shapira taught two different approaches to visualization: 'simple' and 'creative'. The former would be quite straightforward as regards the imagery employed, while in the latter, the more advanced method, the person would give his imagination free reign, utilizing the full gamut of aggadic sources, in creating images relating to spiritual themes.

An interesting system of meditation taught by R. Kalonymus Kalman was described by one of his students who escaped the Holocaust.[31] This is termed *hashkatah* and involves 'silencing' one's thought. The goal is to achieve a state of mind empty of the normal stream of turbulent ideas. An aid to this could be to gaze at the hardly moving hour-hand of a clock. Then one can focus on one single sacred idea, such as "the Lord God is True." After this meditative process, which should lead to an 'indwelling from above', presumably a form of inspiration beyond oneself, one should sing the verse "Teach me, o God, Thy way" (Ps. 27:11), in the special melody taught by R. Kalonymus Kalman.[32]

There is also an ethical dimension to these practices. R. Kalonymos Kalman says that the time of 'silencing' can be utilized for gaining certain religious or ethical qualities. The sacred thought on which one focuses might concern faith, love or fear of God, or the putting right of bad qualities such as laziness.[33]

Another technique of prayer taught by R. Kalonymus Kalman is in some ways reminiscent of Braslav *ḥitbodedut*, in which the individual speaks directly to God, spontaneously creating his

[30] R. Kalonymus Kalman Shapira, *Hakhsharat ha-Avrekhim*, (Jerusalem, 1966), p. 32. See *No'am Elimelekh*, ed. G. Nigal (Jerusalem: Mossad ha-Rav Kook, 1978), *Lekh Lekha*, p. 7b.

[31] See Polen, *Holy Fire*, pp. 5, 159 n. 14.

[32] R. Kalonymos Kalman Shapira, *Derekh ha-Melekh* (Jerusalem, 1991), pp. 406–407.

[33] *Ibid*. p. 407.

own prayer.[34] This is explained in another work left in manuscript by the author, published posthumously with the title *Ẓav ve-Ziruz* (Jerusalem: 1966).

R. Kalonymus first explains how helpful it is to have a friend to whom one can confide one's problems, following an interpretation by the Sages of Prov. 12:25, "If there is a worry in a person's heart...he should speak about it with others" (BT *Yoma* 75a). R. Kalonymus says the effect is "as if a stone were rolled off his heart." Then he continues:

> Now do you have any good friend and companion like your Father in Heaven? [In saying one should tell one's worry to others] the Sages were hinting at Him! So hide yourself in a particular room, if possible for you, and if not, turn your face to the wall, and imagine in your thoughts that you are standing before the Divine Throne of Glory, and pour your heart out to Him in prayer and entreaty, as it occurs to your heart, in any language you understand.[35]

The idea that the reader might not be able to find a room to himself in which to carry out this practice is realistic in terms of the lack of space for private spiritual devotions in the pre-war (and perhaps also post-war) yeshiva environment. R. Kalonymus continues with 'an example' of such individual prayer, written simply in case the reader is not used to this kind of practice; he does not want his text to be treated as yet another text to recite. The prayer expresses the longing for purity:

> Master of the Universe! You brought me out from Naught, and created and formed my entire body, spirit and soul, and You see how great is my longing to stand before You with a pure and unsullied soul, which would sense Your Will and

[34] However, in the nineteenth century collection of such prayers by Rabbi Nathan Sternhartz (1780–1845), *Likkutei Tefilot* (Bratslav: c. 1822; Jerusalem, 1957), each prayer is woven around a teaching by Rabbi Nachman.

[35] *Ẓav ve-Ziruz* (Jerusalem, 1966), p. 6.

> meditate on Your Thought, hearing Your Voice in the depths of her heart. However, my heart is sick within me because it is so sullied, sensing foreign feelings, desiring impure desires....[36]

The prayer continues at length with a heartfelt request beseeching God to grant purity to the soul, so that it can ascend above with longing for the Divine, achieving abnegation and unification with God's Oneness.

THE HALAKHIC ISSUE

From the earliest days of Ḥasidism there had been attacks on the ḥasidic mode of prayer, on a number of counts: the change of *nusaḥ* (prayer rite) from the traditional *Ashkenaz* rite to a version of the Lurianic prayerbook, resembling the Sefardic rite; adding new phrases such as *le-shem yiḥud kudsha berikh hu u-shekhinteh* ("for the sake of the Unification of the Holy One with His *Shekhinah*"); and the times of prayer. We will focus only on the third point, times of prayer, because by the twentieth century issues of *nusaḥ* and the addition of phrases which had been points of conflict as 'new departures' in the 1760s could now be seen as time honored tradition.

The same could almost be said about the time for prayer. However, this remains an equivocal issue simply because the Mishnah, Talmud, and *Shulḥan Arukh* clearly present specific times by which the morning and evening *Shema* and the main daily prayers (*Amidah*) should be said. Prolonged ḥasidic contemplation of any kind is liable to lead to overstepping the bounds of this time constraint. One could say that the time for the morning *Shema* is partially dealt with by reciting it early, before beginning the process of contemplation and prayer.[37] But what about the time for the *Amidah*?

[36] *Ibid.* See L. Jacobs, *Ḥasidic Prayer*, pp. 32–3.

[37] However, there remains the problem that one may be reciting the *Shema* without wearing *Tefillin*. Cf. BT *Berakhot* 14b.

The general focus of ḥasidic contemplation techniques was on the morning prayer. Long periods of study and thought could take one not only beyond the required time for *Shaḥarit* but to a point when, according to the *Mishnah Berurah*, by Rabbi Israel Meir Kagan, (1838–1933), the Ḥafeẓ Ḥayyim, one should first say the afternoon prayer and then recite the *Amidah* a second time as compensation for missing *Shaḥarit* in the morning.[38] Nonetheless, among a variety of ḥasidic schools in the nineteenth and twentieth centuries we find this extreme phenomenon. Less radically, in major Jewish centers today one can generally 'find a *minyan*' in a ḥasidic *shtiebl* well after the end of the time for *Shaḥarit*, although generally before midday. Are the people there because they have been contemplating or engaged in some other specifically spiritual practice? Have they been studying Talmud, Rashi, and *Tosafot*? To my knowledge, no surveys on this point have been published.

How did the *ḥasidim* excuse their practice of praying beyond the required time? At the outset, let us make the point that while the Talmud – considering this as the constantly studied and restudied 'foundation document' of the rabbinic ethos – is very concerned about subtle issues of Shabbat observance and *kashrut* of food, for example,[39] it presents a variety of approaches to the issue of prayer. These include the idea that those "whose Torah study was their trade" like R. Simeon bar Yoḥai would not interrupt their Torah study for the sake of prayer,[40] or, like R. Yehudah, would only pray once in thirty days, while revising their studies.[41] It also speaks, by contrast, of the 'early pious ones' (*ḥasidim ha-rishonim*) who would spend an hour in preparation for prayer, an hour in prayer, and an hour after prayer. The Talmud then asks how, if they did this three times a day, and therefore spending nine hours in prayer, they were ever able

[38] I.e. if after midday. See *Shulḥan Arukh, Oraḥ Ḥayyim*, 89:1, gloss by R. Moshe Isserlis and *Mishnah Berurah*, no. 7.

[39] See at length the second chapter of Tractate *Avodah Zarah* (29b ff.), discussing wine, cheese, and milk of Gentiles and food cooked by Gentiles.

[40] BT *Shab.* 11a.

[41] BT *Rosh Ha-Shanah* 35a.

to study Torah or to work, and answers that since they were 'pious,' they were given Divine help in both areas.[42]

The Talmud also emphasizes the need for great concentration in saying the *Shema* and in prayer, which leads to the idea that if one is not in a sufficiently relaxed mood, one should not pray. Thus a groom before his wedding night is declared exempt from saying the *Shema*, and Maimonides also cites the view that a person who has been on a journey should wait three days before praying.[43] Various Talmudic sages did not pray if they were angry or upset.[44] However, this exacting approach to the inner dimension of prayer was discouraged by leading medieval Ashkenazi authorities such as Rabbi Meir of Rottenberg. The latter is quoted in the fourteenth century *Arba'ah Turim* as stating that since "we" – meaning our later and weaker generation – "do not have such great concentration in prayer," these exemptions do not apply.[45]

In this context we can consider briefly some of the ḥasidic comments on the question of praying after the time stipulated in the *Shulḥan Arukh*. Criticism of the *ḥasidim* on the grounds of praying late is found in early documents, even those prior to 1772.[46] However, early material in defense of the ḥasidic practice is sparse. There is a passage by Rabbi Yaakov Yosef of Polonnoye extolling the virtue of 'silence' before prayer, leading to delay in the actual prayer. Since the silence too is for the sake of the Creator, it too is considered as praise, as the Psalmist says: "For You, silence is praise" (65:2).[47]

[42] BT *Ber.* 32b.

[43] *Mishneh Torah*, *Sefer Ahavah*, Laws of the Recital of the *Shema*, 4:1; Laws of Prayer, 4:15.

[44] BT *Eruvin* 65a.

[45] *Tur*, *Oraḥ Ḥayyim*, 98; see the comment in the *Beit Yosef*. A similar caution voiced in *Hagahot Maimuniot* to *Mishneh Torah*, *Hil. Tefillah* 4:15 is cited in the name of the Tosafists. The idea that "we" suffer from lack of concentration in prayer and therefore cannot aspire to the standards described in the Talmud is included by R. Joseph Karo in his legal Code (*Oraḥ Ḥayyim*, sec. 98, para. 2.)

[46] See the sources listed by M. Wilensky, *H⊠asidim and Mitnaggedim: A Study of the controversy between them in the Years 1772–1815* (Hebrew) (Jerusalem: Mossad Bialik, 1970), vol. 1, p. 38, n. 19.

[47] Jacobs, *Ḥasidic Prayer*, p. 50, citing R. Yaakov Yosef, *Toledot Yaakov Yosef* (Koret**Z**, 1780), fol. 132c.

In the nineteenth century we find a number of responses to criticism regarding the times of ḥasidic prayer. One form of this concerns the special stature of the ḥasidic *ẓaddik*, which places him above time. His prayer is of such spiritual power that it transcends ordinary boundaries. This idea was accepted by the ḥasidic followers: it seemed quite naturally to express the distinctive nature of the ḥasidic *Rebbe*. Thus, for example, in the late nineteenth century Avraham Yiẓḥak Sperlin, author of the well-known *Taamei ha-Minhagim*, after giving a number of examples of ḥasidic leaders who would pray *Shaḥarit* or *Minḥah* well after the stipulated time says "*ḥas ve-shalom* to imagine criticizing them – for them the night shines as does the day" (p. 27).

Rabbi Israel of Ruzhin (1796–1850) is reported to have presented an elaborate schema according to which, originally, in the Garden of Eden, existence was of such a pure nature that prayer was suitable at any time. The sin of the Tree of Knowledge led to a serious coarsening of the atmosphere, but – linking to a well-known *aggadah* – each of the Patriarchs succeeded in purifying a certain time for each prayer: the morning prayer by Abraham, afternoon prayer by Isaac, and evening prayer by Jacob.[48]

Then came the giving of the Torah. Again, existence was purified, and prayer was effective at any time. This blissful state was spoiled by the worship of the Golden Calf, and specific times were again necessary, reinforced by the enactments of the Men of the Great Assembly. Based to this account, R. Israel of Ruzhin said that a pure soul which had held back from the sins of the Tree of Knowledge and of the Golden Calf, i.e. a *ẓaddik*, continues to be beyond time and can pray in an unrestricted way.[49]

Consistent with this approach is the tradition that while R. Israel himself prayed late, he wanted his followers to pray at the correct time. When a group of them began trying to imitate him, he criticized them. His rebuke took the form of a story. Yet the account

[48] BT *Berakhot* 26b.

[49] A. Wertheim, *Law and Custom in Ḥasidism* (Hebrew), (Jerusalem: Mossad ha-Rav Kook, 1960), p. 93, citing Friedman, *Divrei David* (Husiatin, 1904).

includes a sequel which seems to extend the concept of late prayer to the ḥasidic followers as well. Here follows a paraphrase:

A woman would always cook a simple lunch for her husband, and would serve it at the same time daily. Once, she delayed the lunch by an hour, but served exactly the same, simple food. Her husband was upset; he would not have minded waiting for something special, but this dish was no different from the normal meal.

This part of the anecdote stresses the special stature of the *ẓaddik*. His prayer is indeed late – but is like a special dish which is welcome at any time.

Yet the story does not stop here. Rabbi Israel's *ḥasidim*, who had been the subject of this rebuke, came upon an "old man" to whom they recounted the parable of the food. He responded that the rejection of the tardy dish only takes place if the love between husband and wife is incomplete. But if the husband truly loves the wife, he will welcome the food whatever it is and whenever it is served. According to this account, when the *ḥasidim* later told this to R. Israel, he accepted this view. God's love for the individual is so great that He will indeed accept his prayer at any time.[50] The implication is that permission is given to R. Israel's followers to imitate the example of their *Rebbe*.

The idea of the *ḥasid* simply imitating an earlier form of genuinely spiritual behavior is expressed in a story written in the mid-nineteenth century to defend the late prayer of the *ḥasidim*.

The texts on which the work *Vikuḥah Rabbah* is based, first published in 1864, were probably composed by a follower of Rabbi Levi Isaac of Berdichew (1740–1809),[51] although they were later edited by Jacob Cadaner, a Ḥabad follower in the second and third generations of the movement (thus c. 1815–60). An interesting passage in this work discusses questions relating to contemplative prayer

[50] After being silent for a while, Rabbi Israel said that the old man whom they met had told him, Rabbi Israel, the same thing – and also God! From Wertheim, p. 93 n. 56, quoting *Hitgalut ha-Ẓaddikim* by Shlomo Gavriel (Warsaw, 1905), quoted in Buber, *Or ha-Ganuz*, p. 282.

[51] Thus Mondschein in his "*Ha-sefarim 'Maẓref ha-Avodah' u-'Vikuḥah Rabbah*,'" *Alei Sefer* 5 (1978): 174–5, and n. 22.

and indicates that the author felt that by his generation authentic spirituality in prayer was largely a matter of the past, whether for the *ḥasidim* or the *mitnaggedim*.

The earlier generations are described as musicians who knew how to play melodies for the king according to the rules of music, and also knew how to prepare their instruments. Some of these, (i.e. the pre-ḥasidic pietists and kabbalists) played their music early in the morning, because they had very good instruments "made of coral", while others (the early *ḥasidim*) played later after spending a long time preparing their lesser quality instruments. Both groups were acceptable to the king.

The children of the members of these two groups, however, know neither the rules of music, nor how to prepare their instruments. They all produce sounds which are largely false. In imitation of their illustrious parents, some, the mitnaggedim, continue to play early in the morning, and others, the *ḥasidim*, "sleep late" and therefore play later in the day.

As far as the king is concerned, none of these melodies are worth hearing. Despite this sorry situation, there are some of the (ḥasidic!) children who realize that their playing is false. They take this to heart, and spend time trying to learn the rules of music, even though they do not do this successfully, and try to prepare their instruments, even though they do not know how. The king sees this endeavor and accepts it.[52]

The meaning of the story is clear: 'our' generation (when the story was told) merely imitates the earlier, genuinely spiritual, figures. Knowing neither the rules of music nor how to prepare one's instruments, the best one can achieve is a sense of humility at one's lack of competence in performing for the King. This leads to a sincere attempt, despite the fact that objectively it is unsuccessful. Yet the attempt itself has some worth.

This was the way the question was evaluated by some of the *ḥasidim*. We are not considering here the scorn with which this quest for the spiritual was regarded by the opponents of Ḥasidism.

---

[52] *Vikuḥah Rabbah*, (Pietrekov, 1912; reprinted Brooklyn, 1981), fol. 19b.

A collection of relevant material till 1815 was made by the late Professor Mordechai Wilensky.[53] There is obviously room for study of the conflict between *ḥasidim* and *mitnaggedim* after that date. However, as we have suggested earlier, by the time we come to the twentieth century, whatever the rivalries and enmities, the *ḥasidim* were able to feel, at least to some extent, justified by their illustrious forbears. Yet quite apart from criticism by the *mitnaggedim*, questions within Ḥasidism continued on the issue of late prayer and balancing one's individual prayer with the synagogue service.

Thus, moving to the modern West, in 1949 a tract of ḥasidic teaching by the sixth Lubavitcher *Rebbe*, Rabbi Yosef Yiẓḥak Schneersohn (1880–1950), included a letter in which the *Rebbe* stated, in the names of his forebears, how one's individual prayer relates to that of the synagogue service.

> [The previous *Rebbeim* of Ḥabad] defined the *halakhah* for those who asked concerning prayer with the community: how can they fulfill both – to engage in the 'service of the heart' with lengthy prayer, and also to pray with the community? They answered that the meaning of 'prayer with the community' is *at the time that the community is praying* [emphasis added, NL]. They instructed them to hear all the prayers, the saying of *Kaddish, Barekhu*, *Kedushah*, the Reading of the Torah and recital of *Kaddish* [concluding] the communal prayer service. After that they should pray slowly, each individual according to his level of attainment in the service of the heart.[54]

This statement by R. Yosef Yiẓḥak gave clear guidance to the contemplative: be present in the synagogue, participate at a certain level in the public service (through saying *amen*, etc.), but mean-

[53] M. Wilensky, *Ḥasidim and Mitnagdim*. On the *mitnaggedim*, see Allen Nadler, *The Faith of the Mitnaggedim: Rabbinic Responses to Ḥasidic Rapture*, (Baltimore: John Hopkins University Press, 1997).

[54] R. Yosef Yiẓḥak Schneersohn, *Kuntres 2 Nisan 5709* (Brooklyn: Kehot, 1949), p. 99. Collected in *idem.*, *Sefer ha-Maamarim 5709* (Brooklyn: Kehot, 1976).

while be preparing for prayer, probably through study of ḥasidic teachings. Then the ḥasid would pray in his own individual, lengthy, intense way. The passage was reprinted in an important work of seventh generation Lubavitch, the *Sefer ha-Minhagim*,[55] which enabled the widely flung and growing movement to have consistency of custom.

It is interesting that R. Yosef Yiẓḥak's counsel concerning prayer, originally directed at scholarly contemplatives, was partly adapted for use by the *baalei teshuvah*, the newly Orthodox (literally 'repentants'). The person who, reading slowly, cannot keep up with the synagogue prayers, is advised by his Lubavitch mentor to attend the synagogue service from the beginning, but to pray at his own pace.

Another form of conflict regarding contemplative prayer concerns not the time of prayer but the very idea that the individual before one's eyes should dare to aspire to it. An example of this is seen in the background to a letter from the seventh Lubavitcher *Rebbe*, Rabbi Menahem Mendel Schneerson (1902–1994), written in 1952 to the head of the (non-ḥasidic) Yeshivah in Manchester, Rabbi Yehudah Zev Segal (c. 1911–1993). The latter had written to the *Rebbe* with a complaint about some boys from Lubavitch families in the Yeshivah, who were clearly trying to follow the contemplative style of prayer. In other respects, however, they were perhaps not untypical youth of the 1950s, at least in the eyes of their austere *Rosh Yeshivah*.

In his reply the *Rebbe* expressed the belief that the attempt to achieve spirituality in prayer, even if not matched by other aspects of a young person's life, would at least have a generally positive effect. The inner experience in contemplative prayer was a resource which would strengthen their affirmation of traditional values in a period of change. R. Menahem Mendel wrote:

> As for what you write concerning the conduct of certain of the students…that you are not pleased about their lengthy prayer

[55] Kefar Ḥabad: Kehot, 1967, p. 8.

> since this does not match their behavior in other matters.... Perhaps your claims are justified. However, it is clearly apparent to anyone considering the nature of the youth of this generation that for them in particular it is a time of crisis. One therefore has to be very careful not to weaken their power to reject the 'winds' which are blowing through the world....[56]

This brings us back again to the concept of the *baal teshuvah*. It is interesting to note that one of the major *Ḥabad* teachers of *baalei teshuvah*, Rabbi Shneur Zalman Gafni (b. c. 1940), is one of the leading contemporary exponents of lengthy, intensive contemplative prayer. A former student described how day by day he would sit almost immobile in the yeshivah hall of Kefar Ḥabad, wrapped in his *tallit*, engaged for three hours in silent meditative prayer. He also expects attempts in this direction from his students.

One might ask: surely someone who is relatively new to traditional Judaism should beware of such intensely spiritual practices? Now, those who follow Rabbi Gafni into the mysteries of *hitbonenut* (contemplation) have indeed learned to study profound teachings in Hebrew: *Tanya*, *Torah Or* and *Likkutei Torah* by Rabbi Shneur Zalman and other works by later Ḥabad teachers. Yet at some level they may well still be regarded as neophytes. Nonetheless, R. Gafni guides them to levels of experience which in any other traditional *beit ha-midrash* or synagogue would seem quite startling. Perhaps his view is that precisely the intensity of Ḥabad contemplation can help these students affirm their commitment to ideals which challenge directly the secular values in which they had been immersed.

WOMEN AND JEWISH SPIRITUALITY

Having attempted to examine some aspects of ḥasidic prayer and spirituality for males, particularly in pre-Holocaust Europe, we

[56] *Iggerot Kodesh Admor...R. Menahem Mendel*, vol. 5 (Brooklyn: Kehot, 1988), p. 325.

now will endeavor to investigate questions relating to spirituality for women and girls, focusing on the same period.[57] Here too, as a reaction to the secularizing force of modernity, a gradual transformation was taking place. Polish-Jewish girls had not previously been given formal Jewish education. In the second decade of the twentieth century, a new movement for the Jewish education of girls began. This was *Beit Yaakov*, founded by Sarah Schenierer (d. 1935) and centered in Cracow. From there it spread throughout Poland and further afield, involving tens of thousands of girls. This movement is well known, but is as yet insufficiently understood as an example of feminine spirituality. Functioning primarily as a movement of schools for Polish-Jewish girls, *Beit Yaakov* is usually thought of as an adventurous step educationally, which is the way it is described by Shoshana Pantel Zolty,[58] or, interestingly, as a model for Jewish feminism, as it is depicted by Deborah Weissman.[59] However examination of some of the sources relating to this movement indicates that in its pre-war form, for the inner circle of its members and leaders, it is to be seen as a remarkable example of feminine spirituality.

The initial context of early twentieth century Polish-Jewish Orthodoxy is the world of the yeshivah, from which the woman or girl was largely excluded, and of the ḥasidic *Rebbe*. The kind of personal relationship a man or youth might have with a *Rebbe* is seen from the account of Jiri Langer (1894–1943), a young man from Prague and a friend of Kafka. Despite his thoroughly westernized background, in the second decade of the century he became inspired by contact with the Belzer Rebbe, Rabbi Issakhar Dov Rokeah (d. 1927). In the introduction to Langer's Czech work on Ḥasidism, entitled *Nine Gates*, he tells of a waking vision he had of the *Rebbe*[60] and describes,

[57] The following is partly based on Loewenthal, "Women and the Dialectic of Spirituality in Ḥasidism" in I. Etkes, D. Assaf et al, (eds.), *Within Ḥasidic Circles: Studies in Ḥasidism in Memory of Mordecai Wilensky* (Jerusalem: The Bialik Institute, 1999), pp. 7–65.

[58] *And All Your Children Shall Be Learned: Women and the Study of Torah in Jewish Law and History* (Northvale, NJ and London: Jason Aronson, 1993), ch. 9, pp. 263–300.

[59] Deborah Weissman, "Bais Yaakov: A Historical Model for Jewish Feminists" in *The Jewish Woman*, E. Koltun, ed. (New York: Schocken Books, 1976), pp. 139–48.

[60] Jiri Langer, *Nine Gates*, (London: James Clarke, 1961), p. 12.

among other aspects of his five years with the *ḥasidim*, the spiritual intensity of their dancing on a festival, and the way the dance of the *Rebbe*, alone, filled him with awe.[61] He also relates that the *Rebbe* recommended that he study Elijah de Vidas' *Reishit Ḥokhmah*,[62] a compendium of passages from the *Zohar* giving guidance for one's spiritual life.

What access did a girl or woman have to this kind of experience? Comparatively little. In many ḥasidic courts she could meet the *Rebbe* and ask him for a blessing, usually giving a written note called a *kvitel*. She would be filled with awe. But in terms of direct communication, that was as far as it would go. Langer writes about R. Issakhar Dov:

> The saint never looks on the face of a woman. If he must speak to women – as, when he receives a *kvitel* – he looks out of the window while he speaks.[63]

Whether or not the *Rebbe* would actually look at a woman, one should not underestimate the spiritual effect achieved by contact with him. Rivkah Leah Klein (nee Einhorn[64]) describes movingly[65] an interview in Hungary early in 1944 with Rabbi Shalom Eliezer Halberstam (1862–1944) of Raẓfeld, the son of R. Haim of Ẓanz. This was shortly before he was to die in Auschwitz. He gave her a blessing that she, her husband and her unborn child would all survive the war. She describes how some months later, posing as an Aryan on a Hungarian bus, at a crucial moment of danger, when she feared

[61] *Ibid.*, p. 14.

[62] *Ibid.*, p. 16–7.

[63] *Ibid.*, p. 11.

[64] Her father was Avraham Einhorn, Rabbi of Szombathely.

[65] R.L. Klein, *The Scent of Snowflowers* (Jerusalem and Spring Valley, NY: Feldheim, 1989), pp. 81–82. Naturally there are methodological problems in using a text of this kind. The account is written only after many years, with either deliberate or unintentional suppression, addition or other editing, of the material. Nonetheless for certain kinds of information – such as the clues we are seeking concerning the relationship of a woman with a ḥasidic *Rebbe* – the source can still have some use, if treated with caution. See n. 85 below.

she could no longer maintain her disguise and that she and her baby would be killed:

> All at once a tremor passed through me, and a picture quickly flashed through my mind, a picture of a beloved face, so fragile, so thin, almost lost in a long, snow-white beard. The *Rebbe*. The *Rebbe*'s words rushed into my consciousness from the past, and, awed and trembling, I clung to his promise....[66]

According to her account, this vivid memory of the *Rebbe* enabled her to regain her composure, saving her life. Rivkah Leah clearly derived spiritual and emotional power from her contact with this *Rebbe*. In fact she had also seen him several years earlier, when she was a small child; he was visiting the house of her eminent father, the Rabbi of Szombathely, and he gave her a coin which he had blessed.[67]

This level of contact for a woman with a *Rebbe* at this period is possibly rare, a product both of her distinguished lineage and the intensity of the times. For the woman in an average ḥasidic family in the first few decades of the twentieth century, most of the evidence suggests a more distant relationship. It was her father, husband, or brother who went to the *Rebbe*, leaving the women at home.[68] In strong contrast to their brothers, Jewish girls were very likely to attend the Polish *gymnasia* where, despite the intense anti-Semitism they encountered, they would also develop a strong interest in Polish literature and secular values. At home, the "modern" girl would appear at the Sabbath meals in stylish immodest clothing, with her

---

[66] *Ibid.*, pp. 433. Another reference to the spiritual strength of Hungarian ḥasidic girls is in Anna Eilenberg's *Sisters in the Storm* (Lakewood: C.I.S. Publishers, 1992). These girls, coming to Auschwitz in 1944, were able to inspire the other Polish girls through simulating a Friday night or Pesach Seder atmosphere. See pp. 155–7.

[67] Klein, *op.cit.*, p. 80–1. Langer describes a rather similar practice in Belz, *Nine Gates*, p. 10.

[68] This is discussed by Ada Rappoport-Albert, "On Women in Ḥasidism, S.A. Horodecky and The Maid of Ludmir Tradition", in *Jewish History: Essays in Honour of Chimen Abramsky*, A. Rappoport-Albert and S.J. Zipperstein, eds. (London: Peter Halban, 1988), pp. 495–525.

nose in a novel; her father might be shocked, or perhaps, he himself immersed in a page of Talmud which he would discuss with his sons, and would not notice.[69] For her part, the young Polish Jewess regarded her parents as old-fashioned and her brothers, who affirmed ḥasidic Orthodoxy, as fanatics.

BEIT YAAKOV

It is in this context that we wish to examine the nature of the interwar *Beit Yaakov* movement. Our claim is that for its inner circle it represented a strong move toward spirituality, meaning both otherworldly experience and dedicated love. The first point to be understood about *Beit Yaakov,* as is explained by Deborah Weissman, is that while today in Israel, the United States and Britain, it represents the values of enclave Orthodoxy, when it began, it was a radical movement.[70] Its radicalism had two aspects. The fact that it aimed to provide organized Jewish education for girls, which was hitherto frowned upon in Eastern Europe, and also in its goal to reach out to girls moving towards "assimilation" (albeit assimilating in a Yiddish-speaking context) and draw them into a society dedicated to the Eastern European extreme of Jewish observance. In this sense, *Beit Yaakov* was an outreach movement. More radical than the provision of Jewish education for girls was the transformation of the young graduates of *Beit Yaakov* into outreach activists.

Dr. Judith Rosenbaum, later Grunfeld (d. 1998), worked in the Cracow *Beit Yaakov* teachers' seminary with Sarah Schenierer from 1924 to 1929. She describes how fifteen year old Gittel travels with Frau Schenierer to a little *shtetl* where a meeting of women has been organized. By pinning up her hair and wearing a long dress Gittel looks older than she really is.

> …[From] the platform…[Gittel] sees hundreds of faces staring up at her and she hears herself delivering a speech she memorized in the morning…. After she has finished [Frau

[69] See Sarah Schenierer, *Eim be-Yisrael, Kitvei Sarah Shenirer* (Bnei Brak: Neẓah, n.d.), vol. 1, p. 19, and Weissman, "Beis Yaakov," p. 141.
[70] *Ibid.*, p. 139.

> Schenierer] asks the audience whether they are willing to start a school with this girl as a teacher.... There is an enthusiastic response. They enroll their children and contribute to the setting up of the school. Gittel remains behind to be the one and only teacher, while Frau Schenierer takes the next train [back to Cracow]....[71]

Fueling this activism and empowerment was the spiritual relationship of the girls with Sarah Schenierer. How did she induce a teenage girl to go off to a strange townlet somewhere in Poland and found a new *Beit Yaakov* school? Here we see, the sources suggest, the charisma of a spiritual leader.

Sarah Schenierer came from a family of Ẓanz *ḥasidim*. From her own writings and her Polish diary we see her as an intensely spiritual young woman, delighted to receive a set of *Ḥok le-Yisrael*, a kabbalistic anthology of Torah literature, including the *Zohar*, arranged for daily study, with a Yiddish translation. This she studied assiduously.[72] She was fully aware of the rifts in Polish Jewish society and the severe problems caused by the lack of Jewish education for girls. On a visit to Vienna in 1914 she heard a sermon in the Stumpe Gasse Synagogue given by Dr. Flesch, a lecture on Judith (it was the Sabbath of Ḥanukah) and other heroines, given from a neo-Orthodox perspective, in which Jewish history joined with Orthodox practice and talmudic tradition to create an inspiring *mélange*. Dr. Flesch preached the need for contemporary Jewish women to follow in the footsteps of their great forbearers. With this, the idea of teaching the Jewish girls of Poland was born.[73] On her return to Cracow she attempted to reproduce this approach, but found that the older girls either ridiculed her traditionalism or, even if attracted by the ideas, would not modify their behavior.[74] She therefore determined to aim for younger girls, in 1917 creating a school for twenty-five students. Before this, however, she traveled to Marienbad and together

---

71 M. Dansky, *Rebbeẓin Grunfeld* (Brooklyn: Mesorah Publications, 1994), p. 117.

72 *Eim be-Yisrael*, vol. 1, pp. 21–2.

73 *Ibid.*, p. 24; Weissman, "Bais Yaakov," p. 141.

74 *Eim be-Yisrael*, vol. 1, pp. 25–6, 28.

with her brother obtained a blessing for the venture from the Belzer *Rebbe*, the same R. Issakhar Dov. Reading the *kvitel* composed by Sarah's brother "my sister wants to educate daughters of Israel in the spirit of Judaism and Torah" the *Rebbe* gave the blessing: *brakhah ve-hazlaḥah* ('blessing and success').[75] This was, despite the fact that, as Langer informed us, he did not look at women. At first, this was the only support she received. The Bobover *Rebbe*, for example, was against the venture.[76] However, eventually *Beit Yaakov* was adopted by Agudat Yisrael, with the approval of leading figures such as R. Avraham Mordekhai Alter, the Gerer Rebbe, R. Israel Meir Kagan, and R. Meir Shapiro. *Beit Yaakov* schools were set up all over Poland and Lithuania, with fund-raising committees active in Europe, South Africa, and the United States.

My claim is that Sarah Schenierer functioned for her pupils not just as a radical educator, but as a spiritual leader, leading her followers on a path which combined a German neo-Orthodox concept of Jewish education with a feminine version of ḥasidic spirituality. Certain aspects of her teaching and activity enabled her and her followers to maintain this role with the approval of some of the major forces in the religious leadership of Eastern Europe. What is the evidence for this view? Taking first one aspect of spirituality, 'otherworldliness', in which ways do we see aspects of the 'otherworldly' in Sarah Schenierer and her pupils?

Dr. Judith Rosenbaum Grunfeld describes an interesting feature of the religious life of early *Beit Yaakov*, *Yom Kippur Katan*. Observing the eve of the New Moon as a fast day was a kabbalistic practice which became popularized through prayer books such as Rabbi Nathan Hanover's *Shaarei Zion*.[77] Judith Grunfeld writes as follows:

> Sarah Schneirer (!), followed by one hundred and twenty girls, would walk to the Rema's *Shul* in the Cracow ghetto....

[75] Joseph Friedensohn (and Chaim Shapiro), "The Mother of Generations," in *The Torah World: A Treasury of Biographical Sketches*, N. Wolpin ed. (Brooklyn: Mesorah, 1982), p. 165.
[76] See Grunfeld in D. Rubin, *Daughters of Destiny*, (Brooklyn: Mesorah, 1989), p. 135.
[77] There was an edition in Premyshlan: 1917.

> After everyone had [prayed] there, we walked to the graves of...the Rema [R. Moshe Isserlis]...R. Yoel Sirkis...and...R. Yom Tov Lipman Heller. Our *tehillim* in hand, we assembled around the tombstones. The atmosphere of [holiness] and tranquility around the graves of the *ẓaddikim* inspired the young girls.[78]

The conventional mode of observing *Yom Kippur Katan* is by fasting and supplicatory prayers, *seliḥot*.[79] Sarah Schenierer's transformation of this day into a time for her girls to visit the cemetery and say Psalms among the tombstones suggests the touch of inspiration.[80] The visiting of graves (and the laying of wicks) was an authentic aspect of the spirituality of Ashkenazi women, as has been described by Chava Weissler,[81] and there is a section in the collections of the Yiddish *tekhines* called *maaneh loshen* which concerns visiting the graves of one's parents or of *ẓaddikim*. For the twentieth century girls of *Beit Yaakov*, to come with Sarah Schenierer to the cemetery, visiting the graves of *ẓaddikim*, opens a path of spiritual encounter insulated from the grief of mourning. Indeed this itself is a significant kabbalistic practice, as we see from the writings of R. Ḥayyim Vital: it is associated with one of the most intense spiritual practices described in the Lurianic literature, that of *yiḥudim*, in which the soul of the departed *ẓaddik* is bonded with the soul of the living.[82]

The practice of visiting graves was adopted in modified form by the ḥasidic movement. Both in Bratslav[83] and in Ḥabad[84] there were

---

[78] Grunfeld in *Daughters of Destiny*, p. 133.

[79] See *Magen Avraham* sec. 3 to *Shulḥan Arukh Oraḥ Ḥayyim*, sec. 417.

[80] Grunfeld's description suggests that this was seen as an innovation.

[81] See Chava Weissler, *Voices of the Matriarchs, Listening to the Prayers of Early Modern Jewish Women* (Boston: Beacon Press, 1998), pp. 126–46.

[82] See R. Ḥayyim Vital's *Shaar Ruaḥ ha-Kodesh* (Tel Aviv, 1963), pp. 74–5. This is discussed in Loewenthal, *Communicating the Infinite* (n. 11 above), pp. 10–11.

[83] See *Ẓiun ha-Meẓuyenet*, (1948; Jerusalem: Hoẓaot Ben Adam, 1969). This includes compilations such as R. Naḥman of Tcherin's *Sefer ha-Hishtat'ḥut* (Lemberg, 1876) and also Rabbi Naḥman's selection of ten Psalms known as *Tikkun ha-Kelali*, which would be recited at his grave.

[84] *Inyan ha-Hishtat'ḥut* (Lemberg, 1873; Lublin, 1909; Warsaw, 1922, 1928).

significant texts concerning one's thoughts and feelings when visiting the grave of Rabbi Naḥman in Uman or of one of the departed Ḥabad leaders in Hadiẓ, Niezhin, or Lubavitch. However, one feels, the *Beit Yaakov* girls did not need texts: the Book of Psalms itself functioned as a mediator between the realms of the living and the dead, especially given the inspiring presence of Sarah Schenierer herself.

The significance of the experience of visiting a grave for a *Beit Yaakov* girl is seen in an anecdote from the Nazi period in Cracow. The source for this is a memoir written by Pearl Benisch in Israel in the nineteen-eighties. The question of the use of Holocaust memoir material by historians has been discussed by scholars.[85] However, our aims in this paper are limited. We are looking not for simple historical facts, which might seem elusive when different observers give differing accounts of the same events, but for traces of spirituality, which arguably are more resilient.[86]

Early in 1941 a young Jewish girl, Balka Grossfeld, was interned by the Germans in the Montelupich prison in Cracow. For several months two of her *Beit Yaakov* friends managed to bring her kosher food. However, they decided then to try and do something more drastic. They would go to Handke, the official who had imprisoned her, and ask for her release.

It is illuminating for us to discover that before embarking on this very dangerous plan of action, one of the friends, Pearl Mandelker (later Benisch), made a special trip to the grave of Sarah Schenierer in the new cemetry in Cracow on Jerosolimska Street. She finds the cemetery, and is horrified to see the heap of naked bodies in the cleansing room; so many people had been killed that there was no time to bury them properly. Then she walked to the graves, which were still intact.

> I knew my way around and soon found the grave of our teacher, Sarah Schenierer. There I poured out my heart in

[85] See James E. Young, "Interpreting Literary Testimony: A Preface to Re-reading Holocaust Diaries and Memoirs," *New Literary History* 18 (1987): 403–23.

[86] See Young, *op. cit.*: 417, 421.

> prayer over what I had just seen, over the disaster which had befallen our people. I cried to our mother Sarah for help.... "Mother," I cried, "...please intervene with the Court of Heaven. One of your children is in the claws of a beast; she must be helped. Mother, I know you cannot observe her pain and remain unmoved. I know you will do all you can, and with God's help you will succeed." I stepped out of the cemetery, my peace of mind restored.... I headed home with renewed hope.[87]

How was this otherworldly bond between Sarah Schenierer and her disciples fashioned? The memoirs of Judith Grunfeld and others show in addition to her firmness and strength of will, her love and power of intimacy in her relationships with her pupils. Yet another factor too, traditional in the history of Ḥasidism, is also relevant: the power of dancing. Repeatedly, one finds reference to her dancing with her pupils, far from the gaze of any man, singing *ve-taher libeinu*, 'purify our hearts.' One account tells of this ecstatic dancing after the close of the prayers on Yom Kippur:

> We were so caught up in the day's holiness and intensity that, after the fast, instead of running to eat, we began to sing and dance. Where we found strength I cannot imagine, but we just kept on dancing. I can remember clearly how our voices rang out to the tunes of *ashrei ha-ish* and *ve-taher libeinu* and how we danced in circles around and around and around.[88]

This group of girls clearly were experiencing a religious fervor which could match that of their brothers at the court of a *Rebbe*. It

[87] Pearl Benisch, *To Vanquish the Dragon*, (Jerusalem and Spring Valley, NY: Feldheim, 1991), p. 81. Visiting graves continues to be a feature of the life of the modern ḥasidic woman. See Tamar El-Or, *Educated and Ignorant: Ultra-Orthodox Jewish Women and their World*, trans. Haim Wazman, (Boulder, CO: Lynne Rienner Publishers, 1994), pp. 151–3.

[88] Basya (Epstein) Bender in D. Rubin, *Daughters of Destiny*, p. 181.

is not surprising that Judith Grunfeld depicts *Beit Yaakov* in terms of the ḥasidic movement:

> Here among the girls, the inspiration of the chassidic life had found its way into the woman's world. It had formed its own style, softened and differently molded, but it was of the same fiber that made the *chassidim* crowd round their *Rebbe*, made them stand for hours to catch a glimpse of him.[89]

However, on the textual level the studies in *Beit Yaakov* concerned Bible, Jewish law, and Jewish history. Although set up in the wider framework of Ḥasidism, and observing meticulously stringent ḥasidic custom regarding modesty,[90] the curriculum in the *Beit Yaakov* classroom did not have specific ḥasidic elements. This is not surprising, given that even for boys the inclusion of ḥasidic 'spiritual' material in the curriculum was a rarity; Ḥabad's *Tomkhei Temimim* chain of *yeshivot* and R. Kalonymus Kalman's *Daat Moshe* were the exceptions to the rule.

Prayer in *Beit Yaakov*

Deborah Weissman, in her study of pre-war *Beit Yaakov*, notes that the girls were required to engage in formal prayer twice a day, for the *Shaḥarit* and *Minḥah* services, and took full part in the Sabbath morning service in the synagogue.[91] What was the nature of this prayer?

We gain an inkling from an interesting document written by Sarah Schenierer herself, in the last period of her life, when her articles for the *Beit Yaakov* journal were the main way in which she communicated with her disciples.[92] This is an essay called "The

[89] Dansky, *Rebbeẓin Grunfeld*, p. 142.

[90] Apart from any other possible consideration, the intense concern for modesty functioned as a protection for the movement, guarding it from the accusation of being 'modern.'

[91] Deborah R. Weissman, "Bais Ya'akov, A Women's Educational Movement in the Polish Jewish Community: A Case Study in Tradition and Modernity", Master's Thesis at New York University (n.d.), p. 87.

[92] See *Eim be-Yisrael*, vol. 2, p. 21.

Power of Prayer." The author does not claim that the ideas in this are new, in relation to what she has previously taught. Indeed, she suggests that readers will already have heard these ideas from their teachers in *Beit Yaakov*.[93] This makes the essay particularly valuable for us as an indicator of the general expectations regarding prayer in the *Beit Yaakov* movement.

Sarah Schenierer starts with a question: why should we pray? Doesn't God know our thoughts and needs anyway? To this she gives three answers:

1. Prayer purifies one's heart from sin, and exalts one's thoughts to a divine plane. Through this we can strengthen our bond with God and cleave to His qualities. 2. Prayer inspires us with joy in our lot; giving us the power to bear all the troubles of life through arousing in us strong *bitaḥon*, trust in God. It implants in us a strong faith that there will be better times ahead. 3. Since prayer pours into us a fountain of joy, it also reduces our longing for material delights, our desires for worldly matters. Through this we become more devoted to our spiritual concerns, acquiring more *mizvot* and good deeds.

This gently spiritual presentation of the nature of prayer is followed by another question: how can we prepare for prayer? Here Sarah Schenierer describes a serious mode of inner preparation:

> Before we stand up to pray, we should properly inspect ourselves, in order to banish from our heart any foreign thought, any bad intention, any false feeling of jealousy, hatred or pride, and also any feeling of trust in our own power.

This self-examination may lead to the discovery that one has wronged another person. This will call for genuine repentance and asking forgiveness from the one who was wronged.

Further practical aspects of preparation for prayer include giving charity to the poor, ensuring that one's clothes are physically clean, and achieving clearly focused *kavvanah* of the heart towards God. One should think of the meaning of the words one is saying.

---

[93] *Ibid.*, p. 85.

"Prayer should be filled with meaning, and be serious. Better to pray a little, with meaning, than a lot without." She then follows with a series of examples of biblical figures noted for prayer: Abraham, Hannah, Solomon at the Temple, Hezekiah, and so on.[94]

Here we see an intriguing mixture of simple directives and spiritual goals. Sarah Schenierer concludes:

> Now, my precious daughters, remember to be very careful with prayer. Pray much, and may your prayer be pure, with truth and with a full and pure heart. You with your warm prayers, and I with mine, we will ask God for a complete healing. But first we will prepare ourselves through *mizṿot* and good deeds.... May God swiftly send me healing, so that I can be together with you, working for the sake of the glory of God's blessed Name, till we merit the complete Redemption....[95]

Purity, intimacy, and seriousness; a sense of love from Sarah Schenierer to her 'daughters' and from them to her. Fueled by this kind of spiritual power, during the twenty years leading up to World War II, *Beit Yaakov* and her sister movements spread throughout Eastern Europe, attracting large numbers of Jewish girls to schools, Sabbath groups, summer holiday camps, and other activities.

Aḥot ha-Temimim

In the late 1930s there was a further advance in the discovery by girls of Jewish spirituality. Rabbi Yosef Yiẓḥak, the sixth Lubavitcher *Rebbe*, had been continuing the route set by his father, the fifth *Rebbe*, in marshalling women as a force for the strengthening of traditional Judaism.[96] A new development was that, in 1938, R. Yosef Yiẓḥak encouraged the establishment in Riga of *Aḥot ha-Temimim*, a society for girls and young women focusing on the study of Ḥabad

[94] *Ibid.*, pp. 86–90.
[95] *Ibid.*, pp. 89–90.
[96] See Ada Rappoport-Albert, "On Women in Ḥasidism" pp. 508–9, 523–4, n. 82.

ḥasidic teachings.[97] This was a completely new departure. For the most part, earlier rabbinic opinion which had favored teaching girls to study Jewish texts had shied away from the idea of teaching any form of mysticism.[98] There is some evidence that during the nineteenth century a few women from prominent Ḥabad families did have access to mystical ḥasidic teachings, but these were a very tiny handful. R. Yosef Yiẓḥak set up the *Aḥot ha-Temimim* group without apology, simply stating that for the authentic Ḥabad ḥasidim "there is no difference between a son or a daughter" and that, in contrast to conventional practice, one also has to teach girls "the paths of Ḥasidism."[99]

R. Yosef Yiẓḥak appointed three Rabbis as spiritual guides for the group. The program of instruction included discourses, those which make an inner demand (*maamarei avodah*) in particular. In addition, ḥasidic gatherings were to be held,[100] which would help in the internalization of the ḥasidic ethos, and would foster a sense of love and unity among the participants.[101] The members of the Riga *Aḥot ha-Temimim* group were expected not only to study, but also to spread ḥasidic ideals and the observance of practical *miẓvot*. They had the duty to translate (into Yiddish) and disseminate ḥasidic teachings, and to campaign for observance of the laws of family purity and other aspects of Judaism.[102] Thus spiritual study was combined with practical activism.

[97] See *Iggerot Kodesh...R. Yosef Yiẓḥak*, vol. 4, note by the editor (R. Shalom Ber Levin) on p. 62, giving a list of R. Yosef Yiẓḥak's letters relating to the setting up of this organization.

[98] See *Sefer Ḥasidim*, ed. R. Margoliot (Jerusalem: Mosad ha-Rav Kook, 1970), sec. 313.

[99] *Iggerot Kodesh...R. Yosef Yiẓḥak*, vol. 3, p. 469.

[100] *Iggerot Kodesh...R. Yosef Yiẓḥak*, vol. 4, p. 187. This letter also reprimands a father for not finding a way to satisfy his daughter's wish to study ḥasidic teachings.

[101] *Iggerot Kodesh...R. Yosef Yiẓḥak*, vol. 4, p. 391.

[102] *Ibid.*, p.391. The Yiddish letter on pp. 377–87 includes an essay on the theme of the spirituality of each Jew. It was sent to the Riga *Aḥot ha-Temimim* in order to be published and disseminated there (see the editor's note, p. 377). Regarding the demand for practical activism, see p. 385.

Chaya Sima Michaelover

In January 1939, R. Yosef Yiẓḥak sent a letter to Chaya Sima Michailover (or Michaelson), a member of this group, setting out a highly unusual system of meditation. Some time earlier she had been involved in translating a letter by R. Yosef Yiẓḥak from Hebrew to Yiddish.[103] In 1938 this Yiddish translation was published in Riga with the title "On the Moral and Educational Significance of Ḥabad Ḥasidism, a reply by the Lubavitcher Rebbe to a letter from Germany." It is helpful to consider the contents of this letter as providing a form of an introduction to Chaya Sima's spiritual path. In some ways, R. Yosef Yiẓḥak's tract on meditation, addressed directly to her, seems to function as a response to issues which are raised in this earlier letter which she translated.

The "letter from Germany," from a correspondent who has not been identified, asks R. Yosef Yiẓḥak how to bring about a spiritual rejuvenation for "assimilating and enlightened" German Jewish youth, for whom the Jewish religion is "dry", and inquires whether the ḥasidic teachings of Ḥabad could be used for this purpose.

R. Yosef Yiẓḥak's reply presents two contrasting features of the Ḥabad perspective on Judaism. On the one hand there is a strong insistence on the need for practical observance of the *miẓvot*, emphasizing the virtues of simplicity and purity of heart without any intellectualist ramifications. On the other, there is a striking depiction of early Ḥabad Ḥasidism as a path of intense, otherworldly spirituality. The Ḥabad followers of the first Ḥabad leader, R. Shneur Zalman, are described as "spending several hours of the day in *ḥitbodedut* [a term which usually means solitary meditative thought] for a number of days – and especially nights – of the week… each according to his ability."

What was this *hitbodedut*? R. Yosef Yiẓḥak continues:

[103] See the introduction to volume 4 of R. Yosef Yiẓḥak's letters, p. 12, n. 25. The Hebrew letter, dated Nisan 5696 (1936) is in *Iggerot…R. Yosef Yiẓḥak*, vol. 3 (Brooklyn: Kehot, 1983), pp. 532–542. It was published three months later in the Tammuz 5696 issue of *Ha-Tamim* p. 47 (189).

> This *hitbodedut* was not an affliction of the body, nor a melancholy penance, on the contrary, it was delightful for them in a remarkable way, effecting a spiritual joy and a sublime love.... Through this [*hitbodedut*], not only did they move away from the swamp of materiality, but they would ascend into a realm of purity and translucence where they would gaze at the beauty of the divine with a clarity of mind and understanding.[104]

R. Yosef Yiẓḥak goes on to say that some of these early *ḥasidim* lost all personal interest in worldly life; the fulfillment of their sexual responsibilities as married men became the expression of duty and "benevolence" towards their wives, rather than physical desire. These highly elevated *ḥasidim*, says R. Yosef Yiẓḥak, were few in number; but they had considerable influence on the other followers of R. Shneur Zalman, so that all the Ḥabad *ḥasidim* saw the essence of life as "Form overcoming Matter," *tigboret ha-ẓurah al ha-ḥomer*, the spiritual overcoming the physical.

R. Yosef Yiẓḥak writes that this slogan applies to each person according to his situation, "for every person should long for that which is beyond him, and should desire and yearn to rise from level to level in doing good, in thought, in speech, and in action, acquiring good personality traits, and [spiritual] ideas."

Continuing his description of the first generation of Ḥabad, R. Yosef Yiẓḥak goes on to say that this slogan influenced large numbers of both men and women. We will consider below the effect of this interesting comment. As regards the "assimilating and enlightened" Jewish youth of Germany, R. Yosef Yiẓḥak states that while the study of Ḥabad thought is open to them, with its implicit spiritual and otherworldly quest, a *sine qua non* is the practical observance of the *miẓvot*. Thus, says R. Yosef Yiẓḥak, although during the century and a half since the publication of R. Shneur Zalman's *Tanya* the teachings of Ḥabad had spread "world-wide," nonetheless

---

104 *Iggerot Kodesh...R. Yosef Yiẓḥak*, vol. 3, p. 539.

this study requires initial preparation of fear of Heaven and observance of the practical *miẓvot*, which are the basis of the Torah....

This proviso, which is emphasized again at the close of his letter, indicates that R. Yosef Yiẓhak was worried that Ḥabad thought, studied by contemporary German Jews, could easily be treated as a form of abstract philosophy, without being anchored in Jewish practice. It is interesting that in a second letter to the same recipient he does offer to enter into correspondence with anyone who wishes to inquire about Ḥabad teachings, implying that this offer stands regardless of that person's level of observance.[105] However the basic message is that full adherence to the practical *miẓvot* is expected before one embarks on the path of Ḥabad spirituality.

At this point we will not consider the implications of this text as regards the religious rejuvenation of westernized Jewish youth, nor the question of the nature of R. Yosef Yiẓhak's depiction of early Ḥabad Ḥasidism, particularly his inclusion of women in the spiritual quest. Rather, let us imagine the effect of this tract for Chaya Sima Michaelover, the young woman in Riga who is studying, translating, and publishing it in the late 1930s. There is the path of simple, dedicated *action* of the *miẓvot*; and there is another path, entailing *hitbodedut*, solitary meditative thought, the transcendence of material desires, and a constant yearning to rise higher. The text provides a teasing hint that this path might be relevant also for a woman.

A Tract on Meditation – For a Girl

At this point we can consider the direct personal communication between Chaya Sima and R. Yosef Yiẓhak. In January 1939, shortly after the publication of her translation of the letter from Germany, Chaya Sima wrote to him, asking "what should she do in order to fill the emptiness of actions?"

The background of the earlier text helps us understand the force

---

[105] *Ibid.*, pp. 543–4.

of this question. The Ḥabad path is being presented to her in a dual form: simple action of the *mizṿot*, contrasting with intense personal spirituality. Is she completely barred from the latter? Or is it in some way relevant to her? We can imagine her thinking: after all, the text did mention women. As an active member of *Aḥot ha-Temimim*, Chaya Sima no doubt fulfilled the preliminary requirement: she *did* observe the practical *mizṿot*. Yet she longed for more. Could she go further?

The *Rebbe* responded to her request with what amounts to a tract on contemplation in study, imparting a method to 'be bonded with the soul...with the essence' of the teaching one is studying, aiming to achieve an inner ethical transformation.[106] R. Yosef Yiẓḥak employs the term found in the letter to Germany: that Form should overcome Matter. According to that letter, this defined the general goal of Ḥabad Ḥasidism in its first generation. R. Yosef Yiẓḥak presents this to Chaya Sima as the goal for which she should strive.

At the same time he makes the claim that the contemplative system expounded in this tract would link the outermost level of the person, their performance of the *mizṿot* with the inner level, the point at which the soul delights in the unity of the mind with the idea, *iḥud ha-massig ve-ha-musag*.

R. Yosef Yiẓḥak dismisses conventional modes of traditional study which emphasize either covering a great quantity of material or focusing on detailed niceties of the text: why this word is written *plene* and another written defectively, or why a certain two words are juxtaposed. He recommends, by contrast, a mode of study in which one explores the same theme repeatedly, seeking to reach ever more profound levels within it or beyond it. The main content of the tract concerns the method for reaching these depths.

The basis of this method differs somewhat from the standard systems of Ḥabad contemplation, although it is based on a concept which is extensively employed in Ḥabad teachings:[107] the idea that the soul has three 'garments', namely Thought, Speech, and Ac-

---

[106] *Ibid.*, vol. 4, pp. 468–72.

[107] See *Tanya* I, ch. 4.

tion. This relates both to the theme of the garments of the soul in the Garden of Eden, after it leaves the world,[108] and to the concept that the spiritual worlds, *Beriah, Yeẓirah,* and *Asiyah* are 'garments' of the divine, which correspond to human thought, speech, and action.[109]

In R. Yosef Yiẓḥak's tract on meditation, the concept of the three garments of Thought, Speech, and Action is developed into a meditative system, one that is almost reminiscent of the Maggid's teachings, in which these three 'garments' of the soul function as a type of ladder ascending higher and higher. From Action one can ascend to Speech, and then to Thought, which is the most intimate garment. At each level, says R. Yosef Yiẓḥak, there is both 'radiance' and 'vessel.' The vessel of Action functions beyond the person; that of Speech is part of the person, but is revealed to others; that of Thought is part of the essence of the person and is concealed from others.[110] R. Yosef Yiẓḥak has thus presented a kind of mystical ladder, in some ways similar to the three worlds of *Asiyah*, *Yeẓirah*, *Beriah*, and like them, having both radiance and vessel. R. Yosef Yiẓḥak's system, based on earlier sources, introduces a further subtlety.[111]

This is that each level, in typical Lurianic form, includes each of the others. Thus while Thought is the highest level, within Thought there are Thought, Speech, and Action. One therefore seeks to ascend, not only to the level of Thought, but to that of 'Thought' within Thought.

To explain what this means R. Yosef Yiẓḥak introduces a further category: that of *otiyot*, 'Letters'. The letters – i.e. the words or language – express an idea, and function as the 'vessel' for the idea

---

[108] See Moshe Hallamish, "The Theoretical System of Rabbi Shneur Zalman of Liadi (Its Sources in Kabbalah and Ḥasidism)" (Hebrew), doctoral thesis at the Hebrew University, 1976, pp. 227–32. See also *Zohar* I 66a.

[109] Intro. to *Tikkunei Zohar*. See Rabbi Shneur Zalman, *Likkutei Torah*, *Vayeẓe*, 36a.

[110] *Iggerot Kodesh…R. Yosef Yiẓḥak* vol. 4, p. 470.

[111] Regarding the levels of 'Thought, Speech, and Action' of Thought depicted as ascending levels of spirituality, see *Tanya*, IV, sec.19, fol.129a. See also Rabbi Dov Ber of Mezeritch, *Maggid Devarav Le-Yaakov*, R. Schatz-Uffenheimer, ed. (Jerusalem: Magnes Press, 1976), sec. 90.

as it is conceived in the mind of the person. On the level of Action of Thought, the Letters can be 'felt,' they are *nirgashim*, tangible. On the higher level of Speech of Thought, the Letters are no longer tangible, but they are still 'recognizable,' *nikkarim*. On the still higher level of Thought of Thought, the Letters are no longer apparent at all. The person has reached the level of the pure radiance of the Concept, beyond any kind of verbal definition. At this point the person can achieve unity with the Concept as it really is, beyond any veil, bonding with "the Concept as it is in itself."[112]

R. Yosef Yiẓḥak speaks of the delight which is experienced through this form of meditation, which can be carried higher and higher, reaching not just Thought of Thought, but Thought of Thought of Thought, and so on. He suggests that, with practice, this meditative approach can be applied to everything one studies. Further, through this intellectualist form of meditation, an inner ethical transformation can also be achieved. The 'Concept' may concern the attempt to attain an ethical change. By uniting with the inner radiance of the Concept, that change is effected within the person in a genuine way.

It is interesting to note that R. Yosef Yiẓḥak indicates that, while one is ascending this spiritual ladder higher and higher towards the realm of Thought of Thought of Thought, the lowest level of Action is still relevant. The delight of one's union with the radiance at the highest level infuses and 'fills' even the level of Action.[113] Consequently, Action is extended into Action, Speech and Thought, an endless ladder reaching to the highest levels. This constitutes a direct response to Chaya Sima's question about 'filling the emptiness of action.'

This personal guidance from R. Yosef Yiẓḥak to a young woman teaching a method of spiritual meditation is possibly unique in the history of Jewish mysticism. The system presented in his letter to her differs from the standard systems of meditation in Ḥabad, although there are some points of similarity with a letter concerning contemplation which he sent in 1936 to a prominent follower from

---

[112] *Iggerot Kodesh...R. Yosef Yiẓḥak* vol. 4, pp. 470–2.

[113] R. Yosef Yiẓḥak cites the mystical concept of 'filling' a letter by writing it as if it were a word, thus *Alef* is *Alef, Lamed, Peh.*

Riga, Rabbi Haim Mordechai Hodakow.[114] It seems that this system was gradually evolving. The version of it presented to Chaya Sima in 1939 is the most complete form known. Did she put it into practice? Did she share the letter with other girls? Was there a group of female contemplatives? We do not know. In 1940 R. Yosef Yiẓḥak left Eastern Europe and reached the United States. There he continued to promote contemplative prayer in a variety of modes, including the visualization technique of R. Elimelekh of Lizhensk and R. Kalonymos Kalman Shapiro, imagining that one is in the Temple.[115] An *Aḥot ha-Temimim* girls' group had been set up in Brooklyn in 1938, studying *Tanya* and ḥasidic teachings with the esteemed *ḥasid* Rabbi Yoḥanan Gordon. This was a step towards the contemporary Lubavitch girls' schools where mystical ḥasidic teachings are on the curriculum.

Approaching the Border

How close are these developments to the halakhic border? Do they cross it? The question of the halakhic permissibility of women studying Torah – despite the well known adverse comment in the Talmud[116] – has been widely discussed.[117] Our focus will be on material which directly pertains to the subject in hand. The main halakhic position was briefly summarized by Rabbi Moshe Isserlis in his gloss on Rabbi Yosef Karo's *Shulḥan Arukh*. Commenting on the latter's strictures on study by women, with the partial exception of the Written Torah (following Maimonides), R. Moshe Isserlis adds: "nonetheless a woman is duty-bound to study the laws which apply

[114] *Iggerot Kodesh…R. Yosef Yiẓḥak*, vol. 3, p. 525–6. R. Hodakow later became the personal secretary of R. Yosef Yiẓḥak's successor, R. Menahem Mendel Schneerson.

[115] See *Iggerot Kodesh…R. Yosef Yiẓḥak*, vol. 8, p. 200. There was some contact between R. Yosef Yiẓḥak and R. Kalonymos Kalman. In 1933 the latter was a signatory, together with seventeen other prominent Polish ḥasidic leaders, to a *Kol Koreh* letter organized by R. Yosef Yiẓḥak on behalf of the Jews of Russia (*Iggerot Kodesh…R. Yosef Yiẓḥak*, vol. 11, p. 219).

[116] BT *Sotah* 21b. See below.

[117] See Shoshana Pantel Zolty, *"And All Your Children Shall Be Learned": Women and the Study of Torah in Jewish Law and History* (Northvale, NJ: Jason Aronson, 1993).

to a woman."[118] In the late eighteenth century this statement was amplified by the founder of Ḥabad, R. Shneur Zalman of Liadi, in his *Laws of Torah Study* (Shklov: 1794). After stating the well-known strictures against women studying Torah, Rabbi Shneur Zalman continues:

> And nonetheless, women too are duty bound to study the *halakhot* which apply to them, such as the laws of *niddah* and immersing [in the *mikveh*], kashering [meat], the prohibition of *yiḥud* and similar. And all Positive Commandments...which are not affected by time, and all Negative Commands of the Torah and the Sages, which apply equally to them as to men.[119]

This extensive syllabus primarily seems to concern practical law, although there is an anecdote about Rabbi Shneur Zalman imparting ḥasidic teachings to his daughter Frieda.[120] Over a century later, R. Israel Meir Kagan extended the range of women's studies to include rabbinic ethical and inspirational teachings, with an explanation of why this was necessary. Commenting on *Sotah* 21b ("any who teaches his daughter Torah is considered as if he taught her lewdness") he first presents, according to the strict *halakhah*, the areas of the Oral Torah which a woman is duty-bound to study in order properly to conduct her life – *niddah*, *ḥallah*, Shabbat candles, and *kashrut*. As for the Written Law, although in the first place this should not be taught to a woman, if it is, it is not considered 'lewdness.'

This, however, is followed by a further statement relating to the exigencies of modernity:

---

[118] *Shulḥan Arukh: Yoreh De'ah* 246:6. This reflects statements by earlier scholars. See Zolty (previous note), pp. 61–2.

[119] R. Shneur Zalman of Liadi, *Hilkhot Talmud Torah* (Brooklyn: Kehot, 1968), 1:14, fol. 11a. He cites as sources R. Yiẓḥak of Corbeil's *Sefer Miẓvot Katan* and R. Yaakov Landau's *Agur*.

[120] H.M. Heilman, *Beit Rebbe* (Tel Aviv, n.d.; photog. rep. of Berditchev, 1902), p. 114.

> All this applied in earlier times when everyone lived in the same place as did their forebears, and the tradition of one's forebears was very firm for each individual, guiding one's behavior.... In this case we could say that she should not study Torah but should rely on the guidance of her righteous parents. But today, through our sins, when the tradition from one's forebears is extremely weak, and it is also common that a person does not live at all in their locale, and especially as regards those girls who are taught to read non-Jewish writings, it is certainly a great *mizvah* to teach them Pentateuch and the Prophets and Writings, and the ethical teachings of the Sages such as Tractate *Avot, Menorat ha-Maor,*[121] and the like in order that they should internalize our sacred faith [*she-yitamet ezlam inyan emunatenu ha-kedoshah*]. For if not, it is likely that they will turn away completely from the Divine path and transgress all the basic laws of Judaism, God forbid.[122]

In these terms R. Kagan vigorously defended Torah study for women. This contrasts with the attitude of the leading exponent of Hungarian Orthodoxy, Rabbi Joel Teitelbaum of Satmar (1886–1979). The latter totally opposed *Beit Yaakov,*[123] on the grounds of traditional strictures against women studying Torah and also the concern that knowledge of Hebrew could lead to Zionism.[124] In 1930, R. Kagan delivered a sermon to an exclusively female audience in the Great Synagogue in Vilna, an unprecedented event.[125] In 1932, he

---

[121] By Rabbi Yizhak Aboab, fourteenth cent., a famous work of religious edification based on aggadic literature.

[122] R. Israel Meir Kagan, *Likkutei Halakhot* (Jerusalem, n.d.), to BT *Sotah* 21b, ch. 3, fol. 11a–b. This was first published in 1918.

[123] See Y.M. Sofer, ed., *Divrei Yoel: Mikhtavim*, vol. 1 (Brooklyn, 1980), p. 49.

[124] See Rabbi Teitelbaum's *Va-Yoel Moshe* (Brooklyn: 1961; 5th edition, 1978), *Maamar Leshon ha-Kodesh*, secs. 37–39. However, see also sec. 33 which encourages study of the practicalities of Jewish law and ethics.

[125] See Rappoport-Albert, "On Women in Ḥasidism," p. 524 n. 82, citing M.M. Yoshor, *He-Ḥafez Ḥayyim, Ḥayav u-Fo'alo*, vol. 2 (Tel Aviv, 1959), pp. 506–12.

wrote approvingly of the founding of a *Beit Yaakov* school in Pristik. He writes that, due to the prevailing atmosphere of secularism:

> Anyone whose heart is concerned about Fear of God is duty bound to send his daughter to study in that school. All the doubts and queries about the prohibition of teaching one's daughter Torah have no place in our time.... In previous times every Jewish home had the firm tradition from male and female forebears, to walk in the path of Torah and piety, and [for women] to read from the book *Ẓe'enah u-Re'enah*[126] every Shabbat, which is not the case in our time....[127]

However, the question of Torah study for women remained an issue, even in *Beit Yaakov* circles. Deborah Weissman reports on discussions in the pages of the *Beit Yaakov* journal of 1930. One writer recommended study of Torah for girls only in small doses, when the girl is fairly mature, and when the study can lead to good deeds and to becoming a better wife and mother.[128] However, in a later issue of the journal, this view was countered by Mordecai Bromberg, an author of Jewish history textbooks used in the *Beit Yaakov* schools, who expressed surprise that the issue was even raised.[129]

Despite this, and notwithstanding the post-war growth of the *Beit Yaakov* movement, today there are still ongoing discussions in magazines and in Gerer ḥasidic female study groups (conducted by, and largely comprising, *Beit Yaakov* graduates) about the legitimacy of Torah study for women and where it is intended to lead, as is documented by Tamar El-Or in her study of the women living in a Tel Aviv Gerer ḥasidic community.[130]

---

[126] A famous Yiddish collection of aggadic commentary on the Pentateuch, first published in Lublin at the beginning of the seventeenth century, much studied by pious women in Eastern Europe.

[127] R. Israel Meir Kagan, *Mikhtavim u-Maamarim* vol. 2, ed. Z.H. Zaks (Jerusalem, 1990), p. 97.

[128] Weissman, Master's Thesis, p. 91, citing *Beit Yaakov Journal*, no. 49.

[129] Weissman, *ibid.*, citing *Beit Yaakov Journal*, no. 52.

[130] El-Or, *Educated and Ignorant*, pp. 75–9, 89–133.

Thus far we have considered only study of halakhic, aggadic, and ethical teachings. What about Ḥabad mystical teachings, with their kabbalistic foundation, and intensely spiritual practices, such as the meditative system taught by R. Yosef Yiẓḥak to Chaya Sima Michaelover?

While R. Yosef Yiẓḥak, in his organizational activities, letters, and other writings,[131] outspokenly campaigned for Torah education for women, he did not attempt to provide this with a specific halakhic underpinning other than reference to the past practice of Ḥabad leaders.[132] In 1954, his son-in-law and successor, R. Menahem Mendel Schneerson, presented a novel halakhic basis for the idea that girls should study R. Shneur Zalman's *Tanya*, and by implication, other Ḥabad mystical teachings.

This is based on the halakhic principle that a woman should study enough to enable her to observe the laws which apply to her. R. Menahem Mendel comments that these include the six commandments listed in the thirteenth-century treatise *Sefer ha-Ḥinukh* which apply continuously to every man and woman. These are: to believe in God, not to believe in any power apart from Him, to appreciate His Unity, to love Him, to fear Him, and not to stray after one's desires.[133]

R. Menahem Mendel claims that these spiritual attainments are facilitated by ḥasidic teachings. Hence, he states, "also according to the *Shulḥan Arukh* the woman has a duty to study this portion of the Torah." Consequently, and based also on R. Yosef Yiẓḥak's prior example with the *Aḥot ha-Temimim* group, R. Menahem Mendel

[131] See, for example, his *Lubavitcher Rebbe's Zikhroines* (Brooklyn: Kehot, 1965), vol. 2, pp. 135, 168–172, telling of traditions concerning the Torah study of women in the ancestry of the Ḥabad leadership. These anecdotes, which have an obvious contemporary pedagogic intent, were first published in the *Morgen Zhurnal* Yiddish newspaper in the early 1940s. See Ada Rapoport-Albert, "Hagiography with Footnotes: Edifying Tales and the Writing of History in Ḥasidism", in *History and Theory* (Beiheft 27, Wesleyan University, 1988), pp. 119–59.

[132] See his *Iggerot Kodesh…R. Yosef Yiẓḥak*, vol. 3 (Brooklyn: Kehot, 1983), p. 469, stating that in 1879 the fourth generation Lubavitch leader, Rabbi Shemuel (1834–1882), publicly called for increased teaching of "the ways of *ḥasidut*" for girls.

[133] This list appears in the author's preface.

advised the head of the Lubavitch Seminary in Yerres, Paris, who had written with a practical question on this topic, that it is correct to teach *Tanya* to the more advanced female students, and gave advice on how to do so.[134]

The effect of this and similar guidance from R. Menahem Mendel is that in the contemporary Lubavitch educational system, girls are encouraged to study *Tanya* and other Ḥabad ḥasidic teachings and discourses, as well as other areas of the Oral Law.[135] All this can be seen as within the purview of the statement quoted above by R. Kagan, that education of girls should enable them to internalize the sacred faith of Judaism.

A TIME TO ACT...

The history of the traditional European Jewish community's scholars' and leaders' confrontation with modernity, is a fertile field of exploration. One approach taken by Jewish thinkers, including Rabbi Samson Raphael Hirsch, Rabbi J.B. Soloveitchik, and many scholars of Orthodox "*Wissenschaft*," was an apparent quest for an interface of Jewish thought with modern ideals. A rather different path was the creation of a Jewish 'sanctified' enclave signified by a dress code, a distinctive language (Yiddish), and an attention to certain specific details of halakhic practice. In general, this was the route taken by Hungarian Orthodoxy, and, eventually, by most branches of the ḥasidic movement.

In this paper an attempt has been made to investigate another dimension of Ḥasidism in its response to modernity: the reaching into the resources of its own history, and indeed the history of Judaism, for a re-emergence of the personal spiritual quest and experience. This meant the taking of steps that could be considered unconventional, unwise, or even forbidden. Yet the steps were made nonetheless, and were given their own rationale within the context

---

[134] *Iggerot Kodesh... R. Menahem Mendel*, vol. 8 (Brooklyn: Kehot, 1988), pp. 133–4. R. Schneerson recommends not teaching the work in the order it is written, but beginning with the easier sections of the book and with those that relate more directly to the *avodah* of the student, to her personal service of God.

[135] See Zolty, "*And All Your Children*" (n. 58 above), pp. 83–6.

of *halakhah* and the equally vibrant *aggadah*. We thus see again a sequence which has occurred a number of times in the history of Judaism: through crisis and danger that threatens survival, a new advance is made. In the case we have been considering, what this meant is that the secularizing process of modernity provoked some leaders of traditional Judaism to draw on the resources of Jewish spirituality, hitherto restricted primarily to an intellectual male elite, and make them available to both young men and young women, strengthening their commitment to Judaism in a time of change.

13

Without Intelligence, Whence Prayer?

Shalom Carmy

If he forgot it was Shabbat and continued as on weekdays… he should complete the blessing ḥonen ha-daat ("who endows with intelligence"). This is in accordance with the opinion of Rabbi, who said: "I wonder how they could eliminate ḥonen ha-daat on Shabbat. If there is no intelligence, whence prayer?"

(Jerusalem Talmud)[1]

Truly it is not only in man's material ambitions, in which he resembles the beast, that he requires the Torah's measures to circumscribe and order them, but also for his lofty spiritual ambitions, including the foundations and ramifications of prayer, he requires the limits and appraisal of the Torah….

[1] JT *Berakhot* 4:4 (34b).

> *Therefore it is improper for a man hastily to abandon occupation in Torah for the sake of prayer.*
>
> (Rabbi Abraham Isaac Kook)[2]

> *I don't believe in artificial nostrums. Much is affected by the religious atmosphere, suffused with superficial instrumentalism; much is due to the tendency towards ceremonialization – which is, at times, vulgarization, of religion; and much is brought about by the lack of a serious capacity for introspection and examination of the world and oneself.*
>
> (Rabbi Joseph Dov Soloveitchik)[3]

Few human enterprises, leaving aside for the moment those we share with our fellow animals, are as universal as prayer. Common human experiences impel us to worship a Being beyond our comprehension, to praise what we admire, to express our needs in hope of their satisfaction, to be grateful for benefactions received, to cry out in pain and remorse before the One who can ease and reconcile our distress. Yet rarely are our fellow human beings as opaque to us as in the activity of prayer. Reciting our way through the same words and paragraphs as our neighbors, whether alone or in unison, silent or shouting, their thoughts and motives remain firmly closed to us.

Hardly less obscure to us are our own thoughts and motives. For observant Jews, routine is surely one of the motives, and obligation is surely present in our thoughts. Both fully observant Jews and more transient worshippers cherish the hope that prayer will do them some good as well, that it will leave us happier, more elevated in spirit, and more at peace with ourselves. Frequently we enter into the words themselves, as we are instructed to: we perform the gestures of praise, petition, and thanksgiving mapped out in the *Amidah*; we accept the yoke of God and His commandments when reading *Shema*; we confess specific sins and ask for His forgiveness.

---

[2] *Olat Reiyah* (Jerusalem: Mossad ha-Rav Kook, 1948), I, 21.

[3] "On the Love of Torah and Redemption of the Generation's Soul," in *Be-Sod ha-Yaḥid ve-ha-Yaḥad* (Jerusalem: Orot, 1976), p. 419.

And when we enter into the words we are reciting, as part of our entering into the holy words of the prayer, we set aside many of our imaginings of the good we hope for, concentrating instead on the requests and expressions spelled out in the prayers themselves.

Prayer is thus an endeavor that baffles both the categories of the transparently public and the intimately private. Just as surely, prayer, both in its narrow definition as the *Amidah*, and in the broader usage that coincides with the *Siddur*, challenges the distinction between religion as a mode of seeking to satisfy our own desires, however elevated, and religion as the service of the heart, offered up to God in response to His demand, liberated from any aspiration to reward. On the one hand, Jewish prayer is a miẓvah among others, circumscribed by external gesture, performed at regular times, and in a set order. On the other hand, prayer is meaningless unless it wells from the depths of the heart, while standing in the presence of the living God.

Metaphysical dialectic engenders sociological paradox. Even those modern Jews who often complacently settle for the lowest common denominator of halakhic observance, may yet, with urgent pangs of emptiness and regret, rue a desultory *Amidah* as an irretrievable opportunity for spiritual growth, unaccountably squandered. At the same time, we witness individuals and entire congregations, ostensibly committed to maximal halakhic achievement, who are, most of the time, oddly and even militantly lax in their conduct with respect to prayer, awakening periodically to the same burden of guilt and shame that affects their more liberal brethren. Unlike other "duties of the heart," prayer is too ubiquitous and public a feature of our lives to permit perpetual evasion and self-deception. Failure is too frequent to protect our ease of mind. For precisely when our *need* for prayer is greatest, the staleness of a myriad indolent recitations rises to the tongue like heartburn; neglect sputters in our spiritual arteries like rusty water in a disused pump.

Can thinking about prayer improve the quality of our prayer? Why not? One reason that thought about prayer might interfere with prayer is that the two are distinct activities. Praying is praising, petitioning, thanking, and so forth. Thinking about prayer is philosophizing. The contradiction is as patent as Yogi Berra's famous contention that you can't hit and think at the same time. Commenting on R. Hamnuna's dictum that "the time of Torah is separate from the time for prayer" (BT *Shabbat* 10a), R. Kook asserts that Torah provides man with novel intellectual insights. By contrast, "prayer deals not with the discovery of new knowledge and the enrichment of the human intellect with their truth, but with the utilization of already attained knowledge, and to deepen through the power of feeling the imprint of moral knowledge on the powers of the soul."[4] In a narrower connection, commenting on the Mishnah's condemnation of the individual who calls upon God to have mercy on us as on the bird's nest of Deuteronomy 22:6, R. Kook insists on the inappropriateness of introducing theological fine points into the text of prayer: "One is confusing, by calculations of profound wisdom and speculating on reasons for the *mizvot*, the majestic feeling that should be natural and simple and whole-hearted in prayer."[5]

A more sweeping objection to the intellectualization of prayer, in our time, is expressed by Rabbi Adin Steinsalz. What *kavvanah* (intention) do you have when you pray, he asks a prominent *Rosh Yeshiva*: what do you actually think about? And when the scholar replies that he contemplates "the connection between the sentences, the words, the various sections…" says Steinsalz, "I snapped that this is something to do on Shabbat afternoon after the *cholent*."[6] It is treating the prayer as a text to be analyzed rather than an utterance to be appropriated and expressed. The illusion that this scholarship is *kavvanah* becomes an obstacle to genuine prayer.

It is easy for those familiar with these pitfalls, and for others who take for granted a romantic critique of cerebration, to condemn intellectual work as a death of the heart, in the spirit of Wordsworth's "we murder to dissect." And yet, as the *Yerushalmi* states, "if there

---

[4] *Olat Reiyah*, I, 20. Cf. *Ein Ayah* to BT *Shabbat* 10a.

[5] *Ein Ayah* I, BT *Berakhot* 5:104, with respect to the colloquy between Rabba and Abbaye. *Tosafot Yom Tov ad. loc.* ascribes to Rashi a view anticipating R. Kook's.

[6] *Ha-Tefillah ha-Yehudit: Hemshekh ve-Ḥiddush* ed. Gabriel H. Cohn (Ramat Gan: 1978), p. 210.

is no intelligence, whence prayer?" Feelings do not exist separate from the beliefs with which they are bound inextricably. Words take on their significance within the framework of larger verbal structures and rituals. We would not dream of launching into a speech of crucial import without a prior grasp of its structural unfolding and social context. To do so would achieve not an eloquent spontaneity, but a gibbering muddle. No more can one undertake to pray without knowing the order and significance of the *seder ha-tefillot*, without appreciating the intention that our words endeavor to encompass. All this requires familiarity and depth, not ignorance and thoughtlessness. You can't philosophize or halakhicize and simultaneously pray – but you can make yourself ready, and clear the intellectual and experiential space in which *tefillah* can happen.

R. Kook and R. Soloveitchik, the master thinkers of Torah Judaism in our age, both devoted a considerable portion of their theological and halakhic work to prayer. What distinguishes them from their medieval predecessors is their commitment to intellectual reflection as a means of overcoming modern man's alienation from authentic prayer. Their explicit goal is not only to understand prayer as a halakhic and religious phenomenon, or to contribute to the elucidation of philosophical conundrums relating to prayer. They are at least as concerned to evoke the nature of *tefillah* in a manner that will initiate and enhance its proper, heartfelt performance. If, recognizing as we do the gap between thinking about prayer and actually praying, we hope to harness the former in the service of the latter, we are fortunate to resort to their pages and enter into their preocupations.

Our task in this paper is to look at a variety of ways in which the study of prayer is useful, or essential, to a satisfactory, and satisfying, practice of prayer. We will frequently appeal to the work of R. Kook and R. Soloveitchik and, when necessary, attempt to confront, and to surmount, unresolved barriers to the translation of their ideas from paper to experience. It is not my purpose in this paper to report a typical cross section of these thinkers' rich, inexhaustible creativity in this area, or to undertake the detailed line-by-line analysis that their texts often reward. The selection of examples and problems reflects my own concerns – the difficulty in summoning up spontaneity, the advantages and pitfalls of intellectual reflection, the tension between the intimate and the public faces of prayers, the coexistence of the stormy, vigorous life of prayer, and the desire for inner peace through prayer. Nonetheless I hope that my obsessions, filtered through the experience of the great twentieth century interpreters of prayer, will strike a chord in my readers' hearts.

I. DARING TO START – SPONTANEITY AND COMPULSION

Immediately one acknowledges the vacuity of soulless prayer the Satan, as it were, rubs his hands in glee and breaks into a filibustering jig. For how can we address God from within our present torpor? Must one not first attain the proper state of mind, and only then pray? First, then, pray for *kavvanah*. But in order to pray for *kavvanah*, one must already possess the requisite second-order *kavvanah*. Yet this too is elusive unless one has already started along the road that leads to God. The result of this infinite regress is either a paralysis of despair or a comedy of Sartrean *mauvais foi* in which the individual tries very hard to coincide with his, or her, role, down to the physical exertions and facial contortions, but succeeds only in pretending to become what one wants to be. Self-consciousness, it would seem, sucks us deeper and deeper into the spiritual quicksand. Mindless behavioral conformity suddenly looks like a tolerable, albeit unattractive, solution.

Viewed superficially, the psychological obstruction becomes greater in the light of R. Soloveitchik's teaching that *tefillah* requires a *mattir*, meaning that we are permitted to pray only because God has commanded us to pray, and that our speech is acceptable to Him only because the words of prayer are provided for us by Scripture. The difficulty of beginning is compounded by the belief that, in ourselves, we are unworthy to approach God, and that the infinite qualitative distance between man and God is bridged, not in fellowship, but only through the experience of being commanded.

At a deeper level, however, the Rav's doctrine, which seems to impede *tefillah*, ends up facilitating it. Despite our unworthiness, we know that infinite God, for reasons that may well be incomprehensible to us, has chosen to require our prayer, and to hear our personal, self-interested petitions as the fulfillment of His command. We also know that our predecessors, men and women whom we cannot hope to emulate, have cleared the way before us. Prayer, therefore, is not merely an imposition on God's attention, as it were, or an absurd raid on His inarticulable and immeasurable exaltation. It is a duty that we cannot shirk. Imperative thunder casts out inhibition.

By the same token, the knowledge that prayer is a privilege, a psychological necessity that yet is not a right, precludes treating prayer as a casual activity. At the root of our inability to pray seriously we often find an inability to take ourselves seriously, to honor our genuine needs, our joys, our troubles and devotions, as worthy of our own solemn concern. The Rav's insistence that we recognize the tremor of unworthiness, the compulsory invitation that underlies our engagement in prayer, is thus of a piece with his stress on the vigorous, honest assertion of one's needs before Him. Knowing that one requires, and is endowed with, a divine summons to prayer, becomes the starting point for the prayerful enterprise.

The difficulty of initiating prayer is implicitly met by one of R. Kook's key concepts: "the perpetual prayer of the soul."[7] According to R. Kook, the soul ever expresses itself in prayer, even when the prayer is subterranean, so to speak, and surreptitious. Worship of God through Torah and wisdom is a disclosure of this concealed prayer. Actual prayer is its realization, which R. Kook compares to the opening of a flower towards the dew or towards the sun. The prolonged absence of prayer with *kavvanah* causes blockage in the flow of prayer, and this deficiency mends only gradually with the renewal of unobstructed channels. Yet R. Kook cherishes the idea of incessant, unconscious prayer. Proper prayer, he states, "can only arise from the thought that the soul truly prays perpetually."

Why is the belief in unconscious, pre-conscious prayer so important for R. Kook? In the context of the passage under discussion,

---

[7] *Olat Reiyah*, I, 11.

the most plausible explanation is that prayer's constancy identifies the rhythm of worship with the unbroken cadence of the cosmos. Prayer is natural to man and to the universe of which he is a part. At the same time, the prayer that hums through our bodies without interruption ought not to be vulnerable to the metaphysical stutter that threatens to prevent the individual from getting started.

The institution of Psalm 51:17 ("God, open my lips...") as the obligatory preamble to the *Amidah* makes the prayer for prayerfulness part of the prayer itself. R. Soloveitchik's emphasis on the integral place of this verse in the *Amidah* may thus offer a halakhic parallel to the phenomenology we have just derived from R. Kook. The recitation of this verse, acknowledging that our lips open in prayer only when God graciously opens them, inaugurates the prayer itself.

Contrary to the popular notion that informal prayer is more fluent and more authentic, our previous discussion points to the conclusion that a fixed, formal liturgy serves better to counteract the danger of self-conscious paralysis. It goes without saying that genuine participation in an orderly, structured ritual presupposes, at the very least, a tacit understanding of the words, gestures, and shape of the activity.

Standard Jewish worship follows a fixed text. While an Anglican like C.S. Lewis, who tackles the problem of getting started in the first chapter of his *Letters to Malcolm, Chiefly on Prayer*, appreciates the value of an established text in averting meandering, stillborn prayer, we ordinarily associate a proclivity for impromptu prayer, audible and public, with a certain kind of Protestant piety. When Jews get "spiritual," we often perceive this, not always incorrectly, as a rejection of traditional Jewish prayer and a hankering for emotional outpourings we stigmatize as Christian. Above all, as a preference for a framework that does not place so much weight on experiencing the liturgy as it stands, with all its structural and linguistic depth and sophistication.

It is natural that we lament such tendencies as reflexes of ignorance and intellectual shallowness, and that we combat the separation of thought from feeling through lines of reasoning like those utilized throughout this essay. It is even easier to caricature a Christianity of unctuous tones and pious swagger; the preachy hectoring that bullies a congregation while poking an argumentative finger in the divine solar plexus, as it were; the unguarded silliness and the inevitable theological solecisms.[8]

Nevertheless, the Christian practice of formulating prayer spontaneously and out loud, forces the individual to take responsibility for his or her petitions, whatever the embarrassing or unfortunate results. By contrast, the Jew, or any other devotee of a set liturgy, who is unready to fully appropriate the text, is liable to relinquish personal identification with the words that he, or she, utters, and to merge completely into the anonymous gray mumble of civic routine.

Profound tensions run through our spiritual lives in general, and our experience of prayer in particular: tensions between formal structure and untutored spontaneity; between the discriminating consciousness and the unleashing of raw spiritual energy; between the individual and the community; between intimacy and public accessibility. Before continuing our discussion, let me take the liberty of quoting a passage from a contemporary work of fiction. The early sections of David Duncan's novel, *The Brothers K*, depict a family of Seventh Day Adventists some forty years ago. In the following scene, children are invited to improvise prayer at Sunday school. The irrepressible volunteer, as usual, is a hare-lipped girl. Keeping before us her effusion, and the narrator's reaction, may help us to recall how much is at stake in our philosophical exploration of the subject, how startling, wondrous, and terrifying:

> "*Nyelp us to nlove nyou nmore and nmore!*" she prays as Micah laughs outright, "*and nmore and nmore!*" she pleads as girls grab Kleenex, "*and snill nyet nmore!*" she begs as boys fizz up and overflow like jostled bottles of pop. "*Nenter our narts!*"

[8] Do not think that these pitfalls have escaped the notice of Protestant thinkers. See, for example, the introduction to Stanley Hauerwas's volume of *Prayers Plainly Spoken* (Downers Grove, IL: InterVarsity Press, 1999).

> she cries, her voice breaking, her body trembling so violently it makes my chair tremble too. *"Nenter nthem now! Nright now! Nwee are nso nlost, nso nvery nlost, nwithout nThee!"* And even as it occurs to me that this must be *real* prayer – even as I see that what is being laughed at is the sound of someone actually ramming a heartfelt message past all the crossed signals and mazes of our bodies, brains and embarrassments clear on in to her God – when I open my fists I see a face so exposed, so twisted with love, grief and longing, that if she was my sister I would take off my coat, and I'd wrap her up and hold her, and I would beg her never, ever to do this naked, passionate, impossible thing again.[9]

II. HOW DOES REFLECTION HELP?

The exposed face, whose prayer we have just listened in on, belongs to an unsophisticated child, though one should not underestimate how much her vocabulary and cadences owe to the grown ups. As R. Soloveitchik often reminded us, the authentic religious personality never stops identifying with the immediacy of the child's experience.[10] Yet our perspective cannot help but expand towards a greater complexity. On the one hand, our mature emotional palette is, or should be, more variegated and subtle than the child's. On the other hand, perhaps for that very reason, the connection between emotional life and ritual response is less vivid. When, at times, the adult posture towards the world becomes, not childlike, but positively childish, jaded and immature at once, one wonders whether any emotional vitality subsists that can be redeemed in the name of religion. Pampered, worldly wise souls are calloused and anesthetized, in a way that keeps out the love and grief and longing. While underneath the hardness and the haze a mute discomfort reigns, that is to the love, grief, and longing of the striving spirit, like chronic nausea to an athlete's honest agony.

---

[9] David J. Duncan, *The Brothers K*, (New York: Doubleday, 1992), p. 8.

[10] E.g. "On the Love of Torah and the Redemption of the Generation's Soul," pp. 412f.

To overcome this order of spiritual numbness means both to make the individual emotionally sensitive and to refine his, or her, intellect. Early in his *Idea of the Holy*, Rudolf Otto invited the reader to direct his mind to moments of deeply felt religious experience. "Whoever cannot do this," he continues, "is requested to read no farther; for it is not easy to discuss questions of religious psychology with one who can recollect the emotions of his adolescence, the discomforts of indigestion, or, say, social feelings, but cannot recall any intrinsically religious feelings."[11] From a halakhic standpoint, such an ultimatum is ruled out by the obligatory urgency of prayer. The elements of human experience presupposed by prayer must be accessible to the average human being. They cannot be limited to the inner world of the religious virtuoso.

The hallmark of R. Soloveitchik's work on prayer is his full commitment to the double challenge we have outlined. From below, as it were, he has demonstrated that the ladder of prayer can indeed be pitched where all ladders start, in the perennial occupations of the heart. Regarding prayer, as in other areas, R. Soloveitchik was not embarrassed by the fact that the ordinary believer comes to God with mixed motives.[12] Unlike the mystics, he championed a straightforward interpretation of petitionary prayer and its central place in *tefillah*. God has commanded us to request His help with respect to our mundane needs; there is no reason to salvage the ingredient of self-seeking in this by re-describing our entreaties as disguised moves in an occult metaphysical exercise whose true object is the *shekhinah* rather than the speaker.[13] Against the blander apostles of spiritual uplift, he does not shy away from confronting human

---

[11] Otto, *The Idea of the Holy,* trans. J. Harvey (Oxford: Oxford University Press, 1958), chapter 3, p. 8.

[12] See *U-Vikashtem mi-Sham* in *Ish ha-Halakha: Galuy ve-Nistar* (Jerusalem: World Zionist Organization, 1979), p. 160: "The fact that the antithetical experience of love and fear, the flight to God and the flight from God, is rooted in biological nature and in the human psychosomatic state, does not diminish its value and importance."

[13] Of course R. Kook is more attuned to the mystical outlook. See our discussion below, Section IV.

sinfulness, in all its ugliness, as a real setting in which the struggle for holiness takes place.

The building blocks of *tefillah* – praise, petition, gratitude – and the other components of the liturgy, correspond to universal human experiences. Consciousness of depth crises, which is important to the Rav's conception of petition, would seem to require special sensitivity, insofar as this type of crisis does not force itself upon the sufferer willy-nilly, as does a disease or famine, but requires some degree of reflective liveliness. Yet R. Soloveitchik believes that a consideration of boredom, shame, and other general human experiences, provides the needed awareness.[14] No doubt he would endorse the second reason for understanding prayer as petition offered by Karl Barth (with whom the Rav also shares the emphasis on prayer as a commandment): "only in this way is there any safeguard that the real man comes before God in prayer."[15]

The other facet of the Rav's treatment of prayer consists of his elaboration of its halakhic structure and import. *Halakhah* confirms and molds the subtlety and nuance of the prayerful life. Where the uninitiated turns the pages of the *siddur,* indiscriminately wending his or her way from the beginning of the proceedings to the end, the *halakhah* establishes a fixed, meaningful order. As we all know, the *Amidah* is not a jumble of benedictions, but rather a

---

[14] These ideas are developed most systematically in his *Worship of the Heart* ed. S. Carmy, (Hoboken, NJ: Ktav, 2002), chap. 3.

[15] Karl Barth, *Church Dogmatics* III: 4 (tr. Bromiley and Torrance (Edinburgh: T. and T. Clark, 1961) §53, p.98. Some Jewish thinkers (e.g. R. Aharon Kotler, *Mishnat Rabbi Aharon* [Jerusalem: Machon Mishnat Rabbi Aharon, 1982] Volume I, 83ff) have presented the idea that prayer is a privilege rather than a right, without drawing any systematic conclusion. The detailed similarities and differences between the Rav's discussion of prayer and Barth's would make a worthwhile topic for further inquiry, precisely because of the interconnection between the themes. On their respective theories of theological language, against the background of German philosophy, see B. Ish-Shalom, "Language as a Religious Category in the Thought of Rabbi Y.D. Soloveitchik," in *Sefer ha-Yovel la-Rav Mordekhai Breuer*, ed. Mosheh Bar Asher (Jerusalem: Akademon, 1992), pp. 799–821, and Graham Ward, *Barth, Derrida, and the Language of Theology* (Cambridge: Cambridge University Press, 1995), chapter 1.

sequence in which petition must be prefaced by praise and sealed with thanksgiving; the connection of the *Amidah* with the preceding *Shema*, linking redemption and prayer, is likewise essential to the encounter prescribed by *halakhah*.

R. Soloveitchik expanded and deepened such insights. Thus, for instance, *Pesukei de-Zimra* and *Hallel* are not merely two series of Psalms that play a part in different segments of weekday or festival worship. The former is essentially an act of scriptural study, which consists in reading Psalms 145–150, inculcating a theological message about God the Creator that prepares the individual for the main part of the morning service. The latter is the fulfillment of the obligation to extol God on special occasions, which uses Psalms 113–118 as its text; the meaning of the act is praise and thanksgiving, not the fact that sections of Scripture are being read. This fundamental difference is reflected in the different opening and closing benedictions for the two recitals as well as in other details.[16] Or, to take another example, thanksgiving (*hodaah*) appears in the *Amidah* and in *birkat ha-mazon*. In the former, the benediction is accompanied by bowing; in the latter, bowing is inappropriate. Why? Because the expression of gratitude in the *Amidah* takes place in the context of prayer, which entails submission to God, hence bowing. In *birkat ha-mazon* the context is one of thanksgiving after a satisfying meal. Both prayers thank God, but the nature of the thanksgiving cannot be the same in two disparate frameworks.[17]

"Without intelligence, whence prayer?" Intelligence is the path to knowledge of oneself, thorough knowledge of the words and gestures in which one is engaged – without such knowledge, how can one fully discharge the duty of prayer, and how can one find in prayer the resources for spiritual growth? Even if the individual, or the group, luckily avoid major theological or halakhic error, one might as well speak of performing a piece of music that one hasn't studied and rehearsed. One may discharge the halakhic obligation to

---

[16] See *Shiurim le-Zekher Avi Mori*, vol. II, chapter 2.

[17] Based on MS.

pray, but the flavor of prayer will be missing, and a feeling of spiritual malaise and dissatisfaction is one consequence.

The last analogy reminds us that the knowledge of which we speak must be internalized. A student once asked me, regarding the Rav's painstakingly described journey through the first three benedictions of the *Amidah*, how anyone can actually concentrate on the hairpin turns of consciousness implicit in the text?[18] Can one indeed shift from the unworthiness to pray expressed in the preamble, to the confidence of *Avot*, to the sense of awe that dominates *Gevurot*, then to the synthesis of *Kedushah*, the various petitions, and the three blessings of thanksgiving that, according to the Rav, recapitulate, in reverse order, the themes of the opening three? No matter how slow the pace (and whistling past the opportunities for woolgathering that beset artificial prolongation), the task seems psychologically impossible. One cannot pray and stage-manage multiple changes of mood at the same time. The only answer is that repetition and habituation must come to the aid of theological and halakhic understanding. The act of prayer must occupy the foreground of consciousness while the interpretation of prayer, in the background, provides the meaning. As R. Kook remarks more than once in discussing prayer, the sensitive and disciplined imagination, essential for living prayer, is grounded in familiarity and habit.

So far we have examined the kind of ongoing reflection on the human condition and on the liturgical text that usually makes its intellectual mark gradually, slowly seeping into the cracks of our consciousness and bodies until we are able to enact the halakhic distinctions and make the work of the liturgy our own. Sometimes intellectual insight, when it is achieved, is more sudden. So sudden, indeed, that in retrospect it seems too obvious to have required discovery. What we discover, in effect, is not a mystery about the institution of prayer, or about ourselves, but an elementary grammatical truth about the nature of prayer. In such cases we are

---

[18] See "Thoughts on the *Amidah*" in *Ish ha-Halakha: Galuy ve-Nistar* (Hebrew); English translation in *Worship of the Heart*.

liable to underestimate the intellectual nature of the insight. Let me illustrate with two examples:

1) Some years ago, I wrote an essay on petitionary prayer.[19] My analysis was heavily influenced by R. Soloveitchik's view that prayer reflects man's attempt to learn his true needs. Yet, faithful to the Rav's outlook, I rejected a purely didactic theory of prayer, in which prayer is equated with self-analysis. A writer sympathetic with my aims and insights nevertheless imputed to my philosophizing a failure to avoid the didactic approach.[20] Having emphasized adequately, I thought, that the individual is not merely judging himself, but wants God to respond and to help the supplicant to attain his legitimate goals, I was initially unsure as to where I had opened myself to misunderstanding. Upon careful review I found that insufficient attention had been given to the formal act of petition. Honestly presenting one's situation to another person who is benevolent, and able to help, may come close to asking for help, and can certainly be interpreted as a broad hint that help is wanted. But, in grammatical terms, it is not quite a request. Both the text of prayer and the spirit of prayer demand of the individual that he, or she, explicitly address God in petition. If it takes the effort of writing an article, and digesting a critique to grasp this apparently simple point, then so be it.[21]

---

[19] Shalom Carmy, "Destiny, Freedom and the Logic of Petition," (*Festschrift* for Rabbi Walter Wurzburger), *Tradition* 24:2 (Winter, 1990): 17–37.

[20] A. Walfish, "Bet Midrash and Academic World: the Study of the Prayerbook," *Shanah be-Shanah* 39 (1998): 467–504; 475 n. 21. My present discussion of Walfish's criticism and its remediation is indebted to my conversation with him (7/29/99).

[21] The following exchange, between the veteran politician Tip O'Neill and his former schoolteacher, on the eve of his first election, brings this idea home: "Tom, I'm going to vote for you tomorrow even though you didn't ask me to." I was shocked: "Why, Mrs. O'Brien," I said, "I've lived across from you for eighteen years. I cut your grass in the summer. I shovel your walk in the winter. I didn't think I had to ask for your vote." "Tom," she replied, "let me tell you something: people like to be asked." Tip O'Neill, *Man of the House* (New York: Random House, 1987), p. 25. The theological point, however, is not that God "likes to be asked," but that the beseecher should do the asking.

2) R. Ḥayyim Soloveichik's famous analysis of *kavvanah* in prayer defines the act of prayer as awareness that one is "standing before the king," i.e. in the presence of God. Hazon Ish, among his other criticisms, argues that such awareness is implicit in the very fact that an individual enters into the verbal behavior and gestures associated with halakhic prayer; any additional requirement is redundant.[22] It would appear, then, that the consciousness of addressing God, and the conception of God accompanying our address, is so deeply embedded in the grammar of prayer as to render discussion superfluous. Whatever the case might have been when the Hazon Ish annotated his copy of R. Ḥayyim, many traditional Jews are both amazed and inspired when they encounter the following statement by R. Ḥayyim's grandson:

> It is impossible to imagine prayer without, at the time, feeling the nearness and greatness of the Creator, His absolute justice, His fatherly concern with human affairs, His anger and wrath caused by unjust deeds. When we bow in prayer, we must experience His soothing hand and the infinite love and mercy for His creatures. We cling to Him as a living God, not as an idea, as abstract Being. We are in His company and are certain of His sympathy. There is, in prayer, an experience of emotions that can only be produced by direct contact with God.[23]

III. AN EXAMPLE OF REFLECTION ON THE TEXT: ON HEALTH AND WEALTH

The victim of Rabbi Steinsaltz's disapproval, in our opening section, probably did not immerse himself in the intellectual quest outlined above. Although, even if he did, he would still be vulnerable to criticism: the time for study is before, not during prayer. The kind

[22] *Ḥiddushei Rabbenu Ḥayyim ha-Levi* to *Hil. Tefillah* 4:1 and marginal comments of Hazon Ish. On the basis of R. Ḥayyim's position, see also S. Carmy, "I Have Set God Before Me Always," in *Kuttonet Yosef: Memorial Volume for R. Yosef Wanefsky* (New York: Student Organization of Yeshiva, 2002), pp. 427–30.

[23] R. Soloveitchik, *Worship of the Heart*, p. 63.

of inquiry that can effectively be transferred to the post-*cholent* hour would more likely be a localized examination of the text, the extraction of assorted *diyyukim* and homiletical goodies from the lines of the *Siddur.* But the aimlessness of many such investigations and the sinking feeling we often experience when called upon to celebrate the results, or at least nod appreciatively, should not obscure the fact that meaning resides in the details, not only in the structure and theme.

After all that R. Soloveitchik has taught about the importance of petition in prayer, the supplicant must work his way through thirteen specific requests. Petition, in the Rav's understanding, pertains to our needs, about the true nature of which we are more or less deceived. The fixed order of prayer is the Torah's way of educating us to a better comprehension of our true inventory of needs.[24] Ultimately, of course, the text itself cannot tell us what exactly our needs are with respect to our various troubles; that is why we address our personal entreaty to God. Can the careful, word for word, examination of the text, in addition to the investigation of its general structure, yield some insight that will at least channel our thoughts in the right direction?

Let us examine two petitionary blessings: the prayer for health (*refa'einu*) and the prayer for prosperity (*bareikh aleinu*). Prayers for health flourish today, not only in the privacy of the *Amidah*, but also in the spectacular boom in *mi she-beirakh's* and the popularity of public Psalm recitation. Most of the time we are praying for others, frequently for people in whose fate we have no selfish interest. No doubt we are all in need of material well being too, but our prayers in that direction seem less important in the overall scheme of our public spiritual existence. This, despite the fact that in days gone by, prayer for economic sustenance was a most prolific subject of petition, as witness the elective petitions inserted in our *Siddurim.* Popular culture portrays the sobbing ignoramus for whom all prayer, even the most abstruse hymn, boils down to one impassioned mes-

[24] See R. Soloveitchik, "Redemption, Prayer, Talmud Torah," *Tradition* 17:2 (Winter, 1983).

sage: "*Ribbono shel Olam*, give *parnasah*," while the most respectable and sophisticated frankly acknowledge the central place in prayer occupied by this need.[25] Why is it not so prominent in contemporary consciousness, even while prayer in time of illness flourishes?

One outstanding difference between threats to our health and other problems is that physical illness lends itself to objective definition: we know that something is wrong, and we count on others to understand and to empathize as best as they can. Moreover, we are willing to communicate our suffering to others in the expectation, often met, that they will know how to respond. Thus we feel free to publicize our trouble, to ask for the *mi she-beirakh*. The same is true when we are threatened with poverty resulting from a drought or the collapse in demand for the goods we had labored to produce and had hoped to bring to market. Such was the typical experience of our ancestors. In the *parnasah* crises, characteristic of our own situation, by contrast, when one is frustrated on the job or desolate in one's relations to others, the nature of the pain is harder to locate, and we are often reluctant to speak and find relief. In R. Soloveitchik's terms, illness manifests a surface crisis, whereas other difficulties belong to the realm of depth crisis. One might imagine that, when standing before God, we need not bother with precise accounts of our condition: He knows it all. Nor need we feel inhibited before the Almighty. Nevertheless our social habits and confused self-knowledge seem to carry over into our private prayers as well. We will return to this phenomenon later on.

Let us focus more narrowly, for as moment, on the petition for prosperity. To begin with, like our other requests, it is phrased in the plural: we pray for others, not for ourselves alone. But the language of the prayer, at least when looked at from a modern perspective, is oddly muted. Our prayer is limited to "this year and its crop." We beseech the Almighty to bless it "like the good years (*ka-shanim ha-tovot*): good years; not optimal years. When we pray for health, the text does not place similar restrictions on the scope of our petition.

[25] Readers of the Neẓiv will have no difficulty recalling passages in which divine worship is linked to the desire for worldly sustenance. See, for example, *Haamek Davar* to Genesis 2:5, Leviticus 20:7.

In principle, one might pray for endless years of boundless health: nothing in the text discourages us from forming such an intention. The words of *bareikh aleinu*, in contrast, encourage us to set our sights lower.

Now the concrete prayer for health that is uttered by flesh and blood people need not request the optimum. When we, or those close to us, are ill, we often bargain with God. In the act of praying, we often discover what it is that we really want and need, with respect to our bodily integrity and function. Take the diary kept by David Klinghoffer's adoptive mother in her battle with the cancer that eventually killed her:

> "Dear God," she writes, "please help me survive this test!"
>
> "Help me, dear God, give me strength and let me rid myself of the cane. I need you, dearest God, please let me feel your love. Tonight depression again has filled my thoughts."
>
> "How can I calm this turmoil inside me? Only God is my salvation."[26]

Mrs. Klinghoffer is far from being a religious virtuoso. Yet the record presented to us is a model of passion and proportion. The formulas of traditional Judaism, of which she was, in any event, not a regular practitioner, would not have denied her an unchecked hope for total recovery. Someone else in her situation might authentically have prayed for the maximum. The question before us is: can the same be said with regard to our desire for prosperity, for material success?

R. Kook touched upon this problem in a slightly different context. Discussing the appropriate blessings bestowed by a guest upon his host, he notes that these include a wish for the host's exceeding success (*me'od*). The guest should not include himself in this particular request. In principle, wealth can be viewed as a means to greater service of God and the community; it is, therefore, a worthy benefit. In considering one's own needs, however, "each person should take

[26] David Klinghoffer, *The Lord Will Gather Me In* (New York: Free Press, 1999), p. 78.

hold for himself of the middle character and should be concerned that great riches will cause him to deviate from the straight path." Moreover, continues R. Kook, fortuitous, outsize success generally comes about through cleverness at commercial affairs, usually a zero sum game. One may wish that others deserve such favor, but it is wrong to want it for oneself.[27]

R. Kook's interpretation targets two dangers in the desire to gain exceeding wealth for oneself. The second is the likelihood that surpassing enrichment will be at the expense of others. The first is that immoderate wealth, and even more so fixing one's ambition upon it, is corrupting, quite apart from the consequences to others. One cannot help recalling Alasdair MacIntyre's remark on the different translations of Aristotle's term *pleonexia* (excess). When Hobbes paraphrases *pleonexia* as "a desire of more than their share," and others translate it as "greed," they indicate a peculiarly modern attitude, according to which excess is bad only if it interferes with the continuous and limitless expansion of others.[28] R. Kook displays penetrating insight into the mechanism of this category of acquisitiveness, but he also insists on the more traditional Aristotelian suspicion of the intemperate lust for possession. In any event, the text of *bareikh aleinu,* which we recite thrice daily, clearly reflects the ethic of moderation as to material possession. It is fully consonant with R. Kook's more rigorous interpretation, which makes acquisitiveness a vice in itself.

Our close reading of *bareikh aleinu*, in the light of R. Kook's comments, reveals a clash between the value system of most upper middle class congregants and the table of values presupposed by the prayerbook. That the Torah's outlook on the symbolic and practical importance of moneymaking and acquisition is alien to our society should not be astonishing. The great cultural contradiction does not need the confirmation of our literary-theological analysis. We pray because we are sinners in need of forgiveness; we pray because we are

[27] *Ein Ayah,* II, 7:9 (to BT *Berakhot* 46a). cf. Kuzari III, 19.

[28] A. MacIntyre, *Whose Justice? Which Rationality?* (Notre Dame, IN: University of Notre Dame Press, 1988), p. 111f. The Hobbes reference is to *Leviathan*, chapter 15.

self-deceivers in need of enlightenment. The point of our discussion is better to understand the mechanism of that enlightenment.

As we have seen, the reason that *refa'einu* is closer to our hearts than *bareikh aleinu* is that the appropriate language for speaking about illness is readily available to us, while the language with which to approach God with our needs pertaining to material welfare proves more elusive in the social and economic situations prevalent in contemporary middle class existence. We have noted, first of all, that the threat of illness is easier to formulate objectively than the anxieties we experience about prosperity. We must now take this idea one small step forward. In order to discover the language with which to pray about depth crisis, one must have depth, that is to say, inwardness. To the extent that one's psychological life is superficial, meaning that it is nothing but a mirror of the other human surfaces that he, or she, meets, the awareness of depth crisis will always remain mute and unredeemed. One can go through the liturgy, perhaps even manage an appreciative nod at the nice *diyyukim* that, with R. Kook's aid, we made in the text. Alas, the words of the liturgy will not penetrate the person repeating them. Without individuality, no inwardness; without inwardness, no depth.

Individuality, as expressed in privacy, is necessary for another reason. To ask, with reference to material possessions, what my genuine needs are, entails not only self-knowledge, but also self-criticism. According to R. Shimon bar Yoḥai, the *Amidah* is recited silently in order not to mortify sinners confessing their transgressions; this is comparable to the fact that the *olah* (burnt offering) and the *ḥattat* (sin offering) are brought to the same place.[29] Yet, as we have seen,

[29] BT *Sotah* 32b; see *Maharsha s.v. mipnei. Berakhot* 31a and 24b offers different justifications of silent prayer, which I discuss in "Destiny, Freedom and the Logic of Petition," p. 36, n. 26. Uri Ehrlich, *Kol Aẓmotai Tomarna: The Non-Verbal Language of Jewish Prayer* (Jerusalem: Magnes, 1999), p. 175, suggests that the confession of sin is an instance of the kind of situation in which individual expression mandates privacy. This is confirmed by the *Gemara*'s reference to the place of the *olah* and the *ḥattat*. According to my analysis, the categories of petitionary prayer and confession of sin both entail self-questioning and self-criticism; hence they share the requirement of privacy. Note, in support, that the *olah* is not viewed as a sin offering, despite the fact that, according to the same R. Shimon b. Yoḥai, it

the gesture of petition, insofar as it poses to God the question of our true needs, leads us to criticize our false beliefs about our needs. If the plea for enlightenment (*ḥonen ha-daat*) leads off the thirteen petitions of the weekday *Amidah*, the requests for repentance and forgiveness follow straightaway.

We have demonstrated how knowledge of *tefillah*, its structure, its nature, and its wording, helps to create the space in which a meaningful approach to God can occur. We must next consider the experiential and theological relationship between the public aspect of the liturgy and the crucial dimension of inwardness.

IV. THE CONTEMPORARY PREDOMINANCE OF THE PUBLIC

For the human being to carry on an intimate, prayerful, relationship with God, privacy is of the essence. The ceremonialism and publicity that pervade so much of conventional religion are enemies of that intimacy. The trend towards higher behavioral standards of observance, which has made attendance at public worship *de rigueur*, further marginalizes the private reality of the whispering Hannah, mother of prayer. Now I am not seeking to justify solitary fixed prayer as an option equal, or even preferable, to praying with a *minyan*. Putting aside narrow halakhic considerations, which would take us too far afield, I see no reason to question the presumption that praying with the community is, in general, more conducive to *kavvanah*. The pace, to be sure, may be too fast or too slow; the conduct of one's neighbors may be distracting. Religious individuals, including the

---

is brought for sinful thoughts (*Vayikra Rabbah* 7:3; Margulies ed. 1, 153 l.5, also cited by Naḥmanides to Leviticus 1:4). David Hartman mounts a trenchant attack on several aspects of R. Soloveitchik's theology of prayer ["Halakhic Critique of Soloveitchik's Approach to Prayer," in *A Living Covenant* (New York: Free Press, 1985), pp. 150–9]. Hartman argues that the Rav is wrong to base his sacrificial concept of prayer on Naḥmanides' commentary to *Vayikra* 1:9. Naḥmanides, on the *olah*, states that the worshipper must view his own life as forfeit, because of his sin; the sacrifice substitutes for the relinquishing of his life. Hartman concludes that Naḥmanides' idea of self-negation depends on sin. Since the Rav does not refer to sin but to man's creatureliness, his appeal to Naḥmanides is, according to Hartman, illegitimate. In the light of our analysis, however, the lines between

greatest, may on occasion feel an overwhelming need to be alone with God.[30] Nonetheless, the mature individual of good will should be able to filter out potential intrusions and take advantage of the benefits. As R. Soloveitchik says:

> I realize today that praying alone and praying with the community are like two different forms of prayer. Praying alone takes a lot less time, and I do not experience the same depth of emotion as when I pray with the community.... Now that I am accustomed to praying with the community, I simply cannot pray alone anymore. The prayer is not prayer without a *minyan*. I simply do not experience anything when I pray alone, and there is no flavor to such prayer.[31]

Whether one is praying with the community or alone, however, prayer has both a public and a private face. A discussion of *tefillah* that would promote spiritual liveliness, and safeguard the intimate aspect, must, therefore, clarify the divisions between the public and the private.

Note well that the present discussion is about the private and the public aspects of prayer, not about the orientation of prayer to personal needs or communal concerns. The two divisions indeed overlap, but they are logically distinct: to pray for the community in silence is certainly not an odd notion. The normative presence of communal and universal themes in the statutory prayers is taken

---

man's vulnerability, his confusion about his true table of needs, and his sinfulness, are not as sharp as Hartman would maintain. *Olah* pertains to man's sinful situation, but is not itself a sin offering. Hartman, who prefers to downplay both man's helplessness and his sinfulness, is disinclined to go deeply into the interpenetration of these categories.

[30] On R. Kook, see Rabbi M.Z. Neria, "The Lights of Prayer of R. Kook," in *Siaḥ Yiẓḥak*, pp. 155f. Cf. *Olat Reiyah* I, 28 on R. Akiva's solitary prayer. For R. Soloveitchik's own testimony, see "Majesty and Humility," *Tradition* 17:2 (Winter, 1978): 32f.

[31] Aaron Rakeffet-Rothkoff, *The Rav: The World of Rabbi Joseph B. Soloveitchik* (Hoboken: Ktav, 1999) vol. 1, pp. 187–8. See also Rabbi A. Lichtenstein's essay in *Shanah be-Shanah* 39 (1998): 288.

for granted. It underscores the necessity that prayer not become an entirely selfish affair. But this does not bear directly on the intimacy or publicity of the prayerful gesture.

The classic definition of essentially public prayer is found in the following statement of Naḥmanides:

> The purpose of lifting one's voice in prayer and the purpose of synagogues and the merit of public prayer is that human beings have a place to gather and thank God who created them and gave them existence. And they shall promulgate this and say before Him "We are your creatures." This is their meaning in saying: "And they shall call unto God with force – from here you learn that prayer requires voice...."[32]

As I have noted elsewhere,[33] Naḥmanides unites, under one rubric, the prayer of thanksgiving and the panicky pleas of the Ninevites. An emphasis on human creatureliness is common to both situations. This is most appropriately a matter for proclamation, and this is best accomplished through the community's lifted voice. Naturally Naḥmanides does not include other elements of prayer, namely the petitions and confessions, which presuppose the intimacy and soul-searching that can only occur in private.

With communal prayer the norm, even these parts of prayer ordinarily take place in the presence of the community. R. Kook, without alluding to Naḥmanides, extends his doctrine about the centrality of proclamation in the synagogue to embrace the petitionary element as well. He does so by making petition secondary to proclamation. The opportunity to approach God with our personal

---

[32] Commentary to Exodus 13:16 ed. Charles Chavel, (Jerusalem: Mossad ha-Rav Kook, 1960), vol. I, pp. 346–7; see notes 30–32. Cf. "*Torat ha-Shem Temimah*" in *Kitvei Ramban*, ed. Charles Chavel (Jerusalem: Mossad ha-Rav Kook, 1963), vol. I, pp. 152–3. P.W. van der Horst, "Silent Prayer in Antiquity," in *Hellenism – Judaism – Christianity* (Kampen: Kok Pharos, 1994), pp. 252–77, surveys the classical and non-rabbinic Jewish sources. Philo, on his account, wavers on the appropriateness of public praise, perhaps under the influence of his philosophical ideals.

[33] S. Carmy, "Destiny, Freedom, and the Logic of Petition."

requests is, in effect, a concession to human nature. He is in full agreement with the Barthian conviction that the real human being will not appear in prayer unless his or her needs are placed on the agenda. But where the straightforward reading of the Talmud implies that praise and thanksgiving were established as the appropriate prologue and epilogue to the requests, for R. Kook petition is allowed for the sake of the superior proclamatory element, that is for the praise and the thanksgiving.[34]

It would appear from this that for R. Soloveitchik, the gesture of petition has a more robust function in the economy of *tefillah* than R. Kook would grant it. This is further borne out by R. Kook's adoption of the Kabbalistic view that petitionary prayer should ideally transcend one's self-seeking tendencies, and focus instead on Sefirotic illumination.[35] So too R. Kook insists that prayer must be free of any misconception about altering God's will.[36] His anxiety concerning this point indicates more than the desire to extirpate a philosophical blunder; the rejected idea is not only false, but harmful. In R. Kook's own words, it is "destructive of the order of human perfection." Nevertheless, one may subscribe to R. Soloveitchik's general orientation yet accept R. Kook's insight that petition, in the context of communal prayer, also serves the ideal of proclamation.

The previous discussion bridges the theological gap between the privacy of petition, which is rooted in personal need and anguish, and the publicity of communal proclamation. No doubt such insight should affect concrete experience favorably. Yet I fear it would be foolhardy to ignore the danger that a spiritual lifestyle, conducted completely in the glare of communal space, is liable to marginalize those features of religious existence that are predicated upon inwardness and self-examination, and that compel such increasingly unpleasant and ungregarious endeavors as questioning the socially validated system of values and turning upon oneself in remorse and repentance. The triumph of herd morality and the withering away

---

[34] *Olat Reiyah*, I, 260.

[35] *Olat Reiyah*, I, 16.

[36] *Olat Reiyah*, I, 14.

of individuality in Western society as a whole, and in the Orthodox community as well, make this threat especially ominous. Authentic prayer is not the only aspect of religious life imperiled by these developments.

If there is a way out of this impasse, it is not, God forbid, to make the communal dimension shallower – that is the worst thing that can happen – but rather to build up the intimate, individual side in whatever way possible. In considering the problem of our prayer life, the very least we can do is not to become self-congratulatory when we see the external, communally oriented elements doing well, or appearing to do so.[37]

We should also be alert to the risks of complacency, with respect to our communal arrangements for prayer, in all that relates to the social or aesthetic atmosphere. The perennial mistake of the philosopher is to underestimate the value of familiarity and habit in facilitating healthy religious experience. This rationalistic delusion often reinforces our society's appetite for novelty as an end in itself. R. Soloveitchik's evocations of his European childhood experiences, his yearning for absent personalities and timeworn tunes, remind us of the importance of an experiential, sensual, rootedness. R. Kook, for his part, vigorously upholds the integration of imagination and reason. He explicitly relates the rabbinic commendation of the person who occupies a set place in the Synagogue to the power of habit and familiarity to instill a deep emotional identification with the order of worship.[38]

Though the more common error nowadays is making too much of innovation, there is also a danger in relying too much on the enchantment of the familiar. We should not dismiss the value, for prayerful orientation, of traditional associations and melodies. By the same token, however, we should beware of mistaking our feel-

[37] The primary effect of so-called Carlebach *minyanim* is to animate the public, celebratory aspects of prayer. Individuals familiar with full-fledged Carlebachian prayer, where the singing and dancing pervade the entire service, and not only a limited portion of *Kabbalat Shabbat*, inform me that the crescent fervor carries over to the private times as well.

[38] *Ein Ayah*, I, BT *Berakhot* 1:55.

ing of comfort with the traditional performance of the traditional liturgy for passion, confusing the tears of nostalgia with the tears of joy, contrition, and love.[39]

V. PRAYER AND PEACE OF MIND – THE ROAD THROUGH SACRIFICE AND SILENCE

The task of defining "spirituality" is probably hopeless. Words like "spirit" and "spiritual" are elusive enough in themselves; "spirituality," an even more abstract locution, feeds on the unclarity of the more established terms.[40] One might feel safe quoting the view that the "concept of spirituality implies that there is the possibility of progress in holiness, that there is a need of working toward perfection, and that there are certain means and ways of attaining such a perfection."[41] But, as Charles Liebman has recently argued, the contemporary enthusiasm for self-fulfillment via "spirituality" often seems at odds with the devotion to holiness, which entails separation and self-transcendence in the service of the transcendent, commanding God.

The starkness of the conflict, as it pertains to prayer, can be illustrated by contrasting the themes of the *Amidah* with the popular tendency to identify the goal of prayer with "peace of mind." We shall not rehearse what was already said about the intense dialectic

[39] This point parallels C.S. Lewis's remarks on familiarity in *The Four Loves*. People tend to overlook the significance of those personal connections that are grounded entirely in familiarity and regular contact, or, alternately, to overestimate the profundity of their social interaction based on having many friends in this relatively casual sense.

[40] Stephen Smith, *The Concept of the Spiritual* (Philadelphia: Temple University Press, 1988), a survey of this terminology in Western philosophy, does not pick up on the precise connotations of the noun and the adjective in English; Alan Olson, *Hegel and the Spirit* (Princeton: Princeton University Press, 1992) contains scattered historical notes beyond the narrow topic of the book. Nor are the definitions in OED much help. Kierkegaard's definition of spirit in *Sickness Unto Death* is probably unsurpassed for its lucidity (which may not be saying much about other accounts) but does not supply the key to contemporary usage.

[41] Lucien Richard, *The Spirituality of John Calvin*, quoted by John Kelsay, "Prayer and Ethics: Reflections on Calvin and Barth," *Harvard Theological Review* 82:2 (1989): 169–84, 180.

of the first three benedictions, nor the arduous work of entreaty that follows. The last part of the *Amidah*, its culmination, which is technically characterized as thanksgiving, begins with *reẓei*, the plea that God receive Israel's prayer under the aspect of a burnt offering (*ve-ishei Yisrael u-tefillatam*). While R. Soloveitchik's idea of petition as man's quest to understand his true table of needs identifies prayer with "self-acquisition, self-discovery, self-objectification, and self-redemption," the theme of *reẓei* identifies prayer with sacrifice, "unrestricted offering of the whole self.... God claims man, and...His claim to man is not partial but total."[42] R. Soloveitchik calls the tension between these two goals frankly "irreconcilable." What common ground can there be between this paradoxical dialectic and the wild enthusiasm with which many of us greet rumors of medical reports that imply that regular attendance at services lowers the blood pressure?

And yet, who can deny that *tefillah* – and I mean strenuous *tefillah* with *kavvanah* – does bestow upon the worshipper a feeling of tranquility and peace? R. Soloveitchik closes his "Thoughts on the *Amidah*" with the last blessing, *sim shalom*, the prayer for peace. There he exults in a state of mind in which "the fear is forgotten, the dread has disappeared, the *mysterium tremendum* has passed, and in their place arise joy and yearning for the source of Being." The problem in our society is that the peace of which the Rav speaks can only be the fruit of assiduous spiritual exercise: one gains one's life only by relinquishing it. The community Professor Liebman is thinking of is too impatient, and too bent on their own well-being, to take the sacrificial leap. What we need, for such people and for ourselves, in the moments when we falter, is a way of making the promise of spiritual wholeness and peace as vivid as the terror of the sacrifice. What we need is a connection between what we regularly experience, in the absence of a full commitment to the prayerful

[42] "Redemption, Prayer, Talmud Torah," pp. 70f. The Rav once suggested to me that, in his later years, he had come to place greater stress on the sacrificial aspect of prayer. For another theology of prayer founded on the equation of prayer and *korban*, see Maharal, *Netiv ha-Avodah*, chap. 1.

life, and what we hope to experience when that life is vigorous and unobstructed.

Let us turn to a familiar passage that occupies an anomalous place in our liturgy. At the very end of the *Amidah*, after the last blessing has been completed, but before we step back three paces, thus officially concluding the *tefillah*, we read the meditation beginning *Elokai neẓor*: "God, preserve my tongue from evil, and my lips from speaking deceit, and may my soul be silent to those who curse me, may my soul be like earth to all...." This post-*tefillah* meditation is a version of Mar b. Ravina's words in BT *Berakhot* 17a and not part of the body of obligatory prayer. The sentiment it expresses cannot be paraphrased simply by enumerating the specific requests it contains: to successfully refrain from speaking evil; divine protection against one's enemies; understanding of Torah and so forth. There is a common denominator: a yearning for purity of lips and heart. The praying individual asks to be free of whatever would corrupt, or distract, his, or her, inner life. From a literary perspective, the meditation forms a fit closing to the *tefillah*. If R. Soloveitchik is correct in viewing the last three benedictions as chiastic recapitulations of the first three, then *Elokai neẓor* corresponds to "God, open my lips...." In a word, we have here a plea for equanimity, for peace of mind. The goal is achieved by placing ourselves completely in God's hands: we remain indifferent to our ill-wishers because we trust God to confound their counsels.[43]

Unquestionably the peace and calm expressed in these thoughts can best be attained if one has thoroughly internalized the message of the *Amidah* as a whole, and, in particular, the concept of prayer as sacrifice. Only an individual who has confronted the demand to give up everything to God can authentically give up his, or her, frustrations and resentments to Him as well. Only the individual

[43] My revered teacher R. Aharon Lichtenstein discusses the question already raised by the *Or Zarua* (II 89:3) about the recital of *Elokai neẓor* on Shabbat, when petitionary prayer is ordinarily limited. See "The Problem of Shabbat Prayer," in *Siaḥ Yiẓḥak*, pp. 86–105, especially p. 96ff. My account of the meditation surely treats it as a "spiritual" request that would, from many perspectives, be very much in keeping with the spirit of Shabbat.

who has striven to find a voice and redeem his or her legitimate table of needs, and who has also learned to renounce everything for the sake of the divine, can satisfy the need for the silence that is beyond striving. Yet the taste for equanimity is available to us all, and the scent of genuine tranquility may be enough to lead us forward in our strenuous journey to the sometimes-terrifying Source of all peace.

The silence of *elokai neẓor*, in which we withdraw our speech from evil and meaningless pursuits and dedicate it to the holy, exemplifies the gesture of withdrawal and renunciation that defines the sacrificial concept of prayer. But silence and sacrifice come together for another reason. The sacrificial cult is, by its nature, a realm of ritual activity rather than words. It is unnecessary to enter into the question of whether the *Mikdash*, during the *avodah*, was a place of absolute silence.[44] It is enough to consider that a modern visitor to the *Mikdash* would be as impressed by the overall silence as the pilgrims in the "Letter of Aristeas" (92) and that this would stand in conspicuous contrast to the verbal worship to which we are accustomed. An appreciation of the withdrawal from the temptation of mean language is thus connected to an appreciation of the manner in which the world of the *korban* continues to define the world of prayer.

One of the tragedies of our present communal predicament is that many people who are anxious for spiritual fulfillment are also the most addicted to incessant verbalization (in and out of *Shul*). Sometimes I get the strange feeling that the corny jokes, trivial an-

[44] Israel Knohl, "Between Voice and Silence: The Relationship Between Prayer and Temple Cult," *Journal of Biblical Literature* 115:1 (Spring, 1996): 17–30, revives a theory of Yeḥezkel Kaufmann to that effect. Knohl attaches to this suggestion historical speculations that are not germane to our subject. Ehrlich (176 n. 40) suggests that the silent *Amidah* may be an attempt to incorporate this element of the *Mikdash* model. Let us note, at this point, that silence, in this connection, applies in more than one way: actions performed silently, without words, are not the same thing as words recited inaudibly. Nonetheless, there is a psychological family resemblance among the different sounds of silence. For an examination of the phenomenon, in all its phenomenological variety, along classic Husserlian lines, see Bernard Dauenhauer, *Silence: The Phenomenon and its Ontological Significance* (Bloomington, IN: Indiana University Press, 1980).

nouncements, desultory conversations, the booming political orations, and the honeyed attempts at spiritual intimacy, from pulpit and from pew, have more than a whiff of the burnt offering about them. It is as if one were to confess: "Dear God, I may not have the patience to pray properly, and I cannot sacrifice my flesh and blood upon Your Altar. I offer You instead my capacity for chatter, and for You I kill my valuable time." Imagining such sentiments may make us laugh for a moment, but wondering whether we can consistently afford to be smug about our neighbors has an immediate sobering effect.

There may be many causes (read: excuses) for our difficulty in realizing the peace of *sim shalom* and *elokai neẓor,* ranging from the frenetic pace of contemporary upper middle-class life to the quasi-Freudian cult of privacy-shattering discourse that so enraged Foucault. One factor, and the one closest to the dialectic we have traced in this section, is our fear of the sacrifice that the quest for holiness entails. It is not just that we aren't sufficiently committed to God, or that we like our superficial selves too much to strive for something higher. We are also obscurely afraid that the redeeming act of self-renunciation may also destroy something of what is spiritually good in us as well.

R. Kook was not oblivious to this impediment. His remarks illuminate the connection between *Mikdash* and prayer in a new way:

> At the time of wholeness (*sheleimut*), when the *Mikdash* existed, atonement through sacrifices affected only the evil powers; the sacrifice subdued the force of evil but did not act deleteriously upon the good powers of the body and the soul. But now, just as, for the nation as a whole, because of our sins, the exile is an iron furnace to purify the dross, and together with the evil powers which it weakens, it also wreaks havoc with the good powers, so too, the individual who needs to mend the evil powers through fasting, also depletes the good powers by enfeebling body and soul. This is affected by the prayer [of the person who fasts] that it should be as if [one's

> body] had been sacrificed on the Altar and accepted, so as to extirpate only the evil and to fortify the powers of good.[45]

Fear and love, familiarity and terror, serenity and turmoil, intimacy and proclamation, solitude and togetherness, ritual and raw emotion, sacrifice and self-fulfillment. The story of Jewish prayer is one of endlessly intersecting themes and struggles. Our lives wait for the meaning.[46]

---

[45] *Olat Reiyah*, I, 293.

[46] I am grateful for several remarks on the first draft by my revered teacher R. Aharon Lichtenstein. Among many others with whom I have discussed the matters touched on in this essay, let me single out Rabbi Yitzchak Blau, Rabbi Asher Friedman, Rabbi Alex Mondrow, Rabbi Yehuda Septimus, Rabbi Alan Stadtmauer, Bernard Stahl, and Jerry Zeitchik.

Section seven

14

Religion, Spirituality, and the Future of American Judaism

Chaim I. Waxman

The United States at the mid-twentieth century appeared to many to be a highly secular society in which the prospects for the future of organized religion were predicted to be very slim at best. In the mid-1960s, the theologian Harvey Cox's ideas in *The Secular City*[1] were widely discussed, a group of "radical" theologians were proclaiming the "death of God,"[2] and there followed a variety of articles on it in the news media, including the *New York Times* and *Time* Magazine.[3] In 1967, sociologist Peter Berger published his highly influential work, *The Sacred Canopy*, in which he saw secularization in the fact "that the state has taken over traditional functions of the church

[1] Harvey Cox, *The Secular City* (New York: Macmillan, 1965).

[2] Thomas Altizer and William Hamilton, eds., *Radical Theology and the Death of God* (Indianapolis: Bobbs-Merrill, 1966).

[3] See, for example, *New York Times*, 17 Oct. 1965, and *Time*, 22 Oct. 1965.

such as education and social control, and that the rise of scientific understanding as the dominant worldview has brought into question religious definitions of reality."[4] He argued that separation of religion and state, a hallmark of modernity, meant religious pluralism, which resulted in religion's loss of influence over the public sphere and its becoming a commodity in a free-market situation and, thus, subject to "consumer preferences," while the religious institutions became increasing bureaucratized. Berger and Thomas Luckmann,[5] among others, saw religion as playing a role within the private sphere only. And in the private sphere, although he is a staunch critic of secularization theory, Andrew Greeley was forced to admit: "It would appear that a bit of the numinous has worn off, at least in the area of sexuality."[6] If hard pressed, he might well have conceded that it had worn off in other areas within the private sphere as well.

Indeed, major survey research appeared to confirm the secularization of America's public sphere. For example, a series of Gallup polls indicated that Americans viewed religion's influence on American society to be waning.

Table 1: Is Religion's Influence in the US Increasing or Decreasing (%)

	1957	1962	1965	1967	1968
Increasing	69	45	33	23	18
Decreasing	14	31	45	57	67
No difference	10	17	13	14	8
No opinion	7	7	9	6	7

Source: Gallup Poll reported in *New York Times*, 25 May 1968, p. 38.

[4] Peter L. Berger, *The Sacred Canopy: Elements of a Sociological Theory of Religion* (Garden City, NY: Doubleday, 1967).

[5] Peter L. Berger and Thomas Luckmann, *The Social Construction of Reality: A Treatise in the Sociology of Knowledge* (Garden City, NY: Anchor Books, 1967); Thomas Luckmann, *The Invisible Religion: The Problem of Religion in Modern Society* (New York: Macmillan, 1967).

[6] Andrew M. Greeley, *Unsecular Man: The Persistence of Religion* (New York: Schocken, 1972), p. 193.

The secularization was perceived to be so rampant and powerful that Peter Berger predicted that, "By the 21st century, religious believers are likely to be found only in small sects, huddled together to resist a worldwide secular culture."[7]

By the mid-1970s, however, what Berger had earlier portrayed as but "a rumor of angels," had developed into a full-blown societal development in which there was a "new religious consciousness."[8]

The presidential campaign of 1975–76 highlighted Jimmy Carter's experience as a "born-again" Christian, and he was but the most famous of a significantly growing number of newly religious. Indeed, the country was undergoing "the restructuring of American religion."[9] American religious patterns witnessed a marked decline in the strength of liberal Protestantism and a growth in Evangelicalism.[10] The moral majority, which grew in the late 1970s may have peaked and begun its decline in the early 1980s, but there were numerous indications of a rise in religious consciousness. The cover story on the Sunday, February 27, 2000, *New York Times Magazine* featured a religiously conservative Christian family who, together with other Evangelical and fundamentalist Christians, "make up about 25 percent of the American population."[11]

Conservative Christians are, however, clearly a minority, albeit a significant one, and they do not tell the whole entire story of the place of religion in American society. Indeed, some might suggest that America as a whole is a highly religious country. For evidence that it is not the secular one that it was portrayed to be in the 1960s

---

[7] "A Bleak Outlook Seen for Religion," *New York Times*, 25 Feb. 1968, p. 3.

[8] Charles Glock and Robert Bellah, eds., *The New Religious Consciousness* (Berkeley: University of California Press, 1976).

[9] Robert Wuthnow, *The Restructuring of American Religion: Society and Faith Since WWII* (Princeton, NJ: Princeton University Press, 1988).

[10] James Davison Hunter, *American Evangelicalism: Conservative Religion and the Quandary of Modernity* (New Brunswick, NJ: Rutgers University Press, 1983); James Davison Hunter, *Evangelicalism: The Coming Generation* (Chicago: University of Chicago Press, 1987); also see Wade Clark Roof and William McKinney, *American Mainline Religion: Its Changing Shape and Future* (New Brunswick, NJ: Rutgers University Press, 1987).

[11] Margaret Talbot, "A Mighty Fortress," *New York Times Magazine*, p. 36.

and that there has been a sharp increase in religion and spirituality in the country since that time, one need only look at the reading patterns of Americans. As reported by the Religion editor of *Publishers Weekly*,

> in February 1994, the Association of American Publishers, which also tracks the movement of books very carefully, had already reported that the sales of books in the Bible/religion/spirituality category were up 59 percent nationally over sales for February 1992. Earlier, in June 1992, *American Bookseller*, the official publication of the American Booksellers Association, had devoted six pages to this emerging pattern, declaring that "the category's expansion is indisputable." An even earlier Gallup study had projected that the largest sales increase in nonfiction books in the twenty-first century would be in religion/spirituality books (82 percent growth by 2010 over 1987), to be followed at a considerable distance (59 percent) by second-place investment/economic/income tax books. As if in preparation for that predicted pattern, the American Booksellers Association in 1995 opened for the first time a special section of its annual convention and trade show for what it categorizes as "religious/spiritual-inspirational" books.[12]

It is not only in books but in television as well that Americans demonstrate a deep involvement with spiritualism. One highly popular weekly show – indeed, in 1998 it was among the ten most-watched television shows in the country – was *Touched by an Angel*, a show which featured the well-known singer and actress Della Reese as Tess, the angel who oversees the work of her angels in the field, the two most central ones being Monica (Roma Downey) and Andrew (John Dye). Each week, these angels, who look like ordinary humans, helped someone in trouble, undergoing a crisis, or otherwise unhappy, by convincing him or her that God loves them

---

[12] Phyllis A. Tickle, *Rediscovering the Sacred: Spirituality in America* (New York: Crossroads, 1995), p. 18.

and that, if only they seek Him out, He will respond and help them to change their lives for the better.

The numerous references to God and to the mercy he has, even on fallen angels, were completely out of character with American prime-time network television. This was not simply mysticism or spirituality: it was traditional biblical notions about God and His ways, something which the mass media have long avoided. It simply has not been "proper" to mix religion, which had been relegated to the private sphere, into the mass media public sphere in any serious way.

In addition, Andrew Greeley and Michael Hout analyzed survey data from the past several decades and find that an increasing majority of Americans respond affirmatively to the question, "Do you believe there is a life after death?" Between 1973 and 1998, the figures have gone from 77 to 82 percent. In fact, the increases have been across the board, spanning adherents of various religions as well as those claiming no religious affiliation, and have been the greatest among America's Jews.[13]

These figures appear to indicate an abandonment of secularism and a return to religious consciousness and religiosity. In the summer of 2000, Sen. Joseph I. Lieberman, an Orthodox Jew, was nominated as the Vice-Presidential running mate on the Democratic ticket, and he so frequently made reference to God and traditional religion that the was asked, by a number of national organizations, and even a Jewish one, to tone down those references, lest he weaken the separation of religion and state. Be that as it may, his very nomination suggests that traditional religion is viewed positively among the American public. Perhaps there is a real *baal teshuvah* movement apace. After all, there has clearly been an unforeseen and significant rise in interest in Jewish mysticism in recent years. There has been a proliferation of books about Kabbalah and, as a book critic for the *Jewish Week* found, "New titles are coming from Jewish publishers and university presses as well as mainstream commercial houses

[13] Andrew M. Greeley and Michael Hout, "Americans' Increasing Belief in Life After Death: Religious Competition and Acculturation," *American Sociological Review* 64 (December, 1999): 814–815.

Table 2: Percentage Believing in Life After Death, by Survey Year and Religion, US Adults, 1973–1998

	Religion			
Year of Survey	Protestant	Catholic	Jewish	None
1973–1975	82	74	19	44
1976–1980	84	77	27	49
1982–1985	82	75	34	48
1986–1990	84	78	35	49
1991–1994	85	81	52	57
1996–1998	86	83	56	63
Percent Change	+4	+9	+37	+19

Source: Andrew M. Greeley and Michael Hout, "Americans' Increasing Belief in Life After Death: Religious Competition and Acculturation." *American Sociological Review* 64 (December, 1999): 816, based on data from the General Social Survey, 1973–1998.

that only a few years ago would have found the subject too much on the fringes."[14]

Whatever else the rise in spirituality in American culture may signify, however, it does not mean a return to religiosity in the sense of normative, institutionalized religion. As both Robert Wuthnow and Wade Clark Roof argue, contemporary spirituality is largely a search or "quest" by the members of the baby boomer generation and their children to find "purpose" and "meaning" in their personal existence. As Wuthnow suggests, the sacred has been transformed into something fluid. The baby boomers are the first to have "opportunities to explore new spiritual horizons," and, in the past two decades, they sought it within themselves, in their "inner selves," rather than within the church.[15] Based on his analyses of religion and spirituality among baby boomers, Roof argues that Americans'

[14] Sandee Brawarsky, "Into The Mystic," *Jewish Week*, 19 November 1999.
[15] Robert Wuthnow, *After Heaven: Spirituality in America Since the 1950s* (Berkeley: University of California Press, 1998).

ideas and practice of religion is motivated by a search for a sense of spirituality and personal fulfillment. Americans are looking beyond traditional religious institutions and identities and are on a spiritual quest, borrowing different elements from a variety of practices now available to them in the ever-expanding spiritual marketplace.[16]

Some may argue that one ought not to compare Jews and non-Jews, nor try to understand what is happening among Jews by looking at larger social patterns. After all, in a recent article which appears on the web site of Yeshivat Har Eẓion, R. Aharon Lichtenstein suggests that, "We are 'believers and children of believers,' and as such are guided by *Ḥazal*'s dictum that '*Ein mazal le-Yisrael*:' the Jewish experience is not determined and therefore cannot be fully understood by reference to astrological forces, or, in modern terms, by historical causation or sociological categories."[17] This seems to suggest that Jews are immune to larger social patterns and forces.

This is puzzling, especially in light of the assertion by the author of the *Sefer he-Ḥasidim*, and expressed by many others in similar terms, to wit, that Jewish patterns of behavior resemble those of the non-Jews in the host society.[18] The assertion by R. Yehudah he-Ḥasid (c. 1150–1217) says nothing about the special relationship of Israel with God any more than establishing causality in human behavior says anything about free will. As Durkheim observed long ago, "Sociology does not need to choose between the great hypotheses which divide metaphysicians. It need embrace free will no more than determinism. All that it asks is that the principle of causality be applied to social phenomena."[19]

---

[16] Wade Clark Roof, *Spiritual Marketplace: Baby Boomers and the Remaking of American Religion* (Princeton: Princeton University Press, 1999).

[17] R. Aharon Lichtenstein, "Centrist Orthodoxy – A Cheshbon ha-Nefesh, Part 1: The Complexity of Experience" (Lecture 22). Adapted by R. Ronnie Ziegler. www.vbm-torah.org.

[18] "כמו שמנהג הנכרים כן מנהגי היהודים ברוב מקומות" (ר׳ יהודה החסיד, ספר החסידים, ס׳ תתש"א)
"פירוש ברית עולם" (לר׳ חיים דוד אזולעי): "ר"ל כי זה תלוי בטבע הארץ...."
"As is the custom of the gentiles, so are the customs of the Jews in most cases' – because [custom] is a result of the nature of a particular environment…." R.H.Y.D. Azulai on *Sefer he-Ḥasidim*, 1101.

Accordingly, analyses will now be presented of some data from the 1990 National Jewish Population Survey (NJPS), which indicate the levels of religiosity of a major segment of the American Jewish population.[20] Since we are dealing with social science data, Jewishness was determined by the respondent; that is, I selected those who, when asked their current religion, identified themselves as Jewish. The specific data are for the age group known as "baby boomers," that is, those born between 1946–1964. That cohort represented, in 1990, a third of the American population.[21]

For reasons that are beyond the scope of this paper, America's Jews have been and apparently continue to be less religiously traditional in their beliefs than their Christian counterparts. For example, respondents' statements about the nature of the authenticity of the Bible, in NJPS, were compared with almost identical statements by baby boomers in the larger

American population, as found in the 1990 General Social Survey.[22]

These data indicate that Jewish baby boomers are much less likely than their non-Jewish fellows to believe that the Bible is divine.

[19] Emile Durkheim, *The Rules of the Sociological Method*, ed. George E.G. Catlin (Glencoe, IL: The Free Press of Glencoe, 1962), p. 141.

[20] Parts of the discussion that follows are from my book, *Jewish Baby Boomers: A Communal Perspective* (Albany, NY: State University of New York Press, 2001).

[21] Leon F. Bouvier and Carol J. De Vita, "The Baby Boom–Entering Midlife," *Population Bulletin* 46:3 (November 1991): Figure 3, 10–11; Edwin R. Byerly and Kevin Deardorff, *National and State Population Estimates: 1990–1994*, US Bureau of the Census, *Current Population Reports*, p. 25–1127 (Washington, DC: US Government Printing Office, 1995): Table 3, 32.

[22] The General Social Survey (GSS), conducted since 1972 by the National Opinion Research Center, is an ongoing survey of American households with questions that ask about attitudes and practices dealing with a wide variety of topics of social concern. Initially administered annually with a sample of 1,500 interviewees, since 1994 it is conducted bi-annually and the sample size has been increased to 3,000. It asks questions concerning alcohol and drug use, crime and punishment, race relations, quality of life, patterns of sexual relations, and religious behavior, among others. Because it is administered approximately every two years, GSS data are amenable to providing evidence of trends and patterns over time. This is in

Table 3: Baby Boomers' Statements About the Bible, GSS & NJPS, 1990

	GSS	GSS, College Grads.	NJPS
Actual word of God	29.6	21.3	13.6
Inspired word of God	53.9	57.4	36.6
History, moral by men	15.5	18.5	46.3
Other (Volunteered)	1.0	2.8	3.5

Indeed, almost half of the Jews surveyed believe it is a completely human production, whereas only about 15 percent of the non-Jews do, and about 19 percent of non-Jews with at least a college degree do.

Although the question about the Bible was the only one in all of the NJPS which asked about religious belief, other data suggest similar patterns. In the previously cited findings of Greeley and Hout, Jews consistently had lower proportions believing in an afterlife than both Christians and those claiming no religious affiliation (see Table 2, above) Also, Wade Clark Roof's study of the "spiritual journeys of baby boomers"[23] contained a small sample of Jews. Out of the 1375 cases in his sample, only 32, or 2.3 percent, were Jews, too few to allow any definitive conclusions. However, especially since the percentage of the total sample is fairly reflective of the percentage of Jews in the American population, and the pattern of Jewish responses in Roof's study is so internally consistent as well as consistent with the NJPS data, when comparisons can be made, it seems reasonable to infer that we are dealing with a representative empirical pattern here, one in which American Jewish baby boomers are significantly less religiously-oriented than their Protestant and Catholic peers.

Roof's data reveal that more than 84 percent of the Jewish baby boomers in his sample agreed that an individual should arrive at his

contrast to most surveys whose findings are appropriate solely to the particular time of the survey.

[23] Wade Clark Roof, et al. *A Generation of Seekers: The Spiritual Journeys of the Baby Boom Generation* (San Francisco: HarperCollins, 1993).

or her own beliefs rather than to accept them simply because they are propounded by religious functionaries. A smaller percentage of Christian baby boomers – about 75 percent of the Protestants and about 73 percent of the Catholics – agreed. The same percentage of the Jewish baby boomers, 84 percent, agreed that one should follow one's own conscience rather than have one's morality defined by one's religion, whereas even fewer of the Protestants agreed with this than agreed with the idea of arriving at one's own beliefs. Among Catholics, 8 percent more agreed that one should follow one's own conscience than believed that one should arrive at their own beliefs. Jews were least likely to agree that being a church or synagogue member is important, and Jews were least likely to say that either their family or their friends share the same views about religion.[24]

Religion, however, entails not only beliefs but actions as well. As Durkheim put it, religion is "a unified system of beliefs and practices relative to sacred things...."[25] In analyzing the ritual behavior of Jewish baby boomers, as revealed by the NJPS data, two distinct sets of religious rituals are examined. One set is comprised of household rituals, reported by the respondents concerning observance within their households. The second set is comprised of personal rituals, and of these the respondents reported about their own personal observance of them. The findings with respect to household rituals indicate sharp variation.

Table 4 indicates the continued popularity of the rituals of the Passover meal, the Seder, and the lighting of Hanukkah candles. These are regularly observed by almost three-fourths of the baby boomers surveyed. This contrasts sharply with the rate of observance of the other household rituals where less than 20 percent of the Jewish baby boomers reported regularly observing the other three household rituals in the table, lighting candles Sabbath eve and observing the kosher food rituals. This pattern reconfirms the observation of Sklare and Greenblum almost a quarter of a century earlier, namely, that the rate of retention in ritual observance is

[24] I acknowledge and appreciate Roof's sharing of his unpublished data with me.

[25] Emile Durkheim, *The Elementary Forms of Religious Life* (1912), A New Translation by Karen E. Fields (New York: Free Press, 1995).

Table 4: Performance of Household Rituals

	Boomers
Household lights candles Friday night	17.7
Household attends Seder	74.3
Anyone in household buys kosher meat	16.3
Household uses separate meat & dairy dishes	12.1
Anyone in household lights Hanukkah candles	73.3

highest when the ritual "(1) is capable of effective redefinition in modern terms, (2) does not demand social isolation or the adoption of a unique lifestyle, (3) accords with the religious culture of the larger community and provides a "Jewish" alternative when such is felt to be needed, (4) is centered on the child, and (5) is performed annually or infrequently."[26]

The relatively high percentage of those lighting Hanukkah candles is frequently cited by some as an indication of the persistence of Jewish identity and identification in the United States.[27] The data, however, indicate that this interpretation needs to be qualified and that Hanukkah candle-lighting cannot be taken as a reliable index of a family's Jewish identity. There were a small number (46) of cases in the NJPS in which both the head of household and the spouse, one being the respondent and being a baby boomer, were Christian from birth. There are a variety of circumstances which could have led to this, such as reconstituted families in which there is a Jewish child in the household whose other, non-custodial, parent, from whom the household head is divorced, was Jewish, and the custodial parent wishes to maintain some of the rituals of the other parent. Or it may be a reconstituted family in which the divorced spouses, who had been in a mixed marriage, now maintain joint custody, and the non-Jewish parent is now married to someone who is not Jewish. In

[26] Marshall Sklare and Joseph Greenblum, *Jewish Identity on the Suburban Frontier: A Study of Group Survival in the Open Society* (New York: Basic Books, 1967), p. 57.

[27] Charles E. Silberman, *A Certain People: American Jews and Their Lives Today* (New York: Summit Books, 1985).

another case, the head of household and spouse may have a Jewish foster child. Or, they may have a Jewish relative by marriage who lives in the household, such a brother-in-law or sister-in-law. Be that as it may, in 20 percent of those cases, respondents reported that their household attends a Passover Seder sometimes (9.9%), usually (4.7%), or all the time (6.1%), and that they light Hanukkah candles sometimes (10.1%) or all the time (9.0%). These data are based on a very small number of cases, and are only meant to be suggestive. But even in endogamous Jewish marriages, the household practice cannot be taken as an indication of the Jewish religious identity of the household because there can be religious and secular people in the same household. In mixed religious families such as these, it is even more obvious that the household practice is not reflective of the religious identity of all of its members. At most, it may indicate the Jewish identity of some member of the household. However, even that is questionable, since having a Passover Seder and lighting candles on Hanukkah have, in many circles, become American rituals, and not simply Jewish ones. There are an increasing number of Christians, especially Catholics, who hold a Passover Seder as an ecumenical ritual to connote the Jewish origins of Jesus, and there are an increasing number of non-Jewish Americans who light candles on Hanukkah to symbolize their solidarity with Jewish Americans. These rituals have become "Americanized" and are now part of the American ceremonial calendar. In and of themselves, they cannot be taken as indications of Jewish identity. Thus, Arthur Waskow introduces his *Freedom Seder* as follows:

> For us this Haggadah is deeply Jewish, but not only Jewish. In our world we all live under Pharaohs who could exterminate us any moment, and so enslave us all the time. Passover therefore fuses, for an instant, with the history and the future of all mankind. But it fuses for an instant, and in the fusion it does not disappear. The particularly Jewish lives within the universally human, at the same time that the universally human lives within the particularly Jewish.[28]

With respect to personal rather than household rituals, the patterns are also mixed. More than half of the respondents reported fasting on Yom Kippur (although we do not know if this means from sundown on the eve of Yom Kippur until after sunset on Yom Kippur), but less than 15 percent refrain from handling money on the Sabbath.

Table 5: Personal Observance

Fasts on Yom Kippur	58.7
Refrains from handling money on Sabbath	13.4

When we look at the denominational backgrounds of those currently identified with denominations, we find that the Orthodox have the highest percentage of those who now identify with the same denomination in which they were raised. This, however, is not an indicator of the strength of Orthodoxy; on the contrary, it may indicate Orthodoxy's inability to attract adherents. From that perspective, the data indicate that Reform is actually the strongest denomination.

That interpretation is reinforced when we look at the current denominational identification of those respondents who were raised within denominations. As indicated in Table 7, the Orthodox have the lowest rate of those currently identifying with the denomination in which they were raised and Reform the highest. In other words, with respect to retention, Reform is the strongest denomination and Orthodox is the weakest since the latter has the highest dropout rate while the former has the lowest dropout rate.

[28] Arthur I. Waskow, *The Freedom Seder: A New Haggadah for Passover* (New York: Holt, Rinehart, Winston, 1970), pp. vi–vii; also see Jan Hoffman, "Make Your Own Tradition: Redefining Seders for Today," *New York Times*, 10 April 1998, pp. A1, B6.

Table 6: Denomination Raised and Current Denominational Identification of Jewish Baby Boomers

Denom. Raised:	Now Orthodox	Now Conservative	Now Reform	Now Reconstructionist
Orthodox	78.2	15.4	4.0	—
Conservative	6.9	68.0	19.4	70.4
Reform	—	4.4	64.8	19.7
Reconstructionist	—	—	.6	4.3
Other/None	14.9	12.0	11.2	5.6
Total	100.0	100.0	100.0	100.0

Table 7: Denomination Raised and Current Denomination of Jewish Baby Boomers

	Raised Orthodox	Raised Conservative	Raised Reform
Now Orthodox	35.2	.9	—
Now Conservative	45.6	58.8	3.9
Now Reform	18.2	26.0	87.9
Now Reconstructionist	—	2.3	.7
Other/None	2.0	12.0	7.5
Total	100.0	100.0	100.0

Since the figures on denomination raised indicate only a minor diminution within Orthodoxy, with hardly any of the Conservative and none of the Reform becoming Orthodox, it might seem surprising and puzzling that 21.8 percent of the current Orthodox were not raised Orthodox. What may be even more surprising is that the data indicate that fully 10.5 percent of those who currently identify as Orthodox Jews were raised as non-Jews, 7.1 percent as Christians, and 3.4 percent as "Other Religion." No other known source indicates such a high proportion of Orthodox Jews as converts.

Also, the figures on denomination raised are somewhat surprising in light of the publicity given to the phenomenon of "*baalei teshuvah*" or returnees.[29] The NJPS data on the percentage stating that they were raised Orthodox reveal a picture drastically different from the impressions of communal workers, including rabbis, in the Orthodox community, as well as those who have conducted empirical research in that community, all of which indicate that there are significant numbers of such newly-Orthodox. For example, Danzger found that 24 percent of the highly observant in his sample, that is, observers of the Sabbath and kosher dietary laws, reported that they are new to the observance.[30] It seems reasonable to assume that a good percentage of these are switchers to Orthodoxy. More recently, a study of more than a thousand members and former members of the Orthodox Jewish synagogue youth organization, the National Conference of Synagogue Youth (NCSY) found that, out of the 28 percent who said that they were not raised Orthodox there were 21 percent who said they were Conservative in high school and are now Orthodox, and 10 percent who said they were Reform or Reconstructionist in high school and are now Orthodox.[31] These figures suggest a much higher rate of denominational switching to Orthodoxy than the NJPS indicates.

It would appear that further investigation is needed into just what the NJPS respondents meant when they stated that they were raised Orthodox. Did that mean that they were raised as observant in the Orthodox definition of the term, or did they mean that they

---

[29] M. Herbert Danzger, *Returning to Tradition: The Contemporary Revival of Orthodox Judaism* (New Haven: Yale University Press, 1989); Lynn Davidman, *Tradition in a Rootless World: Women Turn to Orthodox Judaism* (Berkeley: University of California Press, 1991).

[30] Danzger, p. 343.

[31] Nathalie Friedman, *Faithful Youth: A Study of the National Conference of Synagogue Youth* (New York: National Conference of Synagogue Youth, 1998), p. 32 and Table 4.1, p. 83.

attended an Orthodox synagogue? The two are very different. Many of the latter may have been part of what Marshall Sklare termed the "non-observant Orthodox," that is, those who are heterodox in personal behavior but who, when occasionally joining in public worship, do so in accordance with traditional patterns.[32]

It is important to note that the denominational patterns of Jewish baby boomers in the New York Metropolitan Area are quite different from the national ones, and this may explain some of the difference between NJPS and the Danzger and NCSY data. New York Jewry has a much higher proportion of Orthodox constituents and is generally more traditional.

Table 8: Denominational Identification of NY Jewish Baby Boomers

	Boomers
Orthodox	13.3
Conservative	28.2
Reform	37.0
Reconstructionist	1.6
Something Else	20.0
Total	100.0

In New York, almost twice as many, 61.3 percent as compared to 35.2 percent nationally, of those who were raised Orthodox are now Orthodox. Among the Conservative the difference is not as great, 60.3 percent as compared to the national 58.8 percent of those who were raised Conservative are now Conservative. For the Reform, the drop is even greater in New York than nationally; 78.6, as compared to national 87.9 of those who were raised Reform are now Reform. How this will impact on American Jewish baby boomers as a whole is not all that clear. We have seen the consistent decline in the proportion of America's Jews who live in the Northeast, and there may have been even greater declines in the New York Jewish population itself. It is, therefore, becoming increasingly important

[32] Marshall Sklare, *Conservative Judaism: An American Religious Movement*, augmented ed. (New York: Schocken, 1972), p. 46.

for both social scientists and Jewish communal planners and workers to distinguish New York's patterns from the national ones. Jews in the Northeast are becoming an increasingly smaller percentage of the American Jewish population,[33] and there is every reason to assume that the same pattern holds, at least as much, for the baby boomer cohort.

As for American Judaism as a whole, Charles Liebman offers an analysis of the increase in ritual among the Orthodox and the flourishing of ceremonial behavior among the non-Orthodox. Rituals, he argues, are *miẓvot*, commandments, whereas ceremonies are symbolic acts which derive from and appeal to personalism, voluntarism, universalism, and moralism. He focuses on the non-Orthodox, who constitute about 90 percent of American Jewry, and details how they are creating a uniquely American Judaism by both reinterpreting and transforming traditional rituals into ceremonies as well as by producing entirely new ceremonies, all of which are performed within the context of the aforementioned modern doctrines or "isms." These "isms," he concludes, "now have become major dimensions or instruments through which American Jews interpret and transform the Jewish tradition."[34]

Contemporary American Judaism is replete with the manifestations of the transformation of Jewish rituals into ceremonies. Perhaps one of the most prevalent is the Bar and Bat Miẓvah – traditionally, a rite of passage, at age 13 for males and 12 for females, at which time the youngster becomes an adult for the purposes of religious observances. In American Judaism, these have been transformed into ceremonious affairs at which, even among Conservative synagogue members, approximately half have a non-kosher

[33] Chaim I. Waxman, *America's Jews in Transition* (Philadelphia: Temple University Press, 1983), pp. 137–38.

[34] Charles S. Liebman, "Ritual, Ceremony, and the Reconstruction of Judaism in the United States," in *Art and its Uses: The Visual Image and Modern Jewish Society*, ed. Ezra Mendelsohn, (Studies in Contemporary Jewry 6; New York: Oxford University Press, 1990), pp. 272–83; Charles S. Liebman and Steven M. Cohen, *Two Worlds of Judaism: The Israeli and American Experiences* (New Haven: Yale University Press, 1990), pp. 123–38.

Bar/Bat Miẓvah reception.[35] Another is the recent introduction of gay marriages, replete with the spouses wearing *kipot* and *talitot*, the traditional skull caps and prayer shawls worn by Jewish males and, more recently, by some Jewish females, as well as the breaking of glass, which traditionally symbolizes the incompleteness of the joy so long as Jerusalem has not been ultimately redeemed.

The initial manifestations of the privatizing and personalizing of American Judaism were in the Ḥavurah, a late-1960s movement which represented alienation from the institutionalized synagogue and its substitution in the form of countercultural prayer and study groups. In one of the few ethnographies of a Ḥavurah, the Kelton *Minyan*, Riv-Ellen Prell provides important insight into its basic objective. As she found, its members sought to synthesize the Jewish religious tradition, as they understood it, with their own modern American norms and values, and the *Minyan* functioned as the place where prayer and study were meant to be experienced in an egalitarian manner.[36] Things did not, however, always turn out as they had been envisioned, as Prell's analysis of the "prayer crisis," members' inability at times to accept or find meaning in certain liturgy, clearly demonstrates.

One of the movement's founder's and its spiritual guru is Rabbi Zalman Schachter-Shalomi, who, having been ordained by the Lubavitch H⊠asidim and also having received a graduate degree in psychology from Boston University and a doctorate from Hebrew Union College, parted with Orthodox Judaism and has developed his own non-orthodox brand of ḥasidic spiritualism which he hopes will bring about a "Jewish Renewal." As he sees it,

> Jewish Renewal is based on the Kabbalah, Ḥasidism, and other forms of Jewish mysticism. These sources support a

[35] Jack Wertheimer, *Conservative Synagogues and Their Members: Highlights of the North American Survey of 1995–96* (New York: The Jewish Theological Seminary of America, 1996), p. 42.

[36] Riv-Ellen Prell, *Prayer and Community: The Ḥavurah in American Judaism* (Detroit: Wayne State University Press, 1989).

> transformational and developmental reading of our current place in history.... Restoration is ultimately not a viable option because of the impact of the paradigm shift.... This expresses itself in the emergent voices of the emerging cosmology, in which old reality maps are scrapped and new ones emerge that are, if not identical, at least parallel to the intuitions and traditions of Jewish mysticism...augmented and at times even reshaped by feminism.... This in turn leads to a kind of healthy planetary homemaking and is concerned about ecology. This also calls for an eco-kosher *halakhah* and ethic. In order to become the kinds of Jews/persons who can effect the needed changes, the intra- and interpersonal work related to meditation and liturgy that are the laboratory of the spirit need to be renewed, and this leads to making prayer and meditation into a science as well as an art. Hence the need for a davvenology that is (1) an art and a science, (2) based on the Kabbalah, and (3) a generic empiricism.[37]

Among Schachter-Shalomi's proteges is Arthur Waskow, who was an early 1960s anti-war activist who adapted Ḥasidism to his social and political ideologies. He is currently a rabbi, the director of a center committed to spiritually healing the world, and is also a leader of the Alliance for Jewish Renewal. He introduced an alternative Passover Haggadah, *The Freedom Seder,*[38] which, as was indicated earlier, transforms the Jewish Seder ritual into a universalistic one. He later created a unique Jewish festival commentary, *Seasons of Our Joy.*[39] In all of his works, he puts a Jewish-ḥasidic-spiritual cloak on his political and social radicalism. For example, in his more recent work, *Down-To-Earth Judaism: Food, Money, Sex, and the Rest of*

[37] Zalman Schachter-Shalomi, *Paradigm Shift: From the Jewish Renewal Teachings of Reb Zalman Schachter-Shalomi*, ed. Ellen Singer (Northvale: Jason Aronson, 1993), p. xx.

[38] Waskow, *The Freedom Seder.*

[39] Arthur I. Waskow, *Seasons of Our Joy: A Celebration of Modern Jewish Renewal* (New York: Bantam, 1982).

Life,[40] Waskow adopts Schachter-Shalomi's concept of "eco-kosher" and argues for expanding the definition of kosher to include not only food but every kind of product that Jews "ingest." Rhetorically, he asks a series of confrontational questions, such as whether it is "kosher" to use newsprint in a Jewish newspaper when it was created by cutting down an ancient forest; whether a bank that invests its money in an oil company that pollutes the ocean is a "kosher" place for either an individual or the United Jewish Appeal to keep accounts? Waskow's views on sexuality are anything but traditional. He asserts a religion that only sanctions sex within marriage is not a realistic one, and he is looking for ways in which Judaism can celebrate all human sexual relationships, whether within marriage or without, whether heterosexual or homosexual.

Schachter-Shalomi and Waskow may be unique, but their influence is significant. They were among the major figures in the neo-ḥasidic and mystical movement that emergeod alongside the *ḥavurah* movement.[41] Most of those involved in the *ḥavurah* movement were not as radical as Waskow, nor as neo-ḥasidic as Schachter-Shalomi, but they were interested in spiritualism in non-traditional ways. It was within that context that *The Jewish Catalog* was written. Patterned after the *Whole Earth Catalog*, a work that was very popular in the 1960s counterculture, *The Jewish Catalog* quickly became a bestseller and a publishing phenomenon in American Judaica,[42] and was the first of two additional such catalogs. In a critical review, Marshall Sklare expressed his disdain for the "new personalism" represented in the work. Although, he asserted, "in most areas of life discussed...the relevant Jewish law is scrupulously reported, where applicable...the dominant stress quickly shifts to the experiential side of the subject in question, the side connected with issues of

---

[40] Arthur Waskow, *Down-To-Earth Judaism; Food, Money, Sex, and the Rest of Life* (New York: William Morrow, 1995).

[41] *Jewish Radicalism: A Selected Anthology*, ed. Jack Nusan Porter and Peter Dreier (New York: Grove Press, 1973), pp. xlii-xliii.

[42] *The Jewish Catalog*, ed. Richard Siegel, Michael Strassfeld, and Sharon Strassfeld (Philadelphia: Jewish Publication Society, 1973).

personal style, of taste, and aesthetic pleasure."[43] It was not just one book that Sklare was reacting to; for him, it was another step in the transformation of American Judaism which had begun in the Palmer, Massachusetts branch of Conservative Judaism's Camp Ramah, then to the *ḥavurot*, and then to the creation of a guide for the privatization of Judaism. It was not this book that disturbed him so much as its further impact on American Judaism. In the final analysis, whether he is correct in his specific criticisms of that volume or not is beside the point; the empirical evidence appears to confirm the transformation, privatization of much of American Judaism. This is even the case, to some degree, within some varieties of Orthodox Judaism,[44] such as those whom Heilman labeled "nominally Orthodox," who are much more selective in their ritual observance and religious beliefs than the "centrist" Orthodox who, in turn, are more selective than the "traditional" Orthodox. Although there are no Orthodox Jews who overtly assert the non-binding character of *halakhah*, nor are there any who overtly legitimate the non-conformity with basic requirements of dietary or family purity rituals or Sabbath observance, there are those, even among them, who are selective in their own personal conformity with Orthodox beliefs and norms. They are those whom I have described as "behaviorally modern Orthodox.[45]

The increased personalism and privatization of not only Judaism but religion in general appears to be a phenomenon which transcends America's geographic boundaries and is, in fact, much more pervasive in other, mostly Western, countries. The political sociologist, Ronald Inglehart, has conducted comprehensive cross-national surveys, and his analyses reveal broad international patterns for which he provides a penetrating sociological explanation. In his

[43] Marshall Sklare, *Observing America's Jews* (Hanover: Brandeis University Press, 1993), p. 82.

[44] Samuel C. Heilman and Steven M. Cohen, *Cosmopolitans and Parochials: Modern Orthodox Jews in America* (Chicago: University of Chicago Press, 1989).

[45] Chaim I. Waxman, "Dilemmas of Modern Orthodoxy," *Judaism* 42:1 (Winter 1993): 68.

analysis of survey data gathered in twenty-five industrial societies, primarily in Western Europe and the United States, between 1970 and 1986, Inglehart argues that "economic, technological, and socio-political changes have been transforming the cultures of advanced industrial societies in profoundly important ways."[46] Following Maslow's need hierarchy, according to which the need for food, shelter, and sex are on the lowest rung and must be satisfied before a person can move up the pyramid to its apex, self-actualization, Inglehart maintains that individuals are most concerned with the satisfaction of material needs and threats to their physical security. "Materialist" values, which are characteristic of economically and otherwise less secure societies, Inglehart avers, are values that emphasize material security. In the area of politics, these would focus on such needs as having strong leaders and order. In the realm of economics, these values emphasize economic growth and motivation for strong individual achievement. In the area of sexuality and family norms, the emphasis would be on the maximization of reproduction within the two-parent family. And within the realm of religion, the emphasis is on a higher power and absolute rules. However, once the basic material needs are satisfied and physical safety is assured, people strive for "postmaterialist" values which entail the satisfaction of more remote needs, many of which are in the spiritual, aesthetic, and interpersonal realms. Their focus becomes self-fulfillment and personal autonomy, rather than identifying themselves with their families, localities, ethnic groups, or even nations. This "culture shift" is manifested in a declining respect for authority and increased mass participation; an increasing emphasis on subjective well-being and quality of life concerns; an increasing emphasis on meaningful work; greater choice in the area of sexual norms; declining confidence in established religious institutions as well as declining rates of church attendance; and an increasing contemplation of the purpose and meaning of life. This shift, which entails a shift from central authority

[46] Ronald Inglehart, *Culture Shift in Advanced Industrial Society* (Princeton: Princeton University Press, 1990), p. 3.

to individual autonomy, has taken place in "postmaterialist" society, that is, the West, in the late-twentieth century.

This has meant that institutionalized religions can no longer count on traditional allegiance, because the ability of religion to locate us and to provide order and meaning is greatly diminished in modern society and culture. As Peter Berger puts it, the intricately interrelated processes of pluralization, bureaucratization, and secularization, which are endemic to modernity, have greatly shaken the religious "plausibility structures."[47] Although "a rumor of angels" prevails,[48] it is but a "rumor" in modern society, and it co-exists with a "heretical imperative."[49] That is, the pluralistic character of modern society impels us to make choices, including religious choices. We are no longer impelled to believe and act. We choose, even when we choose to be religiously orthodox. From the standpoint of traditional religion, that is heresy because, as Berger points out, "the English word 'heresy' comes from the Greek verb *hairein*, which means 'to choose.' A *hairesis* originally meant, quite simply, the taking of a choice."[50]

The growth of fundamentalism and *hareidism* in advanced Western societies in no way disproves Inglehart's thesis. He argues that it is precisely the conditions of postmodernity which foster religious fundamentalism because fundamentalism is typically reactionary and arises as a defense mechanism in reaction to the deep fears and anxieties inherent in the previously described situation. It is, as Inglehart suggests, a reaction to the growth of postmaterialism,[51] and, in most advanced societies, fundamentalists are a minority who can, at most, slow down some of the impact of postmaterialism.

---

[47] Berger, *The Sacred Canopy*.

[48] Peter L. Berger, *A Rumor of Angels: Modern Society and the Rediscovery of the Supernatural* (Garden City, NY: Doubleday, 1979).

[49] Peter L. Berger, *The Heretical Imperative: Contemporary Possibilities of Religious Affirmation* (Garden City, NY: Anchor Press, 1979).

[50] Berger, *Heretical Imperative*, p. 27.

[51] Ronald Inglehart, *Modernization and Postmodernization: Cultural, Economic, and Political Change in 43 Societies* (Princeton: Princeton University Press, 1997), p. 251.

They do not seem capable of stopping it. It may be predicted that the greater the size of the fundamentalist constituency in a given society, the more they will be able to impact on the consequences of postmaterialism in that society.

In their recent study, Inglehart and Wayne Baker found that, although attendance at religious services is declining in postmaterialist countries, including the United States, close to half of the Americans surveyed said that they often think about the meaning and purpose of life, and fully half rated the importance of God in their lives as very high. They found that allegiances to established religious institutions are continuing to decline in postmaterialist countries, but spiritual concerns are not.[52]

Increased personalism and privatization present powerful challenges not only to established religious institutions, but also to all institutions. For Jews, these are challenges to the very unity of the Jewish people. As Charles Liebman has penetratingly analyzed it, the privatization of Judaism enervates the basic nature of ethnic Judaism. The "new spiritualism" thus weakens the basic Jewish notions of peoplehood, community, and solidarity.[53]

The connection between commitment to tradition, commitment to institutions, and commitment to the group are apparent in the intense involvements of the *ḥareidi* community with charity and social welfare, *ẓedakah,* and *gemilut ḥasadim*. For example, a recent major study of volunteerism in Israel found that "nearly forty-five percent of ultra-Orthodox Jews volunteer...compared to fifteen percent of secular Israelis.[54] The greater propensity for charity is not limited to *hareidim*. Indeed, my analysis of American Jewish

---

[52] Ronald F. Inglehart and Wayne E. Baker, "Modernization, Cultural Change and the Persistence of Traditional Values," *American Sociological Review* 65:1 (February, 2000): 19–51.

[53] Charles S. Liebman, "Post-War American Jewry: From Ethnic to Privatized Judaism," in *Secularism, Spirituality, and the Future of American Jewry* ed. Elliot Abrams and David G. Dalin (Washington, DC: Ethics and Public Policy Center, 1999), pp. 7–18.

[54] Netty C. Gross, "Salvation Army," *Jerusalem Report*, 14 Feb. 2000.

baby boomers[55] indicates patterns of charity vary denominationally. Eighty percent (80.5%) of the Orthodox baby boomer respondents reported contributing to Jewish charities, compared with 56.4 percent of the Conservative, 43.5 percent of the Reform and only 40.7 percent of the denominationally unaffiliated. Almost 95 percent (94.4%) of the small number of Reconstructionists in the sample reported that they contributed to Jewish charities. The significance of affiliation within the three major denominations becomes even sharper when family size and family income are considered. Orthodox baby boomers reported larger families and lower annual family incomes than Conservative and Reform baby boomers (an average of about $10,000 a year less than the Conservative and $20,000 less than the Reform). However, 70.8 percent of the Orthodox reported contributing $500 or more to Jewish charities, as compared to 18 percent of the Conservative and 15.7 percent of the Reform. Of the unaffiliated, only 11.4 percent reported contributing $500, and none contributed more than $1,000 to Jewish charities.

Although one might expect that in the Orthodox community spiritualism would correlate directly with level of observance, it appears that the suspicion of spirituality in the *hareidi* community is even greater than it is in the non-*hareidi* community. One obvious reason is that the more religiously conservative a community is, the more behaviorally conservative it is as well. However, *hareidim* are suspicious of new patterns even when there appears to be valid halakhic bases for them. For example, despite the apparent contemporary basis for requiring *tekhelet* in *ẓiẓit*, the *hareidi* community is most resistant to adopting this practice. Perhaps the basis of that suspicion is not solely because it views the wearing of *tekhelet* as deviating from established norms but, also, because it is becoming increasingly prevalent within the non-*hareidi* community and is most widespread within the spiritual "*Habaku"k*" community,[56] a growing community of individuals who are perceived as less than

[55] Waxman, *Jewish Baby Boomers.*

[56] "Habaku"k" is a recently innovated acronym, which stands for new phenomenon of a Ḥabad, Breslov, Carlebach, Kook community.

well-grounded in the world of *halakhah* and who do not readily conform to the dictates of either the halakhic authorities or the communal traditions.

There is not only solid historical precedence for this suspicion; it is rooted in an understanding of the driving force behind much of what passes for spiritualism. As Norman Lamm points out, there is an implicit conflict between *halakhah* and spiritualism. "The contrast between the two – spirituality and law – is almost self-evident. Spirituality is subjective; the very fact of its inwardness implies a certain degree of anarchy; it is unfettered and self-directed, impulsive and spontaneous. In contrast, law is objective; it requires discipline, structure, obedience, order."[57]

It might be further argued that the growing pattern of "shtibelization" is further evidence that even the Orthodox community is not immune to the increasing self-directedness which characterizes much of contemporary society. However, I would suggest that a careful examination of the motivations behind this pattern would reveal that, for many, it is not motivated by impulsiveness and/or self-directedness but by a quest for spirituality that is not necessarily qualitatively different from that of many of Roof's subjects, but is within Jewishly legitimate parameters. The participants in the growing number of Carlebach *minyanim*, for example, are not looking to escape either prayer or the synagogue; indeed, their services are much longer than those in more normative Orthodox congregations. They appear to strive towards greater spirituality within the halakhic framework, even if they do not exude "*ruchnius*" in the traditional *hareidi* sense, with its explicit emphasis on *kedushah*, holiness and separateness.[58]

Given the extent of the contemporary spiritual quest in American society, those seeking to, at least, stem the tide of defection from Orthodoxy if not attract others to it, would appear to be advised to foster and encourage this spiritualism within legitimate halakhic

[57] Norman Lamm, *The Shema: Spirituality and Law in Judaism* (Philadelphia and Jerusalem: Jewish Publication Society, 1998), pp. 6–7.

[58] See Charles S. Liebman, "Post-War American Jewry," p. 23, for a distinction between "*ruchnius*" and spirituality.

boundaries. Judaism, after all, was never solely legalistic. As Lamm avers, "law alone is artificial and insensitive. Without the body of the law, spirituality is a ghost. Without the sweep of the soaring soul, the corpus of the law tends to become a corpse.[59] Wuthnow seems to be suggesting something similar, which he calls "practice-oriented spirituality:"

> Practice-oriented spirituality can best be nurtured by practice-oriented religious organizations that is, by churches, synagogues, mosques, temples, and other places of worship that define their primary mission as one of strengthening the spiritual discipline of their members. Such organizations will strive to give members both roots and wings roots to ground them solidly in the traditions of their particular faith, wings to explore their own talents and the mysteries of the sacred.[60]

[59] Norman Lamm, *The Shema*, p. 6.
[60] Robert Wuthnow, *After Heaven*, p. 17.

The Orthodox Forum
Twelfth Conference

Sunday & Monday, April 2–3, 2000
26–27 Adar II 5760

Congregation Shearith Israel
8 West 70th Street
New York City

LIST OF PARTICIPANTS*

Rabbi Elchanan Adler	Yeshiva University, New York, NY
Dr. Norman Adler	Yeshiva University, New York, NY
Rabbi Yosef Adler	Torah Academy of Bergen County, Teaneck, NJ
Rabbi William S. Altshul	Hebrew Academy of Greater Washington, Silver Spring, MD
Rabbi Assaf Bednarsh	Alon Shevut, Israel
Mrs. Leora Bednarsh	Alon Shevut, Israel
Dr. David Berger	Brooklyn College, New York, NY
Rabbi Gedalyah Berger	Yeshiva University, New York, NY
Rabbi Yitzhak Berger	Hunter College, New York, NY
Rabbi Ari Berman	The Jewish Center, New York, NY
Rabbi Jack Bieler	Hebrew Academy of Greater Washington, Silver Spring, MD

*Current Affiliation

Dr. Rivkah Blau	Writer and Lecturer, New York, NY
Rabbi Yosef Blau	RIETS/Yeshiva University, New York, NY
Dr. Judith Bleich	Touro College, New York, NY
Prof. Alan Brill	Yeshiva University, New York, NY
Mrs. Erica Brown	Jewish Federation of Greater Washington, Silver Spring, MD
Rabbi Shalom Carmy	Yeshiva University, New York, NY
Rabbi Zevulun Charlop	RIETS/Yeshiva University, New York, NY
Rabbi Daniel Cohen	BMH-BJ Congregation, Denver, CO
Mr. Nathan J. Diament	Orthodox Union, Washington, DC
Dr. Yaakov Elman	Yeshiva University, New York, NY
Dr. Roberta Farber	Yeshiva University, New York, NY
Rabbi Daniel Feldman	Yeshiva University, New York, NY
Prof. Steven Fine	Baltimore Hebrew University, Baltimore, MD
Rabbi Menachem Genack	Orthodox Union, New York, NY
Cantor Sherwood Goffin	Lincoln Square Synagogue, New York, NY
Rabbi Jay Goldmintz	The Ramaz School, New York, NY
Rabbi Meir Goldwicht	RIETS/Yeshiva University, New York, NY
Rabbi David Gottlieb	Congregation Shomeri Emunah, Baltimore, MD
Mr. Ira Green	Ranana, Israel
Rabbi Naphtali Harcsztark	Salanter Akiva Riverdale Academy, Bronx, NY
Rabbi Michael Hecht	Yeshiva University High School for Boys, New York, NY
Prof. Jonathan Helfand	Brooklyn College, Brooklyn, NY
Rabbi Nathaniel Helfgot	Yeshiva Chovevei Torah, New York, NY
Rabbi Yehuda Henkin	Jerusalem, Israel
Rabbi Basil Herring	Rabbinical Council of America, New York, NY

Rabbi Robert S. Hirt	RIETS/Yeshiva University, New York, NY
Rabbi David Horowitz	Yeshiva University, New York, NY
Dr. Arthur Hyman	Yeshiva University, New York, NY
Prof. Ephraim Kanarfogel	Yeshiva University, New York, NY
Dr. Eugene Korn	Edah Journal, New York, NY
Dr. Norman Lamm	Yeshiva University, New York, NY
Prof. Daniel Lasker	Ben Gurion University, Beer Sheva, Israel
Rabbi Aharon Lichtenstein	Yeshivat Har Etzion/RIETS, Jerusalem, Israel
Dr. Naftali Loewenthal	University College London, London, England
Dr. Vivian Mann	The Jewish Museum, New York, NY
Rabbi Shmuel Marcus	Young Israel of Fair Lawn, Fair Lawn, NJ
Rabbi Eitan Mayer	Tzion Yehuda, Israel
Prof. Stuart Miller	University of Connecticut, Storrs, CT
Rabbi Adam Mintz	New York Board of Rabbis, New York, NY
Mrs. Sharon Mintz	Jewish Theological Seminary, New York, NY
Dr. David Pelcovitz	Yeshiva University, New York, NY
Dr. Nehemia Polen	Hebrew College, Brookline, MA
Rabbi Zvi Romm	Yeshiva University, New York, NY
Rabbi Bernard Rosensweig	Yeshiva University, New York, NY
Rabbi Michael Rosensweig	RIETS/Yeshiva University, New York, NY
Rabbi Shalom Rosner	Yeshiva University, New York, NY
Rabbi Yonason Sacks	Yeshiva University, New York, NY
Dr. Alvin I. Schiff	Yeshiva University, New York, NY
Prof. Lawrence Schiffman	New York University, New York, NY
Rabbi Kenneth Schiowitz	The Ramaz School, New York, NY
Dr. David Shatz	Yeshiva University, New York, NY
Dr. Michael Shmidman	Yeshiva University, New York, NY

Dr. Moshe Z. Sokol	Touro College, New York, NY
Dr. Moshe Sokolow	Yeshiva University, New York, NY
Rabbi Alan Stadtmauer	Yeshivah of Flatbush High School, Brooklyn, NY
Mr. Marc D. Stern	American Jewish Congress, New York, NY
Prof. Suzanne Last Stone	Cardozo School of Law/Yeshiva University, New York, NY
Rabbi Moshe D. Tendler	RIETS/Yeshiva University, New York, NY
Dr. Chaim I. Waxman	Rutgers University, New Brunswick, NJ
Rabbi Tzvi Weinreb	Orthodox Union, New York, NY
Rabbi Jeremy Wieder	Yeshiva University, New York, NY
Rabbi Mordechai Willig	RIETS/Yeshiva University, New York, NY
Dr. Joel B. Wolowelsky	Yeshivah of Flatbush, Brooklyn, NY
Dr. Walter S. Wurzburger, z"l	Yeshiva University, New York NY
Rabbi Alan Yuter	Touro College, New York, NY
Mr. Gerald Zeitchik	The Ramaz School, New York, NY

Index

A

Aaron, in synagogue art, 201
ablution, ritual, 198–200
Absolute, reaching, 130–131
adam gadol, story of an, 20
Adler, Mortimer, 246
adult education
  and developmental changes, 272
  and discovering meaning, 287
  maintain interest as teacher responsibility, 290–291
adults, reading habits of, 290
affective goals in education, 243
afterlife
  belief in, 494
  Crescas' theory of spirituality in, 178
  perfection in, 172
Agent Intellect, 165, 169–170, 173
Aḥaronim, mixed canon of, 152
ahavah, 30
Aḥot ha-Temimim, 440–441
Akiva, Rabbi
  brevity of prayers, 90
  prayer of, 69–73
Amidah, 67, 72, 74, 80–82, 181, 302–303, 316, 456–457
amoraim, voluntary prayers of, 74–75
animal world, spirituality in, 4–6
animation, by spirit, 40
annihilation, of personal identity, 173
Aristotelianism, Jewish, 176
Ark of the Covenant, 195
arona, 195
art
  ceremonial, 213–231
  Christian, 197
  congregational approval of, in synagogue, 228–229
  and dignity of Torah, 196
  Hellenistic influences on, in synagogue, 202
  sharing, between synagogues, 229
  two-dimensional, not prohibited, 222
asceticism, 132–134
Association for the Reform of Judaism, 333
atonement, 46

Z